AMERICA IN TWO CENTURIES:
An Inventory

This is a volume in the Arno Press collection

AMERICA IN TWO CENTURIES:
An Inventory

Advisory Editor

DANIEL J. BOORSTIN

*See last pages of this volume
for a complete list of titles*

ENGINES OF DEMOCRACY

ROGER BURLINGAME

ARNO PRESS
A New York Times Company
1976

Editorial Supervision: ANDREA HICKS

Reprint Edition 1976 by Arno Press Inc.

Reprinted from a copy in
  The Newark Public Library

AMERICA IN TWO CENTURIES: An Inventory
ISBN for complete set: 0-405-07666-5
See last pages of this volume for titles.

Manufactured in the United States of America

Library of Congress Cataloging in Publication Data

Burlingame, Roger, 1889-1967.
    Engines of democracy.

    (America in two centuries, an inventory)
    Reprint of the ed. published by Scribner, New
York.
    Bibliography: p.
    1. Inventions--United States. 2. United States
--Civilization. 3. United States--Economic condi-
tions. 4. Technology--Social aspects--United
States. I. Title. II. Series.
T21.B77 1976   301.24'3'0973   75-22804
ISBN 0-405-07676-2

ENGINES OF DEMOCRACY

ALEXANDER GRAHAM BELL

ENGINES OF DEMOCRACY

Inventions and Society in Mature America

By

ROGER BURLINGAME

AUTHOR OF
March of the Iron Men

CHARLES SCRIBNER'S SONS · NEW YORK
CHARLES SCRIBNER'S SONS · LTD · LONDON
1940

PREFACE

IN *March of the Iron Men,* I traced the history of that American society which, in 1865, found itself organized into a nation. I tried to show how it had been shaped, dispersed and reshaped up to that point not by wars, treaties or what is called political science but by invention. This is a large word and includes the Federation which was our pattern as well as the cotton gin and the steamboat. But my emphasis was on physical things: on the tools, machines, and processes which made life possible in a raw land; which articulated the expansion across the emptiness, which determined the temper of the people and, finally, helped them toward unity.

Beginning with the earliest seventeenth-century settlement, I saw three movements: first a huddling together in small communities in a desperate effort to transplant an old-world culture, second a wide, fanlike dispersion, third a drawing together of all the parts into a new whole, quite different from the first dream. Invention began, then, in the technologies of building and agriculture. But in agriculture was the westward lure, and invention in transport and communication was a normal consequence. It is my belief that the instruments invented in this phase were the instruments of our eventual union and that, working with an industrial revolution imposed upon us by European conflict, they made that union a fact before, politically, it was recognized. Thus, *March of the Iron Men* was a finished story, complete in itself.

Engines of Democracy, though it follows in the time sequence, is a different story. It is the history of what, in effect, is a different nation though the old political pattern because of its wide adaptability still applied to it. From 1865 the effective forces, technical and social, were all collective tending to tighten the complex. The movement of internal consolidation from the final ocean frontiers, unlike the straight westward advance, did not lend it-

vii

self to simple chronological record. Events did not follow one another in orderly sequence; they were simultaneous in various places and under various compulsions. So in this book, I have been obliged to adopt a horizontal rather than a vertical plan, showing the inventions or technologies which developed under a wide variety of social impulses all moving more or less at once toward what seems to be a final cohesion.

The historian of the next phase of American movement will, I think, take off from this cohesive moment to record a new dispersion, not fanlike or expansive like the last but inside the set physical boundaries; a separation of the social atoms as they move toward a variety of subtler frontiers: the outposts of the mind, frontiers of science, the borderlands of mature human desire where there is fertile soil for abundant social growth.

In my record of the second phase, I have, of course, had to meet the increased difficulties of the technics themselves with an untechnical mind and so have presented the brief descriptions of the inventions as a layman must do in the common terms with which I am familiar. With the additional momentary glimpses I have had of the workings of physical law in the devices of the later inventors, I am more than ever humble before the great mystery which is called Science. During the short intervals when I have approached the shadows, I have given specific credit to each authority who has helped light me along the way. But in general, throughout the book, I have concentrated on social rather than technical aspects.

I have many debts of gratitude. I have been fortunate in having the constant guidance of a truly great editor, Maxwell Perkins, whose suggestions started me on this kind of history. Any author who has ever had the expert and friendly advice of Mr. Joseph Hawley Chapin in the illustration of a volume will understand my deep sense of loss at his death. Yet his work was so thorough and his influence so pervasive that the art department he established is able to carry on today almost as if he were still guiding it. My sincere thanks to his successor, Mr. Atkinson Dymock, who has met many problems in the illustration of this book.

The libraries, as always, have been extremely co-operative. The Sterling Memorial Library at Yale has been a mainstay; its staff has been gracious and kind, generous in the privileges it has granted me. I have had abundant help from Mr. David Mearns and Mr. Donald Patterson of the Library of Congress. The Engineering Societies Library of New York, the Detroit Public Library, the Harvard Club Library in New York, and my home town Library in Danbury have been of the greatest help. Doctor Carleton Sprague Smith and Mr. Robert W. Hill of the New York Public Library and Mr. Jay Leyda of the Film Library of the Museum of Modern Art have given me much patient assistance.

As before, I have depended for much bibliographical information on Mr. Theodore Bolton, librarian of the Century Club, who has devoted hours of his time to some of the most difficult problems of my research. Through the kindness of Mrs. Frank Julian Sprague, I have been able to study the Sprague collection at length and she has given me much of her time in discussing many aspects of her husband's inventions.

For special expert advice, I want to thank Mr. John Mills of the Bell Laboratories, Mr. John Warner, President of the Society of Automotive Engineers, Mr. Charles Chatfield of the United Aircraft Corporation, Major Lester Gardner, Secretary of the Institute of Aeronautical Sciences, Messrs. Fred Zeder and Carl Breer of the Chrysler Corporation, Miss Iris Barry and Mr. Julian Street of the Museum of Modern Art, Messrs. Benjamin Schulberg, Ned Griffiths and Val Lewton, motion-picture authorities, Mr. Edward J. Nally, former President of Radio Corporation of America, Mr. Harry Gage of the Mergenthaler Linotype Company.

My old friend Delmar G. ("Barney") Roos will find many of his ideas here and there in the book—the fruit of our long pleasant talks about life and machines. He has in my opinion the keenest mind and the widest outlook ever connected with automotive engineering. He made it possible for me to visit most of the large automobile plants under the best auspices.

Other close friends have helped me in a variety of ways.

PREFACE

William Dozier made me at home in Hollywood and arranged for me to see the studios in operation. John V. N. Dorr, with whom I have been associated for some years in Connecticut civic activities, introduced me to the Association of the Directors of Industrial Research and enabled me to go to their Corning meeting where I had the pleasure of meeting Doctor Eugene Sullivan of Corning Glass and of being hospitably entertained by an old A. E. F. companion, Glen Cole. Through him I was enabled to study the celebrated machines at Corning and Wellsboro. Mark Barr, a scholar in physical and human nature, on whom I have often depended for the simplification of difficult processes in both spheres, provided me with valuable historical material on several subjects. Merritt Crawford was of immense assistance to me in my exploration of cinema history. As before, Stuart Chase has given me constant encouragement and friendly advice in addition to a quantity of source material.

Mr. Arthur Page of American Telephone and Telegraph introduced me to the Bell Laboratories and furnished me with information on every phase of electric communication. Doctor Nicola Tesla was kind enough to send me some useful data about his own work. I learned much from talking with Doctor Leo Baekeland and Doctor George Soper.

As with my earlier book, Doctor Carl W. Mitman of the Smithsonian Institution undertook a careful critical review of my manuscript. He also directed me to source material and, as my footnotes testify, is the authority for a great deal of information on the lives of inventors.

I am deeply grateful to all who extended warm hospitality to me on the transcontinental trip on which I "discovered" America: especially to my aunt, Mrs. George W. Caswell of San Francisco, to Miss Mildred Cram of Santa Barbara, to Mrs. John Vail and Miss Katherine White of Denver, to Mr. and Mrs. Charles Holmes of Lawrence, Kansas, to Mr. and Mrs. J. Henry Johnson of Kansas City, to Mr. and Mrs. Oscar Payne of Tulsa, and to Mr. D. J. Donohoe and Mr. and Mrs. Donohoe, junior, of Ponca City, Oklahoma, and to Mr. Allan Seager of Pineville, Missouri.

PREFACE

I was extremely fortunate in having as research assistant one of the most brilliant and able young men it has ever been my pleasure to meet. William A. W. Krebs, Jr., of Tulsa and New Haven, has been my constant helper and companion and has shown a sympathy with the intent of this book which made a genuine co-operation possible.

To my wife, as always, I owe most of all. To those many authors who know her as Ann Watkins, I need not explain her critical genius. For me it has been infallible. She has had a difficult time with this book and she has been patient. If I have succeeded in keeping a reasonable balance between my technical and social material it is she who has been responsible. I think of her as a full collaborator in this as in every job I undertake.

CONTENTS

xiii

CONTENTS

Part IV

SPEED

Part V

ECONOMY

Part VI

THE SOCIAL LAG

APPENDIX

Note on Abbreviations: *D. A. B.*, cited often in footnotes, designates *Dictionary of American Biography*, N. Y., 1928–36; *M. I. M.* signifies *March of the Iron Men* by Roger Burlingame, N. Y., 1938.

ILLUSTRATIONS

ILLUSTRATIONS

xvi

ILLUSTRATIONS

ILLUSTRATIONS

AT THE END OF THE BOOK

Part I

THE COLLECTIVE IMPULSE

Chapter One

THE CLEFT DUST

I

MUCH has been said and written in late times about "The American Way." Americans in their new introspection—in that phase of reflection which, in the progress of society, is a likely sequence to an all-absorbing physical effort—are intently seeking some trait or feature, some habitude or essence which they may point to as American and unique. This exercise is becoming increasingly difficult. Here and there, investigators are even beginning to suspect the value of statistics, graphs, surveys, averages, curves, charts, tables and dotted maps. Here and there, Americans are turning to the poets for the ultimate expression of the American way.

It is possible that the poets have done a better job than the statisticians. Readers of Carl Sandburg who have been able to grasp the whole body of his poetry have stopped asking the question. There are brief, haunting passages in the poetry of Stephen Vincent Benét (who, we suspect, has gained a place in American literature which will never be lost) which suggest the American way more finally than the entire effort of the Brookings Institution. "The homesick men," wrote Benét of the first settlers,

> "begot high cheek-boned things
> Whose wit was whittled with a different sound
> And Thames and all the rivers of the kings
> Ran into Mississippi and were drowned.
>
> "They planted England with a stubborn trust.
> But the cleft dust was never English dust."

Then, of the later aspect, he said:

> "And now to see you is more difficult yet
> Except as an immensity of wheel
> Made up of wheels, oiled with inhuman sweat
> And glittering with the heat of ladled steel."[1]

[1]Stephen Vincent Benét, *John Brown's Body*, N. Y., © 1928. Invocation.

3

ENGINES OF DEMOCRACY

We commend the whole of this poem, youthful, rhapsodic, and overmelodious as it may occasionally be, to students of the American way.

There was an American way, simple enough to formulate in the adolescence of the nation, but it has been lost. Like Benét's "cleft dust" it was distinct from all European ways unless we go back to the nomads who, originally, are believed to have trekked into a wilderness Europe from the East or South. The American way was the way of the solitary. The citizen of the United States —a title which had little meaning in the early nineteenth century —was a lonely man. He was not an *individualist* as we now use that battered term—a product of frustration; he was an *individual* complete in himself. The suffix arrived when he was no longer so. Like all "ists" he was then a thwarted person. Remove the opposition and there will be no more fascists, communists, feminists, militarists, pacifists, collectivists. These folk will then become fasces,[2] common, females, military, pacific, gregarious if that is what, by nature, they are.

The American, then, of the pioneer phase, was an integral ego. His non-ego was the forest. With various devices evolved by his brain, he cut the forest, pulled or burned the stumps, settled upon the land and made it easy for his less adventurous brothers to follow him. The technology he had developed in this process then made him collective.

There are dangers in this statement. It is exceedingly dangerous to personify or deify Technology, Invention or The Machine. They are all man-made matters and should not be confused with thunderstorms, earthquakes, falling meteors or the movement of planets over which man has no control. The apparent mastery of the machine over man is due, simply, to his own loss of control in other matters. When we became aware of the great things we could do by the so-called subjugation of the laws of nature we grew so absorbed in this activity that we forgot the equally important exercise of "subjugating" the human laws to a reasonable conformation with our achievement. We became so en-

[2]Literally *bunches* or *bundles*. A natural bundle of men differs from men fighting to become a bundle.

4

grossed in the machine that we neglected all effort to adjust the social mind and human conduct to its development. Furthermore, the machine itself assumed such magnitude that we forgot what it was meant to do. It was then an end, not a means. Having produced it to be our menial, we voluntarily reversed the hierarchy and, unconscious of the absurdity of our posture, salaamed before it.

Having devised, for example, the railroad, as a means to fuller social expression, we ran it amuck over the lives, liberties, and pursuits of happiness of our people. We ran it through the streets of towns. We let its sparks set fields and forests afire. We let it terrify men and children and cattle; human beings scampered like rabbits away from their own creation; it destroyed thousands of lives and dominated millions of others. Instead of the train waiting upon men, men waited upon the train.

Precisely the same thing is happening today with the automobile. Here is a locomotive, far more powerful than those of the early railroad, which rushes through the streets of our towns, scattering the crowds it is meant to serve. After many decades of destruction, we eventually learned to instruct and adjust our railroad engineers and to detour our railroads; we may, in time, learn also to educate our motor drivers and route their machines away from the populous thoroughfares but the triumph of invention will come when technological achievement and human adjustment are simultaneous.

We must consider all these aspects when we say that technology caused Americans to become collective. It is probably just to say that man is, by nature, collective. The solitaries among us are probably sports. Rousseau and the other ideal individualists have never got very far in the proof of the contrary. So, when technology united people in America most of them were probably glad of it in their hearts. In any case, the collective impulse grew by leaps and bounds. In the latter half of the nineteenth century, men habituated in the first half to the extreme of loneliness, rushed into orders, leagues, brotherhoods, lodges, clans, societies, clubs, bands, associations, fraternities, unions, teams, sects and circles. From being an individual complete in himself, it became very difficult indeed for an American ever to stand on his own feet. In his early childhood, he was inducted into a group and told that none of his achievements were to redound to his own glory but to the glory of the group. We became obsessed with the team ideal and everything we did was for the honor of the "dear old" school, college, fraternity, class, legion, rotary, or bigger-business association. In this way, individualism became so difficult that the word "rugged" was finally applied to any one who achieved it.

In spite of all this, however, the long habituation to loneliness has left a nostalgia often evident today. In our West, rugged farmers still resist collective authority when it threatens the individual, and resist it with guns. The word "different" has become common in advertising meaning special, and everywhere the word "home-made" is pathetically applied to mass-produced goods. These may be sporadic or ineffectual expressions but they suggest that the American way, while lost, is not wholly forgotten.

Americans are coming to use collective agencies (technology among them) to fight intolerable collective conditions. Confine a modern American to a city and he will invent contrivances to burrow his way out, under rivers if necessary, to a suburb; he will then invent new transport to move that suburb farther and farther away that he may "own his own home," his plot of land. Confine him too rigidly to that home and he devises a machine called a trailer to return him to the gipsy trail. Organize him too tightly in a factory or a union and he will often voluntarily go out of employment. Provide him with "relief" and he will sometimes cling to it though work is round the corner because relief, paltry as it is, gives him personal liberty which industry does not.

So we see a conflict between the nostalgic individual and his collectivized society. The individual impulse is analogous to that desire which psychologists have discovered in mature men—the craving to crawl back into the mother's womb. The early emigrant was reborn when he came to America and the savage wilderness was his mother. The impulse is unwholesome in itself but the conflict between it and the equally unwholesome extreme

6

collective impulse is healthful to our society. As long as the conflict endures there will be hope for the integrity of America.

2

To trace the origins of the collective phase in technology is easy enough.[3] Men did not venture far into the wilderness before they had invented wagons to transport them and rifles to secure food and defeat enemies. The invention of river boats made a further advance possible. But while wagons and powerless boats would keep the pioneer moving overland and downstream they could not bring him supplies quickly or abundantly enough to enable him to settle. The river boats became collective instruments when, unable to move upstream, they were broken up and towns were built of them. Such communities might have remained isolated and evolved a slow civilization of their own but for the steamboat which established a trade connection with the old civilization behind. The railroad made this closer and more general and by the transport of many goods established the tradition that goods should be manufactured in the old civilization and shipped to the new. At the same time they brought back the raw materials, products of the forest and the soil, so that the establishment of the tradition became firmer.

But by this time the East, deprived of half its labor by the emigration, had invented devices to manufacture independent of human hands and these machines were found not only to accomplish this but to accelerate and increase production. Simultaneously, machines brought by the new transport to the West made possible harvests far greater than the pioneers could use. Thus still more firmly was the convention established that goods should be made in one place and used in another; grown in one place and manufactured and consumed in another. This made separate parts of the country dependent on one another, a collective result.

Now came the matter of thought and opinion. The telegraph and the press achieved a collective result in forming blocs of

[3]The sequence is followed in detail in Roger Burlingame, *March of the Iron Men,* N. Y., 1938, hereafter referred to as *M. I. M.*

opinion, though at this point we find a social lag which held back complete union. In the face of the facts, men's social minds, a lap behind their technological ones, still clung to a belief in the effectiveness of the individual. This had enlarged, to be sure, and the sovereign state had become the unit. But blocs of states in which conditions were alike confused the fact of their unlikeness to other blocs with a sense of independence of those other blocs. In this way the South believed itself independent of the North and West and used the steamboat, the railroad, the telegraph, the press and an improved pioneer rifle to prove it. It took four years of bloodshed plus the normal working of the McCormick reaper and New England textile machinery to show the whole fallacy. The bloodshed alone would not have done it.

Hence the divergence between the individual belief and the collective fact caused the Civil War. This was a social lag; the inability of the social consciousness to adjust with sufficient rapidity to the technological realities. We stand in much the same position today in many respects.

The Civil War was "over" in the military sense in 1865 and at that point our present history begins. We shall see how from there on, the technological factors tended to intensify the collective impulse and tighten the collective scheme already established. In this we were greatly assisted by Europe and, indeed, by the simultaneous advance of science throughout the world.

3

Dickens, in *American Notes* and in *Martin Chuzzlewit* showed the wide gap between English society and American society in the eighteen-forties. Here was the high point of visibility of the failure of the emigrants to transplant European cultures to the New World. In that decade, in which the needle and electromagnetic telegraphs were weaned, the separation was complete. The American, rude, shrill-pitched, individualist and a little drunk with a power that was not yet articulate, was a new product in the world. Paradoxically, however, there was homogeneity among these Americans, at least in the eyes of a middleclass Englishman. Dickens, to be sure, never got far from the

Atlantic fringe. From Pittsburgh west, he might have encountered differences though to him they would probably not have appeared fundamental or profoundly impressive. It was there that we like to think the "real America" was in the making.

It is possible that the likeness among Americans which Dickens saw was merely a common unlikeness to Englishmen. Many occidentals believe that Chinese look alike because they have the common trait of not looking like westerners. His dominant feeling, in America, may have been merely that "the cleft dust was never English dust." Certainly the manner of its cleavage was un-English, especially, as he remarked, when the strange, street-marching railroad did the cleaving. But Dickens was seeing, then, an America he would never see again.

He was seeing an America in which the collective forces, the forces of union were already irresistible. But, more than that, he saw an America which already contained germs of European infection—an America which, twenty years later when he would come again, would have become far more European than the one he was seeing then. And he saw, too, an America whose own germs would, in another two decades, begin to affect Europe. He stood, in short, at the close of the isolation era.

Whatever his bias may have been, he undoubtedly observed certain likenesses among Americans which were there in fact. The British race, then dominant in America, had been reborn. Americans had a common mother who was certainly un-English. This mother was the savage wilderness. Their common traits Americans had inherited from her.

As long as we insist on biological metaphors in these matters, it is far more correct to speak of England as the father than as the mother of America. His children, when they came out of the savage womb, were wayward and gave him trouble; it was difficult to teach them manners and, eventually, it became increasingly difficult to keep them from teaching him their own wild ways. Most of this interplay may be traced to two origins: labor shortage and new communications.

Chapter Two

ENTANGLING ALLIANCES

I

A S THE American people spread, it became increasingly necessary to supply them, as we have shown, from Eastern industrial centers. This centralization of industry, growing more intense as means of distribution improved, immediately met the labor problem. Men moved, industry stood still. But industry without men could hardly function. It was therefore necessary to move other men into the vacancies. For these men there was one obvious and, indeed, unique source—Europe. With a constant stream of Europeans moving by transport which daily improved and enlarged into America, it is hardly plausible, except in the ostrich mind, to maintain indefinitely the hope of complete aloofness from the rest of the world.

The other factor which, while effecting the union of the states, undermined the nation's insular ambitions was the telegraph. Morse was always an artist. He thought in large masses not in the thin lines of national frontiers. Morse did not "invent" the telegraph,[1] but he was willing to paint it over the map of the world, splashing his paint across the most sacred and meticulous boundaries. He was also a cosmopolitan. He knew Europe as well as he knew his own country. Besides all this the "system" which he had built upon the scientific performance of Joseph Henry and the mechanical performance of Alfred Vail was by far the best that had yet been devised for land telegraphs.

Untroubled by any doctrine of isolation, Morse predicted in 1843 "that a telegraphic communication on my plan may with certainty be established across the Atlantic."[2] The year before

[1] *M. I. M.*, p. 474.
[2] Edward Lind Morse, *Letters and Journal of S. F. B. Morse,* Boston, 1914, II, 208, 209.

he had personally laid submarine wires insulated with tar in New York harbor.[3] The prediction on the basis of this slight experiment plus a study of what was known of electrical laws at the time reveals the indomitable temper of this painter. But Morse was already passing middle age, his life had been hard and he was engaged in his busiest activity, the demonstration of the telegraph on land. In the twenty-three years before the prediction could be adequately fulfilled, other men more vigorous and less engrossed would have to share this vision.

Meanwhile, however, various submarine cables were tried for short distances. In 1851 a cable insulated with the new gutta-percha was laid successfully across the English Channel by Jacob Brett.[4] The next year a cable connection was planned from New Brunswick to Newfoundland by Frederick N. Gisborne and it is here that the story of the Atlantic cable begins. The leading American characters in this tale are the Field brothers.

The Fields were an astonishing family. Sons of a Congregationalist minister, they were all brilliant, dynamic men. One was an engineer, one a judge, two were merchants in one of whom business acumen amounted surely to genius. Cyrus Field was not, as many have supposed, a technician or an inventor. Like many American business men, however, he was so gripped by a fancy that he believed the necessary technicians could be wheeled into line to make it a fact. Several technologies owe their development to such men.

When Gisborne's money gave out he came, as people still do, to New York to get more.[5] There he met Matthew Field the engineer. Matthew went to Cyrus with Gisborne's story. Cyrus had already retired from business[6] and had no wish to become entangled in a Newfoundland cable. As he looked at the map, however, his eyes moved across the space between Newfoundland and Ireland. It was, indeed, the shortest line across the Atlantic.

[3]*Ibid.*, II, 182, 183.
[4]George B. Prescott, *History, Theory, and Practice of the Electric Telegraph*, Boston, 1860, p. 175.
[5]1854.
[6]He was, however, only thirty-five. Henry M. Field, *Story of the Atlantic Telegraph*, p. 15 n.

Now if the cable to Newfoundland could be extended to Ireland, he thought, the enterprise would be big enough to attract him. It would, of course, be a mad undertaking in the eyes of the world.

We must recognize here an important difference between the nineteenth-century mind and the twentieth-century mind. In the

Cyrus W. Field
Projector of the Atlantic
Cable

After a photograph by C. M. Bell,
1891

Courtesy of the Bettmann Archives

1850's men still thought in small steps. They found great difficulty in moving from one step to another. Because a submarine cable worked successfully for twenty or thirty miles made the proposal that it should work for a thousand miles scarcely less ridiculous. Nowadays, once a means of communication or transport has successfully traversed a hundred yards we instantly conceive of it as covering the globe. But that is a matter of psychological habit which it has taken many years to produce. The men of the fifties were like the men of the thirties who could grasp a five-mile railroad but laughed and tapped their heads when its builder suggested that it should now be extended to seventy-five miles.[7]

[7]*M. I. M.*, p. 258.

With Field's proposal a great deal of head-tapping began. The bottom of the ocean was very different from the bottom of the Channel. A great body of scientific fact and law which we have, today, at our fingertips was still in embryo then. Out of this ignorance it was difficult to form a concept of an ocean bottom beyond all familiar disturbances being an easier resting

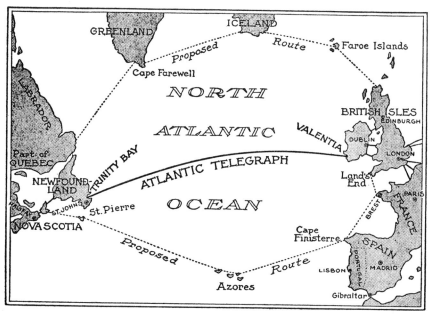

Map showing route of completed Atlantic Cable and two other proposed routes
Redrawn from map in *Atlantic Telegraph* by George W. Bacon, London, 1865

place for a cable than a shallow strait swept by winds and currents.

Field wasted no time. With the instinct of such men he instantly picked the experts who could help him most. One was Matthew Fontaine Maury, head of the Naval Observatory, who already knew more than most men about the bottom of the ocean; the other was Morse who, by this time, had learned much about telegraphy. Maury wrote that the year before the Government had conducted a sounding expedition over the precise line which had already seemed obvious to Field as the bed of the Atlantic cable.

Here, wrote Maury, "the bottom of the sea . . . is a plateau which seems to have been placed there especially for the purpose of holding the wires of a submarine telegraph, and keeping them out of harm's way. It is neither too deep nor too shallow; yet it is so deep that the wires but once landed, will remain forever beyond the reach of vessels' anchors, icebergs, and drifts of any kind, and so shallow, that the wires may be readily lodged upon the bottom. The depth of this plateau is quite regular . . ."[8]

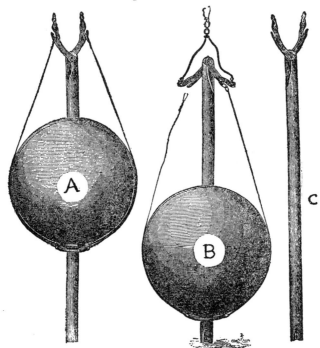

Brooke's
Deep Sea
Sounding
Apparatus

A, shows the instrument ready for sounding. It is very simple, consisting only of a cannon ball, pierced with an iron rod, and held in place by slings. As the ball goes down swiftly, it drives the rod into the ocean bottom, when an opening at the end catches the ooze in its lips. The same instant (B) the slings loosen, the ball drops off, and the rod (C) with its "bite" is drawn to the surface.

From Henry M. Field's "The Story of the Atlantic Telegraph" *Scribner's*

The most important result of the soundings, however, was the discovery that strong currents did not exist at the points where the cable would lie. This discovery was made through a beautiful invention by Lieutenant J. M. Brooke of the United States Navy. The Brooke sounding apparatus was able by a simple process[9] to pick up a bit of the ocean bottom wherever a sounding was made. These bits under a microscope showed tiny shells *intact*. The shells had sunk, through the ages, from the surface and had rested quietly on the bottom. Unless they had rested quietly they

[8]Field, p. 19.   [9]See cut and description.

would not be intact. Currents would have pulverized them, long since, into sand.[10]

Morse, always an optimist where the telegraph was concerned, came at once to talk to Field and reassured him as to the facility with which his, Morse's, electromagnetic telegraph would operate through an Atlantic cable. This was overconfident, technically, as the Morse-Vail instruments proved inadequate to submarine telegraphy[11] but the optimism from a man of Morse's standing must have been of great moral value.

Field, however, was too thorough to accept either of these assurances on their face. He insisted on a new sounding survey which the Government contributed. Then he consulted the English experts on telegraphy. His enthusiasm attracted to him such geniuses as William Thomson, the Scotch professor (later Lord Kelvin) whose invention of receiving and recording instruments made long-range submarine telegraphy a useful practice, and the young telegrapher Charles Tilston Bright, who at twenty-four had probably more technical knowledge than the great visionary Morse ever acquired.[12]

Field then founded the "New York, New Foundland and London Telegraph Company" and, in order not to arouse too much initial popular skepticism, began operations on the practical project of stretching a cable across the St. Lawrence gulf. It is an interesting reflection on the mastery of a large visionary project over a small practical one that when, in 1866, the Atlantic had finally been spanned by the telegraph the connection across the gulf was not yet complete.

Perhaps it was an instinct of isolation which caused Americans, in spite of the leadership of Field, to allow the cable operations to pass so largely into English hands. It is curious, for America had already taken the leadership of the world in land telegraphy. But there were other factors. In America there

[10]Field, pp. 20, 21; Charles Bright, *The Story of the Atlantic Cable*, N. Y., 1903, p. 34.

[11]Edward and Charles Bright, *The Life Story of the Late Sir Charles Tilston Bright*, London, 1899, I, 349, 358 f. Field, Appendix.

[12]Bright, *Atlantic Cable*, pp. 37, 47. See also Edward and Charles Bright, I, 141.

seemed to be no more fluid capital than was needed for internal progress. The conquest of the continent, as we shall presently see, was far from complete. In a large part of the enormous western spaces, communication and transport did not yet exist. Already, American capital was overextended, a fact of which the panic of 1857 was a sharp and alarming index. But perhaps more potent than any of these factors, the United States was on the brink of an internal convulsion which must determine its integrity for the future.

These things all being true and the cable being technically and capitalistically so largely an English effort, why do we devote such space to it in a history of invention in America?

The answer is that we are concerned here not primarily with technics and commercial enterprise but with their causes and their effects in America. We can hardly ignore a movement whose initial impulse came from such essentially American characters as Morse and Field. We cannot escape the technical impetus which the success of the Morse system must have given to the advance of electric communication through the world. But above all this the effect of the cable on the whole history of invention; its effect on American commerce, American internal development, the American "melting pot," and the collapse of American insular tradition is so vital that its laying must stand forever as a landmark in our history.

Another reason for its dominant position in this record is that the interval from the first attempt to the last or, roughly, the decade from '56 to '66 contains so many evidences of the movement of invention into the scientific method. In the story of the Atlantic cable this progress is peculiarly visible.

In 1856 the English government offered a subsidy of fourteen thousand pounds a year.[13] An English company was incorporated, the Atlantic Cable Company, which promised full accord with Field's American company. This was the first great gesture of "hands across the sea"; for the first time almost since the founding of the colonies the hope of a bond of friendship was popularly felt on both sides. It was a technological product; some-

[13]Bright, *Life Story,* I, 120.

thing which the utmost skill in diplomacy could never have achieved.

The United States Congress met the English subsidy in 1857 with $70,000. Both navies offered ships.

2

The story of the laying of the cable forms one of the most thrilling yarns in the annals of the Atlantic. It is a tale of continuous heroism, of furious battle with elemental forces, of persistent trial and bitter error, of ragged nerves and broken bodies, of a fight of faith against the scorn of ignorance. It was well told by contemporary journalists who accompanied the ships.[14]

In the first attempt the English *Agamemnon* and the American *Niagara,* each with its convoy and bearing a half of the cable, set out from Valentia, Ireland, on the 5th of August, 1857. The *Niagara* was to lay her cable halfway across when the *Agamemnon* would splice hers to it and continue to Trinity Bay, Newfoundland. This arrangement included a pretty gesture: the British should bid godspeed to the Americans in parting, but the English were to be met with frenzied greetings by Americans.[15] The first part of the program was carried out with banquets, solemn religious services, flag-waving, and abundant salvos from cannon. The landing ceremonies were not carried out at all.

The *Niagara's* cable parted and sank forever in 2000 fathoms of water on the sixth day out. Nearly four hundred miles of cable had been paid cut and there was no machinery for recovering it. So there was nothing for the ships to do but return to their starting point to meet the jeers of the crowds which had cheered their leaving.

The second expedition left in June, 1858. This time gestures were abandoned and it was arranged for both ships to meet in midocean, splice their cables and move apart, each for her home port.

Meanwhile the paying-out machinery, the electrical instru-

[14]Nicholas Woods, *The Times,* London, quoted at length in Bright, *Atlantic Cable,* Chaps. VI, VII and VIII, and J. Mullaly, *Herald,* New York. John Mullaly, *Laying of the Atlantic Cable,* N. Y., 1858.
[15]Bright, *Atlantic Cable,* p. 62.

ments, and the cable itself had been somewhat improved. We see the trial-and-error method working here. These things were improved; they had not been perfected beyond the possibility of error nor were there any means of knowing beforehand that they would work. Professor Thomson had invented a delicate instrument, the mirror galvanometer, which by a flash of light would register the faintest current. The paying-out machinery was presumably foolproof, but it was far from automatic except in the smoothest weather. In a rough sea, when the rise and fall of the stern of the ship produced variables in the rate of paying out, it was necessary to have men of quick judgment and great skill in constant attendance. The cable was inspected as it was

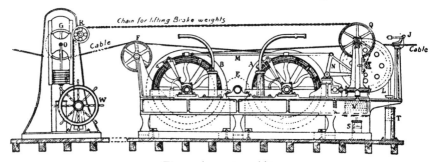

The paying-out machine

Showing a cross section of the machine which was used in the second expedition, 1858

made and submitted to what were considered rigid tests, but a cable is a complex thing and the technologies of metallurgy and insulation were still in their infancy. Physicists of considerable standing still held what we should consider fantastic beliefs about pressures, the condensability of water, strains and, especially, electric currents.[16]

The ships were of that bastard type universal in the fifties which carried sail to supplement fallible engines. The sails being on hand, it was considered extravagant to use steam when not necessary as indeed it was for no ship had adequate coal bunkers.[17] It is, therefore, more proper to look upon the *Agamemnon* and the *Niagara* as sailing ships with what we should call "auxiliary" engines than as steamers with sails ready for a desperate

[16]*Ibid.*, p. 43.   [17]Bright, *Life Story*, I, 240 n.

emergency. Nevertheless, for cable-laying, steam was essential.

Proceeding to the rendezvous the ships moved under sail. It is a great tribute to the captain and crew of the *Agamemnon* that she ever got there intact. The precious cable, weighing over a thousand tons, was a precarious load when she met one of the

The Laying of the Cable—John and Jonathan joining hands
One of the many cartoons which appeared in 1858
From the Congressional Library

worst Atlantic storms on record.[18] For a week the ship was at the mercy of the wind and waves, and men, equipment, and the coal which had burst from its bunkers, were rattled about her like dice in a cup. With the sick bay full, with one man gone stark mad, with every one suffering from exposure, with beams shattered and the hull leaking, the *Agamemnon* finally reached the rendezvous.[19] Under these conditions, the men were hardly in shape for such a delicate operation as cable-laying. Nevertheless, nearly three hundred miles of cable were paid out before it parted and the ships put back to Queenstown.

Forgetting all these hardships, they set forth again less than

[18]The exciting story of this storm was told in detail by Nicholas Woods, quoted by Bright, *Atlantic Cable*, pp. 91 ff.

[19]Bright, *Atlantic Cable*, p. 106.

a month later. When they left England on the 17th of July on the third try there were no ceremonies. No crowds saw them off and no flags waved. Popular interest in the whole adventure was nearly gone. It revived more than three weeks later when a signal was sent over a complete cable from Valentia, Ireland, to Trinity Bay, Newfoundland.[20]

The celebration on both sides of the water lasted for days. Bright and Field were banqueted, given medals, freedoms of cities, cannonades, torchlight processions, and every demonstration of hero-worship that could be devised. Meanwhile, however, the anxious operators at the end stations were sending experimental messages, receiving them with great difficulty, and constantly wondering at the weakness of the currents. Without Thomson's delicate flashing mirror they never could have received them at all. For twenty days[21] this faint whisper continued beneath the fanfares of the celebration until, on September 1, the last message came through. The rest was silence and, overnight, the heroes became villains.

The public of the day seems youthful and fickle enough as we look back upon it. It is hardly imaginable today that the failure of a great experiment in applied science could be met with such universal contempt. On the other hand, it is also unlikely that the effort would be so eagerly followed by the masses of the people. Today such experiments make a quiet progress under the cover of laboratories; they seldom appear at all until it is known beyond the flicker of a doubt that they will be successful.

But in the fifties, in spite of the astonishing demonstrations they had already seen or read about, men were still skeptical about scientific novelties. They had, still, a romantic attitude toward them. They were ready to cheer the incredible new thing —if it worked—just as they would applaud a show of magic or a fine performance on the trapeze. But if it did not work they were equally ready to shake their heads, to shout "I told you so" or to smell out a "hoax."

The day of colossal practical jokes is happily past at least in

[20]Prescott, pp. 181, 182.   [21]Aug. 13–Sept. 1. *Ibid.*, p. 205.

the realm of science. Hoaxes are still practised in the form of rackets and totalitarian experiments but we no longer regard them as funny. April Fool's Day, product of a peculiar phase of humor which reached its apogee in the Victorian era, has gone back to the recess yard of the grammar school where it belongs. But in the 1850's such things were in vogue and men believed that the Atlantic cable was one of them. In English and American papers editorials appeared entitled, "Was the Atlantic Cable a Humbug?" and "Very Like a Whale," and one writer laboriously proved to his own satisfaction that the whole laying of the cable was a myth. "The difficulty," writes Cyrus Field's brother Henry, "of finding a motive for the perpetration of such a stupendous fraud did not at all embarrass these ingenious writers. Was it not enough to make the world stare? To furnish something to the gaping crowd, even though it were but a nine-days' wonder?"[22]

It must have been one of the most heartbreaking periods in the history of invention—that interval between the old magic and the new science. It did not end until Langley's heart broke with his flying machine.[23] Yet in ten years after the first cable, great progress was made away from it.

For seven years no further attempt was made to lay an Atlantic cable. War in the interval interrupted the interest and the availability of money in the United States. When it was proved that the first cable was not a hoax, popular admiration of Field revived but no capital was forthcoming. For these reasons the bulk of the later effort to lay a successful cable came from England.

In the meantime an immense amount of research was done. The first cable had been a terrible lesson to the experimenters. After it we see the new method in invention dominating. In the early sixties it was obvious that there would be no more trial-and-error activity as far as the cable was concerned. In 1859 a commission was appointed in England to make a scientific exploration of every detail of theory and practice. It reported the complete feasibility of an Atlantic cable. Still the capital was withheld. This was extremely fortunate because it allowed fur-

[22]Field, p. 215. [23]See p. 420.

ther time for research. Here we see a curious interplay: the absence of capital actually advanced the progress of invention. During these years, the scientific method gained a secure foothold.

By 1865, the success of several cables in various parts of the world had stimulated English investors. But by 1865, also, knowledge of electricity, electrical invention, engineering technique, and most of the collateral technologies had moved to a point where the likelihood of error was much reduced.

One of these technologies was shipbuilding. In London, an iron

Section of the shore end of the Atlantic Cable of 1865, exact size

From Henry M. Field's "The Story of the Atlantic Telegraph" *Scribner's*

ship had been built of 27,384 tons, 692' x 83' x 58', with paddle wheels and screw propellers, and engines developing over 3000 horsepower. The *Great Eastern* was ahead of her time. Once launched, no use could be found for her until the Atlantic cable companies were ready. By the time they had accumulated their capital, nothing short of this leviathan seemed adequate to their colossal dream. So the *Great Eastern,* by now a white elephant as well as a leviathan, was bought for the cable.

In the electrical field new insulating material, new, beautiful devices for testing currents and discovering faults had been designed. The paying-out machinery was infallible. Everything was infallible but the men.

In the expedition of 1865, two faults were revealed in the cable due, apparently, to sabotage. No motive was ever discovered.[24] The cable broke when the ship was within six hundred miles of its destination. It sank in about two miles of water. At this point a new technology developed which later saved this cable. To grapple for and raise to the surface a cable lost in such a depth was an undreamed-of feat in 1858. It was almost done in 1865. Three times the cable was brought up—once halfway—when the ropes broke. At last there was no more rope and the *Great Eastern* put home.[25]

The story grows duller as it nears.success. This is often true of later technological achievement. Much of the thrill and romance of the older stories was in the mistakes. It is difficult to enthrall the popular fancy with a set of blueprints or test tubes; a laboratory which strangles human error. So the successful laying of the cable in 1866[26] was accepted by the public with a seriousness and realism which revealed the dawn of a new era of thought.

We are not deeply concerned here with the final successful trip of the *Great Eastern* in 1866 or with the recovery of the lost cable which made possible the operation of two Atlantic cables instead of one. We have been concerned with the earlier details because they showed the progress and change of thought; the final phase of the transition which was so vital to our modern civilization. Our interest from this point is in the effect of the new, rapid, international communication upon American society.

3

On one of the decks of the *Great Eastern* stood a bulletin board. Here, every day, was posted the news from Europe. In the first day while the coast line was still visible, in the next day while the thought of men still lingered at home, the full,

[24]Except, as Henry Field suggests, a possible hope of selling short on the London Exchange when the company stock should fall. Field, 280. See also Bright, *Atlantic Cable,* p. 186.

[25]*Harper's Monthly,* XXXL, No. 185, Oct., 1865, p. 668, gives day-by-day account of this expedition.

[26]A concise description of the 1866 voyage is given in *Harper's Monthly,* XXXIII, No. 196, Sept., 1866, p. 531.

clear miracle may not have caught their minds. But as the vast ocean stretched behind them with its world-old tradition of peril and mystery, the continuous flow of words, of intelligent sentences which were written out and posted for all to see must have wrought a revolution in the mind. The difference between these words, this casual conversation and the vague, flickering signals seen on the *Agamemnon* galvanometer was probably greater than that between the telegraphy on the *Great Eastern* and modern radiotelephony.

During the voyage, war broke out between Austria and Prussia. It was a short war. By the time the voyage was over, a treaty of peace had been arranged. Both these intelligences were sent over the new cable. From the moment of landing, news was incessant: London market prices, debates in Parliament and, finally, personal news, business transactions, intelligence of life and death.[27]

As the press made these things familiar, old antipathies disappeared, new relationships grew up. As more cables were laid, immediate contact came also with the rest of Europe. Overnight, Paris styles were adopted in New York, goods were ordered, commerce was stimulated. International disputes were settled by a word of instantaneous explanation. News of American industry stimulated emigration from Europe, helped fill the melting pot.

But the telegraph across the Atlantic had further consequences in the realm of invention. New transport must be devised to keep up with the speed of intelligence. Merchants who cabled orders expected quick delivery. People hearing through the cable of new things in Europe wanted them immediately in America. Often cabled news created an urgent necessity for some one to go to Europe before some emergency was over. Thus, the facilities for transport were multiplied and magnified and competition grew among the nations for the best and fastest steamers.

[27]The first tariff was too high for much personal communication: £1 or $5 per word. By 1872 this had been reduced to 4s. or $1. Bright, *Atlantic Cable*, p. 220. For effect of cable on journalism see W. F. G. Shanks, "How We Get Our News," in *Harper's Monthly*, XXXIV, No. 202, March, 1867, pp. 517 ff.

The news of scientific discoveries and technological inventions, instantaneously transmitted, quickened the pace of progress. An inventor working in England, getting news of the missing link in his device, was able to bring his invention to a quick finish. Knowledge of current demands and markets made dozens of new machines instantly necessary. Patent and copyright systems must be revised, made international. Indeed, a whole new conception and code of international law came into being.

It seems curious, under all these circumstances, that so many Americans still cherished the dream of isolation. This will be easier to understand, however, when we realize that when the cable was laid, the conquest of our own continent was not yet complete. There were still great empty spaces; between the Mississippi and the Rockies there were still unorganized wild lands whose people were red Indians. A civilization had grown up on the Pacific coast, but between this and the East there was still a hazardous overland journey by stagecoaches which were pursued by enemies. It is not surprising that so many preferred the long sea route and, for freight this was of course the only possibility.

And there were still the frontiers. There were remote and lonely outposts which held little communication with the rest of America, not to mention the rest of the world. In such places isolation was a fact, not a dream. And there were enough of them to keep the dream alive for another half century.

We have shown how the dream of disunion endured long after the fact of disunion had ceased to exist. We have shown how the social consciousness of this awoke only after a war had proved the underlying truth—a product largely of technology. In the same way it would take another war, a half century later, to shatter the fantasy of our aloofness from the other nations.

Meanwhile and immediately after the completion of the Atlantic cable, a transcontinental railroad—the project which so tormented Lincoln—became an irresistible necessity.

Chapter Three

TRANSCONTINENTAL

I

WATCHING the march of the American railroad, we are sometimes inclined to wonder about the power of the collective force. For in the two decades following the Civil War individualism seems more rampant than ever in this department. Here, surely, is "high finance" at its top in the world's history and unprecedentedly ruthless; here is the individual running amuck over his fellows; here is the lone wolf prowling in unlimited freedom remote from any pretense of law; here is the quick advance from overalls to Babylonian luxury that seems to be the final fulfilment of the "American dream." Was ever man more lawless or more his own law; was he ever more unmoral and less responsible to society than in this gilded age of the railroad when the riches of a continent lay ripe for his picking and the technological forces stood lined up behind him to help him pick?

Such is the appearance and to keep it, in our minds, properly divorced from the real trend, we must understand the strength of the underlying forces which were all, without exception, collective.

It is well to remember first that finance is often a fictional matter consequent upon and not motivating the facts; that the individualism of the seventies was a reflection of the lapse between technological and social progress and so a kind of mirage —the afterglow of a sun that had set. The technological pattern was one of unity and though it was still large and loose the energy all ran in the directions of standardization and condensation, of contraction and compactness. And every effort even of the rampant individuals themselves contributed to this effect:

in their wildest dreams they were unconsciously allying themselves with a scheme which should limit and finally deny the future liberty of the lonely man.

Thus the adventurer who ruined his neighbor for his own profit was, in fact, merely using his neighbor's property to promote a more binding consolidation. The railroad financier who bought a competing road at a forced price was, in fact, creating an organization which should eliminate the whole principle of free competition for his grandchildren. Yet at the same time he was simply obeying the technological laws with the blindest subservience. Railroads could not function except on a standardized pattern which was, in truth, a pattern of monopoly. The principle of interchangeable parts had become inevitable, and it was obvious in the seventies that many of those parts would be human beings made of flesh and blood, not of tooled metal.

In the purely social province, the man who exploited his neighbor developed among his neighbors the irresistible necessity for defense organization. The industrialist who made machinery work for him designed its interchangeable parts to do his bidding and they did so, but when he applied this principle to animate parts he found them equally interchangeable for their own purposes and, imbued with a will other than his, they soon operated to restrain him. So, though there are many romantic aspects of freedom in the second half of the nineteenth century, yet during the whole period, every individual was actively and continuously engrossed in forging the chains of society. Later in our history we shall come to a point in the technological cycle which suggests that in the second half of the twentieth century a movement the reverse of this may have its inception.

Meanwhile we must follow the rapid process of unification which, more than any other single factor in our history, the railroad advanced. Considering the size, comparative emptiness, and topography of North America at the time of the Civil War, the acceleration of this process seems miraculous. It was, of course, this extreme rapidity which brought about many of the peculiar social and economic troubles with which we are struggling today.

Two important background factors must be borne in mind throughout this study. One is the physical, political, and economic geography of the country. The other is the sharp division which existed—making a far more definite contrast than exists today—between technician and promoter.

This contrast is between realist and romantic, between moral and unmoral, between stern devotion to the god of physical law and blind worship of the gods of chance and gold. There was a place in the sun of that bright, wide age for both of these conflicting religions.

It was an era of sharp values. The highlights were pointed, the shadows dark. Color was in masses, lurid like the hues of a chromo; as we look at it now, there were few nuances. The prevailing shade was glittering gold.

2

The idea of a transcontinental railroad arrived at about the time that the people of America encountered the stunning possibility that the Oregon Country was likely to become a part of the United States. California, at the moment, was still Mexican with a Spanish hangover. Texas, peopled largely by Yankee wanderers and restless adventurers from the backwoods border, was asserting its independence of Spanish ties and yearning toward the sprawling nation to its northeast. What are now Utah, Nevada, Arizona, New Mexico and portions of Colorado were still nominally Mexican, though her hold must have seemed tenuous enough in the secret councils of her volatile government.

There occurred then a social and political vision which was curiously in advance of the technological actuality.

Already, before any steam railroad existed in America, a New Jersey senator had stated the impossibility of statehood for Oregon:

"The distance a member of Congress of this State of Oregon would be obliged to travel in coming to the seat of government and returning home would be 9300 miles. If he should travel 30 miles a day it would require 306 days. Allow for Sundays 44, it would amount to 350 days. This would allow the member a fortnight to rest himself in Washington before he should com-commence his journey home."[1]

This dictum seemed final enough for at least ten years. There has been much controversy among historians on the entirely unimportant point of who then saw the vision and at what precise moment.[2] In the early thirties, while such monsters as the *De Witt Clinton* were scattering their sparks over passengers in open cars on short runs in the East, several newspaper articles called attention to the conceivability of reaching Oregon by railroad. These attracted attention in the period when feats of science roused similar emotions to those felt on watching a smart performance on a trapeze, but it was another dozen years before the vision appeared with any clarity before any one who might realize it.

Meanwhile many things had occurred. The locomotive was doing business and making money in the East and South. A railroad had already threatened the doom of the Erie Canal.[3] Many of the principles which should make the American railroad unique in the world, such as the T-rail, the hooked spike, the flexible locomotive frame or chassis with its swivel-truck, equalizing levers and exterior connecting rods, had been invented. Furthermore, new political and social necessities had developed. Oregon had become a thriving territory, there was an active and reasonable fear that it would presently declare itself an independent nation and, on the other side, the slavery question had become front-page news. Along with these matters and many others came one of the great tragic visionaries of American history. His name, now largely forgotten along with his thankless achievement, was Asa Whitney.[4]

Now there are some who declare that Whitney's vision was seen in light refracted from golden coin, that his whole scheme

[1]Sen. Dickerson of N. J., 1825; John William Starr, *One Hundred Years of American Railroading*, N. Y., 1929, p. 208.
[2]For an excellent discussion of this, well-documented, see Seymour Dunbar, *History of Travel in America*, Indianapolis, 1915, pp. 1321 ff.
[3]*Ibid.*, p. 842.
[4]Not to be confused with the inventor and railroad man of the same name and period.

was designed to benefit Whitney alone and line his pockets with the precious metal.[5] If this be true, he differs little from his contemporaries who made the American railroad a revolutionary force in world history, but in the light of later events his cupidity seems of a modest order. The fact remains that he spent most of his fortune and that his whole achievement was in the realm of psychology. Its effect was nonetheless tremendous.

Early in 1845, Whitney reproduced his vision before the United States Senate.[6] After presenting a summary of the progress already made in transportation, "your memorialist," he continued, "would further represent to your honorable body that he has devoted much time and attention to the subject of a railroad from Lake Michigan, through the Rocky mountains to the Pacific ocean, and that he finds such a route practicable, the results from which would be incalculable, far beyond the imagination of man to estimate. To the interior of our vast and widely spread country it would be as the heart is to the human body. . . .

"Such easy and rapid communication would bring all our immensely widespread circulation together as one vast city, the moral and social effects of which must harmonize all together as one family, with but one interest—the general good of all."[7]

It was necessary in those days (and often still is) to embellish such proposals with references to humanity and the general good before Congress would take the slightest notice of them. Beneath these flowers, however, it seems evident that Whitney was pursuing a collective ideal rather than an individual fortune, especially as in his first proposal he suggested government ownership and operation and in later proposals which, for cogent reasons altered this plan, he suggested a salary for himself of only $4000.[8]

By the time of his second and third memorials, the public had become accustomed enough to extensive railroad building to give an enthusiastic response to the developed plan. Its most attractive feature was a scheme of financing the road by selling

[5]Starr, p. 209. See, however, Margaret Louise Brown, "Asa Whitney," in *Dictionary of American Biography.*
[6]Sen. Docs., 1844–45, III, No. 69.   [7]*Ibid.*
[8]Sen. Misc., 1847–48, No. 28, Sec. 11.

land grants given for the purpose by the Government with no financial cost to itself. But besides the excellent appearance of the proposal *per se,* Whitney was well known as a man who did not let his guns go off half-cocked. He was a successful merchant, he was rich, he was greatly travelled, having spent more than a year doing business in China, and he had explored the very country over which his road would be built.

Yet, though the Senate committees were generally favorable, Congress demurred. It delayed just long enough for the political and economic geography of the West to undergo a complete change.

This was not very long. Within three years of the first proposal, the Mexican War had been fought and won and the immense Mexican territory, which has since been carved into the states of Arizona, California, Nevada, New Mexico, Texas, Utah, and part of Colorado, had been added to the United States. This addition considerably lessened the importance of Oregon, especially when soon after something was washed up in the valley of the Sacramento which completely shifted the western focus of attention. This cynosure was a nugget of gold.[9]

From this point on it was increasingly difficult for Whitney to press his project. The gold rush to California made the need for a transcontinental seem more insistent, but it was no longer Whitney's road. If we should care to play at this point the game known as "The Ifs of History" we should reveal a curious paradox. If the plan for Whitney's Oregon road had been carried out, the transcontinental problem might not have become involved with the sectional controversy of North and South which, at this moment, became violent, and more than a dozen years of delay would have been avoided. On the other hand, if Whitney had been encouraged by Congress to pursue his plans, it is almost certain that, when the change came in the focus of the country's interest, they could never have been financed.

Whitney persisted nevertheless and Davis tells us that "his entire fortune is said to have been spent in the attempt to realize his dream of a Pacific railway, and the 'prince of projectors' to have kept a dairy and sold milk in Washington for a livelihood in his declining years."[10] There is no doubt that his efforts at promotion, circularization, publicity, and Congressional lobbying were continuous and untiring for more than five years and that the effect upon the public of these things, bolstered by the sound technical advices which he brought forth, was to destroy the last doubt in the common mind of the practicability of joining the oceans by rail. And whatever may have been in his mind about a legitimate personal profit from the enterprise, he stands out as a flaming torch of altruism against the group of promoters who were later successful.

In the light of the later behavior of these men, the attitude of Congress toward Whitney was interesting. The last bill for his project, introduced in 1849–50, conceded other possibilities than the northern route. This concession was a reluctant compromise on Whitney's part and made against his deepest beliefs. But he was induced to think that a bill which specified no route would be easier to pass than one which insisted on an adamant plan. Perhaps he felt that if the bill passed, he might later insist on his Oregon dream. But the compromise merely added to his undoing.

Because the bill specified no route, Whitney was attacked as having a deep-laid plan to "dictate terms to states and municipalities desirous of lying on the proposed railway."[11] He was accused of being a stock-jobber, a money maker, a manipulator, and it was said that his railroad would become an irrevocable monopoly. But, as Haney points out, powerful interests and deep sectional jealousies were beneath the opposition.[12]

So, though public doubt had largely disappeared and though public necessity seemed irresistible, Congress was unable to act in the matter of the transcontinental railway. At the beginning of the fifties a political element entered the controversy which

[10]John P. Davis, *The Union Pacific Railway*, Chicago, 1894, p. 33. This is not, however, the story told by M. L. Brown, *op. cit.*, who describes him as dropping the whole effort in 1852 and continuing his life as "a polished gentleman of the old school," taking daily horseback rides over his estate.

[11]Lewis Henry Haney, *A Congressional History of Railways in the U. S. to 1850*, Madison, Wis., 1908, p. 418.

[12]*Ibid.*, p. 420.

was to hold back the technological triumph for many years.

The long-growing jealousy between North and South came into the foreground of every picture when the new Mexican states were admitted.

3

A railroad in mid-century America had two economic aspects, one before and one after the fact. If it ran through a well-populated and wealthy region, its construction would be easier to finance; yet once it was built it could be counted on to bring population and wealth to whatever country it traversed. The question as to what portion of the continent so vital an artery as the transcontinental should cross was thus open to endless debate.

The nation which was in the making in 1850, though a democracy in constitutional form and in spirit, had, nevertheless, from some points of view, much of the look of an empire. Both the South and the West were, in a sense, colonies of the Northeast. The Northeast manufactured, the South and West supplied raw material and food supplies. An industrial revolution having swept the civilized world, the dominating centers were the centers of manufacture. These became also the centers of finance and, as capital became more fluid, money flowed into them giving them a dictatorial power over the economics of the other sections.

The West and South having a common colonial color had stood together against the Northeast on many grounds. Together they had fought a protective tariff which put power into the hands of the industrialists. They might have continued to stand together but for a natural divergence on a single issue. That issue was slavery, and slave labor was simply not adapted to western agriculture under the McCormick pattern. Neither was it adaptable to western diversities of climate or the frontier heritage.

As the country grew in territory, the South wanted the new land determined by the slave issue. A new state which permitted slavery could be counted on to stand with the states whose very existence was believed to depend on slave labor. But some of the new states saw at once the economic impossibility of slavery for themselves, and many of the older western states saw the danger of political dominance in Washington by the slave-state bloc. So came the split between the West and the South. Reluctantly the West gravitated toward the industrial Northeast, drawn by the instinct of self-preservation, and the slave-free issue came into sharp relief as the dominant American conflict.

Naturally the South wanted a Pacific railroad to run through as many slave states as possible and bring wealth to what was already thought of as the southern nation. Southerners saw at the same time the terrible danger to them of creating that wealth in the free states. California's determination to be free made the issue convulsive. It became extremely bitter and it is not surprising that, for ten years, no decision could be reached as to the route of the new span west of the Mississippi.

This delay may have been providential. It gave the technological department an opportunity to make itself equal to the colossal enterprise. When, finally, the Civil War eliminated the advocates of the southern route, the engineers were ready to go to work.

By this time locomotives had vastly improved; they had been adapted to coal; they had acquired a power equal to steep grades. They were flexible enough to take the extreme curves necessary in mountain climbing. The peculiar American road-beds, culverts, bridges, embankments, and so on, had become adequate for the American train. These were quite different from those of Europe.

American railroad building had from the start an economic control. The long distances to be traversed put the solid and straight-line English method out of the question.

The English built their roads to conform to their locomotives. The English locomotive was made to move in a straight line. Its axles were fixed to the same rigid, massive frame that supported the boiler. So if there were curves in the track they must be very gradual. The rails must be at precisely the same level. Thus, in building their roads, English engineers had to cut and tunnel

34

through the hills rather than climb them by spiral or zigzagged track. The expense of such a road would have become prohibitive for long distances.

In America, therefore, the cost of way and track became the dominant consideration. It must be cut to a minimum and the locomotive must conform to the result. The result was a snake-

Locomotive development
Showing flexible frame for curves and uneven track compared with rigid English construction.
Top: American locomotive. *Bottom:* English locomotive
From Charles Barnard's *English and American Locomotives*

like track which wound its way over the mountains and the locomotive became a loose-fitted, flexible machine of great power. It was built to take all the punishment inflicted by sharp turns and by rough, cheaply built roadbed and to spring back into place with no damage. It became a marvel of suppleness and balance and most of the American inventions which went into its making were directed toward the equalizing of weight, the absorption of shocks and a quick adaptability to changes of direction, grade, and unevenness of track. During the fifties most of these inventions were improved.[13]

The main problems, however, of a line of track which should cross four ranges of mountains, many rivers, canyons and other terrific natural obstacles were problems of civil engineering. The building of timber bridges was an art which developed early in the United States. Such highway bridges as the Amoskeag across the Merrimack at Manchester, New Hampshire, in 1792, were great engineering achievements for the period. This one had six spans of ninety-two feet. There was also the Bellows Falls Bridge which crossed the Connecticut with two spans of one hundred and eighty-four feet, begun in 1785 and completed seven years later. Another, in 1803, designed and constructed by a Pennsylvania carpenter to cross the Delaware lasted, as a highway bridge, for forty-five years when it was improved for railroad use and was not finally replaced by iron until 1875. The Colossus Bridge was built to span the Schuylkill (340 feet) in 1812. These older wooden bridges were built with the utmost care and pride of workmanship and only of well-seasoned timber.[14]

As the railroad developed, however, bridges came into such rapid demand that there was not enough seasoned wood to supply it. It was then that the valuable American invention of the Howe truss appeared. This was adjustable to the shrinkage of the wood through a system of bolting. It used, also, vertical iron ties in combination with the timber chords and the timber struts arranged in lattice.[15] It was invented in 1840 by William Howe of Massachusetts, uncle of the famous Elias Howe, inventor of the sewing machine, was patented, and brought him, we are happy to report, a very sizeable fortune.[16] It came into universal

[13]Charles Barnard's "English and American Locomotives," in *Harper's Monthly Magazine*, Vol. LVIII, No. 346, March, 1879, p. 555, gives an excellent comparison.
[14]Thomas Curtis Clarke, "The Building of a Railway," in *Scribner's Magagine*, Vol. III, No. 6, June, 1888, p. 658.
[15]James Robert Mosse, "American Timber Bridges," *Proc.*, Inst. C. E. (London), XXII, pp. 306 ff.
[16]Carl W. Mitman, "William Howe," *Dictionary of American Biography*, IX, p. 298.

use on American railroads during the next thirty years and may be considered one of the indispensable inventions in the development of the railroad in this country. Its greatest drawback was that it was so easy to set afire. Large numbers of them burned. But with the slow development of iron and steel in America, most of the great railway systems which were laid out before 1870 could not have been built without this invention.

Embankment building
Showing how the railroads were, to some extent, able to construct themselves

One fact that early became evident was that a railroad could build itself. Once a mile of track had been laid, trains could be run on it bearing material for the next mile. Timber being cheap, temporary structures were built of it all along the line, strong enough to bear the trains laden with material, though not intended to endure. Thus, in making a culvert, a trestle was built first. This was then covered with earth carried by the construction train. Enormous embankments were built simply by dropping gravel from cars through a temporary wooden bridge. Where a masonry bridge was to be built in a stoneless country, a temporary wooden bridge would go up first; then as the stone was brought by the trains from a distance, the masonry work could be entirely finished without ever interrupting traffic.

Rails, spikes, tools and men were brought by train to the point where the track was to be laid. Sometimes ballast and ties were also brought in this way and often all bridge material. It was only the preliminary work of "location" and grading which the locomotive could not do.

Another singular function of the railroad was to finance its own construction. As soon as a reasonable length of track was laid, it was used for passenger traffic, and the revenue from this encouraged the investors. This system was used also with some of the lock canals.

The civil engineers who finally built the railroad to the Pacific profited greatly from their experience in the Civil War. Here the job of reconstructing wrecked bridges and roads in the shortest possible time taxed the ingenuity of the army engineers to the limit of human resource. The transcontinental was built, largely, by ex-soldiers.

In his memoirs, General Grant describes some of the work done by these men in the war:

The road from Nashville to Decatur passes over a broken country, cut up with innumerable streams, many of them of considerable width, and with valleys far below the roadbed. All the bridges over these had been destroyed, and the rails taken up and twisted by the enemy. All the cars and locomotives not carried off had been destroyed as effectually as they knew how to destroy them. All bridges and culverts had been destroyed between Nashville and Decatur, and thence to Stevenson where the Memphis and Charleston and the Nashville and Chattanooga roads unite. . . .

General Dodge . . . was an experienced railroad builder. He had no tools to work with except those of the pioneers—axes, picks and spades. . . . Blacksmiths were detailed and set to work making tools necessary in railroad and bridge building. Axemen were put to work getting out timber for bridges and cutting fuel for locomotives when the road should be completed. Car-builders were set to work repairing the locomotives and cars. Thus every branch of railroad building, making tools to work with, and supplying the workmen with food, was all going on at once, and without the aid of a mechanic or laborer except what the command itself furnished. . . .

38

General Dodge had the work assigned him finished within forty days after receiving his orders. The number of bridges to rebuild was one hundred and eighty-two, many of them over deep and wide chasms; the length of road repaired was one hundred and two miles.[17]

This cold record covers one of the most intensive activities in the history of American civil engineering. Because it was taken in the stride of war no monument commemorates it. Because it was mere reconstruction of a pre-existing fact, it seems to have had no creative significance. Yet in true history the transcontinental was its normal creative sequel. The Union Pacific Railroad is the existing and immortal monument to the engineers of Nashville and Decatur. General Dodge was its construction chief.

It is ignorant to deny the benefits of war to the history of invention. When we have invented a device to eliminate war we must combine with our invention something to replace its quickening technological impulse. In American history we shall find a period of rapid advance in applied science following every war.

The difficulty is that along with this technological advance there comes, invariably, a social throwback and, often, an economic upheaval. So after the Civil War there was in Washington a brutal dictatorship over the South, with the Constitution gone by the board; in the whole of the southland we see political and economic white slavery as a concomitant of black freedom. We see power concentrated in a handful of men, we see a travesty of democracy, we see vast profits pouring into the pockets of dishonest opportunists whose every act rubs salt in the open wounds of the conquered, and we see the great technological advance itself moving hand in hand with a financial thievery scarcely equalled in our history and seeming to give irresistible impetus to plutocracy.

It is well to remember then that the efforts of the engineer soldiers between Nashville and Decatur were not lost.[18]

[17]U. S. Grant, *Personal Memoirs,* New York, 1886, II, 46–48.
[18]To any one who watched the army engineers at work during the World War it must have been obvious that the "machine age" had not dissolved such human capacities.

4

In more than one way, the transcontinental road was largely a product of the Civil War. For more than a dozen years, the threat of the war had stood in its way. With the secession of the southern states and the outbreak of war, this obstacle disappeared. When the southern senators and representatives were removed from the Congress, the determination of the route was a simple matter. Thus, even with the war in full career, and, indeed, giving to the North a series of highly unfavorable military indices, it was possible to pass through Congress an act incorporating the Union Pacific Company and offering to that organization a large government bounty. The bill was signed by Lincoln on July 1, 1862, during the failure of the Peninsula Campaign and two months before the second Confederate victory at Bull Run. Was it, perhaps, a relief to the tormented President to be able to turn from the sad performance in the war theatre to the practical fulfilment of his early dream?

It is certain that he gave all the details of the bill as careful consideration as if the country were in the midst of a prosperous peace. It provided for a board of commissioners appointed by name. There were one hundred and fifty-eight of these who were to work in concert with five government commissioners. The bill provided for the issue and control of stock and for a government loan per mile of completed track. It provided for a right of way and land grants on each side of it. It laid out the general direction the route was to take. It provided for connection with existing railroads and for a general amalgamation of companies. It arranged that the Central Pacific, a California corporation already in existence, should build eastward to meet the government-created Union Pacific and be equally subsidized.

Steps were taken to alter the bill as soon as it was discovered that it failed to draw the investors' money. It must, the Congress decided, be made more attractive. From that moment the corridors of the Capitol were crowded with lobbyists jostling one another to reach the ears of congressmen. There were lobbies from cities wanting to be on the new line, financial lobbies opposing the stock arrangements, industrial lobbies hoping for favors, and "shysters and adventurers hoping for something to turn up."[19] Most curious of all were the lobbies advocating various track gauges.

It is astonishing to us that nontechnical men, politicians, and legislators should have wrangled so over the gauge of a track. Yet, judging by the debates, it was a matter of life and death to these people whether the rails of the new road be four feet eight and a half inches, five feet, or five feet three inches apart. Countless days in and out of the Capitol were consumed in this argument.

It must be remembered, however, that in 1862 there were at least six different track gauges in general use in the country.[20] So, obviously, certain railroad companies were anxious to have the Pacific road build a track on which their rolling stock might move. We may assume that manufacturers of locomotives and cars were also interested.

Now, the bill of 1862 had given the job of deciding on the gauge to the President. So, in January, 1863, between the Emancipation Proclamation and the reorganization of the Army of the Potomac, Lincoln cheerfully turned aside to discuss matters of inches on a railroad track. No sooner, however, had he given his decision based on extensive research and the advice of the experts than Congress overruled it practically without debate. Lincoln's decision of five feet was given on the 24th of January; Congress, which had specified by law that the President's decision should be final, overthrew it on the 2d of March. The Congressional gauge of four feet eight and a half inches has since become standard for almost the entire world.

The new act of 1864 removed the objections of the earlier act. It was generous beyond the dreams of the first framers. What was originally a loan had become, practically, a subsidy. The Union Pacific and Central Pacific companies were now allowed a parallel bond issue of their own of first mortgage bonds, while the government bonds had a subordinate lien. To all intents and

[19]*Congressional Globe*, 40th Congress, 2d Session, p. 2135, March 26, 1868. Quoted by Davis, p. 125.
[20]Dunbar cites twelve in all including the smallest railroads. *History of Travel*, Appendix C, p. 1393.

purposes the Government had insured the companies against failure.

The subsidies or "bonuses" as they have often been called ran from $32,000 to $96,000 per mile, depending upon the nature of the country to be traversed. The land grants provided in 1862 were doubled. The stock of the Union Pacific Company was made attractive by the device of dividing it into a million shares of a hundred dollars each. Other provisions built this new act into a document before which we stand amazed today; it is a government bolstering of private enterprise on a scale which has never been approached in world history. It was a spur to "rugged individualism" in business and finance which produced one of the last great outbursts of the individualist impulse. We are still suffering from its effect. We are no longer haunted by the ghosts of the lives and fortunes it destroyed. But many of our free spirits chafe under the regimentation it began. From the prodigality of the government-father of the transcontinental has stemmed a very different variety of paternalism.

It would have been scarcely human if individuals to whom such magnificence and protection were offered on a gold platter had failed to take advantage of it for the advancement of their private fortunes. They did so almost immediately. Investors no longer held back when, as an editorial of the period proclaimed, "No bonds issued by any other Company in the country, or, as far as we know in the world, are made so secure by a responsible government."[21] Enormous sums thus came into the unrestricted control of a few persons.

Manipulation of stock, bulls and bears, short-selling were tricks which had often already been used in America. The picturesque Commodore Vanderbilt had built his railroad system in the East largely on the practice of ruining small roads. The Gould-Fisk-Drew triumvirate were already notorious for their games with the Erie which not only brought financial ruin to hundreds of speculators but caused, it was said, many tragic physical accidents.[22] So the public was not unaccustomed to such things.

[21]*Harper's Weekly*, Vol. XI, No. 568, Nov. 16, 1867, p. 723.
[22]Report of the Committee on Railroads, N. Y. State Senate, Jan. 14, 1869.

h corn before the
ppreciate the lux-
sells now in the
while the grades
$12 5c. Not
' as for-
early
een

of
all
est
in
-e-
n-
he
ed
ay,
ns
rt
·h
·h
'e,
rn
sti-

eely
·nd.
1 as
the
sely
ire.
·es
i-
-
y
1
5
e
',
·r
5,
1s
8
·

THE UNION PACIFIC RAILROAD.

ATTENTION has been frequently called in this journal to the marvels of engineering skill accomplished in the construction of the Union Pacific Railroad. No road of its length and magnitude was ever before contemplated, much less attempted; and no such work was ever before prosecuted by the most energetic of men or races, under such adverse circumstances as a war with the barbarous tribes whose country the road traverses, and the present high and unexampled cost of all necessary building materials. Few roads were ever built in a country of greater natural difficulties, for it crosses the two highest ranges of mountains in the country. And yet, in spite of these natural, social, and financial obstacles five hundred miles of the road have been completed in an incredibly short period of time, at once astonishing the scientific and laboring world

But this very material revolution thus accomplished in the construction of the Pacific Railroad is insignificant compared to that commercial revolution which is to follow, of necessity, its completion. When the line stretches unbroken from Omaha to Sacramento, it will affect, not merely the rapid settlement of our vast Western States and Territories; it will not merely influence the tide of German and Irish emigration, swelling it, and facilitating that transfer of energy, industry, and genius from the East to the West which has been going on for scores and scores of centuries; it will not merely affect the cultivation of the wide prairie lands of the West, where corn and wheat grow almost without care, and countless cattle can be grazed and reared without cost; it will not merely develop fully the riches of the vast mining regions of the great mountains, bringing the most extensive mining field of the world within the grasp of the capitalist, the reach of the laborer, the centre of civilization; but it is to affect the trade of all the world, and to pour into the lap of this metropolis and this country the riches and labor of the Old World as well as the New. Ten thousand emigrants from China delve in the tunnels of the road through the Sierra Nevada, and fifty thousand from Germany and Ireland have followed it across the Plains. It will in the same way attract hither the capital of the East, and will make America not merely the short route from Asia to Europe, but the stopping-point, the mart for both Europe and Asia, and Americans will be the merchantmen of the world.

The editorial on the Union Pacific Railroad as it appeared in *Harper's Weekly*, November 16, 1867

hundred miles of the route across the Plains were finished last month; the mountain line across the Sierra Nevada was finished the month before, and the line across the Rocky Mountains and the Humboldt Valley, 419 miles, alone remain to be constructed. This great progress in the work ought to be sufficient inducement to capitalists of the country to invest in the bonds of the Company which are now on the market; but, as if it were not, the treasurer, Hon. JOHN J. CISCO has lately put forward a statement of the financial condition of the Company of the most interesting and encouraging character. From this statement it appears that to meet the estimated cost of the road—$83,445,012—the Company already has in government bonds and land grants, paid in capital, etc., over $85,000,-000, or about $2,000,000 more than the estimated cost. The bonds are in the market, and are being largely invested in, and there is little doubt that the present Company will finish the road in the time promised, but if it does not, the Government, which authorizes and charters the line, must complete it, for the work is now one of such national importance that the people insist upon its vigorous prosecution as positively as they insisted on the prosecution of the late war. It is really necessary to the material reconstruction of the Union, and will add equally to its strength, vigor, vitality, and wealth.

The bonds now thrown on the market are the Company's First Mortgage bonds. The Company is authorized by Congress to issue its First Mortgage bonds in the same amounts as are issued by the Government on the various sections of the road as they are completed, viz.

On the first 517 miles at $16,000 per mile	$8,272,000
On Rocky Mountain region, 150 miles, at $48,000 per mile	7,200,000
On 433 additional miles at $32,000 per mile	13,856,000
Total for 1100 miles	$29,328,000

These bonds bear thirty years to run from last July, and bear interest at the rate of six per cent. per annum *in gold*, payable on the first days of January and July in the city of New York. As they are coupon bonds, the semi-annual coupons will be cashed by any bank or banker throughout the country. Congress has taken more especial care that the interests of the bond-holders of this road shall be secured than has ever been shown toward a similar enterprise. The mortgage is made to Hon. E. D. MORGAN, United States Senator from New York, and Hon. OAKES AMES, Member of United States House of Representatives from Massachusetts, who alone can deliver the bonds to the Company, and who are responsible for their delivery in strict accordance with the terms of the law. To give every facility for the negotiation of the First Mortgage bonds now issued, the Government makes its own bonds issued to the Company a second lien upon the road, with the understanding that the interest, and a part, if not all the principal, may be paid by services rendered at a future day. We may say without danger of contradiction that no bonds issued by any other Company in this country, or, so far as we know, in the world, are made so secure by a responsible government as the First Mortgage Bonds of the Union Pacific Railroad Company.

They were, however, considered not so much immoral as "smart." Thus, even in the sixties, the bacillus of corruption had begun its long inroads on the public conscience.

The directors of the Union Pacific hit upon the happy expedient of creating a "construction company" which it should pay for the work. That the directors of this company which presently

43

appeared under the grand, mysterious, foreign and unpronounce-able name of the Crédit Mobilier of America, should be identical with the directors of the Union Pacific seems to us naïve. It was, however, "smart" in 1865. Far more scandalous things were in vogue, such as the manipulation of army defeats on the Wall Street exchange.

This device, however, was only one of many similar inventions for filling the pockets of the railroad kings. Later, when the transcontinental roads were complete, these monarchs became emperors. In the open they dictated to Congress with an author-ity and on a scale which even the great industrial dictatorships of today scarcely dare attempt in the obscurity of the Capitol's corridors. The infant cities of the West they held in the hollow of their hand. By rate discriminations, by promises and threats of branch lines, by the favoring of certain industries and the devastation of others, by coercion and bribery with passes to legis-lators, they produced a series of swindles which made the Crédit Mobilier look like the job of an amateur bag-snatcher. These operations (which now form a good-sized lore of their own) have been described in detail by many writers;[23] they are beyond our province except where they contributed their strong force to the final collective result which is important to the history of invention. They were products of the heyday of capital. At the time adverse criticism was regarded as pure socialism.

But there was a brighter obverse of the railroad coin. We have mentioned the sharp contrast between these operators and the technicians. The men who did the work of construction were true heroes. The pressure upon them was dictated by the finan-cial conditions which demanded a fast rate of progress. This was achieved by the maintenance of a military discipline on the job. General Dodge carried the army tradition of Nashville and De-catur on into the Union Pacific of which he was chief engineer. His organization provided not only for the efficient march of the construction but also against enemy attack by the plains Indians who rightly saw in the railroad an instrument of their extinction.

[23]Notably Gustavus Myers, *Great American Fortunes,* Chicago, 1910, and Matthew Josephson, *Robber Barons,* N. Y., 1934

TRANSCONTINENTAL

Thus the workers had occasionally to be soldiers in fact and the engineers officers. Their performance in the face of hardships far beyond the comprehension of modern society was equal to that of any army in our history. With the calm self-effacement of the soldier they met the obstacles of terrain, climate, altitude, enemy ambush and mass attack. The engineers met the new daily problems of the "permanent way" with spontaneous intellectual power, inventing as they went the means of traversing mountain passes, canyons, rivers, deserts and plains. Summer and winter the work went on in defiance of tornadoes and blizzards, droughts and torrential rains. To these people the financial disease, the graft, the greed and the power-lust did not penetrate. Though there were lurid tales of vice in the construction towns, of liquor, gambling, whoring—usual in any herd of sweating men—it is hard to believe that their energies were dissipated for long or that corruption ever reached their souls.

The plan was that the two corporations should start at the termini of the projected railroad and move toward each other. The Central Pacific Company was to move east from Sacramento and the Union Pacific Company was to move west from Omaha. The first plan confined the activities of the Central Pacific to the state of California where it was supposed that they would encounter difficulties which would occupy them many years but as they overcame these obstacles in a fraction of the expected time, this plan was modified to provide that each company continue until both met regardless of state boundaries.

The building of a railroad requires a series of steps, the first of which is "location." The "reconnaissance" is made by an advance party of engineers, men capable of looking at a landscape and seeing, in fancy, the railroad upon it. From their sketches, the "preliminary survey" is made with instruments and the map and profile plotted in sections. The "approximate location" with all its curves is then staked out. Plans and specifications for grading, culverts, trestles and bridges are then made. On the transcontinental with its immense land grants, the material for this work could usually be found on the railroad's own land. As this land was explored, valuable mineral deposits were found

45

and the way was sometimes altered from the first plans to pass near them. The presence of useful material was a factor in the location of the road which sometimes outweighed the adverse factor of difficult country.

In construction the graders came first. While they worked, cutting and filling according to the profile, the axemen worked in the woods cutting the ties. The co-ordination of axemen, transportation of material and graders had to be carefully planned in the unforested regions. The graders, followed by the axemen, were followed in turn by the tie layers and these immediately by the construction trains with the rails. These were often drawn, in the advance sections, by horses. The rhythm of all this building was worked out by the army engineers to a degree which eliminated delay.

Rails, locomotives and cars came overland on existing roads to Omaha for the Union Pacific. For the Central Pacific, they had to be carried by water round Cape Horn or via Panama.

Construction began in 1864. The early problems of planning and organization, interrupted, at first, by labor shortage due to the war and delayed by many other matters, were so difficult that in two years only fifty-six miles from the west and forty from the east were laid. The end of the war brought thousands of discharged soldiers to the work. At the Pacific end, Chinese labor was adopted. In 1866, then, there was immense acceleration, track was laid at the rate of a mile a day; this was increased before 1869 so that in places, under the extraordinary inspiration of Jack Casement, who was a kind of Stakhanov of his day, eight miles a day were laid. The job was completed in May, 1869, when the famous gold and silver spikes were driven at Promontory Point.

No story of the transcontinental has ever omitted the account of the celebration when the two locomotives kissed in a bath of champagne. We shall omit it, therefore, except for a single detail which impinges upon the history of invention. The ceremonious driving of the final spike into the laurel tie was telegraphically communicated to a nation which, from coast to coast, quivered with excitement. We are told that a circuit-breaking effected by

the blows themselves rang bells in New York, New Orleans and
San Francisco while the multitudes held their breath.[24] In our
radio-informed world in which the coughs and sputters of heavy-
weight heroes, sweepstake-winners, leaders in beauty contests
and cross-word puzzles are interspersed with the news of war or
crime, depravity, persecution or terror via the dynamic qualities
of a super-laxative, there is a peculiar poignancy in this story.
That men should weep in the streets at a signal which marked
the end of an achievement in engineering is evidence of an emotion far enough removed from our habit to stir us as we meet it
in the record. The bells rang in a new age yet they tolled for
that naïve amazement at technical magic which was passing
forever in the moment.

5

No single triumph of invention so altered the face of America
as did the transcontinental railroad. Along its way came towns
like mushrooms; tentacles from it felt out sources of mineral
wealth and made them exploitable; the great swath of land
which Government had laid along its sides came suddenly alive;
men and women by thousands moved over it from Norway and
Sweden and Germany; wheat sprang out of the ground as if
drawn by the genii of the smoky engine; elevators, gigantic flour
mills, dotting the path, centralized the new industry of food;
the civilizations of the crowded East and still more crowded
Europe were scattered broadcast over the empty land; the Indian
fled and the buffalo vanished; unorganized territory crystallized
into states—political units with written philosophies of government; the whole structure of democracy took form following its
older pattern as the fluid space froze beneath its feet.

These changes did not take place without convulsions. Social
inertia was too strong. The giants took quick advantage of it—
of the laissez-faire legend, for instance, which government had
so wisely followed in the elastic epoch; of pioneer self-law and
devil-take-the-hindmost; of golden opportunity and the divine
rights postulated by a Destiny which would become as time went

[24]Dunbar, p. 1356.

on conspicuously less manifest. But in those days the giants gathered men like sheep about them. To insure docility they drew heavily upon Europe where men were little aware of "equality" or individual initiative. James J. Hill, having created an empire out of railroad land, peopled it with German Mennonites. Whether or not he explained to them the equality postulate of the Declaration they became equal only under him and presently units in a hierarchy. Men like Collis P. Huntington and Leland Stanford bought the state of California lock, stock, barrel, body and soul, out of their railroad earnings and played joyously with their toy, at least until the financiers of the Comstock lode grabbed it away from them.[25]

And then the collective force which, basically, had animated all these games destroyed them. It seemed as if a fluid came out of the very ground the docile sheep were treading, the American ground, the ground of equality. (The farmers of Minnesota, the Dakotas and Iowa are not docile sheep today.) From amazed wonder at the giants they turned to the united hate of men imbued with the democracy of the soil. Out of it came the gigantic force of the Grange.

Secret freight rates were not democratic. Discriminating passes were not democratic. Bribery and intimidation were instruments of plutocracy. Government must intervene. Government created the railroad and government must control it. What is government? We, they replied with surprising awareness, are the Government.

It was at this point that an astonishing discovery was made. The old reliable efficacy of state law suddenly melted. A clause, little invoked, in the Federal Constitution became dominant. The capitalists first forged their own chains by invoking it against the state laws which were limiting them. This was the clause about interstate commerce. As far as the transcontinental went, Congress must be supreme. So Congress must lay down a pattern for the length and breadth of the transcontinental. This was the will of the operators but its benefits to them lasted only until the sovereignty of the people could be transferred to Washington

[25]For the full story, see George D. Lyman, *Ralston's Ring*, N. Y., 1937.

from the state capitals. When this happened the elasticity was gone. A federal pattern must always be more rigid than a set of local patterns. Thus invention completed the destruction of the old league of nations which had been the United States. The railroad began the whole mechanism of interstate commerce regulation which has been tightening, centralizing and standardizing the nation ever since.

The term "transcontinental" was soon pluralized. Within a decade, there were four trunk lines: the Northern Pacific, the Union Pacific, the Santa Fé and the Southern Pacific. The Northern Pacific realized at last the dream of Asa Whitney. The others extended the new civilization longitudinally as well as laterally. Each played its part in tightening the new national scheme.

6

But can we call the transcontinental "an invention"? In a large sense it may be so called and, as a whole, society was its inventor. Technically, it was a great series of inventions, most of them in civil engineering, many of them never dignified by patents. As soon as it was built it created a number of new technical needs. One of them was for better brakes for rolling stock.

George Westinghouse was a born inventor but with his native mechanical genius was combined a vision of large-scale production much like that of Eli Whitney. Thus his invention of the air-brake became quickly marketable: because he invented the means of its manufacture as well as its mechanical operation it came very rapidly into use.

Train-braking, before 1869, was a tedious and dangerous performance. On each car was a horizontal wheel which wound a chain round a staff and so brought the brake-shoes against the circumference of the car wheels. With these brakes, to synchronize the retardation of a train was almost impossible. On passenger trains, the absence of synchronization often caused accidents and at best continual discomfort. On freight trains the difficulty was multiplied by the fact that the only passageway between the cars was over their tops and by the fact that because of a necessary insufficiency of brakemen in relation to the number of cars, a special technique of braking a train must be developed. The freight brakemen moving atop the cars were exposed to many kinds of hardship and danger.

Thus the Westinghouse invention was revolutionary and vital to the success of the American railroad. It worked by changes of air-pressure in reservoirs on each car connected by a continuous pipe to a master reservoir on the locomotive. By a brilliant device called the "triple valve," the brakes were applied when the pressure in the pipe was *reduced,* not when it was increased. Thus if the air pipe which ran under the entire train should be cut by a parting of cars the resultant decrease in pressure in the pipe under the cut-off cars would cause the brakes on those cars to be automatically applied. The engineer controls the braking by opening a valve which allows air to escape from the main pipe: this causes simultaneous braking throughout the train. What actually happened was that reduced pressure in the pipe caused the relatively increased pressure in the reservoirs to apply mechanical action to the wheels.

Westinghouse secured his first air-brake patent in 1869 when he was not yet twenty-three. The automatic brake came three years later. In the development of full automaticity there were twenty patents.[26] He then turned his attention to signalling and here his talent for organization was useful in forming the inventions of others as well as his own into a system. His electrical career seems to have started from this point.

The "block system" was a combination of the telegraph and the semaphore. "Block" simply means a section of track: not more than one train must occupy it at a time. As a train enters it a semaphore is raised against the next train; as the first train leaves the block, the semaphore is lowered. For a long time this system remained subject to human error. As late as 1889, we may read objections to automatic signalling.

Next the air-brake the most useful invention was the automatic coupler. Eli Janney was a farmer, an amateur inventor who thought out his device while watching the switching of cars and whittled it out of wood. It consisted of two knuckles which closed

[26]Henry G. Prout, *Life of George Westinghouse*, N. Y., 1921, Chap. II.

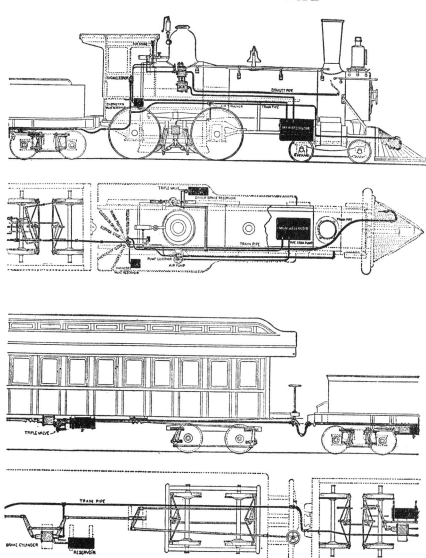

The air brake

Side and top views of Westinghouse air-brake apparatus. The air-brake gear is shown by shaded area, the reservoir and pipes in solid black

upon each other as soon as they came in contact. It eliminated the need of a brakeman risking his life by going between the cars to link them together. Janney's first patent was in 1873 and was improved until the Master Car-Builder's Association (a product of industrial collectivization) adopted it in 1888. It is still the standard coupler.

A multiplicity of devices for safety and comfort came along

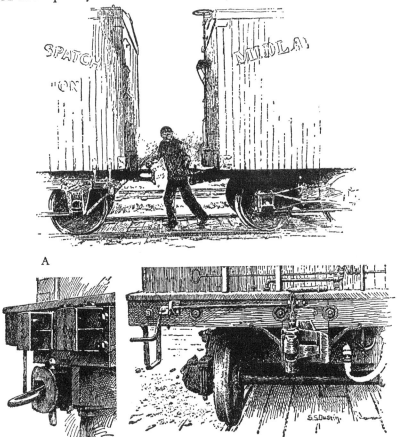

Couplers, old and new

A. The hazardous operation of coupling cars with the link and pin system.   B. Detail of the link and pin coupler.   C. The Janney automatic coupler

rapidly; among them the signal cord, gas lighting, the vestibule, steam heating, the sleeping car, the Pullman, and Wagner "palace" cars. These last were magnificent testimonials to what has been called "The Gilded Age."

7

The record of the transcontinental is probably the greatest story in American history. Any chapter of it contains as much romance as all the wars and politics put together. Its ramifications are infinite, it touches every aspect of society. Through it the nation came into its prime, the old empire disappeared, industry came out of its eastern stronghold, and men and things were standardized from coast to coast. Men at the extremities knew and understood one another in spite of differences in climate and soil—not because of closer physical contact but because they used the same things: their bread and meat and iron came from the same sources.

Iron. . . . Here, indeed, was the *sine qua non* of the new transport. More than anything else the railroad made the demand for it irresistible. As we watch the continuity of iron rails across our land we are in the presence of a new symbol. It is the symbol of rigidity: of strength surely, but a unifying strength. A pattern outlined in this material can be elastic no more.

"The Public be D——d!"

This cartoon shows general reaction to so-called Robber Barons. This cartoon is the result of Vanderbilt's reply to questions on his railroad policy

Daily Graphic, October 12, 1882

Chapter Four

STEEL AND STANDARDIZATION

I

WHETHER the Kelley-Bessemer process was first invented in America or in England is a question of little importance. It was not a process merely for making steel but for making cheap steel. It was designed for commerce and its perfection made steel the skeleton of many societies. That it became the skeleton of America before it was the skeleton of England was due to many things: to the weakness of our still temporary structure and to our desire to make ourselves over; to the urgent demands of transport; to the need of conquering physical obstacles such as rivers, mountain crevasses, and other difficult gaps; to the demands of the interchangeable parts system and machine manufacture, but most of all to industrial rather than inventive genius. The kind of organization which formed the basis of cheap steel in America was a product of individual impulse collectively applied. Its result was collective.

The dates of Kelley and Bessemer in the inventive field prove nothing. The important point in history is the point at which the converters produced a serviceable metal in quantity. This point was about the same in time in America and in Europe, and many other persons had by then played a part in the perfection of the process.

William Kelley was born (significantly) in Pittsburgh in 1811. In that year a rolling mill was built there. The town was already important in the manufacture of iron.[1]

As the boy grew up, this importance increased rapidly. By the time he was fifteen there were five rolling mills, some of them

[1] James M. Swank, *History of the Manufacture of Iron in All Ages*, Phila., 1892, p. 227.

steam-operated, four slitting mills, and fifteen hundred persons, or better than 10 per cent of the population, were employed in the manufacture of iron. We are told that in his youth Kelley had been an eager "student of metallurgy"[2]—a high-sounding word for the science of the period—and certainly his environment favored such a study. It did not prevent him from going into the dry goods business, however, in which, presumably, his wealthy father set him up. We find him, at thirty-five, still in it and belatedly making love to a beautiful girl of sixteen whom he met at Nashville, Tennessee, on a selling tour. Miss Gracy married him and took him to Eddyville, Kentucky, where her father was prosperous in tobacco. There, stumbling over pieces of rich hematite which lay all over the surface of the ground, his metallurgical fever returned with a rush. So he sent for his brother John (also his dry goods partner) and they bought land and set up a furnace.

Iron and steel at that period were still produced in the old way[3] though with improved furnaces and bloomeries. The quantity of carbon contained in the various kinds was still regulated by rule-of-thumb methods, for chemistry, in America at least, was a largely unknown science. Wrought iron was produced by a partial melting in the bloomery with stirring of the bloom to remove the carbon. It was also produced by remelting pig iron while a blast of air oxydized it or combined with the carbon in a gas. This process was becoming more common, as it produced larger quantities but it consumed more fuel. Cast iron and pig iron, which have a high carbon content, were still made in blast furnaces where the iron was melted to liquid and a lime flux combined with the impurities of the ore to form slag. Steel was still made by heating wrought iron in the presence of pulverized charcoal to put carbon into it, either by the blister or the crucible method. The quantity of steel thus produced was very small.

It is superfluous to go into further detail about these processes. We need remember only that the nature of the product depended upon the amount of carbon it contained. Wrought iron, which

[2]John Newton Boucher, *William Kelley: A True History of the So-called Bessemer Process,* Greensburg, Pa., 1924, p. 3.
[3]*M. I. M.,* pp. 107 ff.

was soft and malleable, was made by removing carbon. The hard and brittle cast iron and pig iron were made by mixing fuel and ore and heating the fuel so hot that the iron was reduced to liquid in which state it absorbed carbon from the fuel. Steel was made by the cumbersome process of first removing the carbon to make wrought iron and then putting it back during a reheating.

Now Kelley began with pig iron which he transformed into wrought iron by reheating it while a blast of air removed the carbon. In this process, the iron first melted to liquid then, as the carbon left it, it partly solidified into a paste even in the presence of continuous and intense heat. In other words, iron seemed to be less hot once the carbon was removed no matter how much external heat you applied.

Kelley's mind was reflective and scientific to the point that he asked for reasons while other iron masters accepted facts. Suddenly there came an answer. Carbonized iron melts more easily than decarbonized iron because the particles of carbon between the particles of iron are burning, thus the iron in a sense makes its own heat and a much hotter heat than can be given it by fuel from without.

Kelley's reflective temper at that moment was augmented by the fact that his fuel supply was dwindling. Having exhausted the best ore at the place where he began, he had been forced to move over a better vein where, unhappily, there was no timber for his charcoal, and hauling timber was expensive. He was therefore doubly glad when he suspected that pig iron *contained its own fuel*. Immediately he proved it.

Separating his melted pig from the charcoal as soon as it was liquid, he tried blowing a blast of cold air through it. As he had imagined, the liquid became hotter and the oxidized carbon blew off it in a shower of sparks. Thus he proved that, once the pig was melted, the decarbonizing process could be continued with no additional fuel.

Now the idea of blowing cold air on something to make it hotter was unexpected, to say the least, to men accustomed to Aristotelian thinking. Any one who thought such things was whatever the vocabulary of the day substituted for the later charming vernacular "nuts." Mrs. Kelley, who had always blown upon her coffee to cool it, sent for the doctor.

The doctor she picked was an excellent choice from the point of view of the future of steel in America. He, too, had a reflective and scientific mind and took sides with Kelley, whom he pronounced not only sane but intelligent.

The year of Kelley's first discovery was 1846. Hounded by skeptics and men who called him mad, and distrusted by his own family, he withdrew into the forest where, in secret, he worked at his process. His difficulties were great. Though he produced some fine wrought iron, some of which was used for boiler plates, he seems to have produced no steel. Yet there is no question that he did independently discover the process by which, with the addition of other inventions, steel was later manufactured in quantity.

We must cross the Atlantic at this point. England, at the time, led the world in the manufacture of iron.

2

Henry Bessemer was a true inventor of the old school, versatile, immensely ingenious, with a strong mechanical flair. His inventions ranged from bronze powder used in the manufacture of gilt paint to a seasick-proof dining saloon for a ship. He was also a good business man, so he had the full equipment for success.

He entered the iron field through interest in the manufacture of guns. It was in the course of his experiments with improvements in the quality of metal that, "accidentally" as the storytellers will have it, he hit upon the process that Kelley had discovered some ten years before.

He found, in his puddling furnace, a pig of iron which, apparently, had not melted. Poking it, he discovered that only the shell of the pig was there; that the inside had fused and flowed away. From this he deduced that the outside had lost its carbon and hence gained a higher melting point through contact with the air. It was a short step from there to the blowing of cold air through molten metal in a pot. Seeing that the carbon in the metal burned with a flame and that sparks shot off, Bessemer, aware of the proof of his deduction, was "almost prostrated with joy"[4] and, recovering, designed his converter.

The converter was a great invention in itself. A swinging pot, punctured at the bottom and with air pipes entering the holes, it could be tilted to cut off the blast; the tilting also prevented the metal from flowing out the holes. With such a tool it would seem possible to cut off the air at the precise point when steel was attained and before the metal was entirely decarbonized into wrought iron. Here, however, came the greatest difficulty.

In the interest of clarity we have, as usual, indulged in extreme simplification. The chemistry of iron appears more complex as we approach the varied composition of the ores. They contain—besides the carbon—manganese, silicon, sulphur, and phosphorus in varying quantities. Experiment with a fuller knowledge of chemistry than that known in 1850 has shown the parts these substances play in the qualities of different grades of steel. Bessemer's first experiment in producing steel succeeded because the pig he used was low in phosphorous and high in manganese.

English iron makers were more advanced than the Americans. Ten years had passed since Doctor Huggins of Eddyville had investigated Kelley's sanity. During these years people in general had become more adaptable to the apparent paradoxes of science. So Bessemer had an easier time with scoffers. When he read his famous paper, *The Manufacture of Iron Without Fuel*, therefore, before the British Association for the Advancement of Science, he aroused immediate support. James Nasmyth, an engineer of high standing,[5] went so far as to pronounce the metal resulting from the experiment, "a true British nugget."[6]

With other iron, the process failed. Particularly it failed with iron high in phosphorus. Often it did not even make satisfactory wrought iron. So when Bessemer took out a patent, his

[4]L. W. Spring, "The Story of Iron and Steel," in Waldemar Kaempffert, *A Popular History of American Invention*, N. Y., 1924, II, 16.
[5]Inventor of the steam hammer and other machine tools.
[6]James Nasmyth, *Autobiography*, ed. by Samuel Smiles, N. Y., 1884, p. 372.

licensees, trying to produce commercial steel or malleable iron, protested. Some of the difficulties were later overcome by a change known as the "basic Bessemer process"[7] which worked peculiarly well with high-phosphorous iron. But in 1856 many Englishmen believed the process would never come to anything.

With different irons, Bessemer never knew when to cut off his blast. To stop it too soon left high-carbon iron in the converter,

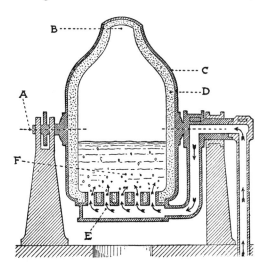

The Bessemer Converter

A. Axis upon which the converter turns when it is tilted to pour out the molten metal. B. Spout. It is from this spout that we see issuing the burst of flame and the outpouring of sparks when the converter is in operation. C. Outer steel casing. D. Lining of siliceous rock or other material. E. Air entering through the holes of the false bottom. F. Molten iron

to leave it on too long often produced over-oxydized metal, brittle, called "burnt iron." It was at this point that Robert Mushet appeared on the scene.

This Scot found that by adding to the molten metal after the blast was turned off a substance called "spiegeleisen," wrought iron could be made into steel. Spiegeleisen contained carbon, manganese, silicon and iron.[8] The manganese removed the surplus oxygen and also toughened the metal, and the carbon completed the old process. So, in the end, the Bessemer process as it was used had to resort to the cumbersome trick of adding carbon to decarbonized iron. With the spiegeleisen, however, this became more exact and scientific, as it was easy to formu-

[7]Lining the converter with substances containing a high lime content—notably dolomite. This invention, however, was not Bessemer's own. It was made by the English chemists, Thomas and Gilchrist.

[8]Also lime, zinc and magnesia.

late the precise percentage needed for various pigs and various steels. Without Mushet, therefore, it is doubtful if Bessemer would have made cheap steel in quantity. Neither would Kelley.

3

Kelley, in ten years, had made little progress. When, however, in 1856, Bessemer applied for a patent in the United States, Kelley objected. Though he had got no patent of his own, he filed a claim for priority and proved it in court. This prevented Bessemer from getting an American patent and gave a patent for the "pneumatic process" to Kelley.

Kelley's patent threw a wrench into the progress of steel manufacture in the United States. Behind it was a little-perfected means of making "refined" or wrought iron. Behind this process stood a man without organizing ability, without industrial talent, with no real concept of quantity production of steel, working in a still largely unorganized country. The transcontinental, the greatest instrument of the country's organization, was not even on paper in the form it should take and sectional antagonism which had brought the forces of industry and slave-plantation to the threshold of war was about to shatter, for a time, all appearance of consolidation in defiance of the factual pattern laid down by applied science.

On the other hand, across the Atlantic, in a nation tightly consolidated by industrial revolution, a center of scientific thought and industrial planning, was the complete equipment for the quantity production of steel. We should not call it complete by present standards but it was ready to produce more metal—of a sort—than the country could, at the moment, use, and it was certainly complete enough to answer America's most exigent demand: indeed, it was peculiarly adapted to that demand—for rails. A rail,[9] rolled from Bessemer steel in 1857, was laid on the Midland Railway and immediately proved the future of Bessemer steel for the arteries of transport.

[9] An analysis of this rail shows a low carbon content, .08% and a higher phosphorus content, .428% than was permissible in later British rails, yet it lasted sixteen years and a million and a quarter trains passed over it. Swank, p. 401.

By the time the Civil War began in America and before the act authorizing the incorporation of the Union Pacific, well-organized companies in England, Sweden, Belgium were using the beautiful Bessemer machinery for quantity production.

During the war certain Americans inspected this equipment, notably Abram Hewitt and Alexander Holley. Hewitt was always skeptical of Bessemer processes,[10] but Holley was won over by his inspection and by his friendship with Bessemer, who generously handed him the "exclusive right" to manufacture by his process in the United States. How he was expected to do this, under the circumstances, is not clear, but it became evident to Holley on his return that he could not legally use these rights in defiance of the Kelley patent.

A curious situation then arose. Though Bessemer could not patent his process in the United States, he did take out a patent on his converter. Meanwhile, two industrialists in America, Ward and Durfee, had bought the right to manufacture under the Kelley patent and had also bought the American rights to Mushet's recarburization trick. Thus Holley was unable to manufacture Bessemer steel without infringing the Kelley patent and the Kelley manufacturers presently found that they could not work effectively without the Bessemer converter.

This paradox appeared in 1865. The war was over, the North was in its fantastic industrial boom, the transcontinental was well under way. The more profound students of the subject were well aware that, as the technology of the railroad advanced, bringing heavier locomotives and cars, and that as industry would demand more and more trains, soft-iron rails, no matter how expertly rolled in England, would not endure. News had reached the railroad men of the new cheap English rail steel. The name of Bessemer was already familiar. But on top of all this, the late magnification of an old economic device had made the situation intolerable.

This was the tariff. It had jumped prodigiously during the war and was still climbing. It was already obvious that if, under it, we must continue to buy steel from England our roads would

[10]Allan Nevins, *Abram S. Hewitt*, N. Y., 1935, p. 132.

61

never have steel rails. In this conflict, then, a compromise was inevitable. This kind of compromise was to become characteristic of our collective phase.

In the case of the sewing machine we have already seen an example of the pooling of patents[11] in the "Combination," a forerunner of the various industrial associations of today. The Kelley-Bessemer paradox was resolved by a consolidation of the two companies. The Holley interests came out far ahead in the deal, controlling seven-tenths of the property. This amalgamation with its smoothing out of the legal difficulties made possible the steel industry in America.

It is astonishing, even considering the factors which abetted it: the post-war boom, the protective tariff and the demands of transport, how rapidly it grew. A glance at the figures shows this. In the twenty-five years from 1867 there was an increase of production of Bessemer steel alone from about 3000 to 4,600,-000 tons. In the statistics, the early importance of transport demands is plainly visible. Of the total of 157,000 tons in 1873, 129,000 went into rails.[12] Bessemer steel was, of course, better adapted to rails than to anything else, and it remained the best process for this purpose.

The extraordinary development of Bessemer steel in the United States, which brought us ahead of England in 1880, was aided by the fact that the ores in the largest American deposits were peculiarly adaptable to the process. Notwithstanding Mushet's invention, iron high in phosphorus and sulphur was never satisfactory for the early Bessemer steel. For this reason, many of the eastern ores were found to be of little value in making iron for use in the Bessemer converters. But the discovery of the immense Mesaba deposits near Lake Superior was contemporary with the introduction of the Bessemer process, so it became profitable to transport these beautifully adapted ores to the East where the iron works already were and where the coal was. Thus the steel industry, as it grew, was widely separated from its source

[11]*M. I. M.*, p. 371.
[12]Victor S. Clark, *History of Manufactures in the U. S.*, N. Y., 1929, II, 89, 245, 247. Depew, I, 325. Iron and Steel Association, *Report to the Secretary, 1875*, pp. 53, 54.

of supply, and this aided the development of rail transport. Continuously, in the nineteenth century, these two activities played into each other's hands.

Bessemer steel, then, was largely rail steel, and as the rails increased they helped the process. But the United States today has a steel skeleton besides the steel viscera of the railroads. What are the other kinds of steel that form these bones and what are the processes by which they are made?

4

Americans developed most of the steel-making processes and reached in this development a high efficiency; few of them, however, were first invented in the United States. Thus Peter Cooper and Abram Hewitt, when they introduced open-hearth manufacture into this country, were obliged to borrow from England, Germany and France.

William Siemens, a native of Germany, most of whose work was done in England, was a great inventor. Disturbed by the waste gases which he saw pouring out of factory chimneys brightly and hotly aflame, he concentrated on conserving and using this material for heat. Thus he evolved the regenerative furnace which forced these gases to combine with the right amount of air in a flame of great heat. The mere burning of fuel even with a strong blast could never produce anything like the intensity of heat derived from the gases. He then made his furnace "reverberatory" by passing the gas from the flame through a chamber which it heated: then by passing new gases through this hot chamber he achieved an even hotter flame when the preheated gas was ignited.

With his brother Frederick, he applied this furnace to the making of steel. This was the open-hearth process. By playing this hot flame over the surface of molten iron in an open basin they could burn out the carbon without unduly oxidizing the metal. The process was not complete, however, until the invention of the Martin brothers of Sireuil, France, was added to it.

A consciousness of steel as a giant was coming rapidly into the visionary minds of the world. It had long been known as a magical dwarf. The instruments of surgeons, the tools of the cabinet-makers, the animate swords of gods and men had long been forged by demi-sorcerers. Even when the magic disappeared, steel-making was an art rather than a science and its quality depended upon the skill of the artist. The makers of cutlery and

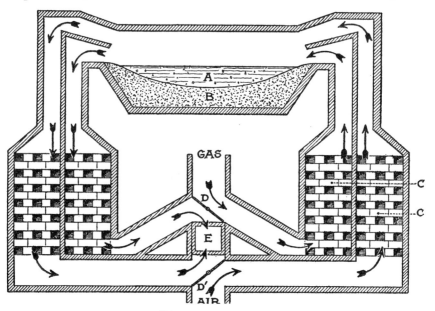

The open-hearth process

A. Charge of pig and scrap iron and a flux of limestone. B. Saucer-shaped lining of magnesite. C and D. Regenerators, consisting of checkerwork constructions of firebrick, for gas and air heating. D and D' Reversing valves. The gas and air unite in a flame over the charge of iron and pass off and then through the firebrick construction which it heats. Changing the direction of the gas and air, with the reversing valves, is the special feature of this process. E. Chimney or outlet

precision instruments were geniuses, gifted from birth; they worked, apparently, not by a formula but by intuition in a manner which the lay mind admired but could not comprehend. Now Bessemer had revealed the giant, a child of science, of chemistry (no longer alchemy), of physics and mechanics and Titan-scaled industrial plans.

In the early consciousness of this new Steel, we find a confusion which often obscures our study. Men were not yet sure that the great ingot or the long rail was the same material as the needle or the awl. Thus we find them—Bessemer himself indeed

—speaking of "malleable iron" when they mean steel, and we confuse it with wrought iron hammered from the carbonless bloom, soft and unresilient, excellent for the horseshoe and useless for the saw, perfect for the nail but feeble for the structural beam. And when Kelley speaks of "refined iron" we are never sure whether or not he means the steel that is such a common thing to us.

But by 1864, the vague sense had crystallized into formulated understanding. In this more articulate phase, it is not surprising to find independent concentrated experiment in various parts of the world. So, in France, we find Pierre and Emil Martin puzzling over the still unsolved problem of determining beforehand the precise chemical constituency of a particular steel and producing it by formula.

Their device was "dilution": dissolving in the molten pig, portions of scrap steel, ore and "sponge" iron. It was the combination of this invention with the reverberatory-regenerative furnace of the brothers Siemens that produced the open-hearth process.

The Siemens-Martin furnace was a much slower process than the Bessemer. It thus had the advantages that samples could be taken from time to time and the flame shut off when the right carbon content was present in the liquid; none of the split-second guess was necessary as with the Bessemer converter, recarburization with spiegeleisen or other ferro-manganese substance was unnecessary (though this was sometimes practised) and over-oxidization did not occur. When the "basic" method of lime-lining the hearth was introduced even the high-phosphorous ores were reducible.

5

The United States at this time was far behind Europe in both science and industry. Certain sporadic excellences had been attained in the older industrial regions: high points in the manufacture of shoes, textiles, rifles, agricultural machinery, in milling, cotton ginning, and in that strange loose-jointed, basket-framed contraption which rattled up and down incredible grades and round switchback curves, the American locomotive. But, on the whole, our nation was still sprawling, disorderly, unkempt, still largely in the process of settlement, still partly savage, partly empty, partly incommunicable, a jumble of corn and tomahawks, frame shacks, fabulous gold mines, frontier saloons, racing steamboats, bewildered niggers; with lone oases like Boston building walls round their culture and the memory of pigs in New York streets.

Yet here and there in the chaos stood great men, geniuses, their minds constructing the new order, their hands itching to mould the raw, strong, rich material at their feet. The gaunt, patient rail-splitter, whose stature none could compass, stood with malice toward none, contemplating the wounded southland with the vision of healing in his quiet eyes, unmindful of the mean death that awaited his first step. Withdrawn deep in his laboratory stood the great thinker, Henry, surrounded by his beloved magnets which had made the world conscious of itself and would one day remove the barrier of distance to the human voice. In a noisy way station the strange raw boy, Tom Edison, sat thinking far beyond the routine messages clicking from the instrument on the table before him—tense, almost bodiless, forgetful of food and sleep, and, in the busier factory centers, restless among the hammers and the heat, the industrial dreamers: the compact little eccentric master of men, Andrew Carnegie, watching the furnaces across the tracks of the Pennsylvania Railroad, the aging but still adventurous Peter Cooper and his brilliant son-in-law and partner Abram Hewitt, all with the full-colored picture in their minds of the America we know today.

Some of these men were impatient with the slowness of their country in industry. Carnegie had not yet seen a Bessemer converter in action—when he did see one in 1872 it nearly prostrated him[13] as it had its inventor—but Hewitt had seen one and was in communication with the Bessemer people in England and so had Peter Cooper in his wartime visits. When Hewitt went again to England in 1867 while Louis Napoleon's magnificent world's fair was exhibiting the marvels of all nations he was startled and humiliated by the advances in Europe.

[13]Nevins, p. 241.

"They beat us to death in France," he wrote to Edward, Peter Cooper's son. "They roll one-inch round iron in lengths of 100 feet. . . . But I cannot begin to make you see the progress. You must come for yourself."[14] He saw here the great Le Creusot works and the operation of the Martin process. He saw the great Krupp plant in Essen where there was "a cast-steel rail fifty feet long which had been bent double, cold, in the middle without a fracture."[15] Also, he "found Bessemer steel being made in all the principal nations. . . . He also saw the facilities for its production expanding with enormous rapidity. Already Europe had more converters than it needed. . . ."[16]

Hewitt was not, however, like Bessemer and Carnegie, prostrated by this machine. Almost at once he saw its limitations: its requirements in composition of pig, "the uncertain quality of each flow or 'cast'."[17] So he focussed his study on the open-hearth. To him, it answered all the questions which the more spectacular Bessemer device evaded. So he arranged to take out a patent for it in America at his own expense and returned to install it in the Cooper and Hewitt works in Trenton. His biographer adds at this point that "the whole tour abroad must have been somewhat painful; for the European industry was ten years in advance of America." It was Carnegie, however, and not Hewitt, who enabled it to catch up and reach so far beyond that by the end of the century, the United States was producing nearly a third of the world's supply of steel.[18]

Andrew Carnegie was one of the strangest characters who ever entered the story of American industry. He must have been a thorn in the flesh and conscience of many an orthodox fortune-seeker of his amoral epoch. Constantly asserting throughout his life that he cared nothing for money, he spent his later years proving this incredible attitude to the great benefit of the English-speaking world. Yet he became the richest man in America in a period of fabulous personal wealth; he established America's greatest industry and led it to its apex of power. From our present

---

[14]Nevins, p. 240. [15]*Ibid.*, p. 239.
[16]*Ibid.*, p. 241. [17]*Ibid.*, p. 242.
[18]Am. Iron and Steel Association *Reports*.

moral attitude we may contrive to look down our noses at certain ruthless episodes in his career and in our sullen moods we may point to him as a creator of certain abuses, but in his day he was surely a paragon.

He shows none of the fixed and continuous concentration of his fellows upon business. He was forever making sallies into the heterodox realms of literature and the arts. He would saunter away from his offices and be gone for months: he would be discovered in Scotland showering gifts on his adored birthplace, or in England dining with Gladstone, discussing history and political science with John Morley and James Bryce, reading poetry with Edwin and Matthew Arnold, rescuing Lord Acton from foreclosure or writing startling articles for the London reviews. Great Britain, to be sure, regarded him somewhat as an escaped *enfant terrible,* for he was insistent in his attacks upon her crown, her royal family and what he considered the nonsensical pageantry which surrounded them, but he was beloved by British individuals and even officials, and British institutions have never manifested reluctance when he chose to benefit them.

No "definitive" biography of him has yet been written, partly because he himself so bewildered posterity by his *Autobiography,* though Mr. Hendrick[19] has given us as good an approach to one as we may need. His immortality is unquestionable in his works: the Institution, the libraries, the medals, the still struggling peace foundation and many others. Perhaps this, along with the steel skeleton of our nation, is all that we require.

His childhood was regular enough in the American formula: it showed the familiar bag of tricks—poverty, hard work, hunger, foreclosure of mortgages, a loving mother, early migration to the land of promise. It is after he "got there," after opportunity's door opened so wide for his entrance that we are surprised. Here, suddenly, the income becomes automatic; he seems hardly even thrifty, and we look in vain for a continuity of ten-hour days. We find him winning by the oddest means, spending fortunes on enlargement in the depths of depressions, his little Scotch face wrinkling into smiles when other great men are dour, fervid with

[19]Burton J. Hendrick, *The Life of Andrew Carnegie,* N. Y., 1932.

a blind faith in something when menaces surround him, yet a confirmed agnostic throughout. The answer probably is in a judgment and mastery of men. As he said himself he had a flair for finding men "cleverer" than he and making them work for him. One of them was William Richard Jones.[20]

In most of the effective and powerful organizations of the world, there is probably a Bill Jones. Sometimes he is the chief's "alter ego," a moon to his sun, who fills in the empty spaces and keeps the continuity of the chief's work. Carnegie's "Captain Bill" was more than that. He was dynamic in himself, a separate ego. There was no "Yes, sir" and "No, sir" about Bill Jones. He was a mechanic and an inventor of sharp, intuitive technical judgment. His economic judgment was just as keen. He could see a whole balance sheet at a glance of his mind's eye and interpret it in mechanical terms. Thus he horrified many of his colleagues by scrapping an entire set of machinery, a whole department, a building, a plant, knowing beyond their comprehension that it was cheaper so. With him began the rapid "obsolescence" of machinery which has become a bugbear of industrialists today. Jones was the first "efficiency" engineer, the first "industrial engineer," the first Stakhanovist, one of the first Americans to combine a complete technical knowledge with a fine business acumen. His heritage was that of Arkwright and Slater but it had come to him across a wide gulf in which the shop and the business office were distinct. Jones did much to break down the distinction, and since his time more and more engineers have needed and had an understanding of business.

Most of all, however, Jones was a captain. He was a veteran of the Civil War in which he had organized units and brilliantly commanded them. He had the army vision of blocs of men moving in unison but he had, too, an eye to the individuals. He managed them ruthlessly enough, yet he inspired them and he was beloved by them. Thus he built up the power of the Carnegie Company and developed its automaticity so that, apparently, it ran itself while the boss took his holidays.

More than in any other specific place, the collective forces are

[20]Asher Isaacs, "William Richard Jones" in *D. A. B.,* X, p. 208.

visible in the growing power of this company and in the inevitable combination which it engendered. This is interesting because, from the start, the steel business was peculiarly subject to uncertainty, to market manipulation, to uneven cadences. Construction is a jumpy activity, fearfully at the whim of financial booms and depressions. In it was always a conflict of long-term fact and short-term thinking. Steel was enduring, but was the use that it was put to enduring? Was the profit enduring? Was it not too easy to overconstruct in a period of shifting needs?

Carnegie's force lay in his concentration on the fact of steel rather than the fiction of profit. He repeatedly said that he cared nothing for stocks and bonds. So, while his rivals played the old games of manipulation, short-selling, inflation on paper and overcapitalization, Carnegie built from year to year on surplus earnings. All this time he kept the vision in which America and Steel were essential parts of the same composition. To him neither could exist without the other; both were fundamental realities. To this religious agnostic they were gods.

So, in the depressions, the shattering panics which marked the terrific growing pains of the quick-maturing nation, Carnegie Steel went right on building. The intervals when others "held off," watchfully waited, cut down, pinched and pared were the periods of Carnegie's greatest expansion. It was then that he bought up plants, built new works, bought ore-fields, railroads, fuel, employed the surplus men. Thus he kept the continuity and it was this which, in fact, built the steel skeleton. So, in effect, he brought his gods to their godhead. To do it he broke the mould of business tradition.

His final power lay, specifically, in the control of all the adjuncts of his trade. He placed no reliance on contracts with other companies to supply his ores, his coal, his transport. Instead, he bought and owned his companies. This kind of control which became characteristic of industrial America in its collective phase knocked down the rivals like ten-pins and caused those which survived to organize in trusts against him.

In time his power became so great that the trusts could no longer endure against him. But Carnegie had other interests. His love of life, of society, of the humanities, half-baked as it was, and his desire to improve mankind exerted a stronger pull on him than the steel magnet. He capitulated and sold out at a price. It was the greatest price that had ever been paid a single man in the recorded history of the world. It required the full exertion and boldness of a Morgan to raise it, for the barefoot bobbin boy of Dumferline had acquired a large comprehension of wealth. He took it smilingly: "Well, Pierpont," he remarked, "I am handing the burden over to you." He then spent the remainder of his life unloading the reciprocal burden of the money to the improvement, as he saw it, of humanity. This was, on the whole, rather a spirited swan-song to the individualist age.

6

If we have passed by Bethlehem or Birmingham or other great centers of independent manufacture for the iron-hearted Pittsburgh, it is because our business is to show trends, not to detail history. The trend here is consolidation and Pittsburgh marks the high point. But the steel itself, whoever produced it, was the greatest consolidating factor of all.

The rails of the nation did not turn from iron to steel overnight. The change at first was surprisingly slow and we find iron rails persisting in places late into the century. Structural steel replaced wood and iron in a scattered and intermittent manner. Nevertheless, from the seventies the pattern was there. No new wooden or iron bridges would be built.

But with steel, it was evident that rivers and canyons would be spanned and on the plans of new systems of communication, short cuts straightened the lines. With steel construction, a certain homogeneity, certain likenesses were certain to come. As a building material, steel set standards: standards of method, dimension, appearance. Cities would presently look alike. So would bridges, signal towers, factories, fences, ships, guns, machines. With steel as a material, interchangeable parts would be more identical, precise, standardized. Machinery would grow toward automaticity and its products, too, would look alike. It would set a rigid pattern in every phase of life to which all softer materials including flesh and blood must conform.

So, indeed, must much thinking. As railroads stretched and straightened, as cities squared, as identical forms repeated themselves, it was easier for thought to move geometrically than to jump the lines. Steel is a definite factor in American conservatism: unity and standardization of thought, the fear of derailment. To use another figure, the mind follows the jig rather than its wayward impulse, for its objective is so frequently a standard form. The steel jig holds the tool more rigidly than ever upon the hard material.

As we continue in our search for technically initiated or guided trends, we shall touch, again, upon the technology of steel. As chemistry was aided by the microscope a whole new science developed and metallurgy will be the subject of our chapter. Along with it, curiously, came the beginning of an opposite trend. With this science, such a variety of forms and uses developed that the pattern again lost its rigidity. A symbol of this is the motor vehicle which followed no rails. With it thought, also, jumped the lines.

Meanwhile we shall move at once to the most immediate effect of the new skeleton material. Consolidation took one predominant form. This form bunched people into fasces from which for many years there was no escape. The railroad centralized. The factory centralized. Steel as a convenient bone structure of this centralization increased the rapidity of consolidation.

The social symbol of the collective impulse is the city.

Chapter Five

THE CITY: CENTER OF UNITY

I

THE BEST civilization is not static. It is a balance of conflicting forces and it is always, if imperceptibly, in motion. It is like a modern steel bridge of the suspension variety, every smallest part of which is continually moving, motivated by opposing forces. Thus, as we have said,[1] the ancient individualist desire in America which was enhanced in the backwoods is a stern opponent of the collective forces, and the soundness of American society will depend, not upon any static accepted forms but upon this conflict. When the conflict stops, we shall fall into the errors of the totalitarian states of Europe. When the conflict stops, so will the United States.

From time before record men seem to have bunched together; from fear, from a sense of strength in combination, from common hunger or need, from the desire to release a suffocating accumulation of ideas (though this is a late development), from countless other causes. It is a biological essential, for instance, that a man should come into reasonable proximity with a woman and an essential to survival that the resultant children should remain, for a period, close to their mother if not their father. So the family is the simplest gregarious form and given two families in limited surroundings (limited especially from the subsistence standpoint), it is unavoidable that they should either unite or conflict. Families presently become large and the tribe becomes, also, a natural form. We may multiply this up to the point where people are bunched or kept together by an outside force: a ruler, a dictator, a political plan or the application of some mechanism; at this point the form may become unnatural and it is from such a condition that many of the "solitaries" like Rousseau have sprung in a kind of back-somersault.

[1]See p. 6.

73

We are concerned here, not with the essential form of the city in civilization or with the history of its development through the ages. This history has been beautifully written.[1a] Our interest must be only in the American city which, of course, reproduced to some extent world development: how invention affected it and it invention, how it was at once a result and an instrument of consolidation, of the collective epoch in which so much invention arrived and how, finally, it may have become, through the application of technical and other forces, an unnatural form for the future.

Congestion began with the factory.[2] It was extremely unwelcome to Americans. They accepted it only when the irresistible forces of invention compelled them and even then they unloaded the worst of its burdens on the shoulders of immense masses of Europeans imported for the purpose.

Whatever the compulsions of the artisan age or commercial activity nothing ever approached the physical cohesion forced by the factory system. In Europe, congestion occurred under the guild program though other factors such as feudal land-holding, political manipulation and so on were also at work. In America, artisans lived where they pleased and worked at home. Work was brought them or they sought it but outside of their separate homes there was no focus. Always, they cultivated a bit of ground. They came and went when and where they pleased. They scheduled their own hours of labor and leisure.

Commerce was more exacting but it was usually more dispersed. Large bodies of men were not forced to labor in concert in one place unless that place be a ship which was transient. Shopkeeping was an individualist matter, its routine was dictated by the acquisitiveness of the owner. The merchant office was often seasonal in its activity or dependent on the coming and going of ships. Even in the more exigent commerce of later times, there was variety and transiency, space and movement, diversion and amusement.

[1a]Notably by Lewis Mumford, *The Culture of Cities*, N. Y., 1938.
[2]In all this discussion we must except the monstrous phenomenon of New York which will be specially treated later in the chapter.

The factory, however, was focal and inexorable. The clock and the machine were its tyrants and stood between the boss and the worker. A force which was no longer personal or human drew people tightly together at a set moment and held them together. A rigid discipline enforced concerted motion and hence physical contact during a dozen working hours. That the habit of this contact should project itself into the hours of leisure was inevitable. But beyond all question of social habit, the centralizing force of the factory compelled congestion.

No one who must report at five or six in the morning at a given point whence he would not be released until dark could have his home far from that point. As industrial plants increased their laboring force by adding foreigners the surrounding area accessible to the workers became more and more crowded.

There came a stage, however, beyond which human beings could no longer adapt themselves. Even low-standard Europeans were not wholly immune to communicable diseases, to bacteria in polluted water or to pulmonary deterioration in the absence of air. It became necessary, therefore, to invent some means of preserving health within the congestion.

Immediately new technological demands were postulated. One was the protection of water, another was transport. From these came the devices for piping, pumping, reservoir-holding, sewerage and sewage disposal, plumbing, paving, the omnibus and the tramway. These were the fundamental urban inventions. Further refinements brought the whole technology of fire protection and prevention, the technico-social inventions of police protection, street cleaning, hospitals and parks and the social inventions of government, education, clubs, amusements and churches.

All these things came to pass in all cities and they are familiar to us as essentials of urban life; the industrial city has been chosen as a take-off into their discussion because in its case the need was so extreme.

First of all comes water, as essential to life as air and usually less accessible under the artificial restrictions which man has placed upon his fellows.

When the industrial city crowded round the factory, the individual well for each family or house unit was no longer adequate. The wells must be larger and each must supply several houses. But as excreta entered the ground as rapidly as the water came out of it, it was unavoidable that the water should become polluted. So the necessity arrived for removing the water supply from the neighborhood of the houses and this process brought a whole new technology with it which involved artesian drilling or reservoir construction; aqueducts or piping, protection and perhaps filtration. This arrived soon in the extreme case of the town not situated on a lake or river.

But even most towns on the lakes or rivers eventually made use of such technology. While a lake or river normally offers an endless water supply, it also offers a repository for waste. The early river factories did not hesitate to dump their waste into the rivers. Thus a town might avoid pollution by drawing its drinking water from a point above that at which its factory disgorged but what about the town farther downstream? Factory pollution soon became a source of inconvenience, disease and death particularly when inorganic chemical poisons entered the lakes or streams.

In a lake or river town, human waste buried in the ground does not as quickly pollute the water supply as it does if that supply comes from wells, but a river invited a sewer system as soon as ideas of sanitation began to enter the American consciousness and anything which "carried away" obnoxious waste seemed desirable regardless of where it carried it. Our industrial towns, therefore, suffered much in their early growth from a failure to understand sources of pure water and sources of pollution. Many of them still suffer though filtration, purification and treatment of waste are now understood, because of the expense of these things and the failure of municipal governments to meet it squarely.[3]

The towns which drew their drinking water from lakes and

[3]For a brief but lucid and specific treatment of these modern conditions, see Stuart Chase, *Rich Land, Poor Land*, N. Y., 1936, pp. 147 ff.

A

B

C

D

A. Pittsburgh and Allegheny from Coal Hill, 1849
From a lithograph by C. Warren Smith and Co.

B. View of West Corington, Ohio, 1830
From C. T. Greve's *Centennial History of Cincinnati*

C. View of Burlington, Iowa.   D. View of Quincy, Illinois
From drawings by H. Lewis's *Early 80's*

rivers were worse off than those which could find a virgin supply in the hinterland. Such a supply necessitated elevation and aqueducts. Ancient Rome, condemning its muddy Tiber for domestic purposes, emulated the Phœnicians and the Greeks in large engineering enterprises and drew its virgin water from remote hills. In a pre-iron age this work implied a quantity of cheap labor. The great masonry aqueduct structures which so impressively bridged the valleys were not, as was once supposed, the result of

Courtesy of Board of Transportation, City of New York

Wooden water pipes uncovered when the subway was constructed under
Fulton Street, Manhattan

ignorance of hydraulics but rather of material necessity as pipes could be made only of lead or bronze.

In America where wood was used for everything, the first water conduits were made from the bored trunks of trees. Recent excavations in New York have unearthed pieces of such conduits in a surprising state of preservation. New York, having a favorable hinterland but no river supply,[4] began its search for virgin water as early as 1832. The industrial towns along the Sound in Connecticut which had similar happy situations were establishing reservoirs in the hills by the mid-century and, in that individualist age, placed the hydraulic work in the hands of private enterprises where much of it still is. The blanket charter of the Bridgeport Hydraulic Company which is, at the moment,

[4]The Hudson is tidal. The so-called East River is, in fact, a strait.

78

astonishing so many students of the law of eminent domain was issued in 1857 and testifies to the abundance of empty hinterland at the period.

The virgin reservoir method was greatly accelerated by the cheap manufacture of iron. With plenty of metal for mains and sewers, the situation of towns on or near the coast with hills behind them presently became ideal as far as water supply and waste disposal were concerned. Unhappily, the majority of industrial towns in America were not so situated.

The classic example of a city hounded all its life by water difficulties is Chicago, lying in a vast plain but at the edge of one of the largest fresh-water lakes in the world and upon a river inlet to that lake. Early in the quick growth of the city, the individual wells became polluted. Water was then hauled from the lake in barrels and sold to the inhabitants. This outrageous enterprise was partially replaced in 1834 by a protected public well and then, as pipes came into use, by pumping from the lake 500 feet from the shore. In 1854 a waterworks stored the pumped lake water in two reservoirs. By this time, however, the lake water near the shore was so polluted that the death rate in the city had climbed to the astonishing figure of 53.9 per 1000. In the following year a newer sewerage system aggravated the pollution and it became necessary to extend the conduits of the water supply farther and farther into the lake. This game was won by the pollution which storms carried a great distance from shore.[5] Eventually, then, the problem had to be met by draining into the river and reversing the direction of its flow, a colossal engineering undertaking which ended by dumping all of Chicago's sewage into the Mississippi to the great alarm of the downstream communities on that river. There, with the addition of new methods of water purification and treatment of waste, the matter rests.

Proper sewerage requires a large volume of water to dissolve and carry the solid constituents of sewage. With cheap manufacture of metals, notably iron, this was supplied via the great American institution of plumbing, which was of strictly urban

[5]Charles Zueblin, *American Municipal Progress,* N. Y., 1902, pp. 103–106.

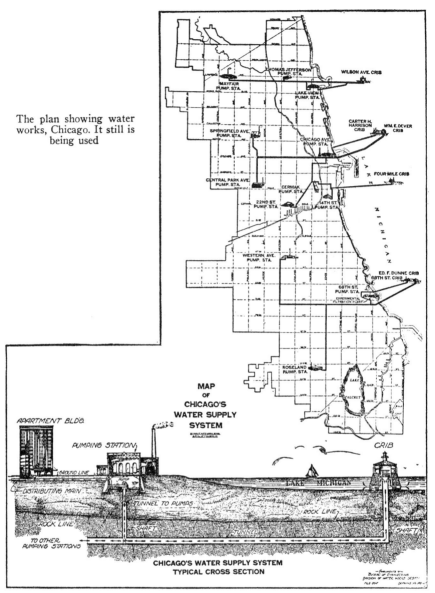

The plan showing water works, Chicago. It still is being used

origin. In Europe, plumbing had become a familiar institution long before most Americans had seen a water pipe. According to Mumford, the water closet was invented in England in 1596 by Sir John Harrington and improved by Joseph Bramah in 1778.[6] The piped sink was long in use in Europe and the piped bath

[6]Mumford, *Culture of Cities,* p. 424.

had been used on and off since Roman times whereas it was virtually unknown in the United States until the mid-nineteenth century. None of these things became usual in America until the

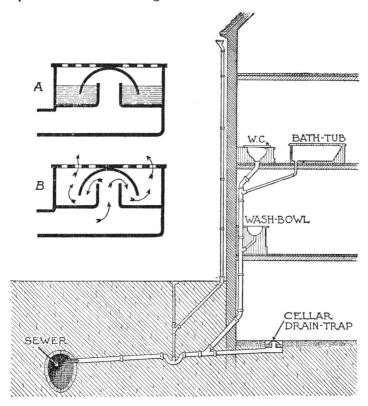

An early attempt at sanitary house drainage

A and B, sectional views of a typical drain-trap. The effectiveness of this system depends upon the basin in the trap staying filled with water (A) so as to block the gases from escaping as they do when the water has evaporated (B)

Redrawn from the book: *Sewer Gas and How to Keep It Out of Houses* by Osborne Reynolds. Macmillan, London, 1872

seventies and eighties. They remained luxuries until mass manufacture in the twentieth century made them universal and the compact, efficient, sanitary bathroom became an American symbol.

We are interested in them here only as they affect water supply in the city. They assisted sewerage and answered the problem of carrying liquid waste "somewhere else" but they also brought enormously increased consumption of water and caused remote pollution. In the future, while bathing is not likely to decline, some more efficient method of disposal will have to replace the present extravagant system which uses billions of gallons of pure water in one place to carry pollution to similar billions in another.

Such abuses were felt only when the number of cities increased and a kind of interdependence developed among them. At first we see one man objecting because his neighbor pollutes his well. Then one section of a city rises against another section for the same reason. Finally a whole city protests at the act of another city so that a community as far, for instance, from Chicago as St. Louis will be up in arms against this remote neighbor because of water pollution. In the same way, New York has enemies on hundreds of miles of coast line where bathing beaches have been affected by the city's offal.

These are all significant indices of a collective result.

3

As congestion reached the bursting point, it was necessary for a city to increase its area. This introduced the problem of transit. While transit was still by wheeled vehicles drawn by horses through the streets, there arrived the earlier problem of paving. Here again if we must seek remote origins we must go back to the Romans whose roads of a stone foundation, two layers of differently graded concrete and smooth stone pavements, survive today in France and Italy. In America, cobblestones were the earliest form of paving and they seem to have existed in Boston and New York in the seventeenth century. Franklin, in the eighteenth, introduced this kind of paving more extensively in Philadelphia. It was borrowed from Europe.

So, too, was the wood block, never as effectively used in the United States as in France and England because American wood blocks were usually round instead of rectangular or octagonal, the spaces between them being filled with gravel and other binding material. McAdam, the Scotch inventor, devised a road made entirely of crushed stone without binding, on the theory that the traffic would complete the road by forcing the irregularly cut stones into a tight mosaic. The "macadamized" road became popular in America even as the pavement of small towns, though it suffered modifications of the original design. One was due to the fact that while the road material when cut by hand formed a satisfactory mosaic without binding material, as soon as it was turned out by machine the stones became so regular in shape that a binding of sand, sand and cement, tar or other material became necessary.

The macadam and wood-block streets were overlapped and finally generally replaced by what was called asphalt. In this the asphaltum which was, in fact, bitumen existing in large natural deposits, performed much the same function that cement performs in concrete. The pavement was made by mixing the hot asphaltum with sand or gravel depending on the surface desired. This was rolled with a heavy steam roller. Asphalt still predominates as street pavement in America. It requires a minimum sub-structure and is easy to repair or cut.

The first local transit was provided by wheeled vehicles dignified beyond their due by the Latin word meaning "for all." In some American cities, notably New York whose shape made the transit problem acute from the start, the omnibus gave abundant opportunity for cut-throat individualism in business and thus its doom was soon sealed. Historians of the mid-century tell of the mad competition of the various omnibus companies so that drivers "recklessly drove over men, women and children in their haste to beat their nearest competitors to waiting passengers."[7] Municipal governments, always behind the facts, were slow in coming to the "regimentation" of a franchise. This had to be pointed out to them by means of a track. On a single track running through a street a free-for-all would be impossible and even if the street should be filled from gutter to gutter with tracks, competition would be limited. And as a track-filled street would cause considerable inconvenience to other traffic the minds of aldermen and councilmen and other city fathers, which bore some resemblance to the single track in question, finally became adjusted to the franchise idea. It was regarded, of course, by

[7] James Blaine Walker, *50 Years of Rapid Transit*, N. Y., 1918, p. 6.

the rugged individuals of the period as dictatorship, socialism, the scrapping of personal liberty and the subversion of constitutional rights but the battered public welcomed it and, under franchises wrought with the usual accompaniment of graft and spoils, the street-car came in.[8]

Steam was manifestly not economical for short hauls so the cars were horse-drawn. The "horse-car" was invented by John Stephenson, an Irish-American living in New York, a carriage mechanic of great ingenuity. His car was operated on the first street-car line in the world on Manhattan Island in 1832.[9] In New York, street-cars and buses overlapped each other for some thirty years.

The street-car introduced a technic which the railroad had not provided. It demanded a rail which should be flush with the street and over which vehicular traffic might move. A rail invented by the French engineer, Loubat, and improved by George Francis Train, the eccentric American Fenian who took the street railway to England, and others, came into use in New York in 1852. Stephenson, who presently became a successful horse-car builder supplying the transit companies of many cities, also introduced certain designs in springs and brakes which carried on into later motorized street-cars.

The sharp topography of San Francisco was responsible for the next step in urban transit. The grades of the streets which still astonish new visitors to this city presented a special problem. It was solved by Andrew Smith Hallidie,[10] an engineer of Scottish extraction, by the cable car. An endless cable moving underground in a conduit furnished the motive power. A device for grappling this cable was suspended from the car and passed through a slot midway between the rails. The slot and the conduit were later used in the second step of the development of the electric car. The cable car was expensive but it became popular, nevertheless, even in cities which did not present the extreme

[8]The question is often asked, Why did the motor street-car precede the automobile? The answer is in a later chapter and is suggested by that chapter's title, "Roads and Rubber."

[9]Carl W. Mitman, "John Stephenson", in *D. A. B.*, XVII, p. 583.

[10]Mitman, *D. A. B.*, VIII, p. 156.

need of San Francisco.[11] It was the first answer which urban transit technology gave to the growing demand for speed.

The peculiar social needs of Manhattan have always pressed transit engineers to their full capacity. They have never caught up with the demand; it is unlikely that they ever will, for reasons which will presently appear. As the city began to grow it was evident not only that every longitudinal thoroughfare would be necessary for transportation but that the spaces above and below the street must also be used. Hence came the peculiar monstrosity of the elevated railway and the more reasonable and convenient device of the subway, borrowed from London.

The "L" is important only in that it introduced steam transportation for a brief interval into the city. For long distances in New York and later in Boston and Chicago it was economically possible. It is interesting in its demonstration of the advancing technics of iron and steel construction. Its greatest usefulness came, of course, with electrification.

It is not commonly remembered that the first serious American proposal for underground transit came in New York as early as 1864. In that year Hugh B. Willson, an avid student of London's suffocating "Underground" opened the year before, promoted a company with a capital of $5,000,000 for a New York subway. The bill for the franchise, however, which must come before the state legislature was defeated in Albany, presumably under the influence of street-transit lobbies. Its defeat stirred New Yorkers to a rage reflected on their *Times'* editorial page. "We wonder," wrote the editor, "how much longer the people of our city will permit themselves to be thus plundered by men who are ostensibly their servants and dependents."[12] The residents of Manhattan continued to wonder in this direction for many years. It was 1901 before subway construction was actually begun, six years after Boston, happier perhaps, in her legislative control, had taken the lead. Meanwhile the technology of electrical transit reached the practical stage.

The problem of how to present the later history of invention

[11]Arthur M. Schlesinger, *The Rise of the City*, N. Y., 1933, p. 91.
[12]N. Y. *Times*, April 11, 1864. Quoted by Walker, p. 14.

in America becomes acute at this point. Electric motive power is, of course, the product of the electric motor but in transportation it must also await the development of the dynamo. Thomas Davenport emerging surprisingly from Brandon, Vermont, had been inspired by Joseph Henry to the point of producing an electric motor as far back as 1837. A decade later, a car was made to run by electricity, but Moses Farmer who designed it depended on a battery for his energy. It was soon evident that this dependence was misplaced and so the electric car like the electric locomotive must wait for the efficient generation of electric power by mechanical means. So, too, the full presentation of the history must also wait for our study of this kind of power through its collateral development via the dynamo.

Meanwhile we must be content with the bare statement that city transit was revolutionized by the third rail of Stephen Field in 1874, the trolley of the Belgian immigrant, Van Depoele, early in the eighties and the "wheelbarrow suspension" and multiple-unit control of the inventive hero Frank Julian Sprague in the same decade. Except in subways and on elevated railroads—antiquities in themselves—we look today upon the surviving relics of this revolution in urban transit as collectors' items. In certain medieval communities, the trolley car still alarms the passing motorist and more frequently abandoned tracks will throw him into a skid but the era is dead and we forget the effect of this revolution which came to the end of its physical career in less than a single human lifetime.

Its results in urban civilization were immense. It extended the city and grouped the residents along its tracks; it centralized the foci of industry and business at its terminals. Many of our cities to this day are monuments to the trolley car: the dispersive automobile has not yet broken the somewhat unhappy pattern it drew. In the cities which adapted their growth to the trolley car, there is overcentralization with accompanying fictional property values and traffic congestion. In the business districts of cities, the centralization about the transit terminals made necessary the amazing phenomenon of vertical congestion. In an automobile age, the skyscraper would very likely never have arisen.

4

The skyscraper made possible by the cheapening of structural steel by the open-hearth process was an invention answering the extreme need of centralization on Manhattan Island. Architecturally it was a triumph and it provided a violent impetus for invention; its social effect was disastrous.

Manhattan was ideal for the skyscraper. The island is almost solid rock. At the outset of true skyscraper construction on a large scale, this was the only reliable foundation. The difficulties of excavation had already been met by railroad engineers with the rock-drill and the explosives of Alfred Nobel. The building is succinctly described by Mumford as "the iron cage and the curtain wall. This," he goes on to say, "translated into colossal paleotechnic forms the vernacular frame and clapboard construction of the old American farmhouse. The outer wall became a mere boundary of the interior space . . . ; instead of the building's being a shell, it became essentially a skeleton—a skeleton . . . with a tough external skin."[13] New Yorkers who watched these earliest buildings as they rose so fast to the tune of the riveters will remember with what astonishment they saw pieces of this "external skin" clinging here and there to the vermilion-primed skeletons apparently without special design with nothing below them for support.

The first building to use this method was not, however, in New York. The Home Insurance Building, begun on this plan in Chicago in 1884, has been called "the father of the skyscraper"[14] because of its construction method, though fire-resistance rather than great height was its motive. Its architect was the distinguished Civil War veteran, Major William LeBaron Jenney.[15] The columns for this building were of cast iron and it used also beams of Bessemer steel as this was before American steel manufacturers had proved the superiority of open-hearth steel for building purposes.

New York's Flatiron Building, designed by Daniel Hudson

[13]Mumford, *Culture of Cities*, p. 209.
[14]*The Octagon*, Jan., 1932, p. 20. Quoted by Mitman, see below.
[15]Carl W. Mitman, "William LeBaron Jenney," *D. A. B.*, X, p. 55.

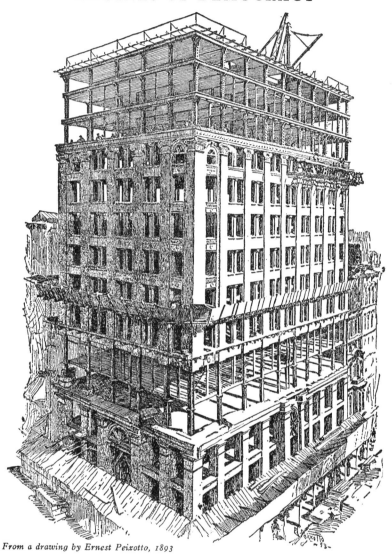

From a drawing by Ernest Peixotto, 1893

The New York Life Insurance Building in Chicago, showing method
of constructing the outer walls

Burnham on the small triangle of land bounded by Broadway,
Fifth Avenue and Twenty-second Street, was regarded as one
of the wonders of the world in 1902. With it, "cage" construction
in steel came into its own. It set the pace for skyscrapers from
that day on.

The skyscraper presupposed other inventions. One was the

passenger elevator invented in 1852 by Elisha Gray Otis and improved by his son Charles but adapted to the true skyscraper when it was electrified by Frank Julian Sprague in 1892. A *sine qua non* of the skyscraper was the telephone, which we are about to meet. The skyscraper soon developed new kinds of heating, plumbing, wiring, tiling, plastering, wall and floor compositions, ventilation and lighting. Like the buildings themselves, these things must follow rigid formulas, they must be mass-produced and interchangeable. The skyscraper can be switched quickly from an office building to an apartment house, to a hotel.[16] The cage form has been used for all these purposes so that it is no longer architecture but engineering and it is now proper to speak of the engineer rather than the architect of a building. With it the ancient idea of adapting, by means of art, a structure to a specific use has disappeared. The skyscraper is perhaps the most adequate symbol we have of the age of mass production, machine production, interchangeability and the collective fact.

Socially, its effects have been almost unmitigatedly distressing. Whatever inherent beauty it may have as a shaft or tower is nullified by its environment: its lack of approach, its baselessness, its dimensional disproportion—for any building must include in its dimensions the space about it. It has created puzzles of traffic and transit which are insoluble unless, indeed, a city can be planned for its skyscrapers in which case the purpose of the building is defeated for it exists only as a means of close concentration of large populations in a small area. It has caused unreckoned hurt to the minds of those who must occupy it and the frantic effort it inspires to get as far from it as possible during the leisure spaces has sapped their energy and wasted their time.

5

The city of New York is a financial fiction. Beginning as a trading post, that is still its main function. For years before the Dutch settled the island of Manhattan, it was used as a convenient rendezvous, a point at which the native producer met the European middleman and from which both departed as soon as

[16]Mumford, *Sticks and Stones*, N. Y., 1924, p. 168.

the deal was consummated. After Peter Minuit bought it from the Indians for a price which became famous when translated into twenty-four dollars, it was owned to the end of the Dutch occupation by a commercial company and its inhabitants were regarded as company employees. Before the end of the seventeenth century it had become thoroughly cosmopolitan and polyglot to the point of some eighteen or twenty languages and these immigrants had introduced mercantile practices from many parts of the world.

In the eighteenth century, the city became the greatest haunt of pirates, privateers and commercial jugglers in the whole of the thirteen colonies—the refuge of men like Coats, Fletcher, Tew and Kidd[17] and the headquarters for the barter of prizes captured at sea. In the Revolution, it was the center of the treasonable activity against the Continental Army and much of the treason was dictated by profit motives. There was, to be sure, an interval during which the island presented a pleasing aspect with many quiet homes and farms and a kind of integrity which appeared to be divorced from wholly commercial dealings but this was already doomed at the turn of the century when the subdivision and sale of loyalist properties had begun the land fiction.

In 1808, the city was "planned." The only guide of the planners was the profit motive; they designed then the deadly gridiron which subdivided existing properties into small rectangles subject to endless speculative stimulus.[18] From that point on, land values had no reality. The buyer thought of his plot not as beautiful or convenient or fertile in itself but in terms of its mythical future value to another supposititious buyer. The land was merely a "security" whose value was subject to daily alteration as the city grew. The result was that the city was never built but only "planned." There was no sense of permanence about any structure. One by one the houses disappeared, prices of property moved beyond the reach of individuals and shelter was rented by the cubic foot.

The extremity to which the New York romance was carried

[17]For an amusing brief survey of their activities, see Rodman Gilder, *The Battery*, N. Y., 1936, pp. 29–34.
[18]Lewis Mumford, "The City," in *Civilization in the U. S.*, Harold Stearns, ed., N. Y., 1922, p. 7.

was, of course, made possible by its geography. A long narrow island cut off on its sides by stretches of water traversible only in boats it could grow in only one direction. As an important natural seaport it must grow. When, with the completion of the Erie Canal, it became the main gateway to inland America its growth was accelerated. At this point the Hudson and the so-called East River played effectively into the hands of the land speculators.

The only possible answers must come through technology. The first answer was the suspension bridge to Brooklyn, a triumph of engineering but soon inadequate. The need was for close-packing about the center of financial activity. The next answer, the vertical movement, again played into the hands of the financiers. The value of a square foot of land must now be multiplied by the number of vertical feet of steel which might be based upon it. There was a wide range of guesses and as the towers grew like weeds the whole center of the metropolis became a fable. Suddenly, New Yorkers became Lilliputians crawling between the feet of vast, indifferent, steel Gullivers. Is it odd that they became blind worshippers of the machine?

In their extremity only the machine could save them. Even it could not save them from the fiction; it could only palliate the cruel facts which were the by-product. The machine burrowed for them under the rivers, threw bridge after bridge across to new land, multiplied the trains, electrified them, piped water for the composite Gulliver for hundreds of miles, lighted him, ventilated him, drained him and made it possible for millions of human maggots to infest him. Thus, with the aid of the machine, man was able to survive, at terrific cost, the ultimate nightmare conjuring of his brain.

This survival is often regarded as beautiful—from the harbor. Its beauty is less evident as we investigate certain residues of the effort. New York, as the gateway, sucked in the mass of nineteenth-century immigration. A quantity of poor folk from Europe stimulated by the more golden chapters of the fairy story got to the gate and could get no farther. Forming a sort of scum round the edges of the magic island, these resident particles rapidly reduced the pleasant fiction to a grim reality. The landowners along these edges found themselves forced to provide for the particles at rates out of all proportion to the story-book value of the land. Just short of the edge spaces, the march of the Gullivers had halted. To get, therefore, some approach to proper fictitious values, the only way was to crowd the human particles into the smallest possible space and to spend the minimum of money on the improvement of their shelters. Here, then, even the machine was balked. To go into the detail of the resultant disease, crime and anti-social behavior in these districts would hardly be the province of a history of invention. In the 1920's, the story-tellers made a beginning of getting around the difficulty by stimulating a demand for river-frontage among the wealthier citizens of Manhattan. In that golden era, it will be

A typical city profile showing the wasteful effort of copying Manhattan.
See text on page 93
Our Cities, Their Role in the National Economy. See footnote on page 93

remembered, arrived also that triumph of the dreamers known as the "co-operative ownership" of apartments.

New York, nevertheless, has provided something without which the nation could hardly exist. Under our economic system the ready flow of capital demands precisely such a fictional center. As a clearing house for the symbols of wealth—the chips in the game—it is essential. It was an instrument in creating our empire of the first half of the eighteenth century and it was fundamental in the creation of the nation which followed that empire. It was the necessary center for the operation of such semi-tangibles as credit. In it was evolved the necessary fiction of our currency.

Just as we use the fictional device of algebra to arrive at numerical solutions, so, in a sense, we use New York as a means of determining values. The simple equation $x - y = z$ may be resolved by assigning values to two of the symbols. If, for instance, we let New York assign the value to x and if z is a reality unobscured by New York, y is determinable.

As a container and distributor of money, New York has drawn to it the arts and sciences. As a convenient gateway it has drawn, too, much of the culture of older Europe. As a center of the nation's lines of communication it has been able to distribute these things throughout the nation especially as technology has come so abundantly to its aid. As a stimulus to technology, it is perhaps unequalled in the world, not merely because it is a financial center but because, in itself, it has postulated such difficult technological problems.

Its future is as indeterminate as tonight's dream. With the dispersive trend which, occasionally, we may scent in the modern air, it may lose its usefulness. It would make, as some one has suggested, a beautiful ruin.

6

Unfortunately, New York, as a fable, has been used as a pattern by many cities which were not forced to such a scheme by their own physical problems. A useful government report has presented the common plan (or lack of plan) in profile form.[19] "This vertical, cross sectional view makes the intense development at the center seem even more grotesque and reveals how really precipitous is the drop from the towering peaks of the skyscrapers, which mark business center, to the encircling belt of much lower, often obsolescent and decaying buildings. . . . Apparently in the small city a single skyscraper can, so to speak, suck up all or most of the demand for office space and create a vacuum of blight all around. The more imposing the skyscrapers at the center, the wider is the area over which they exert a blighting and depressing influence. This is reflected in actual physical deterioration, in accelerated obsolescence, vacant building sites, and in decaying commercial areas and residential slums."[20]

These troubles, however, are beginning to be understood. City

[19]See cut (from *Our Cities* profile).
[20]*Our Cities, Their Role in the National Economy.* Report of the Urbanism Committee to the National Resources Committee, Washington, 1937, p. 6.

planning is, today, a recognized profession and there is much intensive activity in this direction. Though progress may be slow in the face of financial opposition it is probably steady, and the next quarter century will certainly see improvement in housing, slum clearance, parks and traffic congestion, even if the bugbear of government regulation must enter the picture. Again, in our history, we shall be faced with a choice of freedoms and, under intolerable conditions, we may choose the freedom of health, fresh air and space even at the sacrifice of the individual's freedom to amass so-called wealth at the public expense. Our descendants, having a clear view of our collective progress via the machine which we created, will probably be surprised at our calling this choice Socialism.

The technologies which remain in this urban phase are those of fire and police protection, lighting and intraurban communication. The development of the fire engine and of scientific firefighting and prevention makes an interesting and complex study. Limited in a selection of the technologies which have most affected society we must sacrifice many of lesser effect. The action of fire-fighting is negative, in a sense, like military defense. It is not a denial of the importance of these things to select for such a record as this the more progressive inventions. The effort at fire prevention is more decisive than the efforts of engines or ladders. In this, steel construction and the use of fireproof compositions have been the greatest technical contributions. The whole question of lighting must wait on the dynamo, the arc, and the incandescent bulb.

That leaves communication: far too large a subject to be included with other matters in an urban chapter. The telephone is the genius of the American city. An attempt to picture a skyscraper without it would result in a nightmare greater than any that monstrosity has yet produced, but the dream would break down in laughter.

The record of the progress of the telephone, from the first faint whisper in the ear of a man whose life was dedicated to the comfort of deafness to the world network of voice communication today, is probably the most stirring story in the whole history of invention in the world. 94

Chapter Six

"CENTRAL"

I

THE CHARM of the telephone story must not, however, blind us to certain of the device's less happy psychological effects nor to its curious reversal of the normal interplay of necessity and invention. The invention was sporadic, it was as nearly accidental as any invention can be which presupposes such a long progress of the collateral sciences, it answered no specific social need of the moment and it created such a multitude of needs that its inventive grandchildren are fabulous in number.[1]

Rapid communication had arrived via the telegraph a score of years before Doctor Bell's brilliant experiments began. The concept shared by Henry, Wheatstone, Schilling, Gauss, Weber, Samuel Morse and many others had crystallized under the able executive hands of Morse and Hiram Sibley into a practical commercial system. The public had only just had time to catch its breath after the first stunning wonder at this technic (not to mention the restunning by the Atlantic cable) when the telephone delivered a new blow to the solar plexus of American communication-consciousness. Society had not, therefore, had time to articulate or even feel any new necessity. It was possible that such a need might soon have been felt. In 1870 the urban trend had begun. The railroad, especially the transcontinental span, was a great stimulus. Yet, even by 1880, there was no city of a million population in the United States, and in that year more than 70 per cent of the country's people were still rural. It is therefore reasonable to assume that the telephone was a cause rather than a result of urbanization; that it helped bring about the great increase in size, impressiveness, convenience and even glamor of the city which made it such a magnet for rural popu-

[1] For a discussion of the genealogy of inventions, see *M. I. M.*, pp. 51 ff.

95

lation in the last years of the century.[2] At least it is evident that the skyscraper and all the vertical congestion of city business centers would have been impossible without the telephone. Whether, in the future, with its new capacities, it will move to destroy the city it helped to build is a question for prophets rather than historians.

Undoubtedly the skyscraper, preposterous and inconvenient as it may have been in truth, was a factor in the city's lure. It gave the aspect of magnificence "from the harbor," and if we extend that phrase metaphorically inland, so that it covers the plain or the hilly hinterland, the feelings of all "harbor" gazers will be understood. It is not difficult to imagine the boy and girl of the farm, dulled by cows and corn and the inexorable agricultural routine, laying down spade and milkpail under the spell of this mirage and moving somnambulistically toward the dream city. That, at any rate, is what they did in increasing hordes, and chronological statistics show that the urban trend grew in a direct ratio to the growing height of the skyscraper.

That the telephone finally supplied a great need in relieving congestion is certain. To imagine all messages in a modern city being carried by hurrying boys or by cumbersome coded telegraphy would stretch our fancy to the snapping point. On the other hand the fact cannot be evaded that the telephone created much of the congestion it relieved. Unless this means of communication had pre-existed, such extreme overcentralization could not have occurred to the imagination of its developers.

Furthermore, as it is in 1940, once the scheme was developed, the telephone stimulated a multitude of desires. With a telephone at one's elbow, it is difficult not to think of a dozen needs which would be stoically dismissed were it not there. Unfortunately, food, shoes, party dresses, gin, waitresses, automobiles, doctors, friends and other matters cannot be sent over a wire. The telephone, however, gives the illusion that they can. It is all very well to call some one up and say, "I must see you at once" or "That refrigerator must be installed by six o'clock," but it

[2]In fifty years from 1870 the proportion had changed to more than 50 per cent urban. *Our Cities,* p. vii.

seldom occurs to the 1940 telephoner what a complex mechanism is set in motion by his call: a mechanism which involves elevators, power houses, subway trains, traffic lights, internal combustion motors, destructive gas fumes, filling stations, tank trucks, oil wells, an overburdened police force and an entire system of education on automotive and pedestrian behavior.

One of the humane achievements of the telephone arrived later in its progress. This was its penetration into the rural area. Here it relieved the farm wife's monotony and the isolation of the farmer to an extent which has never been measured. From it evolved a new organization of society. The house with a telephone became the center of a small unit. This brought many a friendly visitor. Beyond this center was "Central"—a person in the older days—who became not only the focus of a larger unit but almost a goddess, omniscient. Then, in the long winter evenings, the women would hang on the party line avid for news of a world only a little outside but still outside. For all their abuses these exercises were probably, on the whole, gentling and happy and may have kept as many folk out of the insane asylum as the fury of the city put into it. That the telephone saved more lives through calls to the doctors in the country than it did in the city is also probable. But it established, also, the irresistible necessity for roads and the internal combustion motor.

The hen-or-egg question which the telephone poses is not important enough for further discussion. The results are more definite and calculable than the causes. Technically the subject projects itself into "ether" waves and there, too, another set of social effects is evident, so no attempt can be made to cover the whole matter in a single chapter.

2

"Inventions," says John Mills, "whether of means or methods are, broadly speaking, products of evolution; they arise like brachiopods, Java men, or four-toed horses from antecedent conditions. Given a suitable and general state of scientific knowledge, the induction motor and the telephone, insulin and permalloy, the quantum theory and relativity, are inevitable, although the name of the inventor will depend on accidents of native ability, personal interest, and background of experience."[3]

In our history to this point, the assembly of all these factors has been sometimes difficult. In the transition from an inarticulate to an articulate world, records have been lost, connections are missing; the evolution of an invention and the motivation of an inventor have often been obscure in a society whose communications were, relatively, so slow. We arrange these matters today according to the tempo we know; we are accustomed to graphic presentation of an entire subject with straight easy lines leading from cause to effect, from parts to assembly. That is because of the widened compass of our consciousness, because we see, or think we see, the world at a glance; potentially we know, at any given instant, precisely what is happening in Tokyo and Buenos Aires, in Nome and in Cape Town—a fact which accounts for the recent journalistic confusion between the words "occur" and "transpire"; to the modern reporter the implied acts are simultaneous. Quick communications of sight and sound have created the illusion of a panoramic background, all visible and all audible. The technic of the movie built upon the lapse between the eye and the mind has laid out a pattern of connection among the parts of a story of wide scenic dispersion; gradually the machinery of thinking has adjusted to the scheme making us impatient of detail, eager for mass arrangement, intolerant of anything which breaks the circle of the horizon or the cycle of movement.

The effort to compose the history of certain older inventions into any such whole and visible picture has occasionally led historians and students into error. It is easier, for instance, to give Samuel Morse credit for the entirety of the telegraph than it is to trace the steps necessary to so complex an invention, particularly when the records are incomplete. The result is a story which may delight the reader who likes to think of the history of his country as a series of miracles but is scarcely acceptable to the realist interpreter. Careful investigators have finally supplied

[3]John Mills, book review of *Emile Berliner, Maker of the Microphone,* by Frederick William Wile, *Radio Broadcast,* Vol. X, March, 1927, p. 498.

realities to bridge these gaps; the continuity of the drama has been completed by the entrance of other characters—of such experts as Joseph Henry, Leonard Gale and Alfred Vail—and by the use of a backdrop which reveals the detail of the evolution, the slow march of collateral sciences and impinging technologies.

In the next phase of electrical communication, the materials are more accessible. No doubt the invention which Morse and his collaborators so successfully promoted is largely responsible for this availability. It had already "contracted space" and integrated the scientific world. It had accelerated the tempo of thought and pointed the coincidence of discovery. As a result we have the incidents of the new drama occurring and transpiring on the same chronological plane so that the total effect is well adapted to twentieth-century habits of understanding.

The bare, incontrovertible facts which compose the story of the telephone[4] combine naturally into a drama far more complete and moving than the synthetic romance of the telegraph with all its artificial theatrical effects. The set requires no careful reconstruction; upon it was thrown the clear floodlight of informed minds working within the memory of living man and working by modern methods. That light has never gone out though other, more powerful illuminants have been added; there are no black intervals between the first performance of the play and the performance of today.

In the "continuity" of the drama there are no breaks, no awkward pauses, no forgetting of the lines, no wrong entrances or exits and, especially, no miscasting of the characters to be glossed over by indulgent audiences and critics. It all seems so carefully planned in its coincidences, its dialogue, its "theatre," even its love story, that we find it difficult to believe that it was a natural evolution. Yet as we advance in the history of invention in a world drawn together by easy communications we shall en-

[4]These have all been conveniently assembled in a volume which telephone people call "The Red Book." The entire book is composed of records of a suit for infringement. Bell's own depositions form a complete history of the invention as well as a biography of the inventor. Given under oath, they are as nearly "source material" as we can obtain. The proper title of the book is *The Bell Telephone,* Boston, 1908. The original depositions are on file in the clerk's office, U. S. Circuit Ct., Boston.

counter more and more of these natural dramas in which no tricks or magic, no romantic synthesis are necessary to their completion. Happily, our attitude as audience has changed; the new clarity has made us more avid for truth than for fable, and the increased size of the productions has drawn our attention from the stars to the play.

As an approach to the story of the telephone, Mr. Mills' statement has special value. Using it as a take-off, we should examine first the evolutionary background of the invention and next the equipment of the inventors. Since we are on the subject it might be convenient to regard the background as a switchboard on which the cords of the collateral sciences have come to protruding culminating points and to regard the inventor as the expert who "plugs in" the connection.

3

By 1870, the science of sound showed a long advance since the beginning of the century. The collaboration of musicians, physicists and anatomists had developed it to a point from which the genius of Hermann Ludwig Ferdinand von Helmholtz had carried it into the statement of laws.[5] Sound was now known to be produced by vibration, which was transmitted in waves through the air and produced sympathetic vibration in the air. This vibration caused mechanical motion in the bones of the ear whence it was perceived by nerves running to the brain. Helmholtz had analyzed musical tones and found their composition of fundamental and overtones; he had produced vowel sounds synthetically by means of tuning forks and resonators, and he had used electromagnets to vibrate these forks.[6] By 1870, he had gone on into the study of electrical oscillations and electromagnetic induction, and he was then discussing these matters with a pupil named Heinrich Herz, who would later go on to demonstrate electromagnetic waves in the ether and so lay the foundation of wireless communication.[7]

[5] H. L. F. v. Helmholtz, *Die Lehre von den Tonempfindungen als physiologische Grundlage für die Theorie der Musik,* Berlin, 1863. Trans. A. J. Ellis, *On the Sensations of Tone,* etc., London, 1875.

[6] *Bell Telephone,* pp. 9, 13.

[7] *Encyclopædia Britannica,* 13th ed., XIII, p. 249c.

We get here a glimpse of that part of the background in which lay the science of sound and the science of electrodynamics, and we may see a relation between them. In another part of this background was the technology of communication. The telegraph, especially in America where its use was widespread, had posed a new question—an economic one this time, as this means of communication was in its commercial phase. A message could be sent over a wire to a great distance, but until that message was complete no other message could be sent to the same destination unless another wire was used. As public demand increased and it became necessary to send a number of messages simultaneously to the same receiving station, additional wires had to be installed. It was soon obvious that neither money nor space would be available for all the wire construction that the public would demand of the telegraph service.

The economic question was immediately translated by the technicians into a technical one: How to send two or more messages over the same wire at the same time. By 1870 this problem had attracted several inventors.

Telephony, or the transmission of speech over distances, had been approached in several ways. The word "telephone" was in existence[8] and had been applied to speaking tubes, instruments for use with taut wires without electricity and devices for transmitting music, such as that described by Charles Wheatstone for opening the valves of pipes by the closing and breaking of circuits.[9] In 1860, Philip Reis of Germany was able to transmit electrically the pitch of a tuning fork; he also called his device a "telephone," and when the word was later used for Bell's invention claimed priority on what seemed baseless grounds as there is no evidence that any of Reis' apparatus carried speech; there is, indeed, much evidence to prove that it could not do so.[10]

We must proceed, now, to an examination of the equipment

[8]Frederick Leland Rhodes, *Beginnings of Telephony*, N. Y., 1929, pp. 225 ff.
[9]British Patent No. 2462, Oct. 10, 1860.
[10]Am. Bell Tel. Co. v. Albert Spencer et al. Circuit Court of the U. S. Dist. of Mass., No. 1424. See Opinion of the Court, June 27, 1881. Quoted by Rhodes, p. 55.

of the inventor, a Scot by birth and parentage, who arrived in Boston in 1871 and found a connection among the collateral sciences and technologies by means of which he might make his invention.

4

In the first decade of the nineteenth century, a shoemaker sat at his bench in St. Andrews, Scotland, and recited Shakespeare as he worked. The sound of the words so moved him that he strove to improve his diction as he spoke, reaching for the full value of every speech sound. This exercise presently diverted him from the ancient family trade and he left his bench for the theatre. Finding that speech interested him more than acting he left the stage to become a teacher of elocution, and to this profession he finally devoted his life.

This was Alexander Bell. His son, Alexander Melville Bell, followed him. He learned speech at his father's knee, but in his boyhood he acquired a more scientific attitude toward it. He interested himself not only in the speech sounds themselves but in the way they were produced. He studied the anatomy of the larynx, the vocal cords and the mouth. As a result of intensive study he was able to design what he called a system of visible speech. This was a set of symbols, each representing the exact positions of the mouth, lips, tongue and palate in the uttering of vowels and consonants. From its use, correct pronunciation was possible. It had a wide vogue and was used through Europe and America in teaching elocution and languages and in the instruction of deaf mutes. From it derived the symbols now used in dictionaries to indicate the proper pronunciation of words.

Melville in turn begot a boy and named him Alexander. At eleven the boy adopted the middle name of Graham. Graham Bell, as his biographers usually call him to avoid confusion with the other Alexanders,[11] added to the enthusiasm of his grandfather for the perfection of speech and to his father's scientific flair a sensitive musical ear and a native musical understanding.

[11]Catherine Mackenzie, *Alexander Graham Bell, The Man Who Contracted Space*, Boston, 1928, p. 21.

He added also the attributes of the inventor: an avidly inquiring and deeply reflective mind, an inexhaustible capacity for study and a stubborn persistence.

In his teens, Graham was collaborating with his father in London and in Canada. In 1870, at twenty-three, he took over his father's London work while Melville lectured in America. In the spring of 1871 he was invited by the Boston Board of Education to make experiments with "visible speech" in a school for deaf mutes. A year and a half later, he settled permanently in Boston and opened a school of his own.

Here then was the equipment with which the inventor approached the technology of communication. In the third generation of a family devoted to the study of speech sound, he was ahead of them all in native gifts and acquired skill. Musical, scientific, studious, inquiring, reflective, he was the ideal expert to connect the cords of science which had only just arrived at the proper culminating points. If an omniscient and prophetic God had planned him for this purpose forty years before he was born no more perfect pattern could have been designed for his evolution.

Compare this young man to Samuel Morse, the painter turned amateur electrician on the threshold of middle age. The contrast will not disparage Morse whose executive capacity must not be questioned, but it will point a difference in method which merely removes him from the inventive field. Bell made his connection with his own hands; Morse ordered a set of experts to make his. Bell, in short, was an inventor, Morse was a director and co-ordinator of inventors.

Yet even Bell did not invent the Telephone as we understand it. He simply devised a means of conveying speech sounds by electricity. The fundamentals of his device are still in use today, yet of what value to our civilization would that device be without the other devices, separately invented, which make the integrity of our telephone: the switchboard, the loading coils, the carrier currents, the multiple-wire cables, the administrative organization which society has demanded—without the army of technicians which that demand has called into being? This is evolution and we can no more place the responsibility for our telephone upon the shoulders of one man than we can place the responsibility for the ultimate human organism upon the single sport of the shrew from which it is said to have evolved. Bell himself understood this; Morse, already mature in an era when such matters were still shadowy, did not.

Graham Bell, in Boston, met the demand for a multiple-telegraph; one that would carry a number of messages over the same wire at the same time. His long, silent study of Helmholtz and the science of sound; of Faraday and electrodynamics—a research the extent of which no one can estimate since the storehouse of the subconscious is without dimension—had led him into experiment before he came to Boston. He had, indeed, communicated some of his thoughts to agencies of the English government and had received the usual cold reply from a crank-pestered underling. In Boston, in the intervals of his teaching, the puzzle recaptured his mind. America with a new tolerance toward applied science and with the communication-demand overtaxing the equipment must have been stimulating enough to this boy whose youth she shared. It is not surprising that the peculiarly tormenting qualities of this problem led him away from the deaf.

Yet the mute characters were never wholly off the stage. There were, for example, the engaging boy, George Sanders, whose acute mind transcended the awful barrier of his silence; the spirited girl, Mabel Hubbard, whose whole being defied the blight of her defect. These children played stellar roles. Their devoted fathers were both intelligent men; more vital to the history of invention, they were both rich. They both saw the genius in this teacher of the deaf and their admiration was beyond disguise. So even when they saw the multiple-telegraph drawing him away from their children's interest[12] they followed him, fascinated and eager.

They also saw, being intelligent and practical men, the possibilities of the multiple-telegraph. So, when Bell's income from

[12]Bell had undertaken the entire education of the Sanders boy. Mabel Hubbard he did not teach but he was her father's adviser on her instruction. Rhodes, pp. 3, 16, 27.

teaching fell off, they financed his experiments. There was, of course, an agreement among them. To Bell this agreement remained binding upon him even when he departed from the program it had set by inventing wholly outside its sphere.

We must come now to the work of the expert, avoiding as delicately as we can any missteps that may lead us too far into a foreign province.

4

You can tell all this story to a child and he will probably accept it. Here is an orderly composition of people and things, of time and events, all ready for a thought; the thought came and fell directly into its place in the setting and all the factors of the composition combined to make it a reality. It is an easy story, easy to tell and plausible to believe. But if the child projects his mind beyond the norm, focuses upon the material climax and asks, unexpectedly, "How does it work?" it may be well to remember that it is time for supper. For the only answer to his question is: "When you have learned as much as Bell knew when he made his first telephone you will know how his telephone worked, and when you have learned as much as all the savants of the Bell laboratories now know you will know how the telephone works today, but all of this information will scarcely suffice to answer the question of how it will work the day after tomorrow."

Thus even the technician writing for the lay mind must stop somewhere short of the whole truth. The lay historian can do no more than pose a cause and a result, and to do this he must use such extreme simplification as he has devised to clear the matter for himself. If this simplification raises the hair in horror from the technician's head, the technician must restrain himself, for though he may turn in rage against a simplifying colleague, the social historian wears an armor which will resist him. For the social historian is concerned not with the truths of science but with the truths of society, and all his exposition of machines must be directed toward a clarity of human motivation. Furthermore, the lay writer is in diabolic league with the lay reader in such matters and the technician must respect this conspiracy; otherwise he will find aliens climbing over the edge of his plane and casting mortal shadows upon his godhead.

Graham Bell approached the multiple-telegraph with tuning forks. Now if a set of tuning forks is arrayed at one end of a room and a set of similarly pitched forks at the other, any vibrating fork will set up a sympathetic vibration in the fork which has an identical pitch, but all the other forks will remain still and mute. Further, if the prongs of a tuning fork are placed within the poles of an electromagnet, a current in that magnet will cause the fork to vibrate, and if another fork and magnet are included in the circuit, the second fork will vibrate providing it is of the proper pitch; thus communication may be achieved by vibrating forks. Now if a set of forks of several pitches are in one part of a circuit and a set of forks with corresponding pitches are in another part of the same circuit, two or more forks vibrating at A will cause the two or more forks at B which are similarly pitched to vibrate while the others are silent. As the forks at B may be identified by pitch, two or more messages may thus be sent over the same wire at the same time.

What actually happens is that the transmitting fork breaks the current which the electromagnet sets up every time it vibrates.[13] It is the interruptions which are sent over the circuit. The magnet at the receiving end naturally repeats them. Thus, precisely the same process takes place as with an ordinary telegraph, except that here the breaks are made automatically by the fork instead of manually by the key. They are so rapid that the resulting sound is a hum instead of clicks. Now if we cut a manual key into the circuit, we may break the hum again into dots and dashes. So, Bell made a "harmonic" multiple-telegraph by two circuit breakers, one fast and automatic, one slow and manual.

The next step was substituting "reeds" for tuning forks. The reed could be tuned by lengthening and shortening its vibrating

[13]In Bell's experimental apparatus, a wire from one prong of the fork dipped in mercury which was connected in the circuit; as the wire rose out of the mercury with each vibration the circuit was broken. *Bell Telephone*, p. 13.

end, so it is a more adjustable instrument than a fork.[14] Its flexibility led him into new realms. It led him back into his favorite province of sound variation. The fork was capable of a single sound, a single pitch: the reed was capable of many. Bell's gesture, holding the reed to his ear to tune it, was significant: from that moment, speaking in metaphor, the reed never left his ear. From that moment, dull, codified telegraphy was supplanted in his mind by something else. He was not yet clear as to what it was. But, pressing the reed against his ear, noting its changes when thus damped, he returned to his electromagnets with a change of direction.

The steps of his reed experiments are completely accessible to every student.[15] To detail them here would cause two obstructions: it would dim the pure beauty of the technical story and arrest the movement of the human one. It is sufficient to outline his changes in method. Instead of vibrating the reed by the electromagnet, he reversed the process; attaching the reed to a permanent magnet, he vibrated it by plucking it, and when this was done in front of an electromagnet, a current was set up and the tone of the reed was transmitted to the receiving reed. From here he moved to directing currents of air against the transmitting reed. To us, at this point, he seems very "warm"; it seems as if the step from here to directing the voice against the reed was exceedingly short.

It was, in fact, less simple. There was a series of obstacles. The current generated by the magnet reed was inadequate. The reed, flexible as it was compared with the tuning fork, was still too insensitive. These and other matters stood between Bell and the new thought of carrying speech sounds over a wire. At this point, two startling new inventions impinged upon his newly tuned consciousness from outside.

Rudolphe Koenig had made a laboratory device called the

[14]The lay reader is usually puzzled by this word "reed" which he thinks of as something which grows in a marsh. The musical technician, however, uses this word also for vibrating pieces of metal. Bell's "reeds" were made of clock-spring material. He described them as "blades of steel." *Bell Telephone*, p. 15.

[15]*Ibid.*, Bell, talking to the Court, spoke simply, as though to a child.

manometric capsule. This had a membrane into which one spoke; the vibration of the membrane caused a disturbance in gas contained in the capsule; when a jet from the capsule was lighted the flame rose and fell with the speech sounds. The flame, reflected in a whirling mirror, took a different shape with each sound. This new means of making speech visible fascinated Bell, as it recalled his father's work. The other invention was Leon Scott's phonautograph which not only made speech visible but permanently recorded it. Here a brush was attached to the center of a membrane and at right angles to it. Speaking at the membrane caused the brush to move in a wavy line over smoked glass.

The technically informed reader will now see the collateral sciences moving toward one another. From the tuning fork experiments he catches a glimpse of the electric wave filter which would one day be used in "carriers"; in the phonautograph, he sees the dawn of the phonograph and the sound track. These visions are easy in retrospect. Seeing them, it is difficult not to be impatient of the gaps that remain—all this fumbling with wires, for instance, when the radio waves are so near!

But picture Bell's mind in the dark and watch him as the light begins. First, in the foreground, familiar roads are clear. Then, as the mist rises, their direction changes. Is it thinkable that they shall meet? But it is inevitable. And now, suddenly, their meeting, too, is familiar—as if he had known it from the beginning. This kind of thinking is sometimes called prophecy.

The interrelation of trains of thought is fine and clear from this point. Bell took his new-found toys back to his school, interrupted by the thought (never very remote) that they would work for the deaf and dumb. Conform the phonautograph to the human ear, make its tracings precise. So, again, he met anatomy. Doctor Clarence J. Blake, a Boston aurist, gave him an ear cut from a cadaver for his experiments, and Bell made beautiful tracings. He tried to thrust them into the large storehouse of his subconscious, and he went back to what he called his "telegraph."

It was no longer a telegraph. The threshold of Bell's subconscious was too low. The memory of the membrane of Scott's device and the membranes of the ear kept haunting him. Somehow he must make a reed, a series of reeds, something capable of translating speech sounds into interruptions of electric current.

If Galileo, Descartes, Leibnitz, Huygens and Pascal could all have jumped on trains and gone, in a few hours, to some meeting place their conference might have advanced science by a century or so. In latter-day experiment men do this. In 1875, the great Joseph Henry must have been, in himself, a magnet for electrical experimenters. Indirectly, he had supplied Samuel Morse with the essence of the electromagnetic telegraph. An old man now, secretary of the Smithsonian Institution of Washington, he drew Graham Bell irresistibly. Bell brought him his apparatus and broke down a little as he explained it. No one knows how clear it may have been to Henry, who must have seen more things than he had time to tell. "But I have not the electrical knowledge," said Graham Bell, "necessary to overcome the difficulties." "Get it," said Joseph Henry, jumping across the young man's words.[15a]

So Bell went home, studying, perhaps, on the way. We find him next in a shop where inventors went to get their models made, talking earnestly to a boy just graduated from apprenticeship. This Watson made him an instrument, brought it to him and stayed to watch the experiments: Watson and Bell were inseparable from that moment.

Yet together they made no advance toward Bell's concept. Working with reeds they still tried to transmit delicate and complex vibrations by circuit breaking. Suddenly an accident occurred: the transmitting reed which Watson was vibrating froze to the electromagnet and Bell, with his receiving reed pressed against his ear, knew that something new had happened. In every language the story has been told how Bell rushed from his room to Watson's, shouting, "Don't change anything, let me see. . . ."

Watson wrote that no one but Bell with his musical ear and his long training could have detected the change. When Bell saw the transmitter, he understood. "That strip of magnetized steel," Watson explains, "by its vibration over the pole of its

[15a]William C. Langdon, "Alexander Graham Bell," in *D. A. B.*, II, p. 150.

magnet, was generating that marvelous conception of Bell's—a current of electricity that varied in intensity within hearing distance of that spring."[16] In other words, they had made the discovery that current must not be *broken* by vibration, it must only be made to *vary in intensity.* "That undulatory current had passed through the connecting wire to the distant receiver which, fortunately, was a mechanism that could transform that current back into an extremely faint echo of the sound of the vibrating spring that had generated it. . . ."[17] So, in that instant, the last mist rose and Bell saw the meeting of all the roads. Until then, the electrical road had been still obscure.

Once the new technic had been found of varying the intensity of the current instead of, as in the telegraph, breaking it, Bell lost all interest in telegraphy. An "undulatory" or varying current was capable of transmitting, as Bell soon found, the delicate complexity of vibrations occurring in a membrane when it was talked at. His work, then, from here on was with a membrane stretched over a cylinder instead of with reeds.

To translate the vibrations of the membrane into a varying current, he attached a wire to the center of the membrane. The other end of the wire entered a weak acid solution held in a metal container. Putting this apparatus in circuit with a battery and a receiving instrument having an electromagnet with its armature attached to a membrane he spoke into the membrane of the transmitter. His voice made the wire rise and fall in the liquid, thus varying the intensity of the current as it passed through the liquid to the metal container. The receiver reproduced the sound. Two translations had taken place. In the transmitter speech sound made mechanical vibrations which were translated into variable current. In the receiver, the variations in the current moving through the electromagnet were translated through the armature back into mechanical vibrations which the second membrane threw out to the ear. Over these instruments, Bell spoke no scriptural words, no "What hath God

[16]Thomas A. Watson, "The Birth and Babyhood of the Telephone," in *Proc.,* Telephone Pioneers of America, Oct. 17, 1913. Quoted by Rhodes, p. 22.
[17]*Ibid.*

wrought?" but the simple message: "Mr. Watson, come here; I want you." Thomas Watson heard it and came.

5

In principle these transmitters and receivers have never changed. Granulated carbon was substituted[18] for the acid solu-

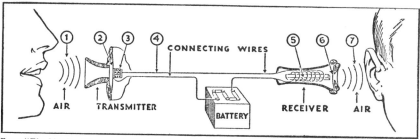

From "The Magic of Communication" by John Mills

A simple telephone circuit

The ear drum or diaphragm of transmitter (2) is set vibrating by the dance of air molecules. Back of the diaphragm is a chamber partly filled with grains of carbon (3); through this carbon chamber and the connecting wires the battery sends an electric current which sets in motion billions of electrons, too small to be seen, around the circuit formed by the wires. The receiver has an iron diaphragm (6) and a coil of wire wound on the magnet (5). The motion of the diaphragm of the receiver is the same as that of the transmitter. The receiver speaks, undoing the magic which turned a spoken word into an irregular procession of electrons

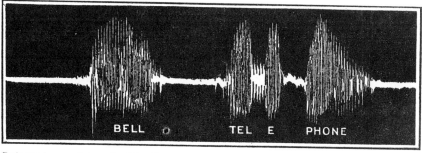

Redrawn from a photograph of the vibration of an electric current when the words "Bell Telephone" are spoken into the transmitter

From "The Magic of Communication" by John Mills, Information Department, American Telephone and Telegraph Company

tion. Metal discs took the place of the membranes. Mechanically generated electricity has replaced the battery current. There have been many refinements from the queer boxes of the seventies to the so-called "French 'phone" we use today. The fundamentals of Bell's invention remain.

[18]Invention of Henry Hunnings, 1878. See also devices of Thomas A. Edison, Rhodes, pp. 78, 79.

Yet, as the officers of the present telephone company in America will soon point out, Bell at this stage had invented nothing which could, in itself, be useful to society at large. Before such benefit could come, a host of inventors must concentrate upon the problems which Bell's instruments presented. The technology of telephony must again approach dangerously near the technology of telegraphy—not to mention commercial approaches. Distance must be overcome, the question of more than one simultaneous message over a wire must be faced again. More im-

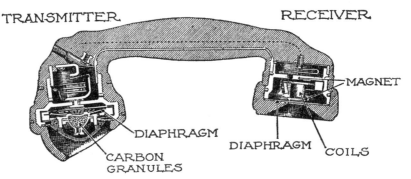

The transmitter and receiver in a hand telephone are separate units as in a desk telephone

From "The Magic of Communication" by John Mills, Information Department, A. T. and T. Co.

portant still, socially considered, were the problems of connections among many speakers and listeners, of the administration of exchanges and finally of the business organization of a complex public utility which must unavoidably tend toward monopoly. Perhaps nowhere in history is there a finer example of collective invention than in the development of the American "Bell System."

Graham Bell lost no time in forming a company. Before the end of the decade, telephonic communication was urgently in demand. This posed the problem of the switchboard. Individual lines between houses could never develop into a social matter or, indeed into a commercial scheme until there was some sort of central exchange.

There was, however, some technical basis for switchboard invention. An ingenious detective named E. T. Holmes had rigged up a system of electrical burglar alarms by means of which indicators in a central office would show which of several Boston business houses a burglar was trying to enter. In New York, offices were using the telegraph to communicate among themselves and there was a switching exchange there. A Chicago company called American District Telegraph had indicators showing the location of persons who had pushed buttons to

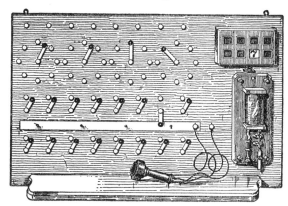

The first telephone switchboard, New Haven, Conn., 1878, which had 8 lines and 21 subscribers

Redrawn from a photograph from *The Birth and Babyhood of the Telephone* by Thomas A. Watson

call a messenger. All of these devices contained elements of a telephone switchboard system.

Bell's company made use of some of these. Telephones were hooked up to Holmes' burglar alarm circuits for daytime use while the burglars were presumably in hiding and people wanted to talk. Crude little exchanges were rigged up in drug stores and must have been highly beneficial to the druggists. Finally, in New Haven, a commercial telephone switchboard was installed in 1878 which handled twenty-four subscribers and employed common switch arms and studs. This is a landmark in history; a more important one, technically, was the "Edison Exchange" opened in Chicago by the American District Telegraph Company in Chicago also in 1878, because out of this grew the multiple switchboard. Here each subscriber's wire ended in a socket on a board. The operator simply made the connections by plugging in a cord which reached from one socket to another. The signalling apparatus was all separate from the board and worked by the old A. D. T. call boxes in another room. These were watched by a clerk. When an indicator showed, he wrote a number on a piece of paper and sent it by messenger to the switchboard operator. The operator found the socket corresponding to the location number, plugged in his own telephone, asked for the number desired and then, with a cord, plugged in the connection. When the subscribers increased to cover a large

W. E. Co. Universal
Switchboard, 1879

Courtesy of the Bell Telephone
Co. Laboratories

surface of board, this became good exercise. The operators were boys; they did much running about. Subscribers, we are told, objected to their manners.[19]

If we should trace in detail the progress of switchboards from this point, our tracing would result in a mere list of names. The switchboard is a complex technical subject in itself to which entire volumes have been devoted. To list the demands would be more in key with our scheme.

These were, first, compression of space occupied by exchange facilities, an important matter in New York, for instance, where

[19]Rhodes, pp. 153, 154.

telephone service multiplied so rapidly. The next was division of operator labor which contradicted the first demand because it necessitated putting an entire switchboard before each of many operators. Otherwise, the running about would be impossible, especially when women (with the elaborate clothes of the period) replaced the unsteady, uncivil, beer-drinking boys.[20] At the same time, signalling must be worked into the switchboard, not managed in another room. Finally, the exchange itself must be multiplied so that there would be a number of exchanges instead of one in a city, and all the exchanges must somehow be hooked together.

The annunciator or signalling process was tied into the switchboard by means of the "jack-knife" switch commonly called the "jack," the invention of Charles E. Scribner who eventually took out more than five hundred patents in connection with the switchboard. Imagine a jack-knife with a hole bored in its side. When the blade is closed, assume that its point rests on a stud. Attach a wire to this and another to the blade's hinge, connect the other ends of both wires to the poles of the battery and an electrical circuit will run through the blade as long as it rests on the stud. But if, now, a plug is put through the hole in the side of the knife's handle, it will lift the blade off this contact and at the same time a new contact will be formed with the plug. Connect the plug with a circuit wire and you have a simple device for opening one circuit and closing another with a single operation. Mount the jack-knives in rows, construct the proper circuits and you have a switchboard panel in which one (the annunciator circuit) is normally closed but in which this is broken and a connection established by plugging in a cord.

If all the subscribers have jacks on the board and also flexible cords on a shelf below, a connection is easy. The plug on the cord automatically stops the signal and makes the connection between subscribers when it is inserted in the hole. This is extreme simplification and leaves out the intermediate connections between operator and subscribers.

Leroy B. Firman solved division of labor by putting a duplicate

[20]*Ibid.*

panel and set of cords before each operator. Thus every operator in an exchange had a complete set of jacks and cords covering all subscribers. This, of course, increased the total space occupied by the exchange but it contracted the space to be covered by a connection and multiplied rapidity of service. This was the principle of the multiple switchboard in use today. An evolution of invention finally made possible the service to large numbers of subscribers in a relatively small space. They were all tricks which became easy as men became more familiar with the extraordinary flexibility of electricity in circuits.

Manual switching involves four or five operations. First, the operator's recognition of a signal by plugging in a connection between herself and the subscriber. Second, the request for the number. Third, the removal of her own connection and the substitution of the second subscriber. Fourth, the use of a listening key to make sure the connection is complete. Finally, the breaking of the connection when the signal comes that the conversation is terminated. In a city, these operations are divided between two exchanges unless the caller and the called are in the same district. Here, the called operator uses trunk line cords to connect the caller with another exchange where the connection is completed.

Upon this system is based machine switching, the technical details of which are beyond our province. In this scarcely credible[21] stage of evolution, a group of relays which we may call, affectionately, "the memory" assumes a certain shape or pattern as a result of impulses sent to it from a subscriber's dial. When the dialing is complete, this pattern sets in motion successive selectors which feel their way up the switchboard panels until each arrives at an automatically "conditioned" point. Each comes to rest at the proper point, is held there by a trip and so completes one step in the connection. At the end of a call, the relays forget the whole business, lapsing back to their normal shape and all the selectors drop home. Fatigue is not discernible but if any nerve in the system snaps, a doctor in the guise of a repair man is automatically notified.

[21]Inability to believe is, of course, confined to the layman who has not had time to trace the steps.

The processes by which an unoccupied "memory" is chosen, the "dial tone" or mechanical "number please" actuated, a not busy panel selected, excessive, unexpected loads distributed and many others form a story of magnitude and beauty well worth investigating. We shall touch again upon "mechanical brains" in other forms. They are less fallible within a formula than human brains and less subject to accident or fatigue. The clock can "tell" time far more accurately than a man and the jigged tool can bore its holes with finer precision than the human eye can measure. It is well that machines have been made to perform these lesser functions so as to release men's minds for higher ones. All formulated thinking should be done by machines. Their work does not detract from the dignity of the mind or threaten its function. They elevate it to new planes by removing the little burdens just as, once, the body was relieved by machines from physical burdens. If we can invent enough thinking machines we may learn, one day, something of the true capacity of the human mind.

6

The telephone—and here the word is used in its largest sense —kept pace, in America, with the closer organization of society. As thought, opinion, business and industry became more and more standardized in the nation, the telephone underwent an inter-urban as well as an intra-urban development. Men in Philadelphia, Buffalo, Boston, were no longer content with the impersonal communication of the telegraph with its coded messages. Now they must ask questions and receive instant answers; they must know not only facts but tempers, dispositions, emotions inherent in the variations of voice sounds. They must use straightforward English in their communications, not translated dots and dashes.

Telephone companies and their technicians tried to anticipate these demands. They could not adequately do so until everything connected with the telephone should come under what may be called a "totalitarian" regime. Monopoly was inherent in the whole telephone idea just as it was in the railroad or the telegraph though it has never been fully realized in either. It was especially so in the telephone purely from the technical standpoint: apparatus, methods must be standardized and made simultaneously available to all parts of the system if technics would keep pace with social collectivization.

A recent investigation of telephone history by the Federal Communications Commission[22] has reported certain methods and practices in the elemination of competition. Ethics in such a large and rapid consolidation of forces must always come under purist criticism. The question, therefore, may always be asked, "Which would you rather have, ethics or a railroad, free-for-all competition or a telephone?" and it contains Jesuitical suggestions. But in the then state of our nation, individual answers could not be considered. The mass answer was a demand for the telephone —a demand which it, to be sure, and not society had created. Thus the organization of the Bell System was merely a part of the whole collective phase. The "greatest good to the greatest number" was the result. If individuals lost opportunity for private profit, if free competition[23] dropped out of existence, if personal "ruggedness" lapsed, so it did in most departments of industrial and commercial activity during this whole tightening of society.

As general manager of the American Bell Telephone Company, formed in 1880, Theodore Newton Vail saw with an extraordinary prophetic clarity the development of a nation-wide telephone system. This prophecy was expressed in the certificate of incorporation of the American Telephone and Telegraph Company formed in 1885 which certified that "the general route of the lines of this association . . . will connect one or more points in each and every city, town or place in the State of New York with one or more points in each and every other city, town or place in said state, and in each and every other of the United States, and in Canada and Mexico; and each and every other

[22]Federal Communications Commission, Proposed Report, Telephone Investigation Pursuant to Public Resolution No. 8, 74th Congress, Washington, 1938, pp. 134 ff.
[23]On telephone competition, see Annual Report of President of A. T. & T. Co., March, 1910.

of said cities, towns and places is to be connected with each and every other city, town or place in said states and countries, and also by cable and other appropriate means with the rest of the known world."[24]

The genius of an organizer like Theodore Vail is as mysterious as the genius of an artist. Perhaps it is more so; the artist himself is more accessible through his work. A work of art—a painting, a sculpture, a book is a complete and relatively static thing subject to endless study and interpretation by other artists. An industrial organization, however, is fluid and in constant motion, in continuous growth; moreover its creation is in a human medium for its moving parts are men and women. It may never be interpreted by any one within it for any broad view of its integrity or wholeness would render such a person incompetent in his function within the organization. It, too, like the painting, should probably be interpreted by the artist for it is life itself but to the artist the material for study is rarely available. Industrialists are jealous of their mysteries; they live in fear of interpretation, for to them the small truths are more vivid than the larger truth, they see the details before the mass, the trees instead of the woods and they tremble lest the public too shall see these things. They are wrong. The public is incapable of seeing anything but the mass and it craves that view; when interpretation is in the hands of the artist, it will see only the blocs of color, ignoring the brush strokes.

It is conceivable that a masterly work of fiction might make clear the genius of a Theodore Vail. It was intuitive in the sense that his entire experience was unconsciously at his fingertips. Combine this intuition with a will which was always many laps ahead of the facts, a flexibility in dealing with his fellow men and a mind capable of forming large, loose patterns which other men under his will can be forced to tighten and articulate— there, perhaps, will be a momentary glimpse of the organizer. But we must see him in action, not in his speeches and his reports, his letters or his commands.

Bit by bit the large number of competing companies which

[24]Rhodes, pp. 196, 197.

presently grew up were induced to co-operate with the American Bell Telephone Company through its new subsidiary, the A. T. & T. The A. T. & T. was designed for the promotion of long-distance communication. As this came into practice closer and closer co-operation naturally became necessary. Obviously the end of the whole matter must be the elimination of competition. This, in an age of individualism, must be slowly attained.

Often the waste of telephone competition was so evident that companies voluntarily capitulated and sold out. In other cases most adroit schemes of control were applied without limiting the sense of a company's independence. But as the network of long-distance telephony grew, so did the need not only of standardized equipment and method but especially of a discipline and esprit de corps like that of an army. That is what we have today: its most amazing aspect is that it exists in an organization which is virtually monopolistic, in which the money incentive is largely absent. Certain officers of today's company find a motive like that of an army in war, a sense of responsibility to the public which resembles patriotism. These same executives might, however, be less pleased with the suggestion that the whole scheme suggests that of a socialist or totalitarian community in which the individual is subordinate to the group and in which, too, the individual money or power incentive is absent. Yet the analogy is difficult to escape. It is often astonishing how fascism or socialism will be adopted wholesale by industrialists who turn pale at the remotest hint of such matters in government.

Possibly it was the fascination of the work itself which held these people together. Perhaps it was the "message to Garcia" motive. Perhaps it was a sense of security which, with the removal of frontiers and the general collectivization of society, became an increasing desire among Americans. In any case, the A. T. & T. has become a symbol of the collective phase, of the trend toward socialization, yet, paradoxically, it has been possible only under our capitalistic system and with a wide base of absentee ownership. Somewhere, then, a profit motive exists but the workers who produce that profit work, themselves, largely without it.

When long-distance communication began, a technical obstacle appeared. Already the ground had proved inadequate as a conductor for telephone conversations, strange and obstructing sounds constantly having been heard. The remedy called for a double wire, but when two wires were placed in close proximity, a phenomenon occurred which technicians call attenuation—"thinning out" of the transmitted sounds. A train of electrical vibrations moving along a telephone wire, like a train of vibrations in the air, consists of successive bunches of electrons interspersed with spaces in which they are not bunched. When two telephone wires run side by side, it happens many times a second that places where there are many electrons in one wire come opposite places where there are few in the other wire. When this occurs, some of the crowded electrons stop moving along the wire in their original direction and seek to fill in the place in the wire opposite to them where there are few electrons; they cannot jump across because of intervening insulation, but they are drawn thus away from their job of pushing along the wire. From the point of view of transmission this is wasted energy, and the impulse received at the other end of the line is consequently weaker. The higher the frequency of the vibration, the more the loss; hence not only do impulses become "thinned-out" but this occurs in such a disproportionate manner that distortion of voice sounds as well as their weakening through attenuation obscures and sometimes makes unintelligible long-distance communication.

There were several possible remedies for this: one was to place wires far apart, another was to increase the size of wires, a third was to "load" the wires or, rather, the circuits. The word load derived from a simplification which has become classic among electrical people. It seems to us inadequate but we will give it for what it is worth.

Tie a long light rope to a post, take hold of the free end and wave it up and down to produce a wave motion in the rope. Now try the same experiment with a heavy rope. It will be found that, while it takes more effort to produce waves with the heavy rope, the waves themselves will be better. Now attach weights at intervals to the light rope and much the same effect will be obtained as with the heavy rope. Why this happens may be learned from a study of inertia in physics.

Experimenters found that by attaching "inductance coils" at intervals along a light wire, capacitance could be counteracted and the electrical wave motion rendered more uniform and complete. This made the light wire capable of as good transmission as the heavy wire even when it was in proximity to another wire. Thus economy was effected and wire weighing 12.5 per cent of the heavier wire could be used. The question was where to put the coils and many trials were failures. The problem was finally solved by a Serbian immigrant, Michael Pupin, who, the histories of invention hasten to tell us, received some half-million dollars for his idea. The answer was a mathematical formula. Under it the coils had the desired effect.

A new system of "repeaters" was later introduced via the vacuum tube amplifier, discussion of which must be postponed until we enter the mysterious realm of communication without wires. The tube amplifier, placed at intervals in the circuit, merely renewed the vibrations so that a series of short intervals was used instead of a long, loaded stretch.

Economy forced intensive experiment on cables which should carry a large number of wires. This finally resolved itself into the effort to carry many messages over a single wire, the ultimate result of which is the coaxial cable.[25] An understanding of this depends on much knowledge of wave filtering but there is a remote analogy in Bell's early tuning-fork experiment. The laboratories have lately evolved a method of cutting quartz crystals in such a way that only certain frequencies may pass through them. These matters also we shall approach again.

The whole business of transoceanic telephony depends upon the use of radio waves, or waves in the so-called ether, for communication. A message originating in an ordinary transmitter is sent over a wire to a broadcasting station where it is translated, so to speak, into a frequency suitable for radio transmission. It travels then without wire to a receiving station where it is re-

[25]Still, at this writing, experimental.

translated and moves over wires to a switchboard and thus to its ultimate destination.

A primary difficulty in this method derived from the fact that many radio receivers in various parts of the world could pick up the message. There was therefore no privacy in this kind of communication. The problem was solved by what is known in telephone jargon as the "scrambling" of speech sounds.

Once we know what happens to speech sounds when they are translated into electrical waves, we may easily juggle those waves so that they will produce gibberish when received back. Thus a sentence caught by an ordinary receiving apparatus will sound something like "ilru umpum glub-glub boo" to the listener, though, when this sentence is received at the proper destination, it will convey in the precise tones of the speaker that "Mabel has run away, you must come back." Perish the thought, of course, that we have rendered an exact scrambling: the telephone companies are careful enough that no decoding shall be practicable and they employ as many as twenty-six scrambling combinations. The experts in New York will amuse the visitor, however, with a rapidly repeated scrambled version of "Mary had a little lamb, etc."—an improbable commercial message.

The scrambling recipe is given by Mr. Mills as follows: "Generate with a vacuum tube a small current of high frequency; modulate it in another tube by the audio-frequency current from a telephone line; amplify the modulation product as required and send it either into an antenna for radiation or into wires for guidance to its destination. At the terminal amplify what is received, if required; select through filters the desired frequency range; demodulate to audio-frequency; amplify to taste and transmit over ordinary telephone lines to appropriate receiving equipment."[26] This seems a fitting climax to present technical discussion. If we have neglected such details as the phantom circuit, overhead and underground wires, cable methods, details of the microphone transmitter and the "cross-bar" it will be because of the limitations already mentioned upon social history.

What, then, in America, has the telephone done for humanity?

[26]John Mills, *Signals and Speech*, N. Y., 1934, p. 261.

7

There are, at this moment, in the United States about five telephone messages to every three letters.[27] The volume of printed matter sent through the mails still exceeds the volume of vocal messages, though advertising for which most sub-first classes of mail are the vehicle has long since also invaded what is called "the air"—actually telephone lines. But whether or not reading may one day be supplanted by listening, there is no question that the ability to convey the voice to a distance has enormously increased the desire of Americans for constant articulation.

We are probably the most articulate nation on earth. At every point, at every moment we rush to express ourselves on any subject which has begun to cook in our minds. The result is a colossal product of half-baked thought, much of it still soggy dough. Speech is so common that we no longer associate it with thought. Watching a person walking along a street tormented by thinking, it is amusing to note the smoothing out of his face as he meets a friend and is released by speech from the burden of thought. How often, then, is a half-matured sentence shot over Bell's beautiful pattern simply in the effort at this release, to attack unexpectedly a remote mind engrossed in its separate problem?

How often, in a business office, is a vital conversation interrupted by an irrelevant buzz, a totally immaterial conversation? Business men have been able to fortify themselves against such invasion only by employing large staffs of intermediaries, a protective army who repeat all day the formulas "tied up," "in conference" or "I don't know when." The privacy of less happily equipped persons is subject to constant invasion unless they care to follow the difficult procedure of ignoring the ring. Privacy, however, is in no department of life a concomitant of the collective phase.

The charge of causing unemployment cannot yet be brought against the telephone. Indeed, it has multiplied employment in a hundred spheres by increasing speed of production and the

[27] Arthur W. Page, et al. *Modern Communications*, Boston, 1932, p. 18.

tempo of business activity. It is true that the automatic switchboard has gradually reduced jobs in one department, yet telephone people declare that the switchboard came in only when it became evident that enough skilled operators could not be found to manage the increasing volume of business. It is interesting that the invention of machine switching came, however, not from motives of economy but because the inventor was a rival in business of a man whose fiancée was an operator. She manipulated the switchboard, so the story runs, to ruin her lover's competitors in business. The business in this instance was undertaking, the inventive undertaker was one Almon B. Strowger.[28]

To offset the discomforts of the telephone there are, of course, a thousand benefits. "How does one measure," says Arthur Page, "the value of a baby's laugh over the telephone?" The telephone has nullified many torments of uncertainty. It has stilled quarrels and, possibly, it has even stopped wars. It has aided in the capture of criminals and prevented crimes. There are benefits too many and too obvious to mention.

Our interest is primarily in its impetus to the collective impulse; its stimulus to invention. A visit to the Bell Laboratories whose work reaches far beyond the actual telephone is satisfying on this point. The system has provided a large playing field for a variety of communication experiment: for radio networks, for photograph transmission, for teletyping, for television.

The story is not finished; it may have no end. No abuse can dim its beauty. No diabolic human control can contradict the truth that the telephone is one of the most obedient and sensitive slaves ever delivered into human hands.

As the collective phase advanced, so did business. In the new tempo, the new multiplication of liaison, old offices must go by the board, old methods be scrapped; to correspond with an advanced factory system must come an efficient office system with new jobs, new division of labor. The first needs, in all commercial transactions, were speed and clarity.

[28]1890. Kaempffert, I, p. 338.

Chapter Seven

BUSINESS COMMUNICATION

I

SPECULATORS ran wild in the fifties and the bubbles blew big. Started by California gold, men everywhere were drunk with the possibilities of wealth. There was no limit to what might be dug or grown, built or merely "financed" in the stupendous empire between the oceans. There were outbursts of extravagance in the cities; men flaunted money and champagne and promoters caught them with wildcat schemes. But it was all sporadic and rampantly individualist; development was spotty, the building was jerry-building, buying and selling were sufficient unto the day; nothing was co-ordinated, not even the railroads, largest structure of all.

Many bubbles were pricked in 1857 and men were ruined; there was panic in the market place. Yet there was only a surface collapse. In the interval, people had leisure in which to think more deeply. They thought more of iron as well as of gold; they thought of coal and oil and other more solid, less glittering material. Suddenly there was war. The fire on Sumter was aimed rather at the boom than the depression.

Had the South realized that its act would make, not break, a great industrial nation, it might not have aimed those guns. Had it known that a war between the particular states involved would have provided the one necessary feeding ground for the twin giants of industry and business in the North, it might have compromised with secession.

Even under the first Northern defeats, the giants prospered. It was their prosperity under defeat that brought the victory and would have brought it sooner or later had Grant and his generals never entered the field. The Civil War was a war of attrition and on it Northern business fattened. It not only fattened but it learned co-ordination for the war brought concert into chaotic enterprise.

Northern bankers waving flags and sending substitutes to fight for them found it exceedingly profitable to finance the Government. Government, thus financed, bought industrial commodities. Industrialists under pressure put speed and large-scale production into their plants. Even agriculture played into industrial hands, supplying food in quantity for the boys in blue, and Mc-Cormick with his reapers did a business that surprised him and must have brought many a qualm to the heart of that loyal Virginian. The sewing machine started the clothing industry with uniforms; shoe factories, flour mills kept pace with gun foundries and munitions works. Fortunes were everywhere available wrapped up in American flags and stock exchanges became indispensable conveniences.

The close of the war, therefore, found the North solid, dominant, and rich in fluid capital. The giants had gained a momentum that nothing could stop. The sectional jealousies which, for so long, had delayed the transcontinental span of rails were finished and the plaint of the South was muffled under martial law. Along the long new lines, energy flowed to the outposts, to the mines, to the farms, back to the machines and the offices behind them—a golden flow.

Once, in the midst of this, the voice of the people was heard. When the railroad kings overreached themselves into their feudal empires, the people, feeling somehow that much of their fighting in the new land had been for liberty, spoke against the menace of serfdom. The Grange spoke in its state capitols and brought forth such a complexity of legislation that the kings themselves went to Washington pleading for the homogeneity of interstate commerce regulation. Washington answered, a little too emphatically for the kings and the freight rates were marked upon an iron rule. From that point the people spoke no more, notwithstanding astonishing grievances, for the rest of the century. Or, if they spoke, their articulation failed to carry. For the most part, every one was deep in his particular golden dream. When the popular voice was heard, at last, again, it was through the thunderous amplifier of Theodore Roosevelt.

In the meantime, in the advance of business and industry, there occurred first a scattering, then a cohesion tighter than before. Standard freight rates and the momentary halt of the plutocratic barons brought back free competition on such a scale that it soon defeated itself. There was no recurrence of going to the Government for aid. The instrument of interstate-commerce control had shown itself as too dangerous a weapon. This time business cured its disease from the inside.

To the layman, no technological complexity can be more puzzling than the eccentricity in the mind of the business man. It is a perennial paradox. We still hear, in 1940, again, the cry for free competition, unrestrained trade, "individualism." Yet freedom in business is, in fact, the last thing that the commercial practitioner really wants. Through the world cycles, the movement is repeatedly away from freedom. The largest and most rapid industrial development has taken place in the eras from which it was conspicuously missing. Standard Oils and American Telephones have no more desire for free competition than had the Banca di San Giorgio in fifteenth-century Genoa. Such matters as Steel or even Motors would, indeed, be ruined by it at this moment. Pooling and price maintenance furnish the very vitamins of success to such industries; gentlemen's agreements, rigid control of advertising policy, common "ethics," mutual benefit associations are the tissue of their structure.

In the seventies, we see an extreme illustration of liberty and we see at the same instant, how intolerable it was to efficient industrialists and merchants of the day. The cure is recorded as one of the great evils of our economic history, yet under it came the standardization which made possible mass production; under it came full exploitation of natural resources; without it, it is scarcely possible to imagine how any of our present structure of industry, distribution or, indeed, society could ever have been realized. At its extreme, it became a political menace and the snake was scotched; it has never been killed.

Free competition in the seventies ran amuck, to say the least. Business was a guerrilla war. Throat-cutting was practised in every department from advertising to delivery of goods. Merchants and manufacturers bought pages of newsprint for the purpose not of exploiting their own goods but of abusing their competitors. Handbills, posters, blared forth the horrors of competing methods, the unscrupulousness of rivals. Men were employed to waylay truck drivers and lead them into saloons while "free-competing" trucks delivered rival goods. Salesmen were seduced, diverted or beaten. Consumers were oversold and producers overproduced. It was all a chaos that seemed to move, inevitably, toward stalemate, and capital was so subdivided that large operations became impossible.

The solution was the octopus that frightened children in the cartoons of the nineties. In every large industry amalgamation began. Lured by the charming legal instrument of incorporation which gave a company the privileges and immunities of a person in law, while limiting the responsibility of the individuals composing it, business leaders formed organizations powerful enough to absorb competitors. Amalgamations were financed by the new powerful banking houses, products of the war. Trusts came into being in both vertical and horizontal planes: the first controlled all raw materials necessary to a given product; the second controlled all manufacture of a given commodity. Some, like the Standard Oil, worked on both planes.[1] The trusts became so powerful that they controlled the lives, the fortunes and the sacred honor of individuals all over the land, not to mention their representatives in Congress assembled.

The trusts, however, simplified and coded standards. They introduced economy, speed, and undreamed-of quantity into production. Had they been organized to reduce rather than to maintain prices they would have conferred unguessable benefit. As it was, the cost of certain luxurious commodities was so reduced that, after the scotching of the octopus, standards of living were enabled to rise. Without the interval of monopoly, many

[1] For a good brief description of the rise of monopoly, see Morison and Commager, *The Growth of the American Republic*, N. Y., 1930, II, pp. 135 ff.

of us might still be riding bicycles or taking tramcars to our work and play as most of Europe does today, or struggling with candles, old oaken buckets and backyard privies. When government intervened, the trusts resorted to subterfuge combination to inhibit freedom but their power was so reduced or their stock distribution so enlarged or restraints and taxes so applied that the public could profit. Monopoly still has, of course, a long way to go toward true benevolence.

The point that must interest us here is that all this combination had a highly centralizing effect upon office management and communication. Consider all this activity focussing and depending for its record and direction upon the old sprawling, pigeon-holed, book-filing, letter-pressing, roll-top-desked, messenger-stumbling, pen-pushing Yankee-merchant offices! Picture the banks of high-stooled bookkeepers bent over their massive ledgers, forever dipping their pens and fingers in the ink "wells," *bêtes noirs* of the nineteenth-century office boy! Think of the legions of amanuenses committing to paper in a slow, beautiful, Spencerian script the infinity of communications and records concomitant of daily operations in a country-wide, amalgamated, five or ten or twenty-million-dollar enterprise! The telegraph brought a new burden and the telephone multiplied this again tenfold. Here of all places in the vast, new collectivizing scheme, there seemed the most irresistible necessity.

The slowness of the answer must be a continual puzzle to historians. It was not due to technological failure, as we shall see. It was not due to a pressure of organized labor, for the white-collars were the last to group themselves in defense of anything. It must have been, then, an extreme lag in one department of society and back of that department in the ever-inscrutable, ever-paradoxical and hence ever-fascinating exercise of the business mind.

The answer, of course, was the typewriter.

2

British patent records disclose a writing machine in 1714, though there is no evidence that any one ever saw it work.

Seventy years later another seems to have appeared in France. In 1829, a machine entrancing to antiquarians was patented in the United States, but as the model was destroyed in the Patent Office fire six years later it had to be reconstructed from data in the loyal family of its inventor. William Austin Burt was a sound technician, as his solar compass proves, and his writing machine contained features such as the type-wheel segment and roller feed which were carried far into typewriter history. From here on occasional efforts appear both in Europe and America, notably the attempts of Littledale in England in 1844. Foucault in France in 1850 and Alfred Beach (1857) in America, to produce writing by machine legible to the blind, and more especially the experiments of Charles Thurber of Massachusetts in 1843 and the real achievement of John Pratt, an American in London, in 1866.[2]

With all these data, the credit-searchers must flounder miserably over the effort to pin the invention to an individual. Most of them have fallen back on the undoubted truth that the machine would have remained forever a toy had it not attained a speed superior to handwriting and they therefore attach the laurel to the inventor who finally did hammer out a model which accomplished this. That he could have achieved it without the struggles of inventors that came before him is a matter of doubt, but there is no doubt whatever that the typewriter would never have become a practical reality without the army of technicians and promoters who followed him.

But there is one solid, incontrovertible yet inexplicable and tormenting fact which throws a highly obstructing technical monkey wrench into this whole historical effort and which, probably because of its obstacle to nice simplification, most of the historians have ignored. The fact is that speed in machine writing was in actual commercial practice over long distances via electromagnetic communication thirty years before any inventor made a machine which achieved it on the spot. In other words what was virtually the commercial teletype preceded the commercial

[2]Herkimer County Hist. Soc., *The Story of the Typewriter, 1873–1923,* Herkimer, N. Y., 1923, *passim.*

typewriter by just about three decades and had a wide practical use in various parts of the world for a good half century before the typewriter became a real necessity. As this was an American invention, it should come under our notice.

Before 1845, Samuel Morse and Alfred Vail had planned a keyboard for sending telegraph messages which looked much like the typewriter keyboard. As a key was depressed, what Morse called a "type" fell from a hopper and slid past a circuit-breaker which made and broke the circuit as it encountered the grooves in the type. At the receiving end, a recording instrument took down the message in code (dots and dashes) with a mechanically actuated pen, pencil or embossing point.

In 1846, Royal Earl House[3] patented an astonishing device which not only printed the record of a message sent by keyboard but printed it in Roman type. In the working of this beautiful machine, a technician may find the kind of step-by-step process which has become so immensely valuable in a variety of later inventions from typesetting machines to automatic telephone switchboards. In House's printing telegraph and its simpler, more efficient successor, the invention of David Edward Hughes[4] in 1855, we may see illustrations of mechanical ingenuity, complexity and delicacy probably ahead of any device of their time and surely beyond the technic of typewriter mechanism.[5]

It may seem surprising that the act of typing at a distance should have answered a more imperative need than that of typing in an office. We must remember, however, that Americans were concentrated on distances and therefore in the printing-telegraph, "telegraph" was the dominant word and thought in the hyphenate and that all the recording processes were secondary and incidental to the main project, which was distant communication. Society, here, decided the need and the technician and promoter answered it together, while the poor typewriter man got no encouragement to develop his toy.

The printing telegraph recorded seventy words a minute—a

[3]Carl W. Mitman, *D. A. B.*, IX, 259.   [4]*Ibid.*, IX, 347.
[5]For full descriptions, see George B. Prescott, *History, Theory and Practice of the Electric Telegraph*, Boston, 1860, Chaps. VII and IX.

good performance by any modern typewriter. The greatest claim put forth by any writing machine during the fifties and sixties was that it could produce type-script "almost as fast as the hand can write."

3

We have discussed elsewhere the difficulty of translating a complex motion of the hand into a simple machine motion.[6] Sewing-machine inventors had struggled with this problem and the machine stitch became a fact because most of them had seen a loom. The typewriter was easier because movable type had been a common medium of communication for three centuries. For this reason few inventors went mad trying to reproduce mechanically the making of letters with a pen. It was natural that an experienced printer should make the critical gesture.

This was Christopher Latham Sholes, the recipient of most of the credit for original typewriter invention. His story has been told so often[7] and with such attention to dramatic color that its detail scarcely needs repetition here. The real crisis in the story occurred when, at a doubtful point in Sholes' progress in his Milwaukee shop where he and his collaborators, Carlos Glidden and Samuel Soule, labored in their inadequate manner, a hurricane named Jim Densmore one day entered. This violent, florid gentleman seems to have looked at Sholes' then model, burst out in a flood of profanity which quite bewildered the gentle Sholes and then backed the machine with his entire fortune.[8]

Under the impetus of Densmore's dynamic violence Sholes produced some twenty-five or thirty successive models, each of which Densmore shipped away to be hammered to pieces by testing operators. The most merciless tester appears to have been a Supreme Court stenographer in Washington, James O. Clephane, whom we shall encounter presently in another technically allied invention. Clephane, already run ragged by his complex recording job, was eager enough for a machine that would combine speed and clarity.

[6]*M. I. M.*, pp. 360, 361.
[7]Henry W. Roby, *Story of the Invention of the Typewriter*, ed. by Milo M. Quaife, Menasha, Wis., 1925. See also our classified bibliography.
[8]Roby, pp. 37 ff.

In 1873, Densmore finally beat out of Sholes the best machine which he believed Sholes would ever produce. James Densmore has been criticized for his treatment of Sholes. We find it hard to agree with the criticism especially after all his money and most of his time had been expended on the idea. Densmore knew that the manufacture in quantity of accurate, enduring, efficient machines had passed the artisan stage. He knew that machines were made, now, by other machines and that men who had sub-

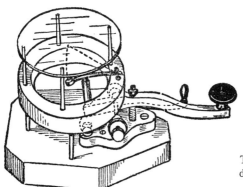

The first Sholes one-letter typewriter, drawn from memory by Charles Weller

stituted the title of engineer for that of mechanic were supervising their construction. He knew that invention had become collective and that many minds must work together under patient, abundant financing before a mechanical device could meet the hard public test. So he persuaded Sholes to sell out his rights and took the final model to the industry which had started the whole system of mass production of machines—the firearms industry. Specifically, he went to E. Remington and Company of Ilion, N. Y. Afraid of his own forceful but blunt articulation, he took with him a silver-tongued gentleman named George Yost to do the talking.

Yost won the day. *Sotto voce,* as they left, Philo Remington remarked to his confidential adviser, Henry Benedict: "It isn't necessary to tell these people that we are crazy over the invention, but I'm afraid I am pretty nearly so."[9]

The Sholes-Glidden model shown to the Remingtons in 1873 had radial type-bars hinged to a disc so that all letters would

[9]Herkimer, p. 58.

strike a common point. It had a sliding paper carriage moving by an escapement as letter and space keys were depressed. It had also a line spacer. It had a "standard" keyboard based on a printer's type case. It used only capital letters. The model was crude and fragile even after all the experiments. The first commercial machine built by the Remington shops six months after the signing of the contract with Densmore added few mechanical features, but it had stability. It was mounted on a sewing-machine stand (another Remington product) and the carriage return was operated by a treadle.[10]

This step brings us out of the first toy stage and should, we may imagine, bring us into the commercial phase. It does not. Like the telegraph, the typewriter must go through a second or "special utility" stage before it could be generally believed or accepted. As the telegraph first excited attention by communicating election news, the typewriter went through years of manuscript-typing, court reporting and other things before business would look at it.

Mark Twain gave it one of his first endorsements. "Gentlemen," he wrote to the Remingtons, ". . . I have entirely stopped using the Type Writer for the reason that I never could write a letter to anybody without receiving a request by return mail that I would not only describe the machine but state what progress I had made in the use of it, etc., etc."[11] He used it none the less—"this curiosity breeding little joker" for his manuscripts.[12]

In 1876, the Remingtons sent a machine to the Centennial Exhibition at Philadelphia. Exhibitions, in those days, were the great hope of all promoters of novelties. Crowds gathered about the machine but the exhibit was financed chiefly by the sale of typewritten souvenirs at a quarter apiece.[13]

4

There are several possible reasons for the resistance of business to the typewriter—none of them quite adequate. The men in the

[10]*Ibid.*, p. 64.   [11]*Ibid.*, p. 71.
[12]*Tom Sawyer* was thought by Mark Twain to be the first typed manuscript. Albert Bigelow Paine, *Mark Twain*, N. Y., 1912, pp. 535, 536.
[13]Herkimer, p. 77.

offices were more conservative than those in factories or ware-houses and the office, presenting its front to the customer, must have, always, an exaggerated dignity. Rapscallions though many of these occupants of desk chairs were, they must present an appearance of the utmost probity in everything they did. A machine would have aroused suspicion at once among cus-tomers; machines may be fixed or juggled. Further, it seemed to come between customer and salesman, to interrupt the "per-sonal touch."

Many persons were insulted by typewritten letters, some sup-posing the senders to believe that they could not read handwrit-ing, others thinking that the letters must be some form of printed circular. Another factor was expense. Writing materials cost but a few cents. Here was a machine that required an outlay of $125 and still did not supply the item of paper. And who was to operate it? Would there have to be a whole new department of experts especially educated to such skilled labor?

The typewriter had none of the productive appeal of the sew-ing machine. It could work no faster than the thought of the operator, and when he stopped thinking it too stopped. It could not make money. It was doubtful if it could save it. True, it wrote fast, but no one wrote letters as fast as that. It was a long time before the ideas of stenography and typewriting came to-gether.

These were some of the problems that faced the Remingtons. They soon abandoned them and turned them over to a sales organization, Wyckoff, Seamans and Benedict. By 1888, the Rem-ingtons were discouraged at the sluggish markets and sold out entirely to their sales company. Wyckoff, Seamans and Benedict had unusual enthusiasm and faith. Once in complete control of the machine, they organized promotion and education depart-ments and, with their first success, competitors arrived.

Sholes, meanwhile, had died. Sentimentalists are inclined to regard his story as tragic, but Sholes was a dreamer; he seems to have had little financial aspiration. All the credit has since gone to him, including a statue, which is, perhaps, more than he deserved. In the usual semifictional inventor's story, backers, stimulators and courageous manufacturers who take all the risks are, for the most part, forgotten.

A great deal has been said about the importance of the typewriter in giving employment to women. But women were already working outside the home in the eighties and nineties. They were in the factories, in hotels, in restaurants, in telephone exchanges. They had come into many jobs along with children when the machine reduced degrees of skill. After the acceptance of the typewriter, businessmen decided that this, also, meant semiskilled labor in the office.

It is true that the typewriter broke into a new, higher class, in which only teaching and nursing were considered respectable female employment, and it is true that the education of women proceeded apace to lift them into the typewriter class. It is also true that the typewriter introduced women for the first time in large numbers to business, with results which no one in the nineteenth century ever dreamed. That men did not foresee these results is profoundly to their discredit.

The more far-reaching social effects of the writing machines and their progeny lay in the total reform of office methods and management that followed in their train. In the reform came efficient division of labor, machine bookkeeping, systematic filing, indexing, multigraphing and a revolution in circularization which became, eventually, a business in itself. The machine's collateral relatives, if not its immediate legitimate progeny, were check-makers, addressographs, mimeographs and calculating machines in a variety defying the briefest inventory in any such space as we have, here, at our disposal. All these made it possible for the office to catch up with the speed of production, transport and commerce outside and materially reduced both its space and its force of workers. They paved the way to the intensive specialization so characteristic of the business world today. With them, agencies and middlemen multiplied with further division and simplification of work.

But the writing machine has never been wholly confined to the realm of business. Temperamental authors could not, for a long time, compose upon it and some cannot to this day; but from the beginning of the twentieth century, editors insisted upon "typescript" (a curious term) and so-called "longhand" must be copied on the machine or face rejection without reading. Here was a demand not for speed but for clarity. In legal work the machine became universal, for the same reason. Eventually it came into the schools and the colleges—especially when it developed its portable form,[14] so that today boys and girls are educated with a minimum of penmanship and many people arrive at maturity with unformed and uncertain handwriting. Only a few businessmen of the nineteen-thirties have been capable of writing even a legible signature, so that the custom has grown up of typing the name beneath it much as we used to inscribe a name and the words "his mark" below the cross of an illiterate.

The necessity of speed brought the typewriter into the telegraph offices when recording machines were momentarily abandoned and messages were read from the sounder. In Europe the printing telegraphs of House, Hughes, Phelps and others, somewhat improved, continued in use and still, in 1940, continue in many parts of the world, but Americans for years preferred to listen to the dots and dashes and hammer out the words on a typewriter. We have returned, in America, to printing telegraphs in variety, from stock tickers to the triumphant teletype, but there was an interval when the typewriter was a necessity in any office which used the key and sounder.

Operation was improved as soon as the touch system arrived and improvements in the machine were based on analysis of the correct motions of the typist. Curiously enough, touch operation did not, for many years, invade one province where typewriting became universal and newspaper reporters of the old school still hammer out their copy with one or two fingers of each hand. But in the city room longhand has scarcely been used in the twentieth century. Here speed is desirable, but clarity, which means speed of reading, is essential. With presses moving at the rate they moved in 1900, editors and compositors could no longer wait to puzzle out the scratchings of a hurried reporter.

[14] 1906.

Fifteen years before, with presses capable of turning out 30,000 papers an hour,[15] they had been obliged to wait not only for this but for the old, painful operation of setting type by hand, a process which had changed very little in four centuries. At such a late day in the history of journalism, when the web press was equipped to turn out such a fabulous quantity of newspapers, this delay must have been well-nigh intolerable. That it had not become so years before; that invention in the field of the press had not forced invention in machinery for composing the type is one of the strange lapses of our history. As we look at it more closely, however, we find a reason in the lag of the mechanical arts, in precision tools, in the progress of true automaticity, in the science of metallurgy which must yet combine lightness and durability. The development of the typewriter was a long step in these directions; indeed, as we look back on the technical aspects, it seems almost inevitable that the typewriter should come first and the demand for the typewriter was, as we have seen, oddly aborted. From the technical point of view, the story is intensely fascinating; so much so, indeed, that the temptation is great to neglect the social forces which must always direct the focus of this record. Let us look, then, at what had happened, since the midcentury in American journalism.

[15]Clark, *Hist. of Manufactures,* III, p. 294.

Chapter Eight

THE ARTICULATE NATION

I

A S THE penny press began in the cities; as the railroad and telegraph aided the news, as news-gathering associations multiplied, the cheap paper vogue became one of the factors of social democracy.[1] At this point another figure crept into the picture.

Benjamin Franklin discovered the astonishing economic possibility that a newspaper might be supported by its advertising. The possibility was not realized in his time and was not fully developed even by the first penny papers. As the circulation of the cheap press grew, however, and as newspaper publishers became aware of the fortunes to be made from the adequate promotion of advertising, papers changed character somewhat. In the free-for-all days, just before the twilight of individualism, the text of a proper newspaper presented a striking contrast to its advertising columns.

Not only did the most dignified papers print the scurrilous attacks of merchants and manufacturers upon their rivals, but they had no scruples about printing the most blatant announcements of quack doctors and useless or dangerous medicines claiming cures for all known distempers. Furthermore, at the apex of Victorian propriety, when the mention of any portion of female anatomy between the chin and the ankle in news or editorial columns would have been highly indecorous; when strenuous campaigns were carried on by the editors against the mildest forms of vice and incontinence; when it was believed by editors and readers alike that the scantiest understanding by children of the mechanics of their conception or parturition would thor-

[1]See *M. I. M.,* Chap. XXI, pp. 383 ff. See also pp. 380 ff. *infra.*

oughly destroy them, the advertising columns ran riot with crude, pornographic discussion of social diseases, sexual impotence, birth control, sex "hygiene" and all the detailed steps which must be taken by the pimply adolescent to make him a Don Juan of devastating proportions. The censorship of these items was exceedingly difficult in an age of free competition; their control was an evidence of the collective impulse. It came at last, and the daily press suffered financially.

The "art" of advertising through all this period advanced little. Advertisements were thrown and crowded together, the desideratum being as many words as possible in the smallest space, so that the eyes of school children were dimmed in the effort to discover their origin in 6-point type and older readers simply gave up trying to read the more respectable announcements. When censorship came, there was an interval when newspaper publishers were hard put to it to find decent advertising to keep up their incomes. Then, with prosperity, with large-scale production, advertising, too, began on a larger scale.

At once newspaper publishers were in difficulties. To carry more advertising the papers must be enlarged. Advertisers were already aware that their announcements must run adjacent to the text of the paper to carry the full appeal. The publishers knew that they must preserve a proper balance of news and advertising to keep their circulation. The material for news text, or what are now called "features," was abundant. But beyond a certain point, display advertising would no longer be able to carry news or editorial matter. The addition beyond this point of a page containing, let us say, a three-to-one or even a two-to-one proportion of news to advertising would impose a cost too great to be met by the advertiser. And this was true simply because the cost of composition of the text was so high compared with all the other costs of the newspaper.

Given ingenious sticks and chases, every simplification of composing-room equipment; given a fantastic speed of fingers, arms and eyes, it was still necessary for the compositor to pick his type from a case and insert it between his leads, to juggle his quads and spaces until the line was justified. When the printing was done or the plate made, he had to pull out the type again and put it back in the compartments from which it came. In the days of fast printing under this system, the hand of a good compositor moved faster than the eye of a layman could follow, yet it was not fast enough to get a large newspaper on the street in time to satisfy a public voracious for news except at a cost which would prohibit the sale of that paper at a price the public was willing to pay. And advertising merely completed the vicious circle.

The complementary arts, therefore, of modern advertising and modern journalism must wait hand-in-hand for the new technician. Advertising, on the whole, fared better. It had other mediums than newsprint.

2

The effort to compose type by machine dates far back in the nineteenth century.[2] The most ingenious devices came, at one point or another, to a standstill, leaving the greatest problems unsolved, and when such machines were put into operation it was found that they did a job so little better than the hand compositor that they were hardly worth their great cost. Yet there was a peculiar variety of inventive mind which kept men at the tormenting puzzle for its own sake—as if, indeed, they could not help it; it was a vice, an addiction, a disease which sent many a thinker to the asylum. Each of them contributed a little; advanced the process a short step so that when collateral technics caught up, the pieces of the puzzle fell so easily into place that untutored men wondered at the long delay. As in so many inventions, the longest step must be a mental catharsis: an elimination which must totally divorce the mechanical motions from those of the human hand.

The problems, as men familiar with printing first saw them, were these. First, a piece of type must be picked from a compartment in a case. Next, it must be carried to the chase or frame from which the impression was to be made and dropped between leads at the right-hand end of a line. Then the machine

[2]For probably the most complete history, see John Smith Thompson, *History of Composing Machines*, N. Y., 1904.

must repeat these complex motions until a second single type be inserted next the first and so on until a full line had run from right to left—a line of characters and spaces. These steps look difficult enough for an inanimate mechanism but they are nothing to what follows.

When the line is complete, it may come to an end in the middle of a word—at the wrong point for a hyphen or leaving no room for a hyphen. The lay reader who does not quite grasp this enigma as we explain it may explain it to himself by trying to typewrite a dozen lines making them all precisely the same length. If he succeeds, his page will contain astonishing violations of orthodox word presentation. The printer solves the puzzle by juggling his spaces; by taking out thick ones and substituting thin ones until the line of type just fills the space and ends at an orthodox point in the final word. However facile practice may make the compositor so that at last he may compose with his thoughts wandering away to wife and babies and budgets, it is nevertheless skilled labor actuated by a high department of the brain; a job far too shaded and delicate to entrust to an inanimate repetitive machine.

The job is called, in printers' jargon, "justification." The next job for the compositor is what is known as "distribution"—putting the tiny types back to bed after they have done their work, each type in its separate room. To conjure before the mind's eye a machine with fingers which will pick each fragment of metal from the chase, and then go searching about through the types' apartment house till it finds the proper room and there release its hold, is a feat which must be reserved for inventors running a high temperature or at least acutely alcoholized. Is it surprising that the doors of the lunatics' haven so often opened for these tired print-thinkers?

So the catharsis must come and thought must begin anew in a clean mind—a mind that must have lapsed back to Gutenberg and the very bottom origins of printing. As long as minds remained fastened on foundry type all experiments must end in some kind of failure: failure of mechanics, failure of speed or economic collapse. It is odd, looking at it from our present knowledge, how long inventive minds clung to these bits of metal in their cases.

Yet the first experiment of which we have adequate record was warm to the final answer. Doctor William Church of Boston made, in 1822, an adjunct to a typecasting machine[3] which caused the type after they had been cast and segregated in reservoirs to drop, at the bidding of the operator who worked a keyboard, into the case at the proper point. Justifying was then done by hand. The type were never distributed after use. They were remelted, and by remelting Doctor Church went a long way in his catharsis. Had he dropped one step in his setting process—the reservoirs—he would have gone farther, leaving only justification to torment the mind.

From this point, in England, France and America we see men racking their brains and, while no machine appeared that could do the whole job, contributions were made which became useful once the catharsis was complete. It is remarkable that before the invention of the typewriter, keyboards were in operation which released a single type from its particular reservoir and allowed that type to move through grooves to the exact spot over the chase from which it might drop into place. And one inventor[4] even reversed this process and by pressing keys caused the types to return from chase to case—a process scarcely more rapid than hand distribution, as the operator must read the type as he went along. In these keyboard inventions, it is enlightening to observe that while the typewriter had not been invented the piano had, and the keyboards of this period were all black-and-white reproductions of the index of the pianoforte.[5]

In Europe several experimenters discovered that by putting certain arrangements of nicks in foundry type, distribution could be achieved by mechanical principles somewhat analagous to those by which one key and only one will open a lock. Nicked type sliding along rods or wires corresponding to the nicks will stop sliding, let us say, when a certain rod comes to an end and will drop at that point. E. R. Gaudens in England and

[3]*New International Encyclopedia*, XXII, 607. Thompson, p. 5.
[4]F. Rosenberg, England, 1843. Thompson, pp. 7, 8. [5]*Ibid.*

Christian Sorenson in Sweden and Joseph Thorne in America all took out patents on such mechanisms. We know little about these inventors and it would scarcely be advisable to investigate their many headaches too closely. It will be well, however, to remember the nicks in the type and it may explain some of what follows if we bear in mind that the greatest concentration on this problem was in America, not in Europe. Why, we wonder? Was it the old "Yankee ingenuity" born in the days of whittling in the long winters on the New England farm, that kept these people at the puzzle merely because it was a puzzle? Or was it the impulse of speed already strong in the forties and fifties? Or was it the terrific urge toward articulation so characteristic of our later society?

Perhaps the overcurious student may find an answer in the lives of men like Mitchell, Alden, Felt, Westcott, Kasterbein, Paige, Richards, Burr, Thorne and MacMillan, who struggled with the problems after 1840. None solved them all. But there was one genius who cannot be passed over in any such summary fashion by any history of invention, social or otherwise. His whole performance was a tragedy. It dissipated many fortunes. Little enough of it has proved useful in the modern setting of type. Yet it is scarcely possible to believe that so prodigious a revelation of the high potentials of the human mind can have contributed nothing to mechanical progress as a whole. And his very mistakes, his whole colossal mistake, indeed, may have brought the turning point on this particular inventional road.

3

James W. Paige came from Rochester in western New York, where much of the Yankee tradition had removed as industry grew. Paige had two attributes of an inventor to a high degree: a scientific mind and an inexhaustible patience. His tragedy lay in the fact that there seems to have been something approaching a vacuum in the economic department of his mind. Usually inventors with this failing are compensated by stern companions —backers like Jim Densmore, who have cool business sense and more understanding of machine practice than machine theory.

Paige's backers were visionaries like Mark Twain, who always had a yen for any mechanical device which might impinge upon his creative product, and others who were subject to pure mechanical hypnosis. Thus a million and a half dollars went into the production of a couple of the most beautiful museum pieces in the entire history of mechanical invention.

Paige took the whole vast problem of setting, justifying and distributing foundry type and solved it without catharsis. The solution worked (in a museum environment) and Paige miraculously survived, which cannot be said of some of his associates. Yet when all was said and done, it must be described, at last, as the most expensive toy ever built.

Perhaps we may be excused from a detailed description of the machine by the statement that two of the attorneys who tried to explain it for the Patent Office records ended their lives in asylums. A few statistics, however, will suggest its complexity.

The invention was conceived in 1872; the first complete machine appeared in 1892. Before the first machine was completed the promoters[6] had spent $1,300,000, and it has been stated that "probably another million was expended before the end came."[7] The first patent application contained 204 sheets of drawings presenting 1000 separate views. Later applications contained 275 drawings, 123 specifications, 613 claims. Patents were pending eight years, during which one death and the two cases of insanity occurred among the examiners. During this time Paige's work was incessant, as it was, indeed, through the whole twenty years of perfection. The keyboard alone took ten years of constant study. The machine when complete contained 18,000 separate parts, 800 shaft bearings and weighed more than three tons. It required only a twelfth of a horsepower to run it.[8]

The keyboard was so managed that whole words could be set at once—the operator using all his fingers. At the end of each line the machine managed the justification mathematically while the compositor went right on composing the next line. A calculating machine did this job by measuring the space oc-

[6]Mark Twain invested heavily in this enterprise. Paine, *Mark Twain*, p. 903.
[7]Thompson, p. 25.　　　　[8]*Ibid.*, pp. 26, 27.

J. W. PAIGE.
MACHINE FOR DISTRIBUTING, SETTING, AND JUSTIFYING TYPE.
No. 547,860.   Patented Oct. 15, 1895.

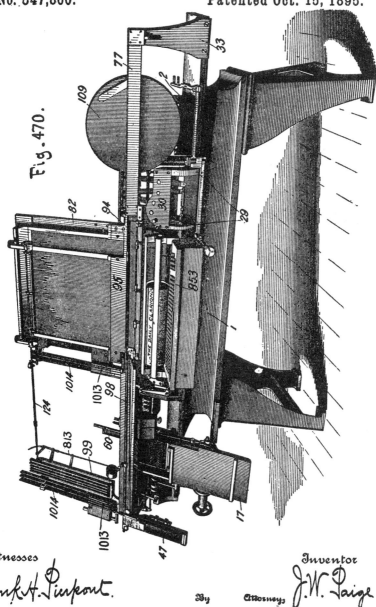

Fig. 470.

Witnesses
Frank H. Pierpont.

By   Attorneys

Inventor
J. W. Paige

cupied by each word as it was set and dividing the empty part of the line into the right number of spaces to be inserted when the time came. This principle reappeared, later, in modified form in the type-casting monotype of Tolbert Lanston. In the Paige machine, separate mechanisms tested the accuracy of the setting, threw out defective type or those which were turned or inverted. Distribution was managed by the nicked-type system. "Automatic stops locked every working part of the machine whenever its mechanism became deranged."[9]

Here, however, came the rub—or one of the rubs. The incredible Mr. Paige must have believed, while he was inventing, that he or some one like him would operate the machine and care for it while it was working. That there was no one like Mr. Paige in the world (and perhaps never has been or will be) became evident during the brief commercial operation of the giant compositor. The mechanism became "deranged" and only the inventor or such of his associates who had retained their sanity could locate the derangement. Repairs were expensive, delays inevitable. But more important than all (and Mr. Paige or Mr. Clemens should have considered this), there was no possibility of putting such a machine into mass or even large-scale production. To accomplish it some 18,000 other machines would have to be invented, each capable of turning out its own particular part in quantity. Having done this, the manufacturer would then have to assemble the 18,000 parts with reasonable rapidity and it would take an even greater mind than Mr. Paige's —if not a group of minds working a lifetime apiece—to put such assembly on anything like a profitable basis. The nineties were not ready for any like performance.

Only two machines were made, therefore, and both soon found their way to museums.[10] It is a tragic fact that as inventive genius moves too far without economic control, there comes a point where the descent is rapid from the sublime to the ridiculous and we are possessed by a horrid fear that an examination of the Paige machines may have given the initial impetus to the long and brilliant career of Mr. Rube Goldberg.

[9]*Ibid.*, p. 27. [10]*Ibid.*, p. 24.

4

We must come now to the catharsis. It was drastic and terrible and entailed great suffering to almost every one concerned. After it, starting from scratch, came one of the most important inventions in the history of the world—an invention probably second only in its sphere to the invention of movable types.

A German immigrant to the United States, a brilliant mechanic, a patient experimenter and above all an artisan of unimpeachable integrity is usually given full credit. Readers of Ottmar Mergenthaler's privately printed autobiography[11] may shed tears over his bitterness against the makers and users of his machine and grow bitter themselves at what they think is his inadequate compensation. It would be wise, however, to give heed to a few other historical and economic factors.

Many tears are wasted over the poor inventors. What happens to their creations? Bought at hard bargains by ruthless promoters, they are launched into mass manufacture by greedy capitalists, patents are wangled, pooled, twisted until at last the creator starves in a garret, alone and friendless, surrounded by replicas of his brain-child. So, according to legend, they perished by the thousand, Goodyear within smell of his rubber, Hargreaves within sound of his jenny, Buick looking through a frosted window and seeing his name on every fifth or tenth (or whatever it was) car that passed below.

For every inventor that dies in a garret, there is at least one who has received far more than he deserved; and every one who dies wealthy has at least a half-dozen collaborators who received inadequate compensation, and for almost every inventor to whom full credit is given there are a dozen or more bitter claimants and most, if not all, of them are right.

As we approach, therefore, the dramatic story of Ottmar Mergenthaler's spectacular achievement, we must be careful never to let him occupy the center of the stage for too long at a time or to divert attention from the other actors in the piece, at least one of whom must be called great.

[11]Ottmar Mergenthaler, *Biography of Ottmar Mergenthaler,* Baltimore, 1898.

James O. Clephane[12] appeared in a significant role in the story of the typewriter. He was a stenographer. He was probably the stenographer *par excellence* in the history of the United States. We may look down upon stenography today—the machine, perhaps, has done that for us—but Clephane took it seriously enough. His job was exigent; he recorded the debates of the Senate and tried to get them into a printed record as fast as a senator can talk.

Clephane, hammering at the Sholes-Glidden-Densmore writing machines,[13] was intent upon this problem. He was constantly stretching out his antennæ for new ideas. It is not surprising that such a man should provide a center for gadget-fanciers. It is more so that this center, once established, became such a magnet for investors.

Perhaps it was the great idea which drew the support. There was much, to be sure, in the persuasive personality of Clephane—a personality to which Mr. Dale Carnegie might well point. But all the subterfuges practiced today in the winning of friends and the influencing of people would have availed Clephane little without his dynamic, irrepressible faith. He had a kind of Napoleonic power that seemed to go with his little stature. Men flocked about him and he led them forward toward the avatar. If any faltered, Clephane would kick him back on his feet. He was harsh, merciless, dominant when the idea was before him.

One of the gadget men was Charles Moore of West Virginia, inventor of a printing telegraph. Clephane started him working on a machine that would print on a strip of paper in lithographic ink. The strip would then be made into justified lines with scissors and the stone which took the ink would be used for making replica impressions. It seems a silly, time-wasting performance but it was a step. Clephane, working from the typewriter, was not encumbered by foundry type.

Moore's machine did not work. Moore protested that he was

[12]The esteemed *D. A. B.* unaccountably omits him. See, however, Thomas Dreier, *The Power of Print—and Men,* issued by Mergenthaler Linotype Company, Brooklyn, 1936, pp. 7 ff., also Mergenthaler, *op. cit.,* p. 7, and all typewriter histories.
[13]See p. 133.

not a good enough mechanic. Clephane answered that they would find a good mechanic. By this time Clephane had influenced people to the extent of some $1500 and a group of enthusiasts had formed the Typographic Company[14]—an institution with vague technical purposes but a very definite social purpose: the quick translation of spoken words into print. So he set out again to find the best mechanic he could lay his hands on.

In Washington, in '76, there existed one of those shops which must have been both a haven and a heartbreak house for many inventors. Besides making models for hopeful mechanical creators, August Hahl, the proprietor, did a sound business in electrical instruments for the Government, which paid, if not better than the inventors, at least more regularly. It was lucky that Clephane picked Hahl's shop, for working in it was Hahl's cousin, the serious, deep-thinking, steady-handed German boy Mergenthaler, a genius of his own kind. The impact between these two giants is echoed in every click of every Linotype[15] in the world today.

They were a long way from the Linotype as they stood in Hahl's shop inspecting Moore's absurd machine. Mergenthaler happily knew nothing whatever about printing and it was this ignorance which administered the first cathartic. "I know nothing about printing," he said, "but I can make a machine that will work for your purpose."[16] He made it and was somewhat bored as he watched it work and saw how wrong the purpose was. He continued to be bored until Clephane came back with another idea. Then, slowly, he took fire and the flame which consumed him gave mechanical composition to the world. It must be remembered, however, that Clephane had supplied the spark and that Clephane, later, did much to fan the flame.

"It is no good, it is no good, it is no good," repeated Mergenthaler to Clephane's spark when Clephane first struck it. Clephane insisted and Mergenthaler, still in profound boredom, made the machine. The idea was to impress letters on papier-

[14]Dreier, pp. 16 f.
[15]The name is a trade-mark and is here capitalized for this reason, though it has crept into the language at last with a lower-case initial.
[16]Or words to that effect. Dreier, pp. 19 ff.

mâché until a mold or matrix was produced into which molten type metal would be poured. There is no record that the serious German laughed when the metal ate into the matrix and became inextricable from it. But he did go home and forget.

He did not forget for long. He could not. The type metal had eaten into his soul. The scar itched. Night after night he would start awake and before his eyes the vague wraith of a machine would form, come true an instant and fade again. Soon he was studying printing in his spare time. Printing, he found, contained one too many operations. The fault went back to Gutenberg. In the machine age, *movable types must be abandoned.*

Yet something must be movable, interchangeable. You would not propose, Ottmar, to carve your sentences on wood blocks in this late machine age? His mind jumped back, now, to Clephane's spark. Clephane had punched molds in papier-mâché. How about punching them in metal? Why not make a mold for each letter and then assemble these molds into a line and cast from them a line of type at a time, a line of immovable type? Movable molds, immovable type. It was a long thought and its pursuit took time.

It was eight years after their first meeting that Mergenthaler showed Clephane his "bar indenting" machine, now known as "Mergenthaler, 1884." It contained a series of bars on each of which was the whole alphabet in mold or female-matrix form. A keyboard shifted each bar up or down bringing the desired letter opposite a casting box. When all the bars were in position they together presented a line of matrices. It could be justified by slipping thin space bars between the type bars. The melted metal, forced into the box and cooled would receive the impression of a line of type.[17]

Mergenthaler was a perfectionist. Having shown his machine to Clephane he instantly lost interest in it. By the time Clephane and his company were ready to put it on the market Mergenthaler had a new model. On it he abandoned the bars, using instead the familiar brass circulating matrix that is used today. The briefest description of this machine shows how it combines

[17]We have omitted unimportant intervening experiments. One bar-indenting machine, for instance, still worked with male matrices and a papier-mâché mold.

the devices of many inventors with the final triumphant device of casting type in the machine, a line at a time.

The brass matrices are assembled in a magazine divided into compartments, one for each letter or character. As a key on the keyboard is pressed, the matrix slides out of its proper compart-

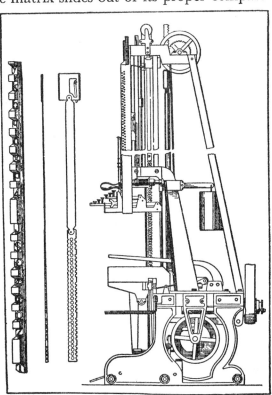

First direct casting band
machine of 1884
From *Biography of Ottmar
Mergenthaler*
Courtesy of Engineering
Societies Library

ment and takes its place in line. As the space key is struck, a spaceband slips between two of the matrices, its end protruding. The spacebands are wedge-shaped. The composition of matrices stops just before the end of the line; the forcing down of the spacebands tightens the line, justifying it with a single motion of a lever. From the complete, justified line of matrices, a line of type is cast by blowing molten metal against it. The matrices are then lifted, the spacebands removed by a simple mechanical motion and the matrices slide along rods to which their peculiar nicks adapt them until, as the rods give out, they drop back into the magazines from which they started. Here is almost exactly the nicked-type idea of Gaudens but carried out not with difficult, tiny, fragile type but with large, solid brass matrices or molds.[18]

It would be impossible to print from a line of type justified in

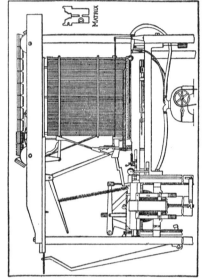

First machine with independent or free mats of 1885

Courtesy of Engineering Societies Library

this way. But it is possible and easy to cast a line of type from matrices so justified.

On a famous July 3 in 1886, Mergenthaler demonstrated his machine in the composing room of *The New York Tribune,* whose owner, Whitelaw Reid, in a sudden brainstorm blurted out the immortal name "Linotype!" as he watched.[19] By this time, Clephane had assembled a formidable group of capitalists —several of them newspaper men—who consolidated all earlier interests and formed a syndicate. Out of it grew the Mergenthaler Linotype Company.

Mergenthaler, at this point, seems to have become cantankerous. The difficulty began with a conflict between his stubborn perfectionism and the desire of the promoters and capitalists to go into production as quickly as possible. Mergenthaler was right but the demand could not be halted. As soon as it was seen

[18]Experts will shudder at our use of this word which has another meaning in Linotype jargon. We are not, however, writing for experts.

[19]Mergenthaler has much to say about Mr. Reid which is scarcely complimentary. As usual we evade the controversy, seeing no purpose to be served by entering it. Mergenthaler, pp. 34, 35.

the Linotype was wanted. Mergenthaler could see always a jump ahead of the promoters and knew that, with the improvements that were inevitable, this year's machine would next year be obsolete. The business men won, Mergenthaler sold out in 1888,[20] and for years newspapers limped along with inadequate and prejudicial machines.

We have then the curious spectacle of the Mergenthaler com-

Ottmar Mergenthaler demonstrating the first commercially successful linotype for Whitelaw Reid, 1886

From a drawing by J. Coggeshall Wilson

pany operating in production, while the inventor whose name it bore retired into his private machine shop where, for the rest of his life, he continued quite independently to make improvements on the Linotype![21] He sold his patents to the company and lived the kind of life he had chosen until, in 1899, he died with more than fifty patents to his credit. His last five years were marred by a terrific struggle with tuberculosis, and this may have helped embitter the autobiography he never finished.

The company went on. It encountered a multitude of troubles due, largely, to lags in the collateral technic.[22] The making of cheap durable matrices was impossible until fine small machine tools for punch-making were evolved and steel-hardening fully developed. The Linotype helped this evolution and the progress

[20]Dreier, p. 33. Mergenthaler, p. 34. [21]Dreier, p. 34. [22]*Ibid.*, pp. 36 ff.

OTT. MERGENTHALER'S RESIGNATION.

BALTIMORE, March 15, 1888.

DEAR SIR:

Your orders of the 10th have come to hand. Regarding the supplies still needed for the completion of the work now on hand I estimate the same to cost about $3,500.

Regarding the reduction of the pay roll at the Camden Street Factory, I can say that within three months the same can be decreased to practically nothing; how much such decrease will amount to from week to week I am unable to tell, as the men will have to be dropped just as they get done with the work on hand.

As to the carrying into effect of the order to close the Camden Street Factory, it is with reluctance that I see myself compelled to leave the same to my successor, and herewith tender to you my resignation as Manager of the company; the same to take effect as soon as convenient, certainly, however, before the order referred to has to go into general effect. The reasons which impel me to this step are generally known to the Board and yourself, and have already formed the subject-matter of a number of communications and complaints on my part to that body or yourself as their representative.

I mention letters of May 18, 1886, March 10, 1887, April 25, 1887 (to Mr. Wm. H. Smith), November 1, 1887, November 14, 1887, and November 24, 1887.

When I was first approached on the subject of giving up my well paying machine shop and to work for the company under a salary I was not at all anxious for such a change, and finally only consented on the condition that I was to be sole manager of the shop and judge of all technical questions, a condition without which I did not see that I could successfully carry out the enterprise to which I was to be appointed.

The contract, dated November 18, 1884, was drawn up in that spirit, and contains a clause which, although in different wording, was supposed to cover that point fully.

Under this contract I have since been faithfully working for the best interests of the company, and have complied with all its provisions to the letter. Under this contract the company did get into possession of its most valuable patents which in good faith I have assigned to the company, although I am sorry to record here that on the company's part most of the provisions are still to be carried out, and that provision of my being sole manager and judge of all technical questions has never, since the advent of the Mergenthaler Company, been recognized, and was, therefore, from the start a point of contention between myself and the Board.

I leave it to the Board to decide whether the company was benefited by such disregard of the plain provisions of the contract under which I consented to render my services, but whatever may be their opinion on this point, I cannot consider any longer to hold a position for which I did not engage myself, and which I never intended to fill.

Force of circumstances, particularly the fact that a large number of worthy people have invested in this enterprise, pinning their faith in my ability to carry it to a successful end, have so far prompted me to continue in charge of a work which I had to perform under so entirely different conditions than intended and under so many needless difficulties; but now I feel that I have complied with every promise ever made by me, and that in now leaving a position which I could not fill satisfactorily to myself and the Board both I am performing but a plain duty towards myself and the company. I leave the company (all reports to the contrary notwithstanding) as a full commercial

success in a condition to economically reproduce their machines in its own factories in numbers large enough to supply the present demands, and with a staff of competent men, who, under prudent management, are able to carry on the business of the company without further direct connection with it on my part.

As to my future relations with the company, I wish to say that I will do all in my power to assist the same in any way I can, always of course provided that the company will carry out the provisions of our contract in the same good faith in which I have carried out mine.

In any work which the company may have done outside of their own shop I should like to be considered on the same basis on which others are, but I should never again, under any consideration, consent to further work under a fixed salary, or to exclusively work for any one concern and excluding all other opportunities.

In entering into the contract with the National Typographic Company it has been part consideration on my part, that by so doing it would open up an avenue for the realization of a long-cherished ambition of mine to become the head of one of the largest commercial establishments in Baltimore. The exercise of my ability as an inventor I only regarded as the route to that end.

The action of the Board in suspending work is tearing down the foundations of the structure, which to build was the result of years, and the collapse of which I cannot witness from within. I prefer to pick up the material thus thrown away and use it in the building of a new structure built upon a different basis, feeling that by doing so I can best serve the interest of the company which is bearing my name, the welfare of which I still have as much at heart as ever.

Thanking yourself and the Board of Directors for the personal deference always shown to me, and feeling extremely sorry that our official relations could not be equally harmonious as our personal ones, I remain,

Yours truly,
[Signed]   OTT. MERGENTHALER.

Whitelaw Reid, Esq.,
President Mergenthaler Printing Company.

So far Mr. Mergenthaler considered this matter as a mere business disagreement. He simply signified his intention of abandoning a position in which he could neither do justice to his own ability nor satisfy the expectations of his superior. He had been given to understand plainly enough that he was not thought to be the right man for the place and therefore thought that his resignation would be a welcome relief to Mr. Reid and the syndicate.

However, the letters received subsequently soon showed that Mr. Reid considered the disagreement a personal one and that he intended to punish Mr. Mergenthaler for the crime of holding views differing from his own on business matters and for the obstinacy he showed in refusing to carry out a policy with which he was not in sympathy and which in his opinion would result in plunging the enterprise into trouble and ruin.

On March 17th, 1888, a letter was received, which with the ensuing correspondence, is here given.

The disagreement

From *Biography of Ottmar Mergenthaler*, pp. 34, 35

made under the direction of Philip Tell Dodge[23] was a tribute to his mechanical genius and his organizing power.

It is not our custom to throw roses to commercial enterprises, but it must be conceded that the company which bears Mergenthaler's name is today one of the most remarkable in existence. The spread of its machines over the entire world has posed peculiar problems of language requiring the services of advanced scholars. The company has retained them and matrices are now made in more than seventy languages, including Burmese, Arabic, Syriac, Armenian, Sanskrit and Hindi. To these in the past decade has been added the difficult Devangari alphabet of India, so that reading is now accessible in quantity to more than 300,000,000 people handicapped before by the difficulty of hand-setting their lingo. This only suggests the reach of an enterprise whose history is inextricable from the world progress of journalism.

5

That newspapers are not the sole product of printing and therefore are not the only users of mechanical typesetting is obvious. It was less obvious forty years ago and for some time after the daily press had satisfied its mania for speed by installing Linotypes, book type was still set by hand. There was a difference in appearance between a page printed from individual type and one printed from line slugs.[24] The difference was observed by readers who paid high prices for their books and publishers would not install the machines.

In answer to this difficulty, there came another type of machine designed not to set foundry type but to cast individual type and set them in line. This was a more remarkable achievement than Mergenthaler's, mechanically considered—especially when it arrived at the justification stage. The Monotype of Tolbert Lanston, however, is a refinement rather than a basic revolutionary invention. It is still abundantly in use for book printing, particularly in England.

The other machines have dropped largely out of competition. What the future holds for the composing-machine industry is

[23]*Ibid.*, pp. 41 ff.   [24]This has been overcome.

somewhat dubious. It is possible that we shall depart entirely from the composition of type, mechanically or otherwise. There are great economies in photo-offset printing.

The new journalism based on machine composition marched toward good and ill in the twentieth century. With virtually unlimited space at their disposal, advertisers rushed into the daily press. To keep its advertisers, a paper must keep its circulation. To increase advertising space, a paper must increase its news and editorial content. Advertising depended on sales. Sales competition was violent; occasionally it came close to war. In Chicago, competition between two newspapers took physical form, men were shot, trucks destroyed, reporters waylaid in the effort to "scoop" the news and be first on the street. The long guerrilla wars of Chicago gangs are said to have had their inception in a newspaper struggle.[25]

In other places rivalry was more orderly and the press grew with dignity in New York, Boston, Springfield, Baltimore, Louisville, Kansas City and other centers where able publishers and editors built monuments to the tradition of clean and truthful journalism. Side by side with this movement, grew the empire of Hearst. The so-called yellow journals, under cover of protecting and magnifying the power of "the people," developed a true cynicism of exploitation on a scale never equalled in history. Power became the sole standard and in the struggle toward that ideal brilliant men capable of greatness became sinners against the light. The yellow press brought on a war in 1898.[26] The infection spread to England and an empire of the press grew into being there which endured beyond its waning in America.

The press wars marked a late flare-up of individualism in America. But levelling influences were at work almost from the moment that machine composition started the race for power. That great collective agency, The Associated Press, and its growing competitor, United Press, created more and more dependence as the text of the news enlarged. With multiplied, consolidated

[25]This statement is based on personal interviews with reporters of the period.

[26]S. E. Morison and H. S. Commager, *The Growth of the American Republic*, N. Y., 1937, II, p. 293.

and efficient communication, scooping effort became wasteful in the city rooms, reporters listened more and more to the telephones, consulted police blotters and shared information. As the text spread beyond news and editorial matter and was forced by advertisers into features—departments, "columns," fiction, comics, women's pages and a quantity of other print which served little other purpose than to increase size and offer new space for display announcements—syndicates took charge and put these matters on a mass production and universal distribution basis.

Advertising enlarged to a point where middlemen became essential and the agencies, serving a quantity of clients, found it desirable to introduce collective control. In the general interest, scurrilous attacks, false statements (in the literal sense) and offensive advertisements must be suppressed. Associations of advertisers came into being for this purpose and new codes of "ethics" were drawn up by means of which falsehood, vulgarity, quackery, obscenity and offenses against taste were so refined and subtilized as to appear true, decorous and decent. In this way "art" came into advertising and as the public became educated to the new forms they became more effective than the old and businesses far larger than the quack-medicine industries were nourished by fears of offensive breathing and perspiring, decaying teeth and ringwormed feet. On the whole, this condition, balanced by increased frankness in other directions, was probably an improvement.

But the economic forces of the collective phase were also at work upon the newspapers. The emperors of the press followed the amalgamation trend. Hearst abolished local editorial policies and diverse politics along the string of his papers that stretched at last from coast to coast. Munsey, Howard, Curtis and the others did the same. The effect was a standardization of thought in tune with mass production of commodities. With a few exceptions, the newspapers became a mere utility, a condition which extended at last into such a plateau of dullness that a new effort became necessary especially when further mechanization began to compete in the air and on the screen. This is reflected today in what is known in press jargon as "rewrite," and the American press is today undergoing reconstruction on the French model with editorial color in the news.

With levelling, the yellow press took something from its betters, but the ochre has run also into the pages of some of the grand old journals. The craze for spectacular news and lurid color has scarcely abated under any influence and it is possibly true that the American press has been the strongest single factor in the spread of American crime. The suggestive power of a contemporary tabloid is beyond the imagination of most of us; it is beginning to be understood by psychiatrists.

Mechanical composition began the impetus which has made the United States, in all the world, the most articulate nation. Inherently, the frenzied desire to express must oppose the collective impulse. The conflict is strong at this moment even within that giant of consolidation, the American press. Above all the economic and commercial forces of the moment, opinion keeps emerging triumphant and free. In the best American papers its freedom seems at times even to shake off the stranglehold of the advertisers. They at all events impose almost the only limitation on its liberty. It is a condition that the rest of the world may well envy. And the historian of the future will find in the copies of those American newspapers whose publishers have been thoughtful enough to print them on rag paper, the greatest compendium of information on the state of the times that exists in the world today.

Mechanical composition brings to a close our record of the collective impulse. The effects of that impulse not only on society but on invention will be visible throughout our book. We enter now discussion of "consolidation." The word is used in its familiar, current military sense: ground is first gained, then consolidated. The wilderness is conquered, the nation is born; the land must now be worked and built upon, the political entity drawn together into a tighter unit.

The first physical factor of that consolidation that we shall encounter is wire. Wire might well be a symbol of American unity. It may, one day, be a symbol of American dispersion. From fence to dynamo to telephone it is integral in our history.

Part II

THE CONSOLIDATION OF POWER

Chapter Nine

WIRE

I

A N ORDERLY overland march of "pioneers" would be expected to settle the country by degrees from east to west as it became accessible to transport and it is natural to think of that settlement as being pushed forever on until, finally, the coast was reached. Always ahead would be the advance guard—explorers not settlers, adventurers whose fluidity of temper kept them moving; men unwilling to stop, consolidate or establish centers until, at last, the ocean stopped them. The advance guard would trace the trails, acquire an understanding of the country it crossed and in its footsteps would follow the settlers, stopping where the prospect pleased, establishing a home and waiting for the impedimenta of trade to catch up. Here is a methodical and orthodox procedure. It is not, however, what happened in America.

As we have seen, other factors intervened. A part of the pioneers moved by sea and found the west coast before more than a handful of overland adventurers had reached it. As ships improved, trade followed round the Horn and fur trade with Indians at one end and Chinese at the other, or barter between Yankees and Spaniards who had moved up overland, northwest from Mexico, while that league of nations known as the United States was in its infancy. When Ohio and Kentucky were still wilderness, scarcely known to white men, brisk business was going on in Oregon and California and the bases were laid for later possession. Then, by the time occasional settlement had appeared on the upper Mississippi, when the new states of Iowa and Wisconsin were almost totally empty and Minnesota a mere agricultural dream, an object so bright appeared in California that the migrants jumped the interval and clippers raced to the coast with the paraphernalia of coastal settlement.[1] So, for a time, the social map presented a curious appearance: California appeared prosperously organized, invasion of the rich prairies just across the Mississippi was under way, wedges from the West pushed by mining fever consequent upon California gold[2] appeared in Nevada and the space between was blank. It remained so until the last quarter of the century.

There was another factor. West of the rich prairies, the nature of the country changed. From an area of adequate rainfall where soil was deep and rich or pastures of apparently infinite extent were lush with grass, the emigrants moved into what the physical geographers call the semiarid or subhumid area later known as the Great Plains. Part of these was desert, capable of supporting only the most abstemious of desert plants, cactus, sage, mesquite; part was covered with coarse grass which supported the billions of bison which, as Hornaday says, were as innumerable as the leaves in a forest.[3]

The bison in turn supported a considerable population of the most violent and savage aborigines of the entire American continent. Their tribes ranged over the whole bison area and the white man from the first was an intuitively recognized enemy with whom there could be no compromise.[4] They contributed the final factor which made the Great Plains a forbidding domain and it is scarcely surprising that the emigrants, heavily armed and nonetheless extremely frightened, hurried across it. Indeed, even when the railroads came, it was decided at once that capital must be provided to span this area completely and rapidly as no stopping place was conceivable in its midst.[5]

Had the emigrants struck this territory some three centuries earlier, there would have been little to fear from the Indians, for it was only from the mid-sixteenth century that they became formidable. It is believed that the great instrument of their power appeared on the scene about 1541.[6] At that period, certain of

[1]M. I. M., Chap. XVIII.   [2]See pp. 505–508.
[3]Smithsonian Institution, Annual Report, 1887, Part II, p. 387.
[4]Walter P. Webb, The Great Plains, Boston, 1936, p. 59. [5]Ibid., p. 274.
[6]Ibid., p. 57. See also Clark Wissler, The American Indian, 2d ed., N. Y., 1922, p. 34.

the Spanish horses brought to America by Coronado and De Soto had run away, reverted to the wild state and produced large herds. The Indians captured them, broke them and finally re-domesticated them,[7] and from this time their culture changed. They presently developed such expertness in horsemanship that both their hunting and war powers grew to tremendous propor-

A buffalo hunt on the plains, from an early print

tions. The horse, says Webb, did for the Indian as much as the railroad did for the white man.[8]

White adventurers presently discovered also that only with the horse could the Great Plains be dominated. Reared on gentler rations, however, and knowing more advanced useful arts, they found little use for the bison, or buffalo[9] as it was more familiarly called, which supplied not only food but clothing, shelter and weapons to the Indian. To the American, the slow stupid bovine existed primarily for his sport and its destruction proceeded with great rapidity as soon as the Plains were invaded and was completed after the arrival of the railroad. The American, being no

[7]Webb says this process was completed by 1784, p. 57. See also A. L. Kroeber, *Anthropology*, N. Y., 1923, p. 387.
[8]Webb, pp. 53, 279.
[9]A misnomer derived from the name of a wild ox native of India. *O. E. D.*

longer in his hunting stage, found the cattle which had escaped from the Spanish country and had herded itself like the Spanish horses, more profitable. With his own horses, he was able to round up these herds in Texas and the border territories and drive them across the Great Plains to good hide and beef markets. This, then, was the first use to which Americans put this vast empty tract. In it grew up the great romance of the open range now so vital a part of American folklore. From the romance came the cowboy tradition, noble enough, perhaps, in its early stage but tenuous and dreary in its later ones.

The fact of the open range was short-lived enough. It was destroyed by new waves of immigration not only from the East but from Europe, by the railroad, by the agricultural impulse. But its death warrant was signed by the invention of a group of Illinois farmers and by the factory in Worcester, Massachusetts, which put the invention into quantity production. With this invention in the van, the giant, Industry, moved west another step, opened the Great Plains to the farmer's use and led to that farmer's further close relations with his Government—not the Government of his vague new state but the Federal center at Washington.[10] The invention has since covered the world in a less happy form and many a pioneer's grandson has cursed it with his dying words as his body was riddled under the cold glare of a star-shell in an alien nomansland.

2

In Nuremberg, at some point in the last half of the fourteenth century, an artisan about whom no one appears to know anything except his single name Rudolf, discovered a new way of making wire. Before this it had been hammered laboriously into shape from raw or forged metal. Rudolf made a rod, pointed the end, inserted the point in a hole in a metal plate, seized this point as it came through the hole with something resembling a pair of pincers and pulled till all the metal in the rod had been drawn through the hole. The result was wire with a circular

---

[10]Frederick J. Turner, *The Frontier in American History*, N. Y.. 1920, p. 257.

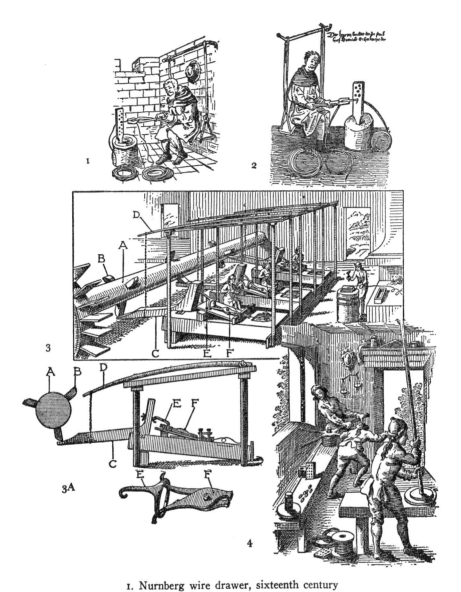

1. Nurnberg wire drawer, sixteenth century
Redrawn from a painting from *Mendel Monastery Portrait Book*, 1533

2. Wire drawer and equipment, Germany, 1421
Redrawn from a painting from *Mendel Monastery Portrait Book*, 1533

3. The last word in wire-drawing machines of 1760

3A. The detail of the machine. Corresponding letters show the important features
of this elaborate machine

4. Wire drawers at work, 1779
Redrawn from an engraving by Em. Eichel, Augsburg, 1779

section. Three hundred years later[11] the process found its way to England and thence it migrated to the American colonies. The principle use for wire in the New World was for "cards," devices by which wool or cotton fiber was combed before being spun into yarn. In 1666, Nathaniel Robinson in Lynn, Massachusetts, petitioned the General Court for aid in his "wyer" drawing and was refused.[12] A year later our old friend Joseph Jenks, the first American inventor of any importance, induced the court at Lynn, "being informed that there are in this towne a sett of tools for wyer drawings, and that there be some in that place that are skillful in that employ," to disburse forty shillings to encourage "those who shall make cards and pins of such wyer."[13]

From that time, we hear little about wire. There were wire mills in Connecticut and Pennsylvania which seem to have been managed somewhat in the fashion of the old ropewalk and the wire stretched out as it was made. A mill in New York City was made 200 feet long for this purpose.[14] In 1831, shortly after Joseph Henry had invented the electromagnetic telegraph and just before Samuel Morse had independently thought of it, the most important figure in American wire history established in Worcester the factory which was to revolutionize the industry.

Ichabod Washburn[15] installed in that factory—then a textile works making wire on the side—new machinery of his own design. A vital part of it was the draw-block, a circular drum which did the work of drawing the wire through the plate and at the same time wound the completed wire upon itself. From then on his output was multiplied by ten, and in 1834 the factory was turned over to making wire and nothing else.

Henry Smith, a literary master who, we may well wish, had turned his fine talent further into history, draws a brief picture of this year, worthy of quoting. It was the stagecoach era and "at times of arrival and departure, from ten to twenty stages were to be seen in these streets [of Worcester] at once; those

[11]1665. J. Bucknall Smith, *A Treatise upon Wire*, London, 1891, p. 2.
[12]Henry Smith, *Fifty Years of Wire Drawing*, Worcester, 1884, p. 5.
[13]Records of Lynn, v. 325, 348, 355. Quoted more fully by H. Smith, p. 5.
[14]H. Smith, pp. 5, 6.
[15]Carl W. Mitman, D. A. B., XIX, p. 501.

of the crack lines gleaming in gold and crimson, and canary yellow, with picked teams, and guided from the box by representatives of the old royal race of drivers.[16] During the year the stages carried 30,000 passengers between Worcester and Hartford. Industry seems to have boomed. Finished iron axles were made for the first time in America. The first gimlet-pointed screw appeared in that year. In Massachusetts was established the first American cutlery works, the first rifled cannon was cast and rubber was first made into clothing[17] (with disastrous results).[18] In New York was put into operation "the first machine for spinning rope yarn directly from the staple without hatcheling."[19] The total American output of wire for the year was 4500 tons.[20]

With his wire factory operating on his own new principles, Washburn established one of the two great wire dynasties of the United States. In 1834, there was little industrial use for wire in this country. Ten years later the words "What hath God wrought?" clicked from Washington to Baltimore, must have brought a thrill to Ichabod when he heard of them. By that time his new processes had driven out British competition and he was able to furnish the new telegraph with all the wire it needed.[21] In three more decades wire was ready to remake the Great Plains.

We must go back now to that country and consider more extensively the various reasons why it remained for so long on the maps as "unorganized."

3

It is a common exercise of the American, if not of the Anglo-Saxon, mentality to turn history into romance as rapidly as possible. In America, the background is brilliantly adapted to the transformation. Often it is a great convenience. Some of the less glorious incidents of our history have thus acquired a glamor. Our long tolerance of the bondage of a subject race which attracted, for years, the surprise of nations based on less democratic theory, has now been mellowed by dance and song and folklore;

[16]*Ibid.*, pp. 8, 9. [17]*Ibid.*, p. 19.
[18]*M. I. M.*, p. 307. [19]H. Smith, p. 20.
[20]*Ibid.*, p. 7. [21]Clark, *Hist. of Manufactures in the U. S.*, I, 518.

the shame we may once have felt is drowned in the Suwanee River. So, too, the destruction of the race whose domain we invaded, not by quick, clean death but by a slow degenerative process, by liquor, disease and confinement, has been absorbed now by the vague romances of the cowboy and the ranger, the Great West, Manifest Destiny and the American Dream. Late debunkers of the Indian myth have led us to conclusions no less romantic in fact; the effort to expose our delinquency has postulated a nobility in the red man which is largely spurious. Indeed, when we come to the Plains, we find the inhabitants not only brutal but sadistic,[22] not only dishonest but expert in the refinements of thievery.[23] So, in these matters, we must try to find a middle way between the myths, remembering always that in the movement of a dominant race across the new land we have merely a repetition of many surges toward civilization, accelerated this time by a more rapidly advancing technology.

With romance coloring our American history, we keep meeting such grandiloquent phrases as the "cotton kingdom," the "cattle kingdom," the "industrial empire" and so on. The grandeur of these titles suggests our later wonder at the magnitude of the things accomplished, as if, indeed, we had lost our power of such achievement. Our concern here is with the cattle kingdom, its brief exuberant life and its death at the hands of agriculture and industry.

As far back as 1846, a herd of wild cattle which were competing in the southern grasslands with the buffalo was rounded up and driven by Texas horsemen all the way to Ohio. In 1856 another was driven to Chicago.[24] They were used then mostly for leather, for which the hard driving did not hurt them. After the Civil War, however, the cattlemen went at the business more seriously for beef. By this time the cattle had increased to a point where between four and five million head were running more or less wild over Texas.[25] Incidentally, immense new urban settle-

---

[22]Richard I. Dodge, *The Hunting Grounds of the Great West,* London, 1877, pp. 417 ff.
[23]*Ibid.,* pp. 401 ff.
[24]Tenth U. S. Census, *Statistics of Agriculture,* p. 965. Quoted by Webb, p. 211.   [25]Webb, p. 216.

ment in the East, extending wherever the railroads ran, had built up a large meat market which could no longer be locally supplied. Invention and industry at this very moment supplied an invaluable medium of transport in the refrigerator car,[26] so the next step was to establish a convenient railhead to which the cowboys might drive their herds. With such a combination, cattlemen and promoters saw fabulous wealth ahead.

The first cattle railhead was at Sedalia, Missouri, but the cowboys had to fight a war against bandits to get there. So the brilliant promoter, Joseph Geating McCoy,[27] an Illinois stock farmer who had left his farm knowing of the inadequacy of midland farms to cope with Eastern meat scarcity, and come west, established the celebrated Abilene as the first true "cow town." McCoy did things on the grand scale. He was a typical American promoter of the expansive days who was never feased by a question of magnitude in operations. He bought the town site, built a hotel and stockyards and advertised the center. In 1867, the year of McCoy's arrival, 35,000 head of cattle arrived. Immediately a flourishing town with all the paraphernalia of the "wild West" center, dance halls, saloons, gambling resorts and brothels came into being. In 1871, 700,000 head were driven there.[28]

Thus the Eastern demand for beef was met. But once the scarcity was overcome, Easterners began to criticize the quality of Southwestern meat. The sinewy wild cattle did not yield the cuts these people had known before the scarcity began. They did not compare with the succulent roasts and steaks that came from domesticated Northern cattle. So the demand fell off and the cowboys resorted to the long fattening periods in country farther north, in the richer grasslands of Colorado, Wyoming and even Montana. Thus the cattle kingdom spread and the Great Plains became the free domain of the cowboy from Canada to Mexico; for the first time this country was of use to white men.

The cattle kingdom, then, was a valuable and necessary stage

[26]1867. See R. J. Wallis-Taylor, *Refrigeration, Cold Storage, and Ice-Making,* p. 365.
[27]Stella M. Drumm, "Joseph Geating McCoy," *D. A. B.,* XI, p. 618.
[28]Tenth Census, *Statistics of Agriculture,* p. 975.

in the consolidation of the continent. For the moment, it filled the gap between East and West. It constituted the first experiment in the unorganized country. It began the extermination of the Plains Indian. But in a rapidly growing nation into which each year there flowed immigration on a scale unprecedented in recorded history; in a land where the collective impulse had, through the railroad, the telegraph, the printing press and industrial machinery, an acceleration which nothing could halt, and under a socio-political doctrine which declared every man the equal of every other, such an oligarchy as the cattle kingdom could be only a stage and a short one at that.

In 1862, the Homestead Law offered a square of land a quarter of a mile to the side out of the "public domain" free to any one who would cultivate it. From that moment, the "boys in blue" already cut off from normal home ties by the war began to dream through their battles of a new paradise at the war's end. In 1865, they started by the tens of thousands on the long, long trail. At the same time, the advance guards of Swedes and Germans in Wisconsin pushed west, Minnesota was staked out and the advance guard stood at the edge of Dakota. Farther south, others followed the railroad across Nebraska. Steamboats racing up and down the Mississippi carried other hordes to convenient starting points on the west bank of the river. On all the trails, the trains of wagons became literally endless. Along the lines, many drivers, here and there, overcome by the beauty or richness of some square of free country, would pull out of the train and stop, but the train moved on. In the early seventies, it arrived at the frontiers of the cattle kingdom.

Now laying out a farm in more or less timbered country is one thing. Projecting it in treeless grasslands is another. The normal beginning for an agricultural settler was a fence. In New England, he built it of the stone he must dig out of his fields before he could plant. In other country, he built it of rails or boards from the trees he must cut before he could sow. But in the Great Plains, the very advantage of not having to dig out stone or cut trees carried with it the disadvantage of having no fence to delineate his farm. Living in an empty country or with neighbors who respected his rights, he might get along for a time without fences—branding his stock and letting them graze in a common pasture, though such a system, at best, appealed little to a thrifty European farmer. But when the roving herds of the cattle kingdom invaded his property, life became truly intolerable.

A few rich men fortunate enough to be near some line of transportation imported timber for fences at terrific cost. Others experimented with hedges. The only hedge material that would grow easily in most parts of the Plains area was the osage-orange plant and for several years the sale and distribution of its seeds made a thriving business. Hedges, however, took time to grow. And all this time there was war between the cattlemen and the farmers as to who should pay the cost of fencing. Should the cattle be fenced in or out? In, said the farmer; it was the duty of the cow owners to control them and keep them off private lands. Out, said the cattlemen; the Great Plains were their domain by right of primary occupation and the open range was their God-given privilege. Had they not laid out, with infinite pains and risk of their lives, the long trails to the railheads and the grazing grounds? But, on the other hand, had not the Government of the United States given land to the homesteaders on the express condition that they cultivate it? And how, pray, could they cultivate it when their crops were trampled and their own peaceful stock was attacked or seduced away into the wild herds? So the war went on, with every one concerned (including the Government)[29] becoming quite desperate until, suddenly, the whole problem was solved forever, in harmony with the normal pattern of our history, by invention and industry in the static centers.

4

In the early seventies, De Kalb, Illinois, was still a village, amid farms; industry had scarcely touched it. In it, at that period, lived two more or less prosperous farmers and a hardware dealer, each of whom had an ingenious flair for mechanics. The three being friends and having common interests, it was natural for them to go together one day to a country fair.[30] There

[29]Report, U. S. Dept. of Agriculture, 1871, p. 497.   [30]Webb, p. 299.

they came upon a curious exhibit. Strung along the smooth wires of an ordinary fence were wooden strips with sharp points sticking out from them. The three farmers examined the exhibit carefully; then each, separately, went home and thought about it.[31]

These gentlemen were Joseph Farwell Glidden, Isaac L. Ellwood and Jacob Haish. The fair seems to have taken place in the summer of 1873, a few months after Henry M. Rose had received a patent for his strips and points. Before the end of the year, both Glidden and Haish had independently applied for patents for barbed wire which dispensed with the strips. In 1874, patents were granted both of them. Ellwood then bought a half-interest in his friend Glidden's patent for $130 and together they converted an old coffee-grinder into a machine for making fences.[32] Privately, at the same time, and probably in ignorance of the activity of the others, Haish began the manufacture of barbed wire according to his own somewhat different design. They all seem to have sold all they could make.[33]

By this time, the town of Worcester in Massachusetts had become a thriving industrial city. The little factory of Ichabod Washburn had undergone enormous expansion under the demands of the telegraph and other electrical inventions. Ichabod had taken a partner and the Washburn and Moen Manufacturing Company was now administered by Washburn's son, Charles Grenfill Washburn, one of the most enterprising industrialists of the era.

In 1875, Charles Washburn began to notice with some surprise the large orders for iron wire which kept coming in from De Kalb. By the spring of '76, he became so surprised that he went to

[31]This, at least, is the story, later denied by Haish. Arthur G. Warren, "Barbed Wire, Who Invented It?" in *The Iron Age*, June 24, 1926, p. 5.
[32]Webb, p. 304.
[33]The whole subject of barbed wire has been given far too little historical attention considering the extent of its social effect. Webb treats it extensively in his Chapter VII. He has used primary sources throughout. Some of these are difficult of access. One, Charles G. Washburn's *History of Barbed Wire*, is still in manuscript in the Industrial Museum of The American Steel and Wire Co., Worcester, but photostats are in New York and other public libraries. We have examined sources used here but we cite Webb as a rule rather than the original source in the hope that the interested reader will look up his remarkable chapter. *The Great Plains* is always accessible.

De Kalb to find out about it.[34] His first meeting was with Haish, whom he offered $200,000 for his patent and factory. Haish refused, believing apparently that a Yankee's first offer could always be raised. He afterward said that if Washburn had gone about the business in an orthodox manner, he, Haish, would have accepted $25,000.[35] Washburn, however, closed the interview and went to Glidden. He bought Glidden's remaining half-interest for $60,000 plus a royalty of a quarter of a cent per pound on wire which might subsequently be sold by Washburn

Facsimile of a letter from Herbert L. Cary, superintendent of the Glidden plant at De Kalb, to his son in reply to a request for a statement relating to the use by Jos. F. Glidden in 1874 of a hand coffee mill to form barbs for his barb-wire fencing
Courtesy of The American Steel Company

and Moen for fifteen cents a pound or over. He arranged that Ellwood should continue his factory for the making of Glidden wire in De Kalb under the condition that Ellwood should sell it only in the West.[36]

As almost always happens in the history of invention, it turned out that several patents for barbed or spurred wire had been granted before Glidden's: notably those of Lucien B. Smith in 1867, William D. Hunt in 1867, Michael Kelly in 1868. There was the usual litigation and a fight between Haish and the Glidden interests which was long and tedious. It had little effect upon the result in the Great Plains and the fact that the wire was made by two or more competing companies probably helped

[34]Webb, p. 308.   [35]Warren, p. 6.   [36]*Ibid.*

in its distribution. The production figures bear simple testimony to the quick spread of the new fencing. In 1874, five tons were produced in the United States. In a quarter century the annual tonnage grew to about two hundred and fifty thousand.[37]

Barbed wire, as it was made after 1876, was of Bessemer or open-hearth steel, a much better material than iron, being more homogeneous, stronger and more durable. Indeed, it is doubtful if iron barbed wire would ever have proved a success. But the Washburn works were ready for Glidden's invention when it came. In 1871 they had installed the steel wire-rod-rolling mill which was the basis of all modern steel wire making.[38] Rapid automatic machinery for twisting the wire and attaching the barbs was presently introduced as well as painting and galvanizing processes. The details of these operations presented no great mechanical difficulties and mass production began at once. We are hardly concerned here with such details.[39]

There was some opposition to the use of the wire in the first years of its production. Cowboys complained that it injured horses and cattle; that these injuries were often fatal. The poor beasts would run headlong into it without seeing it. After a few experiences, horses and cows refused to pass between any two posts lest invisible wire be strung there.[40] To the harassed cattlemen it seems that the animals could never learn to understand its menace.[41] The animals learned quickly enough. The true menace of barbed wire was not to a hide here and there but to the whole existence of the open range and the "kingdom" which lived upon it.

With cheap fences to protect them, the farmers reached farther and farther into the Great Plains. They staked their homestead claims directly across the old cattle trails. Finally, the

[37]Webb, p. 310.
[38]Fred H. Daniels, "Wire-rod Rolling Mills and Their Development," American Society of Mechanical Engineers, *Transactions*, 1893, Vol. XIV.
[39]They are well described in the anonymous article, "Wire, Barbed," in *Encyclopedia Americana*. The machinery was patented by H. W. Putnam, Bennington, Vt., 1876. See Webb, p. 308.
[40]Webb, p. 315. W. S. James, *Cowboy Life in Texas*, Chicago, 1898, p. 108.
[41]There was even a short period of outlaw wire-cutting intended to defeat the progress of the farmers under the new inventions. Webb, pp. 313 ff.

cattlemen themselves found it profitable to fence in their stock and the wild herds grew tame and produced, in consequence, better meat. The multiplication of the railroads with abundant refrigerator cars made the long drives unnecessary. So the picturesque era closed and though some of us may shed a sentimental tear while listening to some lone ranger croon about his "little dogies" into the microphone, no one can seriously regret the translation of the open range with all its wild outlawry into peaceful and productive farms.

Barbed wire did not do the whole job. But it made possible the first advance of true settlers into the Great Plains. As they penetrated into the arid areas, new inventions for irrigation, water supply and "dry farming" must come to their aid.[42] Unhappily, along with excessive plowing, destruction of grass and reckless up-river deforestation came the soil erosion and flood destruction from which the descendants of these farmers are suffering today.

By 1890 the last frontier had vanished, the Indians had been beaten and herded into their unhappy reservations and the "unorganized" territory had been carved into states. From here on western settlement would decrease, the backwash would begin and the search for new industrial frontiers to replace the succession of geographical ones would lead the urban trend.

5

Barbed wire spread not only in the West. Soon it was replacing the old worn fences in the East. It was far more satisfactory. It did not cause the drifting of snow as the wooden fences had done. It adjusted itself by a mere twisting or untwisting to extremes of heat and cold. It did not obstruct the view. It helped conserve timber. Best of all, it was cheap and required little labor.

In 1914, the warring nations of Europe, searching about for new terrors, seized upon this peaceful American invention and tangled millions of miles of it between the trenches. Its presence there brought about a whole new set of military tactics,[43] wire

[42]Webb, Chap. VIII.
[43]"Wire Entanglements," *Encyclopedia Americana*. See also "Artillery," *Enc. Brit.* 14th Ed., 13th Ed. Sup.

cutters and long artillery preparation—the fire being directed at the entanglements—must operate before every raid or advance. What its future will be in this province we must leave to the military experts.

We have dwelt especially on barbed wire because it was an American invention which seemed to have social effects of far-reaching importance. Other uses of wire involve inventions not uniquely American, although in the production of wire for most purposes the United States is still in the lead. The main other uses have been for a multitude of electrical equipment and for telegraphy, telephony and steel cable. Fine wire for scientific and surgical use has been made in America to one four-thousandth of an inch in diameter.

The wire-rope or steel-cable industry was built in this country by a single American family. It began in the Alleghenies when John August Roebling, a wire manufacturer from Germany, made wire rope in Saxonburg, Pennsylvania, for the cumbersome Portage Railway of the 1830's.[44] This "railway" was a series of inclined planes built to draw canal boats, across the mountain ridges. Roebling, in 1840, made a rope of iron wire to replace the hemp rope then in use. In 1848, he established his celebrated plant in Trenton. The railroads by this time had signed the death warrant of Allegheny portage, but Roebling found an endless market for his product in shipyards. Having an engineer's training he presently became interested in the suspension of bridges by iron cable; he built the first railroad suspension bridge at Niagara Falls and died while planning the famous Brooklyn Bridge over the East River from New York. Like Washburn he founded a true industrial dynasty; the company he established in Trenton, the John A. Roebling's Sons Company, "has developed without a break from the little ropewalk in Saxonburg and at no time has it been out of the control of the family—sons, grandsons and great-grandsons of the founder."[45] The big Trenton plant makes almost every variety of wire today.

We associate wire rope with lifting and the suspension of great

44John K. Mumford, *Outspinning the Spider*, N. Y., 1921, p. 19.
45Charles J. Tilden, "John Augustus Roebling," *D. A. B.*, XVI, p. 88.

weights, the towing of vessels or cars—with rough physical jobs in commerce or industry. With its aid glowing ingots weighing several tons are carried through the steel mills, or giant steel cranes do their effective jobs of loading and unloading vessels, or derricks swing steel beams into position to consolidate the structure of a building. We are less inclined to consider this rope as a medium of delicate scientific experiment. Yet in 1938 a tapered steel rope seven miles long was constructed at the geophysical laboratory of the Carnegie Institution of Washington for the purpose of scooping up samples of the ocean's bottom. Doctor Charles Snowden Piggott has discovered through the use of this immense length of wire rope that a greater quantity of radium seems to lie in the red clay of certain portions of the bottom than can be found in any rocks on land.[46] But this is only one of the possibilities that such experiment with wire may reveal. The exploration of ocean bottoms is a significant effort of experimental science.

When Joseph Henry invented the insulation of wire in 1828, he introduced a new technology in electricity.[47] With this protection wire could be made into the coils on which electromagnets depend for their power. With insulated wire he built his "intensity coils" on which electromagnetic communications depend to overcome the obstacle of distance. In 1831, Michael Faraday in England carried Henry's induction theories a step farther and established the principles by which a series of inventors would use insulated wire for mechanically generated electricity and, finally, by a simple reversal of the dynamo, perfect the electric motor.

Neither the dynamo nor the motor was a strictly American invention but Americans have contributed so much to their development, and the social effects of them in America are so wide, that they must take their place in this record of the consolidation of power.

[46]*N. Y. Times,* Jan. 12, 1939, p. 21.
[47]*M. I. M.,* pp. 271 ff. The credit has been disputed.

Chapter Ten

THE WATER CYCLE

I

INDUSTRY in America began, as we have seen, on the rivers. The water wheel, having its origin, probably in remotest antiquity (though many attempts have been made to unearth the first one) came here quite naturally from Europe with the first settlers. The first industry, producing something readily adapted to commercial manufacture, was probably the gristmill simply operated by a water wheel. Something more complicated mechanically was introduced by the sawmill in which back-and-forth-moving saws were motivated by the water wheel plus a crank which translated rotary into reciprocating motion. Fulling mills, flax brakes and various sorts of other industrial devices driven by the water wheel multiplied in the eighteenth century, so what industrial centers there were clustered about the mill-races, natural or artificial, in the rivers.

By the beginning of the nineteenth century, therefore, mechanics had become skilled in the making of water wheels, and masons in the river valleys knew how to build effective dams. Meanwhile other mechanics had perfected a variety of power-operated machines. At the time of Samuel Slater and Eli Whitney a whole factory containing several different kinds of textile machines or machine tools could be run by a single water wheel, and by the time means had been found to keep out floods of foreign manufactures, most of the New England streams and some in the middle states became crowded with such establishments.

From the water wheel a belt or gearing carried the power to a shaft which revolved continuously. From this shaft belts transferred power to the individual machines. A machine was started or stopped by slipping a belt from the shaft on or off its particular wheel or drum. The whole factory could be rendered silent and motionless by throwing the main shaft out of connection with the water wheel. But the water wheel, like Old Man River who drove it, went on a-rolling forever. This was not regarded as wasted motion—you could not stop the river for any economic reason and the only waste was in the wear on the wheel and its bearings.

Then came steam. Its first large use was for transportation.[1] Industry did not need it while it stuck to its rivers. But the new steam transportation, once it started to move overland, showed people many excellent industrial sites nowhere near a river. They were excellent because they were near large bases of raw material: iron mines, fertile grain fields, abundant timber. Almost any site might become excellent industrially for one reason or another now that it could easily be reached by freight-carrying transport. But what to do for power?

It then occurred to industrialists that the steam engine which moved boats and locomotives so effectively might also be useful in a stationary position in a factory. Engines had been thus employed, of course, in Europe for nearly a century in country where there were coal and iron but no swift river. Also the nations of Europe had static, not fluid populations; Englishmen, Frenchmen and Germans had no raw continent beyond the immediate horizon which must be traversed and subdued. So the Europeans had followed a reverse process and taken the steam engine out of the factory and put it on a locomotive or in a boat when the secondary urgency of transport had appeared.

Inside the factory, however, conditions were the same as in the old days. A long shaft was geared or belted to the steam engine's flywheel just as it had been geared or belted to the water wheel. This shaft revolved continuously. To it were geared or belted the individual machines—a drill here, a lathe there, a planer somewhere else—and each machine could be started or stopped by slipping a belt on and off or unmeshing a couple of spurs. But the

[1]Our first importations as well as "made in America" engines were for mines, waterworks, sugar mills, grist and lumber mills. But these were few in number before the steamboat. For a list of them see Frank A. Taylor, *Catalog of the Mechanical Collections* . . . U. S. Nat'l Museum; Smithsonian Inst., Bulletin No. 173, 1939.

engine had to keep on running. When it stopped, the whole factory stopped. As long as a single machine turned, the engine must run. And the engine, unlike the water wheel, must be fed fuel.

It was difficult, therefore, to persuade many of the industrialists that the greater advantages to be derived from another site could compensate for the added cost of power. Some of them must have dreamed, in fitful sleep during their period of conflict between Old Man River and steam, of a shaft long enough to reach from their present dam to a new, alluring factory site a hundred or more miles away, and waked to laugh at the delirious concept. Yet at the very moment of their dreaming, inventors were moving by long, slow experiment toward its realization. Such a shaft, in effect, has come into common use. It is no longer a shaft as mechanical engineers knew shafts in the old days: it is a device less cumbersome, more docile, more simple than any shaft but it has brought us and may bring us more and more back to water wherever we may choose to be.[2]

2

When the classic chain of scientists and inventors[3]—Galvani, Volta, Nicholson, Davy, Oersted, Ampère, Sturgeon and Henry —had completed the connection from Benjamin Franklin to Michael Faraday, the world's understanding of electricity had arrived at a point where it might turn that force to some useful purpose. When Wheatstone and others were able to deflect Oersted's needle at a distance, the first useful purpose was achieved. But when Morse and Vail caused Henry's magnets to move pieces of metal at a distance, many people who watched the movement saw that electricity was here doing actual work. A few saw directly the work of Henry's magnets which, with the proper use of battery current and coils of insulated wire, had lifted weights of more than a ton before the idea of a telegraph had occurred to Morse.[4] The facility with which the magnet was

[2]See, however, A. A. Potter, in U. S. Nat. Resources Committee, *Technological Trends and National Policy*, pp. 259, 260. Also pp. 213, 214 *infra*.
[3]*M. I. M.*, pp. 264 ff.
[4]Not, however, before Henry had himself constructed a working electromagnetic communicating device. *M. I. M.*, p. 273.

Back to water in 1883

Hydroelectric plant of the Portrush Railway in Ireland. Cars on this road began daily operation in November, 1883

operated—by the simple closing of a switch—must have stirred every imaginative observer. Here was a mechanical operation of considerable magnitude which could be controlled by the slight motion of a finger.

Henry, of course, saw the possibilities more clearly than any one else. But Henry, as he was the first to recognize, was an experimenter and discoverer rather than an inventor; his concern was with pure, rather than applied science.[5] For this reason, his quiet work went on for years without attracting any great notice outside of the scientific world and never has he been celebrated like some of the promoters such as Samuel Morse who turned his discoveries into profitable commercial channels. To the men who urged him toward patent application he replied that he did not "consider it compatible with the dignity of science to confine the benefits which might be derived from it to the exclusive use of any individual."[6] Being a true scientist, he had no interest in competition or in establishing claims to priority in his discoveries. His delight was in patient experiment, not in fame.

In 1831, he made a reciprocating machine which operated by electromagnetism.[7] This consisted of a bar electromagnet arranged to oscillate in a vertical plane upon a fulcrum. A permanent magnet was placed under each end of the bar with its north pole uppermost. By means of wires from the coil arranged to make contacts with batteries near the ends of the bar, the current in the electromagnet was automatically reversed as the bar oscillated so that its poles were alternately attracted and repelled.[8] Having made this machine, he described it as a "philosophical toy."[9] While he played with it and other "toys," however, the principles of induction became evident to him. It was the understanding of these principles that made possible the invention of the dynamo and electric motor.

[5]During the late epidemic of popular biographies, this great American scientist has for some inscrutable reason been passed by and a "definitive" life is still unwritten. See, however, J. G. Crowther, "Joseph Henry," in *Famous American Men of Science*, N. Y., 1937, pp. 159–226.

[6]Crowther, p. 182 .   [7]*Silliman's Journal*, 1831, XX, pp. 340 ff.

[8]See cut and Henry's own description, p. 185 *infra*.

[9]"Although," he adds, ". . . it is not impossible that the same principle or some modification of it on a more extended scale, may hereafter be applied to some useful purpose." *Ibid*.

THE WATER CYCLE

At almost precisely the same moment that he did this, Michael Faraday in England discovered precisely the same principles. Much research has been devoted to a question in which Henry was little interested[10]—the question who did it first. "There is a

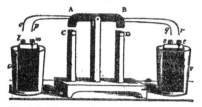

342   *Reciprocating Magnetic Attraction.*

and the galvanic communication formed by the amalgamated ends of the wires dipping into cups of mercury.

The whole will be more readily understood by a reference to the annexed drawing; A B is the horizontal magnet, about seven inches long, and moveable on an axis at the center: its two extremities when placed in a horizontal line, are about one inch from the north poles of the upright magnets C and D. G and F are two large tumblers containing diluted acid, in each of which is immersed a plate of zinc surrounded with copper. *l, m, s, t,* are four brass thimbles soldered to the zinc and copper of the batteries and filled with mercury.

The galvanic magnet AB is wound with three strands of copper bell wire, each about twenty five feet long; the similar ends of these are twisted together so as to form two stiff wires, which project beyond the extremity B, and dip into the thimbles *s, t.*

To the wires *q, r,* two other wires are soldered so as to project in an opposite direction, and dip into the thimbles *l, m.* The wires of the galvanic magnet have thus, as it were, four projecting ends; and by inspecting the figure it will be seen that the extremity *m,* which dips into the cup attached to the copper of the battery in G corresponds with the extremity *r* connecting with the zinc F.

When the batteries are in action, if the end B is depressed until *q, r* dips into the cups *s, t,* AB instantly becomes a powerful magnet, having its north pole at B; this of course is repelled by the north pole D, while at the same time it is attracted by C, the position is consequently changed, and *o, p* comes in contact with the mercury in *l, m ;* as soon as the communication is formed, the poles are reversed, and the position again changed. If the tumblers be

Tullia Pycnanthemoides.   343

filled with strong diluted acid, the motion is at first very rapid and powerful, but it soon almost entirely ceases. By partially filling the tumblers with weak acid, and occasionally adding a small quantity of fresh acid, a uniform motion, at the rate of seventy five vibrations in a minute, has been kept up for more than an hour : with a large battery and very weak acid, the motion might be continued for an indefinite length of time.

The motion, here described, is entirely distinct from that produced by the electro-magnetic combination of wires and magnets ; it results directly from the mechanical action of ordinary magnetism : galvanism being only introduced for the purpose of changing the poles.

My friend, Prof. Green, of Philadelphia, to whom I first exhibited this machine in motion, recommended the substitution of galvanic magnets for the two perpendicular steel ones. If an article of this kind was to be constructed on a large scale, this would undoubtedly be the better plan, as magnets of that kind can be made of any required power, but for a small apparatus, intended merely to exhibit the motion, the plan here described is perhaps the most convenient.

ART. XVIII.—*Description and History of a new Plant, Tullia Pycnanthemoides;* by MELINES CONKLIN LEAVENWORTH, M. D. of Augusta, Ga. (With a drawing.)

TO THE EDITOR.

Waterbury, Ct. May 17th, 1831.

Dear Sir,—I transmit to you a description and drawing of an American plant, which hitherto appears to have evaded the researches of botanists. The generic name which I have bestowed upon it is commemorative, and in compliment to my friend, William Tully, M. D. Professor of Botany, Materia Medica, and Therapeutics, in Yale College, I believe, (with a single exception,) the earliest cultivator of scientific botany, under the Linnæan method, in the state of Connecticut.   Yours Sir, very respectfully,

M. C. LEAVENWORTH.

DESCRIPTIO UBERIOR.

Caulis bi vel tripedalis, quadrangularis, subpubescens, supra medium ramosus ; rami numerosi, axillares, subfastigiati, incano-tomentosi.

Joseph Henry's motor with his own explanation of its operation. (See p. 184)

Facsimile of pp. 342, 343, Silliman's *American Journal of Science,* Vol. XX (1831)

wide opinion," says Crowther, "that if Henry had made this discovery exclusively American, he would have contributed more to the advancement of science in America by this single achievement, than by the manifold contributions that he recognizedly made. He would have given American science an inspiration which might have enabled it to dominate nineteenth-century physics. This, in turn, would have raised the standard of the whole of American culture, and have made American spiritual achievements in the period more equal to the material achieve-

[10]Mary Henry, however, has built a substantial case for her father in her "America's Part in the Discovery of Magneto-Electricity, Part IV," in *Electrical Engineer,* Feb. 10, 1892, pp. 134 ff.

ments."[11] Perhaps this is true, though in the large, the material stage had to come first. The mere existence of a man like Joseph Henry in America was in itself an evidence of the highest spiritual potential. It is possible that his very refusal to force such a claim in the interests of patriotism was the greatest spiritual achievement of all. And, as Crowther later remarks, "from the perspective of the history of science, the question of personal priority is of no importance."[12]

The fact remains that if we are to worship true heroes in America, Joseph Henry must be one of them. Until he attains at least an equal popular fame with a promoter like Morse who made Henry's invention a commercial success, there will be no justice in American hero-worship. In the spiritual realm at least, it is Henry rather than Morse or Edison who should stand as an example to the American schoolchild. Perhaps it is the difficulty of explaining him that has made him so vague a figure in the theatre of our popular education. He made no fortune and wanted none. He had little interest in making friends or influencing people. He put up no fight for personal recognition. The connection between his quiet work in a laboratory and all the powerful machines of modern mass production is contained in courses which are usually "not required" in the curriculum and it has not occurred to many teachers to include it in their lectures on American history.

The principles which Henry and Faraday (and possibly many others) simultaneously discovered were those of self-induction and electromagnetic induction. If two insulated wires are laid close together parallel to each other, a current started in one wire will induce a momentary current in the other wire in the opposite direction. At the instant the first current stops, a momentary current will again be induced in the parallel wire but moving now in a direction opposite to that of the first induced current. This discovery was later turned to advantage in the invention of the telephone and other things. It was especially useful in a matter which will come up later in this chapter.

At the moment, we are concerned with the other principle

[11]Crowther, pp. 162, 163.   [12]Ibid., p. 189.

established by these two scientists, the principle of electromagnetic induction. If one pole of a magnet is moved within a coil of wire, a current will be set up in that wire at right angles to the motion of the magnet. Similarly, a coil of wire turning between the two poles of a magnet would have a current generated in it which would move parallel to the axis of rotation. Here is the clue to a new way of generating electricity. No battery, remember, is required. Nothing but a magnet and a coil of wire is necessary to the induction of this current. As long as either the magnet or the coil moves, so does the current.

It was soon evident to persons watching this experiment that any magnet had a kind of aura about it, a sphere or "field," as it is properly called, of *electrical* influence. But really all that had been demonstrated was the reverse of the electromagnet. In the electromagnet, a current sent through the coil round a bar of iron made that bar into a magnet. Now it was discovered that a bar of iron which was already a magnet could start a current in a coil. In one case electricity induced magnetism. In the other, magnetism induced electricity.

It was natural—indeed it was inevitable—that Henry who had worked so long with electromagnets made with his own invention of coiled insulated wire should come upon this discovery. Faraday, less familiar with powerful electromagnets, is said to have begun his research into induction by watching Oersted's needle. Oersted, we remember, found that a current passing through a wire paralleled to a compass needle would deflect that needle. Faraday, looking at the needle, wondered if it would work the other way.[13] If you deflected the needle by moving it with your finger, would that cause a current to flow in the wire? He tried it but could scarcely measure a current so small. It was only when he had equipped himself with more powerful magnets like Henry's that he could be sure of his discovery. It is possible then, that Faraday first thought of the idea but could not prove it to his satisfaction until Henry had developed better equip-

[13]Rollo Appleyard, *A Tribute to Michael Faraday*, London, 1911, pp. 125, 153–175. Michael Faraday, *Diary*, Dec. 28, 1824. Bence Jones, *The Life and Letters of Faraday*, London, 1870, I, p. 382. See also Mary Henry in *Electrical Engineer*, Vol. XIII, No. 194, Jan. 20, 1892, pp. 2, 53.

ment.[14] It is this sort of interplay of knowledge and experiment that gives such history its beauty—a beauty which disappears when we try to give all the credit to one thinker.

From the discoveries of Faraday and Henry to the invention of the dynamo seems, offhand, a short and easy step. All that is necessary is to keep a coil moving continuously between magnetic poles and you have a current. You are able then to dispense forever with the battery. In practice the step was longer. In the first place certain mechanical difficulties presented themselves. Then a difficulty arose as to the kind of current produced. Men accustomed to the variety of current generated by chemical decomposition in a battery were a little perplexed when they observed the kind mechanically generated by the first dynamos. Questions of kind of current have agitated much of our technical history and have, in certain cases, reached out into social and political realms. We shall discuss these matters in their proper place. Meanwhile, we must look for a moment at another phase of electrical development—a phase peculiarly American.

3

It has often been looked upon as odd that the electric motor became, in America, a focus of attention before the dynamo. The sequence of thought is less curious, however, when we consider the practical or what is sometimes called the "material" attitude of most Americans of the time. They could see an electromagnet energized by the familiar battery lifting heavy weights. The battery, therefore, a simple thing which any one could make, was capable of producing power to do work. It was natural that minds habituated to manual work rather than to physics books should jump over the theory to its application. Remember, we are back in the early thirties now, before much of the "scientific method" had arrived in America.

In 1831, a Henry electromagnet was in use at the Penfield Iron Works at Crown Point, N. Y.[15] Any one who lived near by could go and look at it. Naturally it created a lot of talk in the sur-

[14]A successful experiment in 1831 is reported in a letter. Bence Jones, II, p. 6.
[15]Dorman B. E. Kent, *Thomas Davenport* in *Proceedings,* Vermont Hist. Soc., 1926, 1927, 1928, pp. 216 ff.

rounding rural districts. The talk spread across the Vermont line to Brandon. In Brandon, there lived a young blacksmith whose inquiring mind reached out beyond the everyday jobs of the shop.

Tom Davenport was one of those persons we often meet in the history of invention whose thought, once it has seized upon an

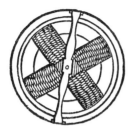

Tom Davenport's motor
From *The Electric Motor and Its Applications* by Martin and Wetzler

object, never lets go. Up to the point at which this boy first saw the Crown Point magnet, he seems to have been a studious, industrious youth.[16] For seven years he had served as blacksmith's apprentice, had saved his money scrupulously toward starting out in business for himself, had finally opened a shop, prospered, married a local girl and built a comfortable brick house. Then, suddenly, one day, he went to Crown Point, saw the magnet and all his docility, industriousness and even his native honesty departed. His whole being clicked at that moment into the conviction that despite hell and high water he must own an electromagnet. The conviction completely possessed him.

Without consulting his brother, he took his brother's horse, traded it for another inferior horse plus cash and with the cash bought not *the* magnet but an extra one the iron works seems to have had on hand.[17] He studied it, learned how it was made and constructed one of his own, using, according to a well-authenticated story, strips of his young wife's precious silk wedding dress to provide insulation.[18] His mind then made a tremendous jump and he built himself a rotary motor.

"This machine," says Mitman, "unquestionably constituted

[16]A frail, slender, touzle-headed boy . . . could generally be found inside the schoolhouse diligently absorbed in his studies," Kent, p. 211.

[17]*Ibid.*, p. 218.   [18]*Ibid.*, p. 219.

a complete embodiment of the principles of the modern electric motor."[19] It consisted of a wheel, the two spokes of which were electromagnets. He mounted the wheel so that it would revolve in a horizontal plane and fixed two electromagnets in the same plane, their poles pointed toward the spokes. By hitching up this apparatus to a battery and repeatedly changing the direction of the current and hence the poles of the magnets, he caused them to repel and attract one another alternately so that the wheel revolved. A commutator and brushes of sorts caused the current to flow automatically in spokes and fixed magnets at the proper moments.

Davenport went on like the typical old-time inventor into a life that was largely tragic. The intensity of his purpose was in the usual constant conflict with inadequate finances. By 1836, he had prepared a model for patent purposes; it was destroyed in the disastrous fire at the Patent Office in December of that year. He made another and received a patent early in 1837. The times were hard during the next decade and until his death in 1851, poor Tom Davenport could never get enough backing to carry out his multitude of brilliant ideas.

Modern industrial corporations are bitterly criticized because they keep inventors on a salary and derive large profits from their inventions. Are such inventors, living in comfort, surrounded by every facility for pursuing their chosen work, less happy than poor, harassed Tom Davenport wasting most of his energy not in technical achievement but in trying to find capital?

Davenport did, however, make several important contributions to applied science before he died. He built a model car which ran by electricity, organized what is said to have been the first electric stock company in America, if not in the world,[20] and made an electromagnetic player-piano[21] (1850).

Contemporary with Davenport were many other motor experimenters in several parts of the world. In Scotland, Robert Davidson built an electric locomotive in 1838. Charles Grafton Page[22] of Salem, a brilliant scientific experimenter, worked from

[19]Carl W. Mitman, "Thomas Davenport," *D. A. B.,* V, p. 88.
[20]Electro-Magnetic Association, 1837, Kaempffert, I, p. 109.
[21]Mitman, *op. cit.,* p. 88.   [22]Mitman, *D. A. B.,* XIV, p. 135.

1838 on electromagnetic machines to replace steam engines. His motors were, however, reciprocating, like the steam engines of the day: the piston being replaced by an electromagnet and the steam cylinder by the magnetizing coil. In 1851, a locomotive designed by him with engines of this sort ran nineteen miles an hour in Maryland and shook its batteries to pieces in the process. Moses Gerrish Farmer, more famous for other inventions,[23] built a model electric railroad train, also run by batteries, at about the same time. By the fifties, however, the chief reason for all the failures was beginning to be apparent and American experimenters realized that they had jumped too far in the effort to turn electricity into power without first learning how to make it. The trouble, of course, was with the battery.

4

In Europe, while all these sporadic attempts were failing in America, patient scientists were establishing some remarkable theoretical truths.[24] What might be called the two-wayness of electricity was one of them. Faraday had asked whether, if the current deflected the needle would a deflected needle induce a current? Finally he constructed a machine which proved it.[25] It was a copper disk arranged to revolve between the poles of a large magnet. By applying brushes, one to the hub, one to the rim of the wheel, he carried off the current. He then put this current through its paces and found that it had the same characteristics as the battery current which, across the Atlantic, Davenport was about to carry, by means of similar brushes, into magnets which would make a wheel revolve. If Davenport had known it, therefore, a few slight changes in his motor would have made it into a dynamo to generate rather than use current.

When inventors made machines on Faraday's principles which

[23]Telegraphy, lighting, electroplating.

[24]For Faraday's experiments see his *Experimental Researches,* London, 1844, pp. 1–60.

[25]The two-wayness of electricity is likewise visible in battery current. Here a current which results from chemical decomposition in the battery will *cause* decomposition in certain chemical substances. On this fact depends electrolysis, a technology by which much chemical breaking down or analysis is carried on.

when they revolved generated a current, they revealed another two-wayness. For as the operation of Davenport's motor *depended on* a continual change of polarity, which is to say a continual change of direction in the current applied to it, so the first dynamos *produced* a continual change of polarity, which is to say a continual change of direction of current. So the current from these dynamos moved first one way and then the other; it was, in short, what was later recognized as the extremely useful "alternating current." It was not immediately recognized as useful because it behaved, with its back-and-forth motion, so differently from the old familiar direct battery current that the inventors made strenuous efforts to overcome its alternation. This was finally done by changing the commutator and brushes— the devices by which the current was accumulated and carried off.

The alternating current dynamo has two brushes bearing on two rings which in turn are in constant contact each with a wire from the opposite end of a revolving coil. As these wires change polarities each time the coil turns, the current in the circuit between the brushes naturally moves back and forth. But by using one ring, splitting it in two and insulating the two parts from each other and then resting both brushes on the ring, each brush will alternately come in contact with one or the other end wire of the coil so that as the coil turns and the polarities change, one brush will always be positive and the other negative, making the current flow always in one direction.[26] This trick of the split commutator seems to have been first applied to the dynamo by Antonio Pacinotti, an Italian vintner who was led away from his grapes by electricity.

The current resulting from Pacinotti's dynamo while direct, moving in one direction only, was not continuous—that is to say it was intermittent, just as we suspect that Davenport's first motor had a jerky, uneven motion. The reason, in Davenport's case, was that there were only two spokes. The jerkiness was overcome when the number of spokes was increased. So, going back to our two-wayness, the jerkiness or intermittency of a

[26]Lancelot Hogben, *Science for the Citizen*, N. Y., 1938, pp. 704–706.

current generated by a dynamo must be overcome by multiplying its spokes or coils and this, in effect, was what was done by the Belgian Zénobe Théophile Gramme who is regarded as the father of the continuous direct current dynamo.

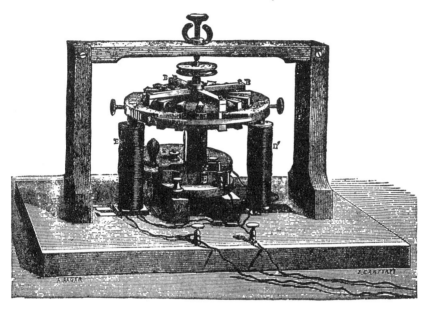

Antonio Pacinotti's dynamo
From *The Electric Motor and Its Applications* by Martin and Wetzler

As a result of the Gramme dynamo, the electric motor was invented all over again—accidentally, as Mr. Martin explains. "At an industrial exhibition in Vienna, 1873, a number of Gramme dynamos were being set up as exhibits. In making the electrical connections to one of these machines, not yet belted to the shaft of the driving steam-engine, a careless workman by mistake attached to its binding posts the ends of two wires already connected to another dynamo actually in operation. . . . To the intense astonishment of everybody looking on, the armature of the second machine began to revolve with great rapidity. When the attention of Gramme was directed to this highly novel phenomenon, he saw that the second machine was functioning as a motor, with current from the first, and that what took place was an actual transfer of mechanical energy through the agency of electricity."[27] We suspect that had poor Tom Davenport been shown the Gramme dynamo before it began to revolve and asked what he thought it was, he would have replied simply, "Why yes, of course, it is a rotary electric motor—like mine, only better made," and he would not have been in the least astonished to see it turn.

The way we have expressed what we have written of these matters may displease electrical engineers. We have simply used terms which seem to us more primary than theirs. The electrician says that there exists between the poles of a magnet a magnetic field. He then says that when that field is cut by a wire which is at right angles to a line between the poles of the magnet a current is induced in the wire. Multiplying the wires into a coil, he winds them about a core, preferably of soft iron and calls the whole business—core and coil together—the armature. The magnet between the poles of which the armature turns in order that its wires shall successively cut the field, he calls the field magnet or more often, simply, "the field."

Further technical explanation of the dynamo and its development, of the "self-exciting" phenomenon discovered in the core by which the field magnets were magnetized and many other refinements of commutators, brushes, materials and so on would not modify in any degree the social effects of the dynamo. They were colossal.

5

Few things are more disturbing to the social historian who wishes to simplify the sweep of history for his readers than variations of tempo. When these are produced by multiplication of factors, by complicated interchangeability of cause and effect, by economic fogs which obscure the sharp, clean edges of technology, by the presence of human weaknesses and inequalities, by the operation of such evasive forces as greed, falsification, ambition, and the desire of men to dominate large masses of their fellows, the effort to arrange the material in any ordered scheme seems well-nigh hopeless. It is in moments like this that we should

[27]T. Commerford Martin, "The Rise of Electricity," in Kaempffert, I, p. 523.

like to fall back upon the poet or the artist whose motive is to present all things and solve nothing.

Tolstoi, seeing, in his bright creative intervals, the impossibility of solutions in a world whose motion was influenced by the incalculable vectors of human passion, gave to that world a better understanding of war than all the strategists and military experts put together though his work is labelled fiction. When, in his less lucid moments, he descended to critical effort and endeavored to solve human problems by direct attack, he precipitated a confusion from which many of his readers have never recovered.

The artist may now be alive who will one day present in the creative manner the impact of science upon society and the complexity of the refractions which resulted. The mathematician and the physicist, however many electrons they may discover dancing about in the human body, will probably persuade no one but themselves toward an understanding. They may see the beautiful Infinity itself, yet, unless they can induce us to follow them as mystics in the blind, faithful manner in which men once followed Thomas Aquinas, they can help us little. It is conceivable that some such rare individual as Lancelot Hogben whose incredible mind seems capable of reaching outside his formulas into remote crannies of human experience may bring a measure of comfort if not understanding to distraught souls caught in the web of the problem. In the meantime, the rest of us must flounder on with our little schemes and diagrams, our footnotes and statistics, our facts and our speculations in the hope that an occasional slant ray of light may penetrate our own consciousness if not that of our readers.

With all the rapid mechanization that we observe going on in the world and especially in America in the nineteenth century, with the apparently steady, inevitable march of the iron men, the echo of whose steps seems to reveal no break in cadence, it was forty years after the Gramme dynamo and eighty years after the discoveries of Faraday and Henry before electrification in America had reached sufficient proportions to constitute a new industrial revolution. The precise specifications of such a revolution we will leave to our betters but the consensus of informed opinion places its opening years as 1910–12.[28] It is, in any case, a fact that we were well on in the nineties before electricity began to impinge to any appreciable extent upon American industrial processes. How shall we account for this delay?

One factor, surely, was the pattern laid down in the early years of our existence by our inherent physical problems. Steam power, when it arrived in the second decade of our federal history, jumped over industry and attached itself to the more immediate necessity of transportation. In the first four decades of the new century it remained, largely, in that province. When the so-called galvanic battery appeared, our era of migration was in full career and the battery, as we have seen, almost immediately jumped on board locomotives and cars with such indifferent success as we have observed. Precisely the same thing happened when mechanically generated electric energy appeared on the horizon. In the seventies, when European scientists and mechanics had finally and after terrific effort evolved machines to generate the kind of current which afterward turned out to be unnecessary for most purposes, American society was still in a state of flux. In our static centers, into which the dynamo came first, we had settled down somewhat but even there our habit of mind was strong enough to make us put our new variety of energy into going somewhere rather than making something.

Thus as far back as 1874, the year after the Gramme dynamo revealed itself so spectacularly and unexpectedly as a motor, we find Stephen D. Field, whose uncle of the same name we have already met,[29] experimenting with an electric railway to be operated by a dynamo via a third rail. In 1880, we find the genius of Menlo Park experimenting, but without important results, with traction. Although the name Edison has since appeared on many traction devices, this use in most cases derives rather from commercial negotiation than from invention. The Edison experiments like all other efforts in this direction became insignificant

[28]Hugh Quigley, *Electric Power*, in Encyc. of the Social Sciences, N. Y., 1931, V, p. 456. Martin Insull, *America's New Frontier*, Chicago, 1929, pp. 11 ff. Harry E. Barnes, *Economic History of the Western World*, N. Y., 1937, pp. 445 ff.
[29]Chap. I.

beside the immense achievements of Frank Julian Sprague, the inventor who has rightly been called the "father of electric traction." A confusion has naturally developed because Edison's company gained control of Sprague's company[30] after which the Sprague name was dropped from the acquired equipment.

Sprague invented the universally adjustable under-running contact system for trolley railways in 1882, the wheelbarrow type of geared motor suspension in 1885 and, ten years later, the multiple-unit system of train control which made possible the effective operation of elevated and subway trains and has since revolutionized suburban traffic on the railroads. In 1887, he made, in Richmond, Virginia, the first complete electrification of an existing street railways system—the largest installation in the world up to that time and followed it in two years by more than a hundred other installations.

In categorical histories of inventions and popular pigeon-holed presentations of the general subject, the name of this astonishing inventor has been tacked so firmly to the trolley car that the social effect of his achievement may have been misunderstood since this variety of transport has largely disappeared from the American scene. The interurban trolley did, to some extent, relieve congestion and disperse the population.[31]

But the combination of the automobile and the electric suburban train produced dispersion from the cities—at least for residence purposes—on an enormous scale. It resulted in a whole new pattern of living of which movement became an essential part. It transported a large part of urban population to more spacious living quarters, leaving the city center to business offices. It is true that it transported the working members of the family to the country for only a part of the day. For the working hours, they must come back. But for the other members of the family it created a home life upon which the city crowding need not impinge. Children could grow up with more freedom, fresh air, exercise and an approach to rural activities. There was dispersion

---

[30]1889. For the opinion then held by Edison directors of the Sprague successes, see First Annual Report, Edison General Electric Co., Jan. 2, 1890.
[31]See p. 86.

Oct. 10, 1931

PERSONAL:

Mr. S. H. Libby,
General Electric Co.,
5 Lawrence St.,
Bloomfield, N. J.

Dear Libby:

I have just received the 1931 back numbers of "The Link" now a G.E. issue, but published, I understand, originally as a Sprague paper.

Hence perhaps you will appreciate my chagrin on noting in the Feb. 20th issue the absence of all reference to Sprague or his work, and the assignment to Mr. Edison of the credit for the development of electric traction.

While the facts stated with regard to the Menlo experiments are probably fairly correct so far as they go, the inference that they were the first, or embodied anything of real novelty, and that what was done was either like or laid the foundation of electric traction is absolutely foreign to the facts.

That this distorted statement should appear in what was originally a Sprague publication, edited by my old associate, and issued under the aegis of the G.E. Co. is warrant for the deepest feeling of resentment and indignation on my part.

Popular applause, commercial propaganda and sentimental gush have helped to build up a legend, largely mythical, to the effect that if Mr. Edison ever had anything to do with anything electrical, no matter how remotely, and regardless of whether he contributed anything of novelty or value, if at any time in the span of human life success was achieved by whatever labor and sacrifice of others, it immediately became an Edison offspring.

Could anything be more unjust to other early pioneers, and to the thousands of able workers in the electric field?

I have time and again told in extended fashion the story of the development of electric traction, both vertical and horizontal, and have tried to give full measure of credit to the many pioneer workers. It is to them and to me - not to Mr. Edison - that the credit for this outstanding industry belongs.

GENERAL ELECTRIC COMPANY

GENERAL OFFICE SCHENECTADY, N.Y.

3 Lawrence St.
BLOOMFIELD, N.J.
October 19, 1931

Mr. F. J. Sprague,
421 Canal Street
New York, N. Y.

My dear Mr. Sprague:

Referring to your letter of October 10, on the face of the evidence, your indignation at the thought I would be guilty of playing you such a scurvy trick was fully justified, but as a matter of fact I am able to prove a complete alibi, that the paper is now prepared for publication and printed in Schenectady, and the entire middle section, consisting of pages one to twelve, inclusive, is written by the Publication Bureau at Schenectady, is the same for all of the papers of the different Works, and is not seen by me or any of the other editors until we receive our completed papers.

The editors located at the different Works prepare only the local material pertaining to their particular Plant, and have absolutely nothing to do with the general section, in one issue of which the story to which you refer appeared.

As further evidence of my continued loyalty to my old employer, if indeed such evidence is needed, I submit a copy of a story written for the Independent Press of Bloomfield, at the time the six story building was completed in 1918.

I sincerely hope that this will remove all doubts as to my understanding of who is the real "father" of the electric railway as at present developed.

Very truly yours

SHL:R

of schools, water, gas and electric supply, sewage disposal, the building industry and politics. Most of this change can be accounted for by electric transportation, the bases of which were laid by Sprague.

Yet, though traction in the eighties was occupying so much

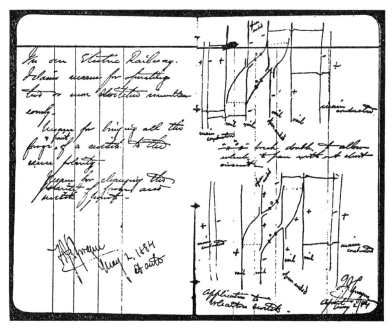

Facsimile of Sprague's plan for his electric railway
From Sprague's note book in the Sprague Collection, New York Public Library

of Sprague's time, he had himself begun to look toward other fields. In the shops of his Electric Railway and Motor Company, there were machines which had no concern with transporting any person or thing. There was, for instance, a stationary motor which ran on direct current at a constant speed. This was an important practical achievement as it adjusted itself automatically to its load within the limits of its specified horsepower. But what was it for, if not to move something along a pair of rails?

As the nineties approached, we find the Sprague company sending out circulars and salesmen to manufacturers with startling statements. The old system that had been in use since the days of the water wheel, these circulars said, was no longer necessary. "The transmission by shafts and belting gives much loss, because of the great weight of machinery that must at all times be kept in motion . . . irrespective of the load on each machine."[32] The circulars produced figures furnished by a mill owner showing that from twenty-five to thirty-nine per cent of the horsepower developed in his mills was used by the shafting alone.[33] With individual motors attached to the machines the load on the generator would come only on those machines which were actually in operation. If half the machines in a factory were idle only half the amount of power need be generated.

But in addition to this saving there was astonishing ease of control. Instead of the cumbersome and always somewhat dangerous operation of slipping a belt on and off a flywheel, a machine could now be started or stopped by a switch that a child might turn. The common industrial accidents which caused the mangling of thousands of workers between wheel and belt need never happen again. Dirt, noise, the smell and dampness of steam pipes would disappear with the shafts. The space required by all such paraphernalia could be turned to some new, useful, productive purpose.

We may imagine industrialists looking at these little circulars with their crude drawings—unbelievably remote from the beautiful promotion "literature" of today—and being profoundly impressed by the bare statements. Yet they must ask themselves a good many questions. The change would mean a lot of scrapping. Would it be worth while? Could they be sure these newfangled motors would not get out of order? Could a thing so small and compact and silent actually do the same work as a big noisy engine? Power, we must remember, in this period was still measured by the average manufacturer, not to mention the layman, in terms of size and "racket."[34] But the most persistent question, we should imagine offhand, must have been: "Shan't I still need my steam engine with all its noise, smoke, dirt and fuel cost to run my dynamo?"

[32]Circular No. 4, Sprague Electric Railway and Motor Co. Not dated but probably 1889. Sprague Collection, N. Y. Public Library.
[33]Ibid.   [34]Meaning, in those innocent days, merely "noise."

A drawing showing principles of operating the overhead system of electric railway

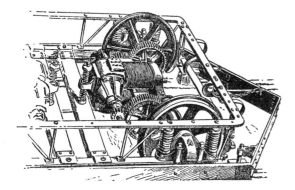

Sprague electric motor attached to street-car truck

From *Scribner's Magazine,*
April, 1890

We give general information as to elevators, pumps (both for air and water), ventilation, blowers, sewing machines, circular saws, printing presses, etc. The different tables and formulæ will be found useful in calculating the power required for these different purposes.

We should be pleased to give any additional information that may be desired, our object being to assist our customers in every way we can; and in these pages we have sought to furnish, as far as possible, intelligent replies to all inquiries that are liable to be made.

We invite correspondence upon all matters pertaining to the general subject, and having had a large and varied experience in the furnish-ing of power for general and special purposes, we gladly place our experience before you. Correspondence can be addressed to our New York office, or to any of our branch offices.

1884.

Facsimile of one of Sprague's circulars showing motor and general text
From Sprague Collection, New York Public Library

The fact was that this question had, in many places, been answered before it was asked. It had been answered by Thomas Alva Edison who had long been attracted by the bright object of the arc light and who since 1879 had almost sleeplessly pursued incandescence. He announced in 1883 that there were then in operation 123 "isolated plants" for lighting purposes.[35] The phrase was fraught with a new meaning. An isolated plant, the Edison company explained, is one in which the owner "furnishes his own power and owns his own dynamos."[36] What, then, is a non-isolated plant?

It is at this point that a new actor is observed on the industrial stage. He has walked on unobtrusively, disguised by incandescent bulbs. His name appeared on the program as Light. Suddenly, in the later eighties, he was found to have a double part. His other name was Power and he carried the new industrial revolution in his pocket.

In 1889,[37] the Sprague company issued Circular No. 3, giving testimonials from the users of Sprague stationary motors. Many of the motors were small and operated by small manufacturers or artisans in cities. They were used for button making, butter churning, coffee grinding, ice cream freezing, meat chopping, organ blowing, sewing, printing, peanut roasting and the making or repairing of jewelry.[38] Did each jeweller, butcher or tailor then have his own steam engine to turn a dynamo which would supply energy to his one-horsepower Sprague motor?

Circular No. 1a[39] answers the question in spectacular typography. "We also wish to show that a New Industry, on a broad and permanent foundation, has been inaugurated, having in view a single object, namely: **THE ESTABLISHMENT OF PLANTS FOR THE GENERATING AND TRANSMISSION OF POWER FOR UNIVERSAL USE AND SALE, IN ALL UNITS FROM A HALF HORSE POWER UPWARD; AND FOR SHORT OR LONG DISTANCE TRANSMISSION

---

[35]Edison Electric Light Co., *Bulletin No. 18,* May 31, 1883, p. 31.
[36]*Ibid.*   [37]The exact date of issue is in doubt.
[38]Sprague Circular No. 3, Sprague Collection.
[39]Probably also 1889. Sprague Collection.

FROM HALF A MILE TO TWENTY MILES**" The writer of this circular used his asterisks and capitals advisedly. His announcement had a significance scarcely equalled in our industrial history.

Clark corroborates the announcement. "In 1889 elevators and machinery at Lowell were operated with an arc-light current carried twenty miles. . . .[40] Before 1889 machine tools were operated by small motors, taking their current from an arc light circuit."[41] The size of the baby giant and his precocity are suggested in the further statement that "in 1888 . . . there were more than 192,000 arc lights and 1,700,000 incandescent lights in use in the United States; 34 electric railways were operating 223 cars; 49 more roads were under construction, and capital was being invested in providing electric services of one kind or another to the amount of over $80,000,000 annually."[42]

The industrialist, therefore, found himself in a novel position. Instead of a dynamo being installed between his steam engines and the machines which made his cloth, lead pencils or shoes, an entire new industry had stepped into the gap. Fuel bought in the open market was no longer an item of his budget and the operation of a prime mover was no longer part of his expense. He must now—if he cared to take part in the changing scheme—buy Power, a kind of long shaft to which he might hook his machines. He must buy it, also, from someone who had absolute control of its supply; he must buy it from someone who sold the same commodity or service or whatever they called it to many other customers—he must share it with cities, railways and private lamp users whose interests were very different from those of a maker of cloth, lead pencils or shoes and who might all have a word to say about its price.

He found, furthermore, that while he had been concentrating on his cloth, lead pencils or shoes, this new industry had been cornered by the technicians. Monopoly, of course, was inherent

[40]It is interesting that this, like the other revolutions, began in the textile industry.
[41]Clark, *Hist. of Manufactures in the U. S.,* II, 380.
[42]*Ibid.,* Clark here cites Am. Iron and Steel Ass'n *Bulletin XXII,* p. 293, Sept. 16, 1888.

in the enterprise of power—at least within any given area. It would scarcely be rational to run a dozen wires to a house or factory from a dozen competing power stations in the hope that a restless customer might be induced to switch from time to time from one to the other. Cheap service would be thwarted by such duplication. It was right, moreover, that such a service be operated by the technicians who understood it and could add their improvements directly as they made them.

If our destiny could remain in the hands of such technicians—the engineers who understand the physical laws—and if those engineers could be held aloof from the business and financial offices which it seems nowadays to be the dominant ambition of every engineer to enter from the moment he gets his diploma, life might be simpler and happier. That our destiny did not remain in such province is a fact which must be considered in all study of the new revolution. It is a curious paradox of human behavior that men having found that by monopoly they can make a thing cheap, often use that very instrument to make it expensive. Because this odd conduct had been observed in other activities, industry was inclined to look upon retailed Power as an object of possible suspicion particularly when it departed from the direct control of technical specialists and entered the more romantic realms of finance.

The industrialist waited to investigate such matters carefully before he electrified his plant. But there were other factors in the delay. To stretch a network of wires over a continent so that every factory, wherever it might be, could, at a moment's notice, demand power and receive it was a large operation to say the least. It involved both technical and economic difficulties on the grand scale. Some of them were met by an astonishing invention known as the Holding Company which was able to centralize and standardize the entire power industry to such a point that by 1935 ninety per cent of the available electric energy in the United States was controlled by fifty-seven companies.[43] As the total output then amounted to about one hundred billion kilo-

[43]Federal Power Commission, *Power Series No. 2*, Washington, 1935, pp. 3, 21.

watt hours, this was a considerable item of our economy to put in the hands of so few men. Besides such dictators, the rulers of the totalitarian states seem amateurs and we may well imagine the facility of control in a political system which should follow the pattern of our so-called private utility chains.

The relations of power utilities to consumers have been the

A Weston "dynamo-electric machine" of about 1889

subject of endless discussion. We are concerned here with the slow march of electric power toward industrial revolution. There can be little doubt that the holding company system was of vital importance in the spread of power distribution and in the reduction of the basic cost of electric energy whether or not the consumer got the full benefit of that reduction. But, as we suggested before, the corporate and administrative effort did not constitute the whole battle. There were also technical problems. Historically they came first. They seem easier, somehow; cleaner and more definite.

6

Electricity is probably the most beautiful, the most versatile, the most powerful and the most docile force that man has ever had under his control. It is at once infinitely strong and infinitely delicate, ranging in its performance from a tiny impulse in an animal brain to the cataclysmic movement of a lightning bolt or the still unknown violence of the smashed atom. We know now, or believe we know, that it pervades our bodies and all inanimate matter. It suggests God; perhaps indeed it is God and would be recognized as Such but for the curious craving of the theologians for the inexact and their fear lest such a force be too little anthropomorphic for the merciful regulation of human conduct. At any rate, we outlanders must all envy, at moments, the electrical experimenter dealing forever with this mystic fluid which comes and goes so long at his beck and call and then, suddenly, eludes him. The fascination such study will exert must be very like the force of magnetism itself, teasing, tormenting, stimulating and disheartening in turn, attracting and repelling, but at the last irresistible.

The current that came out of the first dynamos was alternating and was considered useless. So scientists were tormented until they could find a way of making a good old direct current with no jumping proclivities come out of their generators. Meanwhile, however, the men who wanted to apply electrical energy seem to have forgotten the curious little discovery made by Henry and Faraday which we described as "self-induction." Meanwhile, also, however, there had been much speculation, with economic motives, on sizes and pressures of currents.

A current to do a certain job must be of a certain bigness. But current of a certain bigness requires a certain bigness of wire to carry it and the cost of wire varies directly as its bigness which is to say that a thick wire costs more than a thin one when you are buying it by the mile. Now it was very soon found that although you could run a machine shop with a dynamo in it quite inexpensively, the moment you started putting your shop a mile or more from the dynamo, the thing ran into money. It was at this point in the exploitation of electric power that the exploiters began to look back into the notebooks of the discoverers.

There they found the statement of Ohm's law and notes on some of its consequences.[44] To explain this, the old analogy

[44] If C is current (measured in amperes) and E is pressure or electromotive force (measured in volts) and W is electrical power (measured in watts), then $C = \dfrac{E}{R}$ and $W = EC$, hence $W = \dfrac{E^2}{R}$

of water flowing through pipes is always convenient. If you want to get the same amount of power from water flowing in a small pipe as from water flowing in a large pipe you must increase the pressure because the quantity of moving water is less. Ohm's law says precisely this about electricity: that when you increase the resistance of a circuit you must also increase the pressure of the current to get the same power because the quantity or size of the current is less. The practical men wanted to get current to move long distances over thin (cheap) wires without loss of power. The only solution, then, was to increase the pressure or electromotive force ("E.M.F.") of the current—in other words its voltage.

It was guessed that this could be done by "self-induction" which we have described, by means of the induction coil. The induction coil consists of two parallel coils of wire, the primary and the secondary. Every time a current starts to move through the primary coil another opposite current is momentarily induced in the secondary coil but in a reversed direction from the first secondary current. These induced currents occur, remember, only at the moments of make and break, of start and stop of the primary current. So if your primary current is a direct, continuous current flowing always in one direction you must invent a mechanical way of continually making and breaking it or your induced currents will have no continuity. It was at this point that a new "two-wayness" of electricity was discovered and the immense value of the alternating current (hitherto held in contempt) was observed.

The alternating current behaved just like a constantly made and broken direct current. The simple construction of the first commutators made it come that way (as we have explained) from the dynamo. So, with an alternating current, no mechanism was necessary to produce continuous induced current in the secondary coil.

The trick which turns an induction coil into a "transformer" capable of increasing the pressure, electromotive force or voltage (whichever we please to call it), is extremely simple. If the secondary coil has more turns of wire than the primary coil, then the induced current will have greater voltage than the primary current. A transformer with ten times as many turns in its secondary as in its primary coil will have ten times as many volts in its induced as in its primary current. Thus a current introduced to a transformer may be stepped up indefinitely in voltage simply by increasing the ratio of turns in its coils. Being correspondingly decreased in size or volume it could be run great distances over wires small enough to keep down the cost. Of course, currents with such high voltages are not immediately useful. You could scarcely introduce voltage by the tens or hundreds of thousands into your house for the operation of electric lights. It would even be dangerous to run such high voltage currents as are usual for long transmission lines through cities or populous districts. So another transformer was needed at the other end of the transmission line to step down the current.[45] As the system developed a series of transformers came into use. A main transmission line would enter a transforming station from which a series of lines would extend to substations and from there to still other transformers which would finally reduce voltage to the 220 or 110 units desirable for house lighting and power. With this subdivision, known technically as "distribution," came the economic pattern of wholesale and retail selling of the "juice."

Transformers have now even gone a step farther. Many of us can remember when batteries were part of every household equipment because the current available at the sockets was too "powerful" to operate electric bells, toys, telephones and whatnot. New transformers, capable of stepping down a 110-volt current to comparatively tiny voltage, have eliminated the old exhaustible batteries and now even radio receiving sets using little pressures can be plugged into house sockets.

All this took time. The planning of transmission and distribution was complicated to say the least and it must be admitted that it was extremely haphazard in the revolutionary years. "The engineers," says engineer Samuels, "were so wrapped up in generation and transmission that many of them considered distribution as too lowbrow to merit their attention. Distribution was frequently left to the linesman, purchasing agent, and store-

[45]By the same process reversed.

keeper, and many distribution systems grew up to give the impression of crazy quilts, without any apparent logic either in circuit sizes, voltages, or locations, and sizes of transformers."[46] In this of course it followed the patterns of the American social and economic crazy quilts. It was an accumulation of such patchworks that finally brought the pre-New Deal disaster and the attempted reforms in planning which rugged individuals now regard with horror as "regimentation."

7

In the years from 1880 to 1895 the technical foundation was laid for the electrical revolution. Much of it was brought by a brilliant engineer from the Balkans who arrived in America in 1884. The story is told of him that his father had decided that he was to enter the Orthodox Church but that before he was twenty his own flair for science was so strong that a bitter controversy grew up between them. At the crisis, the Serbian country in which they lived was swept by cholera and the boy on his supposed deathbed exacted the promise from his father that if he recovered he might be allowed to study engineering. The father, in despair and with little hope, conceded and Nikola Tesla was saved for civilization.[47]

Tesla, like a few other geniuses we have met in the history of invention, had the kind of mind which sees through appearance and tradition to the basic reality beneath. Watching an electric motor, he saw, not turning metal but the law by which it turned. He saw the two-wayness of electricity and interchanged the armature and field, making the field revolve. He had seen that commutators and brushes were wasteful, that energy leaked out of them and by his transformation he eliminated them.

While Tesla was thinking out these things in Europe, George Westinghouse in America was expanding from an engineer into an organizer of engineers. Perhaps Westinghouse was the forerunner of that great army of engineers who climbed out of tech-

[46]M. M. Samuels, in *Technological Trends and National Policy,* p. 284.
[47]Eric Hodgins and F. Alexander Magoun, *Behemoth, The Story of Power,* N. Y., 1932, p. 248.

nology into business.[48] It is true that a long list of industrial concerns bore his name and that he held control in most of them and in others in which his name did not appear but it is our conviction that Westinghouse was always more interested in organizing engineering talent than in building financial structure. However that may be, it is probable that he and Thomas Edison did more to make invention collective than any other so-called inventors of the nineteenth century.

In the eighties, Westinghouse never missed an electrical trick. He was forever rushing back and forth between America and Europe, studying patent records and watching experiments in all the great centers of civilization where science was being applied. It would have been astonishing if he had missed the new Tesla motors, patented by 1888. He did not. He bought the rights in that year and from that time his association with the Serbian genius prepared the new revolution.

The Tesla motors were called "polyphase." As this is not a mathematical treatise, we shall be forgiven for not explaining phases. A full understanding of them requires a facility with equations which we do not possess and the expression of their extensive solution would add little to our story of social changes. It is enough to say that the generation of alternating currents in a kind of overlapping succession or fugue was an immense step in the effective use of this kind of current. The results were summed up in a decision upholding some of the Tesla patents. "He first conceived the idea that the very impediments of reversal in direction, the contradictions of alternations, might be transformed into power-producing rotation—a whirling field of power."[49] Tesla began with the motor. The generator followed easily and naturally.

Doctor Henry Prout has summed up the "pre-revolutionary" development of inventions under the Westinghouse organization. "The alternating current transformer is the essential key to transmission of power at low cost. The polyphase motor is the essential key to the reproduction in mechanical form of power trans-

[48]Henry G. Prout, *A Life of George Westinghouse*, N. Y., 1922, *passim*.
[49]Opinion of Federal District Judge W. K. Townsend; Westinghouse Elec. Mfg. Co. *vs.* New Eng. Granite Co. 103 Fed. 763 (Circ. Ct. D. Conn., 1900).

mitted by electricity. In the hands of Westinghouse and his engineers,[50] the crude transformer of Gaulard and Gibbs capable of supplying at low efficiency a few incandescent lamps became in a few years a transformer which could deliver thousands of horsepower at an efficiency exceeding 98 per cent, and the primitive motor brought to America by Tesla in 1888, and loaded to its practical limit when driving a ten-inch ventilating fan, became a motor capable of delivering hundreds and even thousands of horsepower."[51]

8

It will be useful at this point to go back a few years and investigate the great focus on which the eyes of Westinghouse and Tesla and so many other electrical engineers were fixed in the eighties and nineties and which was perhaps the greatest factor in the development of the use of alternating current. Our industrial story began with water. The cycle was completed at Niagara in 1895.

Lord Kelvin, whom we met as William Thomson in connection with the Atlantic cable,[52] seems to have been the first to look at Niagara from a new point of view. An attempt was made to utilize its power in 1877 but the hydraulic technic of the day was inadequate to such a gigantic source of energy.[53] Water wheels had advanced, however, since they ran the mills of our industrial ancestors. The enclosed turbine of Benoit Fourneyron was improved by Uriah Boyden of Massachusetts into an efficiency of 82 per cent when Boyden's turbines were applied to textile mills in Lowell in 1846.[54] In 1880, an Ohio mechanic, Lester Allen Pelton, solved the problem presented by high waterfalls with the celebrated Pelton wheel whose divided buckets made possible a theoretical 100 per cent efficiency.[55] Pelton, who

[50]Notably the celebrated quintet: Albert Schmid, Benjamin G. Lamme, Lewis B. Stillwell, Charles F. Scott, Oliver B. Shallenberger. Prout, p. 153.
[51]Prout, pp. 151, 152.   [52]See pp. 15, 18.
[53]Charles H. Cochrane, "Hydroelectric Development," *Encyc. Americana,* XIV, p. 556.
[54]Philip B. MacDonald, "Uriah Atherton Boyden," *D. A. B.,* II, p. 529.
[55]For the mathematics by which water is designed to leave the buckets at zero velocity, see Thomas H. Beare, "Water Motors," in *Encyc. Brit.,* 13th ed., XXVIII, p. 382.

has been shamefully neglected by American biographers, had driven an ox-team from Ohio to California when, as a boy of twenty-one, he had been thrilled by the gold rush stories of 1850.[56] He had followed mining east to Nevada and had then been dominated by mechanical experiment which he found more appealing than gold. At the Chollar mine of the Comstock Lode the waste surface waters dropped 1600 feet. A mile or so from this fall was a stamp mill which needed power. The cost of coal was prohibitive. Pelton hitched a dynamo to his wheel, which was adapted to the high fall, and generated power to be transmitted to the mill. This seems, not counting an occasional sporadic experiment here and there, to have been the first effective hydroelectric power in the United States.

In the eighties, also, practical engineers were beginning to look at the great falls which had hitherto been admired primarily for its beauty. The practical men were also thinking in a beautiful direction, but their suggestion when they made it aloud was received with horror, and it was said that God would not let them "harness" anything so great and so grand as Niagara. And, during the next decade, God apparently did His best to prevent the hitching, though when it was finished the original beauty was unimpaired, and trippers, if they like, may still watch the waters in the precipitous descent and be awed by the sight without giving a thought to the incidental benefits which have accrued to humanity.

The engineers soon found that the harness need offend no one; indeed, it was obvious from the start that an enormous water wheel stuck (as non-engineers supposed it would be) in the middle of the falls would scarcely do the job. Instead of this, they drilled a hole 136 feet deep about a mile above the falls. At the bottom they placed turbines of the Fourneyron type and, by shafts, connected these directly to the largest dynamos ever built. Now a turbine attached to a 136-foot shaft was a difficult matter to hold in suspension, as it had to be held in order to give the water proper access to the vanes, and it was soon

[56]Even the usually infallible *D. A. B.* has missed Pelton. See, however, *White's Nat. Encyc. Biog.*

evident that a colossal engineering feat must be performed. Engineers, by this time, however, had learned that such problems sometimes solve themselves because of the very magnitude of the forces involved. The weight of the turbine and shaft was

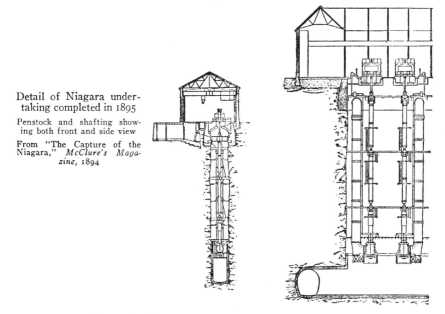

Detail of Niagara undertaking completed in 1895

Penstock and shafting showing both front and side view

From "The Capture of the Niagara," *McClure's Magazine,* 1894

very great, but the force of a 136-foot head of water is also very great. So the trick was done by letting the water bounce back from the bottom of the hole and support the weight upon it. Thus the water, at the same time that it acted (from below) on the blades of the turbine, kept the whole mechanism in suspension, allowing it to turn almost without friction.[57]

By 1895, the three giant generators developing five thousand horsepower apiece were in operation. From then on, the equipment was steadily improved and new inventions have made possible the farther transmission of the power. Meanwhile, seeing the technic by which such gigantic natural waterfalls were brought into new use, engineers began to design artificial waterfalls and the great dams of which we are so proud today are the result of the evolution.

There is current discussion among engineers and power spe-

[57]Cochrane, *op. cit.,* XIV, pp. 556 ff.

cialists as to the economic advantages of water power over steam. While the cost of installing hydroelectric equipment has remained high, the efficiency of the heat engine has vastly increased. In 1884, Charles Algernon Parsons, son of an English peer, borrowing from Hero of Alexandria[58] as well as from the water wheel, invented a prime mover which operated by the direct action of steam on the vanes of a wheel. In 1889, Gustaf De Laval applied a somewhat different technic to the same principle. The steam turbine, refined by the American Charles Gordon Curtis and others, became an astonishingly efficient prime mover dispensing as it did with all of Watt's cumbersome reciprocal motion and its translation. It was well adapted to the running of dynamos.

Using the reciprocating motion but dispensing with the intermediate water-vaporizing stage, the internal combustion engine has also developed great efficiency and may one day become independent of exhaustible mineral fuel and oil. Small Diesel units are in 1940 acquiring popularity as prime movers for generators. Their vogue may be due to the artificial financial difficulties which have been encountered in the power industry and which we shall discuss more fully later.

The low cost of operating all these prime movers is now being balanced against the capital cost of hydroelectric installation. Certain prophets like Herbert Hoover have gone so far as to forecast the early obsolescence of hydroelectric power.[59] Government, however, has found it expedient to sell quantities of water-generated energy as a means of financing flood control, irrigation and conservation, and although much angry criticism has been directed at their efforts. there has been scarcely time for a fair judgment.

This brings us back to the economic conflict. It has been said that the intention of the Federal Government in such immense installations as that of the Tennessee Valley Authority is to show that energy is being sold at too high a price by the private utility systems. In any case, these installations have come after years of bitter protest against the rates charged by power com-

[58]*Circa* 100 A.D. See *M. I. M.*, pp. 51, 52.   [59]*N. Y. Times,* Feb. 3, 1939.

panies. From the time when transmission lines crossing state boundaries carried the matter of power out of state jurisdiction, volumes of "hearings" before committees and commissions have emerged from government presses. The situation has become so complex that groups of experts are required to untangle it. Propagandists like the Edison Electric Institute, much of whose activity is devoted to justifying the private utility systems, point

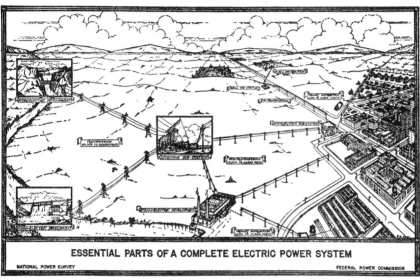

ESSENTIAL PARTS OF A COMPLETE ELECTRIC POWER SYSTEM

Sketch showing modern transmission methods
From Federal Power Commission, *National Power Survey*, 1935

conclusive fingers at national averages, showing that average rates per kilowatt hour have gone steadily down from twenty-five cents in 1882 to 3.41 cents in 1937.[60] The Federal Power Commission, however, has produced a report showing such wide variations in rate according to locality that the averages seem meaningless.[61]

The statement has been made that, given the technological improvement of the past fifty years, energy ought not to cost much more than a cent per kilowatt hour.[62] It has been said that the present high-rate structure has worked such hardships on

[60]Edison Electric Institute, *Rate Book*, 1938.
[61]Federal Power Commission, *Power Series No. 1*, 1935.
[62]Jonathan N. Leonard, *Tools of Tomorrow*, N. Y., 1935, p. 77.

the farmers that as late as 1936 only a little over 10 per cent of the farms in the United States had electric power.[63] It is certain that government power plants and even municipal plants are

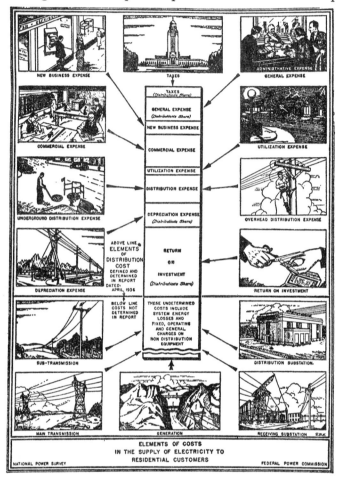

Graphic representation of power costs

From Federal Power Commission, *National Power Survey,* 1935

selling power at rates far below those of the private utilities, but the instant such comparisons are made,[64] the high-geared publicity departments of the utilities angrily retort that public-owned plants are selling below cost. The question of cost for some reason does not seem to be subject to analysis. That private utility cost often includes high salaries to officers, dividends to stockholders of non-operating companies, lobbies in state and

[63]Bernhard Ostrolenk, *Electricity: For Use or for Profit,* N.Y., 1936, p. 128.
[64]Federal Power Commission, *Power Series No. 1.*

federal legislatures and fees to large legal staffs seems evident from a glance at the history of present corporate structures.[65]

On the other hand, great efficiency in repair and maintenance services has been achieved by the close-knit structure of the utilities systems. In the New England hurricane of 1938, this was amply demonstrated by the miraculous speed with which service was restored. This kind of performance is possible only with such a network as the fascistlike systems have constructed. Once the conflict has been resolved between the old philosophy of private property and the new philosophy of public interest something approaching rate justice may result. The difficulty at the moment seems to come from our persistent application of individualist thinking to a completely collective reality.[66]

Our own further consideration of such aspects must await our investigation into both social and technological invention in other fields. Meanwhile the basic industrial change which has come through electric power has had such social consequences that it must command all our immediate attention.

9

The Industrial Revolution of 1910, to which historians have helpfully applied so precise a date, involved other matters than electric power. Quantity production, for example, had begun to change into mass production. The mere division of labor introduced by Arkwright in the 1780's and the system of interchangeable parts begun by Eli Whitney and Simeon North at the turn of the century were not alone adequate to the growing demands of an integrated and socially democratic nation.[67] While Whitney and his followers, abolishing the artisan tradition, found it desirable to make the separate parts of a machine separately and in quantity, each by a process of its own, our later industrialists had found it necessary further to subdivide each of these processes. Thus a gun barrel, for example, which had formerly been finished in a special department by one worker or a small

[65]*Power Series No. 2,* 1935, Chart.
[66]For a brilliant discussion of this, see Thurman Arnold, *The Folklore of Capitalism,* pp. 119 ff.
[67]See pp. 376–381.

group of workers using their machines in haphazard order, must now move along a line of machines each of which shall perform only one small operation. The parts must move in perfect order and as automatically as possible, and must arrive at the end of the line at a point of assembly. In mass production, too, the old division of labor into departments was changed by the new machine lines to a division into steps of a process. Such integration and coincidence were needed as to bring each finished piece into assembly with other finished pieces at the precise moment that the others were ready, so that the motion of producing a complete machine should be continuous and uninterrupted.[68]

Now, plans of this sort had been conceived before electrification became general. But with shafts and belting a proper arrangement of machines was impossible. Under the old system similar machines could be grouped, but the new mass production demanded the juxtaposition of very unlike machines. With each machine connected, however, to its individual electric motor any arrangement became possible.

The application of electricity further increased accuracy, and hence interchangeability of parts. Ease of control reduced the probability of error, but new electrical measuring or gauging devices made possible dimensional accuracies to the ten thousandth of an inch. Finally, electrically operated conveyors realized the revolutionary dream of Henry Ford to bring the work to the man rather than the man to the work.[69] As automaticity increases, the function of the conveyor will become to bring the work to the machine rather than to the man.

Walter Polakov in his fascinating book, *The Power Age,* presents these matters clearly to the layman. He shows the degree of specialization that had been attained (by 1933) when he tells of the Rayon plant using "a spinning frame on which every single spindle, carrying on its top a bucket containing viscose material, is driven by an individual 3-h. p. motor, making 9,000 revolutions per minute."[70] He tells further of the actual entrance of electricity into the machine function rather than its mere use for driving power. Here we see the work of the "electric eye"

[68]Mass production is more fully explained in Chap. XVII, pp. 376–403.
[69]See pp. 395–397.
[70]Walter N. Polakov, *The Power Age,* N. Y., 1933, pp. 94, 95.

actuating mechanical motions to correct errors, throw out imperfect work or produce automatic starting and stopping of motors at precise moments. Since electric power has come into industry astonishing new electrical processes have entered manufacture, such as the method of printing by which metallic ink is made to jump from type or plate to paper, thus substituting magnetism for pressure in printing. And electrolysis and other processes have, of course, changed and enlarged the chemical industries.

The primary social effects of the revolution have come with the use of electric power by individuals. We shall see the profound effect of the new flameless and virtually heatless light in the next chapter. But the home has been utterly changed by electric power. Water supply and plumbing have come to the rural districts through the automatic electric pump which starts by itself as pressure in the house tank lowers. Effective heating has come through entirely automatic thermostatically controlled oil burners and self-stokers which do away with the drudgery of furnace care. Washing of clothes and dishes, ironing, cooking, hot-water heating, refrigeration and food preparation by electricity have taken immeasurable burdens from the shoulders of millions of housewives and all but eliminated the domestic servant. During what is left of the woman's housework she is entertained by music and dialog which come to her via the wall socket. There are of course mitigations to these blessings, among them the utter helplessness of a society which they have made dependent, at the moment when the current fails.

Electric transportation has eliminated much discomfort and attained a speed which transcends the economic limits of steam. The electric elevator has changed the pattern of cities (a doubtful blessing), though later increase of horizontal transport may reshape them. In general, electricity, both through transport and transmission of power, has accelerated the dispersive trend.

The secondary effects of the revolution have been those of mass production. The standardization of every article we use, and to a large extent of our daily activities, has greatly standardized our thinking. The result is collective opinion, collective behavior, potential mass action. Uniformity has become a fetish.

All these things have ripened us for totalitarian organization, the pattern of which has been drawn by the corporate structure of the power interests. But such a pattern is not confined to these primary exponents of the power age. Mass production itself, with its almost inevitable accompaniment of monopoly trend, interlocking association, pooling and so on, has produced an almost irresistible collective formula. Against it the individual must batter in vain. His only hope must lie in some new decentralization which advancing science may bring to relieve the tightness of our present society.

Thus the new revolution has introduced menaces as well as blessings. It has created the industrial dictatorship and our helpless dependence upon it. So far that dictatorship has been benevolent compared with the political variety which in Europe has used its blueprint, though what the future may hold must depend on the extent of government regulation, a kind of menace in itself. The late changes have greatly increased vulnerability in war[71] a threat to which Europe has given too much and America too little attention. But perhaps the greatest menace is in the penetration of the revolution into the integrity of our inner lives.

Man cannot live by Power alone. If he can learn to separate it from his thinking process, to dissociate it from his ego, to relegate it to its proper place as an aid to, rather than a control of, his life, he will survive. At present we have allowed it to determine too much of our behavior. We have fabricated the fiction of its royalty, almost its godhead. In one way or another it has supplanted religion and humane concepts, it has standardized education and limited independence of thought, speech and act. We shall enlarge upon these trends in our chapters on The Social Lag. By understanding the threats and facing the realities, we shall see ahead a happier outcome than we may expect from hiding in their dark and giant shadows.

Meanwhile we must return to our history. To do so will be to step back into a romantic age and inquire into the inventions which arrived in that pleasant ostrich period to make the facing of reality possible.

[71]*Technological Trends and National Policy*, p. 271.

Chapter Eleven

LIGHT

I

AS THE world entered upon its greatest epoch of change under the inescapable motivation of science and technology, we observe a massive effort on the part of society to maintain the *status quo*. Historians have found that effort centered round the English throne. They have taken a diminutive but determined Hanoverian queen as its symbol.[1] In her very person, seated so long on the ever-broadening foundation of empire, she seems to embody all the resistance of Western civilization to the new order. She could not stem the movement but she could and did maintain the static appearance. When the facts altered she hid the facts. From the travail of her own country, heaving with the pains of industrial revolution, she diverted the eyes of her people to the pageant of empire which that revolution had made possible. She taught them to identify themselves with that empire and so forget their own sufferings.

"The poor little street-bred people that vapour and fume and brag,
  They are lifting their heads in the stillness to yelp at the English Flag!"[2]

For sixty-four years, under Victoria, they continued their yelping and so did most of the world. Through her romantic marriage which played such sentimental melodies upon the Teuton heartstrings, through her even more romantic ecstasy of inconsolable mourning, through her unfailing devotion to the absolute in morals and religion and the forms of society she managed to convey a sense of security and unalterable foundation which infected a large proportion of conscious humanity. She was ably assisted in this, of course, by a succession of ruthless

[1]Esmé Wingfield-Stratford, *The Victorian Cycle*, N. Y., 1935; Lytton Strachey, *Queen Victoria*, N. Y., 1921; Horace Wyndham, *Victorian Parade*, London, 1934; Peter Quennell, *Victorian Panorama*, N. Y., 1937; Wanda F. Neff, *Victorian Working Women*, London, 1929.
[2]Rudyard Kipling, *The English Flag*, 1891.

ministers, by masses of sweated workers in northern and middle England, by the peculiar English genius for colonization and by the magnificent effectiveness of the British navy, all of which made possible the continuation of a policy which had its origins in Imperial Rome.

While the British Empire may have kept the peace of Europe less effectively than the Roman, its civilizing effect certainly reached farther. By the end of Victoria's reign, 20 per cent of the population of the world[3] were yelping, under political compulsion, at the English flag. Conveniently, the wealth which England desired had lain largely in the hands of backward peoples so that the colonial policy could be exploited at home as a civilizing mission—"the white man's burden," white meaning English as it still does in the island. But nineteenth-century empire, unlike the Roman, forecast its own destruction, for it included a liberating technology. With understanding of this technology, which turned out to be an inseparable part of the civilizing process, self-determination would come, inevitably, to the subject peoples. At the same time, the ideal of nationality, postulated at home as an essential to order in a highly industrialized state, became irresistible to any people which technology had organized and liberated.

In England, however, while Victoria maintained the static appearance, the process of dissolution was hidden. The ancient class traditions were paraded in the face of a complete basic reversal of society. The land, the church, the aristocracy were brought into high visibility under garish lights which cast deep shadows over the growing power of the factories and the lower groups which manipulated them. When morals declined, manners were substituted. When art declined, ornament took its place. When the nation grew turbulent, orderly empire was paraded and vice-versa. When the sex problem became acute, extra stays, petticoats and flounces were added, floods of fiction provided vicarious sex-lives for hungry "females," the queen gave a new example of chaste connubial bliss and the gas was turned off in the red-light districts.

[3]Spencer Walpole, "English History," in *Encyc. Brit.*, 13th ed., ix, 582.

LIGHT

All this bred the state of mind we call romance—a pretty word for untruth. The infection spread over the world. The Germans, already bathed in the sorrows of Werther and basking now in the warmth of Victorian affection, caught it first. Even the traditionally realist French succumbed under their highly romantic emperor, Louis Napoleon. Italy, thrilled by the fantastic Garibaldi and the glory of *Risorgimento,* was easy prey. Russia, alternately hating and fearing the British power, nevertheless adopted the English manners, elegances and language in her Court, and the Tsarina's apartments, filled with Victorian atrocities, are preserved to this day as horrid examples to Soviet realists.

Synchronous with Victoria's mourning for her beloved consort prince, a wave of nostalgia for the passing order of life swept the Western world. In the churches, prayers were uttered, sermons preached against the new science symbolized by Darwin, the antichrist. Art worshipped "Nature" (God's nature, not Darwin's), and was thrown into a tailspin by the impact of photography which forced it, eventually, into true revolution. Fiction fled into history and avoided all but the most nostalgic of modern aspects. Architecture struggled to revive the Gothic with appalling results. Politics and diplomacy bent all their efforts toward maintaining the dead center of the "balance of power." During this pleasant lavender-colored interval were confined the subterranean gases which exploded so unexpectedly in 1914. When the smoke cleared, the new pattern of the world was revealed.

2

The United States was slow to catch the Victorian infection and was never able to feel its effect all at once. Here the basic conditions were utterly different. The free opportunity offered by the land beyond the horizon prevented any static mood and enforced democracy against the lures of old-world hierarchy. We had our own peculiar variety of romance inherent in the impossibility of the task we had set ourselves. By and large, it was less synthetic: it was the kind of untruth that developed naturally out of physical fact rather than that which is artificially imposed to conceal reality. Our faith was forever in the future, rather than in the past. Our so-called plutocracy which appeared, at one moment, so fantastic, lived on promises which were sound. It was self-destroying as we have seen. Operating in so large a territory it must employ the collective means which eventually killed it. Though it caused suffering while it lasted, the aggravating psychological factor of social oppression so universal in Europe was absent. If an American was poor it was his own fault. The land was large enough for every one. Our industrial proletariat was entirely foreign and inured to tyranny. It was only when it became American, indistinguishable from the pioneer but lacking his tradition, that real trouble began. But by this time, the corporate dictatorship had replaced the old individual plutocracy and all responsibility for poverty had disappeared.

The impact of the Victorian era was felt, for the most part, on the eastern fringe. Here the old urban centers had grown motionless enough to yearn for "culture." There was nowhere but Europe to reach for it. Europe had now settled into her long nostalgia. Thus the stuffy manners and fatigued art which were borrowed (largely from England) by the Atlantic cities and made even more absurd by the application of unlimited money were in violent contrast to the robust license of the frontiers. Victorian morality overlapped and mingled with remnants of Calvinism and expressed itself by crusades against drink and vice and knowledge. Religion, with its deep Hebraic, Calvinistic roots, had been functional in America. It had been superbly adapted to our periods of hardship and scarcity. Now with its function gone and in a new climate of prosperity it easily took on the Victorian color. The orthodox devotions of men like Daniel Drew[4] were evidences of the change. Already, in the sixties, the robust church of our fathers had settled into its long decay in the static centers.

In these centers, also, there had come a need for some sort of pretense to combat the persistent undermining of morality by the new plutocracy. As money poured into great financial whirlpools like New York, the worship of the Golden Calf replaced all other religions. In the interest of this devotion all standards

[4]Bouck White, *The Book of Daniel Drew*, N. Y., 1910.

of honor, decency and humanity were sacrificed. New York borrowed from Victorian dignity to offset this Mammon. A group calling itself "Society" closed its doors against the vulgar rich. A kind of aristocracy grew up which cherished *Mayflower* and other spurious traditions of nobility, but the protest was feeble and of short duration. Boston and Philadelphia with their deeper Puritan and Quaker roots stood out longer.

The sexual aspect of Victorian England was greatly magnified on the coastal fringe and, indeed, in most of America. Here again, however, appeared a new, aggravating factor borrowed, not from Europe, but from our own frontier. In the wilderness, the protection of women had led to their glorification. The sanctity of the family was so necessary to frontier life that affront to a woman became a life and death matter. This led easily to the deification which has been so destructive to our culture.[5] As the attitude filtered out of the frontier and so lost its function, it became biologically damaging in the extreme. The results, multiplied through the generations—mother worship, fear of normal relations with a goddess, concealment of sexual truth, abuse of unmarried mothers as fallen angels, insipid romance, bitter disillusion in marriage, perversions and impotency among men—are filling divorce courts and asylums and bringing fortunes to the psychoanalysts today. Another melancholy hangover of this horror is still visible, particularly in the West where women are regarded as the only fit custodians of the arts, literature, "culture" and education.

For the most part, however, the frontiers felt little of the Victorian impact. Whatever efforts may have been made to gloss over unmannerly behavior on the fringe, the frontiers were usually "wide open." Probably nowhere in the world was there such continuous, unrestrained gambling, drinking, whoring and generally dissolute conduct as in the construction and mining towns of the fifties, sixties and seventies from Memphis to San Francisco, from Omaha to Seattle. Such things, indeed, became inseparable from the later stage of pioneering. The stern old morality of the covered wagon vanished with the railroad. These

[5]Thomas Beer, *The Mauve Decade,* N. Y., 1926, Ch. I.

matters were probably without permanent effect. They were robust and frank without hypocrisy or romance. They were concomitants of hard work in the open. They were necessary by-products of a rapid geographical conquest. It is well to remember them, however, along with the general freedom of the empty land when we read of the "Victorian age" in America.

It may seem that we have gone afield in all this discussion of the *mores* of the Western world which appear to have stemmed from Windsor. What have they to do with a social history of invention in America? How are they concerned with dynamos and engines, telegraphs and machines?

We have discussed them thus fully because of the significance of their destruction by technological forces. In this and the following chapters we must deal with the end of the romantic period; the end, indeed, of much of the romance as we have known it in the world. It will return in other forms. Evidence of its return was abundant in the 1930's in the totalitarian states. The Teutonic mind, like the Anglo-Saxon, will probably always be distressed by too much truth. But the dissemination of falsehood has become increasingly difficult. It can never again be managed in the discreet and gentle Victorian way. It must be done now violently, angrily, with large equipment. It is no longer a matter of turning one's head away, resorting to a smelling bottle, pulling down the curtain, adding an extra flounce, petticoat or furbelow or stepping out of the light. We are hard, clean and naked today. Privacy is not merely outmoded, it is impossible. Our souls are almost as visible as our bodies. Light is diffused and casts no shadows. To counteract such visibility, the most gigantic machinery is necessary—for the old subtleties are futile. If, today, we kill, rape, steal or persecute, the world knows it. We must, therefore, direct our deception toward the motive and explain to the world that while indeed we have killed, raped, stolen or persecuted we have done it for our faith; we must invent a giant religion which will direct that murder, rape, theft and persecution are desirable, necessary forms of worship.

The first force which has destroyed illusion is light. Before artificial light could be directed toward truth men used the sun for this purpose. When the sun proved inadequate in the satisfaction of their eternal curiosity, they invented the lens. With this they saw truth that had hitherto been invisible. Aware next of the power of light to effect chemical change they were able to make permanent record of illumined objects with which to confront new doubters. Combining this property with the lens and with an accelerated control of light and dark they recorded motion in static terms, overcoming the illusion caused by persistence of vision. Reversing this process in a playful mood they made static pictures move and so recaptured some of their vanishing romance.

Impatient with the sun's periodic disappearance, men constructed imitation suns of their own. With them they dispelled the "powers of darkness" and attendant magic. With them they extended the hours of their search for truth. They made their suns powerful, subdued their heat and, adding new collateral light-found truth, were able to penetrate the mystery of the animal body and explore the life function in mid-career.

These things were done not without cost. In doing them, men lost their old God and floundered in the absence of a new one. They lost much reticence and privacy, quietness of mind, subjective meditation. They lost, also, much sleep and many dreams, the blessings of the dark; fatigue and rest must be adjusted anew. Many of these things happened in the so-called Victorian age.

3

From the dawn of human life to the end of the eighteenth century of the Christian era, the activity of man was largely dominated by the astronomical division between day and night. Work was done by the direct light of the sun and at the end of twilight was no longer possible except by the cat-eyed powers of evil. At curfew, then, men retired behind barricades or bolted doors to protect themselves against the prowlers. The prowlers might be real in the shape of wild animals which "saw" with all their senses, human thieves or purely imaginary beings which were natural projections in the mind of the day's long activity. The mind, knowing no curfew, lagged behind the eyes in the recognition of darkness and conjured the shapes which were no longer visible. From this entirely normal mental process sprang all the mythology of ghosts, spirits, banshees, witches and black magic—withal a rich and beautiful creation which has largely disappeared from human understanding.

Men of the very ancient times worshipped a sun-god whose Egyptian form, Ra, has lately been introduced to Americans through the benign influence of the cross-word puzzle. The religion was succeeded by fire-worship, fire being the secondary source of light which men did not yet know derived from the sun's stored heat. When more complex religions arrived, worship was signalized and focused by the burning of oils, liquid or plastic, in lamps and tapers which lighted the shrine of the god. From these glimpses of sacred history we may suspect that worship sprang partly and primarily from fear of the dark.

In the progress of society, artificial light posed a division between rich and poor. Night diversions took place among the privileged classes and were believed by the others to be orgies. They were lighted by resinous torches or by vegetable or animal oils and so dimly that the orgiastic temptation might well have been present. In the medieval period, in Europe at least, work was also done by this light in the Church which controlled much wealth. But the "imitation suns" were usually the property of privileged folk; the masses perforce obeyed the curfew.

Industry and the first industrial revolution began with no better light than this. At sunrise, then, the factories opened; at sunset they closed. In winter the blessing of short days helped balance the curse of the cold. In pre-industrial America, the whittling of the subsistence forms was done by firelight, for wood was cheap and so the evenings might be long. We may suspect the gift of a better eyesight than ours. Later the great whaling industry provided most of the artificial light. It was flickering and smoky, but certain great social leaders like Franklin, who lived a century ahead of his time, put lamps in the streets for the public benefit.

In 1781, Ami Argand, the ingenious Swiss inventor, designed a lamp with a circular wick whose flame was fed by a column

LIGHT

of air within the circle, and so prepared the way for the fine "student" and other brilliant oil lamps which helped to light civilization after the revolutionary discovery of Edwin Laurentian Drake in 1859 which gave the world cheap petroleum.

Drake's first "strike" was one of those momentous episodes which the elder school of academic historians failed to recognize as one of the major determinants of American history. Miss Tarbell eventually reflected upon petroleum as an economic, social and moral phenomenon and her tremendous exposure made America conscious of the giant factor of the new oil in the life of the world.[6] Drake sank the first oil well near the village of Titusville in western Pennsylvania. Five years later this district alone produced more than two million barrels of petroleum a year.[7] Within ten years, whaling was dead and the petroleum industry was organized.[8] We shall return in other places to this colorful American "romance." It is sufficient to remember here that petroleum, from which are derived kerosene and paraffin (not to mention gasoline and a variety of products whose use was not recognized in the sixties), brought light to the remotest corners of the world.

In the meantime, however, William Murdoch had found a new way to get light from coal. It is this of which we must think as we study the Victorian era, for it contributed largely to the romantic aspect we have just considered, for gaslight cast shadows of a peculiar kind.

Illuminating gas was made from the "distillation" or slow combustion of coal. As early as 1807, gaslight invaded a factory in Manchester and from then on the industrial convention of time altered. With gas, the working hours of labor became unlimited. As this new tyranny of the clock was added to that of the industrial machines, strong agitation began for trades unions and a law was finally passed prohibiting labor between 8:30 P.M. and 5:30 A.M. in the textile industries.[9]

[6]Ida M. Tarbell, *History of the Standard Oil Company*, N. Y., 1904.
[7]Allan Nevins, *The Emergence of Modern America*, N. Y., 1935, p. 39.
[8]E. B. Oberholtzer, *The United States Since the Civil War*, N. Y., 1917, I, 255.
[9]1833. Adelaide Mary Anderson, "Labour Legislation," *Encyc. Brit.*, 13th ed., XVI, 10.

229

City lighting by gas followed and had become familiar in England and on the Continent by the time Victoria came to the throne. Consider now the aspect this gave to urban night life. The murky, flickering glow of whale oil or tallow lamps and the will-o'-the-wisp movement of torches and lanterns which had characterized the city night from time immemorial was replaced by vivid blazes of light in some places and what seemed, in contrast, total darkness in others. London and Paris seemed checkerboards of day and night. It was easy to step out of the glare into the blackest of shadow. A municipal government could concentrate the light on what it was desirable to see and conceal the darker alleys and corners. In private life the contrast was even greater. The blaze of London ballrooms did not extend to Whitechapel. There were 500 jets of flame illuminating the toilettes of the Paris opera, but only two or three shone on those of the rue Cadet.[10] Into the glare of the Place de la Concorde, the denizens of the Place de la République might creep for a brief moment of glory, but there would be night in their homes. Light was expensive and controlled. It was fixed and it was monopolized. No one could carry a gas lamp about with him, nor could he make his own in a private generator. It played directly into the hands of England's deepest vested interest next the land— the coal which had started the industrial revolution. And it would help similar vested interests in France and Germany.

Gas posed obviously the threat of change. It altered the life of the middle classes as it grew cheaper and they grew richer. As it became an instrument of industrial tyranny, it helped organize the proletariat. In its earlier stages it endangered life, introduced a new and popular means of suicide. It provided new smells, brought out new colors and obscured others, altered costume and coiffure, modified the technics of the theatre, enlarged the sphere of entertainment and, in its later stages, brought new technics into cooking and heating. It produced the invention of the internal combustion motor and had a considerable effect upon industrial chemistry in increased production of coke and am-

[10]James D. McCabe, Jr., *Paris by Sunlight and Gaslight*, Phila., 1869, p. 665; H. Taine, *Notes on Paris*, N. Y., 1875, p. 36.

monia and on experimental chemistry in the invention of Robert Wilhelm Bunsen.[11]

But gaslight was very different from the light which succeeded it. It gave out prodigious heat and cast shadows. Only in its late incandescent stages, initiated by Auer von Welsbach, did it approach diffusion. It was the diffusion of the incandescent lamps that changed the whole character of light and put darkness under

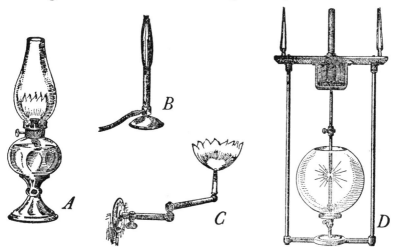

A. Argand circular wick.   B. The Bunsen burner.   C. The gas light.
D. Brush arc-light

the eternal control of man. It was the low heat production of electric incandescence that made possible the multiplication of lamps, their immense scientific and therapeutic value and a whole new technic of illumination. Diffusion through the new character of light and the multiplication of lamps brought the cold, hard definity of the realistic age. Under it the attempt to conceal is futile, but with the passing of concealment has come new understanding of naked beauty. Much pleasant mystery is gone, but so is much hurtful mystery. The exit of manners was followed by the flight of hypocrisy. The revelation of vital facts has revealed the innocence of the life bases. The world may be harder but it is cleaner and frank expression has evolved a new kind of beauty.

[11]The Bunsen burner invented in 1855 has formed a vital part of laboratory equipment ever since.

The diffusion of cool light is based upon a technical experimentation as patient, as persistent and as indomitable as any the world has ever known.

4

Humphry Davy, an English baronet born in the eighteenth century, discovered in 1802 a valuable two-wayness of electricity, namely: that a current *generated* by chemical decomposition of certain materials will, in turn, *cause* the chemical decomposition of certain materials. Every one who touches applied electricity today owes something to Sir Humphry, but his contribution to the pure science of chemistry and through it to the chemical industry is incalculable as a direct result of this discovery. The process is called electrolysis.

Working over it he found that the current would burn up certain metals almost instantaneously. This was due to an extremely rapid oxidization. He found, however, that platinum oxidized more slowly and that, in doing so, it gave much light. Here was an important discovery which led to practical results later when experimenters tried the trick of cutting down the supply of oxygen in which the metal burned.[12] But Davy's most practical discovery came in 1809 when he found that by connecting two pieces of charcoal to the terminals of a 2000-cell battery and then touching and drawing apart the charcoal sticks a flame jumped between them. The flame, which gave a brilliant whitish light, seemed to describe a segment of a circle and so was called the "arc light." It came into a wide use later for lighting purposes and appeared in the Crystal Palace exhibition of 1851 at London and was used sporadically for stage effects.[13] It was never practical for private lighting, even when it was hitched to the dynamo in the seventies, because of its size and expense.

In 1840, Sir William Robert Grove astonished the Royal So-

[12]John W. Howell and Henry Schroeder, *History of the Incandescent Lamp,* Schenectady, 1927, pp. 25, 26. Perhaps the best book for the layman on the whole subject.

[13]Newton's *London Journal of Arts and Sciences,* Vol. 18, New Series, Dec. 1, 1863, pp. 329–331; Vol. 19, March 1, 1864, p. 154; Vol. 22, Oct. 1, 1865, pp. 218, 219.

ciety by illuminating a lecture with incandescent lamps. These, too, used platinum wire electrically heated near its melting point protected from draughts by inverted tumblers. Beyond the astonishment, however, little was accomplished. Large battery current was needed and both current and platinum were expensive. Another Englishman, Frederick De Moleyns, seemed still warmer to the solution with his lamp, patented in 1841, which brought incandescence to pulverized charcoal. J. W. Starr, an Ohioan who died at the age of twenty-five, came still nearer by experimenting with incandescence in a vacuum in 1845. We may skip the work of Staite, Shepard, Roberts, De Changy and others in the forties and fifties. Most of it dealt with platinum or graphite and most of the inventors used as good vacuums as they were able to make with the inadequate pumps of the period.

The most important contribution to electric incandescence was made by Sir Joseph Wilson Swan, a photographic expert, who began his work on carbon filaments in 1860. The English claim him as the inventor of the incandescent lamp. To claim such an invention for any individual is patently absurd, yet most of the evidence gives him credit for the vital factor of the carbon filament. His first lamps used carbonized paper spirals coated with protective liquids, but incomplete vacuum in the glass container caused a breakdown. In 1877, he returned to his experiments. In the interval the new Sprengel pump had been invented and part of the difficulty was overcome. There were other troubles from the gases given off by the filament. Finally, in 1880, by treating cotton thread with sulphuric acid and thus hardening it, Swan produced a good workable filament which gave excellent results.[14]

Meanwhile, however, the incandescent lamp had crossed the Atlantic. Its crossing leads us into the laboratory of one of the strangest and most fascinating characters in American history. It is only necessary to mention the word "inventor" to conjure his name in millions of American minds, yet the very word has changed character to such a point that we can scarcely apply it

[14]Mary E. and Kenneth R. Swan, *Sir Joseph Wilson Swan, F.R.S.*, a memoir by M. E. S. and K. R. S., London, 1929, pp. 58–66.

in the old sense to a person whose activity was in a new era. Its application in this case has often been extremely hurtful. Some day, perhaps, we shall devise a new word more adaptable to the life work of Thomas Alva Edison.

5

We approach this hero with some trepidation and much difficulty.[15] The halo which has attached to him has obscured so much reality that the history of invention will have to be rewritten again and again before all the truth is revealed. We are far too close to him in 1940 to get far into the welter of complex facts beneath the golden glow of the legend. But it is, at the moment, almost sacrilege to suggest that he may not have been the first to think of a hundred technics on which his name is now stamped. All America still kneels at his shrine, eternal flames burn on towers, lamps are switched on and off over earth-girdling circuits to symbolize the blessing of incandescence to civilization, and he is frequently confused with a Creator reported in Genesis I, 3, to have said, "Let there be light." How can we approach such a being in mundane historical record?

The pity of it is that there will one day be a debunking in the fickle American manner and doubt will be spuriously cast on his indubitably great achievements. His legend will soon be ripe for such destruction and it is desirable that sane thinkers establish a few incontrovertible reference points in the interval. There are plenty to choose from.

Edison's genius is spectacular and astonishing enough without making it incredible. The bare factual history of his achievement in the application of science to humble human uses need not be bolstered by stealing the honor from other men—many of them his friends, associates and coadjutors. Yet this theft has been consistently practiced by sycophantic admirers, slipshod newspaper

[15]Frank Lewis Dyer and Thomas Commerford Martin have written with the collaboration of William Henry Meadowcroft what is considered the "definitive" biography, *Edison, His Life and Inventions,* N. Y., 1929. In reading it, however, one is occasionally aware of the halo. A more critical study is the excellent essay by J. G. Crowther, "Thomas Alva Edison, 1847–1931," in *Famous American Men of Science,* N. Y., 1937.

reporters, lazy textbook writers, cribbing historians and commercial promoters to a point where such magnificent figures as Swan, Sprague, Tesla, Brush, Farmer are virtually unknown. It is confidently believed by multitudes of Americans that he was the "inventor" of the incandescent lamp, the electric railway, multiplex telegraphy, motion pictures, the storage battery, the stock ticker and other matters with which he had even less to do and they are abundantly supported in these beliefs by a quantity of otherwise intelligent writers.

Edison's ancestry was immediately British and remotely Dutch. His grandfather was Canadian and hated the United States. His great-grandfather was British colonial and fought against the American provinces in the Revolution. His father moved back and forth across the Canadian border and never seemed entirely sure of his nationality. When at last he settled in Milan, Ohio, he became a prosperous businessman. The myth of Thomas Edison's boyhood poverty which has spurred the ambition of so many poor schoolboys is entirely spurious. It is true that he sold papers and started many business ventures in his teens, but that was because his personal financial demands were so large. Already before his adolescence he had started experimenting and he needed expensive equipment.

As a boy he was studious, stubborn, rugged, enduring, persistent, wholly concentrated and with little regard for the comforts or amenities of life. He was regarded as queer, "addled" and dull, and was taken out of school for this reason. His education from this point came from his mother and through his own effort. His activities as a boy were entirely unconventional and frightened his contemporaries. At eleven, he maintained a sizable chemical laboratory in which all the bottles were marked "poison." This and other doings so terrified neighbor children that he was left alone to work while others played. He seems rarely to have played himself. On one occasion he went swimming with another boy; in complete detachment, he allowed his companion to drown. He went home without mentioning the incident.[16] It is said that a vague sense of guilt haunted him after this for the rest

[16]Dyer, et al., I, 18.

of his life and may have been responsible for the later intensity of his work.[17] It is interesting that this feeling was so vague and so tormenting—probably because of a total incapacity for reflection upon such human matters. Another boy would have suffered with immediate acuteness, then rationalized and forgotten the whole thing. But another boy would not have watched and remained silent. The picture of Edison's profound, inactive concentration upon an accident which was beyond his understanding is remarkable. He was divorced, for the most part, from the emotions which animate and hurt most men. He never greatly loved or hated—he did not, as he might have expressed it, "have time."

He was active enough in the matters which he understood. His mind and hands worked in close synchronization and with great rapidity. Idleness was intolerable to him. He was in no sense a dreamer. He was a kinetic worker. He was capable of carrying on several different kinds of work at once. Because of the itching of his hands for activity and the difficulty of prolonged thinking without a physical accompaniment, he became a trial-and-error inventor, working rarely with the scientific method. This was not invariable; there was plenty of preliminary study, for instance, before he tackled the incandescent lamp. Yet when his work led him into pure science, he abandoned it as in the case of the "Edison Effect."[18] And his remark that he "could always hire a mathematician" was a key to his normal inventive process.

Selling papers on the trains made possible an experimental chemical laboratory on the baggage car. When this caught fire, he stopped being a newsboy and went into telegraphy. Operators were in great demand. He moved about the wide-open frontier in company with gamblers, drunks, and every sort of riffraff, who never diverted him from his work. Yet he had no conscience about his jobs. His work was private. It went on in another department of his brain while he clicked the key and wrote the messages. Sometimes the messages would pile up forgotten while he used the equipment for electrical experiments of his own.

[17]Crowther, p. 326.   [18]See p. 444.

Some of the schemes he devised in this period for automatic telegraphy were intended to keep his mind clear for his private thinking.

By the time he was twenty-one, he had evolved a practical philosophy of invention. "He would not attempt inventions of value to humanity unless there was a definite market for them. This decision was historically important. Edison was the first scientific inventor who clearly conceived invention as subordinate to commerce . . . an important advance in sociology. It made the way for the further advance to the conception of invention as a social product with social responsibilities."[19] It was not, as Crowther adds, confused with any personal desire for wealth. "His behavior shows that he disinterestedly put invention at the service of what he conceived to be the proper social machinery, capitalist commerce."[20] Edison spent most of the money he made for equipment. What he did with the first considerable sum, acquired when he was in his twenties, marked another social advance.

He was really poor when he came back from his frontier wanderings and landed in New York. At this moment (1869) the notorious trio, Gould, Fisk and Drew, were trying to corner gold. Edison went to Laws' Gold Indicator Company which operated stock signals in brokers' offices. He showed an ability in fixing breakdowns which astonished company officers and technicians. He had already devised a stock ticker of his own, an improvement on other inventions. On "Black Friday," the day the gold bubble burst, he kept the apparatus running while men all about him went crazy. Thus he came to the attention of Marshall Lefferts, president of the Gold and Stock Telegraph Company, who offered to buy the rights to his ticker for $40,000. Edison was then twenty-three. He had been friendless and hungry a short time before. With the money, he started the first invention factory.

We must double-star this landmark in the history of technology. Westinghouse and others had instituted laboratories as departments of industrial plants. Edison founded an independent workshop which should be devoted exclusively to invention. By

[19]Crowther, pp. 348, 349.   [20]*Ibid.*, p. 366.

1890, he had a large plant with engines, generators, machine shops, chemical laboratory, library, lecture room and storerooms containing an immense variety of materials. There were eighty expert assistants.[21] Here was frank collective invention; here, for the world to see, was an admission that in the complex state of the new science, the individual inventor could no longer work alone. The invention factory is a familiar institution today and

The Edison laboratory at West Orange in 1890

replicas of Edison's concept may be seen all over the world. It is, perhaps, the happiest invention in recent technological history.

Here, in theory at least, a variety of specialists, abandoning the myth of personal credit, work for the common good of society. Under the present economic scheme, they are usually working also for the good of a corporation. Their inventions may reach society with high prices attached. Whether this is better or worse than if they never reached society at all is a question which we must leave to the philosophers who are attempting to define civilization. Such matters are relative. Prices are subject to adjustment. Perhaps, at the moment, they are rigidly controlled though there are still evidences, here and there, of hot competition. Yet, as we look back over history and see the spotty consumption of technological devices, the deceptions practiced upon the con-

[21]Philip G. Hubert, "Inventors," in *Men of Achievement* Series, N. Y., 1893, pp. 258 ff.

sumer, the principle of "caveat emptor," the unscrupulous under-bidding, geographical price juggling, haggling, bargaining and throat-cutting, not to mention the spectacle of inventors dying in garrets and the long echoes of bitter personal controversy—all characteristic of individualist plutocracy—we may well wonder if, with all our present troubles, we are not better off. In any case, and whatever may happen to economics, it is safe to assume that collective invention has come to stay.

Our present concern is with what went on in the late seventies in Edison's factory. It was an activity which, regardless of the question of who invented what, gave the new cool, cheap, flameless and diffused light to humanity.

6

There is a popular belief that Edison lapsed into a kind of frenzy over the incandescent lamp; that for weeks and months on end he stood in his laboratory working with bare intuition, inaccessible, incoherent, sleepless and unnourished while, in the world outside, a chorus of contemptuous laughter mocked his madness. The late Victorian world loved this sort of wizardry. There was enough of the old magic in it to tickle the nostalgists and enough of the new science to stir the advanced thinkers. Edison stood midway between the mystic saints and Darwin in the public fancy. This fancy created enough of each to satisfy both sides.

The fact was colder. Yet it held curious contradictions. Edison was never won over to the true scientific method, but as we watch the elaborate preparations for his trial-and-error research, there seemed to be little of the old haphazard approach. It is true that scholarly scientists and scientific inventors in England pronounced his achievement impossible. Perhaps this was because of their own economic inadequacy. It is probable that electrical theory was better understood in England than in the United States, but it must be remembered that America had by now caught the industrial revolution and was handling it with wider concepts. Cheap quantity production had already to a considerable extent formed its collusion with democracy. In England, science and economics had come close in the textile mills and in the factories which made basic necessities, but it had not occurred to Englishmen to equip the common herd with such luxuries as electricity. The electrons, therefore, had stayed in the laboratories and the lecture halls.

Edison's whole approach was economic. He was not interested in producing a "marvel." Nor was he concerned with lighting government buildings or palaces. His desire was to give cheap light to the people. The arc light was already a commercial reality. It illumined streets and railway stations. His effort was to "subdivide" this light and, along the circuit, string little, pleasing, docile lamps in houses. This, said the English, could not be done; anyway the houses had gas. Below their utterance was legendary formula: let the masses burn gas and pay the vested interests—even the peerage had dirtied its hands with Northumberland coal.[22] "After all," Gladstone had said to Faraday, looking at a piece of electrical apparatus, "after all, what good is it?" "Why, sir," replied Faraday, "presently you will be able to tax it."[23]

Edison's genius lay in his ability to think in several directions at once. While his hands fingered platinum wire, his eyes could glance up at a graph; in his memory, always vivid while his hands moved, stood whole tables of figures. A cost research assistant could enter at the very crisis of an experiment, tell him that coal was seventy-five cents and the figure registered. As the platinum dropped finally from his hands, eliminated for its cost and its melting point, his mind embraced the cost of gas, its seasonal consumption, its prices, current quotations on iron, copper, coal. As his hands moved into the fragile carbon filament, his mind began to plan gauges of copper wire, dynamos, mains, feeders, loads and a central power station. These matters all came together at the end and met just as the assembly lines of mass machine production bring their completed parts to the central assembly at the proper moment.

The technical problem was this. Incandescence is the result of a current moving through high resistance: ideally in an airless

[22]Hogben, *Science for the Citizen*, pp. 702 ff.   [23]*Ibid.*, p. 707.

EDISON'S LIGHT.

The Great Inventor's Triumph in Electric Illumination.

A SCRAP OF PAPER.

It Makes a Light, Without Gas or Flame, Cheaper Than Oil.

TRANSFORMED IN THE FURNACE.

Complete Details of the Perfected Carbon Lamp.

FIFTEEN MONTHS OF TOIL.

Story of His Tireless Experiments with Lamps, Burners and Generators.

SUCCESS IN A COTTON THREAD.

The Wizard's Byplay, with Bodily Pain and Gold "Tailings."

HISTORY OF ELECTRIC LIGHTING.

The near approach of the first public exhibition of Edison's long looked for electric light, announced to take place on New Year's Eve at Menlo Park, on which occasion that place will be illuminated with the new light, has revived public interest in the great inventor's work, and throughout the civilized world scientists and people generally are anxiously awaiting the result. From the beginning of his experiments in electric lighting to the present time Mr. Edison has kept his laboratory guardedly closed, and no authoritative account (except that published in the Herald some months ago relating to his first patent) of any of the important steps of his progress has been made public—a course of procedure the inventor found absolutely necessary for his own protection. The Herald is now, however, enabled to present to its readers a full and accurate account of his work from its inception to its completion.

A LIGHTED PAPER.

Edison's electric light, incredible as it may appear, is produced from a little piece of paper—a tiny strip of paper that a breath would blow away. Through this little strip of paper is passed an electric current, and the result is a bright, beautiful light, like the mellow sunset of an Italian autumn.

"But paper instantly burns, even under the trifling heat of a tallow candle!" exclaims the sceptic, "and how, then, can it withstand the fierce heat of an electric current?" Very true, but Edison makes the little piece of paper more infusible than platinum, more durable than granite. And this involves no complicated process. The paper is

such closing making a new passage for the electric current and cutting it off from the incandescent platinum. When the latter contracted, as it did the moment the heat was lessened, the lever returned to its normal position and allowed the electric current to again pass through the platinum. By this device the inventor hoped to be able to keep the incandescent platinum always below its melting point. The contrivance is described in his first patent as follows:—

THE FIRST LIGHT.

"Electric lights have been produced by a coil or strip of platinum or other metal that require a high temperature to melt, the electric current rendering the same incandescent. In all such lights there is danger of the metal melting. My improvement is made for regulating the electric current automatically passing through such incandescent conductor, and preventing its temperature rising to the melting point, thus producing a reliable electric light."

FIGURE 1.

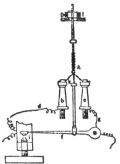

—Fig. 1 shows one form of the device. The incandescent metal is in the form of a double spiral A, the two ends terminating upon the posts b, c, to which the conductors d, E, are connected. A circuit closing lever, f, is introduced in the electric circuit, the points of contact being at i, and there is a platina, or similar wire, a, connected with the lever, i, to the headpiece or other support, i. The current from a magneto machine is connected with the wires E and d. The current then flows from E to the post, c, thence around the platinum spiral to b, and is carried off by the wire, d. Now, when the rod, k, of platinum becomes heated to too great intensity its expansion closes the lever, f, and the current then passes from E, through f, and not through the spiral at all. In this way the lever cuts off the current every time the heat becomes too intense."

Numerous other devices of a similar character were tried and for a while they all worked satisfactorily, but the inventor finally discovered that the constant expansion of the platinum rod k and its pressure upon the lever f bent it so that it became unreliable and it was, therefore, abandoned.

THE SECOND PLATINUM LAMP.

The next regulator was in the form of a diaphragm, which cut off the electric current from the platinum every time the diaphragm was pressed outward beyond a fixed limit by the heated air. The regulation thus produced was so rapid that the eye could not perceive any diminution in the strength of the current. But this also was inadequate in many respects. The next important modification in the light was the substitution for the platinum spiral of finely divided platinum incorporated with non-conducting material. When the electric current was passed through the combination the platinum particles became incandescent and the non-conducting material incorporated with them became luminous and increased the brilliancy. One advantage by this form not previously attained was that a very weak electric current produced a good light.

THE BOBBIN LAMP.

After this followed a device for obtaining more light-giving surface, the platinum being wound in the form of a small bobbin, first having been coated with a non-conducting coating that was not injured by the heat. With this arrangement a new form of regulator was used. The lamp at this stage is shown in figure 2.

heated by the passage of the electric current through it. E is a thin piece of zircon that receives the heat rays thrown off by the reflector, C, which heat rays bring up the zircon, E, to vivid incandescence, making it give out a light much more brilliant than the light of the platinum spiral, C. With this form Mr. Edison tried numerous experiments, and from time to time made many alterations and improvements, but eventually the apparatus was placed in the category of non-successes.

ANOTHER SPIRAL.

Realizing from the first the necessity of the light-giving substance offering much resistance to the passage of the electric current—a necessity in extensive subdivision of the light—the inventor throughout his experiments kept a close watch for substances and forms that gave suitable resistance. In figure 4 is shown a form of lamp disconnected from the regulating apparatus, which largely embodied the above requirement and for a time gave good results.

FIGURE 4.

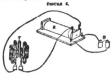

A is a spiral of carbon with two large ends, B, a, connecting with the wires leading to the machine for generating the current. This device was tried for several weeks, but did not, as a whole, give satisfaction.

EVERY MAN HIS OWN ELECTRIC LIGHTER.

Branching off from the line of investigation he had been previously following Mr. Edison at this time began experimenting with a view to having the light produced locally—i. e., arranging for each householder to become his own manufacturer of light, thus dispensing with mains and central stations. The apparatus which he used for this purpose is shown in figure 5:—

FIGURE 5.

R is an induction coil such as are used by peripatetic showmen at fairs and other places when they give electric shocks to inquiring sightseers at so much per shock. It is operated by two cells of battery, B, and wires lead from it to the glass tubing, T, from which the air has previously been extracted, and the passage of the electric current through the tubing gives out a light. This plan is analogous to what is known as the Geisler tube arrangement, the difference being in the form of the tube and the extreme smallness of the bore and also in the degree of vacuum produced, Mr. Edison succeeded by this arrangement in obtaining a light of several candle power with a moderately powerful induction coil. The light, however, was not the one sought after so persistently by the inventor, and so it took its place in that part of his laboratory occupied by inventions not in use.

OSMIUM-IRIDIUM.

Once more Mr. Edison made a departure. He moulded powdered metallic oxides in the form of sticks and subjected them to a very high temperature. In this connection he obtained very fine results from the native alloy of osmium-iridium called iridosmine, which alloy he used in the form of a powder enclosed in a tube of zircon. The electric current passing through the same brought it to a beautiful incandescence.

CARBON AND PLATINUM.

The inventor's next important move was the adoption of carbon in connection with platinum as the substance to be made incandescent. He caused a slender rod of carbon to rest upon another of platinum, the inferiority of contact between the two at their point of meeting producing a resistance to the passage of the electric current and causing the carbon to become highly incandescent, while the platinum attained only a dull red heat. The carbon rod was kept pressing upon the platinum by a weight ingeniously arranged. A dozen or more forms of this lamp were made; but, after all, the inventor was

magnesia and [...]
described, a com[...]
metal and the d[...]
properties. Wit[...]
of 3-16 of an in[...]
standard candles[...]
spiral, not coated[...]
giving a light [...]
the oxide of [...]
wire to a surp[...]
refractory. A s[...]
springy when a[...]
that chemically [...]
and subjected to[...]
to give a light [...]
open arc. Carbo[...]
in this manner [...]
where the carbo[...]
homogeneous as [...]

THE SUB[...]
About this time [...]
inventor—namel[...]
of light from in[...]
candescent subs[...]
sistance to the p[...]
cerning this that[...]
returns the prese[...]
one or two othe[...]
construct lamps [...]
light, shall have [...]
ns."

The lamp, as it [...]
progress, is show[...]

a is the burner [...]
tube, b, by a ro[...]
Within the ca[...]
aneroid chamber, [...]
l, so that the air, [...]
into the aneroid c[...]
flexible diaphrag[...]
with. When th[...]
bobbin, a, become[...]
too highly the air[...]
panded and bulges[...]
and the pin there[...]

The first news story of Edison's incandescent lamp. This sort of build-up for the "Wizard" became common from 1879 on

space. In the presence of air the heated conductor oxidizes, that is, burns up. If it be metal it melts at a given temperature, air or no air. Platinum melts least readily but its point of white glow or useful incandescence is close to its melting point. Edison, like Swan, turned to carbon.

Now, carbon to be solid and substantial must be thick. Thickness gives it low resistance. Therefore a large current must be introduced to make it incandescent. But large current requires thick copper wires. Thick copper wires cost money. Obviously to get a thin copper wire the incandescent medium must be very thin indeed. In other words, the difference between volume (amperes) and resistance (ohms) must be increased. Why not do the trick by increasing pressure (volts)? No, said Edison, we cannot introduce danger to the ignorant masses who will use these lights.

So, now, we see Edison handling his famous cotton thread carbonized for five hours in a muffle furnace. Out came a thing so fragile that even the delicate fingers of Charles Bachelor, Edison's famous assistant (called "Edison's hands"), broke it. Again and again, through three days and three sleepless nights, the threads broke. A jeweller's screwdriver fell against one, another parted as it was being carried to the glass blower's. Finally one got into the lamp, the air was pumped out and the tired men switched on the current. "A beautiful soft light met their eyes, and they knew that the secret of the incandescent lamp was solved."[24] Mr. Jones is dramatic in this sentence but he is optimistic. In theory the solution had come. Edison had used a pump that left only a millionth of an atmosphere (of air) in the bulb. But the filament itself in the tiny interstices of its fiber contained enough additional air to destroy it.

The "frenzy" went on. Cotton thread would not do. Hundreds of times the story has been told of Edison madly seizing everything he could lay his hands on: straw, paper, cardboard, wood splints, tearing up umbrellas, walking sticks,[25] trying everything from tar to cheese.[26] "He experimented with six thousand dif-

[24]Francis Arthur Jones, *Thomas Alva Edison: Sixty Years of an Inventor's Life*, N.Y., 1907, p. 106.
[25]*Ibid.*, pp. 107, 108.   [26]Crowther, p. 388.

ferent sorts of vegetable fibres, collected from all parts of the world. He found that bamboo gave the most durable filaments."[27]

The story runs on that men rushed over the world investigating twelve hundred varieties of bamboo, that one man covered thirty thousand miles and had encounters with wild animals.[28] We find a clashing of dramatic accounts as we explore the history of the "frenzy." They are unimportant. We know that Edison was

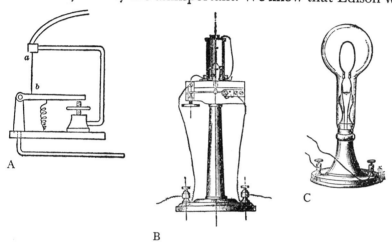

A. Edison's first incandescent platinum lamp (ab is incandescent platinum wire). B. Edison's platinum lamp on column support, 1879. C. Edison's paper carbon lamp

From "Electricity in Lighting," *Scribner's Magazine*, August, 1889

methodical if not wholly scientific, that his mind was dynamic if not wholly intuitive, that he was not subject to the fatigue which limits most men, that his nerves were strong, that his concentration was complete, that his persistence was phenomenal, his faith indomitable and that, in common with all genius, the threshold was low, often non-existent, between his conscious and his subconscious minds.

We shall not try to unravel the confusion of dates and legends. In December, 1879, the announcement was made of a practical lamp.[29] "Several scientists proclaimed Edison's invention to be a fake. Gas stocks, however, dropped in price and stock in the Edison Electric Light Company soared to thirty-five hundred

[27]*Ibid.*   [28]Jones, p. 109.
[29]*N. Y. Herald,* Sunday, Dec. 21, 1879.

dollars a share."[30] The same authority states succinctly what Edison had invented: "a lamp with a high resistance filament of carbon in a vacuum contained in a glass container closed at all points by fusion of the glass and having platinum wires imbedded in the glass to carry current through the glass to the filament. And this was the first incandescent lamp which was suitable for the system of general multiple distribution which solved the problem of the 'subdivision of the electric light.'"

This was not basic invention. It was improvement by economic command of technic. The improvement was responsible for the illumination of the world. But without the labor of many inventors who illumined only their own laboratories and lecture halls, the improvement could never have been made. The reader may now go on playing this good old game to his heart's content.

7

That Edison was no traditional inventor appears in 1880. His plans, worked out by his multithought system, were ready for quantity production of lamps. This approached mass production a few years later when the men in the lamp factory struck and Edison invented a machine to take some of the skilled labor out of their hands. His command of the economics of the transition from quantity to mass production is seen in his price determination. He set a price of forty cents on a lamp that cost $1.25 to make, but this price was to endure through the life of the patent. In five years he had reduced the cost to twenty-two cents but in the same period sales had gone from tens of thousands to millions, so that the vast majority of sales were at a profit. By this time he was through with production—it always bored him once he had designed the system—and he sold his factory.[31]

But at the same time in 1880, he had his plans made for central station generation. While he sold his lamps to "isolated plants" in steamers and factories, he simultaneously completed the celebrated Pearl Street power plant in New York. He seems, in

[30]Howell and Schroeder, *History of the Incandescent Lamp*, p. 58.
[31]Crowther, p. 395.

Top: The first Edison electric lighting station, Pearl Street, New York
Redrawn from a drawing in *Scientific American,* August 26, 1882

Bottom: A New York street lighted by Brush arc-light
Redrawn from a drawing from Alglave and Boulard, *Electric Light,* New York, 1884

these early eighties, to have been everywhere at once. He was down in trenches in the city streets examining his mains. He was in the power house, linking fantastically high-speed steam engines to dynamos with low internal resistance. He would reappear unexpectedly in the laboratory, in the lamp factory, driving his unsuccessful "Judge" locomotive. In the time that it seemed impossible could be left over from these things he was conferring with businessmen like Henry Villard, to whom he would eventually sell out some of his interests, or with managers like Samuel Insull, who would carry others on under Edison ownership.

The Pearl Street plant opened on September 4, 1882, with six "Jumbo" generators of Edison design with a capacity of 125 horsepower each. "When Thomas Edison gave the signal . . . these generators sent forth current along underground lines for a total length of thirteen miles."[32] A night school had been opened to educate its operators. Current was supplied free at this moment to subscribers while Edison was in another "frenzy" inventing a meter. Six months later an electrolytic meter[33] was installed which aroused suspicion. "How do I know I am not being cheated?" But in the six months from June to November, 1883, Edison accounts showed: bills sent out, $36,563.63; money collected, $34,753.17. Cheated or no, the subscribers paid. In the first months other questions came in from skeptics: "Don't you have to use matches?" "Won't it explode?" "Is it safe in a thunderstorm?" and a department called "public relations" was invented to deal with them.[34]

In October, a month after the opening, the news was printed that "the throng of people that pass in the evening down Fulton Street, on their way to Brooklyn, observe with interest that in place of the usual gas lights in several of the stores on both sides of the street, the little glowing horseshoes of the Edison Electric Illuminating Company, each in a small, pear-shaped globe of

[32]National Electric Light Association, *Bulletin,* Vol. IX, No. 9, Sept., 1922, p. 515.
[33]Metallic zinc was removed from one plate and deposited on another as current flowed between them. The plate on which deposit was made was weighed before and after deposit.
[34]*Ibid.,* pp. 515–520.

glass, pendant beneath a porcelain shade, shed an exquisitely soft light upon the goods that formerly were but poorly illuminated."[35]

These things were managed on direct current only. Westinghouse, Tesla and the great Charles Proteus Steinmetz had not yet fully demonstrated the facility with which alternating current might be handled. Edison's increasing inadaptability as he grew older is evident in his refusal ever to consider the use of alternating current in his plants. He had started with the direct and he would keep it despite the proved advantages of the other. He refused to listen to the gentle and patient persuasion of Frank Sprague merely to investigate alternating current.[36] When commercial stations opened using the alternating current, "Edison and his associates placed every conceivable obstacle—political, legal, and financial—in the path of this obvious improvement."[37] But this was a symptom of much of the inflexibility that developed in his later years.

Genius of his sort is not immune to age. He experienced many failures during his later period. The mythology, founded in great achievement, went on, however, gaining momentum and falsehood with every year. He was honored and decorated, a sense of his greatness was forced upon him, he accepted it with reluctance, but no man can resist such pressure. Often when he was given credit for something like electric traction which belonged, *in toto,* to others he seems simply to have refused comment. Perhaps he did not hear—he was deaf from boyhood and usually detached. His intimates call him friendly, warm, cheerful, encouraging. Unhappily, he was led once, along with Ford, into expressions on education, religion, social philosophy, history. It is odd that because a man has succeeded admirably as a practical technician, so many people should put faith in his opinions on cigarette smoking and women's dress or his dicta on God, freedom and immortality. We shall come back, often to Edison. Let us remember that he was a human being.

[35]*The Electrician,* N. Y., Vol. I, No. 10, October, 1882.
[36]Report, F. J. Sprague to E. H. Johnson, Sept. 13, 1886, *Sprague Papers,* Vol. I, Engineering Society Library, New York.
[37]Jonathan N. Leonard, *Tools of Tomorrow,* N. Y., 1935, p. 69.

8

Electric illumination has gone a long way from Menlo Park. The lamps have acquired new shapes, fillings, filaments, plugs. Carbonized bamboo was coated by the Sawyer-Man process. There was the Leigh Powell process for squirted cellulose carbon filament and another devised by Swan. When the lamp got into the General Electric Company (child of an Edison organization) filaments were improved in electric furnaces. Then they were metallized as in the Gem of Willis Whitney and moved on to osmium (von Welsbach), tantalum (von Bolton) and tungsten (developed by many experimenters). The General Electric Company finally applied the name Mazda (from Persian mythology) to the whole of their lamp research. The name means only this and applies to no particular technic.[38] Meanwhile it was discovered that highly rarefied gases would conduct electricity and the filament was dispensed with entirely as in the neon light.[39]

We cannot go here into the uses of inert gases as helium or argon instead of vacuum or into the use of mercury vapor by Peter Cooper Hewitt and others. The so-called glow lamps, whose light comes from a stream of "electrified" vapor, have finally been cheapened to a point where they are in abundant use in factories and for advertising.

With improvement in lamps, generation, transmission and distribution a true revolution has taken place in almost every department of life. Tiny bulbs now penetrate the human body revealing processes and conditions formerly mysterious to doctors. Dentists have been able to explore the mouth and as a result have altered most of their science. Collateral technology starting with the vacuum tube has developed cathode, Roentgen or X-rays invaluable to surgery and medicine, and in this realm, through such equipment, has come the discovery of the electron. Here physics and chemistry have been turned inside out, worlds within worlds have been revealed inside the formerly indivisible

[38]Howell and Schroeder, pp. 100 f.
[39]Hogben, *Science for the Citizen,* p. 749.

atom and each atom has been found to have a kind of solar system of its own. The whole subject of electricity has been re-stated since this discovery. Bacteriology has developed a new world under brilliantly illumined microscopes. Photometry has been able to measure infinitesimal distances. Photography has, as we shall see, not only entered new esthetic spheres but opened a whole technology of measurement and record in scientific ex-periment. The time for scientific research has been nearly doubled since the night has become as useful as the day, sometimes more so.

The technic of the theatre has entered a new phase. The old footlights—the only possible lighting by flame—have disappeared and with them old scenic methods and old make-up technic. Effects of staggering beauty are now familiar. The motion pic-ture, as we know it, has depended on electric lighting. A whole new department of engineering has grown up and the "illumi-nating engineers" have called to their aid experts in optics and color, oculists and doctors, architects and decorators to make lighting more beautiful and more healthful. The home has changed character. Rats and vermin have run from the glare, dirt has become visible and, so, intolerable. The all-revealing light has brought cleanliness of living quarters and of the person. Under the modulated glow women have found new beauty.

The farm has changed character. Light fills the cow barns and stables, no longer setting the straw afire. Hens have been induced to lay more eggs under the continuous blaze of an in-candescent bulb. Prowlers, animal and human, have been scared away.

Devastating light has been shed on crime and the criminal, the debauchee and the degenerate, and but for other technologies which have balanced it in their favor, many sins might have dis-appeared. The new light has proved both a defense and a target in war. It has made over the life of shipboard and general travel. It has made high-speed and abundant motor traffic possible.

Need we extend the inventory? It is already tedious. We began with romance. We have seen old falsehood vanish, new truth and beauty appear. The new light has dissolved neither the warmth nor the glamor of the world. We are on the threshold of a subject in which they will be much present.

It is a truism, we suppose, that men deeply occupied in physical things do not greatly reflect upon life. During such preoccupation the arts lapse. The child is occupied with his growth, with physical concerns. Grooves are made in his mind which we call habits of thought, but the thought itself is based on physical sensation, moves little in the dark silences, seems to originate outside himself. Fancy may be active but sensation rather than reflection is usually the stimulus. The child may sometimes chew the cud of his small experience, but usually the fresh food outside is more alluring.

America was like the child in the first century of her existence. There was too much to do to think. The mechanics of life were more immediate and compelling than its philosophy. Thus art and letters, which are reflections of life, declined as the physical impulse strengthened. Now, in our history, we approach the completion of the physical process. The frontiers are closing, the backwash begins, the static centers are resting a little because better machinery, methods, transport have made production easier. With all this change, wealth has flowed out of the ground and settled in still pools. Leisure has arrived. There is time for thought, reflection, listening and reading, the long delights of the eye, the ear and the mind. Where physical leisure has come we see a craving for such delights; for art, for study, scholarship, learning; for philosophy and poetry, for the reception of abstractions, the contemplation, for example of "pure beauty."

We call this, inadequately perhaps, the "cultural impulse."

Part III

THE CULTURAL IMPULSE

Chapter Twelve

THE PICTURE CYCLE

I

PICTURES have served mankind in two ways: they have answered his need for communication and his need for art. It is likely that the earliest drawings were intended to convey a desire, a record of action or a command to a remote person without relying entirely on the fallible memory of a messenger. As these drawings became common they became conventionalized, losing their character as representations of objects; they became complex in implications, conveying ideas of motion and, finally, sound. As the progress of human evolution is uneven we find, at any given point at which we may stop the motion, a kind of echelon with some men far in the van, while others are still at the points which have been passed by the leaders but struggling to catch up. Thus while, in the Western world, we are using characters which have no significance as pictorial representation to convey the sound of speech, orientals are still using conventionalized pictures to convey ideas, and further back in the movement, tribal communication may be carried on by recognizable drawings of objects.

If, however, we stop the march in 1940 we shall observe an extremely curious phenomenon. As we look at civilization in the United States of America at this moment, there appears a lapse which breaks our orderly simplification. Here, evidently, having learned the ultimate refinement of phonetic code we have found it convenient to abandon it and return to the caveman's method. The bulk of our communication is no longer conducted by characters to suggest speech sound or even by conventionalized drawings to convey ideas—communication which requires intellectual exercise of a complex nature. Our method is to split this process into its two component parts, eliminating most of the cerebral function: we receive our news directly through our senses; either by listening to actual speech sounds or by looking at realistic and sensational pictures. This method has spread, to such extent, from America over the rest of a highly civilized world that we may permit ourselves to suspect that it is an evolutionary advance of a sort: that, after æons of mistakes, we have recognized the rightness of what we call primitive conduct. It is as if, in the course of animal evolution, the will in the human protoplasm suddenly produced a sport with tusks and a tail as better adapted, after all, to cope with its environment.

Perhaps we have made an unwarrantable stretch, in comparing the primitive carving on a bone with the exquisite product of the candid camera or in analogy between the guttural chatter echoing through the jungle and the far-flung sound caught by our superheterodyne magic. Yet the principle is not greatly different. The difference is in the motive behind it. The cave man listened to speech and looked at pictures because he knew no other way of receiving communication; the modern does these things because he has not time to translate written words into ideas. This is, after all, a cumbersome process whose tempo is far behind that of our action. Even for purposes of record, it is, as we shall see, no longer necessary.

2

All of this, of course, has nothing to do with art, the intermediate phase of our subject and the source of the invention we are about to discuss. We enter here a special, rarefied province, a realm feared by the angels, into which, perhaps, we shall embarrass ourselves by rushing. Yet, if we confine our discussion largely to history, to needs imposed by social change and to the invented answers to those urgencies, we shall not greatly transcend our theme.

The word "conscious" may be stretched to imply something more than mere animal sense of being. It implies the capacity for reflection upon things observed, for mental vision of things not seen. Men driven to continuous physical activity—galley slaves or workers upon a modern assembly line—may never become conscious in this meaning. Such awareness requires intervals of waking rest, moments of inaction. During the whole of recorded history, the great mass of humanity has, therefore, remained unconscious in this sense.

As we look over the most recent period, however, we seem to see a broadening of the sphere of consciousness. In the nineteenth century, for instance, we find the arts no longer in the exclusive possession of a small, leisurely aristocracy.

Following the industrial revolution, there occurred a "rise" of hitherto inert elements of the population. As wealth filtered through the strata, bourgeois and even proletarians encountered leisure and hence reflection. Released workers suffered, in new quiet moments, the same craving to possess certain visions and experiences and to preserve them against the passage of time as that which was felt by the cave man when loveliness invaded his opening mind. Thus, at once, the arts extended their field of influence. A picture, for instance, no longer satisfied only the craving of an aristocrat for the possession of beauty or the crystallization of memory; it reached beyond him, now, to the shopkeeper and the mill hand. These persons, however, desired that the picture represent something familiar to them. Thus at the moment that the base of the arts broadened, their character changed.

The bourgeois could not understand the painting which was worshipped by the gentler class with its long heritage of education, its abundant opportunity for study. Nor did its unfamiliar content perform for them the nostalgic function of art. "The ideal type is no longer princely, it is replaced by the features of the bourgeois. . . . The civilization of the Court which found its highest artistic expression in the paintings and pastels of La Tour and Watteau with their volatile, gay movements gives way to the middle-class culture and to the gray, heavy and massive colors of a David. There appears the drawing of Ingres with its precise contours responding to the realistic inclination of the epoch and to the taste of a conventional bourgeoisie, studied in its dignity and aware of its duties."[1]

In England in the Victorian age, artists watched the bourgeois rise and were simultaneously impressed by the decadence of the artificially maintained aristocratic taste. Aware of the realist forces which were opposed by the romantic attitude of the queen and her court, and retching at the imitative painting and meaningless decoration in vogue among the remaining élite, a group of these painters formed, in 1848, the pre-Raphaelite Brotherhood whose slogan was "back to Nature." Their painting, under this motive, was adored by the semiconscious, reality-loving bourgeoisie. In actual fact, however, the "P. R. B.," as it was affectionately called, was caught, like everything else, in the vicious Victorian circle. Its painters had merely moved from one set of untruths to another. They wallowed in a slough of sentimentality from which even the prodigious propaganda of the critic Ruskin could not save them. They were destroyed at last by technological forces.

The chief difficulty of a "back to nature" movement in the mid-century was that most people had only the vaguest notion as to what nature was. The physicists, chemists and biologists were producing evidence in quantity and Charles Darwin was working out his great theory of biological evolution which would distress so many orthodox thinkers when it appeared in 1859, but the artist found such investigation of little value. Thus the boys of the P. R. B., working in their teens to escape from accepted technics, developed the theory that a violent catharsis was the only effective preparation for the observation of nature "as it was." This involved the subordination of perception to the function of seeing; in their painting they must, therefore, try to paint natural objects precisely as the eye received the images and before the mind had a chance to distort them.

Now the distinction between what the eye sees and what the mind sees is exceedingly subtle.[2] Of all the sensory organs the

[1]Gisele Freund, *La Photographie en France au Dix-Neuvieme Siecle,* Paris, 1936, p. 5.
[2]R. H. Wilenski, *The Modern Movement in Art,* N. Y., 1927, p. 86. His whole section on "Human Perception," pp. 82 ff., is well worth reading.

eye seems to be the most elaborately connected with the brain. It is supposed, for instance, that with the eye alone, the full understanding of three-dimensional form is impossible; that here the eye is aided by the tactile sense. A person who merely looks at an object, never touching it or moving around it, thinks of that object as having only two dimensions and if he attempts then to draw it, draws only its outline.[3] It is only by perception, by the combination in his mind of different sensory impressions that he is able to use perspective or the technic of three-dimensional representation of a two-dimensional medium. By limiting themselves, therefore, to mere vision in the horrid fear that mental prejudice might profane the divine Nature, the young men of the P. R. B. found themselves in a formidable position. As a result, their masterpieces have been called "precise and pedantic," "dry and artificial,"[4] "papery," "wan," "feeble dreams," and calculated "to set back the implacable clock of time."[5] Certainly when stood beside the work of either the old masters or the new impressionists, their imagery seems flat enough.

Yet at the very moment of the brotherhood's inception there was in existence an invention which would begin by leading them still further astray and end by showing the public, if not themselves, the error of their ways. This instrument possessed the power of separating vision from perception. It could produce with no aid from the eye precisely the image that is thrown upon the eye's retina before it is perceived by the brain. With it, the artist could discover what nature was without comment, without selection, without the use of other senses. He could then analyze the performance of the mind in relation to this vision.[6] Once he had realized the powers and the limitations of the new instrument, he found that the nature he saw here represented was not precisely the nature he wished to paint or, if he continued to believe that it was what he wished to paint, he came to

[3] J. R. Fothergill, "Drawing," *Encyc. Brit.*, 13th ed., VIII, 552–556. Gives an excellent account of the psycho-physical factors in the understanding of perspective.

[4] Minutieuse et pedante . . . sec et factice," Salomon Reinach, *Apollo,* Paris, 1904, p. 314.

[5] James Huneker, *Steeplejack,* N. Y., 1925, p. 186.

[6] Wilenski, pp. 78–82.

the painful understanding that this mechanical, optical and chemical device could do it better.

The realization of the powers and limitations of the new invention came slowly. Ruskin, on being shown a daguerreotype in 1845, looked at it with stunned surprise, thought with disgust that it had done in a few seconds what it had taken him days to achieve, pronounced it a "glorious" invention,[7] suggested its use by painters and finally heaped contempt upon it as losing the "most subtle beauty of all things."[8] He and others at first confused photography with painting or drawing. This was natural because the process was new. Thus people believed that somehow the camera had the artist's capacity for selection and emphasis and comment. They thought it revealed the true form of objects because it merely recorded relations of light and shade. When they finally understood these things, painting took a new leap forward, artists suspected their perception no more than the old masters had done, and the belief was more generally accepted that "the great artist has not reproduced nature, but has expressed by his extract the most choice sensation it has produced upon him."[9] We shall return to this question. Meanwhile, naturalist art came to an end.

3

It must not be supposed that the graphic and plastic arts had struggled through the centuries without any aid from science or mechanical devices. Lenses were in use in the eleventh century and various tricks such as drawing tables with reference points, gauze-covered frames and so on were used from the end of the fourteenth century. But by this time, also, the celebrated "dark room," called in Latin *Camera Obscura,* was already in existence and all study of the history of photography must go back to this device, for from it derived the optical part of that technology.

The phenomenon of light coming through a small hole in the wall of a dark room and casting an inverted image on the wall

[7]*Works of John Ruskin,* E. T. Cook and A. Wedderburn, eds., London, 1912, III, 210 n.
[8]*Ibid.,* XV, 59, 103; XXVIII, 446, 447.
[9]Robert Henri, *The Art Spirit,* Phila., 1923, p. 78.

opposite was noticed by Aristotle.[10] Its recognition crops up again in the thirteenth century, though meticulous scholars are doubtful if any credit for an "invention" can be given to Roger Bacon and his contemporaries who studied Aristotle's "problem."[11] It is certain, however, that our old friend Leonardo da Vinci used the principle of the camera obscura in his painting[12] and, as it is usual to give credit to this great experimenter for almost any

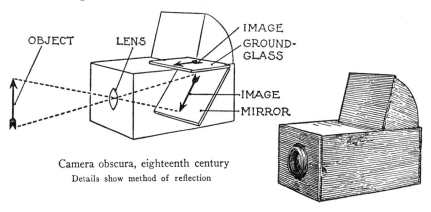

OBJECT LENS IMAGE GROUND-GLASS IMAGE MIRROR

Camera obscura, eighteenth century
Details show method of reflection

invention, there seems no reason why we should not let the bulk of the honor rest with him. To us the much-advertised Giovanni Battista della Porta[13] seems a mere promoter.

Daniele Barbaro describes the use of a convex lens in the hole to make the image clearer.[14] But all this time the *camera* remained an actual room. In 1570, Robert Boyle made a box which served the same purpose,[15] and thus there came into existence the familiar instrument which became, by the eighteenth century, a regular part of artists' equipment.[16] It was simply a box with a lens at one end and a screen of ground glass in the top. A mirror reflected the image to the screen, which was shaded

[10]*Problems*, Sec. XV, c. 5.
[11]Georges Potonniée, *History of the Discovery of Photography*, trans. Edward Epstean, N. Y., 1936, p. 12.
[12]MS. *D*, fol. 8, *recto*.
[13]*Magia Naturalis*, 2d ed., 1589, lib. XVII, cap. 6; Potonniée, Chap. II.
[14]*La Pratica della perspettiva*, 1568, p. 192.
[15]The steps are minutely traced by James Waterhouse, "Camera Obscura," *Encyc. Brit.*, 13th ed., V, 106, 107.
[16]Beaumont Newhall, *Photography, 1839–1937*, Mus. Mod. Art, N. Y., 1937, p. 12.

by a hood. By laying a piece of paper over the screen the image could be traced.

While such tracings were helpful to the study of orthographic perspective and in proportional measurement, and though they became popular among laymen as "true" representations, they were very faulty records. Luminosity and color values were scarcely suggested, and the moods of nature impossible to portray in such a manner; a scene in bright sunlight would look much like a clouded one except that the sunny picture might have more detail. The tracing was a mere silhouette. There was little, therefore, in the tracing from a camera obscura to modify the pre-Raphaelite attitude.

4

Long before history was written, it must have been evident to men that certain substances altered under the effect of light. Notable among these is the human skin, tanning in the sunlight, and when men first wore bracelets or loin cloths they must have noticed photographs upon their bodies in places which the light had not reached. These, however, faded as sunlight was admitted—a difficulty which produced the worst of the struggle with the early heliographic experiments with silver. The "tanning" of silver salts is said to have been first observed by Johann Heinrich Schulze, a German physician who, in 1727, obtained a sun print of a label on silver chloride contained in a bottle.[17] Far more penetrating were the experiments of Karl Wilhelm Scheele, a Swedish chemist, who not only noted similar phenomena but found further that silver chloride was differently affected by rays from different parts of the spectrum.[18] At about the same time a highly suspect story is told of Jacques Alexandre César Charles, a French balloon inventor, obtaining the record of the silhouette of a head thrown on a silver-coated screen.[19]

Experiment now passes to England and we have the first authentic account of the chemical reproduction of an image by

[17]J. M. Eder, *Geschichte der Photographie,* Halle, 1905, cited by Potonniée, pp. 47, 48.
[18]Robert Hunt, "Researches on Light," *Photographic Art Journal,* Vol. I, p. 7 (1851).
[19]Gaston Tissandier, *Photography,* translated from the French, J. Thompson, ed., 2d ed., London, 1878, pp. 10 ff.

Thomas Wedgwood, son of the potter. It is vouched for in 1802 by Humphry Davy. Here nitrate of silver was used and, after making many photographic prints by laying objects, printed papers, etc., on paper coated with this compound (in the manner of the modern blueprint), Wedgwood tried to get an impression from the *camera obscura* and failed.[20] He did, however, get temporary photographs of objects under the solar microscope. The great difficulty was that all these chemical records faded as soon as they were exposed to strong light.

Literally, this was not fading; it was the later darkening of those portions of the sensitized surface which had not been altered during exposure. After the image had been secured, if the whole plate or paper were then brought into bright, diffused light it would darken evenly all over, obliterating the image. The problem, therefore, was to remove the silver salt from all parts of the plate except those portions originally darkened, and to fix the darkened portions permanently so that they could not be further altered. Until this could be done, there was nothing but an idea and practical photography must be deferred.

At the same time, students of theoretical invention are quick to grasp the importance of one unconscious phase of this discovery. Wedgwood had produced a "negative"; that is, parts of the object which were light appeared dark in the recorded image and vice versa. Had Wedgwood realized it, he had here come upon the multiple-record principle of photography: from his negatives any number of "positives" with their values in order might have been made. He did not, however, realize this and such realization seems to us pragmatists to be the very essence of invention.

For this same reason it is difficult for us to give as full credit for the invention of photography to the much-heralded Joseph-Nicéphore Niepce as some writers demand.[21] Niepce, working some fifteen years later, was so distressed by the negatives he

[20]*Journal*, Royal Institution, Vol. I, p. 170, 1802. Quoted by Potonniée, p. 59, fortunately, as the journal is difficult to obtain.
[21]A pompous and angry book by Victor Fouque, *Nicéphore Niepce*, Paris, 1867, translated by Edward Epstean, N. Y., 1936, contains, however, much valuable correspondence. Guided by Potonniée, Note 1, p. 75, and by Larousse and most early histories, we have dropped the accent from Niepce.

obtained that he went to infinite pains to discover a chemical which would keep the true light and shade of the object in the image. He found it, at last, in "bitumen of Judea," which turned white instead of black on exposure, but the bitumen took ten or twelve hours to record an image which somewhat limited its uses for photography. At the same time, however, he made the vital discovery that exposed (whitened) bitumen became insoluble in oil or essence of lavender which dissolved the unexposed portions. His pictures, therefore, were more permanent than Wedgwood's though vague in detail. He then made a startling advance into another field by turning the copper plates on which these pictures appeared into etched plates, from which, in a press, prints could be made—an approach to the idea if not the fact of photogravure.

At this point experiment in the chemical record of light began to spread from the laboratory into the studio. Many of the early experimenters were artists. They were often mediocre painters, men whose gifts were inadequate to their desperate creative impulse. Such a man was Louis Jacques Mandé Daguerre, who worked simultaneously with Niepce and independently of him until Niepce's fearful suspicions were finally broken down, when they worked together.

Daguerre was a scene painter. He produced spectacular panoramas with trick lighting and magic changes which would seem extremely funny and naïve to us but were taken very seriously by the sensation-seekers of the day. They were called the "diorama."[22] Meanwhile, however, while these shows supported him he played with the camera obscura or its twin brother, the camera lucida. As both he and Niepce went to Charles Chevalier, the famous optician, for lenses, Daguerre learned Niepce's name,[23] and having none of Niepce's secrecy wrote him frankly. Niepce replied guardedly to this letter.[24] Daguerre persisted and after

[22]See comment of Terry Ramsaye in his superb history of the cinema, *A Million and One Nights*, N. Y., 1926, I, 15, 16. A book to which, later, we shall often refer.

[23]Arthur Chevalier, *Etude sur la vie*, etc., de Charles Chevalier, Paris, 1862, p. 144. Fouque, p. 63.

[24]Tissandier, p. 38, says Niepce threw it in the fire, but this is not borne out by Niepce's later letter. Fouque, p. 66.

long delays, much backing and filling, "prudence" and subterfuge on Niepce's part, the two got together and signed a partnership agreement. There is something faintly comic about this whole performance. From the correspondence, an acute novelist could draw the complete characters of these vivid and utterly dissimilar Frenchmen who possessed between them such powers

Daguerre's camera and developing cabinet

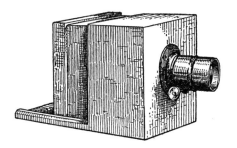
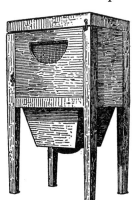

for the development of the new art. Tragedy arrived, however, with Niepce's death (from "congestion of the brain"[25]) in 1833, four years after the agreement had been signed.

Daguerre learned enough from Niepce to go ahead definitely to the full perfection of his beautiful invention. He continued the partnership with Niepce's son Isidore, but on condition that Daguerre's name only attach to the process.[26] Together they tried to commercialize the "daguerreotype." They soon found that patents were futile. As soon as the process was known every one would be practicing it. So they decided to cede the invention to the state and receive pensions in return. Daguerre showed a plate to the celebrated scientist and academician, François Dominique Jean Arago, who was "thunderstruck" and "boundless in his expressions of admiration." There ensued a drama which obscured the recognition of true photography both in Europe and America for about a quarter of a century.

Arago caused the pension bill to be introduced in the Chamber of Deputies. To assure their vote, a proper publicity campaign was necessary. So, bit by bit, the fact of the new invention was

[25]Tissandier, p. 65.   [26]Fouque, p. 116.

allowed to leak out while the details of the process were locked in secrecy. Newspaper reporters were shown daguerreotype pictures and became hysterical in their stories. "What fineness of touch," exploded the *Moniteur Universelle,* "what harmony of light and shade! What delicacy! What finish! . . . In a view of Paris we can count the paving stones—we see the dampness produced by rain; we can read the name on a shop. All the threads of luminous tissue have passed from the object into the image."[27]

From January to August, then, the public was whipped into a frenzy of desire to count the paving stones for themselves and especially to know how the plates were made. It was announced that the full revelation would be made at a meeting of the Academy on August 19. As dawn broke on that day a crowd collected about the Institute.[28] Only a handful could get in but the vast *"foule"* pressed as close as it could hoping some inkling might filter out. The next day the paper of Arago[29] was printed in the news. The process sounded so easy that people stormed the shops for lenses, mercury and iodine, and all over Paris boxes were pointed out of windows, at churches and at paving stones. Within five months twenty-six editions of a handbook of the process[30] were printed in six languages and box-pointing took place all over the civilized world.[31] Daguerre gave public demonstrations[32] and the daguerreotype became a vogue, a craze, *"le dernier cri,"* and was exploited far beyond its deserts and, unhappily, to the long exclusion of superior processes. The generous pensions of the beneficent French Government amounted to $800 (annually) apiece to Daguerre and Isidore Niepce.[33]

Daguerre's process seems cumbersome to us. A silver-plated

[27]Jan. 4, 1839. Quoted by Tissandier, p. 67 n.   [28]Freund, p. 38.
[29]*Comtes Rendus des Séances de l'Académie des Sciences,* Vol. IX, pp. 250–267.
[30]Translated in *Journal* of the Franklin Institute, Phila., Nov., 1839, pp. 303 ff.
[31]Newhall, p. 23.
[32]For an account of one see *American Journal of Photography,* June, 1892, pp. 247–249.
[33]Daguerre's pension was augmented by 2000 francs for telling the secret of the "Diorama." Larousse, VI, 13.

sheet of copper was iodized with the fumes of iodine crystals, producing silver iodide on the surface. On exposure this plate received a "latent" or invisible image. The image was made visible by placing the plate in mercury fumes at a certain temperature.[34] What had happened was a decomposition of the exposed parts of the silver iodide. The mercury fumes condensed upon these parts and not upon the others, thus revealing the lights and shadows with positive relationship between them: the lights being bright and shiny with mercury, the shadows in darker metallic silver.

At this point it appears that Daguerre had not restricted his borrowing to Niepce. The last stage in the process was to dip the developed plate in what was erroneously called hyposulphite of soda,[35] which removed the unaltered sensitizing and made further alteration from exposure impossible. Here was the device of the Englishman John Frederick William Herschel, discovered in 1819—too late for Wedgwood—and one of the most vital inventions in the history of photography.

Daguerre—to what extent assisted by Niepce we do not know or greatly care—made one great step forward in the invention: this was in cutting exposure time by using the *latent* image instead of waiting for the visible one to form. The procedure has been followed ever since.

It must be obvious to the reader that, beautiful, effective and valuable as daguerreotypes might be, photography as we understand it had not yet been invented. With the revelation of the Daguerre-Niepce experiments and the derived process the world became aware that the chemical record of image was possible but it was not yet aware that a further chemical record of that record was a practical, easy matter. In other words, the principle of multiple record was left out of the invention. The nearest approach to this was in Niepce's etched plates, which were inadequate and were not made by a photographic process. Thus you could get one daguerreotype of a landscape or building, but to get another you must point the camera again at the landscape or building and expose a new plate. Meanwhile the view would

[34]167° F.   [35]Correctly sodium thiosulphite.

have changed, subtly, under changes of light and atmosphere.

For the principle of multiple record in photography, we must now go back to England.

5

William Henry Fox Talbot does not belong in the artist category. He was an amateur draftsman and sketcher, but primarily he was a scientist and scholar. He was a mathematician and a chemist; he made important researches in light and color.

Knowing the sensitiveness of silver salts, Talbot tried spreading silver nitrate on paper which had been previously wet with salt solution,[36] and exposing it to sunlight obstructed by objects. He was so interested in the results that he began at once, in the scientific manner, to search for records of similar experiments. He found the story of Wedgwood and Davy in the Royal Society's *Journal*. Here the great discoverer Davy had announced the failure due to inability to fix the image. Such an announcement, says Talbot, "would perhaps have induced me to consider the attempt as hopeless, if I had not (fortunately) before I read it, already discovered a method of overcoming this difficulty, and of *fixing* the image in such a manner that it is no more liable to injury or destruction."[37] This, he explains in a later paper, was "the iodide of potassium, much diluted by water."[37a] It was not as effective as Herschel's "hypo" for which he abandoned it; the process is important only in that it kept him from giving up his experiment.

Talbot was already familiar with the camera obscura and had made sketches with it in Italy in 1833. In 1835, he combined the camera with paper rendered more sensitive by repetition of the sensitizing process, and produced a number of negative photographs. By 1839, he had so interested Michael Faraday in his work that Faraday, having heard rumors of Daguerre's discoveries, urged him to present a paper to the Royal Society[38] in order

[36]Thus forming silver chloride AgCl.
[37]*London and Edinburgh Philosophical Magazine*, Vol. XIV, third series (1839), p. 198.
[37a]*Ibid.*, p. 210.
[38]"Some Account of the Art of Photogenic Drawing," etc., Jan. 31, 1839. *Proceedings*, Royal Society, No. 36, 1838–1839.

to establish priority. At this time, he had not yet discovered that he could get a far quicker exposure by removing his sensitive paper from the camera before the image was visible upon it and then "developing" this latent image. He made this discovery "rather suddenly on September 20 and 21, 1840"[39] according to his own account, though it has been said that he must have borrowed it from Daguerre.[40] From there he went on to the invention of the "calotype," patented in 1841.

Calotype paper was made by washing first in a solution of silver nitrate, then in a solution of potassium iodide. When ready to use, this "iodized paper" was washed in gallo-nitrate of silver made by combining silver nitrate with gallic and acetic acids. After exposure the negative was developed by washing again with the gallo-nitrate.[41] This may or may not have been an improvement on Daguerre's process. The important point is that by it a negative was produced on *paper* instead of a positive on *copper*. The paper being translucent, an indefinite number of positive prints could be made from it by simply laying it over another sensitized sheet and exposing it to the light.[42] Later Talbot waxed the paper on which the negatives were made, making it more translucent[43]—an approach to the glass plates which came into use when sticky collodion was applied to photography.

Unhappily, due to the daguerreotype craze, the calotype was virtually unknown for many years. In the interval, however, at the very moment, indeed, that people all over the world were rushing to obtain Daguerre's shiny plates, a man who was perhaps the greatest photographer of all time was using calotype paper to produce pictures of the most exquisite beauty. It was not until the nineties that these lovely forgotten photographs were finally collected and exhibited to an astonished world. The work which David Octavius Hill, an obscure, mediocre Scottish painter, achieved with primitive cameras and a relatively difficult chemical process still offers a challenge to the photographic

[39]Tissandier, p. 359.   [40]Newhall, p. 34.
[41]*Proceedings* Royal Society, Vol. IV, pp. 312, 313 (1841).
[42]Robert H. Taft, in *Photography and the American Scene,* N. Y., 1938, p. 104, explains that Talbot never thought of this till Herschel pointed it out.
[43]*Ibid.,* p. 107.

artist of today working with Zeiss lenses and lights which capture an image in a millionth of a second. A book of these photographs has been brought out which, in addition to its intrinsic beauty, forms a valuable document of the early Victorian era.[44]

With the Talbot process we come home. Experiment with the first Talbot paper pictures began in America before the name Daguerre had been heard here.[45] Successful paper negatives were made by amateurs in Massachusetts before the Daguerre process was whispered across the Atlantic.[46] This does not mean that such photographs had a dominant vogue here. Unhappily, here too, the exclamations over their beauty and usefulness were drowned by the blare of trumpets that heralded the silvered plate. And there were other factors. Yet true photography containing the principle of multiple record was far more attuned to the dominant note of our American economy.

6

The rise of the lower classes in America was not contemporaneous with that in Europe. Here, indeed, there was no such rise, nor were there, in the accepted sense, any lower classes. This does not mean that we were wholly democratic from the start, though the wilderness had begun its levelling work even in colonial days. But in the sense of being conscious and dominant bourgeois, we were always so.

It is probable that we were more conscious in regard to the arts in our colonial period than later when physical activity became so universal. It is nevertheless true that in the 1840's almost our entire population was in the position which the lower classes of Europe were still struggling to attain. In our infant industries, foreigners were just beginning to replace natives in the duller jobs. Most people in the East had their eyes on the West, to which movement had become continuous. The West, the promise of land, the lure of a new life and the succession of novel experience were great mind openers. Among the actually fluid people there was little opportunity for reflection, but in the

[44]Heinrich Schwarz, *David Octavius Hill*, London, 1932.
[45]Marcus A. Root, *The Camera and the Pencil*, N. Y., 1864, p. 340.
[46]Taft, pp. 111, 112.

intervals of movement and before movement began there was awareness of the quick passage of time and desire for record of experience, for catching and preserving the fleeting moment.

We must not expect much fineness of perception here. That came later as frontiers closed and a sense of permanence began. The emotional records demanded of art were crude enough. Fine painters like Samuel Morse were on the verge of starvation, while lithographic horrors were enthusiastically acclaimed. Only in the oldest centers lived the small cliques who understood good painting, literature, drama and music and they looked to Europe to answer the small demand.

At the same time, the public met with avid and naïve delight anything which was new. Charlatans abounded, displaying novel pseudo-scientific magic, men and women gaped like children at any "marvel" or "wonder." Crowds collected about displays of trick lighting and thronged "museums" or exhibits where mechanical triumphs were on show. Chemistry, so called, was a source of endless delight in all its manifestations. The whole atmosphere of the cities was expectant, receptive, gullible; yet the passing show was not adequate without a souvenir, a news-story, a record of some sort: "something to remember it by."

Could any soil be more fertile for photography? Rumors of the Daguerre wonder blew across the Atlantic all through the spring and summer of 1839. Then, in the fall, came the wonder itself.

Perhaps it was because the silvered plate was so glittering, so "expensive looking," so realistic, so detailed, so splendidly adapted to preserve the image of a son or lover who would be gone tomorrow, but whose memory would remain in a golden and precious form—perhaps it was these properties that gave this cumbersome toy such a hold on the American people. Perhaps it was its trickiness, the fact that it must be held at a certain angle to be seen or the intriguery of its process, that so endeared it. At any rate, we know that it persisted for more than a decade in the face of more convenient, cheaper, more beautiful competitors.

Its immediate penetration went deepest among the scientists and technicians of whom we had, at the moment, some of the best in the world. It is possible that John William Draper, in the thirties, knew more about light and the spectrum than Niepce and Talbot put together, not to mention painter-experimenters like Daguerre. Doctor Draper caught the first faint rumors of the Wedgwood and Talbot efforts and, in 1837, had repeated the Talbot experiments and reached new optical conclusions which made it possible to adjust lenses to human portraiture while Daguerre was still asserting that such a performance was not practicable.[47] The instant the daguerreotype arrived with a description of its process, Draper seems to have been at work with "non-achromatic" lenses to sharpen the image and other chemicals than Daguerre's to shorten exposure.[48]

We do not intend to enter the tedious controversy as to who made the first human daguerreotype portrait. It is as certain as such a thing can ever be that this "first" was American, notwithstanding the wishful thinking of Georges Pontonniée in his strenuously Gallic history.[49] Alexander Woolcott and John Draper may divide the honors as far as we are concerned. Both were New Yorkers. Draper angrily defends his priority, but Professor Robert Taft in his carefully documented history gives the edge to Woolcott.[50] It is significant, in any case, that Americans jumped at once to this phase of the chemical record.

It seems to have been in the spring of 1840 that Draper took his sister Dorothy to the roof, covered her face with flour or chalk, clamped her head in a vise and, directing blue light upon her, took her picture with an exposure of sixty-five seconds. On April 20, in the same spring, a New York paper reported that Alexander Woolcott "executes portraits with an improved Daguerreotype, in an incredibly short space of time."[51] Woolcott worked with an ingenious arrangement of mirrors, described in detail by Professor Taft.[52] Both seem to have added bromine to to their sensitizing material as a quickener.

Our old friend, Samuel Finley Breese Morse, who had by this time tragically abandoned his brilliant talents in art for the pro-

[47]Taft, p. 23. [48]Taft, pp. 29–31.
[49]Pontonniée, p. 202. [50]Taft, pp. 32 ff.
[51]*Evening Post,* April 20, 1840. [52]Taft, pp. 33, 35.

motion of the electromagnetic recording telegraph, now took a hand and helped improve the portrait process. Morse had the advantage of having visited Daguerre himself in Paris before the invention was given to the world. He and Draper got together and opened a commercial studio which may have saved Morse's life during poverty-stricken telegraph years.

The craze spread. Daguerre himself, aware of it, sent a man named Gouraud to America to give lectures and exhibitions, one of which made Philip Hone exclaim, "How greatly ashamed of their ignorance by-gone generations of mankind ought to be!"[53] But, independently, daguerreotypers who were true artists, as far as their medium permitted, sprang up everywhere. Best known of these were Joseph Hawes and Edward Southworth and John Whipple in Boston. The Langenheim brothers in Philadelphia, M. M. Lawrence and the Meade brothers in New York and, perhaps most famous of all, Matthew Brady,[54] who was a fashionable daguerreotyper long before he became a war photographer. "Photo by Brady" was a familiar cachet in the fifties.

But in the small towns, even on the frontiers, daguerreotypers flourished. Spurred by love of gadgetry and "puttering," they learned to play with cameras from whoever would teach them. "The earliest 'portrait takers,' " Taft tells us, "were more besieged with individuals wishing to be trained in the art of portrait taking than they were with clients desiring to have their portraits made."[55] The teachers charged good prices for lessons. And well they might, for prosperity in this new business seemed inescapable. The studios soon became luxurious and magnificent, furnished "seemingly without regard to cost, and merely at the dictation of a refined taste. The piano-forte, the music-box, the singing of birds; the elegant drapery; the beautiful pictures . . . statuary, engravings; all, all seem to impress the visitor with the idea of palace-like magnificence."[56]

But in the country, portraiture was merely added to the accom-

[53]*Diary of Philip Hone*, Allan Nevins, ed., N. Y., 1927, I, 435.
[54]He wrote his own name Mathew B. Brady and could not remember what the B stood for. *D. A. B.*, II, 584.
[55]Taft, p. 39.
[56]*Photographic Art Journal*, Vol. I, p. 359 (June, 1851).

plishments of the jacks-of-all-trades. "Photography, phrenology and biology," writes Ryder, "were all handled from our head-quarters. . . . It was no uncommon thing to find watch re-pairers, dentists and other styles of businessmen to carry on daguerreotypy on the side . . . so it was possible to have a horse shod, your boots tapped, a tooth pulled, or a likeness taken by the same man."[57] By 1850, there were nearly a thousand pro-fesional daguerreotypers and in 1853 it was estimated that three million daguerreotypes were made annually in the United States.[58] Even by 1851, American daguerreotypes were acknowl-edged the best in the world (due probably to better machine "buffing" of the plates)[59] and in the London Crystal Palace Ex-hibition of that year, in which Matthew Brady won a medal, all Europe stood astonished at American examples of the craft. It is significant that the portraits of Daguerre himself were nearly all made by an American, Charles Meade of Boston.[60] By the middle fifties, however, the art was doomed in America.

Meanwhile Talbot's calotype, a means of true photography, became popular among the amateurs. One reason why this was not professionally adopted was that Talbot made the mistake of patenting his process here. The Langenheim brothers, entrusted with the licensing agency, fought bravely for paper photographs, but without success.[61] They were far easier, however, for the amateurs. Edward Everett Hale of "Man Without a Country" and other fame, made paper pictures while he was still an under-graduate at Harvard, assisted by his buddy, Sam Longfellow, the poet's brother.[62] In 1844, Josiah Parsons Cook made remarkable calotypes at the age of fifteen, a truly prodigious feat in that dawn of photography.[63] There were plenty of others who played with cameras to make the fine, soft Talbot pictures.

Yet when, in the middle fifties, the daguerreotype began to die, the calotype did not replace it. It was followed, instead, by the

[57]James F. Ryder, *Voigtlander and I in Pursuit of Shadow Catching,* Cleveland, 1902, p. 20.
[58]Daily *Tribune,* N. Y., April 20 and 30, 1853.
[59]Taft, p. 72.   [60]*Ibid.,* p. 78.   [61]Newhall, p. 36.
[62]Mrs. D. T. Davis, "The Daguerreotype in America," in *McClure's Mag-azine,* Vol. VIII, p. 10 (Nov., 1896), cited by Taft, p. 111.
[63]Taft, p. 112.

most cumbersome, tricky and difficult process ever invented for chemical record. The wet collodion plate had the one great advantage of lending itself easily to quantity reproduction.

7

Collodion is gun-cotton in solution. The solvents are sulphuric ether and alcohol. It has, in itself, no sensitiveness to light. Its value to photography is in its stickiness when wet and because, when it dries, it forms a hard film. In its sticky state it forms a binder to hold the sensitizer to the glass. In it, when wet, were mixed what were called the "excitants," potassium bromide and iodide or ammonia. A glass plate was wet with the solution. It was then let evaporate till sticky, when it was lowered into a bath of silver nitrate. The chemist will understand the reaction which ensued between the excitants and the nitrate. The plate emerged from the bath sensitive; it was exposed while still wet and immediately afterward developed and hypo-fixed.[64]

As the whole of this delicate business must be done in the dark, it took adroit work. We may imagine that in a studio with every device prepared beforehand, with dark rooms ready, with dust and weather kept out, with an ample supply of chemicals at the right temperatures and accurate measuring devices; with the necessary distilled water on tap from a tank; with trained assistants standing by, a skillful photographer might be able to handle such a process effectively. Transfer him now with the whole of his equipment to a battlefield, remote from supplies, at the mercy of heat or cold or rain or storms of dust, not to mention the gunfire of the enemy, and we begin to see the genius of Matthew Brady.

There were other photographers in the Civil War. They did valuable work but Brady was the pioneer, the organizer who made successful war photography possible on a large scale for the first time in history. When the soldiers met a photographer he was always accompanied with a replica of the famed Brady "What is it?"—a dark room on a buggy, which excited universal curiosity and wonder. Brady employed many men and probably

[64]Taft, pp. 118 ff.

a majority of the photographs labelled Brady were taken by others, but he was their inspiration and their planner. He himself was under the ægis of the army intelligence department and he moved about the lines under the orders of the celebrated Allan Pinkerton, who organized the American Secret Service.

Nothing had ever brought home the grim reality of war like these chemical records. Far more sensational and terrific drawings had been made by the news-artists. The public was at once aware of the difference. Many a man and woman who eagerly studied the goriest of lithographic horrors would blanch and faint at the photograph of a corpse. These bare records of the battlefield were often regarded as improper to show to women and children; the worst of them were hidden until a more realistic age.

Here then, with this hardest of all processes, comes the birth of the news picture. Brady could not take instantaneous photographs. As we leaf through this fascinating history, we grow aware of the stillness. The dead were beautifully posed for the camera. In the faces of the living we see that response to the command, "Hold still, please!" It was all news none the less and it is history now, the best of all the histories in many ways. The guns, the fortifications, the engineers' bridges, the technics of earthworks, trenches, shelters, emplacements; of loading, firing, drill, the disposition of troops and, more human, the intimacies of the camp are here in a detail which makes the commentaries of Julius Cæsar seem more than ever difficult reading.

But the Brady photographs were long lost and long forgotten for reasons which will appear in the next chapter. They were collected, finally—those which could be found—from attics, cellars, closets, local and government archives and put in books when that became possible.[65] We have described their taking here, for we are interested in births and Brady photography marked the birth of communication and history by chemical record of light. When this technic joined forces with the technic of printing, such records replaced much type.

[65]*Photographic History of the Civil War*, Francis Trevelyan Miller, ed., N. Y., 1912.

Meanwhile the art with its chemistry and its optics advanced. Photographers everywhere must have sighed with relief when the English physician, Richard L. Maddox, found that gelatin would bind the sensitizing material to glass plates as well as collodion[66] and that gelatin-coated plates could be exposed when dry. There was a new shortening of exposure time with this invention and prophets could see ahead a day when exposure would be rapid enough to stop the clock, so to speak, in the midst of quick action of the subject. But, as silver-salt combinations became more sensitive, the camera itself must become faster. With the old trick of removing a cap from the lens and replacing it, new quick plates would be overexposed.

The subject of instantaneous photography always introduces a strange romantic figure whose name has been inextricably associated with the cinema. The name of Edward James Muggeridge seems to have oppressed the boyhood of its owner. Having early delusions of grandeur and, we suspect, a certain artiness characteristic of the epoch, he changed it to Eadweard Muybridge and, encumbered with this curious alteration, went from his native England to act as a photographer for the United States Coast and Geodetic Survey.[67]

While he was doing this somewhere along the edge of the Pacific Ocean, Leland Stanford, who believed himself (and not without reason) to be one of four owners of the sovereign state of California, got into an argument with a racing friend about the gaits of a horse. According to the usual story, the friend asserted that a horse in motion never had all his feet off the ground at once. The tale has always seemed to us odd, for it must have been reasonably self-evident without recourse to scientific proof that such a phenomenon occasionally occurred: especially, for instance, while the horse was jumping a fence. But Mr. Terry Ramsaye, who has exhaustively studied the arguments, asserts that Stanford's friend meant "at various gaits."[68] These are not specified. At any rate, Stanford took issue, swore that all four feet were frequently off the ground at once and bet $25,000

[66]1871. [67]Carl W. Mitman, *D. A. B.*, XIII, 373.
[68]Ramsaye, *op. cit.*, I, 22.

on his statement. Imagining that photography would prove it—a fancy which shows the growing faith in the power of chemical record—Stanford sought out the expert Muybridge to try it out. Muybridge tried, failed and, according to Mr. Ramsaye, was delayed five years in further experiment as a result of having shot and killed the seducer of his lovely young wife.[69] By the time he returned in 1878, the camera had improved.

It had acquired, among other things, a shutter. Muybridge set up a white background to the race track, spaced out a battery of twenty-four cameras and by an electromagnetic arrangement, caused the shutter of each camera to snap automatically as the horses passed on the track. The result proved Stanford's contention and, incidentally, altered the whole practice of art in the world. Painters and draftsmen of animals in action had, since the dawn[70] of the graphic arts, portrayed their legs in impossible positions.

From here on instantaneous photography grew into a fact. The steps from this point to the magic candid camera which can catch the flight of a bullet are improvements in detail. Along with speed have come the beautiful panchromatic processes by which plates have become sensitive to many colors and show, in blacks and grays, the light relations of the colors to one another. Natural-color photography is a separate field; its experiments date back to the beginnings of the photographic craft and cannot concern us—at least until we have discovered some social effect which black-and-white photography has not produced.

When Muybridge had made his thousands of photographs and published his enlightening books,[71] photography entered a new phase. The world was now ready for the "snapshot."

The social effect of the snapshot is quite different from that of the time exposure. A posed portrait almost invariably reflects posed thought. In the faces of the sitters ("patients," they were

[69]Ramsaye, I, 24 ff., tells the whole yarn amusingly and in detail, but Taft, note 430, p. 509, takes him to task for devoting so much space to it and cites *D. A. B.*, XIII, 373, to show that Muybridge was never married.

[70]In the "dawn" itself, however, the cave men had in some inscrutable manner observed the correct positions. See cut.

[71]Notably *Animals in Motion*, Boston, 1882.

sometimes called[72]) we see the pain of non-motion, varied according to the temperament of the victim, the effort to look one's best, the sense of all the emotions of friends and relatives upon looking at the finished image, the artificial concentration—all of which could be controlled to some extent by the artistry of the operator. There is smugness or synthetic fear, a falsity of some sort in the run-of-the-mill, time-exposure portraits. Many studio photographers have never overcome it.

When the snapshot caught unwary friends, there was none of this. Good and evil showed plain in the sudden capture. Intimate, naïve, fresh, funny, intensely characteristic expressions of faces, arms and legs, opened the mind to new frankness, new awareness of truth, its beauty and its danger. Nothing could be concealed from the snapshot and so it showed the way to what we have called our hard, clean nakedness of today. At the same time, it began the invasion of our privacy. It bared to the eyes of friends and enemies our private meditations and our deeper reticences, our intimate intents, our loves and our hates.

Yet, in America, there seems to have come a dominant warmth and happiness in our play with this device. It came along with the bicycle and is symbolic of the new delicious freedoms of that age. The little instrument goes out into new worlds, on long bucolic rides, its images keep the possession of the rarest moments of sky or scene or friendship; they restore youth in the mind, renew the quick jumps of the heart in breathless meetings, bring the smell of cut hay and salt marshes into city cliff-dwellings, lure us back to quiet bays where once the wild geese flew. We may resent the awful candidness which, in the heartless maneuvers of press photographers, catches us today tipsy or distressed, wounded or dead, but that is another story with other implications. The snapshot age was personal, careless and happy.

It allied itself, of course, with the trend we shall see presently in grander phases: the interplay of democracy and mass production. Even in the pre-Ford era, one man at least seems to have been aware of the trend. He made the snapshot cheap and he made it easy; he made it universal and democratic. The snap-

[72]Taft, p. 43.

shot may not be art, but what is art? Even the snapshot performed one of its functions to opening minds.

The greatest demonstration of this pioneer's genius came with the name of the instrument. "Ko?" queries the released, expectant spring, "Dak" answers the closed shutter with definite finality. The trick of onomatopœia has seldom reached more superb heights.

8

It must be remembered that, in the seventies, a person must needs be deeply in love with the hobby of photography in order to be a successful photographic amateur. There was no simple business of dropping in at a store and buying ready-to-use plates. Nor could such plates, when exposed, be taken to another store and left for development and printing. Only the glass and chemicals, mixing trays, printing frames, could be bought from such photographic supply houses as E. Anthony and the Scovills. The amateur must prepare his own bath, coat his own plates with sensitizer and then develop them. With the wet plates this entailed the carrying of so much equipment that photography could never be *incidental* to other enjoyment. The gelatin dry plates which need not be developed on the spot were much easier, and quite compact little outfits were designed for their use. But the coating of dry plates was even more difficult than that of wet ones. The amateur could be recognized anywhere in those days by the ineradicable stains on his fingers, and housekeepers where he lived were desperate about the condition of rugs and furniture, the smells and the disorder. It was these conditions that George Eastman[73] decided to correct.

If there's such a thing as a "born capitalist," Eastman was one. The stories of his boyhood are less concerned with science and invention than with ingenuity in making money work. He saved it with a skill that is astonishing when we see how adequately, at the same time, he supported himself. During the year '68, when he was fourteen, he saved $39 out of $131 earned, after

[73]Carl W. Ackerman, *George Eastman,* Boston, 1930, is the best biography to date. Eastman, however, was still alive when it was written.

278

paying his board, buying a quantity of clothes and treating himself generously to ice cream. The year following, he had salvaged $42 out of $233 earned, and included gymnasium, a vacation trip, lectures, a magazine subscription and his mother's coal bill in his expenses.[74] By the time he was twenty-three he had accumulated $3600 in this way[75] and he invested it in making photography democratic.

Perhaps it is true that Eastman invented nothing except ways of making a dollar do the work of two and devices for combining other inventions—often profitless ideas in themselves—into gigantic productive schemes. Can we, in justice, deny him credit for invention of a sort, though he rarely claimed such honor for himself? The Kodak was not, perhaps, strictly an invention, but then the Kodak was not an instrument either, not a mere device: Kodak was a whole system of photography.

The wet plate drew him first, but he did not stick to the collodion as so many others had done. He had himself taught photography, bought one of the clumsy outfits and immediately chafed under the burden. He heard that some one had invented dry plates, but he knew that American photographers, their minds all glued together by the sticky nitrocellulose solution, were afraid of them. He resolved to find what was the matter with gelatin.

He saw almost at once that dry-plate coating should be a standardized factory process, not a hit-or-miss dark-room job to be done by a man whose mind should be occupied with the use, not the manufacture, of an artistic medium. It would be as sensible for a painter to weave his canvas. Had no one thought of this? Yes, some one in England had thought of it, but Eastman was not the kind to be thrown off merely because an idea was not wholly his own. He went to England to find out precisely what the other man had thought.[76] He found an English firm producing dry plates commercially in the English manner, expensively, furnishing a few plates as luxuries to people who could afford to pay for them.

Mass production had come close to a fact in many American fields. Eastman saw that this commercial process must come

[74]*Ibid.*, pp. 7 ff.   [75]*Ibid.*, p. 14.   [76]1879, *Ibid.*, p. 28.

under the influence of the American mind—the mentality that worked with quantity and speed. Coming home, he found that a machine could coat the plates more evenly than the hand and do it faster. So Eastman standardized a process for quantity coating with gelatin solution and soon he had a business.

It would be useless for us to go into detail about his vicissitudes. This has been done far better than we could hope to do it by the authorities we have cited. We are more concerned with the formulation of a code which he evolved from error and misfor-

Eastman Kodak, the first camera which introduced to the world the idea that anybody could take pictures

Redrawn from a photograph, courtesy of Eastman Kodak Co.

tune. It was an industrial code, a business code, a thoroughly American code by which he democratized an entire field of human activity.

The first plates revealed defects. They were quick and convenient; they did not keep. Hundreds of them came back from dealers, lifeless after a few months of storage. Long research revealed an inferior quality of gelatin. Eastman took a tremendous step forward at this point, which we may note as posing definite, permanent landmarks in the history of American industry, merely by acknowledging his own ignorance. It is so common nowadays for industrialists to engage experts, specialists, scientists, students in every department that it is difficult for us to remember that this practice had a beginning. Eastman was a pioneer when he hired academic chemists and formed a testing laboratory as a department of manufacture.[77] When experimental chemists came to test materials as a full-time job, the

[77]*Ibid.*, p. 57.

plates acquired longevity along with their speed and convenience.

But in his trial and error conducted in the midst of a rapidly enlarging business, Eastman worked out another rule. There must be an "alternative" for everything. He tried, throughout his process, to keep two different, parallel methods ready at all times, so that if one step in production failed, he could switch to the alternative method. Thinking, one day, in this pattern, the question occurred to him: "What is the alternative to glass?"[78] He had already seen how, when collodion dried, it would peel from the glass in what was then called a "pellicle." Would that be possible with gelatin, too?

It did not work; the pellicle was too insubstantial to introduce into a camera. But by coating paper instead of glass with the gelatin sensitizer, the paper became a photographic material. Then, after it had been exposed in the camera, it could be removed from the paper after development and would then form a negative substantial enough, if carefully used, to print from. Coating long strips of paper thus, the roll was produced—a good strong roll of photographic medium which any one could handle.

The working of Eastman's mind here is plainly visible. He was dividing photography into two parts: an expert part and an amateur part. The making of the roll; its development after exposure, the delicate removal of the pellicle from the paper and the printing from the fragile transparency composed the expert part. The taking of the picture, the mechanical rolling up of the medium to bring new sensitive gelatin before the lens were functions which any one could perform. Now, by standardization, by quantity-production methods, by substituting the scientifically designed machine for the faltering artisan hand, photography was released, for all time, into the realms of the artist and the amateur.

It is probable that Eastman did not even "invent" the famous roll-holder. He put it on the market. At first it was a light-proof frame containing spools. On one spool was a roll of coated paper sufficient for 100 exposures. After each exposure, the turn of a handle brought a fresh section of coated paper before the lens.

[78]*Ibid.,* p. 44.

When the exposures were finished, the holder was removed from the camera, sent by the photographer to the Eastman factory in Rochester and was there developed and printed by experts. The holder, equipped with a fresh roll, was then returned to the customer. Roll-holders were made in sizes to fit any camera.

It was a short step from here to the making of standardized cameras. Now the customer sent his whole camera to Eastman when the roll had been exposed. This seems like a step backward. It had, however, some advantages. The Eastman cameras were cheap, standardized, machine-made and good. With them came the flash of genius—the name, Kodak—and the celebrated rhythmic instruction: "You press the button—we do the rest."

The epochal significance of this brief, sharp sentence can scarcely be overestimated. It is not surprising that it was caught up all over the world to point morals, philosophy and satire, to signalize a new era in every phase of human activity. It was spoken from the stage, it became the title of hundreds of political cartoons, adorned passionate parliamentary debates, was sung in Gilbert and Sullivan opera. It is difficult to think of a "slogan" more powerful as a medium of gratuitous advertising in the whole history of such matters. Yet it was accompanied by its substantial proof. Eastman never failed to "do the rest," and he did it beautifully. Kodak became not only a household word; it was a household fact and its value to humanity cannot be calculated in the ponderable terms in which we reckon the blessings of steel and electric power. The importance of Kodak must be measured by the mystical yardstick of pure joy. It made the passage of time tolerable to the common man.

These things happened in the eighties. All about us, in this decade, we see revolution: the heaving and the travail attendant upon the birth of the mass-production giant. Plenty of time will yet elapse before we recognize the stern features of his full maturity: before the thousand industrial children will spring from his loins. Meanwhile we shall watch him pass through sick and faltering intervals. Society was slow to nourish him to the strength which would demand its recognition of him. George Eastman was one of his most assiduous nurses.

THE PICTURE CYCLE

The loaded Kodak passing back and forth to Rochester imposed a burden which, once the first excitement had abated, began to vex the amateurs. It was evident to Eastman that Kodak system was not yet complete. Still in the back of his mind was the sense that the paper-coated roll with the delicate operation neces-

Jack: Do you think baby will be quiet long enough to take her picture, mamma?
Mamma: The Kodak will catch her whether she moves or not ; it is as "quick as a wink."

A Kodak advertisement in 1890
It put forward their most famous slogan, "You press the button and we do the rest"
Courtesy of the Eastman Kodak Co.

sary to the separation of the pellicle was inadequate to a full Kodak democracy. Also Kodakers were desirous of possessing substantial negatives of their own as well as prints.

As a result of all this impatience, one of Eastman's chemists devised a transparent material and put it on the market. Where he got the idea is a question which has agitated historians and investigators into original inventions. But whether or not the notion of the photographic film was independently conceived by Henry Reichenbach, the United States Circuit Court of Appeals decided, twenty-five years after the fact, that some one had beaten him to it and the Eastman Kodak Company was ordered to pay his predecessor $5,000,000. The predecessor was not a chemist or a manufacturer. He knew nothing about mass production. He was a humble Episcopal clergyman with an experimental avocation.

9

Hannibal Williston Goodwin[79] liked to show photographs to Sunday school students and other parishioners. He had a magic lantern and the art of slide making from glass negatives was in common practice. Being poor, he could not afford to have these jobs done for him and being ingenious and facile with his hands, did them himself in his spare time. As a result his observant, reflective and somewhat scientific mind pondered many chemical problems; among them the Gordian knot which had so distressed Eastman and his experts. He solved it, finally, with a serviceable nitrocellulose compound on which he applied, in 1887, for a patent. The patent was not granted for eleven years but his application, nevertheless, established priority over Reichenbach. The reader is at liberty to review for himself the thousands of pages of records of "interference" litigation between the persistent Goodwin and the Eastman Kodak Company.[80] It is one of the celebrated cases of Patent Office history and attests to the difficulties in which that institution was already, in the nineties, floundering and from which it still suffers. In 1898, Goodwin's patent came through. He tried to put his film into production, but he died two years later. His rights passed, in part, to Anthony and Scovill, heritors of the old Anthony photographic supply house, who carried an infringement suit against Eastman into the highest court where it was settled in 1914.[81] Retroactive royalties were paid to "Ansco" and to the Goodwin heirs.

In view of the importance of the film to another vital American

[79]Carl W. Mitman, *D. A. B.*, VII, 408.
[80]Goodwin Film and Camera Co. v. Eastman Kodak Co., 207 *Fed. Rep.*, 351.
[81]Goodwin Film and Camera Co. v. Eastman Kodak Co., Decision of Judge Coxe, U. S. Circuit Court of Appeals, 213 *Fed. Rep.*, 231.

industry which we shall presently explore, it is our duty to give full credit for the invention to the Reverend Goodwin. It is a pity that he failed to receive his reward in person but this, perhaps, was not psychologically necessary to a man of his faith.

Meanwhile, Reichenbach's film went into quantity production and built the success for Eastman that many of us remember. In 1895 came the final triumph of "daylight loading," by which the amateur was enabled to put in and take out his own film. The business of developing and printing then grew too large for the Eastmans to handle alone. Many professional developers came into the field. A new crop of ambitious amateurs did their own developing. This had become simple with the application of the scientific method to the development process. The two famous experimental scientists, V. C. Driffield and Ferdinand Hurter, had worked out a time basis for development so that the photographer need no longer watch his plate or film to see the image emerge and the Eastmans were quick to provide semi-automatic equipment for the hobbyists.

In the period following the World War we see a shift of amateur photographic interest to Germany. This may have come about through a change of focus in post-war days from industry to artisanship in the temporarily defeated Reich. It is certain that lens development reached a peak of refinement in Germany during this epoch that had never before been approached in the world. This progress brought the so-called "candid" camera—candid meaning simply clear and quick, a generic rather than a specific term—with all its doubtful social implications.

We have dwelt rather upon the artistic and entertaining results of photography than on its large scientific and educational benefits. These, however, will often appear in discussions of other phenomena. The value of photography to astronomy, medicine, physics, chemistry, historical and literary research, jurisprudence, war, crime-prevention, architecture, innumerable industrial processes may, perhaps, never be estimated. Primarily it has brought a realistic attitude to the individual and the social mind. It may have been the predominant factor in the destruction of the romantic age.

To the graphic arts it brought a new phase. Released from the necessity of realism or representation in painting, artists have been able to move farther into the realms of thought; to portray ideas, moods, abstractions, to find new approaches to the emotions. Art may now suggest instead of explaining and its scope in this far field seems truly limitless. It may portray light and color, wind and rain, what we call "the moods of nature" when we mean the moods of ourselves, all these things as they exist in the human mind—composite of thought upon a multitude of sensory impressions rather than the explanation of a single such impression "as the eye sees it."

And photography, with the other arts released to this far wandering, has become truly an art in itself with defined limitations but giving to the photographic artist high creative potentialities of composition and the recognition of sudden aspects of value and color.

We must come back, now, to the point where we began to follow the picture cycle. Here we saw graphic representations used simply for communication—a use to which after countless thousands of years we have now returned with vastly better equipment. But before we can fully understand the possibilities of this new use, we must examine the curiously delayed invention of the photo-mechanical process by which the photograph could be transferred to the printing press and thence go without loss of its detail, its beauty or its color values into the formidable mass production with which we are so familiar.

Chapter Thirteen

PRINTING AND THE ARTS

I

THE SPREAD of communication by radio and pictures has alarmed many casual observers of the American culture. If news, philosophy, religion, political science, literature and the other arts are conveyed to the understanding by sensory impression alone, what chance is there for subjective thinking, reflection, the reasoning processes? It is impossible to read without an active mental operation, yet one can listen to spoken words or look at a picture in almost complete apathy. As the habit grows the mind becomes increasingly passive, purely receptive, like the mind of a child or animal, losing its aggressive function. As the spoken words become more and more complete or the picture more and more detailed, nothing is left to speculation or fancy, inquiry stops, the desire to look beyond the immediate, visible object disappears. All is presented and explained in a broadcast or a movie or a news photograph; thought is served to us pre-digested like a baby's breakfast food.

If we accept this view as ultimate, the spectacle is alarming enough. But while the casual social observer is throwing up his hands in despair, more profound investigators are revealing a surprising parallel movement. While broadcasts and receiving sets are multiplying, so are books. In most American towns the library may still be less continuously crowded than the movie theatre, but it is a rival. The total circulation of magazines intended to be read is still greater than that of magazines designed to be looked at. *The Reader's Digest,* which contains no illustrations and deals, in its text, with every phase of American culture, successfully competes with the "picture book." The eagerness for historical and literary research, for social surveys, political polls, questionnaires, is straining the capacities of libraries, archives and the Post Office. Psychoanalysts are everywhere inducing subjective thinking to what is often believed a dangerous degree, employers are demanding "intelligence quotients" from their humblest employees, white-collar bosses are requiring diplomas giving evidence of from one to four years' reading and university enrollment has increased.

If, now, returning to the history of invention, we will divert our focus momentarily from the colossi of radio-telephony and picture production, we shall find a steady progress in devices for stimulating reflective thought. The American library system is, in itself, a unique and impressive invention. A late addition to library equipment is the film projector, which makes available to a multitude of students old forgotten books, rare manuscripts, ancient inscriptions which but a little time since were locked away in hardly accessible vaults in remote institutions. Laboratory equipment for experiment in pure science is improving daily, perhaps nowhere as rapidly as in America. These things are happening because the demand is irresistible.

One great difficulty in estimating any American aspect is that we do it, as a rule, in terms of great masses of people. When we speak of the romantic movement in France, English eclecticism, German idealism or Spanish decadence, we mean a phase that was felt or understood by a handful of thinkers while the great body of the people remained inert. But when we deal with Americans, we speak of large, popular concepts like "Manifest Destiny" in which the humblest of us share. American puritanism, liberalism, materialism are matters of which we expect our barber or the man at the filling station to be acutely conscious. If we say we are air-minded or car-conscious, we mean that every man-jack, woman, child, waitress, newsboy and street-sweeper participates in these attitudes. This way of thinking colors all contemplation of our folklore and history; the pioneer era, the reconstruction, the "Mauve Decade," the New Deal have all been essentially democratic phases.

We have come into such a view through our thesis of equality. That thesis, however, has not altered the fact of individual inequality which must persist here as elsewhere. Though the thesis may have obviated the slow "rise" of the lower classes which brought social upheaval in Europe, there has, lately at any rate, been unevenness of advancement in different groups. Yet here, our cultural inventions have been accessible to the "dumb," inert, half-conscious people which must compose a large mass in any state, whatever its politics. It is scarcely surprising that there should be an immense substratum demand for such instruments as the radio and pictures which give sensory satisfaction to persons incapable of further mental exercise. Because these folk are in the majority, radio and pictures are said to compose an American menace and "America" is said to be radio- or picture-mad.

It is, of course, inevitable that as the supply rushes up to meet this large basic demand it will spill over into the more sensitive fringes. The delights of sound and vision are attractive to intelligent people as well as to morons or "dummies." The intelligent folk are able, via their intelligence, to adjust these matters in their lives and allot them the proper time and space.

Having seen, then, the presence of other cultural trends, we may proceed to an examination of those inventions which introduced to a large public the visual image of world events and which provided so many people, dull or quick, inert or conscious, with an approach to an appreciation of the graphic arts.

2

The use of woodcuts in printing preceded the invention of movable type. Crude pictures of the saints were printed in presses as far back, probably, as the fourteenth century. Words came to be added as explanations of the pictures, carved on the blocks above or below the drawings.

All this carving was in relief; that is to say, the lines of the drawing were left standing and the spaces between them cut away. When movable type came, it also was carved in relief. Thus a press which printed from raised surfaces came to be known as a "letterpress."

The first wooden printing surfaces were cut with a knife. Later, when more elaborate tools were used, the practice became known as "wood-engraving." This is an exceedingly confusing term as "engraving" in other surfaces than wood employs an entirely different method and requires a different kind of press.

Engraving, properly so-called, came into existence about the middle of the fifteenth century. It was done on metal and reversed the woodcut practice. With a special tool called the "burin," the steel or copper engraver cut his lines into a polished surface. Thus, instead of the lines being left in relief with the spaces between them cut away, the lines were indented or "intaglio" and the spaces between them left untouched. After the surface was inked it was carefully wiped off, leaving the ink in the indentations. Dampened paper was placed upon it and paper and plate were submitted to great pressure in a special press. Thus the ink which had been in the valleys, so to speak, on the plate, appeared in little mountains and ridges on the paper. If we look carefully at an engraving we shall see the ink standing up from the paper surface, high enough, in places, to cast a shadow.

It was difficult to cut into the hard metal and the engraver was limited in his freedom of expression. Then the chemical solvents came to his aid and with them arrived the process of "etching." Certain acids dissolve metals. Some great inventor found that these same acids had no solvent effect upon certain waxes and varnishes. With an ingenuity as astonishing, perhaps, as any we have recorded he thought of covering his plate with a wax or varnish film and making his picture on this "ground," as it was called, rather than upon the metal. The strokes of his tool cut through the ground until the metal was exposed. Then by dipping his plate into an acid bath, the parts of it directly beneath the marks in the ground would be dissolved or eaten away or "bitten" as it is technically called, while that part of the surface still covered by the ground would not be altered. When the biting was complete, the artist washed off the acid, removed the ground and had an intaglio plate from which a great number of effective impressions could be taken.

The etcher, working in the comparatively soft-ground medium, found a new freedom. His work did not stop with the drawing on the ground. As the technic improved, he was able, by the use of added varnish, to stop the biting process in certain parts of his picture while it continued in others. Where he wanted deep black where he let the acid go deep; for a lighter line, he stopped it while the little valley was still shallow. He could get shadows and gray tone effects by making many little lines and dots closer together or wider apart. Etching became a beautiful and expressive art and, beginning with Albrecht Dürer in 1515 and reaching a high point with Rembrandt Van Ryn a little more than a century later, the process was used by painters with delight and with an increasing appreciative public.

Variations of these processes appeared from time to time and were called "dry point," "mezzotint," "aquatint," "soft-ground etching," and so on. They were not useful for book illustration in which woodcuts remained, for the most part, in use. This was because, being in relief, they could be printed on the same press with type and could be inserted into the middle of a type page. Sometimes steel or copper-plate engravings, separately printed, were inserted as illustrations but this combination of two kinds of printing in the same book was expensive. Also, it took much longer to secure good impressions from an intaglio plate than to print from relief forms such as type and woodcuts.

With the widening of the public for pictures which we have seen in the eighteenth and nineteenth centuries, woodcuts were no longer entirely satisfying. There was a desire for quantity reproduction of paintings, for instance, which no form of engraving could quite supply. The technical reason for their inadequacy was that, while woodcuts and engravings could faithfully multiply line drawings, they could never quite reproduce a tone. Shading must be achieved by a multiplicity of lines or dots or marks of some sort. Thus the full realism desired by the rising masses could not be attained in printing.

At the start of the nineteenth century, a new invention met this need. It provided a means of printing which was neither relief nor intaglio. It was the first of the planographic processes and was called lithography because it used a stone instead of a wood or metal printing surface.

It depended on the natural antagonism of oil and water. On a smooth-stone surface a design was drawn or painted with greasy crayon or paint. The surface was then moistened and a roller covered with greasy ink was moved over it. The greasy ink having an affinity for the grease in the crayon adhered to the design, which in turn had repelled the water when the plate was wet. The water, remaining in all other places except where the crayon had drawn, now repelled the greasy ink from the roller so that

The work table of an old wood engraver

From E. G. Lutz's *Practical Engraving and Etching,* Scribners

only the design was inked. By placing a sheet of paper on the stone while it was still wet with ink and water, and exerting pressure, the design could be transferred to it.

The lithograph had a great vogue. The process was cheap and easy, and lithographic prints could be produced in quantity. They were used for advertising, for posters, sensational handbills and cheap wall pictures. For the most part they were scorned by the artists as crude and vulgar. They mark the departure of picture printing from the artistic into the commercial sphere.

PRINTING AND THE ARTS

Lithography, invented by a Bavarian, Alois Senefelder, in about 1800, had come into use all over the world before his death in 1834. Its popularity was due, partly, to its susceptibility to color-reproduction. Because, when skilfully managed, it could provide a fairly exact copy of a painting, it brought replicas of the world's greatest art into the homes of the masses at a cost of a few cents. It reproduced tone as well as line.

Niepce was working with this new trick when he came upon the idea of photography. That still newer and even more exact means of reproducing either art or nature diverted him forever from the inked stone. With the public the two matters remained separate, though both carried strong appeals to the bourgeois taste. It was not, as we have seen, until paper positives made from glass negatives finally drove out the daguerreotype that the public began to think of photography as a means of the quantity production of pictures. When that point arrived, a number of minds impinged upon the possibilities of illustrating books, magazines or newspapers with photographs.

3

In America the desire for news pictures seems to have arrived at about the same time as photography, though no adequate means of reproducing photographs by the printing press was to come until half a century later. Indeed, no news photographs in our sense could be made before the perfection of instantaneous photography. By the time presses were able to reproduce photographs in any verisimilitude, instantaneous photography was already a commonplace. Meanwhile, the picture-craving public had to be content with drawings produced "on the spot" by the news artist. The abortions resulting from a draftsman's tinkering with photographs gave far less satisfaction.

The cheap newspaper became an accomplished fact in the middle forties when the Hoe and Bullock rotary presses put the news into mass production.[1] During the Mexican War, the readers of certain enterprising papers were amazed to see maps showing military operations appearing on the front page. Crude pic-

[1] *M. I. M.,* Chap. XXI.

tures followed. From this time on it was customary to see a news artist along with the reporters at fires, train wrecks, political rallies. The profession of news artist became important and "on-the-spot" sketches multiplied. They learned to work fast in capturing the feeling of quick-moving scenes, and their drawings seemed realistic to newspaper readers of the day. As we look at them now, there is a stiffness and woodenness about them which makes us wonder how they could have been taken seriously until we realize how completely the camera has altered our acceptance of the static representation of motion. Yet so accustomed were the people of the day to certain conventions in the portrayal of the moving figures of men and animals that, if an instantaneous photograph of action had been presented to them, they would have thought it unreal.

There was discussion among newspaper editors then and for many years after as to whether it was dignified to print pictures. When they first appeared they were thought vulgar by the old school of publisher, and some papers kept them off the front page even into the twentieth century. In the meantime the illustrated weekly magazine came into an immense vogue as a news medium.

No modern American historian can afford to ignore the files of the Leslie[2] and Harper[3] weeklies. There is an atmosphere, an emotional content in their news drawings which is essential to a complete understanding of the past American scene. The illustrators of the day were meticulous in their reproduction of detail. Their work was always under a barrage of realistic criticism. A mistake in a strap of harness or in the cut of a garment brought angry letters to the art editor. Thus a modern novelist or a producer of historical plays, pageants or motion pictures can usually rely upon the authenticity of these drawings in the details of costume, vehicles and machinery. On the other hand, almost any eyewitness of an unexpected, fast-moving event will remember incidents which never occurred. However on-the-spot an artist might be, therefore, it was likely that his picture would be finished in the office and there, in the quiet, would creep in

[2]From 1855.   [3]From 1857.

A type of illustration common in both newspapers and weekly magazines. This drawing
shows the arrival of French troops in Piedmont

From *Harper's Weekly*, June, 1859

After the photograph came, the wood engraver tried hard to reproduce the exact effect
of tone values, etc. He showed great skill, as the detail at the right demonstrates

a dozen figures or acts which were the pure figment of his fancy in its effort to supplement defective observation or faulty memory. The public came to expect such creation. Without a camera's evidence, conflicting reports of other eyewitnesses could never be proved. The job of an artist-reporter, then, was to reproduce all static detail (which could be checked) with stern accuracy, while in matters which were evanescent he must give his imagination a fairly free rein. The result was the reconstruction of the atmosphere rather than the facts of an event but with verisimilitude contributed by completely authentic background, properties and costumes. In drawing for the weeklies, the artists had time for this sort of picture.

When news photography first replaced news drawing there was a sense of loss here. The camera supplied accurate detail but it could not compass an entire scene. It could catch the sudden agony of a man who had just been shot, but the chances were that it missed the surprise and horror of the bystanders, the running up of policemen, the escape of the assailant, weeping or fainting women, running children, people offering aid to the stricken man, and many of the supplements which a mind reflecting upon the whole incident would have put in. These things might not have been there in fact, but they were essential to the understanding of people accustomed to thinking without the camera. With the snapshot, much of this would have to be supplied by the imagination. In a way, therefore, the instantaneous photograph made the person who looked at it work harder than the person who studied an artist's interpretation.

The hiatus was filled in two ways: first by the training of the public and second by the enhanced artistry, within his limitations, of the press photographer. He could not, it is true, persuade his camera to record something that was not there but he could, instead of "shooting" blindly, try to compose his scenes. This took quick instinct, long training, immense resourcefulness, complete control in the midst of sudden movement, panic and often great danger to himself. It took, also, to a limited degree, the true artist's sense. He must be on the watch for the grouping of people and things which would more clearly reveal the truth of a situation instead of merely snapping at meaningless, dispersed crowds or isolated individuals. Obviously there was a good deal of trial and error. Out of many "shots," perhaps only one would prove satisfactory, yet as the new art of press photography developed through constant practice, the photographer learned to reduce his waste. Meanwhile the public gained an understanding of the instantaneous photographs and (aided materially by the cinema) learned to relate separate photographs and compose them, mentally, into scenes. We do this so automatically today, schooled as we are in the quick shift from one image-continuity to another, taught from childhood the "story sense" of picture succession, that we forget the long training it required.

The almost universal use of news photographs seems to have come slowly. Even today, in Europe, many illustrated magazines intersperse drawings among their photographs. In America the story-telling comic strip has an undiminished vogue, though there is a departure here from the attempt at strict realism. The principal factors, however, in the delay of press photography have been technical.

4

Illustration via the printing press began, in America as elsewhere, with the woodcut. It was a difficult medium. To carve on a wood block a copy of a drawing or painting took a long time—often as much as three weeks.[4] The wood-engraver was usually an artisan rather than an artist. His attempt at faithful copying of an artist's drawing was likely to bring violent protest from the artist. The first objection was met by an ingenious American, who cut large wood blocks into pieces and parceled out the carving to a handful of wood-engravers, then locked the finished pieces together into a complete printing surface,[5] but this proved prohibitively expensive for newspaper work. The second objection—infidelity to the original—was met by the first impact of photography on printing.

[4]Taft, 420 n.
[5]Taft, p. 420. John A. Kouwenhaven, *Adventures of America, 1857–1900,* A Pictorial Record from *Harpers Weekly,* N. Y., 1938, Preface.

J. D. Brinckerhoff of New York took the revolutionary step of photographing directly on wood in 1855. With the photograph of a drawing to guide them, wood-engravers were able to work faster and more accurately. Yet the woodcut did not stand up under large editions and it was useless for rotary presses. By this time, however, both the stereotype and the electrotype had been invented. By pressing the woodcut into clay a mold or matrix could be made and a stereotype plate secured by pouring molten type-metal into the matrix. Electrotypes were made by forming a wax mold, dusting it with carbon and placing it in a saline bath connected with one terminal of a battery. Also in the bath and connected with the other terminal was a copper plate. Thus, as the current moved through the bath, a film of copper was deposited on the mold. The film or copper shell was stripped from the mold backed up with type metal and mounted on a type-high block and used in the presses.

When, in 1859, photography on zinc was achieved, the further mechanization of picture-printing became possible. This was probably the invention of the Frenchman, Mungo Ponton, who found that albumen containing bichromate of potassium became hard and insoluble when exposed to light. By making a photographic "print" on zinc from the negative of a photographed drawing and then washing away the unexposed albumen, the lines of the drawing would be left standing on the zinc in the hardened, exposed albumen. Now if these lines were coated with an acid-resistant substance, the plate might be placed in an acid bath and the spaces between the lines etched away, leaving the lines in relief.

Perhaps because, in America, wood-engravers had become so expert and formed so large and strong a body,[6] the zinc plate did not come into wide use here until 1880.[7] It and the processes which followed it dislocated an immense number of artisans because, by this time, the printing of illustrations had become one of the great American trades.

A curious reverse process which began with intaglio and ended with a relief plate was the celebrated "swelled gelatin" process

[6]Edwin Bale, "Process," in *Encyc. Brit.*, XXII, 409.   [7]Taft, p. 423.

of David Bachrach, Jr., and Louis E. Levy of Baltimore, in 1875.[8] Unexposed gelatin swells in cold water, exposed gelatin does not. If, then, a print is made on a sensitized gelatin surface which is afterward soaked in water, the spaces between the lines will swell, leaving the lines in intaglio. A plaster mold made from this intaglio surface will be in relief. If this plaster relief mold is pressed into wax a second intaglio mold is produced from which, in the usual way, an electrotype in relief may be made. Finer gradations were obtained with the swelled-gelatin process than with the zinc line cut, because sensitized gelatin swells in proportion to the amount of light admitted to it, but the process was more costly because of the number of steps involved.

It will be noticed that, in all this discussion, we have referred to *photographs of drawings,* and, always, to lines, not to tones. Were none of these processes used successfully in printing actual photographs from nature? Even with all these inventions must we continue to illustrate our magazines by drawings, photographed and then made into line cuts? What, then, was the technical difficulty which stood between a photograph from nature and its exact reproduction in printer's ink? The answer is that only an approximation to exact reproduction of a photograph is ever possible with a printing press. Herein lies one of the fundamental differences between printing and painting, between printing and photography. We have reached an approximation today which fools the naked eye, but even that was attained only by the most laborious effort and by advances in collateral invention.

A drawing is a composition of lines, a painting or a photograph is a composition of masses, which are called tones. A painting made with a brush has solid blocks of color; it uses differences of tone instead of lines to give it color. A photograph from nature contains no lines whatever, merely variations of light and shade.

Now, in printing, tones in their proper gradations cannot be reproduced except when they are simulated by lines and dots. Grays, variations from the blackest black, can be reproduced in

[8]Taft, p. 426.

a press with printer's ink, only if the printing surface is so altered as to intersperse minute bits of white among the minute bits of black. This has always been done and probably always will be by dots or lines.

A great many tricks of etching and stippling were tried to give the effect of the tones. Always the dots and lines were visible as dots and lines, and they robbed the photograph of its realism. To those who thought deeply on the subject, therefore, it finally grew evident that the dots used to give the effect of tones must be so small that the unaided eye could not see them. To make such dots by hand would be far too laborious and costly. Somehow they must be made mechanically. If they could be made automatically on the sensitized plate at the moment the picture was taken, the whole problem would be solved. It was through this sort of pondering that the idea of the "screen" came to inventors.

It seems to have occurred first to that pioneer of photography, Fox Talbot, who tried making photographic prints through gauze. He patented his idea in 1852 but did little experimenting with it. Others took it up and glass screens, ruled with fine lines, were able to break a tone into lines. But the true half-tone plate was an American development which became possible only when Max Levy of Philadelphia invented a ruling machine which would trace lines on glass so fine and so close together that there could be 150 parallel lines to the inch. This was done by covering the glass with etcher's ground and ruling the lines on the ground with a machine which used a diamond point. The lines were then etched with a glass solvent[9] and filled with dark pigment.

A better understanding of the whole history of the process can be gained by first looking at the practice of today before trying to follow the development chronologically, step by step. The modern photoengraver takes a photograph of a photograph, interposing a screen of crisscross lines between his lens and his photographic film (or plate).

The result on the negative will be an arrangement of black

[9]Hydrofluoric acid.

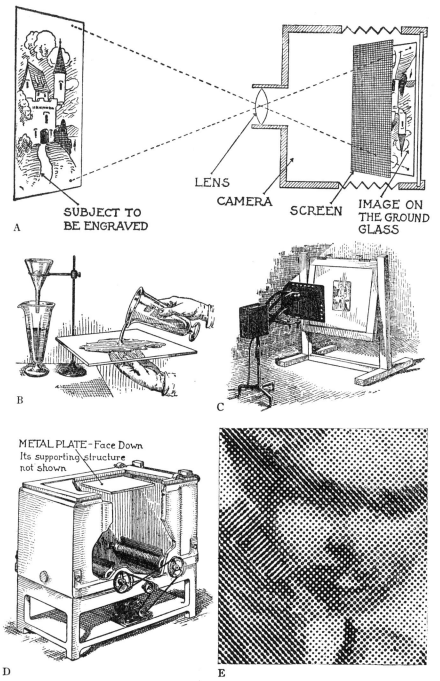

A. Schematic diagram explaining the first step in the making of a halftone engraving.
B. Preparing the photographic plate with a coating of sensitized solution of collodion.
C. With the sensitized plate, developed to make a negative, the image of the picture is
photographically printed on a metal plate. D. The old method of etching the plate in
an acid-filled tray has been displaced by a machine which evenly distributes acid over
the plate by means of revolving paddles. E. A greatly enlarged detail of a halftone
plate showing the different sizes of dots which make up the tone value

dots, large and merging into one another where much light comes through, but small and hence far apart where little light comes through. Naturally much light will come through from the light parts of the photograph—the whites and light grays—and little light from the blacks and dark grays. Now when a print is made from this negative it will correspond with the original: there will be large white dots and small black areas for the light parts and small white dots and large black areas for the dark parts; the grays will have varying black areas.

Why this happens is a question the layman must not ask unless he is willing to make a profound study of light. Stephen Horgan in his description of the process says: "An explanation of the action of the rays of light . . . would require extremely complicated diagrams and such . . . words and phrases as: 'Dioptric image,' 'penumbral effect' . . . 'interference fringes,' 'halation' . . . all of which will be spared the reader."[10] We shall follow Mr. Horgan's example.

The photoengraver makes his photograph print on a zinc or copper plate[11] sensitized with a mixture of glue and potassium chromate. When exposed and the unexposed sensitizer washed off, the plate will have a positive image in dots composed of the hardened sensitizer. Where the original was black there will be dots of hard sensitizer close together on the plate; where it was gray these dots will be farther apart; where it was white there will be empty squares. All this dotted surface is now further hardened by heat and dusted with an acid-resistant resinous material called, in the trade, "dragon's blood," which in turn is heated to make it stick to the dots. All this is done in such a way that only the dots will be protected by dragon's blood, the spaces between them remaining vulnerable to the acid. The plate is put in an acid bath[12] and all the metal is bitten except the dots. What comes out of the bath is a plate ready for printing, made up of dots in relief. When this plate is printed from, the

[10]Stephen H. Horgan, *Horgan's Half-Tone and Photomechanical Processes,* Chicago, 1913, p. 87.
[11]Zinc for a coarse screen suitable for newsprint; copper for a fine screen which requires coated paper.
[12]More lately it is sprayed with acid.

picture appears to consist entirely of tones, and only under the magnifying glass, when the black and white dots are visible, is the deception evident. To the naked eye, a photograph has been perfectly reproduced in printer's ink.

The history of the half-tone process is obscure enough to induce a good deal of caution in assigning credits for the invention. The only certainty is that most of it was American. Stephen Horgan, credited by Taft with making the first half-tone published in an American newspaper,[13] then used a screen on which the parallel lines ran only one way. He made the screen ingeniously enough by photographing a ruled sheet of paper on to collodion film. He then interposed this film between the negative of a photograph and a sensitized metal plate. The result on the plate was lines, not dots, quite evident to the unaided eye when the plate was printed from in the press.

Frederick Ives, by the use of two pieces of ruled glass, made the cross-line screen. This produced dots too fine for newsprint, so most of Ives' half-tones appeared in magazines using coated paper. Ives came, however, gradually to this screen having first used a most ingenious trick called the "V-line"—too complex to describe here though we recommend its study to the interested reader.[14] His slowness in adopting the optical screen was undoubtedly because the Levy ruling machine does not seem to have been invented until 1888. The Levy screen is still used. It has been greatly perfected and the questions of its proper distance from the negative and so on have been scientifically worked out.

Much hand work is still done on half-tones. After the etching bath, hand etching and the routing out of dots which remain in spaces which should appear pure white are done by highly skilled artisans applying acid by the brush and guiding docile machine tools.

It was not until the closing years of the century that photographs began to replace drawings in newspapers and magazines. Meanwhile improvement had been made in paper and ink. News-

[13]New York *Graphic*, March 14, 1880. Taft, pp. 437, 438.
[14]Taft, p. 439.

print still requires a coarse, visible screen but coated paper, which will take a fine screen, has been so reduced in price that excellent reproductions of photographs are possible in the five- and ten-cent magazines of today.

5

Perhaps, if we look carefully, we shall find an even greater social effect of the mass production of pictures than that deriving from news photographs. The art of advertising is a subtle one, resented by many folk—a snaky sort of art whose intent is to separate a man from his money by the most insidious, painless means. That much of it is beautiful, employing technics of loveliness scarcely excelled anywhere in the realm of large production, would be difficult to deny. Would the world be happier if the whole of it were suddenly removed?

Philosophers, economists, sociologists have bandied the question back and forth. Some of them have thought it a pity that the consumer should pay extra for his product because it is expensively propagandized. How cheap everything would be if the costs of advertising, of salesmanship, of many of the more or less fictional functions grouped under the title "service" could be deleted from consumer goods! The advertising man has another story to tell.

In certain "backward" countries, he will explain, women still go out to the pump for their water, still sweep the floors with brooms, wash clothes and dishes by hand; men cut grain with cradle scythes, thresh it with flails. This is not because automatic pumps, vacuum cleaners, washing machines, harvesters and threshing machines do not exist in those lands. They do exist and are for sale at what economists call a "reasonable price," not loaded up with advertising, distribution and service costs. Result: these unhappy men and women do not know of their existence, would have to make long journeys to get them, could not maintain them without competent service men within reach. Thus a large part of the population is denied these great blessings of the new era. Does not civilization march faster if these blessings are first forced upon public consciousness, then brought to the consumer's door, then repaired and finally watched over by a person who is maintained in the "territory" by a great system of which advertising is the life blood? Is not this worth paying for?

The argument is a plausible one. The professional advertising man—a real specialist—may, however, be a little too concentrated on his special problem to appraise all the factors. The careful student of the kind of history whose surface we are here attempting to skim will find a variety of more deeply underlying motivations. If we pursue, for instance, such a thing as "vacuum-cleaner-consciousness," far enough, we shall find it in conflict with class-consciousness, racial heritage, traditions of political and economic oppression, illiteracy, philosophies of press and speech freedom, economic theories of demand and production and an army of prejudices little understood by Americans. Advertising is predominantly an American craft. In the study of anything predominantly American we are likely to find ourselves confronting much unique and special sociology. There are good reasons for the nationality of advertising. They will appear again and again in this record, and are closely bound up with one of the main theses which our book will humbly advance.

The "art" of advertising as we know it scarcely existed before the half-tone. Commercial propaganda of the nineteenth century spread itself rudely over billboards and walls. It was an all-pervading horror, to be sure, but it was invariably a horror. Like most commercial matters it was intentionally ugly, blatantly vulgar. Its active thesis was that you must hit a man between the eyes or in his solar plexus to make him buy. The new advertising may be more evil in its method: the insidious stimulus of fear through a lovely picture may, in the end, be more shattering to our nerves, but the practice offends us less immediately.

In the infancy of advertising a bright young man in a manufacturer's or merchant's office drew the designs, wrote the long, wordy panegyrics. He had not studied psychology or even human nature. He had not worked for years experimenting on the precise "reaction" of perception to Caslon, De Vinne or Roman type design. It would do him no good, for these fonts would not exist in the press where his announcement would be set. He conducted no surveys, researches, canvasses, censuses, compiled no statistics, sent no questionnaires, made no exploration of consumer-consciousness. Advertising was a mere business practice, not a religion as it is today. The bright young man was interested in benefiting his boss rather than humanity. He took his cue, as a rule, from the classic vulgarian Phineas Taylor Barnum, whose naïve ambition was to fool all of the people all of the time but whose practice was so blatant, so obvious and so gorgeous that he endeared himself to the American heart. No other advertiser even approached his heights though they all tried.

With the half-tone, the whole philosophy changed. Nowhere was the bourgeois demand for realism in pictures so exigent as in advertising. A photograph of a lovely young girl displaying impeccable teeth, of a child begging for his breakfast food, a man with a cold, a woman with an aching back made an impact which no flowers of rhetoric could produce. Now, with delicate tones upon the page, with exact reproductive processes waiting to put the most beautiful designs of typography into quick mass production advertisers began to concentrate upon "art." The whole practice passed, thus, from the bright young man to the specialist and, for better or worse, the Advertising Agent came into our civilization. We may credit, if we like, the advertising agent with the mind and emotions of the prostitute. We may speculate upon the neuroses caused by his dwelling upon our little intimate fears and vanities. We may condemn his exaggerations and his emphasis. But we cannot deny that he has garnished his mediums and made his claims, however wicked they may be, easier to look at. And we must concede further that he has provided a large, democratic vehicle for our literary and artistic expressions. In a sense advertising gives us much of our literature just as commerce gives us most of our architecture.

Writers might still write books, even if advertising died. They would have a hard time keeping alive unless the movies became even more philanthropic toward literature than they now are. They could scarcely afford to write short stories or current articles. For, if advertisers withdrew their patronage, the enormous, handsome magazines, which now sell to several million people for a nickel or a dime, could no longer pay living wages to authors to fill their occasional pages of text. For many an author, highbrow though he may be, they keep the pot boiling between his high points of art. These magazines, whether we like it or not, are a vital part of our culture. They are called "Slicks" in the trade. The reason they are so called is because they are printed on shiny, coated paper. The reason they are printed on coated paper is so that they may use half-tones with fine screens.

Side by side, then, advertising and the great American magazines came to maturity. Whether, in their advertising pages or columns, the magazines have reached a higher point of art and interest than in their text and textual illustration is a debatable point. Many a reader of the celebrated *Saturday Evening Post* has confessed that he has never been able to finish a story in that periodical because, as he turned to page 106 to try to follow the thread through the pages where ads ran parallel to text, the ads became too diverting. Thus our memories of current fiction and articles are likely to be inextricably interwoven with streams of automobiles, refrigerators, head colds and bad breath. The radio people have found this confusion useful.

The central factor in all this progress has been the realistic photograph and its realistic half-tone reproduction. The advertisers have staged fine scenes for the camera—photographic plays. A whole new profession has grown up in which actors, cast off by a decaying popular theatre and not quite up to movie standards, have found employment. A close observer may recognize these models as they reappear, first, say, in a Listerine cast, then as leads in Metropolitan Life Insurance or Martini and Rossi Vermouth. Always they are real people doing real things.

The half-tone paved the way for the greatest achievement and refinement of all in picture reproduction: one which today brings the boldest masses of a Picasso, the luminous juxtaposition of pigment of a Manet, the most delicate tones of a Greuze into the possession of the people.

6

Color is an elusive thing. A painter, working in pigments, evolved the theory that the three primary colors were red, yellow and blue. He called these colors primary, because by mixing them the other colors could be obtained, whereas no combination of other shades could produce red, yellow or blue.

Then along came the experimenter with light, the optical scientist, with another theory. To him the primary colors were orange-red, violet and yellowish-green, because, in light, these three combined made white, whereas by the combination of any two of them other colors in light could be produced.

If you will take a beam of white light, which is composed of red, violet and yellowish-green rays, and, by means of filters, obstruct the violet and yellowish green rays, the red rays only will come through. Thus light, coming say from a rose bush blooming with red roses, will, if violet and yellow green filters are interposed, show only the blossoms. The stems, leaves and thorns, being green, will be excluded. A photograph, then, taken of a rose bush through such filters will presumably give an image of the blossoms only, or, if a red bug is crawling up one of the stems, it will show, also, the bug hanging in space.

Now the photographer, understanding these principles and remembering that workers with pigments—printer's ink in our special case—wanted their particular primary colors, red, yellow and blue to work with, tried to get combinations of filters which would make successive photographs of the red, yellow and blue portions of an object. He succeeded. The half-tone process worker was thus able to obtain a plate whose dots were made only by the light from the red parts of an object, another whose dots represented the yellow parts and a third whose dots stood for the blue parts. By printing from these plates in succession on the same sheet of paper, he got all the colors in their natural combination: the result was a full portrayal of all the many shades in which red, yellow and blue play a part.

To make this thoroughly clear, let us go back to the rose bush. While our first photograph, showing only the red part of the bush, may reveal only the blossoms plus, perhaps, a very little besides, the second (yellow) photograph will show a part of the leaves and stems, which, in nature, are green. They show a part, because yellow and blue make green, so there will be some yellow in the leaves. The third, or blue plate, will show more or less of the stems, depending on whether there is more or less blue in them.

Now these plates when printed do not actually mix the inks together. By a precise calculation, the blue dots are printed in the spaces between the yellow dots.[15] If a purplish tone is called for, blue dots are provided between red dots, orange is made by the printing of red and yellow dots side by side. Thus what the eye sees is a juxtaposition of colors rather than a mixture of them—the eye effects the combination. A good magnifying glass held over any colored picture will instantly reveal this.

It is a curious fact that certain artists, the luminists, for instance, like Manet painted in this manner. They held (long before the invention of half-tones) that the best shades were produced by the eye looking at blobs of primary colors next one another. This was based, of course, on the scientific truth that, even when pigments were mixed, colors are reflected to the eye from tiny particles of the individual primary pigments.

As soon as this process was perfected, any painting could be photographed and reproduced in its tone colors. The reproductions we see today are the result of long, patient experiment. The question of "register," of making the dots intersperse instead of printing on top of each other, took laborious trial and calculation. Obviously the details of this history cannot be explained here. Likewise, the four-color process[16] and other refinements must be skipped.

To our brief description we shall only add that this color process must not be confused with color photography, which involves other factors and produces its shades by the combinations of the primary colors in light, not by the primary colors in pig-

[15]This is accomplished by a slight shifting of the screen in making the half-tone negative.
[16]This adds a black plate.

ment. The photographs taken by this filter process are not, themselves, in color. The negatives show only black dots in every case—black dots made by light coming from certain colored parts. The color arrives only with the application of the inked rollers of the press to the copper plates. In color photography the colors appear on the negatives and the shades, being made by light rather than by pigments, use the light primaries rather than the red, yellow and blue of paint or ink.

The printing of half-tones in color has brought about many new inventions in presses and inks. Problems were presented by the necessity of printing on two sides of a page, by the need of great rapidity for mass production, by the use of the rotary-press principle. Quick-drying inks, drying machinery and "wet printing" have all been answers. The problems have been met to the point where the cheapest-priced magazines, some of them weeklies, where enormous circulation requires the most rapid production, now contain pictures in color which are truly beautiful.

If, for the moment, such things have startled people out of reading, it is scarcely surprising. When we have grown habituated to them so that we take them more calmly; when they are no longer bright spectacular toys but, instead, material for reflection, they may lead us back. And they may, moreover, lead the inert into consciousness.

But we have dwelt long enough upon static pictures. Our readers are impatient to see them move.

Two methods the wood engraver used in softening tint edges

From E. G. Lutz's *Practical Engraving and Etching,* Scribners

Chapter Fourteen

WHAT IS TRUTH?

I

THE HISTORY of invention has shown many devices for correcting the errors of the senses. Never, so far, have we seen men deliberately exploiting a defect. Yet the twentieth century brought not only a set of machines for this specific purpose, but an entire industry based on sensory deception.

Perhaps, when it arrived, the photograph hurt us by revealing the truth too abruptly. Pictures, after all, touch the emotions. We have seen how incongruous the snapshot looked to eyes incapable of catching fast movement. No one could credit the queer attitudes of horses half-way through a jump or run. The position of the human body stopped in a phase of rapid motion was grotesque. Perhaps, then, there came a desire to suppress the instantaneous photograph or at least to adjust it somehow to what the eye saw and the mind perceived. At any rate that was what the cinema did.

It laid hold of the exact photograph which our reason had forced us to accept as true and retranslated it into the terms of visual experience. By this time we were fully aware of the eye's deception. Thus, the trick had all the entrancing elements of self-kidding. It met a certain homesickness which the cold, hard photograph had engendered. It brought to a world which was beginning to stiffen under the ruthless disclosures of science a sense of the value of the inexact. It flexed the iron laws. It revived the engaging question, "What is Truth?" at the perilous moment when too many questioners believed they had found a final and boring answer.

In this capacity, the movies promised a valuable function. It was the function of art—of painting, poetry and fiction. It was

the function of reaching toward truth through the illusory media
—the method of the mystic.

As an art form, the cinema held rich promise. From that
promise it has moved consistently away. This is because, instead
of using illusion as a means, it has used it as an end. Because deception was inherent in the medium, it has been thought desirable to make it confuse the verities. Unable to see the value of
the illusory medium in disclosing reality, the manipulators of
the screen pictures have turned them in on themselves, aiming
deception at deception. A fable or allegory is valuable because,
by its fictional device, it points a truth. Yet our present cinema
persists in telling the story of the Garden of Eden and, at the
last moment, laboriously tries to prove that the eating of the
forbidden fruit is a desirable exercise resulting in continued peace
and prosperity for the eater.

The reason for this is, of course, economic. For the first time
in our history we see the cultural impulse in conflict with industrial mass production. The motion-picture industry, like most
of our new world industry, has been tooled for an enormous output. Because the consumption is large, the leaders of this industry have sought the lowest common denominator of taste. But
this industry is unique in one respect. By a pattern of costs, based
on extravagance rather than economy, it has excluded all collateral effort on a higher level. The result is a monopoly of bad
taste unprecedented in commerce.

In a history of the social consequences of invention we cannot
ignore such results. Nor can we be blinded by them to the
cinema's power of sheer beauty to mitigate them, if not indeed
to transport us through them to our benefit. Such beauty as is
created by so-called screen photography develops round itself
a kind of antisepsis, a protection against the meanest bacillus of
intent. Finally, we must achieve and preserve a confidence in
potential values. It is doubtful if any device which contains
within itself such benevolent power can ever become wholly
corrupt.

To appreciate these values, to understand the promise which,
for an interval, seemed to move rapidly toward fulfilment but

which has since lapsed back into mere promise, we must study the brief, rich history of the whole enterprise. Its social effect for better or worse has been inestimably great. In America, it has played a significant part in the new geography whose plan was outlined by the new communications. It has affected the city, the country, the home, the family, love, marriage, education, inner desire and outward aspiration. It is at once a force for standardization and diversification, for concentration and dispersion. It has developed an industrial pattern wholly new in the world. It has created a world of its own as distinct from that of normal earthly life as if it belonged to a separate planet. It has initiated a set of wholly new trades and skills which are inseparably bound to it.

It has altered trends of thought, clarifying some philosophies and annihilating others, posing new cosmic theory, increasing factual awareness at the same time that it confuses perception. Yet outside the human mind it has no existence. Within the human mind it depends wholly upon a mental lapse. If some doctor should find a cure for this weakness, the entire structure of the cinema would fold up overnight, Hollywood would be a ruin and hundreds of collateral industries, technics, crafts and inventions would disappear. We need not be alarmed. Such a doctor would be hanged, drawn, quartered, cooked and eaten before he had treated a dozen cases.

2

Before going into the errors of the mind and eye that deceive us, it might be well to examine briefly just what actually happens inside a projector. It is exceedingly simple. On a long strip of transparent film is a series of photographs. The film moves between a light and a lens. It does not move continuously. It moves by jerks. As each picture is brought into position behind the lens, the film stops moving for a fraction of a second. Then, quickly, it moves again bringing the next picture into position. The period of rest, short as it is, is much longer than the period of motion.

Each picture differs slightly from the one before it—so slightly that, looking at a piece of film we cannot tell the difference unless we examine them closely, carefully. They differ because they are taken by a camera in which a strip of film also moves by jerks. When the camera is pointed at some moving thing it takes a succession of snapshots, each at a different point in the motion of the object. So, for example, in a film of a man walking, a leg will be a trifle higher or lower in each successive photograph.

Why is it, now, that watching the screen we see continuous, uninterrupted motion instead of a jerked set of pictures? The answer lies partly in our optical failure or defect; partly, as we shall later see, in a mysterious performance of the mind.

Our fortunate disease, observed by Titus Lucretius Carus in 65 B.C., was called "persistence of vision." It would be absurd to suppose that Lucretius was the first to notice this phenomenon, but we have credited him with the discovery because he took time to write it down and because his writing is still extant.[1] An image, looked at for a moment, is still seen after it has been removed. Lucretius approached the secret of the cinema, remarking that "when the first image passes off, and a second is afterward produced in another position, the former then seems to have changed its gesture."[2]

Ptolemy, about two hundred years later, made a laboratory experiment, putting spots of color upon a disc and revolving it about its center. The whirling changed the spots into circles in the perception of the observer. Probably no small boy who has played with fire has failed to repeat this experiment. When he pulls a glowing stick from the bonfire and swings it at arm's length, describing a circle, his friends actually see a complete circle in the air. Pinwheel fireworks are built on this principle. We know perfectly well that, in the case of the glowing stick, there is only one point of light, or, on the pinwheel, only four, yet motion gives the illusion of a circular line of an infinite number of points.

The experiments of Ptolemy and the boys are often used to

[1]*De Rerum Natura*, Lib. IV, 65 B.C.
[2]Quoted by Henry V. Hopwood, *Living Pictures*, London, 1899, p. 3. (Still the best book on the invention period though one is now in preparation by Merritt Crawford.)

explain the movies. In fact, however, they demonstrate the exact reverse of the movies. For here we have motion producing the illusion of a static circle, whereas in the movie static pictures are made to give the illusion of motion. Obviously, there are gaps to be filled in. The whirling stick does not demonstrate anything except the fact that vision persists after the image which causes it has moved. Suppose the boy starts his stick at the bottom. By the time it reaches the top of the whirl (over his head) the bottom glow is still visible. So are the glows at all the intermediate points the stick has passed through.

Once we are persuaded of this fact, however, we are ready to go ahead toward the movie.

Philosophers or "scientists," as they came to be called, continued through the ages to speculate on the phenomenon. Historians of the screen, of whom there is a large and increasing number, have followed these thinkers step by step and have caught every whisper on the subject, so it is superfluous to repeat their labors. Early in the nineteenth century, that period of terrific awareness and articulation of every supposed scientific wonder, persistence of vision leaped upon the platforms of societies, institutes and academies and was translated to the agog populace by a set of delightful experimental toys.

Peter Mark Roget, known also for his *Thesaurus,* which has wet-nursed so many literary beginners (largely to their hurt), jumped out of bed one morning in astonishment at a new demonstration of the persistence of vision. Through a Venetian blind he saw a cart moving. The spokes of the wheels were distorted. Hurriedly raising the blind he saw the normal spokes. Lowering it again he understood that what he had seen through one slit of the blind carried over and impinged on what he saw in the next slit. His explanation as he wrote it[3] (with accompanying diagram) was far more complex than this. It aroused the "savants" of England, and, because communications were improving and scientific consciousness coinciding, soon reached out over the studying world. It was important to these people as theory. It is

[3]"Explanation of an Optical Deception, etc.," in *Transactions* Philosophical Society, 131 (1825).

important to us because it recorded the slit principle on which much progress was made.

In 1826 there appeared a toy. John Herschel, Charles Babbage, William Henry Fitton and John Ayrton Paris, all distinguished "natural philosophers," seem to have played a part in its invention. It was a cardboard disc made to spin about its diameter. On one side was a drawing of an empty bird cage. On the other was a drawing of a bird. When the disc was spun, the bird appeared to be in the cage. Delighted with this new evidence of the eye's delay, some of these serious thinkers whiled away their time putting rats in traps, convicts behind bars, riders on horses, plants in pots. Doctor Paris, less engrossed in pure science than the others, made money out of it, appealing to the popular pseudo-scientific fancy by calling his toy the "Thaumatrope."[4] It was still, by no means, a movie. It may be regarded only as an index of a trend of thinking. And it led to experiment.

Michael Faraday bridged the gap.[5] He showed many optical illusions in respect to motion. The wheels moving behind Roget's blinds were his inspiration. Besides proving that motion could be given the appearance of rest, he showed that slow motion could be seen as fast motion. But not until the surprisingly simultaneous experiments of Joseph Antoine Ferdinand Plateau of Belgium and Simon Ritter von Stampfer of Austria was the world convinced that a sense of motion could be excited by the successive visions of a series of still images.

The common mind, which has today reduced all demonstrations of this deception to the charming generic abbreviation "movie," was perfectly willing, in 1832, to accept the terms Phenakistoscope and Stroboscope, applied, respectively, to the scientific toys of Plateau and Stampfer.[6] Though separately devised, they were nearly identical. A disc within a cylinder revolved upon a shaft. On the edge of the disc were drawn pictures. Each picture represented a phase of motion in advance of that of its predecessor—an arm higher raised, a foot farther along in the course of a step. Looked at through the slits, the

[4]*Edinburgh Journal*, IV, 87 (1827).
[5]*Journal* Royal Institution, new series I, 205 (1831).   [6]Hopwood, p. 13.

arms and legs seemed to move. The pictures, of course, were not photographs. Daguerre and Niepce were still, we remember, struggling with their slow, vague silver salts. The pictures were carefully, laboriously drawn. Plateau and Stampfer were the first Walt Disneys.

It should have been evident, here, that something more than mere persistence of vision was at work. Yet this fact was not recognized for some three-quarters of a century, when photography entered the cinema and the new technic of experimental psychology began to play with it.

Suppose the eye does carry the image over from one picture to the next. Will there not always be a click, a jar, an interruption, a jerk or a blur when the new picture is recognized? After all, the eye sees only a series of different pictures, no matter how long each individual one persists. What makes the pictures appear to move within their frames?

Hugo Münsterberg, professor of psychology, began to wonder about this. He watched many experiments which produced the illusion of motion without the aid of persistence of vision. He came to the conclusion that "the perception of movement is an independent experience which cannot be reduced to a simple seeing of a series of different positions."[7] This perception, he believed, was a high, creative function of the mind, separate and special, by no means the sole result of optical tricks.

Ramsaye follows this argument into an exceedingly lucid exposition. Analyzing a foot of modern motion-picture film, he shows that the pictures reveal only about 3 per cent of the motion which actually took place while the photography was in progress. That is because the eye of the camera is open only for three seconds out of every hundred. "The mind can put together eye-reported fragments amounting to 3 per cent and derive from that a sensation of seeing 100 per cent."[8]

None of these experimenters or students has wholly eliminated persistence of vision as a factor in our appreciation of cinema. They have merely shown that it does not explain the entire illu-

[7] Hugo Münsterberg, *The Photoplay, A Psychological Study*, N. Y., 1916, p. 61.
[8] Ramsaye, I, 171.

sion. We may assume that it carries us over the interval in which the pictures are changed. Without it, no doubt, the jar to our senses of the intermediate blank interval would be intolerable, whether or not the illusion of motion was destroyed.

But having added the "high creative function" of the mind to our optical defect, we may feel better about the whole matter. To Münsterberg this very imaginative performance gives the cinema the possibility of being an art form.[9] It is certainly comforting to know that, in spite of the meticulous effort of the producer to eliminate every morsel on which the fancy might chew from his subject matter and its presentation, the imagination of the spectator, in clandestine seclusion, goes right on exercising just the same.

3

The history of the invention of motion pictures is inherently complex. When we speak of the invention, do we mean the camera or the "peep-show" or the projector? Do we mean film or the devices which move it or the lighting behind it, or the lenses in front of it? Do we mean the photoplay, the news-reel, the animated cartoon? Do we mean the sets or the lighting or the studio? Do we mean the sound track or the color filters or the amplifiers?

We must mean all of these things, for they are all parts of what we call the movies today and they had a hundred or more inventors. The disentangling of the facts as to priority in all the fields is a fascinating task for the special historian and we gladly leave it to him.

The undoubted fact that the motion-picture industry has reached its highest development in the United States must not blind us to the fact that its basic technical invention is not wholly or even largely American. Much partisan history, of course, has been written in France, England and Germany claiming priority. Mr. Ramsaye's book, which has been officially endorsed by Edison, assigns much credit to America. But the fact is that the optical joker was being ardently pursued in many lands at pre-

[9]Münsterberg, Chap. III.

cisely the same moment and that most of the pursuers were quite independent of one another. Had they collaborated, we should probably have got our movies sooner and we should very likely have better ones today.

It is evident that the basic principle of the cinema was commercially in use considerably before there was any instantaneous photography. What we call today "the animated cartoon" came first. A multitude of devices with fine names derived from the classic languages stemmed from the productions of Plateau and Stampfer. Among them were the Dædalum and the Zoetrope. But a few inventors carried the animated cartoon a step farther. In 1853, Franz von Uchatius, an Austrian army officer, borrowed the charming two-hundred-year-old invention of a Jesuit scholar,[10] the magic lantern, to throw the animated images upon the wall. Uchatius used a glass disc for his pictures. As it revolved, a shutter with a slit in it framed each picture in succession before the lens and covered the movement of the disc. This was a basic essential for motion-picture projection.

But the truly great nineteenth-century Disney was the Frenchman, Emile Reynaud. Into his Praxinoscope, patented in 1877, he injected a new principle, since forgotten. Instead of seeing the successive pictures, the spectator looking into this device saw their images reflected by mirrors. These mirrors formed a polygon round the central drum of the instrument. Each reflected a picture which faced it from the inside of the outer drum. As the double drum revolved the spectator saw the successive images, not separately and intermittently but merging into one another, and the illumination was never cut off.

Reynaud was not, however, content with his toy. He went on to a projection device which used the same principle. The projector also threw on the screen a stationary scene in which the figures—Snow Whites and Donald Ducks of his time—were made to act. The *"Pantomimes Lumineuses"* which were being shown commercially at the Musée Grévin in Paris in 1892 by Reynaud's

[10]Athanasius Kircher, 1646. Claims have also been advanced for Thomas Rasmussen Walgensten, one of Kircher's coworkers. Maurice Noverre, *Emile Reynaud,* Paris, 1926, p. 36 n.

projector, the *Théâtre Optique,* created a furor in Paris. They were brilliant and lovely with none of the jar or flicker which made most early motion pictures so hard on the eyes. Reynaud's projector used a long film, wound on two reels. From this light was reflected to revolving mirrors and thence to the screen.[11] Effects were sometimes produced by reversing the direction in which the film moved, so that Pierrot, for example, having climbed up a wall, could be made to climb down the other side[12] by merely running the pictures backward.

It is a pity that Reynaud's principle, which has been called "optical compensation,"[12a] has not been used commercially since his time. Today, of course, the standards of the great motion-picture industry could not be made to conform to it without complete, prohibitively expensive retooling. It might, however, at some stage have been introduced. By Disney, perhaps. . . . It would save film. Only some four images were necessary per second to produce his illusion. Sixteen was the standard for the silent film. But there were other advantages, luminosity and continuity among them.

Historically, Reynaud is important. He first *projected* animated cartoons. He gave the first commercial public showing of moving pictures on a screen. But he never tackled photography with any success. By the time he came to it, late in his career, others had gone ahead of him in matters of direction and scenic effect.

Motion-picture photography has a history separate from that of projection. Coleman Sellers of Philadelphia tried in 1861 to synthesize motion from posed pictures. Pictures had to be posed at that date because the cameras and plates were incapable of capturing rapid motion. His Kinematoscope was a paddle wheel looked at through a stereoscope. It must have been pretty bad. One cannot guess at the phases of a movement. What any single phase of a continuous movement looks like has been taught us

[11]See cut. The second lantern projects the set. There is some evidence that the use of the film, or "bande" as it was called, was suggested by Marey. Marey, *Movement*. Trans. by Eric Pritchard, London, 1895, p. 314.

[12]H. Fourtier, *Les Tableaux de Projection mouvementés*, Paris, 1893, pp. 78–83.

[12a]Noverre, p. 93.

Upper Left: Facsimile of program of Reynaud's "Pantomimes Lumineuses." *Upper Right:* Reynaud's Praxinoscope. *Bottom:* The Theatre Optique d'Emile Reynaud

by the instantaneous photograph. Exactly how much it has
taught is evident from a study of the work of Muybridge and
Marey.

Eadweard Muybridge, whom we met a couple of chapters
ago,[13] has been treated by Terry Ramsaye with much contempt.
The fact remains that he did succeed in breaking down movement into its parts and showing these in static photographs.
Whether or not he did it with the assistance of more scientific experience than his own, the photographs were there to show something that had, apparently, never been observed before. Muybridge, in 1883, ranged a series of them, in the form of transparent, positive plates, round a wheel and produced the illusion
of motion. Being given to a certain pomposity in the matter of
names (as his own attests)[14] he called this apparatus the Zoo-
praxiscope.[15] Meanwhile, however, his work had attracted the
attention of a true scientist in France.

Etienne Jules Marey had, since 1870, been working with devices to show the positions taken by various animals in motion.[16]
In 1878, he saw some of the Muybridge photographs which
showed precisely what he had been trying to achieve mechanically and graphically. He immediately got in touch with Muybridge, who brought many photographs to Paris. Marey, after
long examination of them, set to work making some of his own.
But, instead of using a battery of cameras, he used one. He and
his assistant, Georges Demeny, thus made what may be called the
"first" cinema camera. It was not wholly original; he borrowed
from the photographic revolver of Jules Janssen, but he made, on
an octagonal disc, a series of twelve pictures which could afterward give the illusion of motion when revolved in a proper apparatus. By 1889, like several other experimenters, he had
adopted film.[17] His apparatus using film was exhibited at the
Paris Exposition of 1889, where Edison also had an exhibit.[18]
Doctor Marey himself showed it to Edison.[19]

[13]See p. 13.   [14]See p. 13.   [15]Hopwood, p. 51.
[16]Such as, for instance, bulbs attached to horses' feet, etc. See early chapters of Marey, *Movement*. Also *La Machine Animale*, Paris, 1882, 3d ed.
[17]Hopwood, p. 71.   [18]Dyer and Martin, II, 741 ff.
[19]E. J. Marey, *Nouveaux Developpements de la Chronophotographie*,
Paris, 1897, pp. 27, 28.

4

The year 1889 was a highly significant one in motion-picture history. As we look over the careers of various inventors during the eighties, we find them struggling in several parts of the world, with glass plates, sheets and squares of inflexible, more or less transparent, celluloid[20] and variously treated paper. These were either difficult for projection or almost prohibitively cumbersome in a camera which was expected to work fast. After 1889, we find inventors all using a flexible, transparent strip which could be wound on reels. The answer to this mystery is that film had its commercial birth in that year.

It had been invented before this. We have seen that the Goodwin film was invented in 1887.[21] There is evidence also that William Friese-Greene was making his own in England in 1888.[22] At about the same time, Louis Aimé Augustin Le Prince was using what he described as "an endless sheet of insoluble gelatin."

No adequate history of the screen can omit the tragic stories of Friese-Greene and Le Prince, whatever absolute priorities they may or may not establish.

William Friese-Greene, a brilliant if somewhat un-co-ordinated English inventor, devised, in 1889, a practical cinematic camera using film. There is good reason to believe that he made the film himself, but it is certain that he used it before it was available for purchase. The film was advanced in the camera by means of perforations along its edge.[23] A toothed sprocket mechanism accomplished the intermittent motion necessary, bringing the film to rest for each exposure as the photographer turned the crank. On November 15, 1889, there appeared in London a news story telling of the projection of photographs, taken by Friese-Greene, upon a screen.[24] This camera seems to be the first on

[20]Collodion, plus camphor, U. S. Pat., June 15, 1869, by John Hyatt.
[21]See p. 284.
[22]Letter from Will Day to Merritt Crawford, March 12, 1931. (Ms.)
[23]This camera was not constructed strictly in accordance with his 1889 patent, B. P. No. 10,131. Some historians are in error saying that the patent covers perforated film. It does not.
[24]*Optical Magic Lantern*, London, Nov. 15, 1889.

record which contains all the basic essentials of present-day motion-picture photography.[25]

In the course of his career, Friese-Greene also patented cinematophotography in color by means of filters, as well as series stereoscopic photography. The tragedy was that all these inventions came to nothing as far as the inventor himself was concerned. English conservatism has seldom shown to worse advantage. British capital simply refused to be interested and, in 1891, his property was sold for debt. Possibly his brief confinement in a debtors' jail at that time gave the public the final impression of a down-and-outer so that his later remarkable inventions awakened no confidence.

The other tragedy was more spectacular. Louis Aimé Augustin Le Prince, a French-born American citizen, divided the period of his invention between New York and Leeds, England. He began with multiple lenses on the Muybridge principle, but all mounted in a single camera. He went from this to a single lens and what he described as "transparencies" to be moved, intermittently, by a perforated band or ribbon and a sprocket. By 1890 he too had worked out all the basic devices for cinematography and projection. But in that year, having previously established his wife in a comfortable house in New York[26] which he intended to use as an experimental laboratory, and having taken out his first American citizenship papers, he disappeared. He was, at the time, on a visit to France. He got on a train at Dijon, having said good-bye to his brother and was never seen or heard of again. It is an interesting commentary on the attitude toward communications in the period that investigation was not begun for many weeks—until, in New York, he failed to arrive. Then detectives of both France and England concentrated on the mystery with no result. Not a trace of Le Prince or his baggage has ever turned up. Nor could any one discover a motive of suicide or

[25]Will Day, "Great Britain's William Friese-Greene," in *Photographic Journal,* London, July, 1926, pp. 359 ff. Though Mr. Day is mistaken in his belief that Friese-Greene's patent includes film perforation, he seems to have abundant evidence of the actual use of this device by the English inventor before and after 1889.
[26]The celebrated Jumel Mansion.

murder—barring a common robbery. Le Prince was happy, moderately rich, with every promise of future success. It was one of the most complete, one of the least explainable vanishings of modern history.

Le Prince's story has been well told with adequate documentation.[27] Some of his instruments, which he had left in England, are today on exhibition in Kensington Museum. The main reason for introducing him here is that certain details of his process, had they been adopted by the industry, would have improved modern pictures. One was the size of his frames, which were 2⅛ x 2⅛ inches instead of the present universal 1 x ¾ inches. But Le Prince's inventions were forgotten after his personal fade-out, and by the time they were dug up by research, the process of the industry had been standardized and the whole industry tooled accordingly.

What standardized them? Here is the crux of our story. In the pages that follow, the reader may be inclined to regard that standardizing dictatorship as an octopus sucking into itself the fruit of others' labor; of a ruthless giant crushing opposition. Yet standardization had to take place if a mass-production industry was to be established. To avoid much waste of time and dissipation of effort, some one had to be ruthless. It is the old story of the collective impulse necessary to all mass production. If practical invention is to work toward this end, it must be backed by concentration of resources and a technological focus.

5

A piece of Eastman film reached the laboratory of Thomas Edison at some time during the summer or fall of 1889.[28] Edison had been thinking about motion pictures before this. He himself dates his first thought of this in 1887. It would have been surprising if so keen an observer of invention had failed to notice the large number of experiments in this direction which had been going on for more than half a century. But Edison thought of

[27]Merritt Crawford in *Cinema*, Dec., 1930, pp. 28–31. E. Kilburn Scott in *Journal* Soc. Mot. Pic. Eng'rs, July, 1937, p. 46.
[28]Carl W. Ackerman, *George Eastman*, Boston, 1930, pp. 64 ff.

pictures in connection with his phonograph. He wanted, he says, to synchronize sight and sound.

In this connection, he had studied the Zoetrope of Desvignes as well as the photographs of Muybridge. Whether, by 1887, he knew much about the work of Marey makes little difference, for he saw Marey's invention in 1889 and saw in it the value of the use of film. No doubt Edison had thought of film already, for the thought had occurred to almost every one by that time who had sought to make photographs that would move.

Characteristically, the American people in general have assigned to Edison the credit for the entire invention of the cinema. They have been supported in this belief by some historians. Yet Edison, at the time, made no such claim. On the contrary, he specifically included Muybridge, Dickson and Marey as co-inventors.[29] It has since been shown that every element of Edison's camera, mechanical or optical, including his famous "perforations," existed previous to his patents. Yet, as usual, he co-ordinated these matters into something that was fully workable and he brought his product into commerce. In doing it he used his peculiar genius, which so many people have chosen to regard as "wizardry" or magic.

Thomas Edison concentrated, to the exclusion of everything else, on drawing in to himself every scrap of material he needed to launch a technological, commercial venture. Whether this "belonged" to some one else was a question which his mind was not equipped to agitate. If he was asked the question and forced to try to think it out, his articulated response would be that everything "belonged" to commerce, to society, to general knowledge. Having absorbed this material to himself he put his own rubber-stamp of possession on it as a purely practical matter— simply to keep it all under one roof, so to speak, where it could be effectively handled. The academic ethics of all this belongs in another story than ours. We are concerned with the fact that Edison's kind of thinking has made the collective, industrial America of which we seem to be so proud. Let the rugged industrial individualist beware of juggling with this fact, for before

[29]*Century Magazine*, June, 1894, p. 206.

WHAT IS TRUTH?

he can say Jack Robinson (or Herbert Hoover) he will be hoist higher than a kite by his own petard.

Yet as Edison went at the movies we observe a queer lapse in his usual powers. He made up for it in the end by sheer force, sheer octopus sucking, pure dictatorship. These exercises covered some of his lapses and did the trick of establishing certain inflexible rules and regulations. One trouble was that they were not altogether good rules. Another, from Edison's personal point of view, was that their enforcement came too late.

He was busy as a bird dog when the movies first came under his ken. His mind was filled with much bigger and grander things like the crushing of ore. To him, at the moment, any device for making pictures move was just a toy. Yet the recent success of his other toy, the phonograph, prevented him from ignoring its toy possibilities in commerce. So, reserving his own energies for more dignified pursuits, he turned the movies over to an astute and clever inventor in his employ, the brilliant William Kennedy Laurie Dickson.

Dickson was such a lovable person that his friends have forgiven him some of the amazing flights of his fancy which have troubled historians. To weed out the facts from Dickson's accounts of what he thought were about to become facts is a task that has greatly complicated research into the history of the cinema. Yet, between the lines of his record, there appears evidence that he did most of the work on the so-called Edison inventions in this field. This is in spite of Dickson's infallible loyalty to his chief (even after he left his employ), which gives Edison full credit.

Yet occasionally Edison called Dickson to time. From the first, Dickson seems to have dreamed of the screen. Edison would have none of it. Under his toy-complex he wanted motion pictures kept strictly in the money-making toy sphere. There emerged, therefore, from the Edison shops a large, rentable toy dignified by the highly unoriginal name of Kinetoscope. This was in fact a peep-show. One saw movies by gluing one's eyes to an aperture. The commercial kinetoscopes required a nickel in a slot before the pictures should begin to move.

Before a powerful light (which Edison was well equipped to furnish) a strip of film with sixteen positive photographs per foot moved continuously three feet per second. It did not move intermittently. Intermittence was provided by an automatic shutter. It was this shutter process which required such great light power. When other experimenters tried to use it for throwing pictures on a screen, no light could be found powerful enough to do the job.[30]

Along with the kinetoscope came the kinetograph, equally imitative in name. This was the camera which took the pictures. It had to have an intermittent mechanism, for no continuously moving film could be made to record an image. It was made intermittent by the use of an old clock mechanism called the Geneva cross.

In April, 1894, the Dickson-Edison kinetoscope burst upon an astonished public at a "kinetoscope parlor" in New York. It was an immediate success. No one had enough nickels to satisfy his craving to see the little figures jump and dance. What they did made no difference to any one as long as they were lifelike and moved. The peepers were fascinated beyond words at seeing a man sneeze or perform the most meaningless capers.

Meanwhile, the major part of the labor had been in making the films. Edison built his celebrated "Black Maria" at West Orange, said to be the first studio. It was arranged so that it would rotate and thus adapt itself to the position of the sun, for instantaneous photography had not yet been adjusted to artificial lighting. In the Black Maria, Edison staged all sorts of nonsense, performed mostly by the more histrionic or comic of his employees like the celebrated sneezing Fred Ott.[31]

But the public, once tickled by the kinetoscope, became insatiable. With each satisfaction, desire increased and grew complex. So Edison had to stage prize-fights and dances in his Black Maria and soon the public were demanding pictures of real personages in these acts. Edison hired them to come to West Orange and perform. One of these was the popular dancer,

[30]Ramsaye, I, 131, 142.
[31]Ramsaye, I, 57 ff., 82, 83.

Carmencita. So, in the Black Maria, the great American "star system" was first transferred from stage to film.

The inadequacy of the kinetoscope as a showman's device soon became evident to a good many people. Only one observer at a time could see one machine's pictures, and then only by standing in a cramped, uncomfortable position. Edison's little fifty-foot

Interior of Edison's Kinetographic Theatre. A camera and a recording phonograph are shown taking the scene being enacted in the background. Probably an entirely fanciful drawing. It was, however, prophetic

From *History of the Kinetograph, etc.*, by W. K. L. and Antonia Dickson

films did not keep the kinetoscope fans in that position very long as they only lasted about a minute. But why not arrange moving pictures so that a whole theatreful of people could see them at once, sitting in comfortable seats? And then, having got them in their seats, why not give them a longer show than the kinetoscope could provide?

It would have been surprising if projection had not occurred to many people at once. It had already occurred to European experimenters, as we have seen, before the kinetoscope appeared. With the tangible kinetoscope before them and the magic lantern in all their past experience, recurrence of projection invention was inevitable.

In Europe, through some strange lapse of his usual business acumen, Edison had failed to patent his machine. When it was taken abroad, therefore, inventors had *carte blanche* to do what they liked with motion picture invention with no danger of interference from the Edison interests. In London, Robert W. Paul adapted the kinetoscope to projection and was soon packing theatres. In Paris, with the Reynaud tradition in the background, the Lumière brothers, Louis and Auguste, scored an equal success. Later Georges Mélèis invented the photoplay and the true motion-picture studio equipped with scenery, scene-shifting devices and a multitude of tricks for which, being a professional magician, he was peculiarly gifted. Europe, especially France, in these years gained a head start on America in all the technics of the cinema—a head start which was not lost until the World War.

In the United States, the projection field was starred by the Latham family of Virginia and by Thomas Armat. The once bright star of Charles Francis Jenkins, Armat's occasional collaborator, has been somewhat dimmed by later research.[32]

Much space in screen history has been given to Major Woodville Latham and his gay sons, Percy, Gray and Otway, because they were so picturesque. The boys, allegedly wandering up and down Broadway in its age of relative innocence searching out its bars and its beauties, seem to have forecast the mythology of Hollywood in a manner irresistible to popular writers. In contrast to this dissipation stands the fine old figure of the Southern major, laboriously inventing projectors in a little laboratory. The boys, ever avid for schemes to make money, dickered with Edison's aides and arranged for prize-fights for the kinetoscope while

[32]Ramsaye, Chap. XI. There has, however, been much discussion on the subject. For the statements of the two claimants, see *Transactions*, Society of Motion Picture Engineers, Sept., 1925, pp. 70–76 and 109–114. See also Thomas Armat, "Development of Motion Picture Projection," in *Journal Soc. Mot. Pic. Eng'rs*, March, 1935, pp. 241 ff.

the major, ably and probably indispensably assisted by the fine technician, Eugene Lauste, worked on projection. The main Latham contribution was a reel which made possible a greater length of film. The reel necessitated a loop of free film which was cast off by an unwinding mechanism.[33] All the Latham patents were later acquired by Edison.

The whole Latham affair was hampered by intrigue, which moved in and out of the Edison interests. The primary reason for its failure was its domination by the one great technical fault of the Edison mechanism, the continuously moving film in the projector. On the screen, adequate luminosity was impossible unless each picture or "frame" could be brought to rest behind the lens for an appreciable instant. Yet Latham did establish a historic record by giving the first, American, public, commercial showing of screen pictures on May 20, 1895.

Thomas Armat overcame the difficulty. By a cam movement, adapted from a French invention,[34] he arranged "that each picture be given a long period of rest and illumination on the screen, and a relatively brief period of movement from frame to frame."[35] This was the answer to the light difficulty which Edison had missed because he had refused to be serious about projection. With Armat's revelation (scarcely cataclysmic, as so many Europeans had previously disclosed it) Edison grew more serious.

At this period, apparently, no one could be persuaded of the value of any invention unless the Wizard made it. Thus the struggling Armat, though his projection was excellent (for the era), could not get enough publicity to finance it on a large scale. The Edison interests then convinced him that if Edison's name should be attached to his machine, it would instantly capture the public fancy and Armat was sensible enough to agree.[36] Thus the Edison Vitascope came into being and, as the newspapers all rushed to herald this new feat of the Wizard's, the screen picture was launched in America.[37]

[33]The Friese-Greene projector contained both. Day, *op. cit.*
[34]Georges Demeny, B. P. No. 24,457, 1893.   [35]Ramsaye, I, 143.
[36]Ramsaye, I, 224. It must be remembered also that Armat had no camera and therefore must use Edison films.
[37]April 23, 1896, Koster & Bial's Music Hall, N. Y.

Edison's triumph was now complete. As the Vitascope spread it provided much activity for the Edison film production plant. The scope of the Black Maria was enlarged and directors were called in to stage "colossal" outdoor or "location" enterprises. Foreign competition entered with the Lumière and Méliès films. The Edison studios almost burst with such rival productions as "The Great Train Robbery," directed and photographed in 1903 by Edwin S. Porter. By this time, however, there was plenty of domestic activity, more or less controlled by the Edison octopus.

The attempted monopoly was, of course, based on the Edison patents. The old device of the "combination" instituted by sewing-machine inventors[38] and reaching such large proportions in the automobile industry[39] came into use for the cinema. The Motion Picture Patents Company, to which the Edison patents were assigned, operated for years to give privilege to a chosen few and keep out outsiders. Many volumes might be written on nothing but the litigation which resulted. The combination was finally nullified by a decision in 1917 based on an intricate legal technicality. But by this time the Edison patents had been sustained so long that the whole technology was based on them.

By 1900 the period of basic invention was finished—at least in the visual province of the movies. Soon after the opening of the new century, the great industry began in America. As the photoplay arrived from abroad and showed its power vast capital was poured into the hands of producers. The involved competition, fights, litigation, the building up of the huge companies which dominate production today as well as the extinction by fair means or foul of lesser constellations do not belong to our story.

But we cannot leave the invention period without a final correction of popular misunderstanding. Mr. Ramsaye states in italics:

"It is provable that there is not now and never has been subsequent to the year 1888 any motion picture film machine whatsoever of any relation to the screen art of today that is not descended by traceable steps from the Kinetoscope."[40] This state-

[38]*M.I.M.*, p. 371.   [39]See pp. 383-4, 384 n.   [40]Ramsaye, I, 73.

ment is largely true (or was when Ramsaye wrote it in 1926), but it should be clarified by adding, also in italics, *that no basic part of the kinetoscope was original with Edison and that the reason the screen art of today derives so much from it is that Edison by his patents was able to dominate the whole American industry in its infancy.*

So it was Edison, after all, who sold the movie to the great American public.

6

Huge, new and clean, separate and self-contained, lies the walled dream city of the Pacific Coast. You may not see the wall but it is as high as Romance itself and as impregnable. The child of a giant has built the city out of his smooth blocks; in it he can play forever at his make-believe. There he can be boisterous or pensive with his mood; dress himself up as a knight, or soldier, a noble, a beggar, or a thief and strut about in his fancy clothes, shooting off his toy pistols, playing his little games of murder, love, rapine, war, deceit or heroism and no one will be hurt.

As you enter the gates, you leave the world and become a ghost. Your flesh melts and the light shines through you. You are no longer you but only a translucent image of yourself. From now on you will reach the world only through delayed perception; the tricks of men's eyes and minds. You will be gigantic and beautiful, comic, grotesque for the little instant of their watching but yourself is tiny in an inch-wide frame and when the light goes out you will go with it. Your name is a set of incandescent letters, glowing for a while over a hundred thousand doorways in the cities of the world, in desert oases, in mountain villages, in forgotten island ports; but let the child giant turn a switch inside the wall and out goes your name too. When the switch is turned back, new letters will glow in the tubes. You are a memory then (and a beggar to boot).

This phantom city has no precedent in history. To it have flocked the tangible goods and services of the world—to make a story. Food and drink, machines, gold, precious stones, silk and steel; skills, crafts, talents, magic are summoned by the wave of the giant's wand. From Nome to Durban, from Mombasa to Point Barrow throng the slaves, black and white, red, tan and yellow, to be whipped into the pageant of pretense. Where, ever, was there such a Mecca? What solid centers of splendor have ever shown like this great American mirage? Where is the tarnished glory that was Greece, the flickering torches of the Roman empire; where is Xanadu, with its shoddy pleasure palace? Of what avail the labors of the slaves to pile the pyramids or hang the Babylonian gardens? We can do these things overnight in Hollywood. We can sink a ship of ten times the displacement of Caligula's barge and with ten times its tonnage of gold and raise it tomorrow, what is more, for a next week's prop.

Caligula and his ilk, the fiddling Nero and the monkey-shining Commodus, were, in the sweet vernacular of our new dream capital, but pikers. Could any one of them put on an orgy, a chariot race, a pandemonium or a holocaust that would hold a pitch torch to our Klieg-flooded super-spectacles? Would Attila recognize his scourge or Hannibal his elephant march, seeing them thrown from an inch-wide strip of nitro-cellulose today? Such heroes would die of shame and envy at the hyperbole of their immortality.

Phony of phonies, Hollywood! Where but in America could have been built such a titanic plaything? Is it the ultimate avatar of Manifest Destiny? Have we conquered our continent only to step off the edge, at the end of our march, into a sea of romance?

If we should look at it more steadily and microscopically, retracing a brief, garish history step by step, we would see that it is not wholly American. We would see many cold, foreign fingers reaching across our land, not toward glamor but toward wealth. We would see specifically a march of the tribes of Israel following in comfort the hard-won trails of our pioneers. At the end, our dream city seems to change into a Jerusalem built of American gold but housing in its temple an alien calf and with alien money-changers on the steps.

Economically, Hollywood shows its most curious aspect in relation to the real world. Money, there, appears to be in a whirlpool.

Actually, it filters out through tortuous channels into business and industry outside. But the great volume of money paid out to actors, writers, directors, is spent on the spot. Every device known to man to lure away the gold of his fellows has found a place there. There is no thinkable luxurious whim which cannot be gratified within a mile or so of any given studio. Fantasy is expensive. Action in a synthetic world breeds desire that must extend beyond the lots. One cannot be expected to step from the fiction of paradise into real squalor. Furthermore, a star who reaps a daily fortune is expected to carry the illusion of the screen into every detail of so-called "private" life. Actually, there is no private life. Screen stars are more truly possessions of the people than the President of the United States. They are public servants in fact. The world watches their going to bed and their getting up, their baths and their breakfasts, their robing and disrobing. The public demands that these matters be impeccable, superb, for all the world will adore and emulate them up to its little capacity. Thus all the money is spent (like the President's salary) and the city has arranged that it be spent there. The banks of Hollywood have never met Depression.

The labor of these people is as arduous and often as dull as the labor of an assembly line for they, too, are in mass production. No one who has sat through a day of retakes will ever suggest that the working life of a screen actor is one of ease. Such endless, stultifying ennui, one might suppose, could only be relieved by a night of orgy. Yet such relief is obviously impossible under the stern discipline necessary to the performance itself. The only compensation, therefore, is money; the money must be spent for public approval of a private life and hence for the approval of the producer whose fingers never leave the public pulse.

If the public pulse goes down, watching a particular star, a switch is turned and the star's lights go out, one by one, all over the world. It is time, then, for the star to take a quick stock of what is left, if any, in his bank. If ever there is to be another, perhaps lesser, perhaps only "extra" job, a certain fiction known as "front" must be maintained. Appearance, clothes, faces, bodies, must not be let down. So, all over the dream city, you will find ex-glamor girls, sleeping in their parked cars for which there is no gas, creeping into dark boarding houses, starving, but bound forever to the dream city by synthesis of hope. It may be that nowhere in the world is poverty more acute or hope more forlorn.

But behind the stars are other, less extravagantly paid, solider, more continuous and more craftsmanlike labors. The skills of synthesis and pretense seem to reach their apex among the stage carpenters and the technicians in charge of lighting, props, cameras, color, sound. The history of screen sets from Georges Méliès' primitive "Trip to the Moon" to such a modern product as "Gone With the Wind" is fascinating in detail and rich enough to fill many books. They will all, one day, be written. Adaptation to the camera requires an ingenuity quite different from that of the stage. Before the vague, stationary instrument of Méliès, easy modifications of old stage scenery were illusory enough. Relatively speaking, the old cameras recorded very little more than the eye might see from the stalls of a theatre and it is easy to deceive the eye. But as cameras improved in acuteness of lens and sensitivity of film and as they became mobile, following the actors about a set, they recorded detail which could no longer be faked by the brush or by tricks of perspective. In outdoor photography, the real thing could be selected or composed. Yet even outdoors, a critical public soon demanded construction. It became impracticable, also, to move a large company all over the world until precisely the correct background was found in nature. Indoors, of course, construction must always be, and it must be solid, substantial, correct in the last detail, suggesting no deception. Verisimilitude became a fetish and no expense was spared to create it.

It is interesting to observe, at this point, what the screen does which the stage cannot do.

Pictures, when they move, draw the spectator into them. Quite certainly he walks into the perspective depth of a street or room, leaving the fleshed body behind. Even the stage cannot do this, with all its true depth and blooded people. On the stage, the tricks are too ordered and too visible. No casual wind blows across it, no bird flies, bent on its own business. The sky does not alter its mood. No detached causations are fulfilled as in the world. The great triumphs of the screen have not been wrought by the foreground actors alone, but by the curl of smoke from a chimney, the passing of a train outside the story, the natural movement of boughs in the wind, the indifferent lap of waves, all the separate life that goes on in the world behind an event. The "high creative function" of the mind which imagines a set of frames into a continuously moving drama, appreciates such things. So much so, indeed, that since cinema photography has moved largely indoors, directors have resorted to every manner of trick in double exposure and transparency to continue such effects.

The extent in detail, to which set designers have gone, is evident from the examination of the paraphernalia of such a production as "Gone With the Wind." The scenes here were largely from Georgia. An outdoor set reproduced part of the city of Atlanta in the sixties. Researchers had even dug up the real names which appeared on the shop signs in the war period. Every detail of architecture and building had been studied. Buildings were reproduced in true brick, stone frame, lest a critical eye detect a fake. They were so solid that the most microscopic examination of the structure itself could detect no insubstantiality. Yet this was true only for what the camera was expected to record. Behind the front of a house there was nothing—unless a side shot was anticipated. Thus whole new building problems were introduced to the screen architect.

As the picture was in color, the brown California grass had been stained with the Georgian green. The dirt of the roads had been colored a true Georgian clay red. Trees had been brought from Georgia—sometimes only the trunks, for that was all the camera would shoot. Because the California sky is usually clear, clouds had been brought from Georgia and introduced into the final film by photographic legerdemain.

To the casual visitor to the lots, such things seem miracles of invention. Almost, the ingenuity of deception seems greater than that of such workers in machine accuracy as we have seen in this history. On the whole, this visit is more rewarding than any

337

will-o'-the-wisp pursuit of the public or private behavior of the winking and transient stars.

7

Yet star activity cannot be discounted. For from Hollywood are dictated the mores, tastes, desires and habits of thought of unaccountable millions of men and women. Through a deep stratum of the American people, not to mention the rest of the world, scarcely a garment is worn or a kiss exchanged which was not first approved in a Hollywood studio. At least a dozen gods are turned out by Hollywood cinemanthropomorphism every year. No national hero of history stands a chance beside a Clark Gable or a Robert Taylor. Almost every conscious act of millions of adolescents (in age or mind) is patterned on the supposed behavior of such deities—or at least on their conduct before the camera. Their pictures, caught in a rapturous moment, are like icons on the walls of children's bedrooms from the rotting cabins of Arkansas to the perfumed cliff-dwellings of Park Avenue. Untold millions of kids in their langourous teens have been kissed to sleep by a Garbo, a Dietrich, or a Durbin; an Astaire or a Cagney. From table manners to the penultimate motions of love-making, *they have followed* their gods—through hold-ups, gang-wars, killings and into prison *they have followed* them. Unsatisfied with the tricks of persistence of vision to pique their worship, they have followed their gods into their extra-camera lives so that a whole new department of Hollywood has been designed to fabricate such lives out of the frothy material at hand. So, through the magazines, fiction is built on fiction until less than half the world is real.

But the movies have done more. For the lonely farmer they have built a city, warm and friendly but with adventure round the corner: they have given him lights, crowds, movement, noise, the brotherhood of congestion. For the pressed, sweating slum tenant they have opened the empty prairie and the windy sea. To the Eskimo they have showed the tropic beaches and to the plainsman, the forests. They have done more than show—as we have seen, they have drawn him into them.

WHAT IS TRUTH?

Thus the movies have become integral with many lives. Sometimes, dangerously, the fantasy has grown inseparable from the real. The youthful consciousness, particularly, if unsupported by nervous stability, has frequently confused screen crime with real crime, screen love with real love, and results have been disastrous. Parole officers have often traced delinquencies to a picture theatre. Confessions by the dozen may be found in court records that "the movies started me."[41] Boys shoot guns because their gods pointed them. Girls, fired by a cellulose kiss, sink into seduction with the inadequate drug-store clerk. But we have less evidence of the causes of good conduct. We rarely question a lad who has saved a life or a girl who has sacrificed her pleasure for a crippled mother about the inspiration behind these acts. Such things have little documentation. If they had we might disclose the screen there too.

On the whole, the effects of motion pictures have probably been beneficial in spite of the unspeakable guff, twaddle, infantilism, distortion, muling, puking, intellectual and moral perversion which have issued in an unbroken stream from the Hollywood factories. The common mind is unexpectedly selective in its reception. Frequently it will ignore the detail which shocks the "sophisticated" observer. Often it will construct its own moral and miss the studied intention of the picture-maker. Dominated by wishful thinking, it will accept what it desires and disgorge the rest. Sometimes it seems as if the movie-addicted mind possessed high creative powers. Ask the next young person you escort home from a picture to tell you its story. A director or script writer would be astonished at such accounts. An effort to analyze them is being made, at the moment, in a large number of high-school courses in Motion Picture Appreciation.

In education the screen has touched high potentials. With the record of sound added in the projector it is possible to conduct a school without benefit of teachers—or rather, with benefit of the best teachers in the land working in mass production. Fast- and slow-motion movies have proved invaluable in teaching

[41]For case histories, see Herbert Blumer and Philip M. Hauser, *Movies, Delinquency and Crime*, N. Y., 1930.

botany, biology, mechanics and football. Variations of the movies have been useful in medicine and engineering. If producers could be persuaded that every human or social act since the beginning of time was not necessarily dictated by a sexual motive, the movies would be valuable, too, in the teaching of history.

The exact future of the screen is in doubt. Television has posed a threat though not a very real one. A greater threat derives from the low standard of dramatic material based on the producer's underestimate of the common mind. The cinema once before reached a low point in this respect and was saved by the trick of sound. Will it be saved again by a partial lapse into silence? Many serious critics still think the silent film was the true, new art form and that there might be room for occasional non-dialogue pictures, providing the mass-production rigidity could be relaxed. Others see hope in the "animated cartoon" with which the invention began and to which it has come back with new ingenuity in the superb color productions of the Disney factory. Might this be sublimated by the work of great artists into beautiful movement?

It is certain that the movies will be saved. Their hold on the people is unbreakable. It was the movies, after all, that first freed the isolated farm from winter boredom and winter madness. They brought lost people back into the world. They made men friendly even when they made them restless, brought them together in the community of entertainment in the very act of breeding desires that would disperse them. The thumbers along the highways may be seeking some promised paradise of the screen. Yet there are no fewer cars parked round the village green of a Saturday night. Americans will not give up this plaything whether there be sound or silence, art or twaddle. Nor, probably, will the world relinquish Hollywood.

Chapter Fifteen

RECORD OF SOUND

I

SUCH a picture of Hollywood scarcely suggests an industrial town. It is quite unlike Pittsburgh, Lowell, Akron, Wilmington, Syracuse or Youngstown. Yet its commodities cost upwards of $150,000,000 a year to produce.[1] This is a sizeable industry even in this supreme industrial nation.

Hollywood differs from other industrial towns because its products are so different from theirs. Its products, as we have suggested, are dreams. This is not a pretty or fanciful denomination; it is a fact. An economist, we imagine, would classify dreams as services rather than as goods. But they present peculiar problems of manufacture, merchandizing, publicity, price, and they require an unusual variety of skills and labor. In these respects they are unlike steel, soap or the cola beverages. Their value is difficult to estimate in terms of bulk. It is difficult to predict the variations in dream demand of a hundred million weekly dreamers. The producers are harassed by many bogies more or less inherent in their products: kudos, sex-appeal, morality, glamor, which militate against precision of formula. A formula for steel may, after certain experimentation, become standard and rigid. But the compounding of a dream seems to require elusive reagents. One may specify the minims of boy and girl, for instance, in a love dream but the reaction is effected by a substance varyingly denominated as "it" and "oomph," which is scarcely susceptible to precise measurement.

Yet the industry, borrowing from other industrial tradition, has made valiant efforts to establish exact formulas for its commodities. This is not a manner of speaking, it is a literal statement.

[1]Statistical Abstract of the U. S., 1938, p. 804. The figure $165,065 is given for the State of California. We mean "Hollywood" to include all nearby studios. Total U. S., $188,470 (1935).

The word "formula" has been current for years among the picture people. And, looking at picture-making as a large-scale industry selling to a hundred million consumers, how can we reasonably expect anything else? These industrialists must think and talk about salesmanship, marketing, consumer-consciousness, sales-resistance, precisely as if they were dealing in razor blades. Yet because they were not dealing in razor blades or any other interchangeable issue from the jigged tool or the mixing vat, but with something which has no real existence outside the human imagination, the industry has moved through continuous waste sometimes to the brink of disaster.

2

It just escaped going over this brink during the years 1926 and 1927. It was a good time in the world, everything was on what is known in the graphic American language as the Up-and-Up. The great boom was accelerating rapidly toward full career. Stock quotations were climbing, industries were expanding, retail sales were mounting, money was easy—everywhere there was extension and growth. But one by one, all over the land, consumers of dreams began to drop away.

Perhaps they were waking up. Perhaps the actuality was more luring than the dreams. In any case the dark, silent theatres were growing emptier and emptier.[2] Exhibitors perfumed their houses, installed organs, put their little ushers through military drill, interpolated jugglers, songs, dances, "appearances in person" into their shows. It made no difference. Even for the great new American diversion of necking, the theatres were no longer the vehicle. A more mobile one was taking the neckers out into the open air and to remote moonlight parking where they could construct their own more realist, highly competitive dreams.

The chemists in the laboratories of Hollywood rushed to their test-tubes. They shook them, strengthened the mixtures, upsexed them. They sent experts through the factories to inspect

[2]One aggravating circumstance was the great overextension which had taken place. There were far too many theatres.

342

machinery. They listened to the public pulse, somewhat confused now by their own fearful heartbeats, and they turned their switches on the stars. The effort was all futile. Back came the plastic rolls. Spies in the cities watched the theatres fold, saw the dreamers sitting in happy families *at home*.

There were answers enough. It did not take much listening to hear the wails of complaint. The "pitchers" were all the same. Even Adolf Menjou lost his lure after appearing in four successive dreams whose sole difference lay in the costumes and title. The public will take interchangeable cars. It will not take interchangeable romance indefinitely and continue to call it entertainment. But there was another answer.

Since the war, twelve-year-old boys had been tinkering with batteries and wires to catch sound. It arrived first in coded sputterings. Then voices came from the improved contraptions on the table. Vague voices, saying meaningless words often enough, but from far away and with no tangible conductor. It was a thrilling magic. In 1924, it was taken seriously by adults. By 1926 another great dream industry had grown behind the little inventions on the parlor table. It was round these inventions that the spies from Hollywood found the happy families gathered. The little rooms thrilled then, with the diapasons of organs, the wail of saxophones, the scrape of strings. And there were voices. Heard melodies were sweeter.

It seems, looking back on all this change, as if it had taken place overnight. It is difficult to remember any interval between silence and speech on the screen. Between shows, the ghosts acquired, all over the world, the gift of tongues. It was a miracle—another miracle of science, as sudden as all our modern miracles, which become commonplaces the instant they are accomplished. Some one has a brainstorm. He rushes to a captain of industry, stopping, briefly, on the way, at the patent office. The following week, hundreds of millions of people are laughing and crying at brand-new fantasies.

In reality, screen sound has a past as long as screen shadow. In this background are years of patient labor, scores of persistent students, the slow coming together of many collateral sciences.

They were brought to their final meeting place not by science but by society.

3

In the story of the telephone, we have seen something of this background. Before the research of Alexander Graham Bell, men had discovered that sound could be recorded. Bell played for a time with two toys whose origin was involved with the deep complex studies of Von Helmholtz and other European investigators. One was a flame which flickered in a regular sequence in response to speech; the other drew a wavy line on a smoked glass as sound came against its diaphragm. Bell used these devices, which were purely experimental—pieces of laboratory equipment—to help him work out the steps by which sound might be translated into variations in an electric current. The telephone wire carried these variations—alternate strength and weakness of current—over a distance. When they arrived they were retranslated by magnets which, actuated by the current, alternately attracted and repelled, into a comprehensible repetition of the original sound. It is not necessary to repeat the details of this process. We must, however, bear in mind that such a process existed and refresh our memory of its result.

Yet Bell had made no *record* of sound here. He had merely *reproduced* a sound at a distance. On the other hand, Scott, who had made a written *record* of sound on his phonautograph, had found no way to *reproduce* it. It remained for some one to combine record and reproduction; to invent a device which would take the written record, so to speak, and *read it aloud*.

It seems as if no one had ever successfully disputed Edison's invention of the phonograph. It, with the saw gin of Eli Whitney, approaches most closely the ideal of a true, complete "invention" by one man. On the phonograph rests the popular belief in the Wizard's magic. It was a truly incredible popular marvel. With it, for the first time, a machine seemed to come alive, think, understand, *speak*. Somehow, into its wheels and drums, God must have breathed.

Yet all Edison had done here had been purely mechanical. He

344

had not even called in the mysterious force of electricity to aid him. He had simply taken a diaphragm like Scott's and attached to it, instead of a stylus, a needle. As the needle vibrated it traced a wavy line, not on smoked glass but on a plastic substance which would retain the line in intaglio—engraved into it. The brainstorm came when the inventor imagined another needle running through this track, following its curves and waves, and so send-

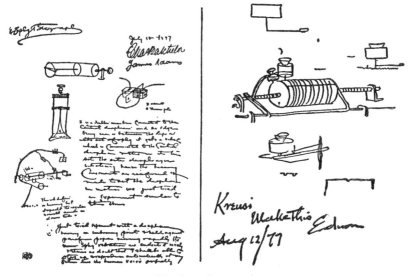

The first phonograph

Edison's original sketch for the phonograph (*left*) and to the right is Edison's first working drawing for the phonograph with Edison's note to Kruesi his modeller, to "make this"

ing the original sound back through the diaphragm. Why not? A sound could make a track. Why, then, could not a track make a sound? Genius is as simple as that. Yet the capacity for thinking in this manner is, truly, a gift which the Creator bestows with astonishing infrequency.

Edison's progress from tinfoil to wax and through other details has been exhaustively followed by historians. There is no need to do it again. The recording line on Edison's cylinders continued to be what is known as a "hill and dale" line. The recording needle cut more or less deeply following variations in the sound vibrations and hence the reproducing needle moving over these hills and valleys bobbed up and down.

In 1887, Emile Berliner invented the lateral line used on the disc records. Here the recording needle vibrated in the plane of the disc, from side to side. The discs soon supplanted the cylinder in popularity, though the hill-and-dale track is still held to have advantages, especially since new technics have found ways of cutting it on the discs as well as on the cylinders. But at the beginning of the century, when the phonograph started on its steep upward curve of sales, the disc using only the lateral track had the immense advantages of better adaptation to mass production and general convenience of handling.

4

The movement of Americans toward an understanding of the arts did not follow the usual path in this direction. As a rule in the history of mankind, wealth has succeeded labor, leisure has followed wealth and interest in the arts has come along with leisure. In all ages men have wanted an accumulation of riches in order that they might stop working. Having got their leisure, they have used it in various delights of the mind or spirit for which the rest of humanity has no time.

In the history of the United States we see a break in this program. At about the middle of the nineteenth century many Americans were inundated with wealth. According to tradition, we should expect a consequent cessation of labor among them. Yet, in fact, generally speaking, the opposite of this occurred. The enriched Americans worked harder than ever. They merely used their surpluses to exploit new sources of wealth and all their energy went into the work of this exploitation. Indeed, when leisure finally arrived in our land it was a consequence of poverty, not of wealth. It arrived when men lost their jobs and Government stepped in with Relief—a device not for maintaining leisure in a class which had originated in wealth but for keeping alive people whose tradition was work after there had ceased to be work to do.

The fact was that Americans (like Nature in the old aphorism) abhorred a vacuum. The habit of filling up empty spaces was so strong they could not stop. As long as a square mile of forest

346

remained uncut, a "section" of ground untilled, a mine undug, a river unspanned or a desert untraversed, the work must go on and wealth, instead of being a means of hateful rest, became always a means to new labor.

Under such conditions it is not surprising that the arts made slow advances. That they made any at all is due, largely, to the fact that the women, inheriting a kind of deification from the frontier, formed a leisure group whose minds, excluded from the gross, physical world, were expected to turn in an artistic direction. But that is a separate story with a tragic ending which need not intrude itself here.

It is significant that music was the first art to make deep inroads into the whole of American society. The attendance at symphony concerts may still be largely female. Yet the understanding of music by women alone could hardly account for the wide spread of musical production in the country. Symphony orchestras are increasing at a surprising rate. Before the war there were seventeen in the entire country.[3] In 1938, there were close to three hundred. Statistics for that year show also more than five hundred schools of music.[4] There are, in addition to these special schools, countless courses of musical instruction in grammar and high schools.

In gratitude for this happy change many Americans genuflect before the god of radio. But let us examine a little more closely into the correctness of this gesture. It is only very recently that the broadcasting studios have gone in extensively for what they call "serious" music. According to their own story they have done this in response to a large demand. By the time they had decided (somewhat tremulously) to broadcast symphonies, there were orchestras all over the country giving surprisingly highbrow programs to large audiences.

It is certain that broadcasts have done a great deal for musical education. No doubt the desire for more and more orchestras, conservatories and school courses increased and spread over a larger portion of the people as a result of radio activity. But the

[3]Dickson Skinner, "Music Goes Into Mass Production," in *Harpers Magazine,* April, 1939.
[4]Pierre Key, *Music Year Book,* 1938.

demand—especially for symphonic music—was not initiated by it.

A symphony is a peculiar thing. Henry Adams tells how, sitting, bored, in a Berlin music hall he had been suddenly "surprised to notice that his mind followed the movement of a Sinfonie. He could not have been more astonished had he suddenly read a new language." Always Adams had expressed his loathing of Beethoven. "He slowly came to admit that Beethoven had partly become intelligible to him, but he was the more inclined to think that Beethoven must be much overrated to be so easily followed. This," he added in his ironic manner, "could not be called education, for he had never so much as listened to the music. He had been thinking of other things. *Mere mechanical repetition of certain sounds had stuck to his unconscious mind.*"[5]

Adams had put his finger there on the only possible means of understanding a symphony. Only by hearing it again and again can one learn to follow the movements. And that is precisely what a considerable part of the American people did during some thirty years of the twentieth century. They listened to symphonies played over and over again, repeating them at will until they had learned to follow them.

But only a monarch or a Pluto rich beyond dreams can command a symphony orchestra to come and play to him and to repeat again and again what it has played. And even the radio once it has given us, for example, the Brahms Number One cannot be turned back to repeat it. It proceeds into César Franck in D Minor or Dvořák's New World. But Edison and Berliner, following the democratic pattern, made every humble citizen a monarch or a Pluto—at least as far as music was concerned.

All over the country and, indeed, in much of the world, in the first quarter of the twentieth century, symphonies in wax were bought and slipped on the machine. Over and over they were played, at the cost of a needle per repetition. First thousands and then millions of people found delight in Henry Adams' experience. Having learned, in their own homes, to follow the movements, they craved to hear them directly from an orchestra.

[5]*Education,* Popular Edition, Boston, 1927, pp. 80, 81. Italics ours.

Always the machines were somewhat defective. Never could the full tone, the full perfection of instrument be reproduced. Thus the new invention, though immensely valuable in instruction and giving a cheap substitute for an expensive performance, because of its defects never replaced the orchestra it tried to reproduce. On the contrary, it stimulated people to go to concerts, increased demand for orchestras and yet at the same time never lost its own popularity. It merely fitted perfectly into a large musical scheme.

Here is an example *par excellence,* of industrial mass production stimulating interest in a true art. Except for printing, it is the only one we know. The phonograph has lowered no standards. It has cheapened nothing. It has not taken a great work of art and diluted it into a sob-story with a sugared ending. It has reproduced the best music of the world, not quite as the best orchestra, singer or chorus might render it directly, yet well enough to teach its values and induce a craving in the listener to hear these things at their pure source.

The radio, still, itself, imperfect, has followed in this train. Yet there is an important distinction between the record industry and the industry of radio entertainment. The broadcaster, like the movie producer, must sell his service to tens of millions of consumers simultaneously. He cannot pick and choose among his ultimate buyers without sacrifice. He must severely restrict his more "serious" programs lest the bulk of his audience, intellectually inadequate to them, be lost. Thus, the lover of symphonies must wait his turn while twenty million or so proletarians laugh over Ma Perkins and Amos 'n' Andy or undulate before the god of swing. His turn may come at an inconvenient moment.

The industrialist who deals in phonograph records is in a very different position. He is able to base his production estimates on two separate markets. He sacrifices nothing by producing for an educated public. He knows the demand in each group and he can answer it exactly. The swing-lovers are not alienated by his manufacture and sale of symphonic records. He is not condemned by the highbrows no matter how large his output of low-grade entertainment as long as he continues to sell them what they want when they want it. On the contrary, they often welcome such an output in the belief that it makes possible a continued production of the best instrumental music.

In practice, however, the reverse of this proposition is usually true. The backbone of the record business, like that of the publishing business, is composed of "standard" works of art. The greatest of the symphonies, concertos, sonatas or solos have a steady sale year after year and are not subject to vogue or caprice. Popular dance and song records have short lives and new production costs are constant. They require what is known in other industries as "retooling," whereas the classics may be stamped out indefinitely from the same die.

The essential difference, of course, is that the movie producer or radio broadcaster must combine industry and showmanship —an extremely difficult combination. The record maker, on the other hand, may adapt his tangible commodity to the ordinary pattern of merchandising. He attained this position at the moment when the old Edison phonograph moved from the public theatre or "parlor," as it was called, into the home.

It is interesting to trace briefly the course of the phonograph record industry through the statistics of its short career. From a value of about two and a half million in 1909, the figures jumped in ten years to a value of some forty-four million. This represented an increase in production of records from twenty-seven million records in 1909 to a hundred and six million in 1919.[6] Then, by 1932, partly because of the depression but largely because of radio competition, there had come an almost incredible drop to ten million records with a value of only about five million dollars.[7] But the greatest surprise in all this history is the fact that since, in 1932, the industry was pronounced dead,[8] the figures have leapt back in 1938 to a production of thirty-three million records with a value of eighteen million dollars, and estimates for 1939 nearly double these figures.[9] Thus the phonograph has not only survived the terrible radio competition but seems to be on its way toward a new peak of its own.

[6]U. S. Census Reports.
[7]"Phonograph Records," in *Fortune*, Sept., 1939, p. 72.
[8]*American Mercury*, Sept., 1932.   [9]*Fortune*, p. 94.

Whether, in the long run, the radio or the phonograph will have the greatest influence on the education of society in the understanding of music is an unimportant question. The recognizable fact, at the moment, is that these two instruments of the quantity production of sound have, between them, created the musical America that we know in 1940.

5

Before following the phonograph to Hollywood and before examining another technology for recording and reproducing sound which is even more closely allied with motion picture photography, a clear understanding of basic technical factors may be gained by studying the devices used to perfect the phonograph itself.

Edison, as we have seen, did not call upon electricity to aid his invention. It did not seem to him necessary. Edison was not greatly concerned with the phonograph as an art vehicle. He called it a "talking machine." To him its importance lay in its ability to reproduce speech. It is true that later he thought of its musical uses—probably when they were called to his attention by others—but in any case, the Wizard himself would probably have been little disturbed by his machine's inadequate handling of a symphony. He was extremely deaf and whatever may have been said by recent worshippers about his love of music, it is reasonably certain that he had little understanding of it.

The old mechanical recording methods captured only a small part of the frequency range of either the human voice or any musical instrument. The old graver could make marks upon the wax representing a range of only from 220 to 3400 cycles.[10] As the sound produced by a singer accompanied by an orchestra might cover a range of from 30 to 12,000 cycles, it is obvious that an immense amount of sound was lost in an old record. Much of this was restored by the imagination of the listener just as it restores such a lot of lost sight to the screen. But the record failed to satisfy music lovers who were able constantly to compare the

[10]Complete vibrations per second.

351

performance of the phonograph with that of an orchestra heard directly.

It was inevitable that the phonograph should eventually find its way into the research laboratories which had been created for improvement of the telephone. Graham Bell had, himself, studied the phonograph early in its career. Since, every device which had dealt with sound had come under the scrutiny of the research department of the American Telephone and Telegraph Company. Meanwhile, also, the technologies which later made possible successful radiotelephony were advancing rapidly.

In the twenties, the parallel technologies came together. Certain inventions had been absolutely essential to the broadcast of sound. The greatest of these, the device for amplifying the electric waves into which sound waves had been translated, was applied to the phonograph in the telephone laboratories by Frank Baldwin Jewett and Joseph Pease Maxfield between 1920 and 1924.[11]

Now, by translating the sound produced by voice or instruments into electrical waves in the old familiar telephone manner, by then amplifying these and finally by communicating them to the recording graver a far superior sound track was made in the wax. This new sound track was able to reproduce frequencies of from 30 to 5500 cycles. But besides this, by a proper arrangement of microphones among orchestra or singers, musicians were no longer forced to crowd about the horns and much larger assemblages were possible. The process, borrowed partly from the telephone and partly from radio, was a means of saving the phonograph industry at the very moment when radio threatened to destroy it.

Today, phonograph recording is done under natural conditions, in concert halls or specially designed studios. The performers are at their ease and, in comfortable positions can, naturally, play or sing better. The recording apparatus catches so many fundamentals and overtones and the phonograph, also equipped with amplification tubes and volume control, reproduces them so faithfully that expert musicians are nearly satisfied. Today the

[11]*Fortune,* Sept., 1939, p. 74.

phonograph has come into abundant use in the music schools and is acknowledged as valuable to practicing musicians.

It was only when an amplification device was added that the phonograph became useful to the cinema. And it was only through amplification that the photographic record of sound on film or the reproduction of that sound in a theatre became practically possible.

There will be, in its proper place, a history of this invention and a detailed description of it.[12] For the moment it is only necessary to know that its function is to step up a variable current by the addition of electrons from an outside source. With it, the electrical impulse into which a whisper is translated gains the strength of that representing a loud shout without amplification. Such strong impulses can perform many tricks with mechanical things like record gravers or light shutters which weak, unmagnified impulses could never achieve.

6

Edison has often maintained that the phonograph first drew him into motion pictures and historians have usually believed this. It has been suggested that Edison, deaf himself, "gave eyes to the phonograph" because he could never get full satisfaction from mere listening.[13] At any rate, the two ideas soon got together in his mind.

In 1894, he synchronized a phonograph with his peep-show kinetoscope and provided earphones. The illusion that the little figures were talking was good enough. The voices were small but so were the pictures. It was only when these pictures leapt upon the screen that the people in them acquired a magnitude out of all proportion to the sound that even the largest horn could give forth. Here, too, in a theatre, came the acoustical problem. As there was no means of delicate volume control, sound could not be adjusted to the size of the theatre or to its acoustical qualities. Edison's experiments, therefore, were all failures once the movies had graduated from the peep show.

An examination of these experiments will, however, correct a

[12]See p. 46.   [13]Ramsaye, 74, 75.

popular error. Many people believe that the talkies were delayed by the difficulty of synchronizing the phonograph with the moving film. Yet this difficulty was overcome by Edison as far back as 1894, and good synchronization was mastered by him and by others in later screen projection. The problem was entirely one of volume control.

When amplification arrived this difficulty disappeared. It is true that much experiment was still necessary in the placing of microphones in the studio and the arrangement of loud-speakers in the theatre, but the basic obstacle was gone. Its elimination in the Bell Laboratories made possible the evolution of a complete system of sound-on-disc synchronization with motion pictures. This, after much effort, the telephone people were finally able to lease to Warner Brothers in the spring of 1926 at the low point of the cinema cycle.

Movie magnates had little faith in sound at that moment. They had seen the earlier failures and the explanation that the radio tube had revolutionized sound performance was far too technical for a movie magnate's mind. The Bell people had been peddling their wares for some time with no success when Mr. Sam Warner was at last persuaded to attend a demonstration. Because he attended it in the company of some of the bankers who were at that time pressing him and because these bankers, having none of the old-time movie producers' prejudices, were electrified by what they saw and heard, he agreed to try it out.

The whole story of the first Warner "talkies," involved as it is with finance and with public caprice, is fascinating in detail. It will, one day, all be told. Meanwhile, the main facts with which we are concerned here are, first, that the Warner sound pictures using the synchronized phonograph plus amplification had an immediate and overwhelming success which brought the silent film to its quick demise, and, second, that, instantly, a competing method revealed itself. This method has a history of its own.

In 1817, Jöns Jakob Berzelius, a Swedish chemist, found that the metal selenium varied its resistance to an electric current when light was thrown upon it. Resistance decreased as the light became more intense. This meant, of course, that the stronger the light the greater the volume of current.

About sixty years later, Alexander Graham Bell based an in-

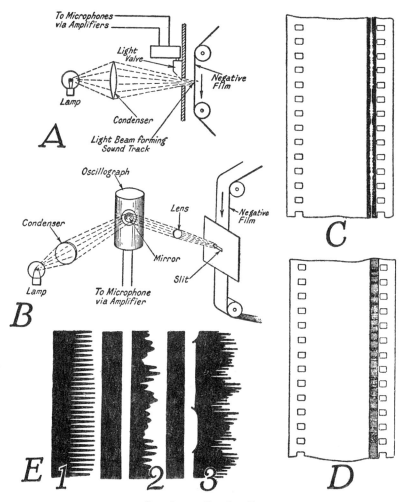

Sound recording for film

A. Variable density recording—the light valve. B. Variable area recording, or better described as "variable contour." C. Variable area positive. D. Variable density positive. E. Example of photophone variable area sound track showing different complex wave form: 1. Bicycle bell, 2. Orchestra, 3. Woman's voice

vention upon this property. The invention was the "photophone," a side step in telephone invention. A diaphragm transmitter when spoken into caused a pivoted mirror to reflect light on and off a distant piece of selenium through which a current was flowing. The flickering light, by varying the selenium's resistance, produced fluctuations in the current and these fluctuations were translated back into sound by a telephone receiver tied into the circuit. Here was a kind of wireless telephone. At a distance, the speaking voice was heard; the distance was bridged not by wires but by a beam of light. At about the same time Francis Blake managed by a mirror device to make a photograph of sound on a moving plate. He made, however, no attempt to translate the photograph back into sound.

Eugene Augustin Lauste, a Frenchman employed for a time in the Edison invention factory, but, later, working independently in France, seems to have spent much of his time between 1888 and 1906 working out a system by which sound could be recorded photographically on a moving film and, from this photograph, run through a kind of projector so that it varied the light thrown on a selenium cell. This projection process caused the same kind of fluctuations as Bell's photophone and Lauste translated them back into sound. Here were all the elements of the final invention of sound-on-film. Yet the invention did not work for any practical purpose. The nigger in the woodpile had not yet showed himself.

The nigger was the radio amplification tube. It was precisely the same nigger that was needed to make the sound of the synchronized disc phonograph fill a theatre and the same nigger that was needed to make an adequate track on the disc. Nearly twenty years was required to bring this fugitive out into the open. The desire to make photographs talk might never have been great enough to accomplish the revelation. But the desire to transmit sound over distances without wires was stronger. Thus amplification developed, slowly, as we shall see later through the study of radiotelephony. Once it was applied to Lauste's photography of sound on film, the talkies arrived.

There are several methods of photographic recording. There is no basic difference between them and they are all simple enough in fundamentals. In them all are four essential elements. One is a varying electric current whose variations are determined

by sound. Two is a tube amplifier which magnifies these variations. Three is a mechanical trick moved by these variations to
throw more or less light upon a moving sensitive film. Four is
the light itself.

In the "variable-area" method light is reflected by a galvanometer mirror on a fixed slit behind which moves the film. A
galvanometer is, in its simplest form, a needle which moves little
or much according to the strength of the current passing around
it. If a mirror is attached to the needle, the mirror will move
little or much according to the strength of current. As the mirror
moves it throws a beam of light on the fixed slit, and this light
covers much or little of the slit depending on the strength of the
current. As the varying strength of the current is a translation
of sound waves, a sound record is made on the sensitive film.
Remember always that if the mirror is to give a faithful reproduction of sound variations, these must be magnified by an amplification tube.

In the "variable-density" method there is no mirror. The light
is focussed directly on the slit. But here the slit is movable. An
amplified variable current moves it by means of an electromagnet.
The slit becomes wider or narrower according to the strength
or weakness of the current. The result on the sensitive film behind the slit is a series of lines all the same length but of varying
thickness. The variations in thickness and thinness of the lines
compose a record of sound.

In reproducing this sound record, a German invention called
the photoelectric cell has replaced the piece of selenium. This cell,
instead of varying resistance, generates a current which varies
in strength according to the amount of light thrown upon it.[14]

To reproduce from a sound film, a positive film is first made
from the negative made as above. This positive is then run between a light and a lens. The lens focuses the light on a photoelectric cell. As dark portions of the film reduce the amount of
light falling on the cell, the cell in turn generates less current.
The variable current generated in this way is now amplified and
is translated into sound by a telephone receiver.

[14]This is the familiar "electric eye" which opens doors, gives alarms, etc.

357

By photographing sound, then, at the same time that images are photographed sound record and visual record are synchronous. They are not, as is commonly supposed, made on the same film. For convenience they are made on separate films. Thus in a studio sound is transmitted to a sound room from the stage microphones, and the sound film is made there while the visual record is made in the camera on the stage. Afterward the two films are combined by photographic printing so that the film that is run through the theatre projector carries the sound track on its margin. The visual projector and the sound projector are encased together. The variable current is carried to loud-speakers (glorified telephone receivers) placed at proper points in the theatre. Thus the perfect illusion that the figures on the screen are speaking, singing or playing the sounds which issue from these loud-speakers is carried out. It has become possible by amplifying devices. These inventions have also made volume control possible so that the projection operator may vary the volume of sound according to the size of the audience and other acoustical factors.

7

The introduction of sound to the movies not only altered the effect of the pictures on the screen but it profoundly altered the studio. The tricks by which extraneous sounds were kept out were developed with the utmost difficulty. The word microphone implies an instrument which takes a small sound and makes it big just as the word microscope implies an instrument which does this to an image. Thus the dropping of a pin on a studio stage may be loud when the record is reproduced. An airplane passing overhead may befog a speech. Today, in spite of the most meticulous efforts, twenty or fifty "retakes" are often necessary because an alien noise has crept in during the "shooting."

The visitor to a Hollywood "lot" will be impressed by the occasional blasts of police whistles that issue from the studios. They mean that all noise in the vicinity must stop. Thus men will be seen everywhere with hammers poised in their hands, ropes will stop moving in their blocks, engines and motors will be shut off.

Only the passing airplanes, so far, are beyond control in these cities within a city.

The Hollywood personnel underwent a complete change. Stars who could register every emotion through grimace or gesture were found inadequate in voice and out they went. New stars were borrowed from the stage. Plays, too, were taken, altered, of course, to fit formulas and technics, the Broadway success was bought at an even more fabulous price than the story had been, adjusted to mass production and produced. The assumption persisted that raw material must be bought (like cotton or iron), for no one in the cinema business has ever assumed the possibility of artistic creation—from scratch—within the industry.

In this way, the magnates of the movies have performed an inestimable service to literature and the drama. In scale, they are by far the greatest patrons of letters that can be found in history. In this respect they are an uplifting influence that the other patrons of this art can scarcely approach. The manufacturers of gum, motor cars, roofing, laxatives, who support the magazines make certain demands on the vehicle of literary mass production which the captains of cinema never even suggest. To write for the mass-production magazines, an author must modify his standards and his material. It is often hurtful to him to distort his forms to suit the taste of three or four million readers. But when the movies buy his stuff it has already appeared in its perfection, with no lowering, no deformity; critics and esoteric readers have seen it pristine as it emerged from the creator's purest consciousness. Then, after its full acclaim as a work of art, it is bought for an enormous sum, run through the mass-production tooling, not by the author but by a proper mechanic, and turned out for the masses in their desired mold. The author, realizing his payment, is able to use it for the devotion to true art; he assumes no responsibility for the distortion of his story, he suffers no mental depreciation from its adjustment, the public enjoys a new film on a familiar pattern, the producer makes money and every one is happy. The fact that the producer could do this same job inside his own shop for a fiftieth of the cost and without buying anything has never occurred, as far as we know, to any one in the business. And we have not the slightest hesitation in setting forth this fact in print, for we have tested the literacy of these gentlemen by an abundance of simple experiments.

As the movie, through sound, drew nearer to the play, critics began to wonder whether it had ceased to be a special art form. Talk in the higher intellectual brackets had just begun to be serious in this connection toward the silent film when sound destroyed it. Truly, the soundless movie had seemed to be an unprecedented vehicle. Here was the unlimited appeal to the fancy of pantomime plus all the tricks of the camera. In the close-up of a subtle actor it seems possible to watch the process of thinking. The faintest gesture will send the spectator down a long, lonely corridor of his own thought. The observers of a silent film may be profoundly creative. Even with an excess of "titles" they must supply most of the dialog.

But the great public has chosen. It has elected sound. Potentials are still high in photographic beauty, in color, in variety of sets. Something has been lost but much has been gained. If the film has moved a little out of the province of art, it has advanced as a medium of education, of description, of propaganda.

As a news vehicle it is, undoubtedly, threatened by television. In the dramatic field this menace still seems far away. A community sense is highly necessary to full dramatic enjoyment. Even the radio has been obliged to provide synthetic audiences in its studios when drama is attempted that the laughter and the applause may be heard. It is probable that with the full visual and audible effects of the stage the theatre will still be desirable. And there must continue to be some means of escape from the home, some community center, unless we are to return, after all our effort away from it, to the subsistence farm.

The story of the cultural phase seems to end here. To approach what has been perhaps the most dominant impulse in our later history—the impulse of speed—it will be necessary to go back a few years and, before we are through with it, to look ahead.

Part IV

SPEED

Chapter Sixteen

ROADS AND RUBBER

ERHAPS it need not be said again that transportation is a *sine qua non* of civilization. It is a curious paradox that without it no appreciable static society can exist. A study of transportation in America, for instance, reveals the use of Indian trails by the European invaders, but their preservation as monuments of civilization depended upon their ultimate use, not as mere paths of movement but as tributaries to static centers. The trail of the nomad leads only one way: to him what is behind is exhausted, he never follows his footprints back. When men first go back upon the trail they have tramped it is to carry something which has been left behind to men ahead, and such behavior implies a static center at one end.

The pioneers of the Iroquois trails traversed a route which could be adapted without prodigious effort to a highway for wheeled vehicles. Along it, white men static in Holland or semi-static at the mouth of the Hudson had taught red men to transport mountains of furs. These Indians, under the remote control of civilization, had chosen the way easiest for their naked feet and burdened backs. The pioneers of the Ohio had picked a way on which at least rafts of supplies could follow if, indeed, the rafts must be broken up and built into shelters at the end of the journey. But neither boat nor wheel could follow the pioneers of the Cumberland Gap without prodigies of adaptation.

Daniel Boone began his trace by cutting direct through the wilderness a path for pack horses. He made detours round the larger trees, but having no thought of wagons did not consider grades, and for many years only the second stage of transportation moved over the Wilderness Road that followed his trace. He came to an Indian path—a war trail—and continued along it with relief, widening it for the pack animals and droves of cattle which would follow and turned at last into a "street" made by the forever moving and gregarious bison. His road was of fundamental importance to the settlement of Kentucky and hordes of migrant folk, moving often in church congregations led by their pastors, travelled over it, driving their cattle, carrying their full supplies in packs on mules and horses. The women went along with the men, and the babies jounced in willow baskets fastened to the packsaddles. These were hardy people, moving thus into the wild lands without wheels.

Wheels existed behind them. In 1755, Franklin had assembled a hundred and fifty wagons for Braddock's unhappy expedition, many of them drawn by four horses.[1] About the same time the Conestoga wagon made its first appearance in Lancaster, Pennsylvania. The wagons were used, however, in these early years only for transport over short distances and in the East. Except for stages running between the large cities of the East such as Boston, Philadelphia and New York, wheeled vehicles were used almost exclusively for the transport of goods, not of people. Men and women walked or rode horses. To drive in a carriage in the eighteenth century was an indication of immense wealth or of physical incapacity.

As Hilaire Belloc points out in his pleasing philosophical essay on the subject,[2] the vehicle creates the highway. Thus, on the Atlantic fringe where business demanded the stagecoach between cities, some effort was made to keep up the roads. The true art of roadmaking was unknown to Americans of the period as, indeed, it was in most of the world since the Middle Ages, when the great Roman art was lost. The best they could do was to use logs in the worst places or fill the deeper holes with sand. Even so, there were periods of the year when overland travel was quite unthinkable.

And, in the West, long after the Conestoga wagon had been adapted to steep grades and mud, the pack horses persisted. This

[1]Franklin, "Autobiography," in Smyth, *Writings*, I, 398 ff.
[2]*The Highway and Its Vehicles*, London, 1926, p. 14.

was partly the result of violent commercial opposition reaching the point of what we should call racket—already showing its ugly head early in the nineteenth century. The pack-horse men had organized. Magnates owning as many as a thousand animals and supplying equipped pack-trains for long journeys fought the wheel with all the bitterness that a modern union fights labor-saving machinery.[3] This helped to keep the Wilderness and Cum-

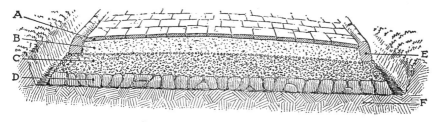

Cross-section of Roman roadway

A. Wearing surface of stone slabs. B. Layer of pounded bricks, tile and lime. C. Rubble.
D. Bottom layer of stones. E. Curbstone. F. Natural undersoil

berland roads and many other routes into the "promised land" virgin to ruts for more than a quarter of a century.

2

The wheel (except in machinery) was confined, therefore, largely to the great static centers. In New York, Philadelphia and Boston the rich and great drove about in equipages which would be regarded as highly uncomfortable today over streets paved with great labor and doubtful skill, and a few enterprising promoters managed astonishing feats of coach and ferry transport from center to center. The postal service into which Franklin injected the first germ of speed laid out a highway route which is still maintained.

Since the fall of the Roman Empire the political and economic position of the highway had been doubtful in many parts of the world. The military need of roads has drawn government attention to highway construction in war time, and dominant rulers like Napoleon have caused government money to be spent on them. In intervals of peace and democracy, however,

[3]Dunbar, *History of Travel*, p. 194.

this burden has fallen upon municipal and county governments, individual landowners or directly, by toll, upon the traffic.[4]

In the vague new United States with its rampant freedom, individualism and angry local jealousies, there seemed to be no way of determining who should pay for the roads. The Continental Congress had voted money for the construction of such military highways as were needed in the Revolution, but no appropriation was made for their maintenance when the war was over. Private capital was spent on the stagecoach roads, some government money went to the maintenance of postal routes and towns paid for their own paving. In a few instances, state appropriations were made for highways: these were always inadequate. The first practical solution of the problem was the turnpike with its levies on the traffic—an imported invention.

From the beginning of the nineteenth century, the turnpike idea spread rapidly. For some thirty years the turnpike companies offered alluring investments to private capital. The roads themselves were bad enough, the rates were high, there was bitter resentment against the system among poor people seeking a promised land, but they furnished the first medium for the covered wagon when settlement in the West began in earnest.

The roads were bad. But consider the difficulties. Here was a virgin country, a forested wilderness. No ancient civilization had flourished upon this land. The cut forest with its pulled or rotting stumps yielded only mud—rich, fertile mud to be sure, but forbidding to the wheel. Only when it froze was overland transport possible, and we must remember always the immense quantity of winter transport which aided our northern settlement. So, in America, the lost art of roadmaking must start from the very beginnings from which it must have sprung on the Campagna marshes.

So it seems to us from our distance as we look across the abyss between. Looking into the abyss, then, we find that Americans did not rediscover that art; that it came, when it did come, from Europe. We approached it, timidly, tentatively, appalled by the

[4]Even in the Roman Empire, the *viæ viales* were made and maintained largely by private capital. J. W. Gregory, *The Story of the Road*, London, 1931, p. 69.

distances. In the 1820's there was real agitation for good roads. In the early thirties many states had highway commissions and state money had been appropriated. Even the Federal Government, emboldened by its dominant attitude toward the western lands, was interested in road improvement. There was real promise of vast activity in highway development. At this point arrived the railroad and stopped the whole of it.

The iron road did, in fact, kill the necessity. That part of the country which was still unsettled continued its settlement along the railroad. The railroad made a gigantic effort to reach those parts which were already settled. Americans became so proficient in railway construction and capital was so drawn to it that all the efforts succeeded. The horse-drawn vehicle was adapted to short distances and was made more comfortable for human transport. But the need of long, surfaced highways disappeared. The rails provided them, and over the rails the steam-drawn trains moved at terrific speed.

The highways, then, fell into natural desuetude, lapsed back into mud and forests. The turnpike companies folded up and were forgotten. Capital, all turned into the railroad and the static centers it had created, could no longer be interested in roads—corduroy, plank, or even, when they arrived, asphalt and macadam. This condition persisted throughout the century and well into the next despite the howls of occasional teamsters, buggy drivers and the late vociferous roar of the cyclists.

It was hardly surprising, then, that the horseless vehicle, demanding a smooth surface for its driving wheels, came into use not in America where mud and wilderness had been conquered by steel, but on the ancient paved foundations of the Roman Empire.

3

On such roads in England in the early nineteenth century one of the inventors of the locomotive was lured to experiment with self-propelled vehicles. Here we find Richard Trevithick in 1801 carrying a load of passengers over a "common road." In 1824, William Henry James produced a practical passenger coach accommodating twenty persons and, five years later, made a second one which attained the astonishing speed of fifteen miles an hour. By 1830 Goldsworthy Gurney was making steam road vehicles commercially. Six years later Walter Hancock established a bus route with steam carriages and, in five months, made more than 700 trips, covering over 4000 miles and carrying some 12,000 passengers.[5]

The other experiments in England, like the abortive earlier attempts of Cugnot in France and Evans in America, have been described in detail in many histories of transportation and histories of the automobile.[6] By 1865, such steam carriages were so common on the English highways that they were regarded as pests, and Parliament passed a law which virtually ended them in England so that in the following thirty-five years (until the law was repealed) automotive experiment was transferred to the Continent.[7]

To us, however, these monsters hardly seem the ancestors of the modern motor vehicle. But for the fact that they ran upon a road surface rather than upon rails they resemble our automobiles no more than the locomotives of the period. To us the true parents of the automobile seem rather to be the internal combustion engine, combining in its cylinder both fuel and energizing vapor, and attaining thus the essential principle of lightness and, at the moment when the pneumatic tire was attached to it, the bicycle.

Without the great discovery which happened to be made by Charles Goodyear in 1839 and the inventions which followed it, the modern automobile is inconceivable. We may think of other means of power than the gas or oil engine. Steam produced on the "flash" principle did operate light engines in motor cars for a number of years. Electricity was also successful (and is still in use) for short distances. But without rubber neither these vehicles nor the roads they moved upon could have long survived. Without rubber, indeed, we should have done better to stick to the steel rails.

[5]James Rood Doolittle, *Romance of the Automobile Industry,* N. Y., 1916, p. 10.
[6]See Classified Bibliography.
[7]Charles R. Gibson, *The Motor Car and Its Story,* London, 1927, Chap. V.

As far as we know this elastic substance enclosing still more elastic air was first extensively applied to the wheels of bicycles. The bicycle, thus equipped, had a far larger social significance than is usually credited to it. It introduced the first idea of individual speed and was the first inexpensive means of rapid individual travel. It brought a medium of exercise which was simultaneously healthful and pleasurable to millions of

The first velocipede

Evolved by Pierre Lallement from an old draisine or "hobby horse" by adding axle-crank and pedals to the front wheel

people. It began, in America, the new agitation for good roads which has culminated today in our great highway system. Besides the pneumatic tire it introduced certain technical principles which were carried on into the motor car, notably ball bearings, hub braking and the tangential spoke. Its makers found it possible to adapt their machinery easily to the manufacture of motor cars, so that we find a number of bicycle industrialists among the first automobile makers.

The bicycle, like its offspring, demanded a reasonably smooth road surface. It originated, therefore, like the automobile, in Europe.

4

The child, mounted on his hobbyhorse, has for centuries imitated the motions of riding. When the horse was mounted on rockers he felt the up-and-down motion of a trotter, when it was mounted on wheels he could achieve the horse's horizontal motion by pushing it forward by striking his toes on the ground.

The hobbyhorse was taken seriously by adults when two wheels, mounted in the same vertical plane, replaced the horse's body and the saddle was hung between them. This machine, invented by a German named von Drais and called, when it was manufactured in Paris, the "Draisine," originally arrived in 1779.[8] It was the first step toward the bicycle. It incorporated the principle that a rotating body tends to preserve its plane of rotation. It had a large vogue in Europe when, by 1816, the cessation of the Napoleonic wars left time for such pastimes and it reached New York some three years later. It was propelled exactly as the child propels his hobbyhorse, by striking the toes upon the ground. It expired, perhaps because this motion was too exhausting.

After it there was a long interval in which there seems to have been no effort toward reviving the bicycle. It reappeared, again in France, in 1855 with a crank and pedals attached to the front-wheel axle. The credit for the invention is disputed, though it is probably due to Pierre Michaux.[9] From this point, the front wheel grew larger and the rear wheel smaller, until we arrive at the "vertical fork" of 1879, the appalling machine used by our grandfathers. That our generations were ever born attests the hardihood and skill of our ancestors in the early days of the "cycling" sport. In spite (or perhaps because) of its danger and notwithstanding its difficulty of propulsion, except on level ground or down hill, this machine really started the bicycle craze which grew to such mammoth proportions after the assembly of inventions by William Pope of Hartford—quite naturally called "the safety."

The safety bicycle had wheels of the same size and used the sprocket and chain invented by a Marseillais named Rousseau.[10] It gradually developed its diamond frame of steel tubes, its spring fork, its comfortable leather seat until it became essentially the bicycle of today. Meanwhile, the pneumatic tire arrived.

The double property of air tightness and elasticity has made rubber one of the most valuable materials in the world. Soon

[8] *Journal de Paris,* July 27, 1779.

[9] Mitman, Smithsonian *Report,* 1934, p. 337.

[10] Mitman, *op. cit.,* gives H. J. Lawson, England, as the maker of the first "safety," p. 338.

after Goodyear perfected the process by which it could retain these properties, an Englishman named Robert William Thomson first used their combination for road transport. He invented what is virtually the automobile tire of today; an inflated rubber inner tube in a fabric or leather shoe, in 1845. That it had almost no use is evident from the fact that John Boyd Dunlop, an Irish veterinarian, reinvented it in 1888 with no knowledge that it had ever existed. Dunlop's patent was for a bicycle tire. In spite of the doubtful validity of this patent, Dunlop, with a capital of twenty-five million dollars, carried his company to success and his tires to the markets of the world. Even in America, where the Dunlop patent was held invalid, competition was not successful until the coming of the automobile.

Here we may look at the series of steps through which the pneumatic-tired vehicle moved to create the highway. To begin with, the nature of the road suggested the tire. English roads were often hard, but they were rarely smooth. The elasticity of inflated rubber absorbed some of the shock caused by the uneven surface. But once the tire became universal on bicycles, another of its properties became evident. This was its gripping effect due to the many small vacuum cups produced by the pores of the rubber as they come into contact with the road surface. As the tire makes this contact, its own surface enlarges, acquiring (but only at the point of contact) the effect of a broader tire. The theoretical result of this was greatly increased speed on the level and increased power through lessened loss of motion on the grades.

This theoretical result, however, became a practical result only upon a smooth surface where the vacuum cups had a chance to do their work. On loose gravel, or on an uneven, pitted road, there was either lost motion or failure to grip. So it was soon evident to the cyclist that a smooth, hard road was essential to the bicycle's efficiency.

The bicycle's possibilities were soon appreciated by Americans. Here was a new instrument of freedom, a magnificent medium of individual expression. The crowding in trains was a collective matter, repellent to the rugged pioneer memory. The horse, for instance, for individual transport had become, since the advent of the railroad, something of a luxury. He must be expensively maintained. He required space or he must be rented from the livery stable, and he was not usually so hired for the transport of a single person for recreation, or a casual errand.

The potentials of the bicycle were intoxicating. It could be kept in some eight square feet of space. It required no upkeep beyond occasional oiling, cleaning and small repairs. On it, one could be as free as the air to escape from one's friends, or to assemble with them, to explore the farthest reaches of the countryside, to know new beauties, to go what seemed unlimited distances at speeds governed only by gravity and surface, to come and go, somewhere, nowhere, at a boy's will. For every one, it was new youth, new health and a new world. It was fully in key with the quickened collective tempo, yet it was essentially, ruggedly, frenziedly individual.

The grown child has overshadowed the beauty of the parent. The motor car, providing the same expression intensified to a point where, like all concerted individual expressions, it has threatened its own independence, has blotted out the fine memory of its sturdy predecessor. We forget, today, the vigorous freedom of the bicycle age when women shed the cumbrous paraphernalia of their lewd disguise, paraded, for so long, under the pretense of modesty, when boys and girls learned companionship with the obbligato of physical work and fresh air, when hidden worlds opened to city-confined souls and the gypsy trail came anew to life.

It was not long, nevertheless, before it was obvious in America, at least, that the gipsy trail would require the attention of Mr. John Loudon McAdam, before it could perform its new function. The ingenious Scot was long dead, when rubber first encountered the morasses known as roads in the United States, but his practice which had brought a renaissance of highways in England was known here. It was a matter now, first of mass desire, secondly, of organization, and finally, most difficult of all, of finance.

To charge a cyclist toll would have defeated the inherent value of the invention. To tax him for the possession of his bicycle was unthinkable in a nation which resented the most necessary taxes. Any organization of cyclists was naturally a democratic and impecunious institution. These organizations did acquire, however, a certain political power from their very size and they presently turned their attention to state agencies.

When we consider the extent of the vogue—the quantity of recreation, camping, racing, "nature" and other clubs which

Amenities of the Erie Canal tow-path
From Thomas Stevens' *Around the World on a Bicycle*, Scribner's, 1887

sprang up, the use of the bicycle for pseudo-scientific expeditions, for police, in the army, for messenger service, for mail, for newspaper delivery and as an adjunct to the telegraph; the long-distance competitions, the road races, endurance contests and an infinity of other matters—we may understand this power. And for finances there were, of course, the manufacturers, who saw the necessity of highways to the extension of their business.

There began, therefore, one of the first great campaigns of mass propaganda (in the sense in which that phrase is used today) that the nation had seen. Unlike the earlier collective drives, morally and negatively motivated like the anti-liquor and anti-vice crusades, this one was practical, positive and realistic; it had, moreover, the force of youth (today the object of such extensive ballyhoo) behind it. Indeed, the bicycle might be looked on as the wedge behind which followed the armies of sport, physical culture, fresh air, girth control, but most of all, triumphant if not flaming youth, which have inundated us ever since and may be observed at their apex in the barelegged processions and carnivals of the totalitarian states.

It is interesting to observe all the familiar propaganda machinery blooming in the nineties; posters, newsprint, mass meetings, societies, committees, lobbies, funds—all for Good Roads. The press took up the cry of the knickerbockered men and bloomered women, and several states revived their highway commissions as a result. If the bicycle craze had continued, it would have brought much change to the highways. The most we can say is that it began the changes; it fertilized the public mind, made people, as we should say, "road conscious," constructed the machinery through which later powers, with a more stable and certain industry behind them, could operate. The propaganda lapsed with the lapse of the bicycle enthusiasm at about the turn of the century at which moment the eyes of the country were turned, with a mixture of curiosity and contempt, upon a new machine.

Curiously, the road propaganda was opposed by many of the farmers. To them the bicycle had the "city-folks" curse upon it. It would bring these aliens into the sacred farm country. It would draw the boys and girls from the soil. It would do something mysterious to hurt the agricultural tradition. Most alarming of all, it might bring taxes down on their heads—taxes to pay for the sport of the city-folks. They opposed good roads with some success.

They continued to urge their poor beasts to strain at mired wagons, content to struggle through the mud if it would offer resistance to anything new-fangled. Their conservatism was ages old the fight of the farmer against change is a tradition whose beginning we can scarcely trace. It is, to be sure, a corollary of much of his strength.

Yet the machine had already entered the farm. One of the devices was a thresher run by steam. Even in the seventies this had been accepted on the farm. This machine was pulled along the roads as a trailer to the engine that ran it. The engine was self-propelled, it looked like a locomotive, it moved slower than a man could walk, but when the harvest came the countryside turned out in excitement to watch its snaillike progress from farm to farm.

There is a story current that a particular twelve-year-old boy, sweating on a Michigan farm and tortured meanwhile by a mechanical flair, was thrown into a frenzy of excitement by the sight of this monster, neglected his work and followed it for days, unwilling to let it pass beyond the reach of his eager and speculative eyes. Legend has it that his name was Henry Ford.

And Paris gave us this
Parisian bicycle costume of 1895
Scribner's Magazine, 1895

Chapter Seventeen

DEMOCRACY AND DISPERSION

I

A VISITOR to Detroit, if he has the confidence of a manufacturer of motor vehicles, will be shown two cars, standing side by side. To the visitor they appear identical.
The main difference between them, the manufacturer will explain, is that one sold off the assembly line for $700, while the
other cost $70,000 to build. The answer is that one is an experi-
mental car built, over a period of many months, by hand. The
other is the outcome of the experiment: it is one of three or
four million products of machine tooling designed to follow the
pattern of the hand-built car. Its assembly, from bare frame to
motion under its own power, took twenty minutes.

Between these two cars stand two Americans, Eli Whitney
and Henry Ford, and a symbolic figure called American Democracy. Each of these figures has a story which, inherently, is so
inextricable from the fabric of American history that we are
perennially amazed at the capacity of historians to separate the
threads. It must be a laborious performance. Yet separated they
are, year after year, as new histories of the United States are
presented to children and adults, to the schools and to the
libraries: histories of wars and politics, international relations
and economic theory, histories of settlement, charters, revolution,
territorial expansion, migration, slavery, union, reconstruction,
tariff, income tax, urban trend, female franchise and World War
minus the story of Eli Whitney and minus the story of Henry
Ford.

Democracy is explained by declarations, constitutions, bills of rights and representation in Congress, but rarely by printing presses, bathtubs, automobiles and radio. The gap between theory and fact, between the blueprint of the mold and the emergent cast, must be supplied by the student and seldom is. The result is a categorical society; and the rigid classification, in our minds, of its various departments is one of the bases of our social unease in the fifth decade of the twentieth century.

If, in the next quarter century, American children become adults without learning the true story of Eli Whitney and his "American system," it will be a far greater educational lapse than if they have failed to encounter the Webster-Hayne debates or have forgotten both the date and the cause of the Missouri Compromise. It is not our province here to give way to emotional hyperbole on such matters but whoever knows that story will forgive our statement that it is a crying shame, an evidence of lazy neglect or gross misunderstanding on the part of our educators that ignorance of it is still so general. For it is an American story, weft for the warp of our dominant national traditions and should be far more appealing to the sturdy young American realist of today than half the nonsense that is told of Betsey Ross, the Boston Tea Party, Grant and Lee at Appomattox, the explosion of the *Maine, "nous voici Lafayette"* or even Ben Franklin's everlasting kite tethered as it is by its spurious moral string to so many American school books. The story is easily available[1] and has even been removed by some writers from the gigantic shadow of the cotton gin, an invention of comparative technical insignificance. It needs frequent retelling.

We shall not retell it here. Its importance to us at this moment of our interpretation derives from its concern with the basis of that mass production of machines which has levelled our standards of living. Whitney, of course, was not planning a physical democracy when he designed his system of interchangeable parts manufacture. Nor did he intend to bring the artisan era to a close by substituting jigs and patterns for the artisan's fallible eye and hand- or power-driven machine tools for his handicraft. The

[1]*M.I.M.*, Chaps. XII and XXII and documentation therein. Joseph W. Roe, *English and American Tool Builders* (2d ed.), N. Y., 1926, Chaps. XI, XII. Burlingame, "Eli Whitney's Second Invention," in *Scribner's*, May, 1938.

fact was, simply, that there were not enough artisans to do the job that had to be done. The demand was for muskets in quantity and the American phrase "in a hurry" had already crept into the language and into the temper of government, if not of people. Gunsmiths had begun to drift west. Had all the gunsmiths in the country been assembled in New Haven and had they worked twelve hours a day they might have filled a government order for 10,000 muskets in two years, but to assemble them would have been impossible for Whitney or anybody else.

But even had they been so assembled, a division of labor on a mass-production pattern such as was in use in the textile mills of England would not have sufficed for the production of fire-arms. Firearms were machines. The parts must fit one another. Had ten men been set to work on barrels and another ten on each part of the lock there would never have been an assembly of parts, for each part, made by eye and hand, would have been faintly different from any other. Gunsmiths fitted these parts as they went along. Each gunsmith, therefore, in such a gathering as we have suggested, would have had to finish one complete musket by himself—barrel, lock and stock—before he could begin on another.

The jig is a translation into wood or metal of a thought. A tool, moving through that jig, multiplies the thought into hundreds of exact replicas. A ruler crystallizes the thought of a straight line. By drawing a pencil along the edge of the ruler, the thought may be identically reproduced in infinite quantity. The eye has here disappeared as a factor. The trembling, uncertain hand has been rigidly held by hard, shaped matter. Expand this simple process, add power, out goes the human muscle and before you stand the mill of Whitney and the plant of Ford.

From the suburbs of New Haven to the suburbs of Detroit, the path of the American System is straight enough in theory. It took Americans more than a century, however, to travel it. On the way, ignoring orderly geography, we shall meet the factory of Samuel Colt at Hartford, those of Wheeler and Wilson in Connecticut and of Howe and of Singer in New York and the plant of the McCormicks in Chicago. We shall meet, also, ore deposits on the edges of Lake Superior, foundries at Pittsburgh, Trenton and Bethlehem. Somewhere along the road, that symbolic wraith, the spirit of American democracy, will begin her march beside us.

Many economists give as the reason for our industrial leadership of the world the abundance of our natural resources. But this is also true of Mexico and Russia, of Bohemia and Spain which only recently, if at all, have had extensive industry. Russia's late achievements would have been still later but for the application of American methods, while in Mexico most industrial development has been under American ownership and control. In none of these countries, except perhaps in late Russia, do we find the same kind of impulse moving through mass production and there it is a synthetic impulse engendered by an enforced ideology. Czechoslovakia, in her brief republican interlude, may have felt it, though only a fractional exploitation of resources resulted.

This peculiar impulse must be added, then, to complete the cause of American supremacy. What is it? We may find a hint of it in the Declaration of Independence and a plan which considers it in the Constitution. In Eli Whitney's time, however, it was still far from social fact. Yet, in the time of Henry Ford, it is not only a social fact but a dominant one.

The automobile was invented, in all of its essentials, in Europe. So were the electric motor, the Diesel engine, wireless communication and many other things which are commonplaces in America today. In the late nineteenth and early twentieth centuries most basic mechanical inventions were European. Many of the tools which have worked so successfully through Whitney's jigs came from Europe. We should expect, then, to find in Europe, the home of all these products and producers, the greatest volume of production.

Yet figures on the production of motor vehicles demonstrate that the United States makes more than seventy-five per cent of those produced in the entire world. If we include Canadian assembly of American-made parts, the percentage rises to eighty. Other high percentages can be found in the production of refrigerators, vacuum cleaners, washing machines and other units dependent upon the electric motor, not to mention radio receiving sets and oil engines. How can this paradox be resolved?

Deeper inquiry shows that, in Europe, there are artificial restrictions on these products. In one way or another, they are kept out of the hands of the masses. The automobile, for instance, is heavily taxed, as is its fuel. In most countries the radio set is taxed. It never occurs to the peasant or factory worker to have electric refrigerators, washing machines or, indeed, electric current in his home because tradition says that such things belong to the upper classes. It is a source of constant wonder to Europeans visiting America to see these perquisites adorning the homes of those living within the lowest-income brackets. The assumption is that all Americans are rich.

This is neither a true nor an adequate answer. A closer approach is found in the assumption of the Declaration that all men are equal. It took, however, a long time for the people as a whole to interpret, realistically, this premise.

One of the most powerful aids toward such interpretation was the cheap press. The penny newspapers not only reiterated the proposition that all men were created equal, but they proved it by making the news (a luxury) available to everybody. This remarkable achievement was made possible by mechanization. The newspaper was a mass-produced commodity which not only spread an ideological propaganda, but carried inherently a demonstration of democratic opportunity. Further, it became a vehicle of advertising and the implication was that any one who could read could buy. This was not true, but the combined influence of equality-inspired potential consumers and advertising managers worked upon the manufacturers to make it true.

The wilderness had, of course, contributed to this evolution. To some extent it had levelled the classes. Whatever might be said of innate equality, or whatever might be felt, in the tighter groups, about economic equality, equality of hardship and equality of opportunity were obvious in the wild lands. There was fertile soil, therefore, for the seeds scattered by the press, and the press, moreover, was levelling in the urban centers where

380

European class distinctions and a European contrast between rich and poor still dominated.

In all these things we see what the late vernacular calls a "build-up" for the story of Henry Ford. In spite of financial inequality, the belief of every citizen that he was somehow as good as the "next man" was communicated to the manufacturer who discovered that he had been looking through the large rather than the small end of his telescope and, reversing it, he saw visions of colossal profit. What he saw, in fact, was socialization, not by distributing the means to buy goods, but by distributing the goods at a minimum price. At his hand stood the pattern of the machinery—a pattern drawn not under a democratic impulse, but under duress of labor shortage. The manufacturer used it to promote social democracy.

Immediately he discovered an economic fact which was incidental to Whitney's necessity. Cheap production on Whitney's pattern means quantity production. In theory, the more you produce the cheaper each individual article becomes.[2] In the artisan age, this theory did not hold true—at least from the point of view of the artisan. It was set in motion by the machinery of mass production—by jig-or-pattern-actuated, replica-producing machines. Under this motion there was, at the same time, enough for every one at a price which almost every one could meet. Given a large market, there was also profit for the producers.

That is why so many inventions have moved from Europe which invented them to America where no class is restricted in their use. That is why the motor vehicle, for example, has remained a luxury in Europe and become a necessity here. There are, as always, other factors. Class restriction is dominant. Alterations have been made in the European class patterns—readjustments along the lines of parties, occupations, inheritance—but, in one way or another, the tradition holds.

We must move, now, into our immediate inquiry and discover what happened when the elaborate assembly of inventions we call the automobile met the mass-production system. The impact has changed the face of our country.

[2]Certain limitations have, in the later enlargement of industry, been imposed on this theory.

Stripped to its bare essentials, the motor vehicle consists of an internal combustion engine, a clutch, transmission gears, a propeller shaft, a differential mechanism, two drive wheels, brakes, two steered wheels and a device for steering them. As an external essential we must add the pneumatic tire. It is not desirable to consider other prime movers than the internal combustion motor for, though the electric motor depending on chemically generated current had a large vogue and the "flash" steam engine a long persistence, only the gas-driven vehicle has survived as a social factor.

Nearly all of these essentials were probably invented in Germany by Carl Benz during the last two decades of the nineteenth century.[3] The pneumatic tire preceded Benz as we know and so did the internal combustion engine, though before Gottlieb Daimler worked on it, it was scarcely adapted to automotive transport.

We need not be surprised, therefore, to see, by 1894, a highly workable car issuing from the shop of Panhard and Levassor in Paris and various contraptions appearing simultaneously on the streets of Detroit, Hartford and New York. England, at this moment, seems to have been still champing at the bit imposed by the Road Locomotive Act of 1865 which required a man with a red flag to walk in front of any automotive vehicle and this law is usually offered by Englishmen as excuse for their slow progress in the field, compared with continental Europe.

The Panhard car of 1894 bears a surprising resemblance to the modern vehicle. In it we see the forward engine, the V arrangement of cylinders, the cooling jackets, the gear box, the gears and the differential, the steering mechanism, the hub-brakes and the separation of body and chassis by elliptical springs. The intervening changes include the multiple-disc clutch, electric lighting and, most important of all, the application of a new metallurgy to all parts.[4] They include, also, the improvement of every funda-

[3]There is an animated controversy here which we shall evade.
[4]See Chap. XXII.

mental device, especially valves, ignition, brakes and tires and radical alteration in body design.

In view of the existence of such a car at this date, it is astonishing what a series of abortions were necessary in America before we had worked out anything approaching its basic effectiveness. A museum of these monsters seems to indicate that, even in the 1890's, we were still in the trial-and-error stage of invention. It would be well, however, to remember again the state of our roads before we judge ourselves too harshly. Again, the cheapness of oats helped conservatism.

It is also curious that at that late period when our study of communications and news shows these matters to be well advanced, so many inventors were working in parallel without contact between them. Hiram Maxim tells in his entertaining little book[5] of how he proceeded naturally from work with explosives to the epoch-making invention of the gasoline automobile in 1892. "I was blissfully ignorant," he writes, "that Benz and Daimler in Germany; De Dion, Panhard and a host of others in France; Napier and a few others in England; Duryea Brothers, Haynes, Apperson Brothers, Winton and others in the United States were working might and main on gasoline-propelled road vehicles. . . . As I look back, I am amazed that so many of us began work so nearly at the same time and without the slightest notion that others were working on the problem."

One American inventor would have been ahead of them all had he demonstrated his so-called invention at the time he first applied for his patent. This was George Baldwin Selden, a patent attorney who, by 1879, had reduced the weight and increased the power of the Brayton[6] internal combustion engine and had drawn plans for a vehicle to be propelled by it. Having applied for his patent in this year, Selden's legal astuteness got in the way of his mechanical enthusiasm. He thought it would be desirable to see a market before he got the patent.[7] In 1895, when the patent was issued after a sixteen-year delay, others had demonstrated

---

[5]*Horseless Carriage Days*, N. Y., 1937.
[6]George B. Brayton, Boston, Mass.
[7]Ralph C. Epstein, *The Automobile Industry*, pp. 277, 278.

their vehicles. His famous patent, however, caused plenty of trouble up to the year 1911 when the court found (apparently to every one's surprise) that the infringers were using the Otto and not the Brayton engine.[8]

By 1895, Charles and Frank Duryea, Ford and Elwood Haynes had built gasoline-driven buggies and tried them out on the road. These, like all American cars for several years to come, followed the bicycle and the carriage in their design. They were "horseless carriages" indeed. Some even had whip sockets in the dash (used, no doubt, when the horse was so frequently called to their aid). The engine was mounted in the rear or under the seat. The wheels were bicycle wheels connected to the engine by chains. Steering was by tiller. Mudguards were not usual, windshields were undreamed of. The first Ford buggy is said to have reached a speed of thirty miles an hour.

The one essential which was found on all cars, regardless of design, was some sort of differential mechanism. Without it, the drive wheels could not make a curve. In turning, it is necessary for the outside wheel to move faster than the inside one. Indeed, the inside wheel must come to a stop in a sharp curve. Any one who has ever worked in the old army infantry drill will understand precisely the action of the wheels of a car as a turn is made. At the command "squads right," the right-hand man in the squad's front line stopped marching and marked time; he acted thus as a pivot. Various devices were used to accomplish this on the horseless carriage. In the chain-drive cars, the differential mechanism was on the divided transverse shaft on which were the two sprockets that drove each wheel separately. With the longitudinal shaft which eventually became standard, the divided rear axle and a simple, bevel-geared device making a double connection between the shaft and the two parts of the axle became universal. It was soon found necessary to house this in a case packed with lubricant.

The clutch was a necessity imposed by the gas engine. A motor driven by explosion is not subject to the delicate control

---

[8]Columbia Motor Car Co. *vs.* C. A. Duerr and Co., 184 *Federal Reporter,* 893. The Selden patent was the basis of a powerful "combination."

possible with steam. In the first place, the engine will not start unless the flywheel is turned over to bring about the initial compression of the gas mixture without which explosion cannot take place. Obviously, the wheels must be disconnected from the engine during this process. Next, the engine cannot overcome the inertia of a static vehicle if the connection is direct; it must be, therefore, through reducing gears. The ratio of the gears must again be changed before speed is possible. Finally, the motor cannot adapt itself to a suddenly increased load and the gears must change again for hill-climbing and braking. The more elastic performance of the steam engine eliminated all transmission mechanism as well as the initial cranking and this convenience maintained the popularity of the steam car. It was driven out at last when the self-starter, improved motor flexibility, greater safety and, more important, increased power without increased weight brought the gas vehicle into the lead on almost every count.

The automobile developed a "craze" long before it had any use except by the rich and by them only as a toy. It was a curious theoretical craze of the sort that, in the twentieth century, derived from much newspaper reading on sports, aviation and other matters. Many an ardent baseball or boxing enthusiast rarely sees a game or a fight; he gets his thrill through communications of the event. Recently he has been able to hear the cheers of the crowd at the moment of action; he approached that point at the opening of the century in voluminous news stories not too long after the event.

Boys and young men, women too—for the bicycle had brought them into such realms—read avidly of the doings at Newport, where a Whitney or a Vanderbilt was daringly experimenting with the nameless new machine. A magazine called *The Horseless Age* racked its editorial brains in the search for nomenclature. The English "autocar," "automotor" and "petrocar" were classified as "abominations," and the American "motocycle" and "autocycle"—note the strong bicycle influence in America—were little better.[9] The editors had prophetic vision about the term

[9]*The Horseless Age,* Vol. I, No. 3 (Jan., 1896), p. 2.

"horse-less carriage," and, indeed, the magazine's own name went by the board when horselessness was no longer a novelty.

Promoters like Ford and Duryea were quick to see the value of the craze, vicarious as it was. So were newspapermen. Playing on the growing frenzy for individual speed bred by the bicycle, races were staged and largely attended. Scoffers with equine jibes may have been in the majority but serious mechanics, engineers, scientific experimenters were also on hand, together with that strong vanguard of every late technological advance, a group of intensely serious boys, a goodly lot of whom would one day be promoters and engineers.

Herman Henry Kohlsaat, publisher of the new Chicago *Times-Herald,* was the first to see the value of a race and he put one on at Chicago on Thanksgiving Day, 1895. It was run through the city streets in melting snow. A Duryea buggy won it, going over the 54.36 miles of course in seven hours, thirty minutes, including accidents and repairs. This race is said to have proved the superiority of gasoline over steam and electricity,[10] though in later years doubt of the validity of the proof must have entered the public mind as races were so frequently won by steam-driven vehicles until, finally, they were put off the course as dangerous. Kohlsaat's first American race had been preceded by the two French races, the Paris-Rouen in '94 and the Paris-Bordeaux in '95 and crystallized in America the excitement aroused by these events. From then on, American races were as frequent as the financial depression of the late nineties would allow and in 1900, American cars were competing for the James Gordon Bennett trophy in France.[11]

Gasoline cars, however, did not immediately assert their superiority over other automotive vehicles in the public mind or market. Between 1896 and 1899 electric cabs and delivery wagons were doing business in New York and other places, steam vehicles were being sold but gasoline cars were not yet being manufac-

[10]Arthur Pound, *The Turning Wheel,* the story of General Motors . . . 1908–1933, N. Y., 1934, p. 37.
[11]*Ibid.,* Appendix I. For steam arguments, see Thomas S. Derr, *The Modern Steam Car and Its Background,* Newton, Mass., 1932.

tured for the market.[12] In 1899, *Cassier's Magazine* reported that a hundred cabs, twenty wagons and from thirty to fifty private vehicles were operating by motor in New York City and that 90 per cent of these were electric.[13]

These steam and electric wagons and carriages did, however, pave the way for gas-car supremacy. They got men (and horses) accustomed to the automobile. It is possible that if these strange anomalies had not looked so provocatively horseless they would have alarmed the horses less, for steam rollers, not as suggestive to the horse of his absence, were looked on in the early asphalt age as necessities. By the fourth or fifth year of the new century, automobiles (the word, like so much of the automotive nomenclature—chauffeur, garage, chassis, came into our language from the French) were no longer novelties or surprises. The horse jokes had been worn pretty thin, the vehicle was creating the highway ahead of it and so moving, timidly at first, out of the city streets; monstrosities, carriages, bastard bicycles were being abandoned for the new (imported) form and the manufacture of the gasoline motor car had been organized.

It is this which must concern us. Stories of the early days of motor transport are alluring enough. Nothing is more fascinating than reminiscence of an era which preceded a revolution. The automobile brought the most profound social change which has ever occurred within a single lifetime. But for us the social implications lie in manufacture; in the peculiar rhythm of democracy and mass production—a rhythm with which no other nation dared ally itself and which has made the United States (with all the attendant faults and pains) unique in the world.

Hero-worship is no part of our business. The genius of one protagonist, however, stands irrepressibly forth. He was no inventor. He was a promoter pure and simple, acutely gifted with understanding of machines and men and their relationship together. His economic touch (in practice) was sharp and sure. His mind, provided he kept on the spectacles of his Idea, saw the full circle of the horizon. He dealt as intuitively with masses

[12]U. S. Bureau of Census, *Manufactures,* 1905, IV, 278; Clark, *Hist. Manufactures in U. S.,* III, 158.
[13]Vol. XIV, p. 599, Sept., 1889, cited by Clark, III, 158.

as with details—masses which blinded, deafened and suffocated other men. He had a sense of motion, of relativity, of continuity which bewildered many an imitator into defeat—as long as his spectacles were on. Once he took them off, he became myopic beyond belief. This with his ruthlessness—but all such men are ruthless—won him derision and enemies. Opinions of him have differed bitterly. By amassing a fortune of incalculable repro-ductivity, he has earned the malice of many men. This is to be expected in any plutocracy with such sonorous democratic over-tones as ours. It need not concern this record.

Our concentration is upon the phenomena of the automotive revolution. Of these he was probably the greatest.

<h1 style="text-align:center">3</h1>

On a farm in the township of Greenfield, some fifteen miles by modern highway from Detroit, this boy grew up. The Civil War was on full blast at the moment of his arrival. These were good farming days and William Ford was deeply attached to the land. Henry's drift from agriculture simply repeated the per-formance of hundreds of American mechanics. He was an obedi-ent, well-disciplined child, but farming and power machinery simply did not go together. When the machine moved into his foreground, Henry had no will to disobey; the machine simply excluded other matters from his mind. The story of the steam tractor[14] is utterly in character. It is easy to picture the boy under its compulsion. His eyes mirror the complete exclusion. Farm, father, duties, animals, simply vanished; the piston moved reciprocally in its cylinder, the steam blew from the valve, the wheels turned, not on the machine, but in his head. His feet moved in reflex like a dog's feet following its master, a mystic's feet following his God. There was an interval when, catching him in a broken connection, his father brought him back from mechanisms, but Henry did not respond to the germ of life in the ground; he set up a sawmill on a fallow acre and his mind worked in the machine.

[14]See end of preceding chapter. Ford tells the story in his autobiography, *My Life and Work*, written in collaboration with Samuel Crowther, N. Y., 1922, pp. 22, 23.

There is no need to waste time on Ford's watches. Like all mechanical boys he took them apart. He repaired them for neighbors. It had nothing to do with his career. What did concern his career was his thought, in his late teens, "that I could build a serviceable watch for around thirty cents."[15] This was the passion that consumed him. It was not, in the usual sense, an inventive passion. "I wanted to make something in quantity."[16] He had long thoughts in those days. He watched labor and saw the result of labor—on the farm, at least—and the ratio was wrong. Somehow machines must be got to working. He started to make a tractor that would pull a plow when it occurred to him that more people would want to buy a car to run on a road. That was the decisive factor with Henry. The longest thought about human labor and human waste could always take its place in the background, when, immediately before him, came a sense of what more people would want. These thoughts stayed, however, in the back of his head—a little torn, a little out of joint from the interruption—and once he had built a car he built a philosophy from such remnants. The car works better.

He built his first in '92. Externally it bore no resemblance to a modern car, Ford or otherwise, being a buggy on bicycle wheels. It had a two-cylinder, four horsepower engine. He drove the car a thousand miles or so, sold it (for $200) and bought it back in the days of his greatness for a museum piece. He built it while he was still with the Detroit Edison Company where began, perhaps, his worship of Thomas Edison. He left the job when a number of enterprising men who approved his car started the Detroit Automobile Company to make it. Henry was chief engineer and a stockholder. He seems to have disagreed almost at once with the others. "The whole thought was to make to order and to get the largest price possible for each car."[17] As Ford's whole life philosophy was to make nothing to order and to adapt public taste to his own, it is not surprising that, in 1902, three years after the founding of the company, he was unemployed.

For three years he "investigated" engines in his little hired brick shop and business on the outside. His economic conclusions

[15] *Ibid.*, p. 24.   [16] *Ibid.*   [17] *Ibid.*, p. 36.

were more remarkable than his technical ones. Usual financing, he found, hitched the cart in front of the horse. Money was borrowed, the interest became a charge on the business, refinancing became necessary, money came before work instead of the work furnishing the money; thus money emphasis came to predominate, the concentration of businessmen was upon stock and bonds instead of on production, and the crescendo of financing was reflected in the cost of the product—the consumer had to pay. This was all wrong: the product was really the important thing, its price must include service to the consumer rather than service by the consumer to the company and every effort of a producer must be toward lower prices.

Whether Henry Ford in the interval of his investigation actually thought all this out or whether part of it was contributed by his later experimental practice, the fact is that in the prime of his career he antagonized many old-school business people by reversing the nineteenth-century formula. From his first production dates a change in point of view. To give him the whole credit would be to erase from history a multitude of potent factors such as government investigations, public resentment roused by exposures like those of Mr. Sinclair and Miss Tarbell, anti-trust enforcement and, indeed, the ever-growing impulse of social democracy. The fact remains, none the less, that his experiments were successful beyond belief and that his contribution to the whole new mass-production pattern was the greatest that has yet been made. He played, of course, into the social democratic impulse at its apex and the public welcomed him with open arms.

It is significant that his autobiography omits all mention of such men as Thomas Malcolmson and James Couzens, who financed and managed the Ford Motor Company at its inception. Without these men, says Leonard, "his name would still be associated chiefly with an unsatisfactory method of crossing a river."[18] This is a historical "if" which might be applied anywhere. Men like Ford find such helpers. There were plenty of Malcolmsons in the country. Ford fought them afterward with his stubborn faith. They left him and he forgot them. His forgetfulness was probably wishful—financing was not in his philosophy

[18]Jonathan N. Leonard, *The Tragedy of Henry Ford*, N. Y., 1932, p. 20.

in any case. Once it was over his faith went on. There were, after all, only $28,000.[19]

Ford's thought moved toward the production of a single model. His collaborators carried him through most of the alphabet, but his faith won out with Model T in the end. In the interval, A, B, C, F, K, N, R, and S were experiments and concessions. He knew the publicity value of speed and conceded it contemptuously in "Arrow" and "999," driven to victory by the daredevil Barney Oldfield. The races were potent factors in the "craze." They put Ford in the headlines. He smiled, perhaps spat, in scorn. These were means to an end. The end was a tough, serviceable, standardized, cheap, middle-class vehicle which "every one" could own. Racing was in the luxury brackets, the sporting parenthesis—sectors of life which Ford despised—but he knew how far those brackets stretched in newsprint, he understood the vicarious fever. Through luxury, then, to necessity, through anything to utility; if he must gain the public confidence by first flashing a toy, well and good. That, at least, is his own story and no one yet has told a better one.

With confidence and money, with the control which it was his first effort to acquire, with his opponents out and the great one-man-show moving toward a dictatorship of which any totalitarian leader might well be proud he was ready for what he calls Production. Production, Ford believes, had never existed in the world before. With the magnificent contempt of men immune to history, he disregards all predecessors: Whitney, Evans, Colt, Singer, McCormick, the whole chain of patient, laborious workers who wrought his assembly lines and all the ramifications of his processes out of the void of the handicrafts. In a colossal blurb printed in the *Encyclopedia Britannica* under the guise of an article on mass production, he writes: "In origin, mass production is American and recent; its earliest notable appearance falls within the first decade of the 20th century," and devotes the remainder of the article and two full pages of half-tone plates to the Ford factory.[20]

Production of the great "T" began in 1909. Frankly designed

[19]Ford, *My Life and Work*, p. 51.
[20]13th Edition, supplement, XXX, 821.

as a utility car, it adroitly followed the oldest Puritan conventions. To overcome any stigma of luxury or pleasure it was made, deliberately, ugly. It was black. No gaudy colors were allowed. No sparkling gadgets. It had not even the dignity of a suit of "store clothes"; it was not a Sunday car, it was a workday car. Gaiety or beauty meant harlotry to Henry Ford and so they meant to the great mass of the pre-war bourgeoisie. Let the sports and the millionaires have their gay vehicles along with their gay women; these were neither the desires nor the perquisites of sober workaday Americans.

The scheme fitted splendidly with the standardization necessary to mass production in the era. Ford would make one model for the rest of time. This one fitted the public: no more experiments were necessary. The market was infinite. And so, indeed, it seemed at the time. No mind in 1910 could conceive of a saturation point. Even twelve years later, after five and a half million cars had been produced, Ford could not imagine a limit. Suppose every family did have a car? There was no reason why they should not have two or three apiece.

There were many things, however, in 1910 which no one could imagine. Wars, revolutions in morals and taste, prosperity, depression, new shuffles and new deals were not in any handwriting on any wall. Americans had little knowledge even of their own history, not to mention world cycles. There was scarcely any self-consciousness. Trends were left to erudite thinkers with thick spectacles in ivory towers—men as alien to the bourgeoisie as they were to the barber. The arts were esoteric if not effeminate. The familiar modern practice in which locomotives, commercial buildings, vehicles or water-closets are designed by artists had not been dreamed. Even the irrelevant rococo decoration of such matters during the Jim Fisk period had been abandoned for "chastity." Useful things were naturally ugly. To beautify them would be to cast suspicion on their utility.

Outside the social, Protestant churches which were concerned almost wholly with practical ethics, matters of the spirit were in the discard. Literature was still suspect. Philosophy meant making the best of things. Music was as yet immune to vulgarization.

DEMOCRACY AND DISPERSION

The higher education had not yet gone into mass production. It was a safe, sane world for the Model T.

In 1914, Ford became a popular hero. Not yet dreaming of the strange antics he would perform a year and a half later on the *Oscar II*, he dreamed only of industrial humanity. On January first, he announced profit-sharing in his plant. Crystallizing in a minimum daily pay of five dollars—a fantasy beyond belief until it was seen in operation—this threw the entire American industrial world into a tail-spin from which it recovered only when it followed his example. He aggravated the distress by installing the eight-hour day.

The public did not share the industrial vertigo. To newspaper readers of the bourgeoisie and even the suspicious proletariat, he became a god. The inflation has since been assiduously punctured. We are not greatly concerned with the controversy as to purity of motive, chicanery or subterfuge. Ford himself admits that the move was preceded by instability of labor in his plant though he does not concede, as Leonard charges, that this instability was forced by revolt against the stultifying effects of assembly-line production.[21] The charge has been made that the minimum pay promise was never, in fact, kept; that Ford took advantage of his rule of a six-months' apprenticeship before profit-sharing to fire men and rehire them as apprentices.[22] Other critics contend that the increase was compensated by a speeding up of machinery —an implication that we shall touch on presently. But for us the only importance of the new wage-scale is its advertising result.

Ford became an idol of the most popular sort, evidence of which was the universal good-natured "kidding" or "joshing," as it was perhaps then called. For six years, this is said to have taken the place of all paid advertising. No show was complete without a "Ford joke." Such jokes were the currency of smoking compartments, saloons and, with modifications, drawing and sitting rooms. The name Ford came into the language with a small f and proceeded thence into the language of the world. The result was profit, production, more profit, lower prices and social democracy until, at last, the fickle public under the strange

[21]Leonard, *op. cit.*, pp. 25 ff. [22]*Ibid.*, p. 29.

393

"immoral" influences of European entanglement, education and prosperity, forced the hero on the threshold of his old age to turn his back on lifelong principles.

The story of how the beloved "Lizzie" became a painted woman has been told too often and too well to need reiteration here.[23] The stream line (now streamlined into a single word) will be discussed more fully later along with the sinister implications of the Turn-in Vogue and its corollary, the Used Car Problem. The fact is, the public of the middle twenties wanted variety, beauty, convenience, speed, gadgetry and "class" in its vehicles. Ford, in making his car a necessity, had got it into the hands of many people who could no longer bother with its primitive and breakable mechanisms. Prosperity contributed to the public reluctance for overalls as a concomitant of automotive transport. Whether this public impulse initiated the demand or whether Ford's competitors presented the answer before the demand was articulated is a nice question.

It is a fact, in any case, that many improvements were made outside the Ford works during the unchanging life of Model T. The baby giant, General Motors, had been born and had employed a promising inventor named Charles F. Kettering to develop the most revolutionary invention in gas-engine history, the self-starter.[24] Packard had introduced force-feed lubrication, Chrysler had adopted hydraulic brakes, several cars were experimenting with four-wheel brakes, Studebaker had found nickel molybdenum steel, Cadillac was playing with thermostatic control of carburetion, Oldsmobile had introduced the beautifying chromium plating, and steel bodies, hypoid gears, rubber engine mounting and other matters were in existence.[25] Some of them were, to be sure, on high-priced cars. Others presently became possible on the cheaper makes whose producers were following Ford methods. But with the prosperity many more high-

[23]Notably by Leonard, *op. cit.*, in his epic Chap. XV.

[24]The first practical electric self-starter was used on the 1912 Cadillac. It was built upon the work of other inventors, such as Clyde J. Coleman, by Charles F. Kettering. Ralph Cecil Epstein, *The Automotive Industry*, pp. 102, 106.

[25]*A Chronicle of the Automotive Industry in America.* Privately printed for Eaton Mfg. Co., Cleveland, 1936.

priced cars appeared. And Ford's immediate competitors, notably Dodge and Chevrolet, were patterning themselves after the expensive cars rather than the Model T. Men like the Dodge brothers, who had worked in the Ford plant, were using Ford's production methods on which, because most of them were adaptations of early processes, Ford naturally had no patent. So the public turned and, from 1923, the sales of the Model T declined at an alarming rate and to save himself Henry Ford had to change his policy.

4

What are those production methods in use today in every large automobile plant with scarcely any variation? They are simply the methods of Eli Whitney and Samuel Colt, improved, co-ordinated and applied with intelligent economy—economy in time, space, men, motion, money and material.

In the artisan age one man finished a whole machine or a group of men worked together fitting parts and making new ones as they went along. In the early production age this work was departmentalized, so that one specialist completed only one part, its shaping, drilling, painting and whatever was done to it. In the late production age, each worker performs only a single operation. It was once considered mass production for a workman to build a whole spring. A spring as made for a Ford of the 1920's was a complex part. It had seventeen leaves. Each leaf was different. Ford designed a "battery" of men and machines for each leaf, all batteries converging at an assembly point. Upon each leaf thirteen operations were successively performed, each by a different man or machine in the battery. Starting with a steel strip, a man placed it in a punch press for piercing and cutting, a conveyor carried it through an oven, a workman took it off, put it in a binding machine, another put it in a nitrate bath and so on.[26]

As such specialization developed, it was found essential to keep each operator in one place, hence the assembly line. Ford soon

[26]Ford, "Mass Production," in *Encyc. Brit.*, 13th ed., supplement, XXX, 822.

decided that all work must be brought to the workman instead of the man going to the work. This was achieved by the endless conveyor belt. With it, the workman never moves. His job arrives exactly timed, waist high so that he need not bend. He does his simple operation and waits for the next piece of work to arrive. He does not have to wait long. "The man who places a part does not fasten it . . . the man who puts in a bolt does not put on the nut; the man who puts on the nut does not tighten it."[27]

In a modern plant there is not one but a multitude of assembly lines. In plan the co-ordination of these lines looks like the vertebral structure of a fish. Its backbone is the main line on which the car is put together. Leading into this are the motor-assembly line, the differential-assembly line and so on, each delivering a finished motor or differential at the main line at the right moment for its placing in the car. Most pleasing of all to visitors are the last operations of filling the gas tank and radiator and driving the car off the line. The complete job from bare chassis frame to motion under its own power takes twenty minutes, but as the cars are built in endless succession on the conveyor, a car drives off the line every fifty seconds or so. Hence five thousand cars are built every eight-hour day. As each contributory assembly line must keep pace with the main one, the scale and degree of co-ordination may be imagined. A chapter ten times the length of this could not begin to detail the operations, so we shall pass at once to the social implications of such mass production, some of which are sinister enough.

Here is no man-boss watching the men, looking at the clock, telling him to hurry. You may appeal to, argue with, rebel against, or sock-in-the-jaw a man-boss, slave-driver though he may be. You may report him for injustice. But the boss of automotive production is a machine. You cannot pray to an endless conveyor belt. You cannot ask it for permission to go wash your hands or rest. It scarcely occurs to you to ask it to "have a heart." In it are neither heart, justice nor injustice. It brings the job and carries it on to the next man whether or not you have screwed on the nut. If you have failed there is no evasion or

[27]Ford, *My Life and Work*, p. 83.

buck-passing, the failure is self-evident, the next man cannot do his job and the whole line is jammed. One failure and the whole Production is reduced. In the flash of an eye a little sin is magnified a thousand times. Your single failure, in short, has gone into mass production.

Henry Ford says that many men do not mind repetitive motions under a mechanical boss.[28] That is all their minds are good for. The mass-production plant provides work for such unskilled men who would otherwise be jobless. There are other opinions. There is the belief that, if this is true, then mass production keeps the whole human level low. Leonard says that, in 1913, "the trolleys which crawled away from Highland Park at closing time were hearses for the living dead."[29] The mere fact, however, of a mechanical boss does not complete the picture. We must remember that the speed of an assembly line is adjustable. It may be quickened ever so little at a time, without the knowledge of any worker. Men may gradually be pressed thus until the speed harasses them into madness. A manufacturer has, therefore, in his hands, a multiple instrument of cruelty which makes the whip of the plantation overseer look like a gentle rebuke. Whether or not he uses it depends upon a number of things. Production is, after all, his goal.

Ford and other men talk much about humanity, about the beneficial effects of the modern factory upon the lives of the workers. Ford—or his company at least—went so far as to investigate the private lives of his workers to make sure they were upright, wholesome and thrifty and issued bonuses in consequence, though that particular paternalism was later abandoned.[30] In the modern plant of one of his rivals we found such a religious atmosphere, at least among the executives, that no one could give us information without prefacing it by extended remarks about the Deity. We found also a college and a night school in one factory giving degrees and jobs in the higher technological reaches.

There is no question, however, that mass production of motors carries with it certain benefits. New methods have vastly im-

[28]Ford, *My Life and Work,* Chap. VII, 103 ff.
[29]Leonard, *op. cit.,* p. 26.   [30]*My Life and Work,* pp. 127 ff.

proved cleanliness. Ford boasts that a man can visit his tire plant in a white suit and remain immaculate, and the claim is true. Great numbers of industrial diseases have been prevented. Good hospitalization is found to be an economy. Each large plant has a special department dedicated to the perfection of safety devices. Eight-hour days and five-day weeks have become standard—not exclusively, however, as a result of voluntary effort on the part of employers. Fresh air, light, lavatory facilities, drinking fountains (with their accompanying energizing salt pills) abound. The worker comes and goes in his own car. Sometimes he gets off-seasonal work in farming. An annual wage scale has been drawn up to correct seasonal exigencies by several manufacturers.

The miseries may be the result of an intermediate stage. We are moving toward the wholly automatic machine. Men are being replaced at every point by machines. This seems right and not a curse as some social philosophers suggest. We shall develop this thesis further in another place. Meanwhile, in our present intermediate stage it is unfortunate that such ammunition has been furnished the Frankenstein school by using the machine as a boss for men. It is unfortunate but it is a necessary and inevitable step.

We seem to have wandered from the automotive vehicle as a factor in social revolution. Yet the car in itself is nothing—or very little. The mere invention of the automobile did not change the face of the country. It was invented in the eighteenth century and very little happened socially. It came into being in the form we know late in the nineteenth and still, for some twenty years, nothing radical occurred. Nearly every change which can be described as revolutionary came about in the quarter century beginning at approximately 1914: in the third, fourth and fifth decades of our automobile's existence, and considerably more than a century after the first invention of automotive transport.

The reason for this is mass manufacture. Until the automobile came into the hands of Tom, Dick, Harry, Jane and Jill, no revolution took place. That is why we have wandered from the invention itself into other more essential devices.

The trend may have been inherent in the vehicle—inherent but dormant. As we saw, the freedom given to the individual by the bicycle was a powerful American lure. The car placed this lure a step higher. Here and there a Jones bought one—a man as good as the next man, equal under the Constitution and his neighbor's envy grew ripe for such a movement as Henry Ford's. Industries, notably public utilities, took the next step with trucks and busses—all paving a way perhaps, paving it certainly in a more liberal sense. The war was no mean factor. From it we emerged into a new world.

5

America of the pre-war years was laid out, socially, according to railroad geography. Nowhere in the world had the railroad developed to such a point and everywhere were the marks of its culture. The vast system had been simplified and co-ordinated to facilitate long "through" journeys, eliminate stopovers and changes for passengers, route freight efficiently and promote speed. This had necessitated great changes in financial control, close interrelation of managements, standardization of freight rates. The whole industrial system depended on the effective handling of the immense bulk of freight. Without it, mass production on any considerable scale could not exist. Every factory must be on a spur. The perfect interplay of this elaborate system with all its mechanical aids, switches, signals, yards; the essential simplification of the labyrinthic complexity of rail—such things were the greatest achievements of the American genius in collectivity to date. The railroads might well be proud. And the people, always awed by the dignity of the giant rhythmic locomotive—colossal, sonorous, deep breathing, yet supple and flexible as a young athlete—the people were proud of their railroads.

Along the steel lines lay the great congested cities. Like magnets they had drawn the people from the wide pioneer dispersion. Had we, in the late nineteenth century, been able to see the whole land from the high air, we should have watched these little bodies, like iron filings moving in jerks over the lines of the railroad fields toward the magnet centers. Every day the trains disgorged their multitude of bewildered boys and girls, men and women, sick in their souls of cows and corn and spaces, into the iron "deepos" from which a trolley car, harassed by its curves, would carry them into a new life, for better or worse.

Along thousands of spurs, smaller, jerkier trains moved through tens of thousands of small towns and villages. At each of their "deepos" stood a line of sleepy horses, hitched to patched buggies, muddy surreys, hotel stages. Leaning against every post and wall stood the bicycles. Occasionally, in 1910, there would be a strange, high, ugly contraption which the horses eyed aslant, uncertain whether it or the train were more alarming. Yet the train, the horses and the men knew, must stick to the tracks and there was no knowing what the new-fangled thing might do. It was surrounded always by a crowd of curious, prophetic little boys waiting for the moment when a hand would seize its crank and startle it into violent explosion. It had neither dignity nor beauty; it was high, hideous and instinct with doubt.

If, in 1910, we should get into one of the horse buggies, we might drive for an hour over mud and ruts and find, at the end, a moribund hamlet with a decayed church, a few sleeping houses, a square brick school, a general store, a post office containing, perhaps, a telegraph key. There were thousands of these dead groupings, forgotten by the railroad world. In them, as in the isolated farms round about, people lived a life so remote and so monotonous that even the notorious assembly line would have been a relief to them. Indeed, from such places, many men were in constant migration toward the machines of production.

Should we take, instead of the buggy, the "contraption" we should be in for a period of high excitement. Whether "she" would get us home was always a live subject of speculation, though if our driver were a good mechanic there was a reasonable expectation of arrival. As long as she moved, the sense of superiority to other men was acute beyond anything the human mind had yet experienced. The first railroad train bound by its track could have been nothing to it. The thrill of power and freedom in the driver, feeling the vibration and violence under his guiding hand, was intoxicating beyond his own belief.

DEMOCRACY AND DISPERSION

Yet if we were thoughtful on this jaunt, we should have noticed the sharp contrast between our powerful machine and the road it travelled on. The hill roads we forced it up had been made by Indians or pack horses and but for widening had been little changed. Over rocks, shale, gullies, washouts we climb, hoping always, doubting much. On every farm, a team of horses was ready, in those days, to go to the aid, for a consideration, of profoundly mired contraptions. It was an age of increasing profanity and, by 1919, the curses were beginning to be heard in state capitols. Roads, yes, but how?—the question still bounced back and forth.

The thrills triumphed over the curses and the boys saw the vision. It was their future. The manufacturers saw and heard the boys. Their gigantic subsidies started the roads. Governments, under the flood of the license revenues, carried on. So the world changed, hope came to the hamlets, new life came to the farms, new markets to the farmers, the cities heaved out of their congestion and spread over the land. The high, ugly monster passed its adolescence, became a necessity, drew down into a low, sleek panther, a demon of speed—a liberator and a killer, but most of all a leveller—both a creature and an instrument of democracy.

But what then of railroad centralization, of American collectivity, whose story we have traced from its beginnings? What of the city, center of unity? What of congested industry, crowded along tracks, worked to the limit of flexibility?

The landmarks are still there. The skyscrapers and the dwindling curves of the profiles down from their heights are landmarks on our road. The cities are still there, huddled about their factories or their commercial monuments. But already the automobiles are gnawing like termites at the bases of our skyscrapers.[31] A new thing, the Metropolitan Area, has come into being. Once a narrow salient bulged out by a trolley line, this is now a wide circle. Buildings are still huddled but people are dispersed. They have sought the grass and the trees for their children and they have found it. Their work may still be in a center but if

[31]This graphic simile was expressed by Mr. Carl Breer of the Chrysler Corporation in an interview with the author.

they live fifty or a hundred miles from it, it is no great matter.

Forgotten hamlets are thriving towns. The remotest farmer is in touch with every aspect of civilization. Large markets for his goods are reached within the hour. The roadside stand, the tourist camp and the filling station have given employment and profit to millions of once-isolated folk. Education, lower and higher, is available without physical effort to every rural adolescent, not to mention his parents newly avid for "culture." Entertainment is only a few explosions away—a quart or so of "gas." The rustic need not migrate to the city; urbanity has come to him. Knowledge and power sweep over the country. The filling-station man on a peak in the Rockies discusses the week's developments in Europe or in Asia with the visitor from New York, who has had every word spoken in Berlin, Tokyo or London thrown against the background of his urbanity from the dashboard of his car.

This is the surface. Volumes could not articulate the profound subsurface revolution. The new industries which automotive manufacture has brought into being as well as changes in productivity of older industries are only part of it. The new opportunities for employment stagger the understanding when the time element is considered. The future of agriculture will be an automotive result. So will the whole geographical arrangement of society.

Such a revolution in the short space of a quarter century is bound to carry with it its disasters. These are usually in the form of social lag or "hysteresis."[32] Cars run today through the congested streets of our cities, leaving destruction in their wake and severely hampered in their own performance. Hitherto insoluble traffic and parking problems have everywhere been posed. The human lag has caused a sinister total of accidents. The social lag has given to the automobile an unjust preponderance of human rights. The revolution has spread a dangerous and purposeless restlessness. A large part of the people has become migratory without destination. The home has been transferred to wheels. The static domestic background has been dissipated. Sexual im-

[32]See Chaps. XXIII, XXIV.

pulses have moved into gypsy trails and many an illegitimate new-born (if not aborted) may be traced to the cozy freedom of a closed steel body. Crime has grown (though detection is catching up by the same instrument). Democracy has spread by "thumbing" into cool disregard of property rights.

What, now, is the future? Will the automobile complete dispersion? Or will it, as a terrifying exhibit in a 1939 World's Fair portended, be confined, like the railroad, to a new kind of track, a "super-highway," hedged in by barriers of concrete and regimented speed? Will it be superseded at last by something else —freer even than itself?

We have brought ourselves, at this point, face to face with this question. It will be answered, at last, not by us but by the whole of society.

Chapter Eighteen

SPEED AND GRAVITY

I

MAN'S CRAVING to oppose gravity, to leave the peopled earth for empty space, has been, from the beginning, a craving to escape. It is essentially an anti-social desire.

It began, we may suppose, when the first human child followed, with his eyes, the bird's flight. Perhaps even the wishful heart of the ape grew wings as he gazed up through the branches at that creature so far above him in space, so far below him in the evolutionary scheme. So, conscious man, one step beyond, knowing that he could do with his brain what any brute of the earth, the sea or the air might do with its body, must have set to work almost before he could record his thought, to devise his wings.

But the desire sprang, certainly, from some sort of social ennui. "If I could do that," the wish moved slowly through his awakening mind as he watched the eagle, "I could escape the persecution of my fellows. I could be alone when I wanted—perhaps forever, if need be." Thus came the association of wings and immortality, echoed by the poets from Homer to Shelley. As men encountered the difficulties of imitating the eagle or the lark, the anthropomorphists endowed their gods with wings. So, for many millennia, to fly was superhuman, wings were a property of deities and their messengers and thus man's effort to fly became sacrilege. As a large part of the civilized world became unified under Christianity, good churchmen came to believe that invention in the direction of flying would surely incur God's wrath.[1] This belief is still held by many persons with, at the moment, considerable plausibility.

But the fancy persisted, indomitable, and it presently acquired an additional anti-social color when it began to concern itself more directly with the wrath of man than with that of God. The man who could fly would be superior to the man who could not. He would not only escape from persecution but he might, once in the air, devise some means of getting even with his persecutors. If society harassed him, he might, from the air, destroy it. The thought must have been immediate and overwhelming at the very inception of what, today, we call "air-mindedness." "If I could fly, I could kill." It was the way of the eagle, to be sure, yet with a subtle difference introduced by the theme of vengeance.

There was little thought of a community of the air in the human concept. The social purposes of the migratory birds are difficult to discover in the history of aeronautics. The craving of the individual to fly could be answered in full only if other individuals were unable to do so. This may be an explanation of why, in a century and a half, the practice of aerostation remained almost wholly in the realms of sport and war. It may be an explanation of why, in 1940, with aviation in a high stage of development, its visible social effects spread so little beyond the effort of man to dominate his fellows on the field of battle or to spread fear among his human enemies.

This statement will be subject to criticism unless the limitations of its definition are kept clearly in mind. Scientists will point to results in pure science attained by means of the balloon, the airplane or the rocket. We must refer them to the sociologist to explain, if he can, what visible social effects have come from the application of any of these discoveries. Aerial photography may hold rich promise but it has not visibly altered the relationships of mankind except in war. Metropolitan planners will describe the alteration in the design of cities as a result of avia-

[1] "God would not suffer such a machine to be successful, since it would create many disturbances in the civil and political governments of mankind," Francesco de Lana, *Prodromo*, etc., Brescia, 1670, Chap. VI. Translation edited by T. O. B. Hubbard and J. H. Ledeboer, *Aeronautical Classics*, No. 4, London, 1910, p. 26.

tion, but as we examine these changes closely we find that they are largely measures of defense. Its sporadic use in forest patrol, the study of flood prevention, insecticide spraying, topography, the control of volcano eruptions and hundreds of other matters have not yet produced visible results in the relationships, organization or work of any large human group. Its use as transport may have quickened the tempo of life, but with what benefit will be problematical until a need can be shown for such quickening —until, as the wags say, we find out what we want to do with the time we save.

Except in war, population has not been dispersed, industry decentralized, congestion relieved to any visible degree by aeronautics. The airplane and the balloon have never been mass-produced[2] and have therefore played no such democratic rôle as that of the automobile. Except to a handful of the population, they have never even been instruments of freedom corresponding to the bicycle or the automobile. It is reasonable, therefore, to state that the social effects of ascension and flight apart from war are, as yet, invisible and lie, if at all, in the future.

This confinement does not, however, justify us in ignoring the invention, because we cannot ignore war. The social effects of aircraft as a weapon are inestimable. Already they have somewhat altered the social geography of the earth and they bid fair, in the next score of years, to alter it almost out of recognition. Probably no inventions since that of gunpowder have spread more terror through the world or engendered in each human heart a more profound distrust of its fellow. They have emboldened men to lie, hardened them to hate, glorified their theft. With aircraft under their control, traitors to civilization have become supermen, competent to break the laboriously constructed morality of human society. Thus mankind, whose component units had hoped through endless millennia to reach heaven by flying, now finds itself in hell as the result of a highly scientific invention. Surely, in 1940, the old thinkers who held that the wrath of God was forever imminent would have ample

2War brought an approach to mass production in 1939 and 1940 but not for democratic reasons. See *Scientific American,* July, 1939.

justification for a belief that that wrath was loosed upon the world almost from the first moment that men successfully imitated the bird.

Such a solution, however, of the world's depravity is a little too simple. At many points in the story of technology we see new inventions as instruments of good and evil, depending upon the human hands into which they fall. The radio will multiply, and the disc record reproduce, the sound of lies with the same fidelity with which they treat the sound of truth. The film will not jam in the camera because it is made to photograph a falsehood. The automobile will give the same performance in the pursuit of a criminal as in the flight of a fugitive from justice. A high-explosive charge will destroy a hundred lives with much the same exactness with which it cuts a path through a mountain to the benefit of peaceful transportation.

So far, men have flown to their perdition simply because it was their disposition to do so. The disposition was there before the wings. There is, however, behind the flying machine, the subtle factor which we have indicated and which is not present behind most other inventions. The anti-social intent was there uncounted ages before the means evolved. Airships and flying machines answered no social necessity but only the lonely, individual yearning for escape and superiority. Even the bow and arrow, the spear and the gun supplied community needs. The balloon and the airplane did not. To some extent, then, the evil (socially speaking) was inherent in the invention.

We like to think that such dispositions will, in time, be overcome by the operation of those forces in human nature which differentiate us from the animals out of which we evolved. If the evil ambitions of mankind in general are to be overcome, the airplane may find brilliant opportunities in more beneficent social fields.

But, whatever these may be, the fact will remain that, technically, the instruments of aeronautics have developed through their war uses. But for the World War of 1914 and the military incentive it bred, the airplane might have remained a plaything, its main use a dangerous sport. Because its military value was so great, governments throughout the world have heavily subsidized its costly technical development. Because of these subsidies great transport lines today cast their shadows over the entire earth. Because fighting is the most difficult exercise in which a plane may engage, extraordinary mobility has been produced.

While the use of the airplane may be held partly responsible for the 1939 European conflict, it is certain that extremely rapid development in technic will be a direct result of war aviation as it was in the years of the craft's infancy. Indeed the future of aviation will be so largely conditioned by this new war that prophecies are, in general, unwise at the moment.

The whole subject must be approached with caution lest our words be obsolete by the time they achieve the flesh of print. Aviation, at the moment, is in the midst of a transitional stage. The entire trend, technical and social, may change within a few years. We will do well, then, to confine ourselves largely to past history. It is fascinating enough.

2

Before we begin any technical investigation into the past, it might be well to define a few terms. The word "aeronautics" has been used to cover the entire field of air activity. More properly, it should be confined to the use of navigable craft. "Aerostation" usually means the use of free or captive balloons not strictly navigable. "Aviation" applies only to the use of heavier-than-air craft.

Because the bird flew constantly over his head, the mind of man concerned itself, first, with heavier-than-air flight. Until past the middle of the eighteenth century, this sort of thinking continued; then some of the thinkers branched off in another direction. Serious reflection began, at this point, upon the fact that certain things rose without wings. The smoke from a fire, for example, indicated such a rising. The particles which formed the smoke might, themselves, be heavier than the air, but, obviously, they were carried upward by something that was lighter.

So, it was thought, was the water in a cloud. If this lighter-than-air matter, whatever it was, could be captured and stuffed in a bag, perhaps it could be used to lift heavy weights such as a man against gravity.

The first inventors who made this thought fruitful were the French Montgolfier brothers, Joseph Michel and Etienne Jacques. They made a bag out of silk, held a lighted paper under the opening and, presently, up went the bag to the ceiling. Some seven months later, in June, 1783, the brothers, in a public demonstration, caused a paper-lined linen bag of 23,430 cubic feet capacity to rise to a height of 6000 feet.[3]

Apparently the Montgolfiers thought that they had discovered a mysterious new gas produced by combustion. The mystery was given wide publicity. It has been stated by eminent authorities that this view was universal and that "all contemporaneous accounts of the Montgolfiers' work . . . give the credit for the ascension to 'Montgolfier's gas' or, as it was likewise called, *l'air alkalin*."[4] This is not strictly true as two contemporaneous letters from Benjamin Franklin testify. "Some suppose it," he wrote on August 30, 1783, "to be only common Air heated . . . and therefore extreamly rarified."[5] In November he wrote after witnessing a spectacular ascent of a Montgolfier balloon: "The Air rarified in passing thro' this Flame rose in the Balloon, swelled out its sides and fill'd it."[6] This American observer, whose comments have been ignored by several historians, was not so easily fooled!

This November event seems to have been the first man-carrying, free balloon ascension in history. The heroes of the occasion were François Pilatre de Rozier (who had just previously attempted the sensation of going up 84 feet in a captive balloon) and the Marquis d'Arlandes. The safety of leaving terra firma in this manner had already been demonstrated by the Mont-

[3]Tiberius Cavallo, *History and Practice of Aviation*, London, 1785, pp. 45 ff.
[4]F. Alexander Magoun and Eric Hodgins, *A History of Aircraft*, N. Y., 1931, p. 25. The celebrated *Encyc. Brit.*, 13th ed., I, 262, has fallen into this same error.
[5]Letter to Sir Joseph Banks, Smyth, *Writings of Benjamin Franklin*, IX, 83.
[6]Letter to Sir Joseph Banks, Nov. 21, 1783, Smyth, IX, 114.

golfiers to their king, Louis XVI, when, in September, a sheep, a duck and a rooster had risen and descended without serious injury. In the gallery of the improved man-carrying November balloon was a small furnace which the two aeronauts were expected to keep alight by throwing straw and wool upon it and thus renew the heated air. The voyage was about nine thousand yards long, lasted between twenty and twenty-five minutes and ended safely.[7]

The Montgolfiers were aided by tremendous popular publicity. Enormous crowds gathered for the demonstrations (as, indeed, they did to see any marvel of science), and from the spectacular nature of the ascensions their fame spread far and wide. It was, of course, a great era in France. Benjamin Franklin's presence there symbolized the birth of democracy coincident with the awakening of scientific consciousness among the masses.

From this point the technics of aerostation advanced rapidly. The gas, hydrogen, had already been produced and weighed and found much lighter than air. At the same time that the Montgolfiers were working, the French chemist, Jacques Alexandre César Charles, whom we met for a vague moment in the story of photography,[8] was busy filling bags with this gas. The hydrogen was made by pouring sulphuric acid over iron filings. It may be imagined what quantities of these substances and what a time it took to inflate the bag, thirteen feet in diameter,[9] which was used for Charles's first public demonstration. This took place in a rainstorm before a crowd of a hundred thousand on the Champ de Mars, Paris. The balloon, carrying no passengers, leaped up three thousand feet and came down fifteen miles away in Gonesse where it terrified the inhabitants. They thought it an evil animal and fled to the priest for comfort.

This ascension took place on August 27, 1783; four months later, Charles and a friend went up in a similar balloon. Scarcely more than a year after that, Jean-Pierre François Blanchard, a native of Normandy, and J. Jeffries, a Massachusetts physician,

[7]Cavallo, p. 86.   [8]See p. 260.
[9]Actually about 500 lb. of acid, 1000 lb. filings. *Encyc. Brit.,* "Aeronautics," anonymous, 13th ed., I, 262.

SPEED AND GRAVITY

by remarkable luck managed to get themselves blown across the English channel in a hydrogen balloon.[10] From this moment France became air-minded. But the vogue for aeronautics spread abroad soon after. By 1790 ascents had been made in England, Scotland, Ireland, Holland, Germany, Belgium, Austria, Italy and the United States, though most of the "firsts" in these various countries are claimed by the intrepid French aeronaut, Blanchard. In 1793, President Washington instigated a subscription of $2000 to finance a Blanchard ascent from Philadelphia, and it is said that Blanchard asked for a personal letter vouching for his innocence of evil intent which he might show to the farmers among whom he should come down. His English was bad, he explained, and he might not be able to explain why he had descended thus from the skies.[11] A hundred and thirty-four years later, Charles Lindbergh, taking off for France, displayed a similar bashfulness and made his solo flight armed with letters of introduction lest he find himself alone and friendless in unfamiliar Paris.

No American seems to have made a successful ascent in America until 1830, when Charles Durant was blown from Hoboken to South Amboy in New Jersey. By this time the balloon had begun its military career in Europe. During the French revolution, an aeronautical school was founded at Meudon. Balloon reconnaissance is said to have brought French victory in the Battle of Fleurus in 1794, and Napoleon tried it in Egypt. It is possible that the moral effect of this novel device was of more value than any tactical results.[12] For good reasons, the captive balloon soon replaced the free one in military work. It was used in the Civil War when news of the fighting was telegraphed from it. Free balloons returned for a brief moment during the siege of Paris in 1870 for purposes of escape and for establishing communications with the outside world.[13] Sometimes they car-

[10]The American financed the expedition. Magoun, p. 41. For description of the voyage, see Cavallo, pp. 180 ff.
[11]Magoun, p. 45.   [12]*Encyc. Brit.*, 13th ed., I, 268.
[13]This has been said to be the first use of aircraft "to carry human beings from the place where they then were to some other place where they wanted to be and which they could not reach as well by any other means." Edward P. Warner, *The Early History of Air Transportation*. A lecture delivered at Norwich University, Northfield, Vt., 1938, p. 1.

411

ried homing pigeons, which flew back to the besieged city bringing news from without. Captive balloons were extensively used
for observation in the World War and, in the War of 1939, for
air-raid protection.

The balloon first liberated the human mind from the fear that,
until he achieved immortality, man could never rise from the
earth. From the time of the first ascension, imaginations played
with extravagant fancies. It was natural that these should reach
their culmination in the grandiose America of the 1870's. For
thirty years John Wise of Philadelphia had believed in the possibility of crossing the Atlantic in a balloon. In 1843, he had
petitioned Congress for a naval appropriation for this purpose.
In 1873, the New York *Daily Graphic* backed him in his project
and, with a balloon of 400,000 cubic feet capacity, he got about
forty miles on his voyage. After his crash at New Canaan, Connecticut, his backers withdrew. He lived, however, to be drowned
at last in Lake Michigan.[14]

Generally speaking, the free balloon only served to exasperate
by granting half of the human desire. Having risen to the wanted
height, men saw no practical use in it. Far from finding a new
god at this altitude, they met the wrath of their old One in
various forms. They found themselves, indeed, almost completely
at His mercy. Control of their travel was far more limited for
practical purposes than that of the master of the sailing ship,
who at least had learned to oppose the wind. The balloon could
not do this with all the attempts at "oars" and wings which were
made. The aeronaut could only control motion up and down by
throwing out ballast and letting out gas. As such bouncing led
to no particular improvement in either social or individual condition and frequently resulted in disaster, free ballooning eventually found its level as a dangerous sport.

With the passing of the free balloon, aerostation took another
technical direction. As the inventive mind moved from the vertical to the horizontal, the gas bag changed its shape. As power
plants improved upon the ground, attempts were made to lift
them into the air. This led, immediately, toward lightness in

[14]Magoun and Hodgins, pp. 79, 80.

engine construction. The result was the power dirigible and, here again, France led the way.

The steam engine presented a difficulty. It is extremely unhealthful to burn wood or coal directly under a bag containing inflammable gas. There was also the question of weight, for a steam engine requires water as well as fuel. Henry Giffard, a French steam engineer, cut through these objections to the first success ever attained with a navigable balloon. His three-horsepower engine weighed 462 pounds, or 159 to the horsepower, which was light for the period, and turned a three-bladed propeller. It was in a boat hung far below his bag for safety. He was able to travel a little more than six miles per hour when no strong wind opposed him.

Giffard was followed by other experimenters using electric motors with batteries but, until at the beginning of the automobile era, when the Brazilian, Albert Santos Dumont, equipped a dirigible with an internal combustion motor weighing about nineteen pounds to the horsepower, no real practical future for the airship was visible. This was in 1891. Ten years later his sixth ship won a prize by following a prescribed course over Paris, a distance of seven miles in less than half an hour.

Airship invention moved, in the early 1900's, to Germany. At this point we see metallurgy coming for the first time to strengthen the lighter-than-air inventions. Aluminum had just been cheapened by the electrolytic processes of Hall and Heroult,[15] and Ferdinand von Zeppelin recognized that it was the proper structural material for airships. The old invention question is revived as we review the work of this brilliant German army officer, whose early career is associated with American union.[16] He was preceded in the "invention" of the rigid airship. He merely made the first one that would fly.

A rigid airship is one which will not change its shape. It has the disadvantage of retaining this shape (as well as its full size) even after it has stopped flying, unlike collapsible balloons and non-rigid airships, and it must, therefore, be housed or it will

[15]See pp. 517 f.
[16]He was a military observer with the Union Army during the Civil War.

blow away.[17] Zeppelin's ships had an aluminum framework covered by cloth. The bags containing the gas were separate: they were within the structure but formed no part of it. The first ship, the *Luftschiff Zeppelin I*, or *LZ–1*, had two sixteen-horsepower gasoline engines and propelled the ship at the astonishing rate of seventeen miles per hour. For the first time, after Zeppelin's flights had been watched, the public became interested and confident in navigable, power-driven, lighter-than-air craft and capital was soon forthcoming for the foundation of a large stock company for their manufacture.

From this time, however, the airship has had a curiously unfruitful and tragic career. Its undoubted success in the early years of the World War as the first minister of *"schrecklichkeit"* contributed little to the improvement of its own technology. It did much more to improve the airplanes and anti-aircraft artillery of the terrified defenders. The terror it spread was, after all, a shock terror—a fear of the unknown, for it did little enough physical damage. But the fear of these raids was such that an immense amount of energy, men and money was spent on defense. As the Zeppelin operated only at night, and as the only really effective defense came from airplanes, and as aviation was not yet adapted to work in the dark, casualties were not entirely the result of bombs. Because of ignorant terror of a comparatively harmless weapon and the consequent damage to morale, England was obliged to keep twelve air squadrons in continuous readiness at home, not to mention some five hundred hit-or-miss anti-aircraft guns. In the end, however, Germany abandoned airships except for scouting; presumably because they cost so much to build. The loss of one Zeppelin, the *L–33* in 1916,[18] brought down in an air raid over England, represented a money loss of $1,750,000.

Since the war, disaster after disaster has attended the use of airships. They have burned and they have buckled, and the

---

[17]Between these two classes is the "semi-rigid" which tries to keep its shape by means of a keel.

[18]For eyewitness accounts of this and other Zeppelin crashes, see Peter Merin, *Conquest of the Skies*, trans. fr. German by Charles Fullman, London, 1938, Chap. XIV.

causes often have been difficult to spot. The latest ships have been all-metal, of enormous size and have used helium[19] rather than hydrogen gas. The increase in size was an essential to speed. The use of duralumin steel in construction was expected to enhance safety, but no entirely satisfactory mathematical calculation has yet been devised for stresses in bad storms.

The lighter-than-air aircraft still has its strong protagonists. It may conceivably have a brilliant future as transport in time of peace. So far its total social effect was contained in the brief reign of terror in England from 1914 to 1917. The destruction of the *Hindenburg*[20] in 1937, after many successful transatlantic trips, was a terrible blow to public confidence in the airship. After the disaster, the *Hindenburg's* pilot abandoned transatlantic navigation though the *Graf Zeppelin*, which he piloted clear around the globe in 1929,[21] had survived. His reason was that the United States had refused to sell helium gas to Germans.

In strictly military work, which we still take the liberty of distinguishing from *schrecklichkeit* over centers of civilians, small airships have been valuable. They were able to cruise over the water in a leisurely manner, watching the movements of submarines and signalling the news of them to destroyers or even dropping projectiles. For such slow maneuvers the airplane was useless.

3

It serves no purpose to confuse a brief history of air invention by recounting the hundreds of records of man's attempt to fly by muscular exercise. Histories of aviation abound with descriptions and old prints of such human angels flapping their wings and becoming genuine angels only at the moment of crash. These things belong in the lunatic fringe of invention. They are incidents of the long catharsis necessary to rid the mind of the delusion that machinery can successfully imitate the dynamic motions of nature.

[19]Inert, non-explosive, non-ignitable.
[20]By fire. She was using, at the time, hydrogen gas as she was at the end of a west-bound trip. She could not obtain the inert helium in Europe.
[21]Time, 21 d., 8 h., 26 m.

Invention in any mechanical sphere may be said to begin only with the discovery of the principles employed in the machine which finally works. Several balloon experiments have been described because they achieved, in practice, the immediate purpose of the inventor or demonstrated certain technics later adopted in all lighter-than-air effort. Hundreds of others have been omitted (as any aeronautical student will instantly observe) because they did not. A dream is not an invention no matter how many patents may be granted it; nothing, indeed, is an invention except a process or a device which works.[22]

The first true approach to flying was made when attention was focussed on the soaring, gliding and landing of the bird rather than its flapping. For while natural dynamic motion is seldom efficiently imitable by machines, a study of shapes and balances as they exist in nature sometimes furnishes useful guides. Thus a long contemplation of the form of the fish proved valuable to the designer of ships, particularly when he came to submersibles. On the other hand, the motion by which it propelled itself could not be efficiently imitated by machinery. Yet again, the means by which the fish was balanced and steered might well be copied.

The wing-flapping theory was exploded by a professor of mathematics at Pisa. "It is clear," said Giovanni Alfonso Borelli, "that the motive power of the pectoral muscles in man is much less than is necessary for flight, for in Birds the bulk and weight of the muscles for flapping the wings are not less than a sixth part of the entire weight of the body." In man, he explained, the "pectoral muscles do not equal a hundredth part of the entire weight of a man.[23] However the specific calculations of Borelli may suffer from modern analysis, he expressed a truth here which should have influenced experimenters through the centuries which followed. He summed up his study with the

[22]The most complete collection of both dreams and inventions in aeronautics we have seen is the 2-volume picture book compiled by Francis Trevelyan Miller, *The World in the Air*, N. Y., 1930.

[23]Joh. Alph. Borelius, *De Motu Animalium*, Rome, 1680–1681, I, Proposition CCIV. The translation here given is by T. O'B. Hubbard and J. H. Ledeboer, in *The Aeronautical Classics*, No. 6, London, 1911, p. 37.

conclusion which later inventors should have used as a starting point that, "It is impossible that men should be able to fly artificially by their own strength."[24] Wastefully, for more than two centuries, the inventors ignored Borelli and flapped miserably to their destruction. Even the educated German engineer, Lilienthal, late in the nineteenth century, could not rid himself of the error.[25]

Yet Otto Lilienthal, in another mood, was one of the first to make a practical approach to true flying. It is an interesting fact that flying began downward rather than upward. Lilienthal carefully studied natural wing surfaces. He tried to imitate the first spring or leap by which the bird leaves the ground but without success. He resorted, then, to gravity to supply the force for his initial effort. Equipped with scientifically designed wings, he jumped from high places or ran down hill for his start, and the wings supported him in the air. As he encountered the wind he was able to soar—to rise higher than the point of his take-off. The same interplay of wind and plane surface, which enables a ship to sail "into the wind" at an angle with the direction of the wind, sent him upward. This was one phase of flight. But it was not fully controlled flight. When the wind dropped, so did Lilienthal, and his device, unlike the bird, contained within itself no means of rising again. Yet this limited success marked a long step forward. It proved that a heavier-than-air flying machine must move upon and climb upon surfaces of air created by itself. Its resistance to the air forms a compactness of the air below it at the same time that its motion produces a partial vacuum above it. The vacuum tends to lift, the compression prevents falling.

Lilienthal's device was the "glider." It was not his original invention. German effort in this direction had been anticipated in England by George Cayley, who conceived the biplane and first stated the basic principles of mechanical flight, by Francis

[24]*Est impossibile ut Homines propriis viribus artificiose volare possint.* Borelius, I, Prop. CCIV. Author's translation.

[25]Otto Lilienthal, *Birdflight as the Basis of Aviation.* Translated (from *Vogelflug,* etc., Berlin, 1889), by A. W. Isenthal, London, 1911, pp. 3 ff.; see also translator's note in preface, p. vii.

Wenham, William Henson and John Stringfellow;[26] in the United States the sensational glides with gliders designed by John Montgomery and launched from balloons did much to convince a skeptical public of the possibility of safe flight. Lilienthal's machines put into practice many of the principles evolved by these pioneers. The untangling of the intricate history of aviation is simplified by focussing on a few successful experimenters whether or not they "originated" the theories on which their success was based. Interest in heavier-than-air flying in America began with the study of Lilienthal's work; hence our emphasis upon him.

Octave Chanute, whose career in the air began at the age of sixty, was a distinguished American[27] engineer. Unlike most early flyers, he brought a mature mind to bear upon invention. Flying, he said, must be approached one step at a time. Granting that a motor would eventually be incorporated in the flying machine, he did not obscure his thought by this phase. We may mark the stage of the catharsis by the absence of flapping from his mind.[28] He concentrated, instead, on balance, taking off here from the work of Lilienthal. Balance in the air was his first objective. If gliding was to remain a sport, the maintenance of equilibrium by shifting the position of the body of its operator (as Lilienthal had managed it) was all very well. It was natural that such supple, acrobatic maneuvering should hardly appeal to the sexagenarian Chanute. "The bird," he wrote, ". . . is an acrobat and balances himself by instinct, but in the inanimate machine the 'equipoise' should be 'automatic' if possible."[29] He designed a biplane, with a flexible tail and a pentaplane with movable wings. He never got as far as powered flight. His longest glide was less than a thousand feet. His importance to this history is, as an English historian has expressed it, that, in heavier-than-air flying, he "definitely transferred the ascendancy from Europe to the United States."[30]

[26]For original source material, see Hubbard and Ledeboer, *op. cit.*, Nos. 1 to 6.
[27]Born in France, 1832, emigrated when six years old.
[28]Octave Chanute, *Progress in Flying Machines*, N. Y., 1899, p. 259.
[29]*Ibid.*, p. 257.
[30]M. J. B. Davy, *Interpretive History of Flight*, South Kensington Science Museum, 1937, p. 121.

4

Chanute, though he objected to certain of Lilienthal's theories, was enthusiastic about the practical work of this pioneer and included in his book, published in 1899, an appendix containing a translation of a large portion of Lilienthal's writings. Whether or not this book introduced Lilienthal to the men who would finally make a successful powered flying machine, there can be little doubt that it added much to their understanding of, and confidence in, the German experimenter. Chanute's was one of the first flying books the Wright brothers read. Another was the work on aerodynamics by Samuel Pierpont Langley. They learned much from the studies of James Means.[31]

At this point in the history of flying in America we begin to see a curious interplay between the flyers and the public. As Chanute began his work the public mind in the United States was fresh toward heavier-than-air flight or "aviation." The only important gliding which had been seen was that with the machines of John Montgomery, a professor, and it had inspired confidence. The many failures of European wing-flappers and half-baked gliders in Europe were largely unknown here. When Chanute, a well-known, mature, distinguished engineer, after a long career of achievement in his profession, took up flying, the public at large was convinced that there was "something in it." But Chanute was wise enough to leave engines out of his practical demonstrations. His belief that engines could come only after means of stability in the air had been thoroughly learned was sound. His belief that the use of small models could not fully and finally demonstrate practicability[32] was also sound. That this renowned technician succeeded, as far as he went, gave an immense boost to the faith of the people.

But this very distinction, maturity and renown which bolstered public trust in the case of Chanute had precisely the opposite effect in the case of Samuel Langley. Langley was secretary of

[31]James Means, *Aeronautical Manual*, 1894–1897; *The Problem of Man-flight*, Boston, 1894.
[32]Although models in wind tunnels have made possible the accumulation of much data.

the celebrated Smithsonian Institution. That such a man should try to fly attracted country-wide interest. Every experiment he made was followed, especially in the press, with eagerness.

Unfortunately Langley reversed the sound methods of Chanute. He put engines into models. The models were large-scale and they seem to have flown beautifully. From this point, because he had given too little time to practical, man-carrying, non-powered gliders, he built a man-carrying machine with an engine in it. The Government had given him fifty thousand dollars for the purpose. This award plus Langley's renown gave the public a promise that his machine would work. When it failed in such presumably expert hands, the public and the press swung to the conclusion that flying was forever impossible—that it was an age-old lunatic's dream belonging in the same category as perpetual motion. Thus, in an instant, the confidence so carefully nurtured by Montgomery and Chanute was wiped out.

Yet this very collapse gave a singular opportunity to the young amateurs of Dayton, Ohio. Because they were totally unknown, Wilbur and Orville Wright were able to pursue their methodical studies in secret. Before the final debacle of Langley, they were strengthened, in this sense, by every failure he experienced. They were actually assisted by the gossip among the few who saw their early trials that they were lunatics and "not worth bothering with." Even at their first demonstration of success, which occurred nine days after Langley's ultimate failure, not a half-dozen people thought it worth while to watch.[33] After the first success, therefore, which had no publicity, they were able to perfect their instrument over a considerable period of time without the handicaps of ridicule at occasional failures or impatience generated by occasional triumphs.

When the Wright brothers first engaged earnestly in the sport of flying, they asked the Smithsonian for books on the subject. In response they got Chanute's *Progress in Flying Machines* and Langley's *Experiments in Aerodynamics*. The Chanute book included, in an appendix, the important parts of Lilienthal's own

[33]"Although a general invitation had been extended to the people living within five or six miles." *Century Magazine,* Sept., 1908. See *infra,* p. 442 n.

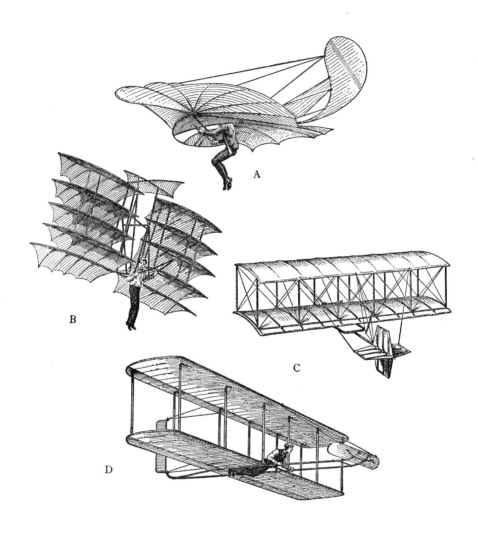

From these came the modern airplane

A. Lilienthal, the great exponent of gliding—in his birdlike craft. B. Chanute "Five Decker" glider, 1896. C. Drawing of truss as Chanute applied it to the glider. D. The predecessor of the modern flying-machine, Wright's glider, 1903. It was from Chanute's glider (C) that the Wrights got their main ideas of construction

writings. Thus the Wrights had for their study the climax of flying in Europe plus the story of how the pioneer Americans had profited by it.

The amateur status of the Wrights has been pointed out by many reporters of their work. Their complete lack of formal technical education, or indeed of any regular education beyond the common schools, has been held up to young inventors as evidence of conquest by trial-and-error as proof that the "school of hard knocks" furnishes the only proper curriculum for an inventive career. This is unfortunate. It dissembles the facts.

"We had taken up aëronautics," they wrote, "simply as a sport. We reluctantly entered upon the scientific side of it. But we soon found the work so fascinating that we were drawn into it deeper and deeper."[34] By 1901, they were in deadly earnest. And by this time, also, they had begun to apply the true scientific method of invention to their work. It is, indeed, difficult to find, in the history of invention, any more sincere, intelligent application of this method than theirs. That they were self-educated in applied science does not mean that they were not educated or that they attacked their problems with haphazard trial. Their invention was the result of study, not of "hard knocks."

The steps by which these unschooled young men arrived at the true scientific attitude give a remarkable revelation of the correct inventional program. As soon as their gliding graduated from the sport stage, they concentrated on books. Gradually, with great reluctance, they were forced to eliminate Lilienthal, Chanute and Langley. "Having set out with absolute faith in the existing scientific data, we were driven to doubt one thing after another, till finally, after two years of experiment, we cast it all aside, and decided to rely entirely upon our own investigations. Truth and error were everywhere so intimately mixed as to be indistinguishable. Nevertheless, the time expended in preliminary study of books was not misspent for they gave us a good general understanding of the subject, and enabled us at the outset to avoid effort in many directions in which results would have been

[34]Orville and Wilbur Wright, "The Wright Brothers' Aeroplane," in *Century Magazine*, Vol. LXXVI, No. 5, Sept., 1908, p. 647.

hopeless."[35] Could there be a clearer exposition of the process of scientific approach?

They then built testing machines—not gliders, but laboratory equipment. Patiently, with repeated tests, they made their own tables of air pressures. "We began systematic measurements of standard surfaces, so varied in design as to bring out the underlying causes of differences noted in their pressures. Measurements were tabulated on nearly fifty of these at all angles from zero to 45 degrees, at intervals of $2\frac{1}{2}$ degrees."[36] Thus they disclosed the extent to which previous tables had been based on guesswork or assumption. The results were revolutionary. "One surface, with a heavy roll at the front edge, showed the same lift for all angles from $7\frac{1}{2}$ to 45 degrees. A square plane, contrary to the measurements of all our predecessors, gave a greater pressure at 30 degrees than at 45 degrees."[37] Only when their tables were complete did they begin the serious building of gliders for practical tests.[38]

Octave Chanute, the thoroughly educated and trained engineer, watched these performances with amazement. He eagerly conceded their results to be in advance of any that had preceded them. "Too much praise," he wrote, "cannot be awarded to these gentlemen."[39] He continued to give them his unselfish, zealous support.

Yet the Wrights reversed the theory of Chanute as they had the data of Langley. They abandoned his automatic stability idea *in toto*. A proper flying machine, they contended, must not right itself; equilibrium must be maintained by the conscious control of the operator. Their machines justified this conviction and, for the first time, the subtle tricks of the air were successfully combated. Then, after exhaustive trial with the wind glider, they slowly, carefully added its power plant.

They were amazed to find that marine propellers were still "after a century of use," largely the product of guesswork. Ob-

[35]*Ibid.*, p. 646.   [36]*Ibid.*, p. 647.   [37]*Ibid.*
[38]The two they had already built belonged to what might be called their amateur period.
[39]Smithsonian Miscellaneous Collections, Vol. 49, No. 1720, Washington, 1907.

serve here the scientific method coming again to the fore as a measure of economy. "As we were not in a position to undertake a long series of practical experiments to discover a propeller suitable for our machine, it seemed necessary to obtain such a thorough understanding of the theory of its reactions as would enable us to design them from calculation alone."[40] Having done this, they report, succinctly: "Our first propellers, built entirely from calculation, gave in useful work 66 per cent of the power expended. This was about one-third more than had been secured by Maxim or Langley."[41] Their eight-horsepower motor brought the total weight to 600 pounds, including the operator.

All the world knows the story of the trial at Kitty Hawk (now a national shrine) just a week and a day after the unbalance of Langley's "aerodrome" had given what seemed the final blow to aviation. It is almost universally believed that then, for the first time in history,[42] a machine, carrying a man, had risen from the ground under its own power and flown. But, on the day after the trial, only five people besides the inventors were aware of this remarkable event. The Wrights had spread an invitation over the countryside. The day was cold and the wind was blowing at twenty-seven miles per hour over the desolate stretch of sand dunes. It was scarcely worth venturing out on such a day to see one more lunatic crash. If the great Professor Langley could not fly, what could they expect of a couple of lads whose careers had begun in a bicycle repair shop in Dayton, Ohio? Thus were the Wrights saved by obscurity and the suspicion of madness for the full development of their invention.

To us today Orville's first little flight scarcely suggests a magnificent spectacle. The machine was in the air only twelve seconds. It did not rise more than ten feet above the earth. A great deal of perfection was necessary.

Two years later, the American public being inert to flying, the news filtered through it to France where there was an "Aero

[40]Wright, p. 648.   [41]Ibid., pp. 648, 649.
[42]There is, however, another claimant for this honor. A book, containing affidavits, etc., was recently published describing the flights in Connecticut in 1901 and 1902 of Gustave Whitehead. Stella Randolph, *The Lost Flights of Gustave Whitehead,* Washington, 1937.

Club." The club started an investigation to see if it could be true. Witnesses were rounded up and cross-examined. Farmers were found who had seen later flights by the brothers near Dayton. "I just kept on shocking corn," one of them said, "until I got down to the fence, and the durned thing was still going round. I thought it would never stop." Another told how a city man, getting off a trolley car, had been stupefied to see a machine fly over the car. "Whazzat?" he is said to have shouted in terror to the farmer. But the farmer was bored. "Just one of them crazy boys. . . . Both crazy and always was. Y'can't go agin nature."[43]

Three years later Wilbur gave exhibitions at Le Mans, France, which surprised the French so that they lost no time in spreading the Wright fame over the world. Six years after that, the new invention was dropping implements of destruction over Europe. Twenty-five years after that it was regularly carrying passengers across the Atlantic.

It seems a far cry from the cat's cradle "crates" of the first World War which terrified their own pilots no less than the enemy soldiers or civilians below to the multi-motored, all-metal giant monoplanes which fly in 1940 in storm and fog and night and can release a two-ton bomb with reasonable certainty of hitting their target, or, in happier times will ride along a radio beam to land a precious cargo in safety. Yet the basic principles of flight have not greatly changed since 1903. The delicate mechanisms which "warped" the fabric wings by bending their edges have been replaced on rigid metal wings by hinged ailerons. The little automobile engine of the Wrights bears a faint resemblance to the two-thousand-horsepower eighteen-cylinder radial engine which propels an American army plane in 1939, nor do the little twin two-bladed propellers, run from the same engine in the Kitty Hawk plane and working in the rear, look much like the great three-bladed hydromatic, full-feathering propellers which meet the varying air conditions of modern flight. Yet power is power and performs the same function. The difference is that there is more of it per unit of weight so that other loads may be increased. A few automatic stabilizers have been added

[43]John Goldstrom, *A Narrative History of Aviation*, N. Y., 1930, pp. 48, 49.

(notwithstanding the Wrights' objections) and a plane can keep on its course while its pilot sleeps. Engines have moved out on the wings, a step which is said to have come in the evolution of bombers to give a better field of view than would be possible with the nose engine.[44] Light, durable metal, whose development will be discussed elsewhere, has made these changes possible.

Though most basic advance seems to have been inspired by military needs, remarkable progress was made in the inter-war years. Between 1920 and 1938 transport cruising speed has been doubled, power-loading decreased by one-third, which means an increase of 50 per cent in power per unit of weight. Average wing-loading has increased 160 per cent. Passenger capacity has quadrupled. Today there is in transport planes an engine rating of 125 to 160 horsepower per passenger as opposed to one of about 50 per passenger in 1920.[45] These technical advances have been made possible, not by the growing number of people wanting to fly, but by government subsidies, direct in Europe, indirect (mail contracts) in the United States. In the background of all commercial flying is the dominant military necessity. It is a curious reflection upon the intermittent progress of the human race that the safety of aviation today is a by-product of the effort to make it dangerous. The survivors of the airplane's destruction will, therefore, be able, eventually, to fly in it without a tremor.

To what extent war uses of aviation have confused the public mind about the safety of transport is difficult to ascertain. If such confusion exists it is highly unreasonable because an economic necessity forces a nation at war to make its military machines as safe as possible and if technic can be advanced sufficiently to provide a reasonable index of survival under the terrific strain of fighting, an immense advance in transport safety can be secured. It is logical to assume, therefore, that the nation which emerges from the struggle of 1939 with the largest air fleet still intact is the one which may be counted on in the post-war era to provide the safest transport.

[44]Edward Pearson Warner, *Technical Development and Its Effect on Air Transportation*, Norwich University, Northfield, Vt., 1938, p. 11.
[45]*Ibid.*, pp. 5, 6.

SPEED AND GRAVITY

The figures which show the increase in passenger miles since air transport began show also the growth in public confidence. Yet this confidence is obviously far below that in other means of transport. If we now set against these figures the low indices of accident per passenger mile of aviation, it becomes evident that some other factor is operating in the mind of the potential traveller. Perhaps this is the spectacular nature of the crashes which still occur. Perhaps it is the unreasonable association of the airplane with appalling war disaster.

Whatever may be said of the uses of aviation in contemporary society, there can be little doubt that the invention of the heavier-than-air flying machine is one of the most astounding if not indeed the greatest of all products of the human mind to date. Its beauty is reflected in the characters of the heroes of its invention. Almost without exception they have been selfless, pure-purposed men, fitter perhaps for schoolboy worship than any group in the history of invention. No slur, as far as we know, has ever been cast upon the careers or intents of Lilienthal, Chanute, Langley or the Wrights.

5

The practice of aeronautics and the technics of aircraft have profoundly affected the study of science and the development of other technologies. The exploration of the stratosphere may approach completion with rocket development. The study of weather has already entered a new phase. Airplanes have been used in botanical and geological research. They have aided both the practice and theory of medicine and physiology. With them photography has found a new use. With them, polar, desert, volcanic phenomena have been abundantly investigated. Their construction has helped to revolutionize technics of metallurgy and power efficiency.

Social promises are visible. The use of planes by individuals and "the family plane" must await new advances in vertical flight and descent as well as drastic reduction in cost. Experts at present refuse to comment extensively on the future of what might be called a "fordplane," which must employ a helicopter principle of vertical ascent and descent. At present it may be said that aviation has scarcely impinged upon the masses (except to kill or scare them). When it does, we may expect dispersion and the relief of congestion. Such dispersion so far has been a negative and artificial result of aviation—astonishing in the extent to which it has been carried in war-troubled Europe.

Air-mail has catered to impatience engendered by the impulse of speed. Its benefits have been sporadic. Transport must carry goods in large quantity before it will have social consequences. One promise in this direction is striking. In Canada, New Guinea and South America, mines, inaccessible to other transport, have been exploited, machinery and ore being taken in and out by airplane. Here the prohibitive initial capital expense of building roads or railroads through difficult country has been entirely eliminated. On the other hand, operating cost of the air transport is extremely high. Whether roads or railroads, difficult as they might be, might turn out cheaper over a long period in which overhead could be spread over continued less expensive operation is still an economic question. In these cases, the fact is that the mines remained unexploited until air transport arrived. But a probable answer in the future will be a lowering of the cost of transport by aviation.

Already costs are being materially reduced, notably by Diesel motors using crude oil. So far planes using these engines have been capable of longer non-stop flight at a somewhat lower speed, but with considerable saving in both weight of fuel per horsepower and fuel cost. A prominent English aeronautical engineer has gone so far as to prophesy that in ten years the fare for a fifteen-hour transatlantic passage will be as low as fifty dollars.[46] As this estimate includes a reasonable profit over and above operating cost and overhead, it seems like a highly optimistic prediction.

Almost the entire ancient art of war has been upset by aeronautics. Secret massing of troops has become impossible except when observation planes and balloons can be annihilated. Since

[46]Personal interview. We have thought it wise to withhold the name of the prophet.

the arrival of the air arm the new technic of camouflage has become a necessity. New tricks of propaganda from the air have aided in demoralizing reserve forces and breaking civilian morale. Machine gunners, infantrymen and spies may be landed by parachute in any part of the enemy country. Bridges, railheads, roads, communications, trenches may be destroyed without the operation of ground forces. Troops may be "strafed" by low-flying machine gunners. Civilian populations must be evacuated from towns. Factories, supply dumps, munitions supplies have become vulnerable. The cost of such attacks and of the effort to disperse populations in danger of them is out of all proportion to the cost of maintaining the air arm. The result is a revision of wartime economy as well as a change in field maneuvers.

The question whether the organization of society popularly known as "civilization" can survive another war would scarcely have arisen without the presence of the air arm. In these years it is trite from repetition. It is our suspicion either that "civilization" will survive or that it will not be worth the salvage. War, as we have suggested elsewhere, contains today all the elements of its own defeat.

Electric communication between flying persons eliminates the possibility of wires. Aviation has therefore been a great boon to the advance of wireless telegraphy and its successor, radiotelephony. This, in turn, has become an arm of war. In the new international conflict, every overtone of war is audible. Whether this newest of all arms will bring the ultimate victory or the ultimate stalemate is not yet predictable. In any case it is a powerful instrument of the new war. It may shorten the social lag which causes it and so bring us peace. However this may be, there can be no question that, in less than a quarter century, it has deeply affected all human relationships.

Chapter Nineteen

WAVES

SCIENCE was once as securely locked up in the laboratories as Scripture was locked in the church. The priests released such of the Bible as seemed useful for social ethics as well as those portions which induced financial support and loyalty to dogma and withheld the rest. The pure scientists, if they had had their way, would have revealed nothing to the vulgar world. There was some reason in their behavior. The scientists, after all, had inherited much of the legacy of black magic. The church was their normal enemy as it had been the enemy of the sorcerer. It cast suspicion upon their experiment. History was full of cases in which the suspicion had crystallized into hangings, stake-burnings and other persecution. For centuries, "philosophers" had been forced to hide their inquiries and their discoveries lest they evolve a cosmos which impinged on that of theology.

When the printing press broke the church's power, a door seemed to open upon a road to truth. The pilgrims upon that road found it foggy enough. They wandered through the obscure dawn of the Reformation with many missteps, leaving the road to err down bypaths into despondent swamps. But at least they were seeking their·own way, led only by what they believed to be the voice of God in their hearts; no longer herded or driven or coerced. In such a mood they were able, at last, to approach scientific as well as religious truth.

We have seen the groping of these people, to whom the printing press and the Reformation had given rebirth, in their refuge in North America. As we now know, the printing press and the Reformation were, in a sense, the progenitors of what we call the New World. In a sense, the Reformation was its father and the printing press its grandfather, whatever rôle British colonial policy may have played as hot-tempered nurse.

There was darkness enough in seventeenth-century America. The Calvinists, possessed of strange intuition, knew that the bone which should endure in the wilderness must be built of tough material. Thus the bigotry, the subjection of the flesh, the cruelty practiced in the name of religion had social consequences which carried through to the last frontier. Yet was not such darkness profoundly inimical to any approach to scientific understanding?

For a time it delayed that approach. Yet even during the necessary delay, while character, strong stomachs and dynamic spirit were building, there was a saving word in the deepest dogma of American Calvinism. The individual was responsible, in theory, only to God. No hierarchy of priests divided or sophisticated this responsibility. No pulpit-thumping by Bradfords, Johnsons, Cottons, Mathers or Edwardses could alter this fundamental. As God, therefore, became synonymous with Conscience, the bigot churches split into congregations and sects and a habit of inquiry became general. Americans in the eighteenth century, then, were ripe for "philosophy."

The torch-bearer arrived on time. With thought cast so far in the future that he seems, sometimes, almost a mystic, Benjamin Franklin possessed the common touch to a degree that will forever bewilder the students of genius. Before the eyes of bigots and faithful, preachers and groping flocks, he led forth and disrobed the ogre of Magic. He did it with simple motions, with a smile and a quiet jest, with the words of the common mind: See, there is nothing to be afraid of—the lightning is there in the sky but it is also here on this table: this little jar does not contain the wrath of God. He offended no one. He did not oppose knowledge to faith; he unified them. He was not hanged, burned or crucified, yet he was the first Messiah of science, the first in all the world to teach its gospel to the multitude in words that could be understood by priests and pharisees, publicans and sinners. In such a temper he went out from America to light the way to a new era in the world.

The Europe which was soon to know the revolutionary power of the steam engine, the railway and magnetic communication welcomed him as no apostle of science had ever before been welcomed. To Frenchmen he symbolized the liberation of thought from both political and theological bonds. Even the children followed him with hope through the streets of Paris as if he had been a saint. Who knows, when he stopped to talk to them in his easy way, how many young inventors, how many builders of a new physical civilization stood in the crowd to stare and think?

When he was gone many philosophers drew back again into the shadows of their workshops. They were still afraid of the masses, in terror of the vulgarization which Franklin had begun. Nor was their behavior wholly unreasonable. Many secrets were still dangerous in the hands of the herd. Many still are. But as science moved on under the stimulus of Franklin and others, it answered too many common necessities to be kept under lock and key. Like the church, science needed money; and the public, no longer blindly faithful, demanded knowledge in advance of payment. The conflict which began is still strong today but violent conflict is a concomitant of progress.

The uses to which radio waves are put today are far removed from the sanctity of the laboratory in which they were first understood. The vulgarity of a hundred broadcast dialogs is scarcely in keeping with the rare concept of their carriers. The broadcast speech of a political dictator is calculated to bring back the darkness which we have worked hundreds of years to dispel. There are times when it seems as if the bogey of magic might better have remained in his den to frighten people with mystery rather than that men should use him against each other. But that is short-term focus. History is full of lapses which, looked at too closely, are mistaken for the long sweep.

Even in 1940 much knowledge is still locked in the laboratory but that is because the common mind is incapable of unlocking the door. The scientists inside are ready enough to demonstrate this incapacity to any one who cares to inquire. A late statement given out by the students of radio waves is as baffling as any theological doctrine ever put into words. Wireless communication, say the new simon-pure scientists, results from a Movement of Nothing in Nothing. Can the mysteries of the Incarnation, the Trinity, the Atonement or even of Transubstantiation approach this in obscurity? Yet this movement of negation conveys thought, laughter and pain. Human bodies have been preserved because of communication without wire; others have wasted away and died and others have gone out to kill. This Nothing has produced most vital effects. Are love, hate, desire, pleasure, a set of zeros? The scientists had better assign values to these matters with reasonable celerity, otherwise their next step may never occur.

2

It is obvious that waves in water or in air do not transport matter from the place where they begin to the place where they end. If you drop a stone in a pond, a wave will start which will eventually reach the shore but the water which was at the point where the stone was dropped before you dropped it will remain where it is. Particles of it will be bumped by the stone and these will bump other particles and the bumpage will continue until finally the shore of the pond is bumped in turn, but presumably each particle, having bumped another, will then bounce back into its original position. This happens again in the air when the pebble is replaced by a sound. Sound is produced by slow vibration and can, therefore, make waves in a logy medium like the air. But when we get up to light, we find an exceedingly rapid vibration which makes its waves in a substance rarer than air. If the vibration is stepped up again above that of light we get to radio waves which must also be bumpings or disturbances in a rarefied medium.

For years, the physicists called this medium the ether, a designation which moderns call "naïve."[1] Radio waves were found to move in complete vacuum so the ether was thrown out and the word "Nothing" substituted for it with that gay disregard of

---

[1] S. E. Frost, *Is American Radio Democratic?* Chicago, 1937, p. 3. Hogben, p. 735, calls ether "an obliging and all-pervading blancmange." But see also James Jeans, *The New Background of Science,* N. Y., 1938, pp. 77, 175 f.

word values so common among these advanced thinkers. "No matter," they will explain if pressed. And what, you will ask, is matter? Words stop at this point and out come pencils and paper, a set of Greek letters, dots, dashes, lines, circles, and snakes with their tails in their mouths, and the public runs back to its receiving sets to laugh and cry at the nothings which, having traversed nothing, there emerge as sounds.

But, given the above definition, we may be excused for a lack of detail in the explanation of how the voices of Hitler, Amos and Andy reach our ears from long distances. We shall confine ourselves, then, largely to history and to the extremely tangible social effects of the mystic non-existents.

Franklin unconsciously started waves in the zero around his Leyden jars and electrostatic machine. If the study of electricity had continued in the direction in which he started it, the waves might sooner have been found and wireless communication might have preceded the Morse and Wheatstone systems. Some technicians think that this would have been the logical sequence, waves being basic and wires a refinement. But Galvani, Volta, Oersted and the rest of the classic chain soon had currents moving through wires and there they stayed, earth-bound, for nearly a century, bringing vast quantities of metal from the mines.

Nevertheless, spark-making machines and Leyden jar condensers were not wholly abandoned in the laboratory. Nor were Franklin's experiments with lightning forgotten. Joseph Henry, working in Princeton in the early 1840's, magnetized needles in his house by lightning flashes many miles away.[2] The needles were in a coil, one end of which was attached to a metal roof, the other grounded. He further made the important discovery that a current induced by lightning was oscillatory. He then strung two parallel wires across the Princeton campus and sent the discharge from Leyden jars through one. Induction occurred in the other though the wires were several hundred feet apart. His conclusion from this experiment was that "distance might be indefinitely increased, provided the wires were lengthened in a

[2]Joseph Henry, *Scientific Writings, Smithsonian Inst.*, 1886, I, 203, 250; II, 334.

corresponding ratio."[3] By 1851 he had actually come to believe that the effect of the Leyden jar spark had been "propagated wave-fashion."[4]

In Europe, the belief in waves grew in the universities. The steps by which they were understood, measured, allied with one another and, finally, manipulated and made useful, involved long research in many branches of science. Each was indispensable, laboriously built upon the one before. Michael Faraday, who laid so much of the foundation of the world we know, must first lay out his "lines of force" before James Clerk Maxwell could apply mathematics to them and devise formulas for the phenomena of static electricity. But while he worked, the checking of Lord Kelvin and the added theory of Karl Friederich Gauss came in to strengthen him so that he was able to arrive, at last, at the vital conclusion that electrical impulses move in waves with the speed of light. From this point on, the analogy of light and electricity in their wave movement became so close that their only difference seemed to be in the rapidity of the vibrations with which they were generated. Thus the sciences of astronomy and optics came to join hands with that of electricity.

While this was happening at Aberdeen, the profound German whom we met briefly in the story of Bell's telephone was studying light and sound, chemistry and electricity, meteorology and mechanics in Berlin. It is strange that the name of Hermann Ludwig Ferdinand von Helmholtz is so rarely mentioned in the history of radio. His inquiry, from such a broad foundation, into electrical oscillations brought him to a meeting-place with Maxwell which resulted in the final theoretical step from which the practical experimenters took off—the demonstration of the truth of all the theory. It is a fine showing of the judgment of the true scientific mind that Helmholtz did not take the step himself though the impulse was there and it was strong. He entrusted it to the next generation: to his laboratory assistant and favorite pupil, Heinrich Hertz.

Hertz did not at once carry on the torch. Subconsciously, too, the impulse was working beneath all his other work. It gathered

[3]*Ibid.,* I, 250.   [4]*Ibid.,* I, 302.

to itself Maxwell's knowledge and theory. When, in 1887, he set up a spark gap and, at a distance from it, a wire ring "detector," he was ready. The sparks leaped the gap, and a current moved in the detector. Wireless communication thus jumped back to the Princeton campus and Henry's Leyden jars but now, in the cycle, was the power of knowledge. Now all the laborious research between the two experiments was justified. There would be no guesswork in the new movement.

Meanwhile, practical men had been at work. The unscientific but skilful guesser Edison, whose finger in every inventional pie is always discovered by the historians, picked up what have later been described as "wireless messages"[5] from a locomotive moving between telegraph lines. Though he rushed, as usual, to the patent office[6] with his tin-foil "detector," only garbled signals from a dozen simultaneous telegrams were ever received.

In America, also, Alexander Graham Bell had laid some of the foundation of modern radio practice and, at the same time, had moved round the edge of wireless communication.[7] Still closer approaches had been made, in England, by William Preece and Oliver Lodge and William Crookes, famous for his work with vacuum tubes. Over all these people had moved waves of wishful thinking. From the time of the first success of the Atlantic cable,[8] when the expense of metal for communications reached such large proportions, the hope had been agitated that, one day, wires might be dispensed with. After all, Steinheil in the early days of the telegraph had used the earth as a conductor.[9] Bell had sent messages without wire through water. What, people were asking, was the matter with the air? Thus a psychological necessity was created for the invention. This reached its climax when Sir William Crookes, in 1892, put the thoughts of so many scientists into words comprehensible by the lay mind.

"Rays of light," he wrote, "will not pierce through a wall, nor, as we know only too well, through a London fog. But the

---

[5]Gleason Archer, History of Radio to 1926. N. Y., 1938, p. 53.
[6]Application filed May 23, 1885; Pat. No. 465971 issued Dec. 29, 1901.
[7] Potomac experiments, 1882.
[8]See Chap. 1.   [9]1838.

electrical vibrations of a yard or more in wave-length of which I have spoken will easily pierce such mediums. . . . Here, then, is revealed the bewildering possibility of telegraph without wires, posts, cables or any of our present costly appliances. . . . What remains . . . to be discovered is—firstly, a simpler and more certain means of generating electrical waves of any desired wave-length . . . secondly, more delicate receivers which will respond to wave-lengths between certain defined limits and be silent to all others; thirdly, means of darting the sheaf of rays in any desired direction. . . . Any two friends living within the radius of sensitivity of their receiving instruments, having first decided on their special wave-length and attuned their respective receiving instruments to mutual receptivity, could thus communicate by timing the impulses to produce long and short intervals on the ordinary Morse Code."[10]

The prophecy produced astonishment in a world just entering upon the age of miracles. In the nineties many of the later triumphs of science were still believed impossible. In this decade, the respected Professor Langley was to be subjected to a barrage of ridicule and abuse—was even to come under the suspicion of madness for his heroic effort to fly. Yet there were engineers and other technical men in many lands who were not thrown off balance by the bold surmise of Crookes. Notably there was a boy inventor who would one day be crowned with all the laurels which should have been shared by Franklin, Henry, Faraday, Gauss, Maxwell, von Helmholtz, Hertz, Preece, Crookes, Kelvin, Bell, Lodge, Heaviside, Hughes, Branly, Fitz-Gerald, Elihu Thomson, Chunder Bose, Augusto Righi, Popoff and many others.[11]

He was eighteen when the article by Crookes appeared. It would be difficult to imagine a clearer statement of what remained to be done to turn a well-established theory into useful practice. But the brilliant young Italian had even more tangible

---

[10]Sir William Crookes, "Some Possibilities of Electricity," London *Fortnightly Review*, CCCII, n.s., pp. 174, 175 (Feb. 1, 1892).

[11]For a fuller list, see G. G. Blake, *History of Radio Telegraphy and Telephony*, London, 1928, one of the most useful guides to the early history which has come to our attention.

demonstrations with which to work. His professor, Righi, at the University of Bologna had invented a piece of laboratory equipment still more sensitive and visual than the detector of Hertz. Guglielmo Marconi started with plans and tools which many an inventor of the past might well have envied him and he worked in an atmosphere of conscious public desire which was well-nigh irresistible.

3

To understand the true necessity of this invention, we must put ourselves to sea at the moment of the changing centuries. When men and women walked up the gangplank of a ship, they left their worlds. They entered, for an interval, a life of pure romance in which no familiar reality could touch them. Death, disaster, pain might come to their homes but, until the ship touched port, there would be peace in ignorance. Fanciful minds might paint dread pictures, but many of them would be in vain. It was usual for crews and passengers to abandon themselves to the mental protection of the sea through the long unknowing days. Good things, too, might happen at home and the fresh air of a fair voyage conduced more readily to the hope of these.

On the whole, perhaps, the stay-at-homes had the worst of it. On the always mysterious ocean, disaster was more apt. We remember the magnificent common prayer in the churches to "Eternal God who alone spreadest out the heavens, and rulest the raging of the sea." Men and women were commanded to His protection with utter resignation. Some of them might never be heard from again. The mystery was ultimate.

For only the briefest intervals, since men first sailed in ships, had this darkness been illumined. We have seen how, when cables were laid, the ships had kept in touch with land and we have seen the impact of this first miracle on the minds of crew and passengers. But once the cables were laid, the mystery closed again over the ocean between the terminals. It waited, through the century, for Marconi to dissipate it forever.

Marconi realized the dream. However vivid it may have been in

the minds of his predecessors, there is no doubt about that. That
he did it with other men's tools from other men's blueprints does
not alter the final fact.

Still in his 'teens working in his home garden, Marconi followed the suggestion of Crookes and introduced a Morse telegraph key into a circuit broken according to Hertz practice by a
spark-gap. Next he set up a "coherer" invented[12] by Edouard
Branly to detect the signals. The coherer was a tube filled with
loose metal filings which stuck together when the radio waves
caused an induced current to flow through them. The ingenious
Branly had devised an automatic hammer which would tap the
tube and thus decohere the filings after the current had passed.
With this equipment he played, for a time, until it was evident
that the limitations of distance were very definite and he knew
that he must introduce something original if there was to be a
practical invention.

The new step was the aerial. The Hertz oscillator which caused
the spark jumps was grounded at one end while the other was
projected high in the air. With a revised coherer the apparatus
worked for distance and the steps from that point were improvements. The basic invention was complete.

Marconi was one of those occasional inventors to whom fate
was kind. Because his invention was soundly conceived in an age
when the applications of science were in vogue, he was soon able
to enlist capital. The capital came from England to which he
had wisely moved for his larger-scale experiments, but when he
went home with a new commercial company in his pocket, so to
speak, the Italian navy was ready to give him unlimited assistance.

These things happened from '96 to '98. Marconi was still in
his early twenties. He had, as yet, little fame but large financial
promise and a multitude of minds and hands reaching out to help
him. His greatest help came from the mysterious sea. In 1899, an
experimental Marconi apparatus on an English lightship sent out
what we now call SOS signals for aid to helpless ships. Lives were
saved, the fact was tangible, it was news; demand increased and
with it came fame. It is often forgotten today that this first valu-

[12]1892.

able demonstration of wireless telegraphy took place in the nineteenth century.

What is remembered more vividly is that thirteen years later every conscious mind in the civilized world knew that the mystery of the sea was ended. On April 14, 1912, signals moved over an icy, starlit sea to tell distant captains that an unsinkable ship was sinking. Help came in time to keep the greatest marine disaster in history from being unmitigated tragedy. In the ports of the world, men wept that night at the name of Marconi; his name and *Titanic* are forever inseparable.

But two years later, when the War came, the voices of William Hohenzollern and Edward Grey were not heard at a hundred million firesides to proclaim Der Tag, or a Drang Nach Osten or the going out of the lamps of Europe. These messages must yet be coded, decoded and put into still another code called print before they could confuse or illumine an anxious world. Had they been broadcast, could they have been sandwiched between blended cigarettes and creamy shortening, they might have delayed the war for years or nipped it clean. But voices must wait with music for new inventions—many of them American. We have contributed much to human intercourse since Marconi first sent Morse's dots and dashes to clear the mystery of the sea. Whether the mysteries of society and human relationships, of love and hate and war are any nearer solution is, at the moment, an arguable question. Whether the frequencies of the waves called nothing can ever be completely in phase with the equally imponderable harmonics of the human mind will present an engrossing problem for our social inventors of the future.

4

We have released ourselves from the explanation why the jumping of sparks across a gap makes possible the movement of waves in all directions (like the waves from a stone dropped in a pond) from the terminals. That they are waves at all in any ordinary sense is a convenient assumption. A highly theoretical measurement from crest to crest of these waves is called wave-length and this depends upon the number of times an oscillating current moves back and forth. The sparks jumping the gap are not, apparently, what produce the waves but are incidental to their production; unless the circuit were interrupted by such a gap, the thwarted and desperate electrons composing the current in the terminals would not behave in a manner calculated to disturb the zero which surrounds them. So we must accept the fact that wavelike motion occurs in the distressed zero; that bumpage occurs over immense distances unimpeded by walls, earth and whatnot and that definite measurements may be made of the motion.

The definition with which these measurements are made accounts, of course, for their intelligent reception. Thus a receiving instrument tuned to one "frequency" will receive only the waves sent out at that frequency. At the sending station, ingenious devices called condensers determine with great accuracy the frequency at which waves will emanate and another condenser in the receiving instrument will cause response to that frequency when it is properly tuned. Frequency is measured in cycles, a cycle being one complete jump of an oscillating current which lands it back where it started. High frequency makes more waves per second and hence a shorter distance between crests or wavelength; low frequency makes fewer waves with longer length between them. For great distances higher frequencies and shorter waves are desirable; thus European voices come to us measured in millions (mega) rather than thousands (kilo) of cycles. It is all scarcely more complex in principle than the responding hum of a tuning fork when a certain note is struck.

But what is the difference between sending code and sending speech by this method? First, it is the difference between the telegraph and the telephone; second, it is the use of a mathematical relation of waves rather than a wire. We have studied the telephone instruments. When we cut them into radio transmission and receiving circuits, we use the radio waves to carry the electrical waves (or varying impulses) produced by speech. They will carry them all right providing the two kinds of waves have measurements which are in proper mathematical relation with each other. Never mind how. The radio engineer explains it, but not in English. He uses Greek letters, lines, pluses and minuses, not words.

It is only necessary to remember that extremely high frequencies are needed and extremely delicate sensitive receiving and reproducing instruments. Here are the induction generators to make the unbelievably rapid movement of zero in zero and improvements on the microphone transmitter[13] and the Bell receiver. But there is a third need and here comes the most useful invention of all—the device which results in the magnification of sound.

Amplifiers do their job in the mysterious interval when speech or musical sound exists only in translated form—in the electrical waves we met in the telephone wires. In effect the amplifier increases the force of the wave-bearing current so that impulses which start little and weak as a result of tiny sounds hitting a delicate diaphragm become powerful enough to vibrate a large steel plate and thus give forth the voice of a giant. We saw amplifiers in the talkies. They were invented for radio.

Reginald A. Fessenden, a professor in the University of Pittsburgh, and Lee de Forest, one of the long, honored line of Yale inventors, were the American pioneers in radiotelephony. Fessenden was experimenting with telephone instruments soon after the wireless telegraph became a reality. As early as 1901 he was able, with what he called the electrolytic detector in circuit with a telephone receiver, to hear faint voice sounds. But the sparks, jumping across the gap at the transmitting station, made such a noise that nothing was intelligible. He determined, then, either to make the frequency so high that the sparks would be inaudible or else to do away with the sparks altogether. So he began to study alternators. An alternator is merely a dynamo which generates an alternating current. If he could move one fast enough, he believed that radio waves would emanate from the generator itself. His aim was a frequency of 100,000 cycles, meaning that the current would change its direction 200,000 times a second. As electric light generators produced only a 120-cycle

[13]Invented by Emil Berliner, 1877.

442

current, it is evident what an apparently fabulous task he was undertaking. Impossible, chorused the usual band of skeptics.

Yet, as the new century came in, there were fewer skeptics about everything. A kind of shift had taken place in which the public, which for centuries, according to popular historians, had called almost every inventor a lunatic, were now more willing to believe than the scientist. Even flying, that last stronghold of the madman, had been followed with interest and hope up to the diastrous failure of Langley in 1903. With wireless communication a commonplace fact no miracle seemed to the people impossible. Furthermore, there was a special fascination in snatching messages out of the air.

Lured by it came the great army of boys, a factor which must never be forgotten in the history of radio. By the second decade of the century uncountable thousands of kids tinkered with wires and tubes, dividing their parents between exasperation and sympathy. Savagely, the children brooked no resistance, could not be thwarted or distracted. School was neglected at least until departments of physics were drawn into the craze and then teachers of electrical subjects worked all night lest they find themselves taught by their pupils. There must have been a sharp decline, in these years, in the curve of what is known as "mischief"—for which no time was left. There are, today, many thousands of adolescents entering their teens who have forgotten more than this historian will ever learn of the mysteries of the waves.

This movement of youth was bound to have its effect. It was to become disastrous at last to wireless communication and the confusing operations of the amateurs were legislated off the air. Meanwhile, however, men listening in the intense concentration of their sons' workshops heard the desperate calls of ships sinking at sea as well as the signals of remote boy friends and they, too, were lured from business and golf. More important still was the large trade in equipment which grew up to cater to the young men's needs, for here came capital and serious equipment. Thus the great investigators such as Fessenden and de Forest were not, as were so many inventors of the past, deprived of funds.

Fessenden, backed by two indomitable capitalists, Thomas Given and Harry Walker, suggested to the powerful G. E. that the sky was the limit and through the brilliant connivance of their Ernst Alexanderson an alternator evolved which achieved the impossible in frequencies and which could generate continuous waves without the noisy handicap of the spark-gap.

While these matters were in progress, there came an English invention, an adaptation of an earlier American discovery, which resulted in the celebrated amplifier known as the audion tube. In 1883 Edison, working on his incandescent lamp, found that the carbon filament when hot seemed to give off electricity. Putting a second electrode positively charged in the bulb negative electricity jumped to it from the filament. But when the second electrode was positive none jumped. Edison remarked upon the phenomenon as curious, but naturally, at that time, saw no use in it.[14] An Englishman, J. Ambrose Fleming, who was acting as scientific adviser to an Edison company in London, was, nevertheless, fascinated by it, whether it had a use or not. Much later, the use appeared. By 1904 Fleming, who like so many electrical investigators had become interested in wireless, used this "Edison effect" to rectify oscillating currents from radio waves. It would let through currents moving in one direction while not passing those which moved back. Still it was not an amplifier. It was merely a detector. It added nothing to the current.[15]

By this time the electronic theory had been accepted. According to this, currents consisted of very minute electric particles called electrons. Fleming's device was a valve which let the electrons pass one way but when they tried to return the valve was shut against them. De Forest took the Fleming valve and inserted in it a grid which was attached to a radio antenna. It thus changed from positive to negative with the oscillations from the radio waves and so became the valve. Through the other electrodes, now, de Forest was able to introduce a strong current from outside, so increasing the number of flowing electrons. This was an entirely new invention which simply made use of Flem-

[14]See p. 236.
[15]The Fleming Valve was patented in 1904. See cut p. 445. For detailed description, see Hogben, p. 755.

ing's adaptation of Edison's lamp as basic equipment. This was the truly vital step necessary for radio telephony and is, today, in some form, a step in all electrical reproduction of sound. Audion tubes could be added indefinitely in a receiving apparatus so that impulses representing sound could be multiplied millions of times. Hence, in the loud speaker, the sound would be multiplied. But the de Forest tubes which he, like Fleming, had originally

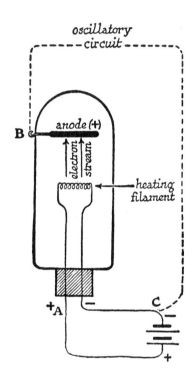

The Fleming valve

When the positive end of filament A is connected with plate B a current flows between A and B, as shown by putting a galvanometer in series with A and B. If instead B is included in the oscillatory circuit, current will only flow in the latter when B is positive. Hence the plate acts as a rectifier

invented as detectors, did not become effective amplifiers for telephony until Irving Langmuir and Henry Arnold had perfected their vacuums.[16]

It is a commonplace now that enormous crowds can be brought within the range of a speaker's voice, not by radio transmission, but by mere amplification. In certain cases the social effect of such amplification is more immediate and violent than that of

[16]The legal fight between them with A. T. & T. backing Arnold and G. E. behind Langmuir has become one of the classics of the patent prize ring.

radio. Propaganda sent out to separate homes has not the contributory stimulus of mob psychology. Each individual in a vast assembly, able to see the speaker, derives a sense of community from the physical presence of other listeners and spectators. The listener to the same speech emerging from the home radio has no such consciousness of unity or solidarity. He is, furthermore, distracted by the small, familiar happenings of the home about him. By the time he has joined the friends who have heard, separately, the speech his emotions may have been cooled or altered by private thought or diluted by other business. It is thus possible that more mass support has come to a power-politician like Hitler through mere amplification to crowds of a hundred thousand which are in his presence than through broadcasts to fifty million.

The vogue for amplification has extended in all directions with occasional unfortunate results. Amplifiers have been placed on musical instruments, for example, and tricks of volume crescendo are practiced which frequently distort all intent of the composer. Speech through amplification acquires sometimes a magnitude out of all proportion to the words spoken. Voices shout at innocent pedestrians from doorways and windows and trucks, rudely invading the privacy of the mind. False impressions are created by mere amplification. On the whole, however, a desirable instrument has been placed in men's hands and the questions of damage or danger must be turned back to the men who use it.

But still another use was found for the magic tube. We have seen it now as a detector and as an amplifier. Suddenly, and apparently nearly at the same time, three engineers saw that it could be made into a generator of waves. They were de Forest, Langmuir and that extraordinary inventor who may in the future do more for broadcasting than all the others put together, Edwin Armstrong. The tubes could not replace powerful alternators at the transmitting end but with a new mathematical system called by the beautiful name of heterodyne, which Fessenden had lately invented, generators of a sort had become necessary at the receiving end as well. Heterodyne combined the waves from the

446

transmitter with waves generated at the receiver and from the combination got a "beat note" of low enough frequency to be audible.[17]

To get this generation, experimenters had used cumbersome arcs and such devices. When the vacuum tubes became generators, the problem was instantly simplified, for such tubes could be hidden away in any set.

After all these vital steps had been taken, more than ten years passed before the birth of the great industry which controls so much of our entertainment, our thought, our opinion. The years were checkered with a complexity of patent litigation which fills volumes of court records. There was a struggle for control whose story is, in parts, far from pretty. America's entry into the World War caused all radio transmission, amateur and otherwise, to be taken over by government. But after the war, when the amateurs became conscious of radio-telephony as well as noisy dots and dashes, they brought up before those corporations which had finally achieved patent control the question whether the new inventions had an entertainment value.

It was a perplexing question. Obviously the amateurs were being vastly entertained at the moment and had been for years. But the young men—30,000 of them by 1920—formed scarcely a large enough group to interest big business. Also, they were specialists, assembling their own receiving sets from gadgets sold at department stores, electrical shops. A little money was made, to be sure, from the gadgets. But how about the general public?

Suppose finished receiving sets were made and sold. Suppose, then, something were provided for their owners to listen to? News, music such as de Forest had already broadcast? Would the sale of sets pay for these things? The hastiest calculation proved they would not.

There came then that curious question which was not asked about inventions which answered an irresistible need. The wireless telegraph was a true child of necessity. Broadcasting was

[17]Assume that waves generated at the transmitter have a frequency of 300,-000 cycles. Now if those generated at the receiver have a frequency of 301,000 cycles, the combination will produce a "beat" of 1000 cycles or the difference between them.

not. What was it for? Who would listen to it? Where would they listen? If they listened at home what possible profit could any one make? And would they, in any case, listen at home—the general public that is, apart from the gadget tinkerers? The social trend seemed to show clearly that they would not.

America, in the years just before her entry into the World War, had entered what appeared to be a new period of transition. The home fires were going out. In the cities, packed now by the long migrations from the land, apartment radiators no longer held the young people as the hearth had done. The ford, spelled by then with a lower-case initial, drew boys and girls away from the fetid air. It and the movie palace were showing the way to new sex freedom. The new, dark, silent theatres were drawing people also from the farms. The monstrous American institution of the quick lunch was replacing the home kitchen and, in the process, vitiating taste and deteriorating stomachs. Sandwiches, hot dogs, banana splits, hamburgers, predigested cereals, "Adam and Eve on a raft," "two three-and-a-halfs buttered," "open-face" and "turn-its"—a thousand gastronomic inventions were better adjusted to the rising temper than the laborious products of the home ovens. Automats,[18] cafeterias, counters dispensed with service.

America's war still further scattered the younger generation, more definitely divorced them from the home. When it was over, the restless boys could not be confined to three rooms and a kitchenette. Apartments were no longer adequate even for birth or death or sickness. Post-war babies came into the world in hospitals, the sacred tradition of "birthplace" evaporated. Funeral parlors were equipped for the reception of corpses before they were cold. Doctors ordered people to hospitals for hives and ingrowing toenails. Love, at its inception, got into a ford, parked in the darkness, or received its stimulus from the movies.

Yet the community was held together by the pattern of public entertainment. The theatre, warm, cozy and darkly free, had become the evening refuge. Even the old folks were fleeing the barren nest to seek it.

[18]These, however, were imported—a German invention.

These facts were noted by certain enterprising promoters. Experiments with the amplifier and the loud-speaker, which could multiply sound millions of times, led to the thought of a new kind of theatre—a sound theatre with voices and music caught from the air to fill an auditorium packed to capacity with a paying audience. News, orchestral programs, could be cheaply put on by radio. This would fit the new social pattern which was alarming sociologists. If the home had disappeared, such promoters thought, why not ally ourselves with the trend and increase the mediums of community entertainment?

The fallacy in the argument lay in the tense used of the verb "to disappear." The home had not disappeared. It was merely disappearing. A factor which was ignored or seemed insignificant to the theatre promoters was holding it against total disintegration. For while the moon-calves went movie-mad or ford-mad or boy-meets-girl mad; while the "lost" generation in the postwar chaos took to speakeasies and divorce, the twelve-year-olds stuck to their magic at home. So the new industry was started by the promoters who watched the boys.

Prominent among the boy-watchers was the corporation known as Westinghouse Electric. In the spring and summer of 1920, its vice-president, Harry Davis, and one of its research engineers, Frank Conrad, held many boys (from twelve to seventy) fascinated by shooting words and music from the antennæ of a new experimental station at East Pittsburgh. While Conrad watched the boys, Davis watched Conrad. The amateurs listened avidly and wrote and telephoned for more. Doctor Conrad ran out of talk and sent music from phonograph records. He ran out of records and borrowed some from a store. The store asked him if he would kindly mention the name of the store in his announcements of the music.

Doctor Davis observed all this and, presently, he also noticed an advertisement in a Pittsburgh paper offering for sale receivers suitable for picking up the Conrad programs from the air. Thus, in his mind, the Great Idea was conceived. As Mr. Davis stated it, later, in a lecture to the Graduate School of Business Administration of Harvard University, the idea was that radio's

449

field was "really one of wide publicity, in fact, the only means of instantaneous collective communication ever devised."[19]

The inspiring words of Mr. Davis's Harvard lecture only suggested, however, the magnitude of the true problem which had been solved. For years the power of radio had been predicted. But the difficulty was that broadcasting seemed to present only the intolerable possibility of giving the public something for nothing. Foreign nations were moving toward the solution in a traditional manner: government ownership of broadcasting stations financed by taxes. But government ownership and taxes were bogies in America, terrifying to every citizen. There must be some other way. Promoters, standing on the brink of a gold mine, had had their nerves shredded trying to devise it. Mr. Davis's brainstorm provided the whole answer and he became, thus, an inventor of the first order.

Advertising, at this period, had become almost a religion in the United States. It had already entered the realms of arts and letters, architecture, transport. It controlled the lives of millions of people, posed ideals (however phony in fact) of truth and purity, created fictional characters dear to American hearts, entranced the children, introduced hundreds of imbecile activities—puzzles, contests, lotteries, coupon-collection—into thousands of homes. Advertising was essentially a *home* force. It dealt with kitchens, bathrooms, clothes, soap and the most intimate whispers. It inspired fear, jealousy, hatred, envy as well as occasional happier emotions. Via the magic waves it brought home back to the tinkering boys.

5

Historians, avid in their search for "firsts," have seized upon the communication of the Harding election news in November, 1920, as the first public broadcast. As we have seen, it was far from the first broadcast and it was in no large sense public. Only those people who were able to assemble a collection of gadgets and their friends were able to hear it. Nevertheless it was widely

[19]H. P. Davis, *Early History of Broadcasting in the Radio Industry,* ed. by David Sarnoff and Anton de Haas; Chicago, 1928, p. 194.

noticed in the press, and it started the ball rolling. As it was broadcast by the Westinghouse station, KDKA, it could be followed by the announcement that the Westinghouse company was manufacturing sets for the market. It brought more customers than its promoters had expected. Thus, from the sale of sets it was able to finance a program and it was content to start on this basis, so long as the general advertising scheme was in the background.

On the same basis Westinghouse in the course of the next year started three other stations: WBZ, Springfield, Massachusetts, WJZ in New York and KYW in Chicago. General Electric, also able under the outcome of the patent fight to manufacture sets, started WGY at Schenectady, and in 1922 A. T. & T. came along with WBNY, predecessor of WEAF, in New York. But it was not until late in 1922 that the success of broadcasting seemed to justify the soliciting of general advertising. Then it was A. T. & T. and not Westinghouse which made the first sale. The first general advertising broadcast (apart from announcements of radio equipment) was an address on advertising by the president of the William H. Rankin advertising agency. It is said to have brought in ten telephone calls and fifteen fan letters.[20] Later Mr. Rankin sold one of his customers a chance to talk about cosmetics over WEAF, the vehicle being a recital by Marion Davies. An offer of her autographed photograph brought ten thousand replies. No further proof was needed that the industry had started in earnest.

In 1922, the number of receiving sets in use was estimated as sixty thousand. In 1923, this figure jumped to a million and a half. In four more years it reached six and a half million or one set for every twenty inhabitants of the country. But the years from '22 to '27 were frantic ones, which followed the pattern of all revolutionary enterprise in our history. While from the start in other countries government regulated broadcasting, in the United States the Government tried to keep its hands off to the bitter end in order to conform to *laissez-faire* tradition. Under it competition ran riot and at precisely the moment when the scientists,

[20]Frost, *op. cit.*, pp. 90 f.

were trying to abolish the ether, broadcasters discovered that it had definite limitations. Everywhere, as stations multiplied, zeros were being effectively blanked out by other zeros: soap and Shakespeare failed to come through because gum and Gershwin were in the way.

The only legislation which existed was a law applying to wireless passed in 1912 before radiotelephony was in practical existence. This required sending stations to have licenses. There was no limit to the number. Licenses were issued by the Department of Commerce and the secretary, Herbert Hoover, brought up in the rugged school, tried bravely to steer a course between freedom and dictatorship which would have defied description even by Lewis Carroll. The public, driven to distraction by *laissez-faire,* brought pressure on Congress. So did broadcasters and advertisers. Yet it was not until 1927 that full, stern regulation went into the statute books and a commission was created to administer it.[21]

America's broadcasting kilocycles, decided by international conference to run from 500 to 1500, were divided into ninety-six "channels." Canada got some of these for her exclusive use and shared others with the United States. Thus was empty space neatly divided by government plan. The division permitted the licensing of between six and seven hundred stations, after which the door was closed. The commission demanded continuity during normal listening hours, specified equipment and stated minimum power requirements in watts. The granting of licenses had, of course, a geographical basis.

In all our history there has been no clearer case of the necessity of government regulation and federal planning. Yet the control has never become heavy-handed. Censorship has been, for the most part, rigorously withheld. It is not, to be sure, greatly needed. Normal advertising censorship is fully adequate. It is one thing to offend a citizen. It is another to offend a potential customer. Thus the commercial programs have been kept as pure as the soaps, as sterile as the antiseptics. Offenses to æsthetic

[21]Federal Radio Commission, changed in 1934 to Federal Communications Commission.

taste are less important, as this is not accepted as a perquisite of the listening and purchasing masses.

The fascinating story of litigation, of patent complexities, of cynical corporate wrangling, of little enterprises going to the wall, of public protest, of the formation of the beautiful networks, of the magnificent technical contribution of the Bell system to simultaneous nation-wide programs—only possible to a totalitarian monopoly of this magnitude—of the scheme of "sustaining" programs with which the stations fill out their legal hours, of all the internal politics and economics of the industry, would take years of any one's time merely to read through. In the Federal Communications Commission, which has replaced the radio commission established in 1927, many men and women devote their lives to its study. Plenty of problems seem to remain unsolved. The new technics of Major Armstrong, which we shall presently brush, may help. Meanwhile radio remains the most democratic commercial institution we possess.

6

It is difficult yet to estimate the social effects of anything of such magnitude. Wild guesses are hazarded every day. The opinions of a hundred million people are said to have been as standardized as a set of parts for a sewing machine. People are presumably forgetting how to read: books, newspapers, periodicals are on the way out. Thought is so levelled that there is the same emotional response to the fall of Warsaw as to a new nosedrop. A new obbligato of continuous, meaningless noise has become essential to daily life. Brain muscles are becoming atrophied since thought is predigested and furnished free along with insidious commercial propaganda. Children are confusing health foods with honor, courage with dog biscuit, spiritual growth with regulation of their bowels. Presidents are steam-rollered into office under the emotional pressure of "fireside talks." Adolescents are driven into frenzies by continuous jazz. Privacy is inescapably invaded because, however definitely you may switch off your own radio, your neighbor's goes on.

Some of these guesses are true. Some suggest mere changes of degree or size or acceleration. Yet much mitigation comes from the magnitude of the broadcasting enterprise, its necessary variety. Commercial programs have acquired a kind of basic uniformity but many sustaining programs breed diversified speculation. It would be difficult for standardized opinion to issue, for instance, from the fairly presented discussions of Congress in 1939 on neutrality. A radical plan for redistribution of wealth may come through tonight, but the highly conservative voice of some captain of industry may shatter it tomorrow. The noise of a continuously functioning receiver may injure our own or our neighbor's nerves but it tends toward the building of a selective mind, and if all the talk of a day enters the subconscious, standardization of opinion will be difficult.

Reading and writing do not seem to be disappearing. Never have the mails been so full of written opinion as since radio broadcasts have stimulated it. Fan mail may be vacuous but it is an effort to express. The impossibility of orally "answering back" a radio speaker or entertainer has driven thousands of men, women and children to their pens and typewriters. Here is thought newly expressed in the written word by an army of people who twenty years ago never took a pen in hand from New Year's to Christmas. From the station end, too, come reams of printed matter, because hundreds of broadcasts, inadequate in themselves, are supplemented by pamphlets. Meanwhile what decline there may have been in newspapers, magazines and books is very likely a healthful one.

The complaint against advertising has rational causes. The complaint of a father a few years ago that his daughter was allowed to join a "secret" radio club only on condition of first swearing to tell the truth, to obey her parents and to drink a cup of a certain health beverage every day is a reasonable one. Such things are more immoral than obscenity. The scarcely altered voice with which Gabriel Heatter used to describe a European calamity and a suit of Rogers Peet clothes was shocking to many sensibilities. Yet advertisers are sensitive to these things when they are pointed out, and a highly critical vocal minority has produced many reforms.

The fan mail movement must be taken seriously. It has made a channel through which the people have learned a new vocality. With the habit of protest or applause expressed to broadcasters, similar comment addressed to the political representatives of the nation has been easy. Communications to Congress from individuals have increased in conformity with increase in fan mail. Thus it has been a contributing factor in the great awakening which was coincident with the great depression. In itself, of course, it must be accepted as minority opinion, as the articulate listeners form only a fractional part of a radio audience, and in many cases minority opinion is what assails Congress in the flood of communications which daily pours into the capitol. But minority rights compose one of the main supporting pillars of our political structure. The indirect effect, therefore, of radio broadcast and reception upon American democracy has been profound indeed.

But American democracy reaches far beyond government and politics. It filters into every interstice of society. It embraces industry, commerce, finance, for all the fight these institutions have consciously made against it, and this embrace has been tightened by radio broadcasting. If industry and business have hoped, by their invasion of the fireside, to strengthen their dictatorship, they have been badly fooled. On the contrary, they have placed themselves in an exceedingly vulnerable position. The new intimacy with the public which they have enforced has frequently bred contempt. While they have increased sales they have invited careful scrutiny of their publicity and salesmanship. Awakened Americans who can take, leave or ignore a printed advertisement are likely to be intensely critical of the intruding voice at the hearthstone. If the voice is too shrill or too honeyed or if its utterances are suspect, protest will follow, letters will find their way to headquarters, and industrial captains who, every day, are coming to look more and more like sensitive plants, will shiver in the wind. For flanking the industrial fortress on the other side is Government, which dispenses the free ether, and commerce has, through radio, immensely enhanced the intimacy between the Government and the people.

Furthermore, commerce has, through radio, entangled itself with many alien forces from which it should have kept aloof if it would strengthen its dictatorship. It has got itself uncomfortably hitched to politics through the sponsorship of controversial broadcasts or, indirectly, by the sustaining programs which it has made possible and necessary. It has mixed itself inextricably with imponderables like taste, moral and æsthetic. It has tied itself by the tail to the exceedingly dangerous dynamism of education. By crashing the gates of the home party it has forced the people to reply in kind and storm its own sanctum.

To understand how radio has worked toward democracy in America while it has done the opposite elsewhere, it will be convenient to compare American and European methods. Government ownership or stern control in Europe has dictated taste or opinion. Commercial control in America has invited controversy. Government control in Europe has posed a direct opposition between government and people. Commercial control in America has centered the conflict between people and attempted industrial dictatorship, with the Government as friendly referee. European systems have thrust government to the front of the stage; the American scheme has made it a backdrop in accordance with our peculiar concept of popular sovereignty. Government broadcasting in Europe has tended to narrow opinion to a single view; commercial broadcasting in America has found it necessary to admit many views in order to increase audiences.[22]

These statements apply to the most democratic nations in Europe. The extraordinary tightening of totalitarian power in the fascist and communist states has, largely, radio broadcasting to thank. In 1939, we saw the adroit manipulation of opinion in defiance of fact which characterized the broadcast speeches of power politics, among these absolutism. Yet here the dictators were often struck by curious boomerangs which returned to their doorsteps through forces inherent in radio technology. Cables and telegraphs might have been controlled so that external prop-

[22]On this question see H. V. Kaltenborn, "An American View of European Broadcasting," and C. F. Atkinson, "A European View of American Radio Programs," in *The Annals* of the American Academy of Political and Social Science, June, 1935, pp. 73–90.

aganda might have been separated from internal. The words intended to obtain the consent of the governed in Germany might never have come, for instance, before the awful judgment of the United States. Again, under older communications systems, a powerful maritime nation was able to control the channels of propaganda as England did in 1914 by cutting the cables between Germany and America.

Radio in international politics presents many paradoxes. Though it seems to be a powerful instrument in unifying peoples toward war, it frequently disrupts war's diplomatic patterns. Undoubtedly radio was partly responsible for the long delay of the war of 1939. It promoted wide discussion of the kind of secret maneuvering which brought the war of 1914 to its unexpected outbreak. It prevented clandestine mobilization. It made the issue of war or peace a popular issue. It increased government's fear of its people. It made the masses articulate. After the war started it had a profound effect on the neutrality of many nations because they were thoroughly informed on the issues. It has probably done more toward unmasking war and revealing its true sordidness than any other single instrument of our present civilization.

7

What are the portents of radio for the future? The frequency modulation system invented by Major Armstrong—an invention which imposes variations in frequency rather than in intensity upon the waves into which sound is translated—has been hailed as "the staticless radio." Yet its social significance does not lie in the fact that it automatically rejects static and background disturbances, but rather in its adaptability to an immense number of new channels. It has been estimated that, as the system operates on the ultra-short-wave band, "in ten megacycles . . . fifty powerful FM stations could be set up in one city," while, in another ten, "another fifty less powerful stations could be erected in small towns around the city; and this grouping could be duplicated (except as it is an economic fantasy) every 200 miles or less across the country on the same wave-lengths without interference between stations."[23]

Certain moss-covered corporations are fighting Armstrong's radio because of the obsolescence it would cause in existing radio sets. Yet it will undoubtedly prove useless, if Armstrong's claims are justified, to try to stem such a revolution. With such a magnification of our present huge system, what will be the social consequences of radio in the future?

One will certainly be dispersion. Already the isolated farmer has been made independent of post and press and of his automobile in matters of news, opinion and entertainment. Men and women in the most remote places are nearly as well informed on world events as the denizens of our tense cities. Since radio has brought the city into the rural districts, there is probably now less desire to move away from the land (other things being equal).

While newspapers will not go out of existence, they may well become a cultural rather than a communication medium. If this happens, they will return to the status they occupied at their inception in colonial and early federal America when news was not available to them.[24] They will still be needed for extended comment because they work in space rather than time, and time seems to be an inexorable limitation of broadcasting.[25] But if news usurps more and more of radio's limited time, entertainment must suffer accordingly, and whether the "fans" will permit this is doubtful.

With an increase in broadcasting channels, there should be an improvement rather than a deterioration of program quality. The air will then be free to educational institutions, to many "highbrow" broadcasters. The fact that Major Armstrong's transmission costs less to operate will play into the hands of more esoteric studios. There will be a selective opportunity on the dial

[23]Revolution in Radio," in *Fortune*, Oct., 1939, p. 88. See also "Staticless Radio" in *Scientific American*, May, 1939, p. 291; *Wireless World*, London, May 11, 1939, p. 443.

[24]*M. I. M.*, p. 386.

[25]Elmer Davis, "Broadcasting the Outbreak of War," in *Harpers Magazine*, Nov., 1939, p. 580.

The Armstrong Principle shown in these two simple graphic charts. *Below:* Each messenger boy shown represents a musical tone (or equivalent radio impulse) as it travels from transmitter to receiver. If one of these single impulses is "hit" or "tackled" by a discharge of electricity in the atmosphere, we hear interference, "static"

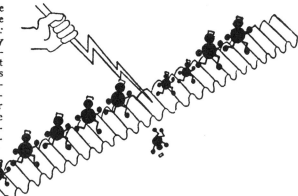

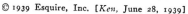

Right: Large messenger boy represents a powerful tone. Medium-size boy represents average tones. Small boy represents low-powered tones. *Below:* Diagram explaining the working of the Armstrong transmitter. Instead of one boy carrying a single tone to receiver, the load is divided among them. Boys move in wave form nonexisting in nature, thus are hard to hit. If one boy gets hit, the others carry the tone nearly complete to the listener.

© 1939 Esquire, Inc. [*Ken*, June 28, 1939]

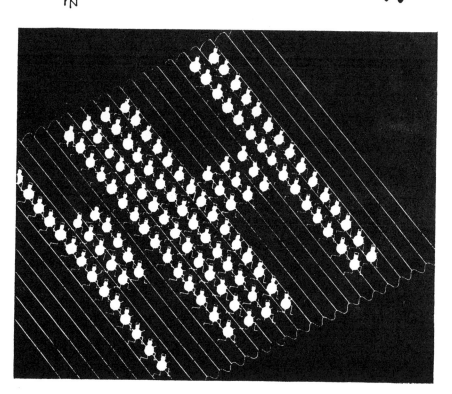

which will shatter the present uniformity or standardization or dullness through competition of "quality" material.

In this discussion we have studiously avoided television. The invention is nearly as old as radio, yet almost twenty years after radio became a commonplace in America, television is still, largely, in an experimental stage as far as society is concerned. For many years after the technology was perfected, the questions "What is it for?" and "Who wants it?" have prevented its entrance into commerce. In this respect it is one of the most curious phenomena in the history of invention. In respect to social effect its influence, to date, is nil.

We have included radio in the section of this record which is dedicated to the impulse of speed rather than in that which follows the cultural impulse. The invention of telegraphy without wire answered the need for more quick communication only possible if the cost of the carrier could be cut. The first demonstrations of its effectiveness came in the rapid response to calls for help from the sea. Its greatest value to date is in the multiplication of intelligences so that events can be brought to the attention of millions of consciousnesses almost at the moment of their occurrence.

The full cultural consequences of radio must lie in the future. In America commercial control has so far undoubtedly lowered its value as a cultural instrument in the sense in which printing, photography and the phonograph have been such instruments. In the same field, its standards in general may be lower than those of the cinema. For the most part, commercial broadcasters have sought the lowest common denominator. With exceptions, such as the broadcast of symphony orchestras, its work toward raising cultural standards or even maintaining those of pre-radio periods has been through "sustaining" programs put on without advertising, at the expense of the networks.

The story of radio brings to a close our history of the speed impulse. A concomitant of this impulse has, necessarily, been waste. With the first consciousness of waste came the impulse of economy. The movement toward conservation was as we shall see a laggard one in American history.

Part V

ECONOMY

Chapter Twenty

CONSERVATION

I

WHEN the last frontier closed in the 1890's a few realists made a rough sort of inventory and uttered the astounding pronouncement that the natural resources of the United States were not inexhaustible. This was such an affront to American tradition that the investigators were thought unpatriotic. Miners and lumbermen, who had organized their enterprises into large corporations which paid excellent dividends to absentee stockholders, were particularly grieved by such an un-American suggestion.

Yet the foreboding persisted in stern, unromantic minds. Generally speaking, doubts like this gain a hold in times of depression and lose it on the upswing. The early nineties were bad times. In these years the first Forest Reserve was created. There was another depression around 1907 and Theodore Roosevelt was able to gain the public ear for the first serious suggestions on economy applied to forests, land and water.[1] It was difficult to call the beloved Colonel either un-American or socialist, yet the "interests" fought him bitterly. The first Roosevelt, though he had romantic intervals in some departments of thought, was not deceived about natural resources. His effort toward economy was on a large scale. In Gifford Pinchot he had a fighting aide.[2]

There was another lapse after Roosevelt, though Wilson's administration began with battles against waste. The World War interrupted them. Thrift is not easy in wartime. When this one

[1]Message of President Theodore Roosevelt, Dec. 3, 1901.
[2]Gifford Pinchot, *The Fight for Conservation*, N. Y., 1910.

463

began in Europe, new frontiers of opportunity appeared in the United States. America's entrance into the war bred new romanticism, which carried us over the first difficult post-war period into the halcyon twenties, when conservation was forgotten by the people.

It was not forgotten by the experts. The army of them which the first Roosevelt had mobilized, though ineffective in the apathy of fictional prosperity which now supplemented genuine wealth, went right on studying terrain and strategy. These men and women had become fascinated and no wonder. They saw beneath the surface into the science which must underlie any national economic scheme. They understood the poverty of the ground on which the orgy was in full swing. They saw clearly into the dungeon beneath the banquet hall. If any real basis of American prosperity were to be saved, a fourth dimension must be added to the three in which the exploitation of the physical country was already operating. The first two dimensions had been those of expansion. The third was depth, supplementing the surface yields. The fourth must be science.

The depression of the opening thirties prepared the people for the realistic demands of a new, revolutionary political administration. There was still a confusion in the public mind between money and physical wealth, a normal result of the decade of fictional values. Quite naturally a program of extensive spending of money was alarming at a moment of such evident ruin. Yet, as the public became educated to certain basic conditions which underlay much of the nation's unrest, it admitted the wisdom of the large outlays in one direction at least. Except where there was a conflict with ancient business traditions, few Americans quarrelled with the second Roosevelt about his efforts to save the land on which the nation stands and from which it derives its sustenance. The effort of the new administration in this direction has all been centered upon introducing the fourth dimension. This chapter and the two which follow will concern themselves with applications of science to the use of natural resources.

2

The experts who had multiplied in the silent army, occupied for three decades in strategic study, were ready by 1930. In the stunned interval of the depression they flooded the country with spectacular accounts of their findings.

The product of mines and oil wells had been and was still being wasted on such a scale that the end of such resources was actually in sight. But still more disastrous was the total disappearance of millions of tons of soil. A large part of the arable land was gone beyond recovery. Much of what remained was going fast. They drew a picture of the country as it would look within the lifetime of our grandchildren. It was a picture of famine.

Why? They asked the rhetorical question and answered it. Because of the belief of our ancestors that there were no limits to the physical wealth of America. Because under this delusion they had raped the land. Because they were encouraged in their ravages by a *laissez-faire* economy, a hands-off government which, nevertheless, had followed a profligate land policy. Because government, terrified lest it interfere with the hallowed rights of the individual in his private property, had permitted that individual to collectivize the forces of destruction in gigantic lumbering, mining and agricultural corporations or combinations.

The collective forces, assisted by rapidly advancing technology, had denuded the forests, torn up the grasslands, flooded and polluted the rivers, abolished the wildlife. The experts blamed the railroad builders, the highway builders, the city builders, the planters and the farmers. They came at last to the beloved pioneers, the men and women who had settled the big river basins, the prairies, the Great Plains, who had pushed the nation west to the Rockies.

The statements of the experts were all true. No fair-minded reader of the whole story could dispute any of them. Even when they pointed out that there was no "alibi" in the plea of ignorance, the historical record bore them out. At the very start of the Federation, knowledge was abundant, there for the asking.

Washington, Jefferson, Madison, Ruffin and other highly influential persons understood soil conservation.[3] John Quincy Adams fought for the protection of the forests.[4] Visitors from abroad were shocked by wasteful American agriculture and constantly printed their protests.[5] Robert Barton of Virginia talked in vain for years about scientific farming, inspiring no one but the Mc-Cormicks, who introduced machines to abet the waste.[6] The Germans and Swedes, who settled so much of the West, came from lands where conservation had long been practiced, so any suggestion of ignorance there must be discounted.

So all these "conquerors" of a continent whose conquest brought defeat for the soil were sinners against the light. If the exposition of their sins acts as a deterrent to future generations, then the end and result will be beneficial. At the same time, the historian must accept these abuses as incidental to a large political and social pattern, and in such a view the sense of sin is somewhat tempered. He must remember, in looking back over the evolution of a continent-wide political domination, the importance of the time factor.

If the pioneers had proceeded by all the best available technics to conserve land resources in the places which they settled, we might have, today, some twenty nations instead of one. There might still be large, scarcely expanded areas between them. Stretches like the Great Plains might have remained unorganized, inhabited, in 1940, by savage tribes. Such a continent might be a desirable place to live in but it would not be the United States we know today.

As it was, the lure of virgin land drawing men away from land which had been abused was the basic cause of our rapid expansion. If the forests had not been cut to make rafts, steamboats, railroad ties, plank roads and, finally, houses, the expansion could not have taken place. The large spaces to be covered imposed a necessity of speed which precluded scientific forestry. The transcontinental railroad, an urgent necessity to a continent-wide political United States, laid out the geography of towns

[3]Stuart Chase, *Rich Land, Poor Land*, p. 98.
[4]*Ibid.*, p. 297.   [5]*M. I. M.*, p. 218.   [6]*Ibid.*, pp. 227 ff.

and farm lands, and undoubtedly laid it out wrong from the conservationist's point of view. But having drawn the pattern and at the same time sketched the plan of continent-wide industrial revolution, it was unavoidable that enormous masses of people should move upon its tracks, build cities along them and exploit the adjacent land for all it was worth. Indeed, the circle becomes more intricately vicious here, for it was only through such exploitation that the railroad could be financed rapidly enough to achieve a coast-to-coast national integrity. This meant more forest-cutting, more quick, careless plowing, more eventual erosion.

Delay in the process would have caused national dissolution. Our history is dotted with attempted secessions, the embryos of separate national schemes. But for the industrial integrity of the North, the South would have been lost to the nation in the sixties. A Pacific republic was averted just in time by the railroad and by rapid, wasteful exploitation of mines.[7] Still earlier there was talk of an independent nation in the Louisiana Territory, which abated when thousands of rafts floated down the Ohio and the Mississippi to establish connection with the Atlantic fringe. Waste accompanied all of these salvages. It was an inevitable product of Manifest Destiny.

Perhaps a continent-wide nation achieved at such cost is not worth while. Perhaps we should be happier if, like Europe, we had gone more gradually at our building. To glance at Europe from 1914 to 1918 and again in 1939 and in 1940 suggests doubts. There seem to be advantages in a unified political commonwealth stretched between the oceans.

At any rate, there it is, and with it a tragic Dust Bowl, washed-out farms, naked, gullied hillsides, a dearth of wild life, polluted rivers, springtime floods. It does no good to say that if we had not cut the trees we should have no towns to be washed away. The vice is rotary and the whole of our civilization is caught in the whirlpool. Our concentration, therefore, must be not on who started the circle but on the best means of striking a tangent. It is a consolation to know that nowhere in the world has such a colossal mechanism of salvage been set up as in the United

[7]See p. 504.

States. Some things are forever lost. Others may, in time, be restored. Still others which we now possess may be retained.

2

There are two kinds of erosion. One is caused by water, the other by wind. Erosion may occur without the intervention of man. Over a large part of the earth, however, this has been prevented by plant life. The erosion with which the conservationists are most concerned is man-made.

A plant is a hydraulic machine. It draws water in through its roots and "transpires" it from its leaves. The transpired water drawn upward by the sun is held for a time suspended in the form of vapor; condensing, it falls as rain or snow, after which the process is repeated.[8]

Roots perform another function. Forming a network in the ground they hold the water, keep it from running away. This is a first-line reserve for later drinking. A second line of reserve is established by water slowly seeping down through the root labyrinth into the subsoil below and finally into an underground artesian lake. Thence it may bubble up into surface ponds, lakes, rivers from which, eventually, it finds its way back to the sky. From such a lake, also, it may be drawn up through drilled wells to supply men and their animals.

If a surplus falls on the ground it moves slowly over the leafy labyrinth of plants to a river, which carries it away to nourish remote places. Meanwhile, the watered and nourished plants grow, wither in their time, decay upon the ground and form humus for new growth. The humus, fibrous, absorbent, rich in plant food, accumulates for centuries and becomes what is known as topsoil.

The story of man-made water erosion is extremely simple. Men cut the trees on a hill and pull or burn the stumps. In any case the roots cease to function and soon disappear. When water falls on the hill, there is nothing to hold it. It is drunk by nothing,

[8]The "hydrologic cycle" is well described by Chase, Chap. V; Katherine Glover, *America Begins Again*, N. Y., 1939, pp. 92, 93; G. V. Jacks and R. O. White, *Vanishing Lands*, N. Y., 1939. Chap. XIV.

its flow is interrupted by no tangle of roots, it runs over the surface. This cheats both the soil and the artesian reserve. Below the timber line the rushing water may encounter thick grass

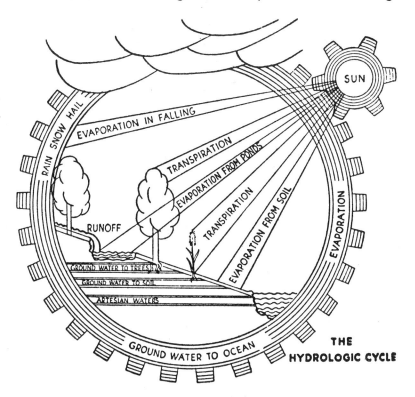

The great wheel

The total water on the planet is believed a fixed quantity but runs through a perpetual cycle. Evaporation and transpiration are followed by precipitation and infiltration—rivers carrying the run-off back to the ocean for subsequent evaporation

and there be dispersed and perform its normal functions. But if men have also plowed out the grass, there are no roots to disperse it. Here men may have employed art and plowed their furrows at right angles to the rushing stream in which case some of the water may be held in little reservoirs to nourish the crops. But if they are extensive farmers like the pioneers, they have plowed up and down the hill creating channels instead of reservoirs. In these the torrent gains momentum. As it erodes the furrows it takes the topsoil with it. It deposits this in the river which, now swollen by many such free torrents, carries it to the sea where it is forever lost to man. Millions of acres of topsoil —the accumulation of centuries—have thus been transported in the course of a few years into the Gulf of Mexico. But some of it, too, has stuck in the rivers in the form of "silt," raising the level of the river and ruining power enterprises.

The story of the Dust Bowl is equally simple. Vast stretches of grassy plain have been recklessly plowed. There are no more grass roots then, to hold the water in its natural reserves. In a region where the rainfall is slight, a drought follows. The plains are wide and flat and hence constantly wind-blown. The winds blow the dry topsoil, which now has nothing to hold it in place, from Kansas or Oklahoma as far east, sometimes, as Vermont.

A natural question arises at this point. Why do the farmer's crops not hold the soil as the grass has done? There are several answers. One is that the roots of clean-tilled crops like corn are too far apart to form thick networks as native grasses do. But the main reason is that between harvest and planting, the fields are bare.

These two activities, deforestation and careless plowing plus the highly important one of overgrazing,[9] are the main causes of land loss. They have other effects, too, such as the destruction of cities from flood, and dust pneumonia. But there are other causes of land loss. There are forest and prairie fires, factory fumes, concrete pavement, river poisoning, destruction of wild life, excavation, exhaustion from the overcultivation of certain crops, and improper attempts at flood control. These subjects have been abundantly treated by specialists. We can do no more than summarize them here.

A handful of statistics suggests the extent of the damage already suffered. Out of our total area of about two billion acres, about seven hundred million, or some 37 per cent, are slightly eroded and must be watched. "Moderate" erosion, which means that a good deal of soil is already lost, is operating on a still larger acreage—about 41 per cent. Some 12 per cent of the land suffers

---

[9] This has been especially true in the Southwest where the cattle kingdom began.

severe erosion and only a fractional salvage is possible here. Three per cent has been wholly destroyed and cannot be recovered.

These figures were published by the Department of Agriculture in 1938.[10] They had been compiled somewhat before that, so it may be assumed that there has been considerable destruction since that time. How much is suggested by the single estimate that about three billion tons of topsoil are annually washed away from overgrazed pastures, cultivated or barren fields.[11] The destruction follows no simple arithmetical formula. Erosion breeds more erosion at an undetermined rate. This rate grows more rapid as more and more topsoil disappears. Bigger gullies carry more water, lead more water into land which is still good. The momentum can be slowed down only if the methods used against it are on as large a scale as nature's means of destruction.

An enormous If is posed by the Department of Agriculture. If present practices are continued, 61 per cent of our present crop land will be progressively destroyed. This leaves only 39 per cent which may be safely cultivated under prevailing practices—a bare hundred and sixty million acres. Certain land not used at present may be reclaimed by irrigation or otherwise adjusted to crops. This brings the total which may safely be cultivated by current methods to a little more than two hundred million acres—less than one half of the total crop area now being exploited.

That is the black cloud which now hangs over American agriculture. It seems to annihilate our fond hopes for an agricultural revolution, a "back to the land" movement, the new opportunities for "chemurgy." Fortunately the cloud has a silver lining. It is visible only when we begin to take seriously the Department of Agriculture's giant IF.

If, adds the department, the *best* known practices are applied to the land, the cultivable area could be increased to an acreage even greater than the total under cultivation today.[12] The difficulty is that the If involves many old American traditions, customs,

---

[10]U. S. Dept. of Agriculture Yearbook, 1938, pp. 5, 6. The Yearbook is entitled *Soils and Men*.

[11]*Ibid.*, p. 7.   [12]*Ibid.*, p. 6.

faiths; among them are rugged individualism, more ingrained, perhaps, in the farmer than in any one else; notions of private property and states' rights and ignorance of the new concept of the public interest. Incidental among these are price structures, corporate ownership, industrial impingement, obstruction by utilities, absentee stockholders and many other collective factors.

To preserve the delicate balance between a democratic pattern and large public necessity is an extremely difficult task. A nation like the U. S. S. R. can force certain measures upon the people at a sacrifice which, happily, is inconceivable to Americans. It is our practice to bring about reforms by education, a process which entails no loss of social liberties. An American, educated in public needs, will voluntarily make the kind of concession to government control which under the super-states is imposed from above.

It is certain that the farmer, by himself, cannot effect a reform. He must have the co-operation of his neighbors. Thus, in the Great Plains, a farmer who "lists" or deep-plows his land against dust will accomplish nothing unless his neighbor does likewise. When the dust starts to blow on his neighbor's acres, his own efforts at conservation are lost. In such an area it is all or no one. This means regulation for salvage and is much like fire ordinances in a city.

The degree to which American farmers have shown themselves amenable to instruction in soil conservation is a proof of the fundamental soundness of our scheme. Freedom, after all, can derive only from a voluntary alliance with natural law.

The farmers are learning the "best practices." These are less difficult, in fact, for the individualist farmer than for the large corporation which must pay dividends to absentee stockholders. If large blocs of land can be transferred to individualist farm-owners and if corporation-owned land can gradually be eased into the hands of government, with the eventual intent of returning it (after its repair) to true private ownership, much of it can be saved.

But behind the efforts of the farmer in contour-plowing, strip-cropping, rotation, grass and tree culture there must be a secure background of engineering. None of these careful tricks will avail much if a swollen river tears over them every spring, destroying, with its billions of gallons of wasted water, the farmer's buildings and his stock. Nor, in the arid lands which, nevertheless, have extremely fertile soil will the farmer prosper unless he can control and tap the rivers. Such a region exists on the coastal plain of southern California, and because its extreme necessities have mothered a host of engineering inventions which form the background of water control, it simplifies understanding of conservation to look at it first.

<h2 style="text-align:center">3</h2>

For centuries the wild Colorado River has been looked on by man as something to be approached with extreme caution. Hundreds of intrepid explorers have been washed away through its mammoth canyons simply because they tried to cross it. Navigation in any of its seventeen hundred miles of flow has been abandoned. Its only practical use has been to furnish a strip of natural fertility along the banks of its lower basin in the California desert and artificial irrigation through the Imperial Valley by a canal starting near the river's mouth in Mexico and thus subject to political difficulties.

But after farming began in occasional places along the Colorado, the river became every year more exasperating. Drawing down to a trickle in the parched summer, it would rise to terrible proportions in the spring so that the farmer was forever between the devil of drought and the deep sea of flood. It irked him no end to see water enough to keep him happy for a full year wash by him in a few weeks, carrying his property with it. And the coastal cities, too, skimping through the summer on domestic water, grew angry at the spendthrift Colorado. Was there not some engineer smart enough to hold back part of this water and distribute it evenly over a suffering land?

There were plenty of them by 1920. It seemed, by that time, that there was nothing beyond the talents of the best engineers. But all the problems did not lie in the engineer's province. American tradition had it that engineers were hired by private capital;

473

that vast enterprises of this sort were initiated by corporations for profit. When corporations looked at the Colorado they were worried about capital, profit, the time factor. How, then, about state governments? But the Colorado affected seven states and each of them had a different opinion of its usefulness. Arizona, for instance, could scarcely be expected to spend millions of dollars to enrich California and thought the Colorado, which had helped carve her precious Grand Canyon, was more valuable for other purposes.

So a group of Californians, in 1922, jumped tradition and called on the Federal Government, thus inviting paternalism, centralization and many other dread bogeys. We may imagine how distressing conditions had become when we see them driving good Republicans to such a step in the middle of a prosperous era.

Naturally, the Swing-Johnson Bill, which followed, was carefully worded.[13] The harnessing of the Colorado, which the bill proposed, must, first of all, be self-liquidating. This was to be managed by the sale of the by-product, electric juice, over a period of fifty years, the total cost to be covered in advance by contracts. Second, construction must be done by private companies under contract to the Government. Third, there must be no competition with private enterprise. Fourth, states' rights must not be infringed, so at least six of the seven states in the Colorado basin must ratify the act.[14] The protected bill was signed in December, 1928, by the retiring Calvin Coolidge.[15] Work began in 1930, the second year of the administration of the first engineer-president, Herbert Hoover.

The Boulder Canyon project was, perhaps, the most difficult engineering feat ever attempted in America.[16] It consisted of three dams, a canal, reservoirs, power stations and lesser adjuncts. The largest (Boulder) dam would meet the full flow of the Colorado in Black Canyon—nearly a quarter million cubic feet per second—turn it back into a lake 115 miles long and, under perfect control, let enough water through to provide an evenly

[13]H. R. 5773, 70th Congress.   [14]*Ibid.*, Sec. 4 (a).   [15]45 Stat. 1057.
[16]For a popular description of the whole project, see Ralph B. Simmons, *Boulder Dam and the Great Southwest*, Los Angeles, 1936.

flowing river for three hundred miles below. Incidentally, the controlled water would develop nearly two million horsepower and furnish more than four billion kilowatt hours annually to go toward liquidation. The dam itself was to be 726 feet high, almost a quarter-mile long across the river from Arizona to Nevada and about an eighth of a mile thick at the bottom.

A hundred and fifty miles below Boulder Dam a second dam (Parker) would divert enough of the river to deliver domestic water to thirteen cities including Los Angeles, and three hundred miles below Boulder Dam still another would send enough water through an eighty-mile All-American Canal to irrigate the whole of Imperial Valley.[17]

A proof of the extent to which invention had adopted the scientific method by 1930 is in the fact that work on Boulder Dam was continuous and was completed in five years. There was no stopping to admit failure and try something else. The Colorado was thoroughly harnessed on paper before the first blast. Moreover the job was timed so that the concrete was ready-mixed at the exact moment it was needed (three and a quarter million cubic yards of it), the machinery was there to be installed not a second too late.

The first job was to throw the wild Colorado out of its course, to lead it gently into tunnels so that the bottom above the dam site would be dry. The tunnels were fifty-six feet in diameter and some 4000 feet long; there were four of them, blasted through solid rock. The blasted rock was carted away to crushers and concrete mixers, where it was made into the material of the dam. Railroads built along the precarious sides of Boulder Canyon carried the material, on time, from point to point; giant cables swung it across the river. Where the railroads could not go, motor trucks could and did.

The workers were as disciplined as an army, as automatic as soldiers in close-order drill. A model city was built for them, a clean, air-conditioned city which defied the scorching heat. To it the shifts returned for their rest. But day and night the work

[17] U. S. Dept. of the Interior, Bureau of Reclamation, *Boulder Dam* (Circular).

never stopped; hot sun or darkness did not alter the comings and goings of the workers.

One day the great wall was finished; the angry Colorado was let flow back, the torrents dashed out their fury against the concrete and bounded back through the dark canyons until among the naked hills stretched a peaceful lake, deep, navigable, giving healthful recreation to the people of two states and a refuge for wild fowl in a spot which had been as forbidding as the circles of Dante's Inferno. The view of it today from the dam is scarcely real, for heaven, here, has flowed into hell.

The huge penstocks, turbines and generators were in place when the engineers saw fit to lead the Colorado into its new job. Carefully they measured flow, lake and river content, temperatures, salt, silt, revolutions of machines, electric pressures. They looked upon their work and saw that it was good. So did the people of dozens of cities in three states, exulting in plenty of new cheap light and power. So did the farmers of the Imperial Valley, where the canal would carry peaceful waters to make an oasis in the dreadful desert two million acres big. So did the water consumers of Los Angeles. The farm lands stretch over the rich soil, ignoring rainfall, ignoring flood. The farmers may build today in security—the force of the Colorado is with them, not against them.

The Boulder Canyon project is a triumph of American invention. On a still larger scale, though scarcely more difficult as an engineering enterprise, the Columbia River is being controlled by Grand Coulee Dam. On a smaller scale, reclamation projects are dotted over the country. The inventions involved are children of the sternest necessity, proofs, indeed, of the hackneyed adage. From the purely technical point of view, the waste of a century seems worth while. From such inventions a future may grow into reality which will make us forget the whole of the sinful past.

4

But experiments in such arid or semi-arid regions are remote from the experience of Americans accustomed to diversified country and the normal changing seasons of the temperate zone.

The struggles with the Colorado and Columbia rivers seem combats with exotic, unreasonable nature rather than with the man-made destruction of good, natural farm land. To the majority of Americans, therefore, the regional planning in the great humid basin of the Tennessee River seems nearer home. Here we find higher than average rainfall, large diversity of country, land adapted by nature to forests and farms. Once heavily wooded, the rich loam held the water and the river moved gently. When the forests were cut, there were great tracts of good farm land. It was planted, however, with exhausting crops like cotton and tobacco which began the depletion of plant food. Erosion followed. The flooding of the river, a normal consequence of tree destruction, wrought its usual havoc among towns and farms.

By 1930, the devastation of much of the valley had made such progress that an attempt to redeem it seemed courageous indeed. The experts knew that, here, erosion must be stopped in mid-career, that correction must be applied on a large scale or the valley would presently become a desert. Then engineers, studying the river, estimated the size of an engineering project to give adequate water-control and here again, as in the West, it seemed obvious that only a great federal undertaking could achieve true conservation.

But the vision of such experts had grown. The pioneer concept that nothing was impossible in America was a part of their heritage. The rest was experience and scientific understanding based upon it. If nothing was impossible to the expanding, creative energy of the pioneer American, then nothing was impossible in salvage and economy to the American technology of the 1930's. There was still a political hurdle. It was jumped by the administration whose primary job was emergency salvage.

There was a vague background of effort by the department of government which concerns itself with Inland Waters to make the Tennessee navigable. This, surely, was a federal job, and the new planners wisely took off from this prerogative. But once navigation was achieved, the collateral opportunities loomed large before the eyes of the conservation technologists. Why not turn the entire valley into a vast laboratory, a demonstration ground from which the whole country might learn to recover desperate regions? But what about the people, citizens of a democracy? The people, it appeared, were as desperately in need of salvation as the land. But to rescue people in a democracy was a ticklish business. The administration understood this and contemplated no charity, no paternalism, no socialization. The plan was intended simply to provide the people with certain normal basic opportunity to which citizenship and taxes entitled them. Part of that opportunity was education. Given it and given certain fundamental physical controls which they were unable to organize without expert administration, they would then have a start *in salvaging themselves.*

The inhabitants of the rural areas in the Tennessee Valley were a sad people. They were a discouraged people.[18] Year after year they had watched their farms slide away. Poverty had driven them into dark, stinking cabins. Their self-respect was as patched as their clothes. Many of them were tenants working depleting and depleted cotton crops for the barest subsistence. A hundred dollars a year provided a moderate budget for a sizeable and growing family,[19] even if there were a few perquisites not reckoned in cash. Degradation, degeneracy, ignorance follow poverty and discouragement. These developments were well under way in the Tennessee Valley.

Under the Tennessee Valley Authority some 40,000 square miles were set aside for regional planning.[20] For flood and navigation control of the Tennessee and its tributaries, ten dams have been estimated as necessary. Two of these already existed for power purposes, one being the celebrated Wilson Dam at Muscle Shoals which operated an explosives plant during the War. (The chemists at once saw the possibilities of this plant in making fertilizer.) When the others are completed, a nine-foot navigable channel will run through the Tennessee River for a distance of

[18]Chase, Chap. XV.

[19]Average annual cash income of 4000 families moved from the Norris Dam site. Chase, p. 267.

[20]TVA Act of May 18, 1933 (48 Stat. 58), as amended by act of Aug. 31, 1935 (49 Stat. 1075).

530 miles.[21] This will create a true waterway from Knoxville to the Ohio where only a highly capricious stream ran before. It will be a national, not a local benefit. Apart from navigation, the undertaking will reduce floods as far away as the Lower Mississippi Valley, with resulting benefits estimated at close to four hundred million dollars.[22]

Local improvement is largely a by-product of the dams. They

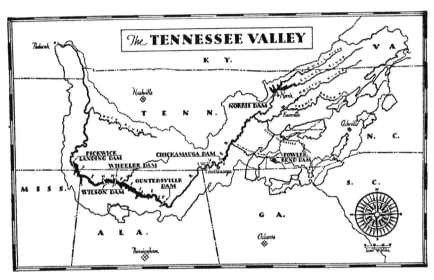

Plan of Tennessee Valley project showing seven great dams

Morris Dam, 265 feet high, 1872 feet long; Gunterville Dam, 80 feet high, 3980 feet long; Wheeler Dam, 72 feet high, 6335 feet long; Wilson Dam, 137 feet high, 4860 feet long; Pickwick Dam, 107 feet high, 7715 feet long; Chickamauga Dam, 104 feet high, 5685 feet long; Fowler Bend Dam, 300 feet high, 1265 feet long

have provided electrification in districts which would never have been reached by private enterprise. So that dark, cold houses are now lighted, powered, heated, equipped with cooking and refrigerating facilities at minimum cost. They have created lakes for recreation, the preservation of wild life, water storage. They furnish power to a valuable fertilizer plant.

When these benefits were achieved, both technical and social experts got to work. The hollow-eyed farmers watched skeptically the experiments in diversified farming, soil study, treating with

[21]TVA, Annual Report, 1938, p. 14.   [22]Ibid., p. 17.

phosphates (mined in the region), terracing, reforestation, preservation of fruits and vegetables, sorghum processing, tobacco curing, bookkeeping. Slowly—for they had known much bitter experience—they became fascinated. They wanted to try these things on their own land. More and more of them became "Test-Demonstration farmers." Test-Demonstration served two purposes: first it improved the farmer's own condition, second it provided an enlightening spectacle for his neighbors. This was voluntary, not enforced. Presently, therefore, in communities which had been dead or dying for years, there sprung up intense activity: for the first time meetings, committees, clubs, county organizations brought isolated folk together.

The Civilian Conservation Corps was turned loose in the region. Under TVA supervision, they planted some sixty million trees. By 1938, farmers had become interested in reforestation and in that year planted more than a million and a half on their own farms. By the end of the fiscal year, 1938, tree-planting had protected 6300 farms covering 950,000 acres.[23]

Social inventors were busy, too, in the new, hopeful tract. As a result good schools have been established, effective medical service, education in sports and recreation are operating. In some of our enlightened communities we sometimes deplore over-organization in these directions. No one who has known the scattered solitary families of the Tennessee Valley can fail to understand the normal hunger of such people for social activity. TVA gave it a start and the people have carried on under their own leaders.

5

The planners of TVA have encountered a difficulty in tabulating "self-liquidation" on a balance sheet which did not embarrass the planners of the Colorado project. Their imponderable figures do not easily reduce to dollars and cents over a definite period. There are a lot of curious items on their books.

Item: clean, healthy children in good schools. Item: mental

[23]*Ibid.*, p. 51.

activity, release from the eternal boredom of impoverished soil. Item: home-owning farmers. Items: a good, diversified diet, light, washing machines, heat, electric ranges, refrigerators, community interests, recreation, amusement. Item: education for thousands of people in the preservation of fruitful land. Item: the return of self-respect to a large degraded population.[24]

Because TVA has concentrated so hard upon such things they have neglected their publicity department. Against it an extremely talented lot of propagandists have operated under good pay from utility companies. Ineffectually trying to combat this army, untrained enthusiasts have talked about "yardsticks," forgetting how literally such a word will be taken up by the enemy—applied wholly to electric power. As a result of this uneven conflict, many a businessman in New York and Chicago thinks the entire TVA is one dam erected for the sole purpose of competing with private enterprises occupied in generating electricity. It is not altogether fair to blame him. He has been subjected to a skillful, interested attack from one side only. Habitually, he will utter the most fantastic improbabilities as established facts. His education will take longer, in the end, than that of the Tennessee farmer.

The controversy, however, is not part of our story. Our focus, as always, must be on the social history of invention in America. We have had a brief glance at the background of conservation, the control of river water. This is a background of engineering. In the foreground are simple farming methods for which machines and implements have already been designed.

Part of the Dust Bowl can probably never be reclaimed. But the dust can be anchored by grasses. This will prevent the desert from spreading. Other parts of the Great Plains area, threatened by the Dust Bowl, are being conserved. By 1936, "foreground" farming practices had been applied to 600,000 acres there. One hundred and fifty-five thousand were being strip-cropped—a strip of grass between crop rows. Two hundred thousand acres

[24]For discussion of the educational program in the Tennessee Valley, see Maurice F. Seay, "Adult Education," in *Bulletin* of Bureau of School Service, U. of Ky., X, 4, June, 1938.

were being plowed on the contour to conserve rainfall and impede wind. More than 3600 miles of terraces had been built to hold the moisture on 65,000 acres. Some 200,000 acres of grassland were carefully controlled to prevent overgrazing. Behind this improvement were 2100 dams in the Great Plains region, providing storage of 32,000,000,000 gallons of water.[25]

In the report of the Great Plains Committee, a chapter on Attitudes of Mind is highly revealing. Here are the destructive attitudes: that man conquers nature; that natural resources are inexhaustible; that habitual practices are the best; that what is good for the individual is good for everybody; that an owner may do with his property as he likes; that expanding markets will continue indefinitely; that free competition co-ordinates industry with agriculture; that values will increase indefinitely; that tenancy is a stepping-stone to ownership; that the factory farm is generally desirable, and that the individual must make his own adjustments.[26] All our land troubles today may be traced to one or more of these legendary beliefs.

The present of the farmer in America is hard. The future is hopeful. He has much to look for in the chemical laboratory.

[25]Great Plains Committee, *The Future of the Great Plains,* Washington, 1936, p. 135.
[26]*Ibid.,* pp. 63–67.

Chapter Twenty-one

SYNTHESIS

ENTERING the chemical laboratory we find ourselves in a room with a view. Looking from the many windows, we are aware that we have reached the ultimate pinnacle of our technological civilization. From nowhere in our world is the scene of the past and the future so clear, the visibility so high. On one side stretch the endless green pastures of the future, secure on their high plateau; on the other is the steep ascent we have climbed, the rocky, bloody path out of the dark valley. Along that path, man, the most dubious experiment of evolution —thin-skinned, weak-muscled, clumsy-footed, soft-toothed, dyspeptic man, has won all the battles with hostile Nature. Has he not, indeed, subdued every possible enemy?

Not quite. In the chemical laboratory, once he has surveyed the charming prospect of his victory, he turns to face the greatest enemy of all. Across the retorts and tubes and machines on the table he suddenly observes a thin-skinned, weak-muscled, clumsy-footed, soft-toothed and dyspeptic antagonist and he is seized with terror. He forgets the pleasant prospect outside. His whole concern is how he may come to grips with this hostile creature, this one being who has behind him the same conquests, who must share the same reward. For the chemical laboratory, in which was conceived the reward of all the valor, has brought man closer than all other agencies put together to his ultimate enemy, himself.

On one side of the room a group is busy over the elixirs of life, the fluids of increase, the anodynes to pain. They are mixing restoratives for the exhausted earth; they are re-creating lost wealth. Across the tables another group is equally intent on toxic compounds which will destroy life and on combustible mixtures which will blast the green pastures to barrenness. In time the concentration in the room grows so intense that no one remembers to look out the window. The compounders of the elixirs are wholly concerned with restoring what the toxic workers have destroyed. The past and the future disappear, all focus is narrowed down to the little circles of light cast by the two lamps of the present and the workers are racing against the time when one of the lamps shall go out.

It is a source of perennial astonishment to poets and philosophers that men, having "conquered" the supposedly inimical forces of Nature, have done so little with themselves. This is easier to understand once we realize how we have gone about the two contests. Our successful "fight" with Nature has not, in fact, been a fight at all. Nor have we, in reality, "subdued" anything. The forces of gravity or of electricity are just as strong as they ever were. We have not shot at them, poisoned them or starved them. On the contrary, we have studied them in order to find out how we might ally ourselves with them instead of opposing them. To do this we have drawn up a set of rules which we obey. If we disobey any of them we are certain to get hurt. We do not defy gravity by jumping out of the window. We simply make use of a valuable supporting material, the air, to climb upon and then call what we have done a "subduing" of gravity. If we had really subdued it or defied it, we should be in a bad spot indeed for our existence on earth depends upon it. Nor have we "chained" the lightning. We have only designed a path for the electrical force in the direction of our use; thus it may move our machines instead of wasting.

If we had studied human nature in the way that we have studied physical force, our present warfare against our fellows would have a different character. If we should investigate the properties of Germans, British, Slavs, Jews, Negroes or Mongols under the laboratory conditions that elucidate the properties of calcium, sodium, nitrogen, vanadium or sulphur, we might lead them into useful channels. As it is, these undirected human elements wander constantly into explosive mixtures. Lately, in their wanderings they have picked up the equations of the chemical laboratory and applied these to the mixture with results which threaten destruction to both humanity and science. A German and a Frenchman react unfavorably enough in simple combination; in the presence of such reagents or catalysts as guncotton and gasoline not a trace of human precipitate remains.

The argument has been advanced that man's study of human nature is an effort to lift oneself by one's boot-straps. To study men, there must be supermen. But why not? Such creatures have dotted history; they seem to be all about us today. Some philosophers believe that evolution will proceed from now on through a series of human levels. If a group of supermen should apply the cool scientific method of the chemist or the biologist to the levels below them rather than the trial-and-error experiment of power politics, a working social order might be possible. But they had better begin soon before the basic material is lost.

Meanwhile, the history of the race between science and society, as it might be called, is exceedingly interesting. The aid which man's struggle with himself has given to technological advance is so unquestionable that it has led many observers to believe that war is "a good thing." The answer to the question whether or not war is a good thing cannot be reduced to simple, arithmetical terms. War has the property of enlarging itself and it has, also, remarkable reproductive powers. It is also destructive in the sense that it changes matter into forms useless to society. Thus, while a given war gives an immense boost to science, its successor, by applying those advances to itself, becomes doubly or trebly destructive. Eventually an infinite quantity may be added to scientific knowledge by means of war, but if war becomes correspondingly destructive there may be nothing left to which the knowledge may be applied. This might delight those so-called pure scientists who have retained enough laboratory equipment and material to carry on, but it would turn society into a junk pile.

For the purposes of the present inquiry into constructive chemistry, however, it will be wise to assume that society will survive.

Granting survival, we may look forward to a physico-social revolution on so vast a scale and of such inherent beauty that the mind of today can form only the faintest image of it. It has already begun in the chemical laboratory. If the supermen, disguised for the moment as social inventors, will go hand in hand with the chemists up the green pastures a benefit will accrue to humanity which will justify all the bloodshed of all the wars since the invention of gunpowder.

2

The application of chemistry probably began when primitive man lit his first fire. From that point it has marched side by side with most invention. Its study was essential to the first production of metals by means of heat. Thus it aided in the construction of tools and machines.

Laboratory chemistry stemmed from the wish of King Midas. The laboratory was founded with a profit motive. If various metals known as "base" could be turned into metals known as "noble" there would be an approach toward getting something for nothing. Gold had already acquired its fictional significance. Thus alchemy may be placed in the category of synthesis, though it bore little resemblance to the synthetic chemistry of today.

From alchemy, which disheartened so many of its devotees, laboratory chemistry passed into a more serious, a "purer" phase. This was analysis, a research into the materials of which substances were composed. When a material could not be further analyzed it was called an element. Finally, when analysis was complete it was found that the substances could be restored by combining the elements in certain proportions and under certain conditions.

Experiment of this sort yielded the most curious results. Compounds came from the combination of certain elements which bore not the remotest resemblance to any of the elements which composed them. What were known as "properties"—smell, color, odor—seemed to disappear in combination. A classic example of such metamorphosis appears when hydrogen, carbon and nitrogen, three essentials of life, are combined in certain proportions to produce the deadly poison popularly known as prussic acid.

These results led to long speculation as to the physical composition of matter and it was decided that all matter consisted of indivisible particles which might as well be called atoms.

A patient inquiry by several indefatigable minds evolved, at last, what was known as the atomic theory of the composition of matter. It is not difficult to understand. Thousands of boys and girls have completed freshman years in the most indifferent educational institutions with a useful understanding of the application of the atomic theory. It has been grasped by artistic and stock-market minds. But it is one of those occasional theories whose intimate operation must be seen to be believed and we can think of no adequate method for compressing a laboratory with all its flames and fragrance between the covers of a book.

For all its workableness over many years, the atomic theory was never literally true. Like much mathematics, it simply posed a set of what Einstein has called "as ifs." They were useful as long as they balanced one another and were discarded only when the study advanced and some of them were found out on a limb, no longer capable of being fitted, so to speak, into the context of a sentence. At that point the atomic theory was replaced or supplemented by another. Whether the new one is literally true is a question which must be left to future generations; we only know now that it works in the new experiments and we feel, too, that it is harmonious in itself apart from all application.

We have no direct concern either with the old atomic theory or with the one which replaced it in dealing with inorganic matter. Our only reason for introducing it is to show what a shock came to experimenters when they tried it on organic substances and this brings us to the historic distinction between organic and inorganic chemistry—a distinction which had religious and social as well as technical significance.

In the early nineteenth century, it was respectable enough for chemists to play with metals, acids, minerals in general. They were dead things and no longer impinged upon religious convictions. On the other hand, blood, bone, leaves, flowers, wood, protoplasm were products of the life force and not subject to inquiry as to the secret of their making. This was God's province and the suggestion that they might be evolved in a cold laboratory was horrifying in the extreme. Such inhibitions, however, did not deter the scientific mind which had already infringed the Divine patents on lightning and other matters.

It is interesting that synthetic organic chemistry began with one of the lowliest products of the animal body. When Friedrich Wöhler in 1828, suddenly, out of minerals, without the aid of kidneys or bladder, produced one of the main constituents of animal urine, he was startled to say the least.[1] The discovery opened the door on a vista of such magnitude that it took many years for the chemists themselves to comprehend it. If urea could be produced in the laboratory, why not any of the other products of plant or animal life? Was not, perhaps, the animal or the plant itself a laboratory? Was there not, in every tree or flower, oyster, dog or man a chemical factory which extracted and combined elements with results which could be imitated in the chemist's own laboratory?

Wöhler, however, was used to shocks. A short time before he opened the door on the vital laboratory, he and his friend Justus von Liebig had run head on into failure in practice of current theory. The atomic theory had implied that compounds were produced by the combination of certain quantities of elements in certain proportions. A compound whose molecules contained the same number of elemental atoms would always have the same properties. Thus a substance, each of whose molecules contained two atoms of hydrogen and one of oxygen (H_2O) would always have the properties of water: it would be wet, colorless, odorless, tasteless, weigh a certain amount, dissolve certain things, boil and freeze at certain temperatures and evaporate under certain conditions. A compound, each of whose molecules contained one sodium and one chlorine atom, would always be $NaCl$, common salt, would taste salty, would dissolve in water, would make people thirsty and would preserve meat. In short, it was *quantity* of elements, *numbers* of their atoms which determined the nature of a compound. A compound, in an instant, could be changed out of all recognition, but *only by adding or subtracting atoms to or from the molecules.*

This was all very well while the chemists worked with simple matters like water, salt and various acids and kept their fingers out of the subtler works of God. But Liebig and Wöhler soon progressed beyond such child's play. They did not hesitate, for

[1]Alexander Findlay, *A Hundred Years of Chemistry*, N. Y., 1937, pp. 19, 21.

instance, to handle the complex, divinely evolved alcohols. When Liebig mixed an alcohol with silver nitrate it nearly cost him his life, but he carried on with his dangerous resulting silver fulminate which explodes almost at a touch. The shock came when he found that this terrific compound had precisely the same formula (expressed in the old atomic terms) as silver cyanate, whose properties were utterly different.[2]

When Liebig and Wöhler consulted about this, checked and rechecked, there seemed to be something wrong with the atomic theory. It could not be wholly false, for certainly the compounds did contain the proportion of elements stated in the formulas. But it was obviously inadequate. There must be something missing. The composition of a carbon compound must be determined by quantity plus something else.

Many patient successors of Wöhler and Liebig discovered that the something else was arrangement or architecture. The atoms, besides being correct in quantity and proportion, must stand in a certain design within the molecule to form one of these delicate, complex, elusive carbon substances.

Let us consider an extremely simple analogy. Let us compare a drink with a painting. Consider the drink to be like a simple inorganic compound, the painting a complex carbon compound produced by what used to be called the "vital force."

The drink, say, is made of gin, vermouth and ice in a glass. The painting is made from several kinds of paint on canvas. If you will mix an ounce of gin with half an ounce of French vermouth and a handful of cracked ice in a glass you will have what is known as a Martini cocktail. If you will mix so many grams of yellow ochre, so many of cobalt blue and so many of ivory white and pour the result on a square of canvas you will not have a picture, certain modern schools of painting to the contrary notwithstanding.

The steps by which the chemists moved from recipes to pictures make one of the most fascinating stories of modern science. The picture-making evolved from long speculation over the formulas and much of the graphic system was worked out on

2Findlay, p. 21.

paper before it got into the laboratory. The architectural nature of the organic molecules made this possible. Thus the atoms became like pieces in picture puzzles: the chemists found where they fitted to make the complete picture of each substance. But they found, too, a strange interchangeability among these parts so that when one picture was finished it could be changed into a different picture simply by removing one or two pieces and replacing them by others.

The first step toward the graphic formula or piece puzzle came with the discovery of radicals. A radical is a set of atoms which stick together to form one piece. Certain atoms in the carbon compounds have a powerful cohesiveness; they cannot easily be torn apart so when the chemists found these they regarded each of them as a single piece in the puzzle and found that they could be interchanged with single atoms. Charles Gerhardt, knowing that the hydrogen atom in many compounds was easily displaced by a radical, began writing formulas in a new way.

He took a simple inorganic compound like water and made it, for the purpose of argument, into a picture puzzle. Instead of writing the formula H_2O he made a design of it: $\left.\begin{array}{l}H\\H\end{array}\right\}O$. Now he found that by replacing one of the hydrogen atoms with one of the newly found radicals such as the ethyl radical C_2H_5, his picture became $\left.\begin{array}{l}C_2H_5\\H\end{array}\right\}O$. He recognized this as ethyl alcohol, which always before had been written C_2H_6O. If, in this, he now replaced the second hydrogen atom with the same ethyl radical he got $\left.\begin{array}{l}C_2H_5\\C_2H_5\end{array}\right\}O$, namely, ethyl oxide or ether. He did the same trick with a pure hydrogen molecule, getting, in succession, $\left.\begin{array}{l}C_2H_5\\H\end{array}\right\}$ which is ethane and $\left.\begin{array}{l}C_2H_5\\C_2H_5\end{array}\right\}$, butane. Out of hydrochloric acid gas he got ethyl chloride and out of ammonia he got three compounds because ammonia, NH_3 has three pieces of hydrogen instead of two. He did these things on paper, not in the laboratory, but it was a step toward the understanding of design and it showed how inorganic compounds could be altered to make organic ones.

The next step, called valence, was worked out by Edward Frankland and Archibald Couper of England and the German August Kékule.[3] Frankland found that certain atoms naturally grouped themselves with certain numbers of other atoms. Applying this to organic chemistry, Kékule found, for instance, that carbon always liked to combine with four other atoms or radicals and that hydrogen and most of the radicals were happiest in combination with one other atom. So he drew a picture of the carbon atom with four hooks on it, each hook reaching out for

an atom or radical $-\overset{|}{\underset{|}{C}}-$ and he drew hydrogen with one

hook, H—, and radicals such as OH with one hook, OH—, so that the complete picture of ethyl alcohol looked like this with two carbon atoms reaching out their hooks; joining hooks with each other in the middle and picking up atoms and a radical with the others:

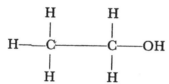

Now this picture tells a story which the old alcohol formula C_2H_6O did not tell. It tells that one of the O's and one of the H's are stuck together in a radical.[4] Without this picture we might suppose that C_2H_6O was the formula for methyl ether whose picture is

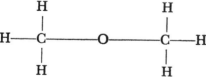

It would be highly desirable, as we can see, to look at the pictures before drinking these substances.

[3] For a detailed history of these developments, see Findlay, Chap. II.
[4] James B. Conant, *The Chemistry of Organic Compounds*, N. Y., 1939, p. 8.

Such paper chemistry was exceedingly useful as a start, but much experience in the laboratory was needed before the complex designs could be worked out. In the laboratory, the hydroxyl radical OH, for example, was found to be extremely snobbish. Only one of them would attach itself to a carbon radical at the same time and thus this sort of thing

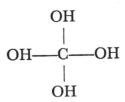

was simply "not done" in the organic world. Thus a compound which was known to contain several OH's must be pictured as having enough separate C atoms so that only one could attach itself to each—like this for glycerine:[5]

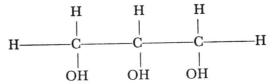

So the pictures grew more and more complex and the pieces were found to be interchangeable only under the right conditions. As the chemists grew brave enough, at last, to go into the aromatic compounds, they were able to evolve the startling benzene ring and to work out the architecture of the most elusive works of God. Eventually, the picture puzzles were no longer two dimensional; sculpture replaced painting and the subject of "chemistry in space"—three-dimensional architecture—drew the experimenters into a world of undreamed beauty.

With such analysis, the step to synthesis was easier and presently the actual compounds were built from the paper designs and hundreds of thousands of substances formerly made by blood and sap, heart-beats, breathing, leaves, kidneys, glands, sunshine, air, water, soil were created in the laboratory. Thus we have got silk, indigo, perfumes, medicines, resins, sugars and alcohols from

[5]Now called glycerol in the laboratory.

492

coal, a mineral, and from other supposedly dead things has been created the food of plants. So, too, have plants and animal products been worked up into substitutes for metal like the plastics so that gear-wheels may be made from soy beans or the control devices of the automobile from sour milk. By smashing— by main force—the structure of hydrocarbons we have learned to produce gasoline from crude petroleum.[6] Here the molecules have literally been split apart and their atoms have rejoined in new combinations. The result is a gasoline of such high octane that it can be used in higher compression and hence fuel-saving motors.

Has magic left the world with the disappearance of the old sorcerers and witches, the soothsayers and the alchemists? Where would such folk stand in the chemical laboratory today? Shall we tremble now before the new magicians, the chemists, and finally duck them, put them in the stocks, hang them and burn them as the old Puritans are said to have done to practitioners of the black magic? It seems sometimes as if some of the war-makers (who need them most) were doing precisely this.

3

This magic, slowly and patiently worked out in England and in Germany, was a long time in reaching the United States. It did not seem to impinge upon American economy. In this broad land we appeared to have everything we needed. We took the materials of what we ate and wore out of the soil, often forgetting to put anything back. Why should we feed the exhausted ground? There was always more, fertile ground to work upon. What we needed from without we were able to import by simple adjustments of tariff patterns.

But in Europe there were difficulties. England and Germany were far from self-sufficient. Germany, moreover, beginning what Mussolini has called her "dynamism" in the nineteenth century, was indulging in wars. This increased her material requirements at the same time that it shut her up inside her own frontiers. France, where Louis Pasteur helped move chemistry into its

[6]This is called "cracking" in the industry. It is achieved by heat.

sculptural or three-dimensional stage, must practice strict economy because there was no way for her to get additional land and resources, and the threat of dynamic Germany imposed the need of conservation for war also upon her. So we should expect synthesis, which is an economy process, to progress furthest in these countries. It was natural for such countries to try to synthesize the materials of which they had a surplus into materials of which they had a shortage.

Germany had coal and good miners, but as industrialization increased, the synthesis of organic materials from coal helped spare the land and cut down on necessary imports. The investigation of coal tar, a product of the distillation of coal in a closed retort, had been carefully studied by several Germans and at least one chemist from the great coal country, England,[7] even before structural or graphic formulas had been invented. This study opened the door to a labyrinth of riches. Later, when the picture puzzles developed, it was easier for chemists to find their way down the wonderful coal corridors of benzol, toluol and phenol to the colors of the rainbow, the anodynes of human suffering and the material of death.

The English boy, Perkin—he was only seventeen at the time—is credited with making the first aniline dye, though his discovery was so accidental that it hardly comes into the realm of true synthesis.[8] It was made with no understanding of structure and his aniline was derived from indigo. Yet his process led other chemists into deep thought. This was in 1856. In 1868, the Germans, Carl Graebe and Karl Theodor Liebermann, produced a genuine synthetic red dye called alzarin and Perkin made an improvement on their process. It was derived from distilled coal tar. It was true madder and its commercialization put thousands of French acres which had been dedicated to this plant out of production. Here was a material for German industry which had been imported from their cool neighbor and which now could be made from their own abundant coal.

But the great German dye industry which developed soon be-

[7]William Henry Perkin.
[8]Pointed comment on this accident is made by the late brilliant Edwin E. Slosson in his classic, *Creative Chemistry*, N. Y., 1920, p. 73.

came a museum and a laboratory for the creative chemists. With their picture puzzles in hand, they found perfumes and flavors in the treasure house of the coal mines. As the atoms and radicals were shifted about, the designs showed disinfectants, medicines— carbolic acid, aspirin the anodyne, phenacetin the fever fighter. Fantastic changes occurred. Salicylic acid, from which comes aspirin, was found when combined with the poisonous methyl (wood) alcohol to yield the innocent flavoring of chewing gum, oil of wintergreen. But most provocative of all to German economists of the opening twentieth century were the architectures of crude toluol, nitrobenzol, picric acid, naphthalene, for from these came not only colors but explosives.

Germans were jealous of their growing industries. Had they concentrated sternly on their productive chemistry, they might have made themselves largely independent of the outside world in industrial materials. But the legacy of Bismarck was "dynamism." The Hohenzollern heirs and the military caste were not content to leave the chemists to their productive enterprise. They had not enough faith. They feared the chimeras of "encircling" France and England and felt covetous eyes on their industries, their trade. They believed still that raw materials lay outside. So they turned their chemists from the synthesis of industrial lifeblood to the creation of compounds that would break the iron ring.

The chemists designed the astonishing process by which nitrogen is drawn from the air in order to make explosives. As the inevitable war came on, they juggled some of their ethylene and aniline pictures into diagrams of poison gas. But such was the general level of knowledge in the world, evened out by quick communications and the interdependence of scientists, that, immediately, their opponents did the same. In peace, the great German chemical cartels had been able to dominate world trade. But once the opponents of Germany were forced, through war, to imitate the German chemists while, at the same time, the British navy stopped German commerce, the advantage was lost. In the post-war exhaustion of central Europe, the chemical domination passed from Germany. It passed to the United States.

Perhaps because of industrial peaks in other fields, this was the logical place for it. Our habit of quick organization made possible a colossal poison gas plant, constructed overnight. We had more fluid capital, more available resources than England and France, bled almost white by the war and obsessed by war problems. Explosives factories, poison plants can be converted rapidly enough, once the picture-puzzles are understood, into factories for dyes, medicines, resins, fertilizers, perfumes, flavors. Rationalists may balance the ethics of the seizure of more than four thousand German chemical patents by the United States as a war prize with the ethics of the use of poison gas. The facts remain. It is not entirely accurate, therefore, to state that "we got nothing out of the war." We got the chemical industry.

An economy of abundance had made this less necessary to us than to the nations of Europe. Yet in the process of our expansion, a peculiar situation had developed in our strange, unplanned, sprawling and wasteful economic·empire. It was a logical consequence of the march of the iron men.

4

We have followed the change in America from colonial agriculture to industrial empire. We have seen industry drive out the subsistence farm and the segregation of the agricultural population in virtual colonies of the South and West. We have seen the concentration of power in the industrial and financial Northeast. As it moved westward out of the fringe, carried by the railroad, it pushed the farmer before it. Gradually, industry absorbed more and more of his land and its gigantic magnetic attraction sucked away his labor.

This, of course, was the normal progress of "civilization." It had happened in England when industrial revolution had shoved the farmer off into the colonies. But Britain was a political as well as an economic empire. When economic empire developed in the democratic United States, the problem was not the same. Politically the farmer had the same rights, the same liberty, the same vote as the industrialist. Economically, his independence disappeared.

Under the impact of industrial civilization, his lot grew steadily worse. He was obliged to fight the heroic battle of the Grange to keep himself from feudal serfdom under the railroad barons. Then the value of his products was manipulated and juggled on industrially motivated exchanges until everyone seemed to be making money out of them èxcept himself. Every happy turn of fate which brought fortune to the industrialist seemed to bring disaster to the farmer. The improvement of his technic, the mechanization of his harvesting brought the bogey of "over-production"; his prices, in terms of the manufactured products of industry, dropped to a point at which his standard of living fell below that of the factory worker. As a result of this, boys drifted away to the cities where work was easier and pay higher and, by the early years of the new century, this drift had altered the whole social hierarchy and political control of the nation.

More and more the farmer came to rely on export trade. In the World War, he saw a rainbow; for a brief interval it was bright in the sky. Prices soared to undreamed heights but they dropped quickly enough in the post-war chaos when the hungry nations of Europe, frightened by war debts and new tariffs, turned to their own fields for food. As the American farmers, in the post-war inflation, borrowed right and left, the momentary rainbow disappeared and the blackest clouds of all came in its place. These clouds burst in the industrial boom of the twenties when the purchasing power of the dollar increased and the farmer realized that his debts were in the terms of the inflated period.

Meanwhile, one of the farmer's large markets had vanished. Since the war, some nine million horses and mules had been replaced by automobiles. This threw thirty million acres out of production for horse and mule feed—which had been the fuel for his power plant. If these acres could immediately have been turned into crops to feed automobiles, no great harm would have been done. But the industrialists had devised another fuel for the internal combustion engine. It came out of the ground, to be sure, but not by means of agriculture. The farmer was forced to buy this fuel with cash. Incidentally, its use left him less manure to put back into the land.

Thus the farmer was put still more at the mercy of industry. The self-sufficiency of the farm cycle had been interrupted by a new, outside element. Now he must buy the horsepower he once got out of his field. From an industrialist he must buy the fertilizer he once got out of his horse. At the same time, the new power enormously increased his production. Yet the human stomach had not enlarged. On the contrary, people had learned, on the whole, to eat less. Their diet had changed. Instead of vast quantities of salt pork and bread, products of corn and wheat staples, they now ate many varieties of fruit and vegetables, and population was no longer increasing on a large scale; there were few more mouths to feed.

Today, the farmer is a virtual ward of government. Government's ingenuity has been strained to its limit to provide tricks to replace normal economic laws. Government has tried the old Wall Street game of cornering farm produce to jack up prices. It has adjusted freight rates, investigated rural electrification, engaged in laboratory experiment on soil, pests and disease, attempted to control floods and erosion, irrigated land. At the very moment when it has reclaimed millions of acres of desert, it has been forced to limit production, startling the world by instructing the farmer to burn or plow-in his crops, to slaughter his stock. It has granted large subsidies for bucolic relief and most of the expense has been paid by the city dweller. It has bought quantities of mortgaged land and rehabilitated the tenant farmers by giving them acres and houses on a plan of long-term payment. Yet all of these devices have not greatly quieted the distress; boys and girls, descendants of once prosperous farm families, are thumbing their way back and forth across the continent, whole families are migrating in their jallopies to vague destinations in the Steinbeck manner and great tracts of land are going fallow or lapsing into pasture.

Our American problem, then, appears to be the reverse of that which so many nations of Europe are trying to solve through chemistry. When Germany synthesized organic materials out of coal it was to spare her soil. Today her chemists are working on "ersatz" food—nourishment synthesized out of inedible material. Our question is whether we can synthesize enough "dead" material out of food to save the overproducing farmer.

SYNTHESIS

The miracle-working chemist has shown the permament rainbow over the farm. He has adjusted his diagrams to the synthesis of the plastics from milk and soy beans. He has found that gears, fountain-pens, airplanes, film, lubricants, paint, glue and thousands of other industrial products may be made from cellulose and cellulose may be made from farm wastes. Corn and sweet potatoes can be made to yield starch. Oats yield furfural, an invaluable chemical product. Tung nuts provide essential ingredients of varnishes and lacquers. There seems to be no limit to the potential value of what was once produced only for food to the non-food-producing industries.

One of the greatest of these is alcohol. It has been found that a ten per cent addition of ethyl alcohol to gasoline improves the gasoline as fuel for internal combustion engines. If a ten per cent blend became universal, some twenty million acres might be put into corn and Jerusalem artichokes. If engines were designed to use a higher percentage of alcohol the farmer might again grow much of the fuel for his power plant. But the alcohols are also vital to many other picture-puzzle products. Instead of deriving alcohols from coal as Germans might be forced to do, it would favor our economy to get them from the farms.

If all these new processes were fully developed and if we could induce our industrialists to use them instead of those which exhaust our resources of coal, petroleum and metals, the farmer's independence would return. Furthermore, there would be scarcely enough land to provide the material. But the chemist has provided also for this contingency. By the conversion of corn stalks, wheat, straw and other farm waste into paper and building material, the forests can be saved and the forests in turn will help to conserve the land. By this means plus fertilizers derived from atmospheric nitrogen (the same process which was developed by Germany for explosives), plus the physical controls which we discussed in the last chapter, almost endless land may be made productive. The yield of the earth is perennial. Under intensive cultivation it is not exhaustible.

Whether such an economy will be practiced depends on the will of industrialist and farmer to submit to planning. This is still a bogey in free America. It is feared because it is a European practice made necessary by confinement. It would be less feared by Americans if it were realized that here it is made necessary by expansion. Our problem is one of abundance, not of scarcity.

But there are other factors. One is individualist greed. That such greed is appeased by collective means makes it no less individually motivated. For all of our surplus of food material, many Americans are close to the starvation line. Complex price structures, subtle manipulations, corporate picture-puzzles, flexible like those of the chemist, perhaps, but less generally beneficial, stand between many Americans and their food. Gentle, intelligent, democratic planning might dissipate such obstacles. Regimentation by design is better than regimentation by neglect or by necessity. The thumbers along the roads, the tenant farmers of Oklahoma, the share-croppers of Arkansas, the occupants of Relief and all the unemployed are regimented today. The limits to their liberty are as "un-American" as the controls of government planning.

The war has thrown many rugged individualists into the isolationist camp. Given present conditions in Europe it is a desirable place to be. It would be well for these people to look to the creative chemist for their salvation, because he can make us largely independent of foreign trade. Already he will show them our largest raw material import, rubber, in synthesis from minerals. If autarchy is desirable, only the chemist can approach it. There are those who think that the main causes of war are economic. If this is true, and if the diagrams of synthesis could be adequately applied to the "have not" nations, a new way might be found to preserve a civilized order of society.

We have presented, in the agricultural dilemma, one of the largest current American problems. A part of the solution lies in the chemical economy. Another part will come from the conservation of such vital material as we have inherited from the wilderness. Can we win back what we have wasted and can we protect our future against new waste? Whatever steps we take in that direction will involve, first of all, the sacrifice of that traditional American desire: to have our cake after we have eaten it.

Chapter Twenty-two

METAL

ECONOMY came, at last, to the metals and the scientific method was applied to that broad base of "manifest destiny" in America. It came by devious routes, not primarily because metals were scarce. It came with mass production when fragile luxuries were translated into tough necessities. It came when transport grew too heavy (or too light) for our steel, when space grew too crowded, when the factors of weight, strength and power must be juggled to fit our economic schemes. It came when the technologies became complex and the needs of democracy enlarged.

But first there was waste. First there was bigness, the magnificent sprawling plan that slowly drew together into rigid lines and changed us, in the process, from an empire into a nation. Nowhere in our history is the working out of our continental integrity so clear as in the interplay of metal between West and East during our formative years. Nowhere does romance run so high; in no phase of our growth does that translation of fiction into fact, which has led so many ecstatic historians to talk of the "American dream," appear with such vividness. Here, from the mines, rises the djinn of the American nation which, with the passing of the years, we see grow palpable and hard; the true out of the myth, the thing out of the thought. Here is alchemy, indeed, with gold transmuted into steel.

We know today what we could not have guessed in the formless fifties, that our destiny (called manifest) was inherent in the third dimension of our geography. In the late forties, our destinies seemed imperial. The South was deepening in colonial color. The outposts of what was called the West were outposts of agriculture and, as the East began to turn industrial, they too seemed destined for the status of colonies. Some of them, indeed, might even break off from the tenuous federation to become separate nations.

But even in the East, in these years, the promising new industries languished. As we look back at them from our hilltop they seem scarcely solid enough for the nucleus of empire. True, they were supplying the West with many manufactures for which the West paid in surpluses from the farms, but it is doubtful if either East or West could have survived without heavy imports from Europe. And the industries were not expanding fast enough. Without capital they could not expand. Potential wealth was not enough. Capital was frozen. It was congealed in land, slow-moving in cumbersome goods. Exchange was largely in kind, credit was dubious, currency was based on imported specie,[1] banks were mostly small depositories and unproductive.

It was a moment almost of dead center. America seemed to be waiting for an explosion violent enough to throw the great American engine into new motion. It came, as every boy and girl who has been to grammar school knows, in 1848. The mere occurrence of such an explosion was not enough to seal our destiny. But the precise geographical position of that explosion could not have been more vital to our national movement if an all-wise planner had put it there.

Gold was found in the valley of the Sacramento in California. It was found by immigrants from the United States. Within a year it had split the eastern population. It lured the arrogant and the greedy, the men who, inflated with the pride of "liberty and freedom," were above ordinary work and sought the quick easy wealth which they felt to be their right in the magnificent New World. But it lured, also, men with true grounds of discontent, men caught in the growing congestion of cities, in the web of experimental laws, men innately unfit for farming.

Thousands of them rushed round the Horn or across the Isthmus of Panama. They did not go for purposes of trade. They went for gold. Other thousands, moving overland, skipped all the rich midland country in their rush for gold. The result was a solid nucleus of citizens of the United States west of the Sierras, oc-

[1]Clark, *Hist. of Manufactures in the U. S.,* I, 285 f.

cupying land at the extremity of the continent. How many decades would it have taken, in the normal course of territorial
expansion, for such a settlement of the Pacific coast?

At the same time, this single event by no means achieved continental integrity or destroyed the imperial pattern. The Cali-

The lure to gold

Advertisement of steamboat transportation to the gold mines of Idaho,
St. Louis, 1863

From the original in the State Historical and Miscellaneous Library,
Helena, Montana

HO FOR THE YELLOW STONE

AND THE

GOLD MINES

OF IDAHO!

A NEW AND VERY LIGHT DRAUGHT STEAMER WILL LEAVE

SAINT LOUIS FOR BIGHORN CITY!

THE JUNCTION OF BIGHORN AND YELLOW STONE RIVERS,

SATURDAY, APRIL 2D, AT 12 O'CLOCK M.

Parties taking this route save 400 miles river transportation and over 100 miles land
transportation. Bighorn City being by a good wagon road from Virginia City 200 and from
Bannock City 206 miles.

I WILL ALSO SEND TWO LIGHT DRAUGHT SIDE-WHEEL STEAMERS

TO FORT BENTON

One leaving at the same time, and the second about fifteen days later. I am prepared to
contract for Freight and Passage either to Bighorn City or Fort Benton.
refer to W. B. DANCE, JAS. STEWART and E. WALL, Virginia City, or to M. HARDEVILLE, Bannack City.

For Freight or Passage apply to JOHN G. COPELIN,
Care JOHN J. ROE & CO., St. Louis, Mo

fornia nucleus was inconceivably remote from the federation
which, in 1850, established a paper connection with the new
community. The existence of the gold by itself could not have
held it to the nation. On the contrary, the gold began at once to
work for autonomy. Californians made their own laws in that
time with little control from outside—special outlaw laws enforced at the muzzle of a gun. To bind California to an orderly
national scheme would take a stronger metal than gold.

But the gold in California through its mighty fictional power
produced that metal in the East. The industrial boom of the fifties
was an immediate effect of this mythology.[2] It is true that some
of the actual gold found its way into general circulation. Between

[2]Davis Rich Dewey, *Financial History of the U. S.*, N. Y., 1936, p. 257.

'50 and '60, the Government coined more than three times as much money as in the sixty preceding years,[3] so, of course, specie in the banks increased. But this could not account for the orgy of speculation, the frenzy of investment following the gold rush. This was based on extended credit due to the facts and rumors of Midas wealth. These created fluid capital which flowed into the railroads which themselves were extending fingers toward the wealth. The railroads demanded iron. Iron was the metal that would seal the promise.

Yet even with all these elements present the pattern was not yet complete. There was still talk of a "Pacific Republic," there were fears of the southern sympathies in free California. The vast lands between the Mississippi and the Rockies were almost wholly unorganized, partly unexplored. Now that the migrant hordes were skipping over them there might not be time to gather them into a national whole. One-way expansion was not rapid enough. To conquer the continent, emigrants must move toward each other, in two directions simultaneously toward the middle, like tunnellers boring through a mountain.

If the gold supply of California had held out, Californians might have remained for years complacently behind their high Sierra wall. But in the middle fifties the gold ran low. Though San Francisco was growing like a giant mushroom and nurturing such Napoleons of promotion as Stanford, Ralston, Flood, Sharon and O'Brien, the boys in the valleys were returning to camp day after day with empty pans. Gold had been squandered, stolen, gambled, dispersed. Evidences of actual poverty were present even in the dream city of the Golden Gate. Prospectors, driven by want, were wandering afield up and over the Sierra wall.

Meanwhile eastern plans for a transcontinental railway were miscarrying.[4] At the same moment overextended credit threatened collapse in eastern industry.[5] The collapse came in '57 and with it a second dead center arrived. The increased discontent of the South with its now thoroughly colonial status and its desire

[3]*Finance Report,* 1861, 221, Table 15, cited by Clark, I, 286.
[4]See p. 31.
[5]J. F. Rhodes, *Hist. of the U. S.,* III, 51 n. Dewey, pp. 263, 264.

to break off and create a new nation was the greatest menace of all to American national integrity. Never in history had the need for a new explosion been so urgent. It came with the tremendous news from Sun Mountain in the desolate Washoe territory just east of the Sierras.

If it is hyperbole to say that Nevada saved our destiny in '59 it is not a long stretch of the truth. There were, as always, many factors, but if we try placing the Comstock Lode in various other positions we can see how critical was its occurrence in the Nevada hills. If it had turned up farther east, Californians might not have reached it before the Easterners who were marching west. If it could have occurred in the Great Lakes region we might have become an empire with the South broken off, with the agricultural states west of Wisconsin as colonies, with California a dominion headed for autonomy or drawn southward. This is the game known as "the ifs of history," and it is played here only to emphasize a point.

As it was, the gold and silver in Nevada, within easy reach of the experienced California gold hunters with San Francisco as a base of operations, started the eastward push. If we tune our ears to the echoes of the opening sixties we will catch the dominant ballyhoo about the Central Pacific Railroad in California.[6] There was scarcely a speech that did not stress the importance of the road going at least as far as the new mines. The mines would finance its first construction. From there it could go on to meet the eastern rails in their westward march. Meanwhile men swarmed over the Sierras to the fabulous riches of the Washoe deposits.

The news, flying east over the new telegraph, started boom number two in eastern industry. Gold or the promise of gold, silver and its rumor, fictional metals at best, flowed east into the iron works where rails were in the making. From Pennsylvania, where the great expansion began, to California where it ended, Allegheny iron would flow back enriching all the land between, making it accessible to the two-way migration. Between the two pushes the middle country would be caught in a vise from which

[6]Samuel Bowles, *Across the Continent*, Appendix.

it could never escape. For it all fear of colonial status was ended.

But what, now, of the unhappy South, left out of all this scheme? Ten years earlier it might well have escaped to nationhood. Western farmers might have supported its secession. Even five years earlier it might have fought its way to freedom. But in '62, while Lee's armies were winning their victories, the first bill for a transcontinental railroad through the northern

THE NEW STATE OF NEVADA.

By the President of the United States.
A PROCLAMATION.

Whereas, The Congress of the United States passed an act, which was approved on the 21st day of March last, entitled "An act to enable the peopl of Nevada to form a constitution and State government," and for the admission of such State into the Union on an equal footing with the original States.

Whereas, The said Constitution and State Government have been formed pursuant to the conditions prescribed by the fifth section of the act of Congress aforesaid, and the certificate required by the said act, and also, a copy of the Constitution and ordinances have been submitted to the President of the United States:

Now, therefore, be it known that I, ABRAHAM LINCOLN, President of the United States, in accordance

Lincoln's proclamation admitting
Nevada to the Union
From *The New York Times,* October 31, 1864

states was signed by the President. Rich California was in the lobbies of the Capitol, pressing it, because Nevada was in its mind. With its passage the industrial boom, re-created by Nevada treasure, leapt to new heights across the country. Hundreds of McCormick reapers were turned into the fields of Illinois and Indiana to cut grain for the Union armies. The new garment industry based on the inventions of Howe and Singer made their clothes. New railroad equipment furnished their transportation.

Thus, in 1864, the year that Nevada became a state, the year that construction began—from the West—on the transcontinental, the year that the first Bessemer steel was made in America, the fate of the South was sealed. The magnetic field thrown across the fortieth parallel from the Alleghenies to the Sierras was too strong for it. It was a field between gold and iron, a field of prosperity. Along it lay the promise of security. Is it surprising that it drew people as well as wealth to the support of the cause of Union?

506

METAL

So crystallized the American dream. So, for the first time, in the sad Nevada hills, the true destiny became manifest.

For that reason pilgrims along the road of American history cannot ignore the faded shrine east of the great Sierra that seems to divide heaven from hell along the Nevada border. Up from Sacramento the mountain rises green with virgin timber to the crown jewel of Lake Tahoe; beyond Truckee it is as barren and gray as the circles of the Inferno. Windswept and sterile, the conical mountains of shattered rock repeat their awful death imagery until, suddenly, the shrine appears like a mirage of life in their midst. It is rotting and it will rot on until the mountains absorb it and the winds sweep out its dust and Virginia City will be a memory, a funny picture in a quaint old book. But it is there today, peopled with the ghosts of a nation's youth, a symbol of the wealth and the waste, the energy and the greed, the cruelty and the faith that made America.

The streets of Virginia City[7] ran blood and champagne in the sixties. Life was a game of roulette with pistols on the squares. It was naïve and debauched, comic, wanton, profane, fanciful; its values winked and swirled like a lamp in the eyes of a man far gone in drink. Each day saw a new millionaire shooting off his joy in the street from a gun in each hand, but night found him begging at the bar from the man who had jumped his claim. It was a life of children playing with passions beyond their grasp. Men came out of stolen shafts to weep at the antics of Ada Mencken or the trills of Jenny Lind at the Opry House; suffused with this glory they would stand all night at the Crystal Bar and shoot their man "for breakfast."

The stories in the books grow tiresome from the packing of silly and sordid detail. But there is nothing tiresome about the ghost city itself. Its tawdry glory is mellowed by decay. In the relic is no sense of the ashes of a Sodom. It is no longer possible to see it in isolation as a complete episode, a finished event. Virginia City is, rather, the dead camp of a still living army. Here

[7]In addition to the diverting Lyman books already cited, see Dan de Quille, *History of the Big Bonanza*, Hartford, 1877; C. B. Glasscock, *The Big Bonanza*, Indianapolis, 1931; Mary McNair Mathews, *Ten Years in Nevada*, Buffalo, 1880; Mark Twain, *Roughing It*.

it won its first victory, raped the forbidding hills of their treasure, paused after the battle for a frenzied, momentary celebration in blood and wine and moved on to build a nation with its loot. This final memory remains, the debauch is forgotten or it is comic in its faded relics, and the descendants of the miners, who come in air-conditioned coaches to see the naïve magnificence of their ancestors, are more likely to feel pride than shame.

2

It seems a far cry from the bonanza[8] orgies of the sixties and seventies to the smooth efficient engines of democracy which pump the lifeblood of our economy today. In the interval, gold and silver seem to have disappeared. The silver has lost its glamor along with its price; the gold, we know, still exists but it is hidden from our view in a concrete vault in a Kentucky mountain. There are economists who worry about it, thinking that as nation after nation edges off the gold standard, it may lose its value: that, as the human mind grows more and more realistic, it may survive only as an antique along with the other toys our great-grandparents once played with and be of little more worth when the vault is opened than the earth which contains it.[9] Some planners would have us exchange it, before it is too late, for more useful metals like tin and antimony, nickel, platinum, radium, vanadium, whose value is less picaresque.

But if the gold has gone from our economy, its effects are still visible. To the metallic flow which began in the sixties were presently added copper and lead. The rails which it helped to lay across the continent changed from iron to a tougher alloy of iron and carbon. The transcontinental spans quadrupled. Today they are crossed by locomotives streamlined with still another alloy. The anatomy is still there, enlarged, but with its bones grown out from the original spine. Its base is still iron.

We have seen the magic alloy of iron and carbon move from the stage of sorcery to the stage of quantitative chemistry. In the new stage, steel, made cheaply in large quantity according to

[8]Technically, a bonanza is a mass of decomposed rock containing ore in large quantity.
[9]Stuart Chase, *The New Western Front*, N. Y., 1939, p. 96.

what were believed to be precise recipes, replaced wrought iron and, especially, wood. As transport grew heavier steel necessarily replaced wood as a structural material for bridges. As buildings grew higher from the necessities of congestion it was necessary there too. As machines, which we have seen multiplying because of labor shortage, performed more duties they too must be built of steel.

For a long time steel, the scientific carbon alloy, bore well the stresses of the enlarging nation. It entered every phase of life. It carried us about, supported our offices and our homes, turned out the quantity of cheap goods we consumed. When mass production arrived, it seemed to be a fundamental element of our democratic machinery. Yet when mass production arrived and began to produce unheard-of luxuries for the masses, the first breakdown of carbon steel occurred.

The landmark, so to speak, of this collapse was the automobile. There was plenty of mass production of machines before the appearance of the automobile. But sewing machines, harvesters, revolvers and many lesser gadgets could be made of materials on which the strain was moderate and easy to estimate. Such material could be machined by a steel slightly harder than itself, but still steel produced by the accepted methods of juggling heat and carbon. Also these mechanisms were relatively simple.

At the same time there was complaint about some of the gadgets. Fastidious folk preferred the more or less handmade European manufactures to the products of our own fast-moving factories. American mass-produced machines sometimes flew apart at critical moments, under unexpected strain. This difficulty became acute with the democratic bicycle.

When the automobile made its first appearance in America revolutionary metallic changes were not, at once, indicated. The more or less experimental vehicles of the early nineteen hundreds were handmade luxuries. Their vital parts could be slowly and carefully shaped with tools which could be made to hold their edges by sufficient lubrication. When the complex car was finally assembled, its owner regarded it as a fragile toy with which to occupy his leisure hours, and the necessary care and thought which he must devote to it were part of the fun. When he shifted gears he must remember how easily they were "stripped," he must never forget his careful lubrication, he must think about a hundred things which never occur to the driver of 1940 and which seem, indeed, beyond his comprehension.

By 1910, the luxury cars were good artisan products. They were solid, heavy, slow, serviceable, and under proper care (a foregone conclusion) they would last "forever." The average driver was almost as good a mechanic as the average garage man is in 1940. But about this time the astonishing project was conceived in the mind of Mr. Ford of making cars which could be owned and operated by "ordinary folks."

With the enlarged market, mass production required extremely economical management. To supply the demand work must be accelerated. Skilled labor must be replaced by machines or by processes split into little steps. The machines must work faster than before. They must be lighter per unit power, less bulky in order to fit into a mass-production floor-plan. Replacement of machine tools worn down by speed or parts too light to stand the quick motion demanded of them became an item of cost. These machines were no longer working on the little levers of a sewing machine to be run by a gentle seamstress or on the relatively clumsy mechanism of a reaper whose parts might be out a good-sized fraction of an inch without making any perceptible difference in the amount of grain cut in a day. They were working on cylinders tough enough to withstand violent explosions which must be bored and drilled and otherwise machined to the thousandth of an inch, on hardy, tight-fitting pistons, on stout axles, smooth, accurate hubs, bearings, gears.

It was in the factory, then, rather than in the product that carbon steel first broke down. The Ford, which became known as Lizzie, was a slow, workaday job, enduring but not subject to severe, sudden strains in its ordinary performance. Hills, bad roads were approached in low gear, curves were taken slowly as, even in 1940, they must be on a dirt road. Breakage was more likely in body parts or springs than in delicate engine mechanism.

But in Lizzie's heyday, roads improved. The luxury market was broadening. The people who wanted to drive fast were no longer confined to the rich, sporting group. Lizzie's competitors were getting lower in price and getting into the hands of drivers who did not want to bother with repairs. As these competitors (still costlier than Fords) multiplied on the roads, traffic problems arose. Fast-travelling cars must be brought to quick stops. With better roads their drivers were tempted to approach curves with less consideration of centrifugal force. It was then that carbon steel broke down in the product.

Eventually the scientists reduced the costs of materials to a point where, with mass-production methods, fast, shock-resisting cars could be made for only a little more money than Lizzie. By this time the general tempo of life had accelerated to a point where most people were willing to pay the difference for the higher speed.

At this point an interesting economic question was asked by the manufacturers. The new fast cars looked, at first, as if they would last forever. If this were true, was it desirable that the materials should be so good? The question was answered, almost immediately, by the public. As soon as the new cars came into the hands of fast-driving Tom, Dick and Harry (not to mention Tom junior), the post-war, reckless younger generation with hip-flasks and park-love—the question was answered. Forgetting oil, grease, tire-air, water, valve-grinding, battery-charging; ignoring centrifugal force, gravity, torques and vectors they quickly satisfied the manufacturers as to the longevity of alloy steels. Motoring in the late twenties and thirties taxed the resources of science—in the United States at least—as severely as the average war.

Science has met it remarkably well. With nickel, chromium, aluminum, copper, vanadium, molybdenum and tungsten; with plastics, lacquers and adhesives; with anti-knock gasolines, lubricants and rubbers, science has met the appalling demands of the automobile industry as well as it has met any practical urgency. It has, to be sure, been well paid for the job and it has profited largely in less ponderable ways.

ENGINES OF DEMOCRACY

The time has come for the question: What are the new scientific methods which have been applied to metals? And what, indeed, is an alloy?

3

These questions involve complexities which laymen can only remotely approach. They involve profound study of heat and of the three-dimensional chemical architecture mentioned—but only mentioned—in the chapter on synthesis. To attempt anything more than a long-distance view, the social historian who is interested primarily in human responses to technology would wantonly insult the men and women who have spent their lives in cloistered laboratories pursuing this difficult subject.

There have always been alloys. An alloy is the combination of two or more metals in such a way as to produce a compound which possesses properties different from those of its constituents. (In the case of steel, metallurgists have got around this definition by calling carbon "semi-metallic.") In ores, one or more metals often exist in juxtaposition. Heat causes them to combine. Thus early smelters of iron sometimes accidentally produced an alloy with manganese, lead smelters got an alloy of lead and antimony, copper smelters got brass and bronze. These being accidental combinations difficulties were experienced when experimenters tried to repeat them with deliberation. No one knew why a real alloy sometimes evolved from the mixture and sometimes did not, so that successful metal-workers were looked on as magicians. This was peculiarly true in the case of steel, perhaps because it made effective weapons. But beyond the middle of the nineteenth century, though a long trial-and-error process had worked out the quantities of metals in alloys and the temperatures at which they combined, no one could say why such combinations changed the properties.

In 1863, it occurred to Henry Sorby, in England, to look at meteoric iron under a microscope. He did this not so much because he was interested in iron as because he was interested in meteorites.[10] In the seventies and eighties, there was occasional

[10]*Proc. Royal Society*, XIII, 333 and British Association *Report*, 1865, Part I, p. 139.

microscopic examination of iron and steel, but it was not until 1893 that announcement was made of a new science based upon it. Two Frenchmen, Albert Sauveur and F. Osmond, presented important papers, in that year, to the Chicago meeting of the International Engineering Congress. Sauveur, at the time, was in the employ of the Illinois Steel Company.

"Metallography," Osmond called the new science. "It is," he explained, "the natural development and scientific transformation of the uncertain art of the interpretation of fractures."[11] Steel broke, evidently, even in 1893, and this student wanted to find why. What he saw, under the microscope, was a structure of crystals. By examining shapes, sizes and other properties of the crystals, he believed that lines of weakness or faults could be spotted. Sauveur believed that "from the size of the grain of the steel under consideration and its chemical composition, we could infer what its heat-treatment has been, and this would indeed be a very valuable piece of information and might explain many failures which chemical analysis had left unaccounted for."[12]

Because chemical analysis had dealt primarily with quantities? This was found to be true, we remember, when chemists first experimented with complex organic compounds. Was it true also of the metals? Did questions of architecture, structure enter here also?

We must be careful of too close an analogy. We are concerned here with the crystals of which all metals are composed. Those were what the metallographers saw through their microscopes. They saw changes in the look of those crystals after heat treatment and they saw changes when other elements like carbon were added to iron.

When the X-ray presently was added to the microscope, a three-dimensional study of the crystals became possible. Now it was evident that each crystal was composed of atoms arranged, as Leonard, in simplified language, has explained it, "like eggs in a crate."[13] It is easier to break up a crystal, therefore, along the straight lines between the eggs than to break it

[11]*Trans.*, Am. Inst. Mining Engineers, XXII, 244 (1893).
[12]*Ibid.*, p. 551.
[13]Jonathan N. Leonard, *Tools of Tomorrow*, N. Y., 1935, p. 108.

diagonally. These lines were therefore called "planes of weakness" or "slip planes." When a ductile metal is bent or otherwise deformed, the atoms have slipped past each other along these planes.

These planes do not occur between crystals but inside them. The boundaries between the crystals are rigid and hard, and a slip plane changes its direction when it reaches the boundary. If, therefore, the boundaries can be multiplied the slip planes have to change direction oftener. This happens when the crystals are smaller, as in a "fine-grained" metal. In such a metal, then, a long slip does not occur. The metal, in other words, does not bend or dent easily.

Regularity of crystalline structure and bigness of crystals, evidently, make a metal softer, more ductile. There are various heat methods of making crystals smaller. How do we make their inside structures less regular? Eggs in a crate are regular. We can slip a piece of cardboard between the lines, lengthwise and crosswise. But suppose we pack eggs and golf balls[14] all in together. We will have a harder time, then, with the cardboard. That is why a harder metal is produced by interspersing atoms of iron and carbon or iron and nickel (because the atoms are of different size[15] like the eggs and golf balls) than either the iron or the nickel or the carbon by itself.

This interspersion occurs at certain temperatures and is known, after cooling, as "solid solution."[16] An alloy results and, because the atoms of each element have combined in a new structure, the alloy possesses different properties from those of the elements which compose it. Sometimes a "catalyst" other than heat is necessary. A catalyst is something which causes two elements to combine but does not, itself, exist in the compound. Heat is a catalyst, so is an electric current. So is the minister who marries a man and a woman.

In the steel alloys often an extremely small quantity of another metal is sufficient to produce a large increase in hardness or

[14]Leonard tries oranges and lemons, *op. cit.,* p. 110.
[15]This is extreme simplification. The effect of "size" in atoms is achieved by stronger or weaker attractions.
[16]A similar effect derives from the dispersion of hard particles among softer ones. This is called "slip-interference." Leonard, p. 115.

tensile strength due to alteration in structure. Two per cent of nickel added to steel increases its tensile strength about 12,000 pounds to the square inch.[17] If 1.25 per cent chromium is added to a 3.25 per cent nickel steel, great tensile strength and toughness result, and such an alloy is used for case hardening. For fine hand tools chromium alone may be added—one-half of 1 per cent to a 1 per cent carbon steel. Ball bearings, which must be hard and durable, take about 1 per cent of chromium.[18]

Vanadium may be used in much smaller quantities than nickel with similar results. A combination of vanadium and chromium with steel gives an alloy suitable for automotive forgings requiring great strength, toughness and "resistance to fatigue."[19] The list is infinite. As many as five different metals have been added to carbon steel to make an alloy for special purposes.[20]

Mass production makes use particularly of what is known as "high-speed" tool steel, speed here meaning the rate at which it has to work. A drill or cutting tool gets hot if it must turn at high speed, or if the work which it cuts is revolved extremely rapidly. When it gets hot its edge is likely to bend because its crystalline structure alters. Metallurgists (or metallographers) by intensive study of microphotographs evolved a steel alloy with 18 per cent tungsen, 4 per cent chromium and 1 per cent vanadium which could become red hot without losing its hard structure. But perhaps the greatest triumph was when they left out the steel altogether and produced a nonferrous tool metal of 18 per cent tungsten, 32 per cent chromium and 45 per cent cobalt which was most heat resistant of all![21]

These materials and others take care of the problems presented by the automobile and much mass production. But the growing complexity of technics in other departments of industry and science posed other problems. Many uses of steel demand that it shall resist corrosion. To answer this, larger quantities of nickel and chromium were added. A high quality of stainless steel for

[17]Thomas T. Read, *Our Mineral Civilization*, N. Y., 1932, p. 48.
[18]H. M. Boylston, *Introduction to the Metallurgy of Iron and Steel*, N. Y., 1936, Tables, pp. 454, 459.
[19]*Ibid.*, p. 466.
[20]Tungsten—vanadium—chromium—cobalt—molybdenum.
[21]*Fortune*, Nov., 1939, p. 76. The trade name of this alloy is Rexalloy.

cutlery uses from 12.5 to 14 per cent chromium.[22] The electrical industries are interested in the fact that a steel alloy with 24 per cent of nickel is nonmagnetic, while with 78 per cent its magnetic permeability is tremendous. With 36 per cent, the alloy is virtually impervious to changes of temperature as far as expansion and contraction are concerned, and is therefore useful for measuring instruments.[23] Experts with the microscope are constantly at work, and not a year goes by without new contributions to new needs. More than thirty-five hundred industrial establishments in America are using metallographic equipment in laboratory work on metals.[24]

4

But alloy steels are not the only alloys which have proved useful to twentieth-century development. Americans have made important contributions in the nonferrous fields, not only in alloy-making which is highly scientific cookery but in getting metals out of their ores. Of these, one is significant enough to demand brief comment here.

When men first succeeded in raising themselves away from contact with the earth, the problem of weight became suddenly acute. We have plenty of stories of balloonists pitching their valuable possessions—instruments, food, even clothes—overboard. When the airship came along and motive power was installed, frantic efforts were made to evolve an engine which could be at once light and powerful. When the engine came, a more durable structure than a cloth bag was thought desirable to support it. We have looked at the rigid airships of Zeppelin and Schwarz.[25] Schwarz's was all-metal. Zeppelin's had a metal skeleton. The metal was not iron.

The Wright brothers supported their precious power-plant (not to mention their even more precious bodies) on wings of cloth and wood, and so, indeed, did intrepid fliers at the start of the first World War. But as the plane became a practical means of transport it, too, took on a metal structure. The metal

[22]Boylston, Table, p. 454.
[24]Figure for 1936. Boylston, p. 415.
[23]Read, p. 49.
[25]See pp. 413 ff.

was not iron. Iron and steel were no longer efficient or economical for such ethereal purposes.

The lightest of the useful metals—lustrous, malleable, resisting corrosion, with high conductivity of heat and electricity—lay hidden in the earth during the millennia when copper, iron and lead were mined and used so extensively by the human race. It was isolated in 1825 by Hans Christian Oersted, hero of the deflected needle,[26] by heating anhydrous aluminum chloride with amalgam of mercury and potassium. Here it is in equation:

$$Al\ Cl_3 + 3K \longrightarrow Al + 3K\ Cl;$$

an expensive business producing tiny bits of a truly precious metal. Twenty years later the adroit Wöhler did little better using straight potassium. Another twelve years passed before Henri Sainte-Claire Deville, stimulated by Napoleon III, who was thinking in terms of military armor, cut the price of aluminum from a hundred to twenty-seven dollars per pound by substituting sodium for the potassium and adding sodium chloride to the aluminum chloride. About thirty years after that, the price had been brought down to four dollars and aluminum was being commercially produced in England, but in the entire period from 1825 to 1889 world production totalled less than a hundred tons.[27]

In 1885, in Oberlin College in Ohio, a twenty-one-year-old student administered a severe purge to the metal accumulations of sixty years on the subject of aluminum. He forgot the chloride and focussed on the oxide which the others had abandoned as too difficult to reduce. Yet the oxide was abundant. The trouble with it was that it had a high melting point.[28] The boy was stubborn about it. The oxide was the thing, unmeltable as it was. Charles Martin Hall graduated from college without solving the problem. But in college he had had a sympathetic teacher who was probably a great man besides. Frank Fanning Jewett continued to watch and encourage the young man. How much he contributed to the brilliant result will probably never be known.

[26] *M.I.M.*, pp. 264 ff.
[27] Harry N. Holmes, *Fifty Years of Industrial Aluminum*, Oberlin, 1937, p. 5.
[28] 2500° C.

In any case, Hall came to believe that the oxide might be dissolved in something which had a lower melting point and the aluminum metal brought out of it by electrolysis, Sir Humphry Davy's simple process of passing an electric current through a chemical solution. He hit upon cryolite as the solvent. He was twenty-two when he made his successful experiment with this process.[29]

There are reasons enough for the long delay. Electrolysis before the middle eighties was an expensive operation. But equally important was the absence of social demand for aluminum. Aluminum was pretty, but what was it for? As it was, when the Pittsburgh Reduction Company was formed in 1888 for making it by Hall's process, a large part of the company's activity was devoted to educating the public to its uses.

In Europe the Frenchman Paul Héroult hit upon a process nearly like Hall's two months after Hall's successful experiment, and eleven years later David Schwarz was able to build his all-aluminum airship. From that point on, Zeppelin developed his aluminum framework.

But to any one who is familiar with aluminum in its pure state, it is evident that a mere reduction in price was not the only necessity before such uses could be possible. Aluminum is light but it is also soft. It shrinks 7 per cent when it is cast. Its strength is far below that of steel or iron. Obviously its use in the pure state must be limited to kitchen utensils and gadgets. But by the time these came in to wide use and new, sterner demands loomed on the horizon in the shape of airships and other matters, students of the alloys had made considerable advance.

The technics of aluminum alloys are fascinating to any bystander in the borderland between science and industry. Zinc, copper, silicon have played their parts. The "modification process" of interspersing tiny crystals of silicon is vividly described by Doctor Frary.[30] An alloy with magnesium, another exceedingly light metal, has proved useful in airplane construction. Today some of the aluminum alloys are as strong as steel and

[29]*Ibid.*, p. 10.
[30]Francis C. Frary, "Aluminum" in *Modern Uses of Nonferrous Metals,* C. H. Mathewson, ed., N. Y., 1935, p. 21.

only a third as heavy. They form the wings of war and peace, the pistons of automobile engines, the masts of racing yachts, the bodies of passenger coaches, dining cars, tank cars on railroads. They are used for electric cables, dam bulkheads, steamship funnels, army canteens, sauce-pans and bottle tops.

Aluminum is the most abundant metal and the third most abundant element in the earth's crust. Even Deville realized that every clay bank was an aluminum mine. The United States produces more of it than any other country—indeed, except for Germany, nearly three times as much as any other country.[31] Certain aspects of the producing monopoly in America are less pretty than others and much criticism has been aimed at the company which succeeded Hall's. It is possible that aluminum will eventually feel the competition of magnesium, of which the United States has a plentiful supply in Michigan brine.

5

From this summary is evident the kind of economy which has been practiced in the use of the metals: it was, for a long time, an economy based on efficiency rather than on conservation. There has always seemed to be an adequate abundance of iron in the United States. But when the nonferrous metals came along in the steel alloys, there was a new stock-taking. We need not worry too much about copper and lead. But looking at our tabulated resources we come to a drop at chromium, nickel and tin, uranium and vanadium and blanks opposite some of the lesser metals. We import twenty times as much nickel as we produce, six hundred times as much tin and more than a hundred times as much chromium.[32] What the war of 1939 will do to these figures is doubtful.

But there are ways of conserving metals. A few years ago worn-out cars were left to rot in enormous dumps, which scarred the landscape. Today scrap metal is salvaged from the carcasses. When the dumps began to disappear, there was a popular belief

[31] 1937, 133,000 metric tons; Germany, 127,500; U. S. S. R., 45,000. U. S. Dept. Interior, *Minerals Yearbook,* 1938.
[32] *Minerals Yearbook,* 1938, Tables.

that the old metal was all going into high explosive shells. But the statistics show large recoveries from discarded metals in recent years. In 1937, about twenty-two million tons of scrap went into new steel. There were recoveries of about half a million tons of copper, nearly three hundred thousand of lead, a hundred and fifty thousand of zinc, sixty thousand of aluminum, twelve thousand of antimony and smaller amounts of the others.[33] Various new methods make possible the use of low-grade ores. So, obviously, our period of waste is over, at least as regards the metals.

America has made the most of its "mining kingdom." Here again, if there had not been waste in the beginning, there might have been an end result of less grandeur. It is instructive to see that the waste was greatest with the fictional metals, least with the realistic ones. By watching the progress from gold to steel we may trace the mental movement from romance to realism.

The gold may not return. The iron will go on. If the supply grows less, we need not be greatly disturbed, the chemists may find a way to make a better substitute from the products or the wastes of the farm. Conservation of resources is largely a process of using interchangeable materials with wise and planned economy. Its failure is due to greed, war, individual desires for power at the expense of the group or, simply, neglect. It seems reasonable to believe that America is outgrowing some of these vices.

The undirected habit of invention is, in itself, wasteful. We need some new machines, some new technologies, we do not need others. If those we do not need are forced upon us by habits of invention artificially stimulated by advertising and the ballyhoo of salesmanship, there will be waste of time, effort, money, nerves, energy and material. It is time to take stock of what we have and of what we truly, as human beings, want. In this way only may we learn to pause in headlong "progress" and reduce that lag of society behind technology which is responsible for most of our disease today.

[33]Exact figures given in *Minerals Yearbook*, 1938, pp. 465 ff.

Part VI
THE SOCIAL LAG

Chapter Twenty-three

THE STREAMLINE HOAX

I

AN AIRPLANE, moving wholly in the air in three dimensions, heads into the air stream. It is propelled by gripping the air with its propeller. The resistance of the air makes its upward motion possible, it climbs upon the air as a train climbs upon the track, a car upon the road. Thus, always the air is resisting it; always an air stream flows round it and past it. The several streams flowing over and under, by the sides, form what are known as the "stream lines"; they enclose a space of dead air which acts as a drag on the craft. Thus design must be adapted to the easiest flow of these streams with as little obstruction as possible, and the space of dead air they enclose in the craft's "wake" must be small.

A branch of mathematics known as aerodynamics grew up round the problems posed by the motion of bodies through the air. Countless thousands of experiments with models in wind tunnels built a mass of data. Finally, a design was worked out on the mathematical basis to overcome superfluous or "parasitic" air resistance, and the effort at the perfect design was called streamlining. To the lay public the streamlines became the lines of the craft.

Students of design studied birds. Then it was assumed that a drop of liquid falling through the air would take a shape offering the minimum of resistance, so the students studied quick photographs of falling drops. The public, learning these things, became entranced. It saw æsthetic values in copies of efficient nature. It became poetic about the falling drop, calling it the "tear drop." It sighed over its new vision of the bird.

These people failed to note, however, that the horse, the deer,

523

the cockroach, the mouse and other creatures which moved rapidly over the ground had somewhat different designs. What are called streamlines are hard to find in these demonstrations of an efficient evolution. This did not deter the public from believing (when it was suggested by adroit propagandists) that the design of the airplane applied to railroad trains and motor cars would achieve wonderful results of speed and saving of power.

In any good world's fair we shall find a pretty exhibit showing two car models moving in the kind of wind tunnels designed for airplane experiment. At one end of the tunnel is a fan supplying the wind. One model is of a modern streamlined car. The other is of an old car built for comfort. As the two cars are pulled toward the fan a dial will show the great effort required to drag the old car, the small effort needed to pull the new one. But a small boy, watching the exhibit, might easily impair it by saying to the demonstrator: "Please, Mister, will you try it again and put the fan over here, at the side?"

If trains and cars always headed into the air stream, as an airplane does, streamlining would be effective for cars and trains. But they do not; neither do they move wholly in the air or use its resistance to climb and propel themselves. If there are strong cross currents, hindering eddies are created to leeward. In any event, dead air is boxed between the car and the road. Propulsion is achieved through the contact of wheels with the ground. Thus, the design of the aircraft does not achieve the same result.[1]

It is true that a train or car moving at an extremely high rate of speed under the right air conditions may have its effort reduced by an "airflow" design. If speed is great enough so that air streams are created by the motion stronger than all other currents, there is a saving of fuel. It is also gained against a strong head wind. But as soon as conditions cease to be ideal, the power saving is compensated.

The public, however, soon became enamored of the idea. The automobile manufacturers did what they could to help it along. Sober, solemn engineers were invited to lecture and write about

[1]Leonard, *Tools of Tomorrow*, 203 ff.; 225–227. Nat'l Resources Committee, *Technological Trends*, p. 193.

how, for hours, they had watched the birds, measured them, dissected them to discover precisely the design best adapted to a road-bound vehicle whose working average would be somewhere below thirty miles per hour on doubtful surface. The spectacle of these serious gentlemen lying on their backs in such research was fascinating. Under the stimulus, car owners forgot about comfort, space, utility. They felt in duty bound to try for the speed for which the car was designed. But twenty million people all trying this on the same roads can scarcely be expected to give their cars a fair test. So the speed became merely an ideal, and many thousands died for it.

If streamlines had stopped with cars, however, they would have lost much of their symbolism. But, in the 1930's, they spread to buildings, houses, furniture, other things which are rarely required to combat air resistance. Inherent in a building are its static properties. To sacrifice space, comfort, interior efficiency, solidity, in order to give it the outside look of something perpetually in rapid motion, is likely to engender restlessness in the inmate. When this was done the streamline reached its full symbolic significance.

It represents the subjective ideal of speed divorced from utility. Not only can the ideal speed never be attained, but it is self-limiting. The ideal of speed, when it became general, defeated speed itself. The unharnessed ideal produced haste, notorious in the old adage. The dimensions in which speed should operate having been ignored, rotary motion resulted. Rushing into flight with our streamlined bodies, we struck the bars of the cage which was still there because we had forgotten to remove it.

All this was normal enough. Intense concentration upon technical progress which moved too fast for us to follow nevertheless impelled us to follow. We did not see the obstacles in the way, obstacles imposed by a social scheme which had only just adapted itself to earlier, now obsolete technologies. The scheme was still there in the foreground. Technics, however, were already scampering over the horizon. Our position in relation to them is what we call the social lag. The desire to catch up is normal enough but its gratification is disastrous.

In America the social lag is everywhere evident. Its acute stage here is due to the extreme rapidity of technological advance. Nullification of human purpose has become a commonplace, accepted as necessary to machine worship. We are like mystic flagellants, suffering for an ideal. We endure our fasting and our hair shirts that speed and the machine may prosper.

Some of us remembering our old cities know that in the 1890's we reached our destinations more quickly in horse-cars or on foot than we did in the automotive busses and taxis of the 1930's. No spectacle of medieval congestion could equal a New York rush hour in our streamlined era in discomfort and savagery. A Roman, watching the human cattle being herded into a subway train, would marvel at the efficiency with which men were led to the slaughter. Where, he might ask, in his sanguinary excitement, is the Coliseum? But, no, this is speed, to save an hour. But what intense activity will occur in the hour saved?

Men standing at a bar, "killing" time. Women and children fretting over a game, a puzzle, a contest, to kill time. Men and women quarrelling because supper is not ready, but quarrelling later because the evening is so long. They must get a new radio to help kill it. There is more time to kill because the subway, the stove, the can of condensed, cooked food all worked so fast. Because, in a jiffy, the telephone brought the cans from the grocer. Well, the telephone will serve, too, to kill the time saved. We must call up Tom, Jane, Junior. They too will be killing time. What shall we do tonight, we have an hour to kill? Books, papers, magazines are slow. Even the radio is slow. If we are to do a good job killing time, we must do it fast. We might go out in the car.

Millions of people killing time in cars. Give him the horn! This car has power enough to pass every other car on the road! What does that snail think he is doing? Out for the air. In a streamlined, this year's model, with a supercharger. . . . No, it's the car ahead that's the trouble. Now we've missed the light. A cigarette, please, to keep us from doing nothing. Lighter's on the dash. Broken? Well, it's time to turn the old bus in, anyway. It's economically sound to turn them in every two years. The new model has a hydramatic drive, there'll be nothing to do with your hands. What, then, shall we do with our hands?

2

It is economically sound to turn in our car every two years for the new model. The calculation is easily made; after two years the car "runs into money." Two years is its economic life. But its actual life is seven years. It is provable that the average car continues to perform adequately for seven years before it becomes dangerous. The average proves that many cars last longer than this. Others, of course, smash up. But after two years, repairs, new parts, new tires bring operating expense higher than that of a new car. Tires alone will almost justify a turn-in.

But if tires alone will almost justify a turn-in, then there must be a considerable discrepancy between the cost of tires to the manufacturer and the cost of tires to the car owner. The new car comes equipped with four new tires. If these tires cost the manufacturer any reasonable proportion of what it costs the owner to go out and buy them, he could scarcely afford to put out a new, tire-equipped car at a price which would make a turn-in almost worth while on account of tires alone. Obviously, also, spare parts, repairs must cost the owner a good deal more than it costs the manufacturer to make and assemble everything new. There seems, somehow, at this point, to be a nigger in the economic woodpile.

Further search reveals other dark little boys hiding in the shadows. When the two-year-old, economically unsound car is turned in, a surprisingly large allowance is made on the new car. Does the dealer then take the unsound machine and throw it on the junkpile? Not, as a rule, if he can avoid it. He seeks some one whose economic education has been neglected, sells him the old car and takes one which is still less sound, economically, in partial payment. This process goes on until some three cars or more have been exchanged (depending on the dealer's astuteness), at which point the dealer for the first time realizes the profit on the new car.[2] Thus many millions of cars are constantly

[2] "The Used Car," *Fortune*, June, 1938, p. 40.

operating on the roads in defiance of sound economic principles.

It seems evident that some one, in the chain of events, must take a loss. The dealer claims most of it and there seems to be justification for his claim. He must, after all, house the turned-in cars often over long periods. In many climates winter interposes an interval between the new-car market, artificially stimulated by an "auto show," and the used-car market, stimulated by early spring warmth. This means housing. But the dealer has other expenses: repairs, paint jobs, the turning back of speedometers, high-powered salesmanship. So the dealer complains, but discreetly, lest he lose his "franchise," his right to sell new cars and the privilege of having them dumped upon him at the whim of the maker.

This economic activity has a background which is somewhat involved with the streamline hoax. A visitor to any of the large Detroit plants will find himself markedly unpopular if he mentions the used-car problem. If he suggests that it might be met by a cut in production, he will arouse antagonism. "Will you halt progress, then?" he is asked. "Will you stop invention, technological advance, industrial growth, employment?" It is easy to make such an attitude appear unpatriotic or anti-social.

But we must examine that word "production." Spoken in the angry tones of a cornered manufacturer, it may be a mere abstraction. In itself, production is not necessarily a desired end. A specific production may be excellent, for it fills a social need. It is met, then, by a specific consumption. On the other hand, a production for the purpose of enriching a group, and for which desire must be artificially stimulated, is another matter. Thus abstractions which easily lend themselves to religious or patriotic appearance are often dangerous.

Production of private passenger automobiles bears an interesting relation to consumption, particularly in America. There arrive points at which the market stops expanding. If a market is surfeited, say, in 1940, with cars having a seven-year life, what happens to production in 1941? It may be assumed that each year enough cars will have their seventh birthday to keep the market steady. But this does not work out in practice because of the speed with which the democratic pattern in America was drawn. An immense market for cars developed more or less all at once. The resultant production initiated a momentum difficult to stop. The religion of the manufacturers (as well as other, practical, considerations) precluded the thought of decrease even when the market disappeared. Thus artificial stimulus must be applied.

It was brought to bear on many human or social tendencies. One was changing fashions. Cars were easily adjusted to the clothes formula and here the streamline ballyhoo was highly effective. Another was social hierarchy. The old hierarchy differentiated between the owner of a Rolls-Royce and the owner of a Ford or Dodge. But as mass production improved the cheap car, and as the light, cheap car proved its serviceability, this distinction disappeared and an age factor took its place. Thus the new hierarchy distinguished between a new car and a used one, a car two and a car seven years old. Mileage, it may be remembered, does not figure largely in class distinction.

Years of depression and various other turbulences had levelling effects hard to combat. It was in this period that the economic hoax appeared. It was worked out simply enough by means of price maintenance. It could easily be destroyed by competitive practice among tire-makers, various jobbers and retailers. Even repair-men could help dissipate it but this danger was avoided by combining shops and dealers and then bringing such pressure on dealers that they were obliged to charge high prices for repairs or go out of business.

But hundreds of other artificial stimuli were resorted to. Each model must differ from the previous year's. Knee actions, automatic chokes, magnetic gearshifts, free-wheeling slipped in and out. As the insides became so perfect that nothing could improve them, the outsides altered. Headlights skipped about from hood to fender. Radiators spread to the fenders, running boards fell off, windshields split. Ease of operation became a fetish. Gearshifts were put up on the steering wheel, vacuum tricks made them susceptible to the touch of a baby's little finger, doors were made to close themselves. Gadgets multiplied on the dash, cigarette lighters gave way to machines ejecting a cigarette already lit. These little tricks kept consumers awake even when the prodding of the economic impulse failed. It failed, sometimes, when the cash gave out. It required cash to be economically sound. But this difficulty, too, was met by the instalment plan. Anything, including financial ruin for dealer and consumer, was better than that Production with a capital P should stop.

The shot-in-the-arm method has spread through most of industry and commerce. This year's sewing machine is more streamlined than last. It will look well beside the new car, the new ice-box. Mrs. Jones' sewing machine, though it sews, is not streamlined at all. Anyway our sewing machine is broken. Five minutes' work with a screw driver will make it as good as ever. But the man who came with a screw driver—from the company —said it would be cheaper to buy a new model. Soon other screws would go. The new model has eliminated these screws by streamlining. We might mend it ourselves, of course. But who has time to be a jack-of-all-trades, mend a sewing-machine here, an oil burner there, a pump somewhere else? That is what Service is for. Service says don't bother, get a new model. Only a cent and a half every two hours for a year.

That is the streamlined way. It saves time (providing more to be killed) and it keeps production going. Production brings progress and progress brings invention, therefore technology cannot lag. Only society lags, weighed down by debt, rotary from restlessness, slowed by its own speed, beating its wings against old cages as each new bright object appears. The life metaphors are profoundly mixed.

3

But is not social lag inevitable? Must not inventors go on, led from discovery to invention, from science to its new application? The inquiring mind cannot stop. And how can society be expected to adapt itself instantly to each new technological step?

It cannot and it should not try. But invention, instead of applying every new scientific discovery, can adapt itself to the human steps. If there were an invention to satisfy every true human necessity, the inventors would be kept busy enough—indeed there would needs be more of them than ever. If inventors should concern themselves only with true human necessity then society would lead, technology would follow, there would be no social lag.

But the inventors are watching the scientists rather than humanity. Whenever there is a new scientific discovery, a dozen or a hundred inventors spring up to speculate on how it can be applied. They do not look about them to make sure that such an application is needed. They invent first and they or some commercial organization which they have attracted "create" the need. To create it requires a large staff of psychologists called salesmen; if these are gifted enough to create a fiction in enough minds, the invention sells. The more it sells, the more complicated, debt-laden and encumbered social life becomes.

There are, of course, offsets to the process, reactions. One of them is natural social resistance. Many automotive engineers, for instance, have wanted for years to put the engine in the rear, giving better visibility and simplifying a great many problems. But this has been defeated (partly by the streamline hoax) because people have built up a concept of automotive æsthetics which leads them to believe that a rear-engined car would be "funny-looking." There has been the same kind of reaction from styles in clothing and houses. Women, in many activities, would always have been better off in trousers but society, for centuries, would not have it, supposing it to be indecent. The makers of fine, steel prefabricated houses cannot sell their product today because it is "funny-looking."

The zipper was invented in 1893.[3] No one at that time could see the slightest use for it. The tempo of life was relatively slow. People dressed, undressed and did the other things for which zippers are now used, in a leisurely manner, enjoying the leisure. By the time tempo quickened, the invention was forgotten, being dug out only in the streamline era when it performed other functions as well as speed, such as smoothness or streamlining. It is a magnificent time-saver in the 1940's, having an extensive use in

[3]By W. L. Judson, Chicago. *Fortune,* Sept., 1932.

the theatre (lagging behind the movies) and for the binding together of great carpets.

More properly, the safety razor adapted itself to the tempo. It came with light, with cleanness, with realism when, at the same time, the speed requirement eliminated the barber. It created no need. Its electric successor on the other hand required the most strenuous effort to overcome resistance because there was no conceivable need for this sort of power-mower. Nor for an electric tooth-, hair-, clothes- or shoe-brush.

It has been said that the great urgency of modern times is for less rather than more inventions. But that is true only because the word invention has been restricted. A cheap, solid building admitting the maximum of sun and air is an invention and it is desperately needed. A cheap means of eliminating grade-crossings on railroads would be an immense boon to society. A city plan to eliminate skyscrapers would be an invention of major importance. Elasticity of price-structures, adjustment of farm surpluses, uniformity of divorce regulation, socialization of medicine might be far-reaching inventions. Psychiatric treatment of criminals, elimination of slums, annual wage-scales in seasonal industries, fair taxes, restriction of outdoor advertising, gentling of police methods are all useful inventions. With them we could do without electric-eye door openers, television or hydramatic drives bought on the instalment plan in the effort to be streamlined.

For the social inventors there is endless opportunity. Their work need not be opposite to that of the scientist. On the contrary, if they will ally themselves with natural law as the regional planners are doing, they will be obliged to follow him closely. But both for them and for the technologist there must be a change of attitude. They must study humanity first. That is what, in the end, invention must be for and it is its only excuse.

The machine must play its part in any future invention. Inventors may begin, therefore, with the slogan that the proper study of the machine is man.

Chapter Twenty-four

THE FRANKENSTEIN DELUSION

I

A S LONG as the machine was understood as an aid to human labor, it was hailed as a blessing to society. As it became automatic and replaced human labor it took on a new significance. In America, where workers were few in relation to the work to be done and where most of them were deeply engrossed in the soil, the labor-replacing machine performed a service which was recognized as necessary, releasing men for the duty of adapting their environment. In other countries, where there was a surplus of working population, the labor-replacing machine seemed to aggravate the already burdensome problem of unemployment and roused a bitter antagonism.

The fear, of course, proved groundless, at least during the industrial revolutions, for the machine so enlarged the industrial frontiers that the demand for labor increased. Moreover, the machine provided work for unskilled labor which had been unemployed in the handicraft and artisan period. But it imposed other burdens. The factory system placed what appeared to be a machine boss over the workers. Responsibility and command shifted from the master to the clock. The coordination of machines collectivized the workers. A worker attached to a machine was no longer an individual. The failure of his machine would throw the entire factory out of gear. Thus, to some extent, he became a machine himself. In any event, the machine became for him an ideal: the more machinelike his performance, the better the performance of the whole factory. The result was stultifying, at least to the more conscious workers. It must be remembered, always, however, what

533

an extremely low level of consciousness prevailed among the surplus population which suddenly found itself at work in the new factories.

It does not require much serious reflection to realize that however automatic a machine may be there must always be a man somewhere behind it though he may be as invisible as the announcer whose voice is amplified in the railroad station. A man designed the machine and the machine simply reproduces his thought with endless repetition until it is turned off. If it is a manufacturing machine, it produces endless solid replicas of some one's fancy. It can do no more than this; it can neither initiate thought nor engage in a reasoning process. There must be a man to decide when it is to go on and off and though he may not even turn the switch, he has specified beforehand the conditions under which the switch is to be turned. If those conditions should be artificially or erroneously produced, the machine cannot recognize the difference. A thermostat intended to communicate with an oil burner when room temperature reaches a certain point will communicate also if the sun happens to shine directly upon it or if the wall it hangs on catches fire. A trip in a road laid to record the passage of cars will record hundreds of nonexistent cars if a mischievous child discovers and plays with it. Behind the machine is a human brain; the more complex it is the more brains probably stand behind it.

But as machines became more automatic, the men behind them were farther and farther removed until people watching the machines forgot about the men. Because it is man's tendency to endow all sorts of things such as animals and gods with human attributes, people came to think of the machine as having a will, whims, fancies, desires and failings. It became customary to speak of the "tired" locomotive, the "capricious" or "temperamental" motor, "stern" or "stubborn" steamships or looms.

Machines had acquired these fictional qualities long before Mary Shelley wrote her youthful little fantasy called *Frankenstein*;[1] the conflict between man and the machine was already

[1]Published 1818.

recognized. But *Frankenstein,* coming as the factory system was working into its oppressive stage, was seized upon as an allegory showing the *victory* of the machine.[2] From that time on, man was thought of by many thinkers as the servant or slave of the machine.

For the next hundred years, machines reigned as gods in their own right. They soon became evil gods. They made the world materialistic, hindered the growth of the spirit, stultified, were "heartless," greedy; they were monsters with "maws," they were malicious, possessed of subtle intents and men and women were sacrificed to them. Yet in all this time the machine did nothing but what men intended it to do, namely, to take severe burdens off human shoulders and give thought a means of reproducing itself.

Collective philosophy expresses itself in abstract terms. Thus it became usual under the extreme collectivization wrought by the factory system, to refer to Man and The Machine without specifying what man and what machine. The machines along the assembly lines may be stultifying but the reaper or the thresher or the automatic electric pressure pump which delivers water to the bathroom are not stultifying. These devices relieve men of back-breaking labor and give the spirit a chance. Truly the modern Frankenstein school cannot studiously believe that men forced all day to their last ounce of energy by axes and wooden plows, by the transport of water, by tanning, shoemaking, butchering or a thousand other means of mere survival, that women tied to their spinning, weaving, brewing, pottery or whatnot had more time and strength for spiritual contemplation than their twentieth-century descendants!

Yet certain men, it is true, used machines to exploit other men, used children to tend semi-automatic machinery because it had shouldered the skill the children lacked; made machine-made light an excuse for longer hours; used the clock unmercifully as

[2]The monster in the story was not, as many suppose, a mechanical robot. "The dissecting room and the slaughterhouse," says Victor Frankenstein, "furnished many of my materials." Into the synthetic man thus created, Frankenstein, by some unexplained chemistry, became "capable of bestowing animation upon lifeless matter." Ed., N. Y., 1933, pp. 45, 48.

a master. They were always capable of stopping the clock, disconnecting the dynamo or slipping off the belts but they did not do this until certain other men forced them to it with complex economic consequences.

Attitudes, however, went astray. Men who regarded the machine as a means of profit forgot its function as a means of release and, for a while, in the profit effort, especially as frontiers widened and competition grew hotter, attached more and more men to machines instead of less and less. Labor, when it organized, tended to abet this process. It worked for the employment of more men at shorter hours and its overexertion in this direction started a reaction: factory operators preferred to deal with machines rather than with men; thus the replacement of men by machines which already seemed an economic desideratum was helped along by labor itself.

In America when frontiers, geographical first, and then industrial, began to close, there came the dread bogey of technological unemployment. As machines came in, men went out and, because social inventors had stopped thinking of the machine as a means of release, found themselves destitute. How much actual blame for unemployment can be laid on the shoulders of those who replace man by machines is still problematical. That there has been severe dislocation is undoubted. But whether jobs still exist, still multiply, in other fields, provided only the technologically unemployed could be guided to them will be a study for the historian of the future. Whether, also, many free, imaginative Americans with diversified thought and capacities above their station would not rather be unemployed and on relief than chained to a truly stultifying semiautomatic machine is another question which statistics cannot answer.

In any case, social attitude is fundamentally to blame. That men released by mechanisms should find themselves without occupation for their newly freed spirits shows a profound failure in social invention.

2

In a rightly planned society, it would be reasonable to expect some such action as the following:

SCENE

A Technological Laboratory, a TECHNICAL INVENTOR *at work. Enter* SOCIAL INVENTOR.

S. I. (*desperately*) For God's sake, invent more machines.
T. I. What for?
S. I. To release more men and women.
T. I. How many do you need?
S. I. As many as you can give me. A million, say, by this time next year.
T. I. What do you want them for?
S. I. To carry out my social plans. I must have people to do work which machines cannot do. I need designers, builders, artists, musicians, teachers, preachers, entertainers, city planners, people to educate in the activity of thinking. I need a great many workers to help improve the general condition of humanity.

If this dialog should suddenly occur today, T. I. would look at his visitor with a fishy eye and send for a specialist who was trained to handle such fixations. Or, if he cared to do the humoring himself, he might say:

"But my dear man, these factory workers are low-grade people."
"Precisely. I want to make them higher grade according to the evolutionary scheme."
"But you can't take people whose minds are numbed by repetitive motions and turn them into teachers and whatnot overnight."
"Not overnight. Nor do I expect all of them to be teachers or thinkers. I have, however, an immense amount of work that has to be done and by weeding out and grading these released people, I can gradually develop my plan. Certainly, as long as they continue to make repetitive motions, their minds will be useless. Those motions should be made by machines which have no minds."

This sort of conversation is, of course, apocryphal in our modern America. Such dialogs do not occur. If they did, the social inventor would be accused of treachery to his cause. He would be upbraided for inhumanity. It would be said of him

537

that he was trying to create unemployment. He should rather oppose the invention of anything which would throw these men and women "out on the street to starve." Meanwhile he must hurry to devise jobs, any jobs, random, haphazard, immediate jobs to take care of those who, on the street, are already starving as a result of machines. He must struggle, in other words, to catch up with technological invention. This haphazard struggle, reaching first for one straw, then for another, then at a bit of drifting wood to keep from sinking—this panic struggle is so engrossing that he has no time for the careful planning of a social future.

The answer is that the dialog here presented should have taken place long ago and that it should have been constantly repeated ever since; that the social inventor should have remained always a jump ahead of the technician instead of a stumble behind.

But, even today, it is conceivable that constructive social invention is still possble. Even at this late day, there may be steps for the social inventor to take which are larger and better directed than those he is now taking in the effort to regain his lost leadership.

If we consider what might be available for suddenly released workers, a number of things may occur to us. The most spectacular release in recent years has been that of the Negro cotton pickers effected by the new Rust machine picker. At first the social inventor is stunned by this blow; the Negro cotton picker is not of a high order of humanity and scarcely lends himself to spiritual advancement. He can do nothing, apparently, but pick cotton. Yet as long as he continues to pick cotton he will remain in a low stage and human evolution will be indefinitely retarded.

But suppose we think more exhaustively about the spiritual capacities of the plantation worker. Looking at our present American culture, we see that much of our music is derived from Negro folk lore. That is because the plantation Negro knew how to sing and still does. And, what is more, there is scarcely an American who does not love to hear him do it.

Is there any reason why Negro choruses on the grand, American scale should not be organized to tour the country? Organized, professionally, that is, with a profit motive? Would not a great moving band of a thousand or five thousand plantation singers attract huge audiences wherever they went? Their training, given so general an aptitude, need not be difficult. It is doubtful if they need be highly paid. The work would be more profitable than Relief and would stimulate more self-respect than picking cotton. Their performance might be instructive as well as entertaining and it might draw people from other sterile forms of entertainment which exist at the moment *faute de mieux.*

Americans are avid for music. Nothing suggests this more forcibly than the annual Bach Festival at Bethlehem in Pennsylvania. The church in which it is held contains only a small fraction of the crowd which listens. The church is surrounded by a sea of people which seems to have no boundaries—people trying to hear the singing of Bach. But Bethlehem is a thoroughly industrial town. The singers are mostly puddlers and other workers in the steel industry. Would they rather sing, perhaps, than puddle for their living if puddling could be done by machines and the singing made a full-time job? We should have no less steel and far more delight to our senses. The social inventor might investigate such matters before the machines are invented. He might well go to Bethlehem and say to a technician, "See here, these people can sing; I know of a million people who would like to hear them. How soon can you release them to me?"

Rebuttal is possible at this point, in the explanation that music is already mechanized and that methods of mass production have, indeed, taken over the whole function of entertainment. Yet this is inadequate. The thrilling sense of community in a vast audience can never be replaced by radio music. As it is, the studios have found it necessary to supply synthetic studio audiences to help out their entertainers—to laugh and applaud at the proper places and thus try to carry this community sense to lonely listeners.

But there are other ways of using released men. The Civilian

Conservation Corps is one. The social inventor will do well to interest himself in conservation. He might also look into the matter of "chemurgy" which we have discussed. Shall we not presently need a million or more men to handle these things?

There are jobs which machines cannot do alone that are necessary to the welfare of society. Some of them are manual jobs but they are not necessarily stultifying like the work on an assembly line. If they were done they might create other work higher in the scale. At present, they are not done at all though millions are unemployed. There are houses to be designed and built, cities to be replanned, an appalling tradition of sewerage and sewage disposal to be replaced, rivers to be purified, water supplies revised, traffic planned and controlled, rerouting of roads around the cities, parking systems devised and constructed, grade crossings eliminated, trees and gardens planted, parks built. Some of these things are being done. To do them all more machines must be invented to release more men and women.

If we can accept the belief that we need more rather than less machines, we shall need more engineers. Automaticity imposes new problems of design. Dies, for instance, must multiply as handicraft disappears from manufacture. Are we educating men now to be our future engineers? Are there not many men on Relief who, turning away from technological employment, might welcome technological education? Might not some of the industries, foreseeing the need of new technical development, profitably use some of their capital to *pay men wages while they learn?* Such an astonishing performance is dependent only on a point of view.

The point of view is, after all, a logical one. The most casual study of evolution has shown that man entered the world poorly equipped, physically, to live in his environment. Yet with his advanced mental power he designed tools which made it possible for him to adjust the environment to himself. As the tool was an extension of the arm, so the machine is an extension of the tool.

Thus our incessant movement toward use of the machine is a natural, not a perverse one. Our logical environment is not, therefore, the forest, but rather the network of power, machine transportation, electric communication, mass production in which, more and more, we find ourselves. Our movement toward such things has been a movement toward human nature, away from animal nature.

Lately we have moved, no doubt, too fast in this direction. The result is that we have "over-adjusted" environment. Technological advance has produced an environment toward which we have always aimed but which we have achieved too soon, before we were ready for it. Because the machine was so necessary to us we have reached the conclusion that the machine is all we need.

But man is not as simple as this. He is differentiated from lower forms of life not only by his ability to use tools. He has other qualities such as kindness, pity, tolerance, a sense of beauty, the capacity for abstract thought, the ability to plan, imagine, forecast and envision, which are not evident in the lesser animals. Nor can he teach these things to the machine. The machine, therefore, can never dominate him. Only his attitude toward it can hurt, hinder or destroy his society.

Chapter Twenty-five

CONCLUSION

THE HISTORY of the United States is fundamentally a history of invention. In itself, the United States was a new thing when it was devised. The federation with which it began was one of the greatest inventions in the history of the world. A scheme so elastic, so uninhibited that it was capable, at last, of embracing the greater part of a continent and assimilating in that embrace people of every race and condition on the planet is a device which transcends the farthest reaches of technical design.

Yet invention could not stop there. Like so many inventions, the pattern of the federation imposed necessities. It imposed necessities of collectivization, consolidation of power, culture, speed, economy and, as a concomitant of the fulfilment of these needs, there came the social hysteresis which is the bitter cause of today's unrest.

But the unrest still does not disrupt the scheme. Nor will it, if history is understood with all its interplay of social and technical forces, and if thought for the future is based upon that understanding. We are not "overreaching ourselves" for the first time. We have done it before in the days of our grand expansion. We did it when gold was found in California, but the railroad pulled us back into the scheme. We did it again when the octopus of the railroad stretched itself over the good land and wound its tentacles about the free people. But the scheme saved the people from the railroad—a little forgotten word about interstate commerce, which some long dead framer had thought to include. There are other forgotten words still there, waiting for the emergency.

Under the scheme, we have outlived every nation but one. Only England today is older, politically, than the United States. Today Europe, in her social turmoil, is looking back with searching eyes at the days when a Pennsylvanian congress gathered and Boston Harbor was "black with unexpected tea."[1] Is there not for

[1] Thomas Carlyle, *The French Revolution*, Book I, Chap. II.

her, even in this belated time, a hope in what followed that American turmoil? Cannot Europe too hope for a scheme of federation, of united sovereign states which will stretch and tighten, give and take, assimilate and resolve as technics and society move within it?

It will differ from ours. It will lack, always, the peculiar factor of the wilderness. It will be a re-carving of old society, not a growth of new society on the empty land. It will have, here, certain disadvantages but it will have advantages as well. More experienced in the social complex, it will avoid many of our raw mistakes. Already it has handled the machine invasion better than we have. With a Scheme for reference its future mistakes may dwindle away to unimportance.

For us, in the future, the danger is in neglect of the pattern through misunderstanding of the way in which it grew. If we borrow too heavily from Europe in social invention we shall invite disaster. Our plan for the future must be our own plan, based, step by step, upon the past. We must destroy nothing until we are sure it had not an origin somewhere in the wilderness. At the same time we can ignore none of the intermediate phases. A wilderness philosophy could have little bearing in 1940. Yet the philosophy of 1940 is American only if it is derived in some manner from one which may be traced back to our peculiar beginning.

Many American conflicts which seem distressing are fundamentally healthful. Such, for instance, is the conflict between the individual and the collective concepts. A victory for one or the other would be hurtful. Such is the conflict between industrial dictatorship and political democracy. An armistice between these two might result in what, in the 1930's, was called fascism; the victory of one or the other might spell slavery or famine. While the balance is even, the nation is sound.

Whatever inventions the future is based upon must be our own. If their origin is not American, they must be adapted to the maturity of our scheme, just as the railroad was adapted to its adolescence. So we shall survive and grow again.

BIBLIOGRAPHY

ACADEMY OF MOTION PICTURE ARTS AND SCIENCES, Research Council, *Motion Picture Sound Engineering*. A series of lectures presented to the classes enrolled in the courses in sound engineering given by the Research Council of the Academy of Motion Picture Arts and Sciences, Hollywood, California. New York: D. Van Nostrand Company, Inc. 1938.

ACKERMAN, CARL WILLIAM, *George Eastman;* with an introduction by Edwin R. A. Seligman. Boston: Houghton Mifflin Company. 1930.

ADAMS, HENRY, *The Education of Henry Adams;* an autobiography. Boston: Houghton Mifflin Company. 1927.

America and Alfred Stieglitz; a collective portrait, edited by Waldo Frank, Lewis Mumford, Dorothy Norman, Paul Rosenfeld and Harold Rugg. Garden City, N. Y.: Doubleday, Doran & Company, Inc. 1934.

AMERICAN ACADEMY OF POLITICAL AND SOCIAL SCIENCE, *The Motion Picture in Its Economic and Social Aspects . . .* Editors: Clyde L. King and Frank A. Tichenor. Philadelphia: The American Academy of Political and Social Science. 1926.

AMERICAN INSTITUTE OF MINING AND METALLURGICAL ENGINEERS, Petroleum Division, *Transactions,* "Petroleum Development and Technology." New York. 1924.

American Journal of Photography and the Allied Arts and Sciences. New York: Seely & Garbanati.

American Journal of Science. Edited by Benjamin Silliman. New Haven: S. Converse.

American Mercury. New York: A. A. Knopf.

AMERICAN SCHOOL OF CORRESPONDENCE, *Telephony;* a comprehensive and detailed exposition of the theory and practice of the telephone art, by Samuel G. McMeen and Kempster B. Miller. Chicago: American School of Correspondence. 1912.

AMERICAN SOCIETY OF MECHANICAL ENGINEERS, *Transactions.* New York.

AMERICAN TELEPHONE AND TELEGRAPH COMPANY, *Annual Reports.* Boston: A. Mudge & Son.

BIBLIOGRAPHY

ANDERSON, NELS, and LINDEMAN, EDUARD C., *Urban Sociology;* an introduction to the study of urban communities. New York: A. A. Knopf. 1928.

ANTHONY, ARTHUR BRUCE, *Economic and Social Problems of the Machine Age.* Los Angeles: University of Southern California Press. 1930.

APPLEYARD, ROLLO, *A Tribute to Michael Faraday.* London: Constable & Co., Ltd. 1931.

ARCHER, GLEASON, *History of Radio.* New York: American Historical Society, Inc. 1938.

ARMAT, THOMAS, "Development of Motion Picture Projection" in *Journal,* Society of Motion Picture Engineers, March, 1935, pp. 241 ff.

ARNOLD, THURMAN WESLEY, *The Folklore of Capitalism.* New Haven: Yale University Press. 1937.

ASHBY, N. B., *The Riddle of the Sphinx.* Des Moines, Ia.: Industrial Publishing Company. 1890.

ATKINSON, C. F., "A European View of American Radio Programs" in *Annals* of The American Academy of Political and Social Science, June, 1935.

ATLANTIC TELEGRAPH COMPANY, *The Atlantic Telegraph.* A history of preliminary experimental proceedings, and a descriptive account of the present state and prospects of the undertaking. Published by order of the directors of the company, July, 1857. London: Jarrold and Sons. 1857.

BACHELLER, IRVING, "Keeping Up with Lizzie," *Harper's Magazine,* October, 1910.

BARBARO, DANIELLO, *La Pratica della perspettiva di monsignor Daniel Barbaro* . . . opera molto profittevole a pittori, scultori, et architetti. Venice: Camillo & Rutilio Borgominieri, fratelli. 1569.

BARBER, HERBERT LEE, *Story of the Automobile,* its history and development from 1760 to 1917, with an analysis of the standing and prospects of the automobile industry. Chicago: A. J. Munson & Co. 1917.

BARNARD, CHARLES, "English and American Locomotives" in *Harper's New Monthly Magazine,* Vol. LVIII, No. 346, March, 1879, p. 555.

BARNES, HARRY ELMER, *Economic History of the Western World.* New York: Harcourt, Brace and Company. 1927.

BEARD, CHARLES AUSTIN and WILLIAM, *The American Leviathan;* The Republic in the Machine Age. New York: The Macmillan Company. 1930.

BEER, THOMAS, *The Mauve Decade;* American Life at the End of the Nineteenth Century. New York: A. A. Knopf. 1926.

BELL, ALEXANDER GRAHAM, *The Bell Telephone;* Deposition in the Suit Brought by the United States to Annul the Bell Patents. American Bell Telephone Co., Boston. 1908. (Known among telephone people as "The Red Book.")

BELLOC, HILAIRE, *The Highway and Its Vehicles.* London: The Studio Limited. 1926.

BENÉT, STEPHEN VINCENT, *John Brown's Body.* New York: Doubleday, Doran and Company, Inc. 1928.

BERNARD, L. L., "Invention and Social Progress" in *American Journal of Sociology,* XXIX, 1923–24, 1–33.

BLAKE, GEORGE GASGOIGNE, *History of Radio Telegraphy and Telephony.* London: Chapman & Hull, Ltd. 1928.

BLUMER, HERBERT, and HAUSER, PHILIP M., *Movies, Delinquency, and Crime.* New York: The Macmillan Company. 1933.

BOGART, ERNEST LUDLOW, *An Economic History of the United States.* New York: Longmans, Green and Co. 1922.

BOGEN, JULES IRWIN, *The Anthracite Railroads.* A study in American railroad enterprise. New York: The Ronald Press Company. 1927.

BORELLI, GIOVANNI ALFONSO, *De Motu animalium.* Ed. novissima, ab innumeris mendis & erroribus repurgata. Additæ sunt post finem partis secundæ Johannis Bernouillii . . . Meditationes mathematicæ de motu musculorum. Lugduni Batavorum, apud Petrum Vander Aa. 1710.

BORELLI, GIOVANNI ALFONSO, *The Flight of Birds.* London. Printed and published for the Aeronautical Society of Great Britain by King, Sell & Olding, Ltd. 1911.

BOUCHER, JOHN NEWTON, *William Kelly.* A true history of the so-called Bessemer process. Greensburg, Pa.: the author. 1924.

BOUTHOUL, G., *L'Invention,* Paris. 1931.

BOWDEN, WITT, *The Industrial History of the United States.* New York: Adelphi Company. 1930.

BOWDEN, WITT, *Technological Changes and Employment in the Electric-lamp Industry.* Washington: U. S. Govt. Print. Off. 1933.

BOWLES, SAMUEL, *Across the Continent.* A stage ride over the plains, to the Rocky Mountains, the Mormons and the Pacific states, in the summer of 1865, with Speaker Colfax. By Samuel Bowles. New ed. Springfield, Mass.: S. Bowles & Company. 1869.

BOYLSTON, HERBERT MELVILLE, *An Introduction to the Metallurgy of Iron and Steel.* New York: J. Wiley & Sons, Inc. 1936.

BRADFORD, GAMALIEL, *The Quick and the Dead.* Boston: Houghton Mifflin Company. 1931.

BRIGHT, CHARLES, *The Story of the Atlantic Cable.* New York: D. Appleton and Company. 1903.

BIBLIOGRAPHY

BRIGHT, EDWARD BRAILSFORD, *The Life Story of the Late Sir Charles Tilston Bright, Civil Engineer;* with which is incorporated the story of the Atlantic cable and the first telegraph to India and the colonies. Westminster: A. Constable and Co. 1899.

BRODERICK, JOHN THOMAS, *Forty Years with General Electric.* Albany, N. Y.: Fort Orange Press. 1929.

BROOKINGS, ROBERT SOMERS, *Economic Democracy.* America's answer to socialism and communism: a collection of articles, addresses and papers. New York: The Macmillan Company. 1929.

BROWN, CECIL LEONARD MORLEY, *The Conquest of the Air.* An historical survey. London: Oxford University Press. 1927.

BROWN, NELSON COURTLANDT, *A General Introduction to Forestry in the United States,* with special reference to recent forest conservation policies. New York: J. Wiley & Sons, Inc. 1935.

BURLINGAME, ROGER, *March of the Iron Men.* A social history of union through invention. New York: C. Scribner's Sons. 1938.

BUTLER, EDWARD, *Evolution of the Internal Combustion Engine.* London: C. Griffin & Co., 1912.

BYRN, EDWARD WRIGHT, *The Progress of Invention in the Nineteenth Century.* New York: Munn & Co. 1900.

CAFFIN, CHARLES HENRY, *Photography as a Fine Art.* The achievements and possibilities of photographic art in America. New York: Doubleday, Page & Company. 1901.

CAMERON, ALEC MUNRO, *Chemistry in Relation to Fire Risk and Fire Extinction.* London: Sir I. Pitman & Sons, Ltd. 1933.

CARMAN, HARRY JAMES, *Social and Economic History of the United States.* Boston: D. C. Heath and Company. 1930.

CARVER, THOMAS NIXON, *This Economic World,* and how it may be improved. New York: A. W. Shaw Company. 1928.

CASSON, HERBERT NEWTON, *The History of the Telephone.* Chicago: A. C. McClurg & Co. 1910.

CAVALLO, TIBERIUS, *The History and Practice of Aerostation.* London: the author. 1785.

Century, The, Illustrated Monthly Magazine. New York: Scribner & Co., 1870–81; The Century Co., 1881–1930.

CHANUTE, OCTAVE, *Progress in Flying Machines.* New York: M. N. Forney. 1899.

CHAPIN, F. STUART, *Cultural Change.* New York. 1928.

CHARTERS, WERRETT WALLACE, *Motion Pictures and Youth.* A summary. New York: The Macmillan Company. 1933.

CHASE, STUART, and TYLER, MARIAN, *The New Western Front.* New York: Harcourt, Brace and Company. 1939.

548

BIBLIOGRAPHY

CHASE, STUART, *Rich Land, Poor Land*. A study of waste in the natural resources of America. New York: McGraw-Hill Book Company, Inc. 1936.

CHATBURN, GEORGE RICHARD, *Highways and Highway Transportation*. New York: Thomas Y. Crowell Company. 1923.

CHEVALIER, ARTHUR, *Etude sur la vie . . . de Charles Chevalier*, Paris. 1862.

Chronicle of the Automotive Industry in America, 1892–1936. Prepared for private circulation by Eaton Manufacturing Company in celebration of its Silver Anniversary. Cleveland. 1936.

CLARK, VICTOR SELDEN, *History of Manufactures in the United States;* with an introductory note by Henry W. Farnan. New York: Published for the Carnegie Institution of Washington by the McGraw-Hill Book Company, Inc. 1929.

CLARKE, THOMAS CURTIS, "The Building of a Railway" in *Scribner's Magazine*, III, 6, June, 1888, p. 643.

CLEATOR, PHILIP ELLABY, *Rockets Through Space;* the dawn of interplanetary travel. New York: Simon and Schuster. 1936.

CLEMENS, SAMUEL (Mark Twain), *Roughing It*. Hartford, Conn.: American Publishing Company. 1872.

COLE, ARTHUR CHARLES, *The Irrepressible Conflict, 1850–1865*. New York: The Macmillan Company. 1934.

COLES, LEONARD ARTHUR, *The Book of Chemical Discovery*. London: G. G. Harrap & Company, Ltd. 1933.

COLLINS, ARCHIE FREDERICK, *The March of Chemistry*. Philadelphia: J. B. Lippincott Company. 1936.

CONANT, JAMES BRYANT, *The Chemistry of Organic Compounds*. New York: The Macmillan Company. 1939.

CORBIN, THOMAS W., *Marvels of Mechanical Invention*. An interesting account in nontechnical language of modern mechanical inventions. London: Seeley, Service & Co., Ltd. 1922.

COREY, LEWIS, *The Decline of American Capitalism*. New York: Covici, Friede. 1934.

COYLE, DAVID C., "Balance What Budget?" *Harpers Magazine*, October, 1937.

COYLE, DAVID CUSHMAN, *Brass Tacks*. Washington: National Home Library Foundation. 1935.

CRAWFORD, J. B., *The Crédit Mobilier of America*. Boston: Charles W. Calkins & Co. 1880.

CRAWFORD, MERRITT, "L. A. A. Le Prince" in *Cinema*, December, 1930, pp. 28–31.

CRESSY, EDWARD, *Discoveries and Inventions of the Twentieth Century*. New York: E. P. Dutton and Co. 1930.

BIBLIOGRAPHY

CROWTHER, JAMES GERALD, *Famous American Men of Science*. New York: W. W. Norton & Company, Inc. 1937.

CROWTHER, SAMUEL, *America Self-contained*. Garden City, N. Y.: Doubleday, Doran & Company, Inc. 1933.

DANIELS, WINTHROP MORE, *American Railroads;* four phases of their history. Princeton: Princeton University Press. 1932.

DASHIELL, BENJAMIN FRANCIS, *The Beginner's Story of Radio*. Cleveland, O.: The Radex Press, Inc. 1935.

DAVIS, ELMER, "Broadcasting the Outbreak of War" in *Harper's Magazine*, November, 1939, p. 580.

DAVIS, JOHN PATTERSON, *The Union Pacific Railway*. A study in railway politics, history and economics. Chicago: S. C. Griggs and Company. 1894.

DAVIS, WATSON, *The Story of Copper*. New York: *The Century Co.* 1924.

DAVISON, CHARLES, *A Manual of Seismology*. Cambridge: The University Press. 1921.

DAVY, MAURICE JOHN BERNARD, *Interpretive History of Flight*. A survey of the history and development of aeronautics with particular reference to contemporary influences and conditions. London: H. M. Stationery Off. 1937.

DAY, WILL, "Great Britain's William Friese-Greene" in *Photographic Journal*, London, July, 1926, pp. 359 ff.

DENNIS, LAWRENCE, *Is Capitalism Doomed?* New York: Harper & Brothers. 1932.

DENNIS, LAWRENCE, *The Coming American Fascism*. New York: Harper & Brothers. 1936.

DEPEW, CHAUNCEY MITCHELL, ed., *One Hundred Years of American Commerce* . . . A history of American commerce by one hundred Americans, with a chronological table of the important events of American commerce and invention within the past one hundred years. New York: D. O. Haynes & Co. 1895.

DE QUILLE, DAN. See Wright, William.

DERBY, E. H., "Transportation by Railway and Ship Canals" in *Harpers New Monthly Magazine*, Vol. LX, No. 358, March, 1880, p. 579.

DEWEY, DAVIS RICH, *Financial History of the United States*. New York: Longmans, Green and Co. 1934.

Dictionary of American Biography, under the auspices of the American council of learned societies . . . New York: C. Scribner's Sons. 1928–36.

DODGE, GRENVILLE MELLEN, *How We Built the Union Pacific Railway* and other railway addresses. The author. 1910.

DODGE, RICHARD IRVING, *The Hunting Grounds of the Great West*. A description of the plains, game and Indians of the great North American desert, with an introduction by William Blackmore. London: Chatto & Windus. 1877.

DOOLITTLE, JAMES ROOD, ed., *The Romance of the Automobile Industry;* being the story of its development—its contribution to health and prosperity—its influence on eugenics—its effect on personal efficiency —and its service and mission to humanity as the latest and greatest phase of transportation. New York: The Klebold Press. 1916.

DOOLITTLE, WILLIAM HENRY, *Inventions in the Century.* Philadelphia: The Linscott Publishing Company. 1902.

DOYLE, GEORGE RALPH, *Twenty-five Years of Films;* reminiscences and reflections of a critic, with a foreword by Alexander Korda. London: The Mitre Press. 1936.

DOYLE, GEORGE RALPH, *The World's Automobiles, 1881–1931.* A monograph on fifty years of car-building. Windmill Hill, Ruislip, Middlesex: the author. 1931.

DREIER, THOMAS, *The Power of Print—and Men;* together with the text of "A Salute to the Modern Newspaper," produced and broadcast by the National Broadcasting Company. Brooklyn: Mergenthaler Linotype Company. 1936.

DUNBAR, SEYMOUR, *A History of Travel in America.* Being an outline of the development in modes of travel from archaic vehicles of colonial times to the completion of the first transcontinental railroad; the influence of the Indians on the free movement and territorial unity of the white race; the part played by travel methods in the economic conquest of the continents; and those related human experiences, changing social conditions and governmental attitudes which accompanied the growth of a national travel system. Indianapolis: Bobbs-Merrill Co. 1915.

DYER, FRANK LEWIS, MARTIN, THOMAS C., and MEADOWCROFT, WILLIAM H., *Edison, His Life and Inventions.* New York: Harper & Brothers. 1929.

Economics, Sociology and the Modern World; essays in honor of T. N. Carver, edited by Norman E. Himes. Cambridge: Harvard University Press. 1935.

EDER, J. W., *Geschichte der Photographie.* Halle. 1905.

EDISON ELECTRIC INSTITUTE, *Rate Book,* 1938. New York: Edison Electric Institute.

EDISON ELECTRIC LIGHT COMPANY, *Bulletins.* 1883.

Electrical Engineer, The. A weekly review of theoretical and applied electricity. New York: Williams & Co. 1892–99.

Electrician, The. New York, October, 1882.

BIBLIOGRAPHY

ELLIOTT, WILLIAM FRANCIS, *Sound-recording for Films.* A review of modern methods, with a foreword by Paul Rotha. London: Sir I. Pitman & Sons, Ltd. 1937.

Encyclopædia Americana. Chicago: Americana Corporation. 1939.

Encyclopædia Britannica, The. Thirteenth Edition. This is a reprint of the Eleventh Edition with Supplement added. New York: Encyclopædia Britannica, Inc. 1926.

Encyclopædia of the Social Sciences, editor in chief, Edwin R. A. Seligman; associate editor, Alvin Johnson. New York: The Macmillan Company. 1930–35.

EPSTEIN, RALPH CECIL, *The Automobile Industry;* its economic and commercial development. Chicago: A. W. Shaw Company. 1928.

EVANS, ARTHUR F., *The History of the Oil Engine.* A review in detail of the development of the oil engine from the year 1680 to the beginning of the year 1930, with a foreword by Sir Dugald Clerk. London: S. Low, Marston & Co., Ltd. 1932.

FARADAY, MICHAEL, *Experimental Researches in Electricity.* New York: E. P. Dutton & Co., Inc. 1931.

FIELD, HENRY MARTYN, *The Story of the Atlantic Telegraph.* New York: C. Scribner's Sons. 1892.

FIELD, RICHARD MONTGOMERY, *Natural Resources of the United States.* A basis for economic geography. New York: Barnes & Noble, Inc. 1936.

FINDLAY, ALEXANDER, *A Hundred Years of Chemistry.* New York: The Macmillan Company. 1937.

FORD, HENRY, and CROWTHER, SAMUEL, *My Life and Work.* Garden City, N. Y.: Doubleday, Page & Company. 1903.

FORD, HENRY, and CROWTHER, SAMUEL, *My Life and Work.* Garden City, N. Y.: Doubleday, Page & Company. 1922.

FORNEY, M. N., *Catechism of the Locomotive.* Railroad Gazette. 1875.

Fortnightly, The. London: Chapman and Hall. From 1865.

Fortune. New York.

FOUQUE, VICTOR, *The Truth Concerning the Invention of Photography;* Nicéphore Niépce, his life, letters and works, translated by Edward Epstean. New York: Tennant and Ward. 1935.

FOURTIER, H., *Les Tableaux de Projection Mouvementes.* Paris. 1893.

FRANKLIN, BENJAMIN, *The Writings of Benjamin Franklin;* collected and ed., with a life and introduction, by Albert Henry Smyth . . . New York: The Macmillan Company. 1905–07.

FRANKLIN, HAROLD BROOKS, *Sound Motion Pictures,* from the laboratory to their presentation. Garden City, N. Y.: Doubleday, Doran & Company, Inc. 1929.

FRANKLIN INSTITUTE, *Journal.* Philadelphia. 1826–19—.

BIBLIOGRAPHY

FREUND, GISÈLE, La photographie en France au dix-neuvième siècle; essai de sociologie et d'esthétique. Avec vingt-quatre photographies hors-texte. Paris: La Maison des amis des livres, A. Monnier. 1936.

FROST, S. E., *Is American Radio Democratic?* Chicago: The University of Chicago Press. 1937.

Frustration of Science, The, by Sir Daniel Hall, J. G. Crowther, J. D. Bernal and others . . . foreword by Frederick Soddy. London: G. Allen & Unwin, Ltd. 1935.

GENTHE, ARNOLD, *As I Remember.* New York: Reynal & Hitchcock. 1936.

GIBSON, CHARLES ROBERT, *The Motor Car and Its Story.* A description of the strange vehicles invented before the motor car, the struggles & adventures of their inventors, with an account of the evolution of the petrol motor car & a simple explanation of the manufacture of modern cars & of the scientific principles on which they work. London: Seeley, Service & Co., Ltd. 1927.

GILDER, RODMAN, *The Battery.* The story of the adventurers, artists, statesmen, grafters, songsters, mariners, pirates, guzzlers, Indians, thieves, stuffed-shirts, turn-coats, millionaires, inventors, poets, heroes, soldiers, harlots, bootlicks, nobles, nonentities, burghers, martyrs and murderers who played their parts during full four centuries on Manhattan Island's tip. Boston: Houghton Mifflin Company. 1936.

GILFILLAN, S. C., "Who Invented It?" in *Scientific Monthly,* XXV, 1927, 529–534.

GLASSCOCK, CARL BURGESS, *The Big Bonanza.* The story of the Comstock lode. Indianapolis: The Bobbs-Merrill Company. 1931.

GLOVER, KATHERINE, *America Begins Again.* With a foreword by Stuart Chase. New York: McGraw-Hill Book Company. 1939.

GOLDSTROM, JOHN, *A Narrative History of Aviation.* New York: The Macmillan Company. 1930.

GOODALE, STEPHEN LINCOLN, *Chronology of Iron and Steel,* edited by J. Ramsey Speer. 2d ed. Cleveland, Ohio: The Penton Publishing Co. 1931.

GOSLIN, MRS. RYLLIS CLAIR (ALEXANDER), and GOSLIN, OMAR P., *Rich Man, Poor Man;* pictures of a paradox; a publication of the People's League for Economic Security. Editorial committee, Stuart Chase, Henry Pratt Fairchild and Harry A. Overstreet. New York: Harper & Brothers. 1935.

GRANT, ULYSSES SIMPSON, *Personal Memoirs of U. S. Grant.* New York: The Century Co. 1886.

GRAS, NORMAN SCOTT BRIEN, *Industrial Evolution.* Cambridge, Mass.: Harvard University Press. 1930.

BIBLIOGRAPHY

GRAVES, RALPH HENRY, *The Triumph of an Idea;* the Story of Henry Ford. Garden City, N. Y.: Doubleday, Doran & Company, Inc. 1934.

GREAT PLAINS COMMITTEE, *The Future of the Great Plains.* Washington. 1936.

GREGORY, JOHN WALTER, *The Story of the Road;* from the beginning down to A.D. 1931. London: A. Maclehose & Co. 1931.

GRIFFIN, CLARE ELMER, *The Life History of Automobiles.* Ann Arbor: University of Michigan, School of Business Administration, Bureau of Business Research. 1926.

HACKER, LOUIS MORTON, and KENDRICK, BENJAMIN B., *The United States since 1865.* New York: F. S. Crofts & Co. 1932.

HALE, WILLIAM JAY, *The Farm Chemurgic;* farmward the star of destiny lights our way. Boston: The Stratford Company. 1934.

HALL, CYRIL, *Seven Ages of Invention.* London and Glasgow: Blackie & Son, Limited. 1930.

HAMILTON, GEORGE, *Epistle from the Marquis de la Fayette to General Washington.* Edinburgh: Mundell & Son. 1800.

HAMILTON, WALTON HALE, *Price and Price Policies* (with Mark Adams, Irene Till . . . and others). New York: McGraw-Hill Book Company, Inc. 1938.

HAMLIN, TALBOT FAULKNER, *The American Spirit in Architecture.* New York: Yale University Press. 1926.

HAMMOND, JOHN WINTHROP, *Charles Proteus Steinmetz,* a biography. New York: The Century Co. 1924.

HAMPTON, BENJAMIN BOWLES, *A History of the Movies.* New York: Covici, Friede. 1931.

HANEY, LEWIS HENRY, *A Congressional History of Railroads in the United States to 1850.* Madison, Wis. 1908.

HANEY, LEWIS HENRY, *A Congressional History of Railways in the United States, 1850–1887.* Madison, Wis. 1910.

Harpers New Monthly Magazine, Editor's Historical Record (department). "Transportation," Vol. XLVII, No. 280, September, 1873, p. 631.

Harper's Weekly. A journal of civilization. New York: Harper & Brothers. 1857–1916.

HARRISON, H. S., "Inventions. Variations and Mutations in Invention. Analysis and Factors of Invention" in *Man,* XXVI, 1926, Nos. 74 and 101; XXVII, 1927, No. 28.

HASLETT, ARTHUR WOODS, *Radio Round the World.* Cambridge: The University Press. 1934.

HAYS, WILL H., *See and Hear.* A brief history of motion pictures and the development of sound. New York. 1929.

BIBLIOGRAPHY

HAZARD, ROWLAND, "The Crédit Mobilier of America." A paper read before the Rhode Island Historical Society, Tuesday evening, February 22, 1881. Providence: S. S. Rider. 1881.

HELMHOLTZ, HERMANN LUDWIG FERDINAND VON, *On the Sensations of Tone as a Physiological Basis for the Theory of Music*. Translated with the author's sanction from the 3d German edition, with additional notes and an additional appendix, by Alexander J. Ellis. London: Longmans, Green & Co. 1875.

HENDRICK, BURTON JESSE, *The Life of Andrew Carnegie*. Garden City, N. Y.: Doubleday, Doran & Company, Inc. 1932.

HENRI, ROBERT, *The Art Spirit*. Notes, articles, fragments of letters and talks to students, bearing on the concept and technique of picture making, the study of art generally, and an appreciation, compiled by Margery Ryerson. Philadelphia: J. B. Lippincott Company. 1923.

HENRY, JOSEPH, *Scientific Writings of Joseph Henry*. Washington: Smithsonian Institution. 1886.

HERKIMER COUNTY HISTORICAL SOCIETY, *The Story of the Typewriter, 1873–1923*, published in commemoration of the fiftieth anniversary of the invention of the writing machine. New York: Press of A. H. Kellogg Company. 1923.

HODGINS, ERIC, *Behemoth;* the Story of Power. Garden City, N. Y.: Doubleday, Doran & Company, Inc. 1932.

HODGINS, ERIC, *Sky High;* the Story of Aviation. Boston: Little, Brown and Company. 1929.

HOFFMAN, PAUL G., and GREENE, JAMES H., *Marketing Used Cars*, with a foreword by C. A. Vane. New York: Harper & Brothers, 1929.

HOGBEN, LANCELOT THOMAS, *Science for the Citizen*. A self-educator based on the social background of scientific discovery. New York: A. A. Knopf. 1938.

HOLME, CHAS., ed., *Art in Photography*. New York. 1905.

HOLMES, HARRY NICHOLLS, *Fifty Years of Industrial Aluminum*. Oberlin, Ohio. 1937.

HONE, PHILIP, *The Diary of Philip Hone*, 1828–1851, edited, with an introduction by Allan Nevins. New York: Dodd, Mead and Company. 1927.

HOPWOOD, HENRY V., *Living Pictures;* their history, photo-production, and practical working, with classified lists of British patents and bibliography. London. 1899. Only this edition contains the full material on the early invention period.

HORGAN, STEPHEN H., *Horgan's Half-tone and Photomechanical Processes*. Chicago: The Inland Printer Company. 1913.

HOWELL, JOHN WHITE, *History of the Incandescent Lamp*. Schenectady, N. Y.: The Maqua Company. 1927.

BIBLIOGRAPHY

HUBBARD, T. O'B., and LEDEBOER, J. H., *The Aeronautical Classics,* No. 6. London. 1911.

HUBERT, PHILIP GENGEMBRE, *Inventors.* New York: C. Scribner's Sons. 1896.

HUEGY, HARVEY WILBORN, *The Financial Policies and Practices of Automobile Finance Companies.* Urbana: University of Illinois. 1938.

HUMPHREY, EDWARD FRANK, *An Economic History of the United States.* New York: The Century Co. 1931.

HUNEKER, JAMES GIBBONS, *Steeplejack.* New York: C. Scribner's Sons. 1922.

HUNT, ROBERT, "Researches on Light" in *Photographic Art Journal,* I, 6 (1851).

HYDE, HARFORD MONTGOMERY, *Air Defence and the Civil Population.* London: The Cresset Press, Ltd. 1937.

INSTITUTE FOR EDUCATION BY RADIO, *Education on the Air . . .* yearbook of the Institute for Education by Radio. Columbus, Ohio, State University. 1930.

INSULL, MARTIN, *America's New Frontier.* Chicago. 1929.

IRON AND STEEL ASSOCIATION, *Report.* 1875.

JACKS, G. V., and WHITE, R. O., *Vanishing Lands.* New York: Doubleday, Doran and Company. 1939.

JAMES, W. S., *Cowboy Life in Texas,* or 27 years a maverick. A realistic and true recital of wild life on the boundless plains of Texas, being the actual experience of twenty-seven years in the exciting life of a genuine cowboy among the roughs and toughs of Texas. Chicago: M. A. Donohue & Co. 1898.

JEANS, SIR JAMES HOPWOOD, *The New Background of Science.* New York: The Macmillan Company. 1933.

JEANS, SIR JAMES HOPWOOD, *Science and Music.* New York: The Macmillan Company. 1937.

JOHNSON, EMORY RICHARD, *American Railway Transportation.* New York: D. Appleton and Company. 1908.

JONES, BENCE, *The Life and Letters of Faraday.* London. 1870.

JONES, FRANCIS ARTHUR, *Thomas Alva Edison.* New York. 1907.

JOSEPHSON, MATTHEW, *The Robber Barons;* the great American capitalists, 1861–1901. New York: Harcourt, Brace & Company. 1934.

KAEMPFFERT, WALDEMAR BERNHARD, ed., *A Popular History of American Invention.* New York: C. Scribner's Sons. 1924.

KALTENBORN, H. V., "An American View of European Broadcasting" in *Annals,* American Academy of Political and Social Science, June, 1935.

KEIR, ROBERT MALCOLM, *The Epic of Industry.* New Haven: Yale University Press. 1926.

KENNEDY, E. D., *Dividends to Pay*. New York: Reynal and Hitchcock. 1939.

KENNEDY, JOSEPH PATRICK, ed., *The Story of the Films*, as told by leaders of the industry to the students of the Graduate School of Business Administration, George F. Baker Foundation, Harvard University. Chicago: A. W. Shaw Company. 1927.

KETTERING, CHARLES F., *The New Necessity*, Century of Progress Series. Baltimore: Williams and Wilkins Co. 1932.

KOUWENHOVEN, JOHN ATLEE, *Adventures of America, 1857–1900*. A pictorial record from *Harper's Weekly*. New York: Harper & Brothers. 1938.

KROEBER, ALFRED LOUIS, *Anthropology*. New York: Harcourt, Brace and Company. 1923.

KROWS, ARTHUR EDWIN, *The Talkies*. New York: H. Holt and Company. 1930.

LANSING, MARION FLORENCE, *Great Moments in Science*. Garden City, N. Y.: Doubleday, Page & Company. 1926.

LAUT, AGNES CHRISTINA, *The Romance of the Rails*. New York: R. M. McBride & Company. 1929.

LEEMING, JOSEPH, *Peaks of Invention*. New York: The Century Co. 1928.

LEONARD, JONATHAN NORTON, *Tools of Tomorrow*. New York: The Viking Press. 1935.

LEONARD, JONATHAN L., *The Tragedy of Henry Ford*. New York: G. P. Putnam's Sons. 1932.

LEWIS, NELSON PETER, *The Planning of the Modern City*. A review of the principles governing city planning. 2d ed. rev. New York: John Wiley & Sons, Inc. 1923.

LILIENTHAL, OTTO, *Birdflight as the Basis of Aviation*. A contribution towards a system of aviation, compiled from the results of numerous experiments made by O. and G. Lilienthal, with a biographical introduction and addendum by Gustav Lilienthal, translated from the 2d edition by A. W. Isenthal. New York: Longmans, Green & Co. 1911.

Literary Digest, The. New York, Funk & Wagnalls. From 1890.

LOEB, HAROLD, and ASSOCIATES, *The Chart of Plenty*. A study of America's product capacity based on the findings of the national survey of potential product capacity, with a foreword by Stuart Chase. New York: The Viking Press. 1935.

London, The, Edinburgh and Dublin Philosophical Magazine and Journal of Science. London: Taylor and Francis. From 1798.

LOW, ARCHIBALD MONTGOMERY, *Recent Inventions*. New York: T. Nelson & Sons. 1935.

BIBLIOGRAPHY

Lucretius (Titus Lucretius Carus), *De Rerum Natura*, 65 B.C.

Lyman, George D., *Ralston's Ring*. New York: Charles Scribner's Sons. 1937.

Lyman, George D., *The Saga of the Comstock Lode*. New York: Charles Scribner's Sons. 1937.

McCabe, James Dabney, *Paris by Sunlight and Gaslight*. A work descriptive of the mysteries and miseries, the virtues, the vices, the splendors and the crimes of the city of Paris. Philadelphia: National Publishing Co. 1870.

McClure's Magazine. New York: S. S. McClure, Limited. 1893–1929.

MacIlvain, K. M., *Sound-picture Recording and Projection*. Scranton, Pa.: International Textbook Company. 1931.

McKee, Henry Stewart, *Degenerate Democracy*, introduction by Lionel D. Edie. New York: Thomas Y. Crowell Company. 1933.

MacKenzie, Catherine Dunlop, *Alexander Graham Bell*, the man who contracted space. Boston: Houghton Mifflin Company. 1928.

McMahon, John Robert, *The Wright Brothers*, fathers of flight. Boston: Little, Brown & Company. 1930.

Magoun, F. Alexander, and Hodgins, Eric, *A History of Aircraft*. New York: Whittlesey House, McGraw-Hill Book Company, Inc. 1931.

Marey, Étienne Jules, *Movement;* translated by Eric Pritchard. New York: D. Appleton and Company. 1895.

Mathews, Mary McNair, *Ten Years in Nevada*. Buffalo: Baker, Jones and Company. 1880.

Mathewson, Champion Herbert, ed., *Modern Uses of Nonferrous Metals,* published for the Seeley W. Mudd fund, by the American Institute of Mining and Metallurgical Engineers. 1st ed. N. Y. 1935.

Maxim, Hiram Percy, *Horseless Carriage Days*. New York: Harper & Brothers. 1937.

Mergenthaler, Ottmar, *Biography of Ottmar Mergenthaler* and history of the linotype, its invention and development. Baltimore, Md. 1898.

Merin, Peter, *Conquest of the Skies;* the story of the idea of human flight. London: John Lane. 1938.

Meteyard, Eliza, *A Group of Englishmen (1795 to 1815)*. Being records of the younger Wedgwoods and their friends, embracing the history of the discovery of photography and a facsimile of the first photograph. London: Longmans, Green and Co. 1871.

Miller, Francis Trevelyan, ed., *The Photographic History of the Civil War*. New York: The Review of Reviews Co. 1911.

Miller, Francis Trevelyan, *The World in the Air*. The story of flying in pictures. First historic collection of official prints and photographs from government archives and private collections recording five thousand years of man's struggles to conquer the air. Associate in aeronautic history, Joseph Olin Howe, in collaboration with Frederick A. Barber of Historical Foundations, with a board of international authorities. New York: G. P. Putnam's Sons. 1930.

MILLS, FREDERICK CECIL, *Economic Tendencies in the United States;* aspects of pre-war and post-war changes, with an introduction by the Committee on Recent Economic Changes. New York: J. J. Little & Ives Company. 1932.

MILLS, JOHN, *Signals and Speech in Electrical Communication.* New York: Harcourt, Brace and Company. 1934.

Modern Communication, by Arthur W. Page, H. D. Arnold, and others. Boston: Houghton Mifflin Company, 1932.

MOLEY, RAYMOND, *Are We Movie Mad?* New York: Macy-Masius. 1938.

MONTMASSON, J. M., *Invention and the Unconscious,* translated by H. S. Hatfield. New York. 1932.

MOODY, JOHN, *The Railroad Builders.* A chronicle of the welding of the States. New Haven: Yale University Press. 1921.

MORISON, SAMUEL ELIOT, and COMMAGER, HENRY STEELE, *The Growth of the American Republic.* New York: Oxford University Press. 1930.

MORRIS, RAY, *Railroad Administration.* New York: D. Appleton & Co. 1920.

MORSE, EDWARD LIND, *Samuel F. B. Morse,* Letters and Journals. Boston: Houghton Mifflin Co. 1914.

MULLALY, JOHN, *The Laying of the Atlantic Cable.* New York. 1858.

MUMFORD, JOHN K., *Outspinning the Spider.* New York. *c.* 1921.

MUMFORD, LEWIS, *The Brown Decades.* A study of the arts in America, 1865–1895. New York: Harcourt, Brace and Company. 1931.

MUMFORD, LEWIS, *The Culture of Cities.* New York: Harcourt, Brace and Company. 1938.

MUMFORD, LEWIS, *Sticks and Stones.* A study of American architecture and civilization. New York: Boni and Liveright. 1924.

MUMFORD, PHILIP S., *Humanity, Air Power and War.* An essay upon international relations. London: Jarrolds, Limited. 1936.

MÜNSTERBERG, HUGO, *The Photoplay;* a psychological study. New York: D. Appleton and Company. 1916.

MURCHISON, THOMAS C., *The Romance of the Development of the Automobile.* Shrewsbury, Mass.: The Museum of Transportation. 1933.

MUYBRIDGE, EADWEARD, *Animals in Motion.* An electro-photographic investigation of consecutive phases of muscular actions by Eadweard

BIBLIOGRAPHY

Muybridge (3d impression). Commenced 1872. Completed 1885. London: Chapman & Hall, Ltd. 1907.

MYERS, GUSTAVUS, *History of the Great American Fortunes.* Chicago: C. H. Kerr & Company. 1910.

NASMYTH, JAMES, *Autobiography.* Edited by Samuel Smiles. New York: Harper and Brothers. 1883.

NATIONAL ELECTRIC LIGHT ASSOCIATION, Bulletin IX, September, 1922.

NEFF, MRS. WANDA (FRAIKEN), *Victorian Working Women.* An historical and literary study of women in British industries and professions, 1832–1850. New York: Columbia University Press. 1929.

NEVINS, ALLAN, *Abram S. Hewitt;* with some account of Peter Cooper. New York: Harper & Brothers. 1935.

NEVINS, ALLAN, *The Emergence of Modern America, 1865–1878.* New York: The Macmillan Company. 1928.

New International Encyclopedia, The, 2d ed. New York: Dodd, Mead and Company. 1930.

NEWHALL, BEAUMONT, *Photography;* a short critical history. New York: The Museum of Modern Art. 1938.

Newton's London Journal of Arts and Sciences; being a record of the progress of invention as applied to the arts. London: W. Newton. 1820—.

NIXON, ST. JOHN C., *The Invention of the Automobile* (Karl Benz and Gottlieb Daimler), preface by Rudolf Caracciola. London: Country Life, Ltd. 1936.

NOLEN, JOHN, ed., *City Planning.* A series of papers presenting the essential elements of a city plan. New York: D. Appleton and Company. 1916.

NORDHOFF, CHARLES, "California: How to Go There and What to See by the Way" in *Harper's New Monthly Magazine,* Vol. XLIV, No. 264, May, 1872, p. 865.

NOVERRE, MAURICE, *La vérité sur l'invention de la projection animée.* Émile Reynaud, sa vie et ses travaux. Lettre-préface de M. Victor Collignon. Brest: L'Auteur. 1926.

OBERHOLTZER, ELLIS PAXSON, *A History of the United States since the Civil War.* New York: The Macmillan Company. 1926–37.

OGBURN, WILLIAM FIELDING, *Social Change with Respect to Culture and Original Nature.* New York: B. W. Huebsch, Inc. 1922.

OGBURN, WILLIAM FIELDING, *Social Characteristics of Cities.* A basis for new interpretations of the role of the city in American life. Chicago: The International City Managers' Association. 1937.

OGBURN, WILLIAM FIELDING, *You and Machines.* Washington, D. C.: National Capital Press, Inc. 1934.

BIBLIOGRAPHY

OGBURN, WILLIAM FIELDING, and GOLDENWEISER, ALEXANDER, ed., *The Social Sciences and Their Interrelations*. Boston: Houghton Mifflin Company. 1927.

Optical Magic Lantern Journal and Photographic Enlarger. Edited by J. Hay Taylor. London: W. Fawcett and Co. 1890–1903.

OSTROLENK, BERNHARD, *Electricity: for Use or for Profit?* New York: Harper & Brothers. 1936.

PACH, WALTER, *The Masters of Modern Art*. New York: B. W. Huebsch, Inc. 1924.

PAGE, ARTHUR and others, *Modern Communication*. Boston: Houghton, Mifflin Company. 1932.

PAINE, ALBERT BIGELOW, *Mark Twain*. New York: Harper and Brothers. 1929.

PARK, WILLIAM LEE, *Pioneer Pathways to the Pacific*. Clare, Mich.: Clara Aire. 1935.

PARTINGTON, JAMES RIDDICK, *A Short History of Chemistry*. New York: The Macmillan Company. 1937.

PERLMAN, WILLIAM J., ed., *The Movies on Trial*. The views and opinions of outstanding personalities anent screen entertainment past and present. New York: The Macmillan Company. 1936.

PHILOSOPHICAL SOCIETY, London, *Transactions*.

PHILP, CHARLES G., *Stratosphere and Rocket Flight* (Astronautics; a popular handbook on space flight of the future, including a section on the problems of interplanetary space navigation. London: Sir I. Pitman & Sons, Ltd. 1935.

Photo-Era Magazine, the American journal of photography; an illustrated monthly of photography and allied arts. Wolfeboro, N. H.: A. H. Beardsley. 1921–1932.

Photographic Art Journal, The. New York: W. B. Smith. 1851–53.

POLAKOV, WALTER NICHOLAS, *The Power Age;* its quest and challenge. New York: Covici, Friede. 1933.

Popular Science Monthly, The. New York: D. Appleton and Company. 1872–19—.

PORTA, GIOVANNI BATTISTA DELLA, *Magia Naturalis*. 2d ed. 1589.

POTONNIÉE, GEORGES, *The History of the Discovery of Photography*, translated by Edward Epstean. New York: Tennant and Ward. 1936.

POUND, ARTHUR, *The Telephone Idea;* fifty years after. New York: Greenberg. 1926.

POUND, ARTHUR, *The Turning Wheel*. The story of General Motors through twenty-five years, 1908–1933. Garden City, N. Y.: Doubleday, Doran & Company, Inc. 1934.

561

BIBLIOGRAPHY

PRENDERGAST, FRANCIS E., "Transcontinental Railways" in *Harper's New Monthly Magazine,* Vol. LXVII, No. 402, November, 1883, p. 937.

PRESCOTT, GEORGE BARTLETT, *History, Theory, and Practice of the Electric Telegraph.* Boston: Ticknor and Fields. 1860.

PRIBICHEVICH, STOYAN, "In an American Factory" in *Harpers Magazine,* September, 1938.

PROUT, HENRY GOSLEE, *A Life of George Westinghouse.* New York: C. Scribner's Sons. 1922.

RAMSAYE, TERRY, *A Million and One Nights.* A history of the motion picture. New York: Simon and Schuster. 1926.

READ, THOMAS THORNTON, *Our Mineral Civilization.* The Williams & Wilkins Company, in co-operation with the Century of Progress Exposition. 1932.

REINACH, SALOMON, *Apollo.* Paris. 1904.

RESEARCH COUNCIL ACADEMY OF MOTION PICTURE ARTS AND SCIENCES, *Motion Picture Sound Engineering.* New York: D. Van Nostrand Company, Inc. 1938.

RHODES, FREDERICK LELAND, *Beginnings of Telephony,* with a foreword by General John J. Carty. New York: Harper & Brothers. 1929.

RHODES, JAMES FORD, *History of the United States from the Compromise of 1850 to the End of the Roosevelt Administration.* New ed. in nine volumes. New York: The Macmillan Company. 1928.

RICKARD, THOMAS ARTHUR, *A History of American Mining.* New York: McGraw-Hill Book Company, Inc. 1932.

RICKARD, THOMAS ARTHUR, *Man and Metals.* A history of mining in relation to the development of civilization. New York: McGraw-Hill Book Company, Inc. 1932.

ROBY, HENRY W., *The Invention of the Typewriter,* edited with historical introduction by Milo M. Quaife. Menasha, Wis.: George Banta Publishing Company. 1925.

ROE, JOSEPH W., *English and American Tool Builders.* McGraw-Hill Book Co. 1926.

ROOT, MARCUS A., *The Camera and the Pencil;* or, The heliographic art, its theory and practice . . . together with its history in the United States and in Europe. Philadelphia: M. A. Root. 1864.

ROTHA, PAUL, *Celluloid;* the film today. New York: Longmans, Green and Co. 1931.

ROYAL INSTITUTION OF GREAT BRITAIN, *Journal,* October, 1830–November, 1831. London: J. Murray. 1831.

ROYAL SOCIETY OF LONDON, *Proceedings.* London. 1932–19—.

ROYAL TYPEWRITER COMPANY, *The Evolution of the Typewriter.* New York: Royal Typewriter Company, Inc. 1921.

BIBLIOGRAPHY

RUSKIN, JOHN, *The Works of John Ruskin,* edited by E. T. Cook and Alexander Wedderburn. London: G. Allen. 1912.

RUTHERFORD, ERNEST RUTHERFORD, *The Newer Alchemy;* based on the Henry Sidgwick Memorial Lecture delivered at Newnham College, Cambridge, November, 1936. New York: The Macmillan Company. 1937.

RYDER, JAMES FITZALLAN, *Voigtländer and I in Pursuit of Shadow Catching.* A story of fifty-two years' companionship with a camera. Cleveland, Ohio: The Cleveland Printing & Publishing Co. 1902.

SABIN, EDWIN LEGRAND, *Building the Pacific Railway.* The construction-story of America's first iron thoroughfare between the Missouri River and California, from the inception of the great idea to the day, May 10, 1869, when the Union Pacific and the Central Pacific joined tracks at Promontory Point, Utah, to form the nation's transcontinental. Philadelphia: J. B. Lippincott Company. 1919.

SCHLESINGER, ARTHUR MEIER, *The Rise of the City, 1878–1898.* New York: The Macmillan Company. 1933.

SCHLESINGER, ARTHUR MEIER, *New Viewpoints in American History.* New York: The Macmillan Company. 1922.

SCHWARZ, HEINRICH, *David Octavius Hill,* master of photography, translated from the German by Helene E. Fraenkel. New York: The Viking Press. 1931.

Scientific American, 75th Anniversary Number, Oct. 2, 1920.

SEABURY, WILLIAM MARSTON, *The Public and the Motion Picture Industry.* New York: The Macmillan Company. 1926.

SELDES, GILBERT VIVIAN, *An Hour with the Movies and the Talkies.* Philadelphia: J. B. Lippincott Company. 1929.

SENNETT, A. R., *Carriages Without Horses Shall Go.* London: Whitaker and Co. 1896.

SHANKS, W. F. G., "How We Get Our News" in *Harper's Monthly Magazine,* Vol. XXXIV, March, 1867, pp. 517 ff.

SHANNON, FRED ALBERT, *Economic History of the People of the United States.* New York: The Macmillan Company. 1934.

SHEARD, CHARLES, *Life-giving Light.* Baltimore: The Williams & Wilkins Company in co-operation with the Century of Progress Exposition. 1933.

SHELLEY, MARY, *Frankenstein.* First published, 1818. Edition quoted in text, New York: E. P. Dutton and Company. 1933.

SHOTWELL, JAMES THOMSON, *On the Rim of the Abyss.* New York: The Macmillan Company. 1936.

SHOTWELL, JAMES THOMSON, *An Introduction to the History of History.* New York: Columbia University Press. 1922.

BIBLIOGRAPHY

SHOTWELL, JAMES THOMSON, ed., *The Origins of the International Labor Organization*. New York: Columbia University Press. 1934.

SIEGFRIED, ANDRÉ, *America Comes of Age*. A French analysis by André Siegfried; translated from the French by H. H. Hemming and Doris Hemming. New York: Harcourt, Brace and Company. 1927.

Silliman's Journal of Science, see *The American Journal of Science*.

SINCLAIR, UPTON BEALL, *The Flivver King*. A story of Ford-America. Pasadena, Calif.: The Author. 1937.

SINCLAIR, UPTON BEALL, *Upton Sinclair Presents William Fox*. Los Angeles, Calif.: The Author. 1933.

SLOSS, ROBERT THOMPSON, *The Book of the Automobile*. A practical volume devoted to the history, construction, use and care of motor cars and to the subject of motoring in America. New York: D. Appleton and Company. 1905.

SLOSSON, EDWIN EMERY, *Creative Chemistry;* descriptive of recent achievements in the chemical industries. New York: The Century Co. 1919.

SMITH, ARTHUR DOUGLAS HOWDEN, *Commodore Vanderbilt;* an epic of American achievement. New York: R. M. McBride & Company. 1927.

SMITH, HENRY, *Fifty Years of Wire Drawing*. Worcester, Mass. 1884.

SMITH, J. BUCKNALL, *A Treatise on Wire*. London. 1891.

SMITH, WALTER S., *A Book on Capital and Labor*. Treating of the scientific, economic and social conditions that exist in the United States at the present time. Allegheny, Pa. 1908.

SMITHSONIAN INSTITUTION, *Annual Report* of the Board of Regents of, the Smithsonian Institution, showing the operations, expenditures and condition of the institution. Washington: Govt. Printing Office. 1847–19—.

Social Changes. Chicago, Ill.: The University of Chicago Press. 1929.

SOCIETY OF MOTION PICTURE ENGINEERS, *Journal*. Easton, Pa.: Society of Motion Picture Engineers. 1916.

SOULE, GEORGE HENRY, *A Planned Society*. New York: The Macmillan Company. 1932.

SPEARMAN, FRANK HAMILTON, *The Strategy of Great Railroads*. New York: C. Scribner's Sons. 1904.

SPRAGUE, FRANK JULIAN. Manuscript Collection. In New York Public Library.

SPRING, LA VERNE WARD, *Non-technical Chats on Iron and Steel,* and their application to modern industry. New York: Frederick A. Stokes Company. 1917.

STANLEY, DOUGLAS, and MAXFIELD, J. P., *The Voice, Its Production and Reproduction.* A treatise on voice training, production and re-production. New York: Pitman Publishing Corporation. 1933.

STARR, JOHN WILLIAM, *One Hundred Years of American Railroading.* New York: Dodd, Mead & Company. 1928.

STEARNS, HAROLD EDMUND, editor, *America Now.* New York: Charles Scribner's Sons. 1938.

STEARNS, HAROLD EDMUND, editor, *Civilization in the United States;* an inquiry by thirty Americans. New York: Harcourt, Brace and Company. 1922.

STEINMETZ, CHARLES PROTEUS, *America and the New Epoch.* New York: Harper & Brothers. 1916.

STEVERS, MARTIN D., *Steel Trails;* the epic of the railroads. New York: Minton, Balch & Company. 1933.

STOKES, I. N. PHELPS, *Iconography of Manhattan Island,* 1498–1909. New York: Robert H. Dodd. 1926.

STRACHEY, GILES LYTTON, *Queen Victoria.* New York: Harcourt, Brace and Company. 1921.

SUMNER, G., *Folkways.* New York. 1907.

Survey, The. New York: The Charity Organization Society, 1897–1912. Survey Associates, Inc. From 1912—.

SUTHERLAND, GEORGE, *Twentieth Century Inventions;* a forecast. New York: Longmans, Green and Co. 1901.

Swan, Sir Joseph Wilson, F.R.S., A Memoir by M. E. S. and K. R. S. London: Ernest Benn, Limited. 1929.

SWANK, JAMES MOORE, *History of the Manufacture of Iron in All Ages,* and particularly in the United States from colonial times to 1891. American Iron and Steel Association. 1892.

TAFT, ROBERT, *Photography and the American Scene;* a social history, 1839–1889. New York: The Macmillan Company. 1938.

TAINE, HIPPOLYTE ADOLPHE, *Notes on Paris;* transl. with notes by John Austin Stevens. New York: H. Holt and Company. 1888.

TALLEY, BENJAMIN BRANCHE, *Engineering Applications of Aerial and Terrestrial Photogrammetry.* New York, Chicago: Pitman Publishing Corporation. 1938.

TARBELL, IDA MINERVA, *The History of the Standard Oil Company.* New York: McClure, Phillips & Co. 1904.

Technological Trends and National Policy. See U. S. NATIONAL RESOURCES COMMITTEE, SCIENCE COMMITTEE.

TENNESSEE VALLEY AUTHORITY, *Facts Book.* Norris, Wheeler and Wilson Projects. Norris Dam. 1934.

TENNESSEE VALLEY ATHORITY, *Tennessee Valley Authority, 1933–1937.* Washington: U. S. Govt. Printing Office. 1937.

BIBLIOGRAPHY

THOMPSON, JOHN SMITH, *History of Composing Machines.* A complete record of the art of composing type by machinery . . . also lists of patents on composing machines, American and British, chronologically arranged. Chicago: The Inland Printer Company. 1904.

TISSANDIER, GASTON, *A History and Handbook of Photography,* transl. from the French of Gaston Tissandier; edited by J. Thomson London: S. Low, Marston, Low & Searle. 1876.

TOWERS, WALTER KELLOGG, *Masters of Space;* Morse and the telegraph, Thompson and the cable, Bell and the telephone, Marconi and the wireless telegraph, Carty and the wireless telephone. New York: Harper & Brothers. 1917.

TROTTMAN, NELSON, *History of the Union Pacific;* a financial and economic survey. New York: The Ronald Press Company. 1923.

TURCK, J. A. V., *Origin of Modern Calculating Machines.* Chicago. 1921.

TURNER, FREDERICK JACKSON, *The Frontier in American History.* New York: H. Holt and Company. 1921.

U. S. COAST AND GEODETIC SURVEY. *Magnetic Declination in the United States,* 1930, by Daniel L. Hazard, chief magnetician, Division of Terrestrial Magnetism and Seismology. Washington: U. S. Govt. Printing Office. 1932.

U. S. DEPARTMENT OF THE INTERIOR, *Report of the Secretary for 1867.*

U. S. FEDERAL COMMUNICATIONS COMMISSION. *Proposed Report, Telephone Investigation* (pursuant to Public Resolution No. 8, 74th Congress). Washington: U. S. Govt. Printing Office. 1938.

U. S. FEDERAL POWER COMMISSION, *National Power Survey.* Principal electric utility systems in the United States . . . 1935. Washington: U. S. Govt. Printing Office. 1936.

U. S. NATIONAL RESOURCES COMMITTEE. RESEARCH COMMITTEE ON URBANISM. *Our Cities;* their role in the national economy. June, 1937. Report of the Urbanism Committee to the National Resources Committee. Washington: U. S. Govt. Printing Office. 1937.

U. S. NATIONAL RESOURCES COMMITTEE. SCIENCE COMMITTEE. *Technological Trends and National Policy,* including the social implications of new inventions. June, 1937. Report of the subcommittee on Technology to the National Resources Committee. Washington: U. S. Govt. Printing Office. 1937.

U. S. Statistical Abstract, 1938. U. S. Govt. Printing Office. 1939.

VERMONT HISTORICAL SOCIETY, *Proceedings.* Montpelier, Vt. 1860–19—.

WALKER, JAMES BLAINE, *Fifty Years of Rapid Transit, 1864–1917.* New York City: The Law Printing Company. 1917.

BIBLIOGRAPHY

WALL, EDWARD JOHN, *The History of Three-color Photography.* Boston, Mass.: American Photographic Publishing Company. 1925.

WALLIS-TAYLOR, ALEXANDER JAMES, *Industrial Refrigeration, Cold Storage and Ice-Making.* Edited by R. J. Cracknell, with a chapter on small commercial and household refrigerating plants, being the 7th ed. revised and enlarged, of "Refrigeration, Cold Storage, and Ice-Making." London: C. Lockwood and Son. 1929.

WARNER, EDWARD PEARSON, *Technical Development and Its Effect on Air Transportation.* A lecture delivered by Edward Pearson Warner, Sc.D., under the James Jackson Cabot professorship of air traffic regulation and air transportation at Norwich University, February 23, 1928. Northfield, Vt.: Norwich University. 1938.

WARREN, ARTHUR G., "Barbed Wire, Who Invented It" in *The Iron Age,* June 24, 1926, p. 5.

WASHBURN, CHARLES G., *History of Barbed Wire;* manuscript in the Industrial Museum of the American Steel and Wire Company, Worcester, Massachusetts. There is a photostat of this manuscript in the New York Public Library.

WEBB, WALTER PRESCOTT, *The Great Plains.* Boston: Houghton, Mifflin Company. 1936.

WEEKS, LYMAN HORACE, *Automobile Biographies.* An account of the lives and the work of those who have been identified with the invention and development of self-propelled vehicles on the common roads. New York: The Monograph Press. 1904.

WELLER, CHARLES EDWARD, *The Early History of the Typewriter.* La Porte, Ind.: Chase & Shepard, printers. 1918.

WELLS, LOUIS RAY, *Industrial History of the United States.* New York: The Macmillan Company. 1922.

WHITE, BOUCK, *The Book of Daniel Drew.* Garden City, N. Y.: The Sun Dial Press, Inc. 1937.

WILENSKI, REGINALD HOWARD, *The Modern Movement in Art.* London: Faber & Gwyer. 1927.

WILGUS, WILLIAM J., *The Railway Interrelations of the United States and Canada.* New Haven: Yale University Press. 1937.

WINGFIELD-STRATFORD, ESMÉ CECIL, *The Victorian Cycle,* with an introduction by Henry Seidel Canby. New York: W. Morrow & Company. 1935.

WISSLER, CLARK, *The American Indian;* an introduction to the anthropology of the new world. 2d ed. New York: Oxford University Press. 1922.

WOOD, FREDERIC JAMES, *The Turnpikes of New England,* and evolution of the same through England, Virginia and Maryland, by Frederic Wood. Boston: Marshall Jones Company. 1919.

BIBLIOGRAPHY

WRIGHT, ORVILLE and WILBUR, "The Wright Brothers' Aeroplane" in *Century Magazine*, Vol. LXXVI, No. 5, September, 1908, p. 647.

WRIGHT, WILLIAM, *History of the Big Bonanza*. An authentic account of the discovery, history and working of the world-renowned Comstock silver lode of Nevada, including the present condition of the various mines situated thereon; sketches of the most prominent men interested in them. . . . By Dan De Quille (William Wright). Hartford, Conn.: American Publishing Company. 1876.

WYNDHAM, HORACE, *Victorian Parade*. London: F. Muller, Ltd. 1934.

WYSOR, HENRY, *Metallurgy*. A condensed treatise for the use of college students and any desiring a general knowledge of the subject. Easton, Pa.: The Chemical Publishing Co. 1908.

ZUEBLIN, CHARLES, *American Municipal Progress;* chapters in municipal sociology. New York: The Macmillan Company. 1902.

BIBLIOGRAPHY — CLASSIFIED INDEX

BIBLIOGRAPHY—CLASSIFIED INDEX

BIBLIOGRAPHY—CLASSIFIED INDEX

EVENTS AND INVENTIONS

EVENTS	INVENTIONS
1866 Civil Rights Act.	1866 Atlantic cable, Cyrus W. Field, New York. Compressed air rock drill, Charles Burleigh, Massachusetts. Iron tank cars, Pennsylvania.
1867 Purchase of Alaska.	1867 Paper from sulphite pulp, Benjamin C. Tilghman, Philadelphia. Twine binder, John F. Appleby, Wisconsin. Typewriter, Christopher Latham Sholes, Wisconsin. Automatic gear cutter, William Sellers, Pennsylvania. Micrometer caliper, Joseph R. Browne, Lucian Sharpe, Rhode Island.
1868 Fourteenth Amendment to Constitution.	1868 Dining car, G. W. Pullman, Illinois. Lawn mower, A. M. Hills, Connecticut. Chilled plow, James Oliver, Indiana.
	1869 Celluloid, J. W. and Isaac Hyatt, New Jersey. Air brake, George Westinghouse, Pennsylvania.
1871 Chicago fire.	1871 Collecting cylinder for printing press, Richard March Hoe and Stephen D. Tucker, New York. Welt machine, Charles Goodyear, Jr., Daniel Mills, Auguste Destouy, New York.

EVENTS	INVENTIONS
1872 Re-election of Grant.	1872 Loose-leaf filing, Amherst College Library, Massachusetts. Automatic air brake, George Westinghouse, Pennsylvania.
1873 Panic.	1873 Automatic car coupler, E. H. Janney, Virginia. Cable street-car, Andrew Smith Hallidie, California.
	1874 Barbed wire, Joseph F. Glidden, Illinois. Electric railway, Stephen D. Field, California.
	1875 Refrigerator car, G. F. Swift, Illinois.
1876 Centennial Exposition, Philadelphia.	1876 Telephone, Alexander Graham Bell, Massachusetts. Mimeograph, Thomas A. Edison, New Jersey.
	1877 Microphone, Emile Berliner, District of Columbia. Phonograph, Thomas A Edison, New Jersey.
	1878 Telephone switchboard, Charles E. Scribner, Illinois.
1879 Resumption of Specie Payments.	1879 Compressed-air shield tunnelling, C. D. Haskin, New York. Cash register, James J. Ritty, Ohio.
	1880 Half-tone process, Stephen Horgan, New York.
1881 Assassination of President Garfield.	1882 Trolley car, Frank J. Sprague, New York.
	1883 Shoe last machine, Jan Ernest Matzeliger, Massachusetts. Overhead lumber skidder, Horace Butters, Michigan.
	1884 Linotype, Ottmar Mergenthaler, District of Columbia. Skeletal Steel Construction,

EVENTS AND INVENTIONS

EVENTS	INVENTIONS
1884 Cleveland elected.	William Le Baron Jenney, Illinois. Electric passenger elevator, William Baxter, Maryland.
1885 French gift of Statue of Liberty.	1886 Oil flotation ore refining, Mrs. Carrie J. Everson, Illinois. Electrolytic reduction of aluminum, Charles Martin Hall, Ohio. Electric welding, Elihu Thompson, Massachusetts.
1887 Interstate Commerce Act.	1887 Photographic film, Hannibal Goodwin, New Jersey. Vestibule passenger car, H. H. Sessions, Illinois. Monotype, Tolbert Lanston, District of Columbia. Lateral-cut recording, phonograph discs, Emile Berliner, New Jersey.
1888 Great Blizzard, New York.	1888 "Kodak," George Eastman and William H. Walker, New York. Telautograph, Elisha Gray, Illinois. Adding machine, William Burroughs, New York. Induction electric motor, Nicola Tesla, New York.
1889 Johnstown Flood.	1889 Automatic telephone switching, Almon B. Strowger, Missouri.
1890 Sherman Anti-Trust Law.	1890 Clincher pneumatic auto tire, William Erskine Bartlett, Massachusetts. 1891 Electric automobile, William Morrison, Iowa. Carborundum, Edward Goodrich Acheson, Pennsylvania. 1892 Portable typewriter, George C. Blickensderfer, New York.

EVENTS AND INVENTIONS

EVENTS	INVENTIONS
1893 Finanical depression.	1893 Zipper, W. L. Judson, Illinois.
	1895 Multiple unit system, electric train control, Frank J. Sprague, New York.
1898 War with Spain.	
1900 Gold Standard Act.	1900 Loading coil, long distance telephony, Michael Pupin, New York.
	Autoplate stereotype machine, Henry A. Wise Wood, New York.
1901 Assassination of President McKinley.	1901 High-speed tool steel, Frederick W. Taylor and Maunsel White, Pennsylvania.
	Lag-bed tractor, Alvin O. Lombard, Maine.
	Multigraph, American Machine Sales Co., Ohio.
	1903 Mercury vapor arc, Peter Cooper Hewitt, New York.
	Airplane, Wilbur and Orville Wright, Ohio.
	Electric auto starter, Clyde J. Coleman.
	Steel-alkaline storage battery, Thomas Alva Edison, New Jersey.
	Bottle machine, Michael Joseph Owens, Ohio.
	1904 Casing-head gasoline, A. Fasenmeyer, Pennsylvania.
	Safety razor, King Gillette.
1905 Russo-Japanese Arbitration.	1905 Nickel refining, Ambrose Monell, New York.
1906 San Francisco earthquake and fire.	1906 Deflocculated graphite, Edward G. Acheson, Michigan.
	Sound track for films, Eugene Augustin Lauste, New York.

EVENTS AND INVENTIONS

EVENTS	INVENTIONS
1907 Panic.	Crystal detector, radio, Henry H. C. Dunwoody, New York.
	Radio telephone, Reginald A. Fessenden, Massachusetts.
	1907 Audion tube, radio, Lee DeForest, New York.
1909 Discovery of North Pole by Peary.	1909 "Bakelite," L. H. Baekeland, New York.
	High-frequency radio generator, E. F. W. Alexanderson, New York.
	1910 Gyro-compass, Elmer Ambrose Sperry, New York.
1912 *Titanic* disaster.	1913 Mercury-steam turbine, William Leroy Emmett, New York.
	Poulsen arc, radio, Valdemar Poulsen, New York.
	Cracking process, gasoline, William M. Burton.
1914 Panama Canal opened to traffic.	1914 Regenerative circuit, radio, Edwin A. Armstrong and Lee DeForest, New York.
1915 Sinking of *Lusitania*.	1916 Gas-filled incandescent lamp, Irving Langmuir, New York.
	Alexanderson multiple tuning, radio, E. F. W. Alexanderson, New York.
1917 Entry of U. S. into World War.	
1918 World War Armistice.	
1919 Prohibition Amendment ratified.	
1921 Washington Disarmament Conference.	
1924 Army Air Corps round-the-world flight.	1924 Cellophane, Dupont Company, Delaware.
1927 Lindbergh flight.	
1929 Stock Market collapse.	1929 Polaroid, Edwin H. Land, Massachusetts.

INDEX

INDEX

352; sells first radio advertising, 451; symbol of collective phase, 128; totalitarian aspect of, 120
American way, 3, 4
Americans,
individualism of, 8, 26 ff.; lawlessness of, in 1850's, 26; likeness among, 9; power of, 8
Ammonia,
chemical formula, 490; in photography, 273; production of, 231
Amos 'n' Andy, 349, 434
Amoskeag River, 36
Ampère, André Marie, 182
Amperes, relation to voltage, 207
Amplification,
false impression created by, 446; of music, 446; vogue for, 446
Amplifier,
effect of on oratory, 446; invades privacy, 446; in mob psychology, 446; vacuum tube, necessary to sound film, 356 ff.; vacuum tube, in phongraph, 352, 353; vacuum tube in radio, 442 ff.; vacuum tube in telephone, 122
Anchors, interference with cable, 14
Anglo-Saxon mentality, 169
Annunciator, telephone, 115
Antenna, grid attached to, 444
Anthony and Scovill,
acquire Goodwin rights, 284; photographic supply house, 278; sue Eastman Kodak Company for infringement, 284
Anthropomorphism, 206, 404
Antimony,
508 ff.; recovery of, 520
Apartments,
co-operative, 92; modern, inadequacy of, 448
Ape, desire of for wings, 404
Apperson Brothers, 383
Appomattox, 377
Aquatint process, 291
Aqueducts, masonry, 78
Aquinas, Thomas, 195
Arabic, language on linotype, 157
Arago, François Dominique Jean,
reads paper on daguerreotype to French Institute, 264; thunder-struck by daguerreotype, 263
Arc-light, 231 ff., 245
Architecture,
Gothic, Victorian, 223; photography in, 285
Argand, Ami, invents circular wick, 228, 229
Argon, 248
Aristocracy, custodian of arts, 255, 256

Aristotelian thinking, 56
Aristotle *Problems*, 259, 259 n.
Aristotle recognizes camera obscura principle, 259
Arizona,
Boulder Dam in, 475; Mexican, 28, 31
Arkansas, share-croppers in, 500
Arkwright, Richard, division of labor, 217
Arlandes, Marquis de, first balloon ascension, 409
Armat, Thomas,
designs intermittent mechanism, 331; designs movie projector, 330 ff.; relations with Edison, 331
Armature, 194
Armenian, language on linotype, 157
Armstrong, Edwin,
contributions to vacuum tube generator, 446; invents frequency modulation system, 457; new technics, 453; patent litigation, 458
Arnold, Edwin, 68
Arnold, Henry, perfects vacuum in deForest tube, 445
Arnold, Matthew, 68
Art,
American understanding of, 346 ff.; broadening of, 255; decadence of, 256, 257; decline of in Victorian era, 222; denied to masses, 255 ff.; effect of instantaneous photography on, 276; effect of leisure on, 255; effect of photography on, 257 ff.; graphic, 253 ff.; mechanical aids to, 258 ff.; middle class interest in, 255 ff.; naturalist, 258; nostalgic function of, 255; photography in, 286; plastic, 258; possession of aristocracy, 255, 256; rarefied province, 254 ff.; relation of movies to, 311 ff.; reproduces nature, 258; study in America, 250; what is?, 278
Artichokes, Jerusalem, 499
Artisan age, 74, 533
Artist,
ability to explain technology, 195; perception of, 258
Artists, news, 293 ff.
As ifs, 487
Asphalt pavement, 83
Asphaltum, 83
Aspirin, 495
Assembly line,
beginnings, of, 218; machine-boss, 396, 397; object of, 218, 395, 396; stultifying effect of, 255, 396, 397, 540
Associated Press, 158
Astaire, Fred, 338

Astronomy, photography in, 285
Atlantic cable,
1857, 17; 1858, 17–21; 1865, 22, 23; 1866, 23; celebrations, 20; considered a hoax, 20, 21; effect on business, 24; effect on commerce, 16; effect on immigation, 16; effect on international disputes, 24; effect on invention, 24; effect on press, 24; effect on transportation, 24; English efforts in, 15, 16, 21; English investment in, 22; English subsidy of, 16; final success of, 23, 95; first communication by, 20; first success of, 20, 21, 436; grappled for, 23; inspection of, 18; instruments, 15; insulation of, 22; lapse of interest in, 20; paying-out machinery, 18, 22; plans for, 11; predicted by Morse, 10; research in, 21, 22; route of, 13; sabotage of, 23; skepticism about, 12; soundings for, 13, 14; threat of Civil War to, 16; U. S. subsidy of, 17; weight of, 19
Atlantic Cable Company, 16
Atlantic coast, 9, 467
Atlantic Ocean, shortest line across, 11
Atom,
smashing, 206; solar system in, 249; supposed indivisibility of, 486 ff.
Atomic theory, 486 ff.
Atonement, mystery of the, 433
Audience, synthetic radio, 360, 539
Audio-frequency current, 123
Austria,
early balloon ascensions in, 411; war with Prussia, 1866, 24
Authors, temperamental, 137
Automat, 448
Automobile,
accidents, 402; actual life of, 528, 529; as time-killer, 526, 527; brakes, 382; chain-drive, 384; chassis, 382; clutch, 382, 384, 385; combination with electric train, 197; compared with locomotive, 5; craze, 385 ff.; cylinders, 382 ff.; dealers, 528, 529; description of in 1910, 400 ff.; differential, 382, 384; dispersive factor, 400 ff.; economic life of, 528, 529; electric, 382, 386, 387; experimental, 376; future of, 403; headlights, 249, 382, 529; knee-action, 529; mass-production, 376 ff.; mud-

INDEX

INDEX

guerreotype, 267; in America, 270 ff.; invented by Talbot, 267; patented in America, 272; popular among amateurs, 272
Calvinism, 224, 431
Camera,
automatic, 276; candid, 254, 276, 285; effect of on pre-Raphaelite painting, 257 ff.; eliminattes error, 257 ff.; improvement in 1870's, 276; movie, Demeny's, 322; movie, Méliès', 336; movie, mobile, 336; movie, sprocket mechanism, 323 ff.; news photographers, 296, 297; not selective, 258
Camera obscura,
box, 259, 260; invention, 259, 260; meaning, 258; principle, 258–260; tracings, 260
Canada, automobile production in, 379
Canals, construction of, 38
Cannon, first rifled, 169
Cape Horn, 46, 163, 502
Cape Town, 98
Capital,
American, overextension of, 16; fluid, 504 ff.; frozen, 502; investment of in electric services, 203; to span Great Plains, 164; sub-division of, 129
Capsule, manometric, Koenig's, 107, 108
Car, refrigerator, 171, 177
Carbolic acid, 495
Carbon,
compounds, 489 ff.; essential of life, 486; granulated, in telephone transmitter, 111; iron content of, 55 ff., 508; oxydization of, 56 ff.; in spiegeleisen, 59
Carburetion, thermostatic control of, 394
Cards, wool, 168
Carnegie, Andrew,
adventurousness of, 68; autobiography, 68; biography of, 68; birthplace of, 68; character of, 67 ff.; childhood, 68; dreams of, 66; English attitude toward, 68; first sees Bessemer converter, 66; founds steel industry, 67; immortality of, 68; interest in literature, 68; monopolistic control, 70; poverty, 68; religion, 70; unorthodox behavior of, 70; wealth of, 67, 68
Carnegie, Dale, 150
Carnegie Institute, 68, 179
Carnegie, libraries, 68
Carnegie Medal, 68
Carriages, luxuries in 18th century, 364
Carrier, wave, 108

Cars, railroad,
38, 49; coupling of, 51, 52; heating of, 52; lighting of, 52; sleeping, 52; vestibules, 52; wheels, 49
Cartoon, animated, 318 ff., 340
Carving, primitive, 254
Cary, Herbert L., letter on barbed wire, 175
Casement, Jack, 46
Caslon type, 305
Cassier's Magazine, 387
Catalyst, definition, 514
Catharsis, mental, need of in invention, 143 ff., 415 ff.
Cattle,
destruction by, 173; domestic, 171; injured by barbed wire, 176; pioneer, 364; Texas, 166 ff.
Cattle drives, 170 ff.
Cattle kingdom,
170 ff.; end of, 176, 177
Caveman, pictorial communication, 253, 254
Cayley, George, designs biplane glider, 417
Celluloid, invention of, 322 n.
Cellulose products, 499
Census, errors of, 311 ff.
Centers, static,
dynamos in, 196; manufacturing in, 7; transportation from, 363 ff.
Central Pacific Company,
bond issue, 41; construction plans, 45; subsidy, 40
Central Pacific Railroad, financed by Nevada mines, 505
Cereals, predigested, 448
Chain, bicycle, 370
Chains, utility,
advantages of, 205; comparison with totalitarian states, 205; cost of to consumers, 216, 217; efficiency of, 217; structure of, 217
Chain-drive, automobile, 384
Champ de Mars, Paris, 410
Chanute, Octave,
astonished by Wright brothers, 423; bases experiment on Lilienthal principles, 418; begins flying at 60, 418; comment on bird-flight, 418; distinguished American engineer, 418; influences American public toward aviation, 419; Progress in Flying Machines, 418, 418 n., 419, 420; skepticism of small models, 419
Characters, pictorial, 253
Charcoal, in smelting, 55 ff.
Charlatans, in America in 1840's, 269
Charles, J. A. C.,
alleged photographic experiments, 260; balloon in-

ventor, 410 ff.; first balloon ascension, 410
Charleston, S. C., 38
Chase, printer's, 141
Chattanooga, Tennessee, 38
Check-writer, 137
Chemical industry, electrolysis in, 219
Chemistry,
as entertainment, 269; early history, 486, 487; elements, 486 ff.; inorganic, 487 ff.; knowledge of in 1850, 58; metals, 513; organic, see Organic chemistry; photography in, 285; quantitative theory, 488 ff.; starts with Midas wish, 486; synthetic, 483–500; in war, 483 ff.
Chemurgy, farm, 471, 540
Chevalier, Charles, optician, 262, 263
Chevrolet cars, 395
Chicago,
death rate, 1854, 79; elevated in, 85; sewage disposal, 79; water supply, 79 ff.
Child, occupied with growth, 250
Children, effect of radio on, 453
Chinese,
labor, 46; likeness among, 9
Chlorine, in common salt, 488
Choke, automatic, 529
Chollar Mine, 212
Christianity, world unified under, 404
Chromium,
in automobiles, 394; supply of, 519
Chromium-nickel-steel, 515
Chromium-steel, 515
Chromium-vanadium-steel, 515
Chromium-vanadium-tungsten-steel, 515
Chrysler cars, 394
Church, attitude toward science, 430
Church, Dr. William, 144
Churches, Protestant, social, 392
Cinema, see Movies
Cinemanthropomorphism, 338
Circuit,
interrupted, for wireless sending, 441; phantom, 123; radio receiving, 441, 442; radio transmission, 441, 442; resistance of, 207; telephone, 106 ff.
City,
American, 73–94; amusement in, 74, 75; in civilization, 74; clubs, 75; commercial, 74; congestion in, 74 ff.; effect of factory on, 74; expanded by trolley car, 86; fire department, 75, 94; government, 75, 83, 84; hospitals, 75; industrial 74

583

INDEX

photography in prevention of, 285

Crookes, William, comments on radio principle, 1892, 436, 437; Marconi should share credit with, 437; vacuum tube inventor, 436

Cross-bar, telephone, 123

Crossword puzzles, 47, 228

Crown Point, N. Y., iron works in, 188, 189

Crowther, J. G., comments on Joseph Henry, 185, 186

Crucible method, steel, 55

Cryolite, in aluminum process, 518

Crystal Palace Exhibition, London, 1851, 232, 272

Cugnot, Nicolas, early automotive inventor, 368

Cultural impulse, 250 ff.

Culture, American yearnings for, 224; middle-class, 255 ff.

Culverts, railroad, 34, 37, 38

Cumberland Gap, 363

Currency, based on imported specie in 1840's, 502; gold, 503 ff.

Current, audio-frequency, 123

Current, electric, in animal brain, 205; in cable, 18, 22; failure of, 219; induced, 186 ff., 207, 208; induces magnetism, 187, 188; pressure of, 206, 207; in selenium, 354, 355; size of, 206, 207, 355; in telephone, 106 ff.; undulatory, 110, 353 ff.; see also Alternating current, Direct current

Curtain wall, 87

Curtis, Charles Gordon, perfects steam turbine, 214

Cutlery, manufacture of, 169

Cycle, farm, 497, 498; picture, 253 ff.

Cyclists, stimulate road improvement, 367

Cylinders, automobile, 382 ff.

Czechoslovakia, end of, 379; wealth of, 379

Dædalum, 319

Daguerre, Louis Jacques Mandé, difficult relations with Niepce, 262, 263; government pension, 264; independent inventions, 262 ff.; partnership with Niepce, 263; scene painter, 262

Daguerreotype, American, best in world, 1851, 272; astonishes Arago, 263; developing, 265, 266; effect on Ruskin, 258; end of in America, 272; especially attractive to Americans, 269; first commer-

cialization of, 263 ff.; first news of in America, 268 ff.; in French Chamber of Deputies, 263, 264; obscures true photography, 263; process explained, 264–266; public announcement of, 263, 264; public response to in France, 264

Daguerreotype portraiture, 270 ff.

Daguerreotype studios, 271, 272

Daguerreotype teachers, 271

Daguerreotypers, American, 271 ff.; rural, 271, 272; training of American, 271

Daily Graphic, New York, 1873, 412

Daimler, Gottlieb, automobile inventor, 382

Dakota, advance guard in, 172

Dakotas, farmers of, 48

Dams, power, 180

Dark, blessings of the, 227

Dark room, photographic, 273, 274

Darwin, Charles, "antichrist," 233; conflict with orthodox thinkers, 256; theory of biological evolution, 256

Darwin theory, 256

Davenport, Thomas, 86; blacksmith's apprentice, 189; boyhood, 189, 189 n.; electric stock company, 190; industry of, 189, 190; marriage, 189; model car, 190; patents, 190; player-piano, 190; tragedy of, 190

Davenport, Mrs. Thomas, silk wedding dress incident, 189

David, painting of, 255

Davidson, Robert, 190

Davies, Marion, autographs photograph for radio fans, 451; in early broadcast, 451

Davis, Harry, lectures to Harvard business school on broadcasting, 450; studies broadcasting, 449

Davis, John P., 31, 32

Davy, Sir Humphry, 182, 232 ff.; photographic experiments, 261

Dayton, O., home of Wright brothers, 420

Deaf, instruction of, 102 ff.

Decarbonization, 56 ff.

Decatur, Tennessee, 38, 39, 44

Decentralization, hope of, 220

Deception, sensory, 311 ff.

De Changy, incandescent lamp inventor, 233

Declaration of Independence, equality thesis, 48, 379 ff.

deForest, Lee, acquires capital, 443, 444; contributions to vacuum

tube generator, 446; pioneer in radiotelephony, 442

Deforestation, 177, 465 ff.

DeKalb, Ill., farming village, 173, 174

De Laval, Gustaf, invents steam turbine, 214

Delaware River, 36

Delinquency, juvenile, effect of movies on, 339

Demeny, Georges, makes movie camera, 322

Democracy, effect of automobile on, 377 ff.; effect of bathtub on, 377; effect of mass-production on, 380 ff.; effect of printing press on, 377, 380; effect of radio on, 377, 453 ff.; usual explanations of, 376, 377

Demodulation, 123

De Moleyns, Frederick, 233

Densmore, James, character of, 133, 134; first meeting with Sholes, 133; promoter, 145; takes Sholes' typewriter to Remingtons, 134

Department of Agriculture, U. S., soil statistics, 471

Derricks, 179

Der Tag, 440

Descartes, René, 109

Desert, Great Plains, 164

Desert plants, 164

Desk, roll-top, 130

De Soto, see Soto

Detector, electrolytic, 442; wireless, 436 ff.

Detroit, Mich., automobile manufacturing center, 376 ff.; early automobiles in, 382

Devangari alphabet on linotype, 157

Deville, Henri Sainte-Claire, cuts price of aluminum, 517

De Vinne type, 305

De Witt Clinton, locomotive, 29

Dial tone, telephone, 117

Dickens, Charles, 8, 9

Dickerson, Senator, of New Jersey, 28, 29

Dickson, William Kennedy Laurie, credited by Edison with movie invention, 326; loyalty to Edison, 327; movie inventor, 327

Dictatorship, industrial, 220

Dies, manufacture of, 540

Diesel motor, see Motor

Diet, change of American, 498

Dietrich, Marlene, 338

Differential, automobile, 382, 384

Dimensions, eye's grasp of, 257

Dining saloon, seasick-proof, Bessemer's, 57

585

INDEX

INDEX

INDEX

INDEX

tery over man, 4; ruling, 300; thinking by, 117, 534; worship of in New York City, 91; obsolence of, 69

Machines,
automatic, perfection of, 218; dish-washing, 219; harvesting, 304; ironing, 219; manufacturing, 7; textile, 8, 180; threshing, 304, 375; washing, 219, 304, 380, 481

MacMillan, typesetter inventor, 145

Madder, 494

Maddox, Richard L., 275

Madison, James, knowledge of soil conservation, 466

Magazine, illustrated, 294 ff.

Magazines, American,
advertising in, 306, 307, 359; articles in, 306, 307; circulation of, 287; five-cent, 307; "slicks," 307; stories in, 306, 307; ten-cent, 307

Magazines, mass-production of, 310

Magazines, printing of, 310

Magnesium,
in airplane construction, 518, 519; in Michigan brine, 519

Magnet, permanent, 187

Magnetism, induced by electric current, 187, 188

Mail, U. S., comparison with telephone, 124

Malcolmson, Thomas, finances Ford Motor Company, 390

Man, physical weakness of, 483 ff., 540

Manchester, England, factories in, 229

Manchester, N. H., 36

Manet, painting of, 307

Manganese,
in iron ores, 58; in spiegeleisen, 59

Manhattan,
first street-car line in, 84; geography of, 83, 90, 91; skyscraper in, 87 ff.; social needs of, 85

Manifest Destiny,
Hollywood? 334; inherent in third-dimension of geography, 501; popular concept of, 288; romance of, 170; waste a product of, 467

Manometric capsule, Koenig's, 107, 108

Manufacture of Iron Without Fuel, The, by Henry Bessemer, 58

Manufacturing, in static centers, 7

Marconi, Guglielmo,
assisted by Italian navy, 439; background, 437, 438; boyhood, 437, 438; com-

pletes basic invention of wireless telegraphy, 439; fate kind to, 439; obtains capital, 439; places apparatus on English lightship, 439; works with tools of others, 439

Marey, Etienne, Jules,
given credit by Edison, 326; meets Edison, 1889, 322, 326; relation with Muybridge, 322; study of motion, 322

Mark Twain,
backs Paige typesetter, 146, 148; letter on typewriter, 135; types manuscripts, 135

Marriage,
effect of movies on, 313; disillusion in, 225

Marseilles, bicycle inventions in, 370

Martin Chuzzlewit, 8

Martin, Emil, inventions of, 63, 65

Martin, Pierre, inventions of, 63, 65

Martin, T. Commerford, explains reversal of dynamo, 193, 194

Martini and Rossi, 307

Maryland, electric locomotive in, 1851, 191

Massachusetts, manufacture of cutlery in, 169

Mass-production,
automobile, 376 ff., 509 ff.; conflict of with individualism, 6; democracy of, 217; departments, 218; division of labor, 218; economy of, 381; effect of electric power on, 218; emerges from quantity production, 217; Ford writes on, 391; high-speed steel in, 515; inadequacy of steel in, 510 ff.; interchangeable parts in, 217, 218; magazines, 310; movies, 325 ff.; newspaper, 293, 380; of machines, 218, 378 ff., 509; specialization, 395; standardization in, 219; stimulated monopoly trend, 220; in U. S. S. R., 379

Master Car-Builder's Association, 51, 52

Mathematicians, approach of to infinity, 195

Mather, Cotton, 431

Matrices, type, 152 ff.

Matrix, stereotype, 298

Matter, physical composition of, 486 ff.

Maury, Matthew Fontaine, 13

Mauve Decade, 288

Maxfield, Joseph Pease, 352

Maxim, Hiram, 383

Maxwell, James Clerk,
applies mathematics to

Faraday's lines of force, 435; Marconi should share credit with, 437

Mayflower, tradition, 225

Mazda, generic term for lamp research, 248

Meade, Charles, photographs Daguerre, 272

Meade Brothers, New York daguerreotypers, 271

Means, James, books studied by Wright brothers, 419

Measurement,
electrical, 218; proportional, 260; scientific, 249; wave, 441

Meat choppers, electric, 202

Mechanization, American, in 19th century, 195

Medicine,
photography in, 285; socialization of, 532

Megacycles, meaning, 441

Méliès, Georges,
invents photoplay, 330; *Trip to the Moon,* 336; uses stationary camera, 336

"Melting pot," American, effect of cable on, 16, 24

Membrane of ear, 109

Membrane, phonautograph, 108, 109

Membrane, telephone, 110

Memphis, Tennessee, 38, 225

Mencken, Ada, 507

Menjou, Alolphe, 343

Menlo Park, electric railway experiments, 196

Mennonites, German, 48

Mercury,
use of in daguerreotype, 264, 265; vapor, 248

Mercury-potassium almagam, 517

Mergenthaler, Ottmar,
autobiography, 149, 156; boredom of, 151; employed by August Hahl, 151; invents bar indenting machine, 152; invents Linotype, 154; patents, 155; persistence of, 151 ff.; sells company 1888, 155

Mergenthaler Linotype Company, 154 ff.

Merrimack River, 36

Mesaba, ore deposits, 62, 378, 379

Mesquite, 164

Messages, multiplication of telegraph, 101

Metal,
chemical analysis of, 513; crystals, 513; economy in, 501 ff.; fatigue of, 515; geographical interplay of, 501 ff.; grain, 514; heat-treatment, 513; recovery of, 520; scrap, 519, 520; structure of, 513 ff.

594

INDEX

INDEX

INDEX

THE "GREAT EASTERN"

Top. Launching of the *Great Eastern*
Bottom. The *Great Eastern* on the ocean

From " Pictorial History of the Great Eastern"

THE PROGRESS OF THE CENTURY.
THE LIGHTNING STEAM PRESS.   THE ELECTRIC TELEGRAPH.   THE LOCOMOTIVE.   THE STEAMBOAT.

Top. Receiving the Message, September 2, 1866, over the recovered 1865 cable. *From the painting by R. Dudley, courtesy Smithsonian Institution. Bottom.* The Progress of the Century, Currier and Ives print. *Congressional Library*

The beauty of Manhattan is forgotten in the congestion of its canyons and subways caused by these towers. The Flat-iron Building (*left*) was one of the pioneer New York sky-scrapers. The photograph shows the "cage" method of construction. Below is a hopeful plan for tomorrow which, by its semicircular motif, works toward centralization. Un-happily the planner could not quite forget the skyscraper tradition

Top. Railroad building on the Great Plains. *Courtesy of the Hudson Historical Bureau*

To the right. General Dodge, the builder of the Union Pacific

Below. The Twentieth Century train on its 16-hour run from New York to Chicago

William Kelly

Peter Cooper

Andrew Carnegie

Abram S. Hewitt

PIONEERS IN STEEL

Center. The original Kelly converter

"In most of the effective and powerful organizations of the world there is probably
Page 69

Top left. Molten pig iron being poured into open-hearth furnace. *Top right*. Besse
blowing off. *Center*. Bill Jones. *Bottom*. Cold-rolling operation

Professor Bell lecturing to an audience at Salem, Mass. The inventor
is illustrating his demonstration by means of a telephone placed before
his audience and communicating with his laboratory at Boston fourteen
miles away. "*Scientific American,*" *March 31, 1877.* Bell's First Telephone. *New York Museum of Science and Industry.* Portrait of Bell in 1876

THE SWITCHBOARD

Top. It required half a dozen rude, beer-drinking boys and as many minutes to answer a signal call. A contemporaneous picture of the Cortlandt exchange, New York, 1879. *Above.* In 1933 a close-up of a long-distance operator. *To the right.* A modern exchange

THE TYPEWRITER

Christopher Latham Sholes, inventor of the modern typewriter

A. Sholes' typewriter of 1873. The letters are arranged nearly as they are in the standard keyboard of today

B. Patent office model of the machine patented July, 1886, by Sholes, Glidden and Soule

Left. Sholes' daughter. The first typist

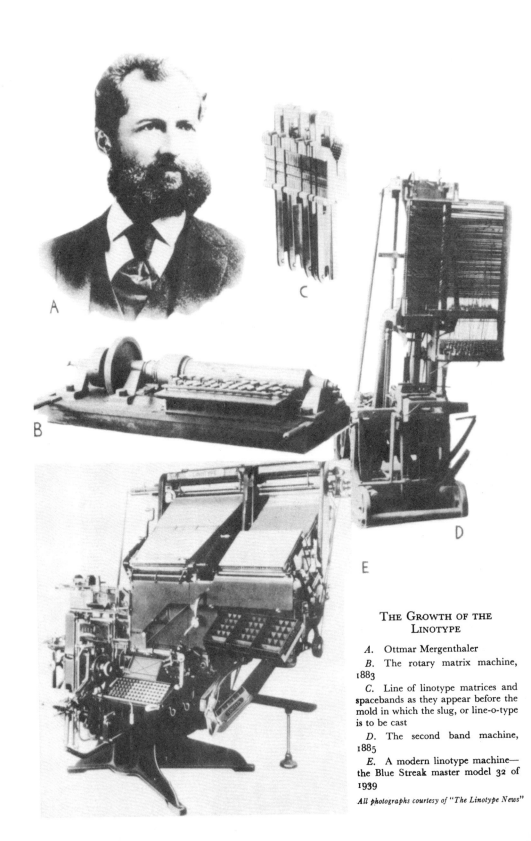

THE GROWTH OF THE LINOTYPE

A. Ottmar Mergenthaler

B. The rotary matrix machine, 1883

C. Line of linotype matrices and spacebands as they appear before the mold in which the slug, or line-o-type is to be cast

D. The second band machine, 1885

E. A modern linotype machine— the Blue Streak master model 32 of 1939

All photographs courtesy of "The Linotype News"

Top. The open range. *From "McClure's Magazine," 1894*

Center. Double strand of barbed-wire fencing. This is the original barbed wire as made by Joseph F. Glidden in 1874. *Courtesy of United States Steel Co.*

Bottom. Part of the famous "coffee mill" used by Glidden to form barbs. *Courtesy of United States Steel Co.*

GEORGE WESTINGHOUSE

One of the first American engineers who was also a business executive

FRANK J. SPRAGUE

A. First Sprague Multiple Unit System
B. The Pelton water wheel

GEORGE WESTINGHOUSE

One of the first American engineers who was also a business executive

FRANK J. SPRAGUE

A. First Sprague Multiple Unit System
B. The Pelton water wheel

Top. The open range. *From "McClure's Magazine," 1894*

Center. Double strand of barbed-wire fencing. This is the original barbed wire as made by Joseph F. Glidden in 1874. *Courtesy of United States Steel Co.*

Bottom. Part of the famous "coffee mill" used by Glidden to form barbs. *Courtesy of United States Steel Co.*

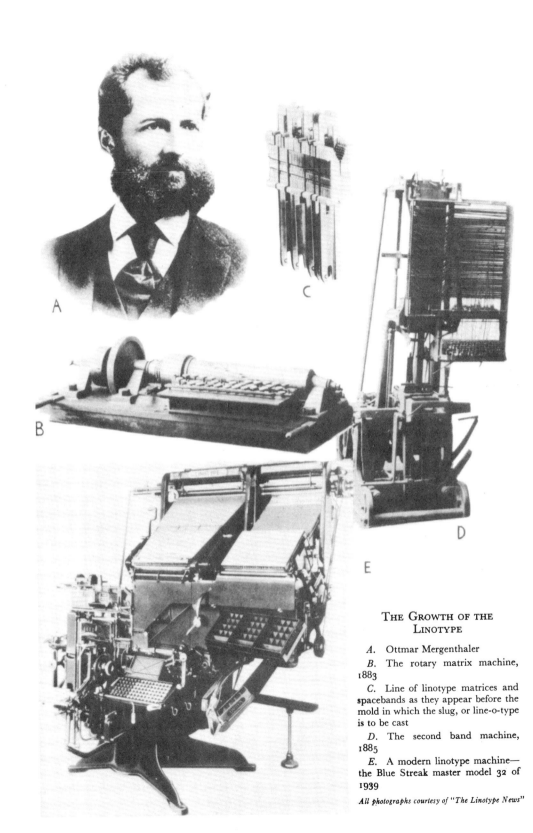

THE GROWTH OF THE LINOTYPE

A. Ottmar Mergenthaler

B. The rotary matrix machine, 1883

C. Line of linotype matrices and spacebands as they appear before the mold in which the slug, or line-o-type is to be cast

D. The second band machine, 1885

E. A modern linotype machine—the Blue Streak master model 32 of 1939

All photographs courtesy of "The Linotype News"

THE TYPEWRITER

Christopher Latham Sholes, inventor of the modern typewriter

A. Sholes' typewriter of 1873. The letters are arranged nearly as they are in the standard keyboard of today

B. Patent office model of the machine patented July, 1886, by Sholes, Glidden and Soule

Left. Sholes' daughter. The first typist

THE SWITCHBOARD

Top. It required half a dozen rude, beer-drinking boys and as many minutes to answer a signal call. A contemporaneous picture of the Cortlandt exchange, New York, 1879. *Above.* In 1933 a close-up of a long-distance operator. *To the right.* A modern exchange

All photographs courtesy of American Telephone and Telegraph Co.

Professor Bell lecturing to an audience at Salem, Mass. The inventor is illustrating his demonstration by means of a telephone placed before his audience and communicating with his laboratory at Boston fourteen miles away. "*Scientific American,*" *March 31, 1877.* Bell's First Telephone. *New York Museum of Science and Industry.* Portrait of Bell in 1876

Top. Railroad building on the Great Plains. *Courtesy of the Hudson Historical Bureau*

To the right. General Dodge, the builder of the Union Pacific

Below. The Twentieth Century train on its 16-hour run from New York to Chicago

William Kelly

Peter Cooper

Andrew Carnegie

Abram S. Hewitt

PIONEERS IN STEEL

Center. The original Kelly converter

"In most of the effective and powerful organizations of the world there is probably a Bill Jones."
Page 69

Top left. Molten pig iron being poured into open-hearth furnace. *Top right.* Bessemer converter blowing off. *Center.* Bill Jones. *Bottom.* Cold-rolling operation

The beauty of Manhattan is forgotten in the congestion of its canyons and subways caused by these towers. The Flat-iron Building (*left*) was one of the pioneer New York sky-scrapers. The photograph shows the "cage" method of construction. Below is a hopeful plan for tomorrow which, by its semicircular motif, works toward centralization. Un-happily the planner could not quite forget the skyscraper tradition

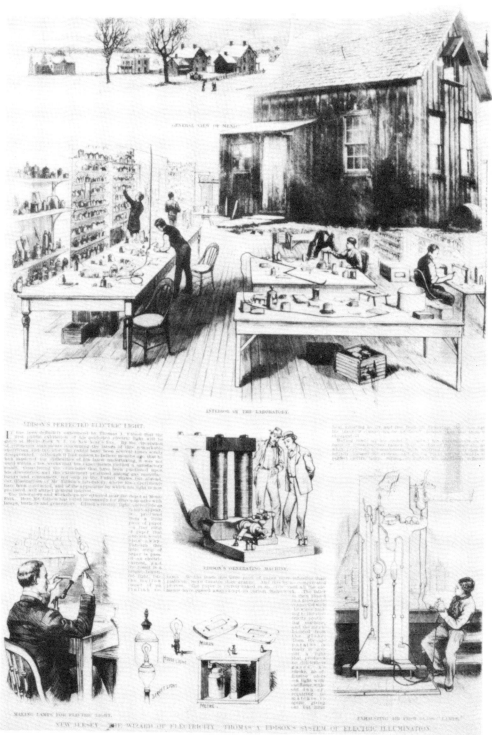

Top. The first incandescent lamp factory. Menlo Park, 1880

The scenes of the interior of the "wizard's" Menlo Park Laboratory where the first experiments were made. *Page from "Harper's Weekly," 1882*

LA DAGUERREOTYPOMANIE

DAGUERREOMANIA

Two early French cartoons showing the public frenzy. *Top.* Nadar, the first aerial photographer. Daumier lampooned Nadar and the popularity of photography by predicting that the day would come when every house in Paris would quarter a dark room and a crazy camera fan. *Bottom.* Maurisset's imagination went even further

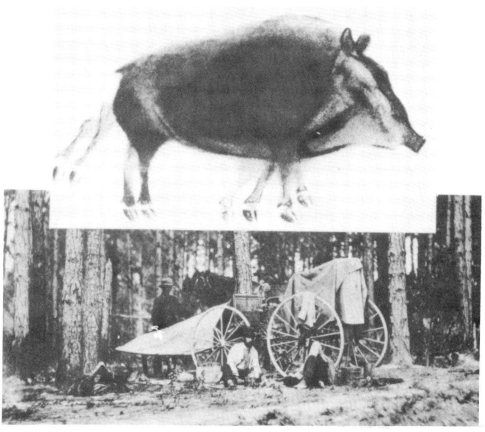

STEPS IN THE PICTURE CYCLE

Top. The celebrated Altamira cave pictures show that the eye of primitive man saw motion as the stroboscope catches it today (*see next page*). *Center.* Brady's Photo-out-fit in front of Petersburg, Virginia. *Bottom.* Muybridge battery of cameras with which he made his horse pictures

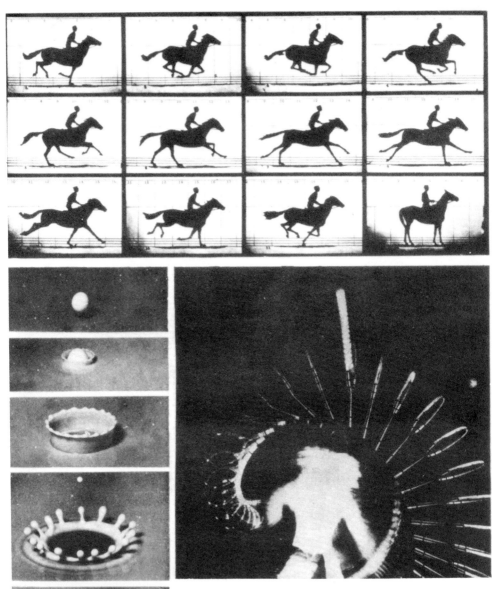

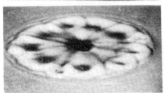

The horse in motion. Muybridge's first series of photographs

To the left. A drop of milk

Right above. All action caught in one shot, by means of the stroboscope

Both photographs courtesy of Harold E. Edgerton

THE GROWTH OF THE MOVIES

Top. Praxinoscope of 1882. *Center.* Edison's studio, the Black Maria. *Bottom.* The modern
studios in Hollywood use many acres of land and many buildings

Top. The kinetoscope, phonograph and graphophone arcade in San Francisco. *Courtesy Museum of Modern Art*

Bottom. Modern motion-picture theatre which holds an audience of 6200. *Radio City Music Hall*

THE BEGINNING OF SOUND RECORDING

Edison and his first hand-turned phonograph, 1877

Lower left. The telegraph repeater with which Edison was experimenting at the time that the idea of the phonograph occurred to him in 1877. *Lower right.* Model of Edison's phonograph which was exhibited in Paris in 1888

Top. Scott's "phoautograph" of 1857. Though this is sometimes called a precursor of the phonograph it really had little in common with the phonograph or talking machine as it could only register sound. It could not reproduce it. *Below.* The first publicly exhibited gramophone of Emile Berliner. Emile Berliner, the inventor of the lateral-cut disk, now used on most phonographs. *Bottom.* Interior of modern studio for making records. *Courtesy of RCA-Victor*

ROADS

A. *Top.* Model showing the early Roman road construction. *B.* In 1910 many cars came to stops like this. This was still the "get a horse" period. *C.* In 1937 the Bureau of Public Roads called this the modern superhighway. But in 1939 the superhighway was giving way to (*D*) the "highway of tomorrow." It scarcely suggests increased freedom

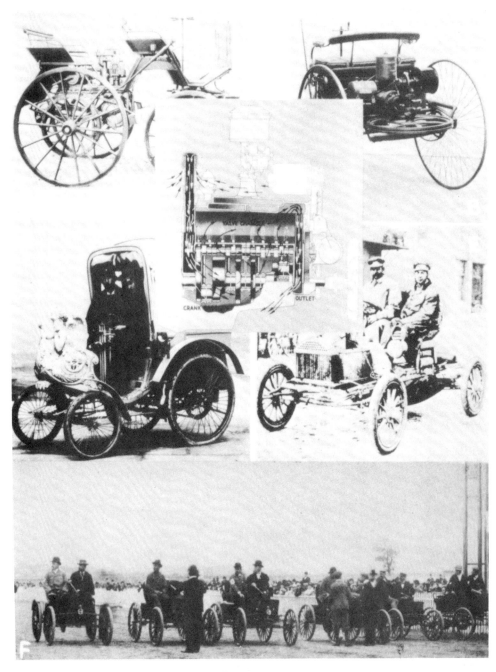

BEGINNINGS

A. The Gottlieb Daimler car of 1884. The modern car was rendered possible mainly by this car. *B.* The Benz car of 1885. *C.* Cross-section of a 1939 Ford V8 motor. *D.* In 1899 the French added sex appeal to the car. *E.* The Buick of 1904. *F.* Start of an automobile race in 1898. John Jacob Astor was one of the entrants in this race

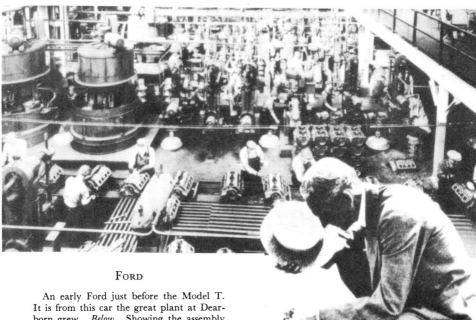

FORD

An early Ford just before the Model T. It is from this car the great plant at Dearborn grew. *Below.* Showing the assembly line in the foundry machine shop. *To the right.* Henry Ford among his soy beans

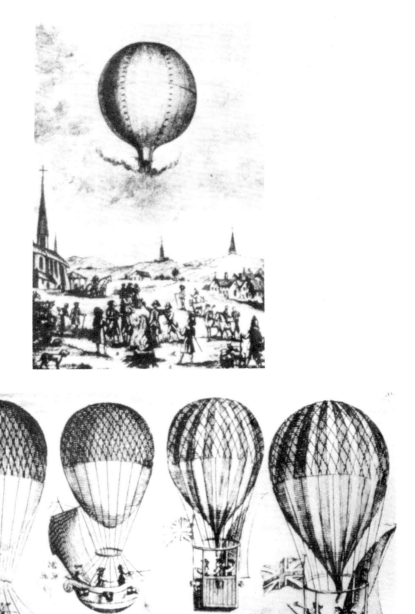

LIGHTER THAN AIR

Top. Montgolfier balloon of 1783. *Bottom.* In the next year (1784) the English cartoonists prophe-
sied "War in the Air" for the 1800's

The Langley machine. *Courtesy of Smithsonian Institution*

An early Wright plane was the first airplane to be owned by the United States Army and in fact the first plane to be owned by any government in the world

The China Clipper, modern transocean flying boat

Digging up St. James's Park, London, for air-raid shelters

PROGRESS IN RADIO

Top left. The Leyden jar. *Top right.* The farmer early took advantage of the radio. This photograph shows a farmer with an early crystal set, getting either his market or weather report. *Center.* The interior of a modern radio studio. *Bottom.* The master control room. Through this exchange the various studios are connected with the nationwide networks

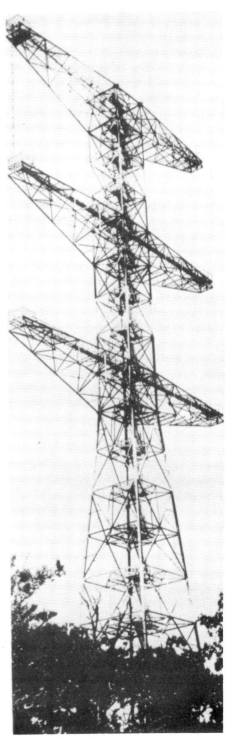

Toward Frequency Modulation

A. Modulation unit
B. Intermediate stages
C. Power amplifier (40 K.W.)
D. The radio tower

Photographs courtesy of Major Edwin Armstrong

THE DEATH AND REBIRTH OF SOIL

Top. Destructive cutting followed by fire has completely destroyed this forest and soil erosion has started. *Center.* This was once grassy meadow land. Deep gullies have drained the meadow. Sheet and gully erosion have removed all of the top soil. *Bottom.* Major correction during erosion showing sloping operation by bulldozer

ECONOMY OF WATER

Boulder Dam at night. This photograph was taken during **construction.** *Right.* Boulder Dam from above. *Below.* The Norris Dam

Top. Dust and sand start gathering

Left. An orchard under irrigation at Orland, Calif.

Bottom. At one time this was sand and dust. Now it can truly be called the Fertile Valley, Yakima Valley, Washington

Top. Cartoon of the days of the Gold Rush; "The Air Route." *Courtesy of the University of California Extension Division*

Center. Virginia City, Nevada Territory, 1861. The famous Comstock mining town. *From the Anson Phelps Stokes collection, New York Public Library*

Bottom. Gaiety in Virginia City in the 'sixties. *From an old drawing*

1 Soy Beans Mancho Variety	8 Oil for Binding Sand Cores
2 Soy Bean Meal	9 Soy Bean Resin
3 Soy Bean Oil	10 A. Wood Flour B. Stearic Acid C. Colors
4 Glycerine	11 Soy Bean Molding Powders
5 Fatty Acids	12 Plastics
6 Phthalic Anhydride	13 Soy Bean Enamel

7
Soy Bean
Oil Resin

THE "CHEMURGIC" FARM

Top. Industrial uses of the soy bean. *Bottom.* The Ford soy bean oil extractor. As the beans are fed in at the lower end, rollers crush them and they move into the long, inclined cylinder, in which, by means of a rotary screw, the bean flakes are given a thorough washing in high-grade gasoline, which releases the oil. At the top of the incline the oil passes into a container and the bean meal goes into a compartment where steam cleanses it entirely from trace or odor of the gasoline. The meal is then ready to be made into plastic

AMERICA IN TWO CENTURIES:
An Inventory

An Arno Press Collection

American Association of Museums. **A Statistical Survey of Museums in the United States and Canada.** 1965

Andrews, Israel D. **On the Trade and Commerce of the British North American Colonies, and Upon the Trade of the Great Lakes and Rivers.** 1853

Audit Bureau of Circulations. **Scientific Space Selection.** 1921

Austin, E. L. and Odell Hauser. **The Sesqui-Centennial International Exposition.** 1929

Barnett, James H. **The American Christmas.** 1954

Barton, L[eslie] M. **A Study of 81 Principal American Markets.** 1925

Bennitt, Mark, comp. **History of the Louisiana Purchase Exposition.** 1905

Bowen, Eli. **The United States Post-Office Guide.** 1851

Bureau of Applied Social Research, Columbia University. **The People Look at Radio.** 1946

Burlingame, Roger. **Engines of Democracy:** Inventions and Society in Mature America. 1940

Burlingame, Roger. **March of the Iron Men:** A Social History of Union Through Invention. 1938

Burnham, W. Dean. **Presidential Ballots, 1836-1892.** 1955

Cochrane, Rexmond C. **Measures for Progress:** A History of the National Bureau of Standards. 1966

Cohn, David L. **The Good Old Days.** 1940

Cozens, Frederick W. and Florence Scovil Stumpf. **Sports in American Life.** 1953

Day, Edmund E. and Woodlief Thomas. **The Growth of Manufactures, 1899 to 1923.** 1928

Edwards, Richard Henry. **Popular Amusements.** 1915

Evans, Charles H., comp. **Exports, Domestic and Foreign, From the American Colonies to Great Britain, From 1697 to 1789, Inclusive;** Exports, Domestic, From the U.S. to All Countries, From 1789 to 1883, Inclusive. 1884

Federal Reserve System, Board of Governors. **All-Bank Statistics, United States, 1896-1955.** 1959

Flexner, Abraham. **Funds and Foundations:** Their Policies, Past and Present. 1952

Flint, Henry M. **The Railroads of the United States.** 1868

Folger, John K. and Charles B. Nam. **Education of the American Population.** 1967

Handel, Leo A. **Hollywood Looks At Its Audience:** A Report of Film Audience Research. 1950

Harlow, Alvin F. **Old Waybills:** The Romance of the Express Companies. 1934

Harrison, Shelby M. **Social Conditions in an American City:** A Summary of the Findings of the Springfield Survey. 1920

Homans, J. Smith, comp. **An Historical and Statistical Account of the Foreign Commerce of the United States.** 1857

Ingram, J. S. **The Centennial Exposition.** 1876

Institute of American Meat Packers and the School of Commerce and Administration of the University of Chicago. **The Packing Industry:** A Series of Lectures. 1924

Leech, D[aniel] D. T[ompkins]. **The Post Office Department of the United States of America.** 1879

Leggett, M. D., comp. **Subject-Matter Index of Patents for Inventions Issued by the United States Patent Office From 1790 to 1873, Inclusive.** 1874. Three vols.

Magazine Marketing Service. **M.M.S. County Buying Power Index.** 1942

Martin, Robert F. **National Income in the United States, 1799-1938.** 1939

McCullough, Edo. **World's Fair Midways.** 1966

Melish, John. **Surveys for Travellers, Emigrants and Others.** 1976

National Advertising Company. **America's Advertisers.** 1893

Peters, Harry T. **America On Stone:** The Other Printmakers to the American People. 1931

Peters, Harry T. **California On Stone.** 1935

Peters, Harry T. **Currier & Ives:** Printmakers to the American People. 1929/1931. Two vols.

Pownall, T[homas]. **A Topographical Description of the Dominions of the United States of America.** Edited by Lois Mulkearn. 1949

Reed, Alfred Zantzinger. **Present-Day Law Schools in the United States and Canada.** 1928

Reed, Alfred Zantzinger. **Training for the Public Profession of the Law.** 1921

Rogers, Meyric R. **American Interior Design.** 1947

Romaine, Lawrence B. **A Guide to American Trade Catalogs, 1744-1900.** 1960

Scammon, Richard M., comp. **America at the Polls:** A Handbook of American Presidential Election Statistics, 1920-1964. 1965

Smillie, Wilson G. **Public Health:** Its Promise for the Future. 1955

Thompson, Warren S. **Population: The Growth of Metropolitan Districts in the United States, 1900-1940.** 1947

Thorndike, E[dward] L. **Your City.** 1939

Truman, Ben[jamin] C. **History of the World's Fair.** 1893

U.S. Bureau of the Census, Department of Commerce. **Housing Construction Statistics: 1889 to 1964.** 1966

U.S. Census Office (12th Census). **Street and Electric Railways.** 1903

Urban Statistical Surveys. 1976

Wayland, Sloan and Edmund de S. Brunner. **The Educational Characteristics of the American People.** 1958

Woytinsky, W. S. **Employment and Wages in the United States.** 1953

U.S. Census Office (1st Census, 1790). **Return of the Whole Number of Persons Within the Several Districts of the United States.** 1802

U.S. Census Office (2nd Census, 1800). **Return of the Whole Number of Persons Within the Several Districts of the United States.** 1802

U.S. Census Office (3rd Census, 1810). **Aggregate Amount of Each Description of Persons Within the United States of America.** 1811

U.S. Census Office (4th Census, 1820). **Census for 1820.** 1821

U.S. Census Office (5th Census, 1830). **Abstract of the Returns of the Fifth Census.** 1832

U.S. Census Office (6th Census, 1840). **Compendium of the Enumeration of the Inhabitants and Statistics of the United States.** 1841

U.S. Census Office (7th Census, 1850). **The Seventh Census of the United States.** 1853

U.S. Census Office (8th Census, 1860). **Statistics of the United States in 1860.** 1866

U.S. Census Office (9th Census, 1870). **A Compendium of the Ninth Census.** 1872

U.S. Census Office (10th Census, 1880). **Compendium of the Tenth Census.** Parts I and II. 1883. Two vols.

U.S. Census Office (11th Census, 1890). **Abstract of the Eleventh Census.** 1894

U.S. Bureau of the Census (12th Census, 1900). **Abstract of the Twelfth Census of the United States.** 1904

U.S. Bureau of the Census (13th Census, 1910). **Thirteenth Census of the United States: Abstract of the Census.** 1913

U.S. Bureau of the Census (14th Census, 1920). **Abstract of the Fourteenth Census of the United States.** 1923

U.S. Bureau of the Census (15th Census, 1930). **Fifteenth Census of the United States: Abstract of the Census.** 1933

U.S. Bureau of the Census (16th Census, 1940). **Sixteenth Census of the United States: United States Summary.** 1943

U.S. Bureau of the Census (17th Census, 1950). **A Report of the Seventeenth Decennial Census of the United States: United States Summary.** 1953

U.S. Bureau of the Census (18th Census, 1960). **The Eighteenth Decennial Census of the United States: United States Summary.** 1964

U.S. Bureau of the Census (19th Census, 1970). **1970 Census of Population: United States Summary.** 1973. Two vols.